Political History of Belgium
From 1830 onwards

Political History of Belgium

From 1830 Onwards

Els Witte
Jan Craeybeckx
Alain Meynen

ASP

Cover design: Frisco, Oostende
Book design: Style, Hulshout
Print: Drukkerij Van der Poorten, Kessel-Lo

(Academic and Scientific Publishers nv)
Ravensteingalerij 28
B-1000 Brussels
Tel. ++ 32 2 289 26 50
Fax ++ 32 2 289 26 59
E-mail info@aspeditions.be
www.aspeditions.be

ISBN 978 90 5487 517 8
NUR 680
Legal Deposit D/2009/11.161/073

CONTENTS

Introduction 9

CHAPTER I – *E. Witte*
Breakthrough of a Liberal Constitutional State (1830-1848) 19

The 1830 Revolution 21
The National Congress and the Constitution 24
The Military, Financial and Diplomatic Consolidation of the Nation 28
The Suppression of Internal Opposition 31
Domestic Post-Revolutionary Politics 34
The Promotion of Catholic Interests 39
Social-Economic Policy 40
The Role of King Leopold I 45
The Liberal Anti-Clerical Opposition 47
Early Socialism 50
The All-Liberal Government of Rogier and Frère-Orban (1847) and the Revolutionary Events of 1848 53
Freedom of Language, Gallicisation and the Resistance of Language Lovers 56

CHAPTER II – *E. Witte*
The Triumph of Liberalism (ca. 1850-1884) 61

Economic and Social Changes 62
The Liberal Party's Economic and Social Policies 66
The Labour Movement 73
Middle Class Social Progressiveness 76
The Liberal Freethinkers and Anti-Clericalism 82
Ultramontanism versus Liberalism 85
The School War (1879-1884): pivotal point in the clerical vs. anti-clerical conflict 89
Petty Bourgeois Flamingantism 92

CHAPTER III – *E. Witte*
The Expansion of Democracy (1885-1918) 97

Social and Economic Democratisation 97
The Labour Movement Moves into the Social-Democratic Camp 101
The Social-Democratic Programme 106
The Breakthrough of Christian Democracy 109

The Democratisation of Voting Rights and Social-Political Integration 114
State Intervention in the Social Sector 119
The Battle for the Farmer's Vote 123
Catholics vs. Freethinkers 125
Cultural Flamingantism 129
Colonialism and Militarism 135
The Impact of the First World War on Domestic Policy 138

CHAPTER IV – *Jan Craeybeckx*
From the Great War to the Great Depression 143

The Beginning of the Era of Universal Single Suffrage and the New Political and Social Relations 143
The Loppem Agreements (11 November 1918) and Their Political Fallout 146
King Albert and His Governments 150
The Political Parties 154
Pressure Groups, Employers' and Labour Organisations, Social Dialogue and Social Legislation 164
The Flemish Movement and the Language Laws 171
Foreign Policy up to 1936: the end of imposed neutrality 176

CHAPTER V – *Jan Craeybeckx*
From the Great Depression to the Second World War 183

The Short Rule of Leopold III (1934-1940): the executive in a fragile parliamentary democracy 183
The Political System During the Great Depression 185
Consensus vs. Social Conflict: the road to an initially corporatist social pact 190
The Right-Wing Movements in a Divided Catholic World 197
Belgian and Flemish Fascism Before and During the Second World War 201
The End of the Collective Security System: the policy of independence and the Second World War 208
Occupation, Collaboration and the Resistance Movement 216

CHAPTER VI – *Els Witte*
Restoration and Renewal (1944-1950) 221

The Balance of Power During the Liberation Period 221
Economic Reconstruction and Social Cooperation 230
The Elimination of the Extreme Left and the Extreme Right 234
The Royal Question 239
Integration into the Western Bloc 245

CHAPTER VII – *Els Witte*
Conflict and Conflict Management in the Religious-Philosophical Sphere 249

The School War and School Pact (1950-1959) 250
Pluralism, Secularisation and 'Socio-Cultural Catholicism' 256
The Federalisation of Education and Culture 260
Moral Themes as Political Issues 264

CHAPTER VIII – *Alain Meynen*
Economic and Social Policy Since the 1950s 271

The Organisation of Economic Expansion 273
The General Strike of 1960-1961 277
Economic Policy in the 1960s 279
The Development of the Collective Bargaining System 281
The Resurgence of Labour Resistance and the New Social Movements (1968-1973) . 285
The Crisis of Crisis Management (1974-1981) 290
1982: the Breakthrough of Neo-Liberalism 296
The Neo-Liberal Labour Policy (1982-1987) 302
Post-reformism, Competitiveness and Participating Management (1988-1992) 306
Racism and the 'New Social Issue' 313
Recession, Tentative Recovery and Budget Deficit (1991-1997) 319
The 'White' Crisis 323
Legitimacy and Economy (1997-1998) 328
Counter-Globalism 333
Globalisation and Wage Norms 340
Flexibility and Wage Cost 344
The New Economy 350

CHAPTER IX – *Els Witte*
Increasing Tension Between the Communities and the Creation of a Federalised Belgium 361

The Main Players: The Flemish and Walloon Movements 361
The Third Conflict Area: Brussels 369
Consequences of the Linguistic Legislation Strategy: drawing the linguistic border (1962), the language compromise of Val Duchesse (1963) and the Leuven Vlaams conflict (1968) 374
Federalism Gains Ground: the constitutional reforms of 1970 and 1980 376
Voeren and the Brussels Fringe: levers in the creation of the federalised state (1988) 380
The 1993 Saint Michael Agreement 385
Liberal-Socialist-Green and Liberal-Socialist Governments Continue the Devolution Process (1999-2005) 388

CHAPTER X – *Jan Craeybeckx & Alain Meynen*
Decolonisation, Relations with Zaïre-Congo and Foreign Affairs 393

The Decolonisation of Belgian Congo (1960) 394
The Relations Between Belgium and Zaire 395
Belgium and NATO 400
Belgium and Europe 406

CHAPTER XI – *Els Witte*
Mechanisms of Post-War and Present-Day Political Systems 413

Pacification Democracy 413
New Politics 417
Parties and Elections 420
Changing Relations Between Government and Parliament 432
Justice and Politics 439
The Role of the Monarchy 442
Media and Politics 445
A Unique Kind of Federalism 449

ANNEXE I
Electoral Balance, 1847-1991 457

Composition of the Different Directly Elected Representative Bodies in Federalised Belgium (1995-2004) 460

ANNEXE II
Chronological Overview of Governments Since 1830 463

Bibliography 471

List of Abbreviations 497

Author index 505

Subject index 511

Introduction

International interest in Belgian politics has increased considerably over the past few years. Belgium is host to countless multinationals and their international staff. The headquarters of multinational organizations, NATO among them, further add to the international dimension of the country. As the capital of Europe, Brussels has become a prime pole of attraction. In the Brussels region alone, some 15 percent of the population consists of non-Belgian European Union citizens.

English is the main language of communication for most of these foreigners. It should not come a surprise that Brussels has several English-language secondary and high schools. Meanwhile, the legion of Brussels-based foreign journalists is increasing at a rapid pace.

For all these people, it is beyond doubt that there is a need to understand the complex political situation of the host nation. It is a cliché to claim that contemporary history offers an excellent introduction to understand the current political developments. Up to now, there was no such publication. The authors are convinced that this translation of their overview of Belgian political history can fill this void and become a successful book. A lot of attention is focused on the second half of the 20th century, including the recent developments of the 1990s and the beginning of the 21th century.

This publication has, over the years, become a standard reference book in Belgium, and especially in Flanders. The seventh, completely updated, edition was published at the end of 2005[1], twenty-five years after the first edition was brought on the market by the Standaard publishing house. In 1990, it was co-edited for the first time by the Brussels university press. The book is widely used in education. It is an appreciated reference book in colleges and universities and it is a handy guide for politicians, civil servants and journalists. The public at large has also gained access, partly through

1. E. Witte, m.m.v. J. Craeybeckx en A. Meynen, Politieke geschiedenis van België van 1830 tot heden, Antwerpen, 2005, 584 p.

the ECI book club. At the end of the 1980s[1], it was translated in French and became successful in francophone Belgium.

The chief author is Els Witte, a contemporary history professor. She has published many books, articles and contributions about varying aspects of Belgian politics in the 19th century and the second part of the 20th century. She has written the seven chapters that cover those periods. She is a member of the Belgian Royal Academy and was rector (1994-2000) of the Dutch-language Brussels university (Vrije Universiteit Brussel). Her colleague Jan Craeybeckx, who also is an eminent historian and member of the Academy, has centered his efforts on the period between the two world wars. Alain Meynen, a contemporary history specialist, wrote the chapter on social economic policy since the 1950s.

The publication does not want to limit itself to a factual account of Belgian history. Its chief goal is to draw the main outlines of the political process that led to the current situation. This approach has given the book a great sense of coherence. The interpretation of the concept of 'politics' is based on the premise that political events are closely associated with the economic and social changes. It goes beyond saying that the essence of politics is power. Because of this, the analysis of the issues that have an immediate impact on power is a central theme. The book also systematically focuses on the power elites and on the means they use to consolidate power. The traditional institutions – parliament, government and political parties – are strongly influenced by pressure groups.

The structure of the book is based on a thematic approach, although chronology is not disregarded. The chronological divisions in the book were chosen to highlight the cohesion of the different themes. The book should allow the reader to form a personal opinion on the political developments in Belgium. The historical dimension allows ample room to form an opinion on the forces that created, and rule, Belgian politics. The authors did not only rely on their own research, but also culled information and ideas from published articles, academic publications and ongoing research. Comments from other colleagues were also taken into account.

Now, let us take a look at the book's contents. The choice of 1830 as the starting date for the opening chapter is clearly based on the birth of the nation. At the same time though, several other socio-political developments materialized and would determine political developments: the emergence

1. E. Witte & J. Craeybeckx, La Belgique politique de 1830 à nos jours, Brussel, 1987, 639 p.

of Belgium's industrialization and the breakthrough of the liberal parliamentary and constitutional state through the 1831 constitution, which became a model for other liberal nations. It is not exactly right to claim though that 1830 was the key date in the development towards an industrial-bourgeois secular society. The seeds of the secular society already were imbedded in an earlier period. The same can be said for the bourgeois power structure, for which the reigns of Napoleon I and William I were of the utmost importance. Where necessary, the book refers to the pre-1830 period, when Belgium was at first part of France and later part of the United Kingdom of the Netherlands.

The second dividing line and the point of departure for the second chapter can be situated around 1850. The bourgeoisie had taken over power by then and the political foundations of economic liberalism were already firmly in place. Liberalism was in its prime, and not only at the socio-economic level. It was evident in parliament, in government, and it had repercussions at the religious-philosophical level. Liberalism created a progressive middle class movement that began contesting the powers of the upper classes. The movement began to center on the social issues and on the suppression of the Flemish-speaking population. Links were established with the socialist proletarian movement, which was growing fast during those years. As of the mid-1880s up to the Great War the social issue totally dominated political life.

The third chapter mainly covers this broad social issue. The proletarian movement that demanded political power to ease the plight of workers, and the bourgeoisie, which had monopolized power and was not about to relinquish it totally, started to find some common ground. A compromise between the two laid the foundations for Belgium's political order. The bourgeois parliament was expanded to give larger sections of the population the opportunity to defend their rights in the legislature. For the bourgeoisie, it meant that the menacing forces of proletarian resistance were channelled through parliament. The liberal foundations of the nation were safeguarded even though it came at the cost of the bourgeois monopoly.

Even though the foundations were established long before 1919, the direct political consequences of this new situation would only become clear after the Great War. Belgium went through such drastic change that it can be argued that those days around 1920 established the political fundamentals that would last through much of the 1960s. There is a host of evidence to show that a new era began after 1919. The parties adapted themselves to a more democratic parliament after the introduction of the single vote for men in 1919. The division of electoral power between the different parties was established. The role of the monarch and his relationship with parliament changed. The pressure groups representing labor and the employers were institutionalized and mediation between the social groups produced its first results. The Flemish emancipation movement gained new impetus following a hesitant start. The fourth chapter takes a close look at all these issues. Many of those developments were temporarily interrupted by the Great Depression in the 1930s. As so often, the depression caused a shift to the right within the existing parties and even more so in the fascist groups and parties. It also completely dominated the government's economic and social policy. Even Leopold III's foreign affairs policy ahead of World War II cannot be detached from the effects of the Great Depression. The special situation that led up to the war and World War II itself are so irrevocably linked that they are treated as one in chapter five.

Contrary to what might be assumed, World War II did not bring about such fundamental changes as the Great War had done. The political balance, such as it was in between the two wars, soon reasserted itself. The war, though, did have other consequences – the measures against collaborators, the Royal Question and changes in the existing parties come to mind. The sixth chapter centers on this transitional period and takes a close look at both the further growth of the prewar structures and the legacy of World War II.

It is still difficult to assess the different stages in Belgium's history since the 1950s and this is why the thematic approach was stressed even more for the most recent period. The seventh chapter deals with the religious-philosophical conflict. The struggle between catholics and freethinkers dominated the 1950s and spawned Belgium's second 'school-war'. The resulting 'school pact' further institutionalized the compartmentalization of society and boosted the catholics' clout. With the 'Golden Sixties' came an increasingly secular society and increasing religious-philosophical pluralism, which blunted the cutting edge of the conflict. The fight for the liberalization of abortion legislation confirmed the pluralist character of society. From the nineties onwards, secularization on the individual level gradually grew stronger, allowing other ethical questions to be liberalized as well. This process was speeded up under the socialist-liberal(-green) governments.

The Keynesian state is the focus of the eight chapter. The 1950s and 1960s mark the full development of the welfare state and the collective bargaining economy. It went hand in hand with fierce social strife, highlighted by the general strike of 1960-1961. The economic crises of 1970 and 1980 showed the system to be dysfunctional and led to a neo-liberal social economic policy. That policy was instrumental in restoring profit and in boosting the growth of the Belgian economy in the late 1980s. Those good days though yielded little for the overwhelming majority of workers. In the analysis of the 1987-1996 period, the link is shown between, on the one hand, the new production system that had emerged with its competition ethics, its new management structures, technological developments and massive unemployment, and on the other hand the exclusion of many from the structures, the new social question, the competitive positions on all levels and the new racism with its extreme-right variety. In outlining the essentials of the 1996-2006 period, most attention goes to the following themes: the relationship between the moral legitimacy crisis of 1996 and the socio-economic policy, the consequences of the European budget logic, the function of globalisation, the meaning of flexibility and wage standards, the function of the agency population, the continuing dismantling of industrial structure and the further development of a service economy, the re-emergence of the specific Belgian development concerning economic performance during the 'new economy' and the 2001 crash, and a new cycle of neo-liberalism.

The theme of the ninth chapter is the tension that has dominated relations between the two main language groups. Riding the economic success of Flanders since the 1960s, the Flemish Movement at first centered its efforts on improving the protective language laws in Brussels and the communes on the linguistic border. With the Walloon Movement adding its influence, the efforts increasingly took a federalist turn. But the process slowed down because of a dispute over the role of Brussels in a new federal state. Slowly but surely, Belgium turned from a unitary nation into a federal one in four stages: 1970, 1980, 1988 and 1993.

Federal Belgium became fully operational in 1995, with the regions and communities charting their own course on the socio-economic and socio-cultural levels. However, the process of federalisation did not stop, as the analysis of the Lambermont and Lombard agreements and the hot dossier of the splitting of the Brussels-Halle-Vilvoorde community shows.

By way of conclusion, the last chapter looks into the core institutional and political mechanisms that have dominated the past decades. Themes that keep coming back are the so-called pacification democracy, the characteristics of the party system, the dominant electoral trends, the changing relationship between parliament and government, the position of the monarchy and the increasing role of the mass media.

Since the end of the eighties, the model has clearly been influenced by 'new politics'. We attempt to indicate and contextualise its characteristics and try to trace its influence on the way the parties function, on the electoral system, the legislated and executive powers, administrators, the judiciary and the mass medium. The characteristics of Belgian federalism and the way in which it influences the political model are other obvious topics in this final chapter.

This book uses the 'fault line model' to investigate the areas of conflict. It is well known that recent Belgian political history is dominated by three intertwining problems – the socio-economic, the religious-philosophical and the language dispute. The origins of the three tension areas date back as far as 1830 and it is the reason why they have been the points of departure for this historical analysis. The labor vs. capital conflict came to a head around the mid-19th century. The capitalist process of industrialization and the subsequent system of social exploitation spawned the labor movements, which succeeded in partly changing the political institutions. This development progressively created Belgium's current capitalist society, which is characterized by the continuous consultations between its participants.

The origins of the conflict between the proponents of a society based on church and religion and the backers of a secular society based on rational humanism without church interference go back even further. Unlike the social economic controversy, it was not always the focus of political decision making and the conflict lay dormant for long periods in between crises. Ever since the French Revolution, a seesaw battle marked the shifting fortunes of the clerical and secular forces. The post-revolutionary years after 1830 marked the restoration of clerical power after a regression under the Dutch and French regimes. When the bourgeoisie and the socialist labor movement came to the fore, so did anticlericalism and secularization. The catholic movement started its recovery with the first 'school war' of the 1880s and built on this momentum up to World War II. After the war, the conflict flared again until the 1959 'school pact' settled the burning issue of education. Since, tension has been far less apparent. The clerical vs. secular conflict, which has now caused tensions for well over 150 years, has left its marks on the political institutions, most notably when it comes to compartmentalization, or 'verzuiling' of society.

The roots of the third conflict, the language issue, do not nearly go as deep. As long as Flanders was an economic backwater compered to industrialized Wallonia, the Flemish movement made little headway. It could not challenge the bastions of 19th century francophone nobility and bourgeoisie. The first successes of the Flemish emancipation movement came at the turn of the century, when the economy of Flanders finally began blooming and when political democratization started to have an impact. The collaboration of the Flemish nationalist wings of the movement during both wars had an adverse impact on its development in the post-war periods. Linguistic fever rose quickly during the 1960s when Wallonia's economic decline coincided with Flanders' economic boom. It gave the conflict a new dimension.

The book also systematically analyses the relationship between the executive and legislative powers, even though the issue has been strongly influenced by the three key areas of tension. The Belgian monarchs have, at certain stages, dominated foreign policy. There are examples galore – the attempts of Leopold I to beef up the royal powers, the colonial policy of Leopold II, the policy of territorial annexation that Albert I supported in the wake of the Great War, the role of Leopold III before, during and after World War II, the impact of Baudouin I on ethical issues. These are all aspects that indicate the importance of this fourth conflict area in Belgium's political history.

To conclude this introduction on the book's different themes, the paragraphs that illustrate Belgium's impact on European and even world history have to be highlighted. The birth of the Belgian nation in 1830-1831 cannot be dissociated from the balance of power that the Great Powers, most notably Britain, sought at that stage. The position of Belgium was part of that throughout the 19th century. It impeded a fully independent foreign policy, but because of its geographical location, Belgium could not avoid being smack in the middle of that. After World War II, Belgium proved that a small nation can have an important mediating role in international policy. Belgium also had a stake in the construction and development of western

Europe within the U.S. sphere of influence. A few years later, Belgium's place in the world was inextricably linked to establishment of SHAPE on its territory. In the second part of the 1960s, Belgium helped smoothe the way for the rapprochement between Eastern and Western Europe.

Belgium's role in the economic history of Europe and the world also should not be underestimated. Belgium was the first country on the Continent to become a modern industrial nation. As of the mid-19th century it occupied a prime position in the global marketplace and by the end of the century, it had become a strong competitor on foreign markets, even well beyond Europe. Belgian industrialists were doing business in Russia, China, the Americas and the Middle East. A powerful colonial empire was built during the same period. Belgian colonialism had a unique characteristic: the monarch was the driving force behind the nation's move into Africa and it was an initiative that served Belgian capitalism extremely well. The decolonization of Congo during the 1960s became an international issue because the central African nation was the world's largest producer of copper, zinc, uranium and radium. The neo-colonial regime of Mobutu received the full backing of the United States and France. Belgium did its utmost to maintain firm links with its former colony. But as Belgium's economic stake in Congo decreased, policy changed. Meanwhile, Belgium had had an important role in the construction of the European economic market. The Benelux economic union became the model of the Common Market. The European Economic Community set up base in Brussels in 1958. The choice of Brussels as the main capital of Europe was a logical development and boosted Belgium's international position. This book offers a coherent historical analysis on this issue.

This introduction shows that Belgium's unique history has depended on the close interaction between different conflict areas and on the interesting social and economic development. Interest in Belgium's historical development, which remains a remarkable phenomenon, has spilled well beyond the national borders. Scores of foreign (notably U.S. and British) economic and political historians, political scientists and sociologists have studied parts of Belgian history. Although it was impossible to provide an exhaustive bibliography, we did try to give an overview pointing out the most directive and representative books and articles.

As we already mentioned, this overview goes as far as the beginning of 2006. The reader will find no information on the federal elections of 2007, on the financial crisis of 2008 and its impact on the Belgian economy, on the failure of the state reform discussions, nor on the regional and European elections of 2009. At the moment it is still very difficult to get to grips with these evolutions.

Chapter I

Breakthrough of a Liberal Constitutional State (1830-1848)

It is no easy task to draw clear, defining lines in the sands of history. Even the 1830 revolution, an obvious point of departure, was not the clear-cut watershed in the political struggle. It is beyond doubt, obviously, that the revolutionary days of September and October 1830 marked a turning point in the policy of the North and South of the United Kingdom of the Netherlands, as it was formulated since 1814 under King William I. They were proof that the policy of assimilation imposed by the North was defective, even though the causes of these limitations by far preceded those autumn days. This is not the place to elaborate on all the factors leading to the failure of the 'amalgam'. As such we will only mention that the historical development of social and cultural patterns in the North and the South differed so much that it made integration, or even the absorption of the South by the North, very difficult.

Yet the nature of the shock of the 1830 events was not such that it could be considered the only decisive moment in the transfer of power. Neither the outcome of the September battles in Brussels, nor the instauration of the provisional government and the National Congress marked the end of the Belgian revolution. Even though the foundations of independence and the new regime were laid then, another decade would pass before there was any real consolidation on a national and international level. Peace with the neighbouring nations had to be restored, a financially viable state structure had to be created, constitutional rights had to be ensured, internal opposition against the new state structures had to be suppressed and Belgium had to be officially inducted in the list of European nations. This coming of age was only completed in 1848. As such, the 1830-1848 period can be treated as one single historical period.

If we take a step back and assess the political development of the Southern Netherlands from a much wider perspective, it becomes clear that 1830 was far from a decisive year. Instead, the 1830-1848 years can be seen as a transitional period during which the remnants of the ancien régime were gradually adapted to modern trends, characteristic of the emerging bourgeois industrial era. The slow but certain decline of the ancien régime had already been going on for decades. Its main characteristics are well-known: it was based on an agrarian economy, exploited by the land-owning aristocracy and Church, and a merchant-capitalist sector and the traditional cottage industry completed the economic scene. On a social-political level, this produced a class society, with two privileged classes – the aristocracy and the clergy. The bourgeoisie, though far more numerous, came third and could not count on privileges. Church and religion held a tight control on all sectors of society, helped by a monarch ruling by the grace of God. Ancient, regional constitutions marked the boundaries of the (absolutist) power of the monarch.

Industrial capitalism gained a foothold around the turn of the century and with it came a new social-economic class that would boost the traditional bourgeoisie. It is widely known that the different stages in the French Revolution and the subsequent Napoleonic rule were instrumental in the political recognition of the bourgeoisie and the overthrow of feudal and clerical structures. The annexation of the region by France and the subsequent rule of William I, led to the bourgeoisie, in particular the industrial bourgeoisie in Belgium, being backed by the authorities. At the same time, the political foundations of a secular society unshackled from religious control were established. The Church lost countless possessions and the concordats between monarch and pope granted the clergy a function as keepers of the established order, which was subsidised by the state. The industrial and financial capitalists profited greatly from the enlightened despotism as practiced by William I. But it was opposed by the group of (mainly intellectual) citizens, who wanted to defend the political interests of the bourgeoisie.

Against this background, the 1830 revolution had an ambivalent role. Some wanted to use the revolution to slow down the rise of a modern, mechanised industry and restore the political powers of the Church and landowners. The bourgeois intellectuals who led the revolution, on the other hand, made sure that the key principles of the liberal society were anchored in the constitution. The political tensions between those two groups – who together ended the regime of William I – dominated the first two decades of Belgium's political agenda, right up to the mid-19th century when the industrial bourgeoisie finally imposed itself.

The 1830 Revolution

In order to gauge the impact of the 1830 Belgian Revolution, an orientation on the general, economic, social and political of this political upheaval is necessary. During this period, Belgium was in the midst of its transformation from an agrarian society into a fledgling industrial nation. The textile plants in Ghent and Verviers were almost fully developed and the steel factories and coal industry around Liège and Hainaut were developing fast. In part, this development was a consequence of William I's incentives. The powers of capitalism took control of these sectors at the start of their development. The merchants in the major ports cashed in on the industrial trend and also profited from the colonial trade with Dutch East India. Industrialisation was changing a country where the non-mechanical sector (in the hands of merchant entrepreneurs) thrived and the agrarian structures dominated. Land property was still the prime choice of investment and the majority of the population was employed in the agricultural sector.

In a country with such economic conditions, aristocratic and bourgeois landowners still carried a lot of clout, as was evident from the political setup during William's rule. The First Chamber of the States-General belonged to the aristocracy and this class also had quite some influence in the Second Chamber. Some members of the emerging industrial and commercial high bourgeoisie had already become part of the political elite ahead of 1830 and the economic policy proved that William treated them as such. These two influential groups were not swayed to participate in the revolution by any economic motives. On the contrary, as will be shown later, the industrial and commercial high bourgeoisie did not want any change in government at all and would even become the core of the Orangeist opposition.

The Belgian revolution was, mainly, a lower bourgeoisie and middle-class uprising, as is evident from numerous indications. This middle class was to be situated between the aforementioned higher class and the lower social strata of the population. In spite of often considerable differences, these people all bore the same grudge – they felt excluded, for very diverse reasons and to different extents. The status and financial situation of some of them was well above the mere working class, yet not high enough to exert any political power; others considered themselves qualified to have a say in the political system. In other words: they were citizens high enough on the social ladder to be able to distance themselves from the real oppressed masses, and at the same time enviously observe the political game of the powerful.

It was a heterogeneous group of upwardly mobile citizens, including intellectuals, teachers, wealthy craftsmen, journalists, civil servants, merchants etc. They provided the vanguard of the 1830 revolution with their demands for social and political reform. The only way to gain a political foothold was to break William's authoritarian leanings and the power of the establishment, in order to allow their own social class to gain participation and to develop politically. The intelligentsia turned the complaints into concrete demands, including sovereignty of the people, a parliamentary system with ministerial responsibility, the recognition of key rights, etc. These middle-class intellectuals had grown up in an environment where they had found an ideological reinforcement for their ambitions – as far as liberal and democratic ideas were concerned, they could go back to the late 18th-century revolutionary era.

The cutting edge of this middle class resistance relied on support from other sectors that shared some of the grievances. It is clear that merchants, small entrepreneurs and craftsmen from the non-mechanised, traditional sectors (textile, brewery, milling, refinery and distillery industries) all added their weight. They criticised their heavy tax burden and the government subsidies for the new, mechanised industries. But this group did not have any real political power either. Analysis of the petitions addressed to the government from 1828 onwards shows that backing for the opposition could also be generated from this middle group.

As far as the landed gentry is concerned, enough indications exist to assume that part of them chose the side of the revolutionaries. The interests of agriculture and land ownership had not been given the attention they had hoped for under William I's rule. Moreover, the monarch had thwarted most of the ambitions of the higher clergy. Within the constraints of the Concordat, William and the church had fought bitterly over the constitutional recognition of the different religions, his secular education policy and the appointment of bishops by the monarch. Within part of the clergy and some of the Catholic lay circles (largely coinciding with the class of the landowners) the idea had taken root that the recognition of freedom of religion and education could harbour the tactical means of avoiding government control. Through a parliamentary regime, clerical supremacy in a largely Catholic society might be restored. So the tactical interests of the liberal middle class and the Catholic forces dovetailed and Catholics and liberals confirmed this in the famous 1827 'Unionist' alliance, also known as the 'monster alliance'. There is no underestimating the role of the Belgian clergy in the opposition to the government.

The same can be claimed of the working class. The economy was in a rut, trade and industry were stagnating. Ever-increasing mechanisation, successive crop failures, soaring price and a harsh 1829-1830 winter all combined to further impoverish the population and enlarge the group of paupers dependent on help. These circumstances created an atmosphere in which a resistance group could easily mobilise a disorganised, discontented mass and temporarily enlist it for service in a nationalist movement.

There is no danger of exaggeration in the claim that the intellectual middle class was the core of revolutionary action in 1830. It created action groups and established opposition networks where the input of newspapers was instrumental. In every single city, it controlled resistance committees. They prepared larger protest actions, including petitions, during which they gained support of large sections of the non-intellectual part of the population. Their political know-how showed when they used the social unrest of August 1830 to fan the fires of revolution. They were just as successful in gaining control of the local militia, which was supposed to suppress revolt. They both brought down legal authority and set up an efficient opposition from within the weakened institutions. They developed revolutionary centres of power, which produce a counter-elite. When the institutions of William disintegrated, they took control and after the retreat of the Dutch army, they showed frantic activity in order to secure their power.

Yet the Belgian revolution was hardly decided on the barricades or in Brussels' city park in September 1830. In fact those September days saw mere street scuffles and the Dutch army was not really beaten by the revolutionaries. The Dutch command withdrew its troops to avoid a bloodbath that would have ended any prospect of peaceful negotiations between the government and opposition. In a last attempt to hold on to his southern possessions, William I sent the Prince of Orange to the port city of Antwerp, but because he wanted to keep the throne for himself, this strategy failed. Attacks by the revolutionaries on the citadel resulted in a shelling of the city, which blew up the remaining political bridges between North and South. William's indecisiveness and his strategic and tactical mistakes, characteristic of his reaction to the revolution, undoubtedly played a role in the course of the revolutionary process.

It was the political motivation on an international level, however, that were decisive. As William was not able to solve the crisis, the solution of the conflict turned into an international affair. The United Kingdom of the Netherlands, when it was created in 1814, was intended as a buffer state to contain France and the nation quickly came under Britain's sphere of influence. The French revisionism, obviously, wanted to see The United Kingdom of the Netherlands disappear, and so France backed the Belgian revolt. The European powers, though, and Britain in particular, feared that yet another war would bring chaos and anarchy to the continent. So they sought to prevent the Belgian revolt from turning into an international conflict. An independent and neutral Belgium seemed the best solution to avert war and the new nation would be able to take on the role of strategic buffer zone against France. On top of that, a spirit of liberalism united several international decision-makers. They backed the creation of a new liberal state where industrial and financial capitalism would be allowed to blossom; their backing is a further explanation as to why Belgium had become a politically viable concept for the international community in early 1831.

The National Congress and the Constitution

The 1831 constitution was the immediate political result of the revolution and it was a compromise between the landowners and clergy on the one hand and the liberal middle class on the other. The conservative forces were willing to adapt to the inevitable changes in society but this willingness was aimed at retaining the organic link with the past and preventing radical change. The liberal middle class, in spite of their desire for systematic, radical reform with a view to its expansion, showed restraint, a typical reaction of early liberalism. They still needed to negotiate with the landed gentry, and had to accept the sizable political power of the 'enlightened' aristocracy.

This was evident during the election for the constitutional parliament – the National Congress. Ahead of the revolution, an indirect electoral system based on wealth had limited the electorate. The group of voters appointed the much more limited electoral college, which limited the immediate political impact of the electorate. The system was changed to a system of direct elections, but voters had to pay even slightly more electoral taxes than during the reign of William I. The poor may have been useful to fight the revolution, but their independence was considered too limited for them to be part of the 'legitimate' power structure. This kind of thinking also excluded the lower middle class and even the intellectual revolutionary leaders from that group were only allowed a role in the voting process through the backdoor of an electoral derogation based on intellectual capacities. This concession also gave priests, university graduates, doctors and lawyers access to the ballot box, apart from the wealthy.

The composition of the National Congress reflected the economic and social-political situation. The aristocratic landowners and the intellectuals, mainly lawyers, dominated at the expense of wealthy merchants, industrialists, bourgeois landowners and entrepreneurs. The revolutionary Unionists, who had been voted into the Congress by well-organised, usually clergy-led electoral associations, held the overwhelming majority. Those who opposed the creation of a Belgian state were in a minority. The conservative and Catholic groups outnumbered the anti-clerical wing. The democrats in either ideological camp were no match for the conservative and moderate forces. The Belgian constitution was a result of this balance of power.

There was a large consensus to contain the powers of the monarchy, especially in the wake of William's absolutist reign. Even the aristocracy, eager to act as a stabilising force, wanted to contain the absolutist ambitions of the monarchy. This solidarity between aristocracy and bourgeoisie gave the bourgeois intellectuals in the Congress enough room for manoeuvre to push through their vision of constitutional reform, in line with the ambitions of their own class. Several provisions in the constitution limited the royal powers and established the solid foundations of a liberal nation. They included the constitutional arrangements to contain the monarchy, the institutional balance of power between the legislative, executive and judicial branches, the principles of ministerial accountability towards the legislators and the co-signing by ministers of laws and royal decrees.

The bourgeoisie was convinced that by serving the self-interest of the wealthy, society as a whole would profit. This principle made sure that the rights to self-determination and economic autonomy became a central part of the constitution. It applied to the free-market principles of the economy and to political freedoms as well. They came to symbolise the belief in man's limitless capacity to govern society. It was essential that those rights be safeguarded in the constitution. The parliamentary system would have to make sure those rights continued to prevail. Parliamentary negotiations and discussions were core concepts in that system, underscoring the strong belief of the liberals that reason in the end would be able to reconcile the different interests within society. It was up to parliament to cast those civil interests in rational terms and to unite them into one common denominator. Parliament's supervisory role was aimed at scrutinising any state intervention and preventing the interests of the bourgeoisie being jeopardised. The State was called on to police society and protect, guard and expand the interests of the wealthy. Public opinion, created within the 'legal' country, needed to be drawn into the parliamentary discussions and political decision-making, using the same rational terminology. This called for an appropriate legal framework, on all levels of society; a logical result of this principle was to make freedom of speech, freedom of association and assembly and freedom of the press into constitutional rights. The liberal bourgeoisie insisted on freedom of the press because it considered a free press – as a forum of discussion – a necessary addition to the parliamentary system. Each of these freedoms was guaranteed in the 1831 constitution; as such, the liberal members of Congress had succeeded in founding a modern, civil society, much more liberal than the United Kingdom of the Low Countries.

It did not mean that Belgium's early liberalism was revolutionary or democratic. It was 'revolutionary' in September 1830 because it entered an alliance with republican, democratic and nationalistic resistance groups. But these groups were soon reduced to a minority within the Congress, allowing the moderate early liberals to safely distance themselves. During the revolution itself, these groups had been readily embraced and even necessary. But Belgian liberalism could do without these democrats in laying the foundations of a bourgeois nation. A conservative social policy had its advantages for the Belgian liberals: it did not only give voice to a particular interpretation of liberal principles, but it also met the demands of the conservative allies and the European states, whose support they did need.

The liberals and the conservatives were equally fearful that the proletariat would threaten the existing order and push Belgium into a more extremist corner. Belgium's new leaders immediately took action to counter the development of a so-called people's democracy. The Congress emphatically rejected the concept of democratic republicanism, preferring a moderate constitutional monarchy instead. Furthermore, it also settled on a monarch who was acceptable to the major European powers. Prince

Leopold of Saxe-Coburg, a relative of the British royal house, did not upset the balance of power. Belgium's initial candidate, the Duke of Nemours, would have shifted that balance too much France's way and Britain would never have been able to accept that. Leopold was also welcomed by the conservative aristocracy and the high clergy since he was not at all known in European court circles as someone who wanted their powers curbed – after all, he was an emanation of those groups himself. His relations in financial circles, moreover, were a guarantee that he would encourage the expansion of the capitalist bourgeois class.

The new constitution scrapped the legislative chamber reserved for the aristocracy, but the bicameral system did have its conservative, aristocratic touches. The Senate was to be the conservative counterbalance for the Chamber since only the wealthiest (i.e. members of the landed gentry) could gain a seat there. The physiocratic idea that only landowners could be representatives and that other possessions did not sufficiently bind the ordinary citizen to the state structure, was only rejected with a tiny majority in setting up the election criteria for the Senate. The Senate's high electoral tax – fifty times higher than the minimum electoral tax – made sure that the idea was put into practice, though. The Chamber of Representatives, on the other hand, was the domain of the liberal bourgeoisie. But even there, property was the all-important yardstick. The minimum electoral tax was constitutionally set at 20 guilders: only those who could lose a certain wealth were allowed in. Congress rejected suffrage based on intellectual capacities and intellectual maturity gained no-one entry into the political process. So property was the liberal citizen's only guarantee to safeguard his political freedom; the constitutional concept of equality was reserved for members of their own class, and social and political equality only existed in as far as it did not threaten the social position of the bourgeoisie.

The same principle also applied to other laws which, in line with the constitution, stopped short of being truly democratic. A heavy tax burden severely curbed freedom of the press, limiting the scope of the fourth estate to the wealthy. Freedom of association meant little as long as the working class was not allowed to join in an alliance. Electoral taxes for elections for the Chamber of Representatives were sometimes three to five times the constitutional minimum and limited the electorate to about 1 % of the population.

So the legislative achievements of the Congress turned out to be a carefully balanced compromise that reflected the cooperation between aristocracy, landowners and bourgeoisie on the one hand, while the democratic forces were kept far from political power. Understandably, this mock democracy provoked a lot of bitterness among the revolutionaries from the lower classes, who had been kept politically impotent.

The Belgian church authorities, though, had little to worry about after most of its aspirations were reflected in the constitution and subsequent laws. The Catholic majority and moderate liberals, who could accept a society based on Catholic morals, aimed at keeping the established order and confirming the system, had made sure of that. The clergy obtained the advantages of the separation between Church and State yet suffered few disadvantages. It was guaranteed an expansion of religious services and, at the same time, charity and education were exempt from state control. The state also subsidised the Church's infrastructure and paid the clergy as stipulated by the Concordat. The Church was forced into one fundamental concession – the freedom of expression. It was a key issue for the liberals and an ideological consequence of the right to self-determination. The scope of this constitutional provision cannot be overestimated. It was essentially a rejection of the Constantine notion that united Catholicism, morals, law and public order into one inseparable whole. It opened the constitutional door to the secular society feared by the Church, even though this prospect was far from a realistic one in a country as Catholic as Belgium, especially as the political situation allowed the Church to redevelop its institutions and reclaim much of its political clout. This prospect probably explains why the Belgian bishops, against the official Vatican policy, which still held on to the old provisions of the ancien régime, assumed a fairly flexible and conciliatory position. It was clear that the Church had made a major step forward compared to the difficult situation under Dutch and French rule.

So the Congress had succeeded in reconciling the positions as far as the relation between Church and State was concerned. But it would prove much harder to defend the construction against external and internal opposition during the 1831-1839 period.

The Military, Financial and Diplomatic Consolidation of the Nation

In the summer of 1831, the European powers tried to push through a solution for the Belgian question by backing Leopold's candidacy to the throne. A few days after Leopold's coronation on 2 August, William I attacked the new kingdom. The Dutch king had lost his southern possessions through violence, and now he was trying, by force, to improve his international diplomatic position at a time when an armistice still had to be signed. The weak and ill-disciplined Belgian troops needed the help of the French army to drive back the Dutch during the Ten-Day Campaign. Because the French soldiers withdrew from Belgium immediately afterwards, France avoided an open conflict with Britain. The Belgian defeat forced the London Conference to impose a new, and much tougher, treaty on Belgium. Apart from mandatory neutrality, this Treaty of the XXIV Articles forced Belgium to cede parts of its Limburg and Luxemburg provinces. It also was a severe economic blow since Belgium was forced to accept an unfavourable division of national debt and custom duties on the river Scheldt that linked Antwerp with the sea. William, however, refused to sign this treaty, even though it was favourable for him.

The Belgian government, fully realising the weak negotiating position of the new kingdom, had no such hesitations and signed. This diplomatic defeat outraged some hawkish patriots and, in an attempt to appease them, the government demanded that the Dutch army immediately withdraw from Antwerp and the fortresses on the Scheldt. The European powers, with the approval of Leopold I, at first rejected this. But when it appeared that William refused to open peace negotiations and that the French conservative government would be getting in serious difficulties if pro-Belgian feelings were not recognised, the issue was reconsidered. Britain preferred the risks of a fight over a fortress in Antwerp over a new European conflict.

The evacuation of the Antwerp fortress did not yield any fundamental changes. The Dutch army continued to occupy the other fortresses on the Scheldt, Belgium continued to hold on to all of Limburg and Luxemburg and William still did not want to sign the Treaty of the XXIV Articles. In short, there was still a state of war. The Belgian government persevered in its efforts to conclude peace negotiations and following difficult diplomatic talks with Britain, France and the Netherlands, the government was rewarded on May 21, 1833, when an international convention guaranteed Belgium an advantageous status quo as long as the Dutch refused to sign the Treaty. There would be no resumption of hostilities and the blockade of the river Scheldt was lifted. Belgium's parliamentary opposition was placated and softened its hawkish stand.

As the years went by, Belgium's international position improved, especially after the 1833 convention boosted its self-confidence. So when William finally offered to sign the Treaty in March 1838, after almost five years, protests rang out against the loss of parts of Limburg and Luxemburg; one had become accustomed to their inclusion in the country. Leopold, the government and parliament were all intent on negotiating a more favourable treaty. But France and Britain did not back Belgium's territorial claims on all of Limburg and Luxemburg and certainly did not want to risk a new war over this. The European powers did not want to go beyond granting Belgium a better deal on the division of national debt. Belgium's financial sector also wanted to avoid a territorial conflict over the two provinces. The threat of war had hurt stocks and undermined business. In spite of the protests of Belgian patriots and the Church, which did not want to lose Catholic Luxemburg, and passionate debates on the issue in parliament, government and parliament were forced to sign and ratify the Treaty of the XXIV Articles in 1839. After nine years of diplomatic efforts, the Belgian nation was a *fait accompli*.

The important stake of the financial powers in consolidating the Belgian state has already been mentioned. The need for credit was obviously extremely high in those unstable years after the revolution and Belgium's leaders, who were not affluent themselves, tried to obtain political support from their poor followers by lowering taxes and offering government jobs. The revolutionary leaders took the importance of each social group into account and there were special measures targeted at both the industrious middle and lower classes. To suppress social revolt, the authorities set up a costly employment program and awarded subsidies to private companies. The threat of war called for extra expenditures (setting up an army, acquiring arms, paying damages) and influenced state income negatively. The initial contacts with the Société Générale bank, which had been under the control of William, added to the financial problems. The wealthy landowners and the high bourgeoisie were unwilling to offer the new rulers financial support. Patriotic loan programs were utterly unsuccessful. Local investors did not line up to fund the new nation, so the government was forced to look elsewhere.

It found a friend in the Société Générale; once pro-Belgian executives were running the bank, it adopted a positive attitude towards the new State. The company and Leopold I brought the government leaders in contact with the Rothschilds, one of the most powerful banking families. The impact of the financial sector on European politics should not be underestimated and almost all major nations were, in one way or another, indebted to international bankers. In this specific Belgian question, the Rothschilds' interests were served by two factors: as providers of government loans, they backed the creation of a new nation, and so they were hardly against Belgian independence; moreover, peace and the European balance of power made sure their interest rates stayed high. In return for their financial backing, the Rothschilds forced Belgium to remain a political dove. The 1831 and 1839 loan programs both stipulated that. Belgium had solved its financial problems, but the Rothschilds were to control the credit sector of the new nation. It is beyond doubt that the financial situation affected the diplomatic negotiations during the 1830-1839 period.

The Suppression of Internal Opposition

The outcome of the revolution left many disgruntled. The republican democratic forces in particular led the opposition against the new groups in power during the first few months after the revolution, since the limits on voting rights and the concessions to the conservatives kept effective political power among the privileged few. Their hopes for a new society in which the lower middle class would be part of the ruling establishment were quickly dashed by the constitution.

These unionist revolutionaries, including well-known revolutionaries such as L. De Potter, P. Van Meenen, L. Jottrand, E. Ducpétiaux, A. Gendebien and A. Bartels, had been among the most belligerent before, during and after the September days of 1830, and they were unwilling to let their ideals fade away. Soon they realised they would be denied the fruits of their revolutionary actions by a National Congress that was more than willing to abandon the republican and democratic principles. Many understood they would have to resort to more than mere legal means to pressure the Congress. By adding a patriotic touch to their complaints, they gained the support of a few thousand followers. By June 1831, when Congress was to vote on the choice of Leopold, the protesters even had a plan in the works for a republican coup. It was bound to fail, and did. The Congress, representing the legal forces, was overwhelmingly royalist, with only a smattering of members who were openly republican. The revolt was badly prepared and the march on the capital from a few provincial cities turned out to be a huge fiasco.

It was the last, ill-fated attempt to give the new regime a more republican and democratic outlook. The democratic minority had been unable to affect the compromise between Catholics and the moderate liberals, but this did not mean the final exit for the democratic efforts. Hawkish patriots would protest each time territorial issues came to the fore – and actually managed to raise some support – especially when Belgium accepted the Treaty of the XXIV Articles in 1838. The democratic wing included some liberal and Catholic legislators and it was the core of an active minority in parliament trying to hang on to revolutionary traditions against the policy of the moderate unionists – with precious little success on the diplomatic level. This small group of republican democrats wanted to establish a more equitable social order and kept close links with similar groups abroad, especially in France.

The anti-Belgian opposition was a lot more dangerous and packed more economic clout. During the first decade, the anti-Belgian movement had an immediate impact on the domestic political situation and its influence disappeared only after the 1839 signature of the Treaty. The founding principle of the movement was one common idea: the independence of Belgium was to be rejected. The new State was considered a utopian construction, neither economically nor politically viable for modern industry. According to them, the situation that had resulted from the revolution had to be contained and ended as soon as possible.

It was unclear, though, what kind of new society the counterrevolution would offer as an alternative. The movement's majority was Orangeist and it sought full economic reunification with the North. At first the Orangeists wanted the Prince of Orange on the throne. After Leopold became Belgian monarch, they backed an economically unified but administratively separated United Kingdom of the Netherlands under William I. In Belgium's francophone south, the Reunionists wanted to become part of France again. The conflicting strategies were mainly the result of conflicting economic interests. The Verviers wool and Liège arms industries, and the Borinage coal producers were all largely dependent on the French market for their exports, and as such had great expectations from a new integration into France. The Orangeist party, on the other hand, included many merchants and industrialists that had flourished under the union with the North; the entrepreneurs who had enjoyed William's subsidies harboured the same sympathies. This explains why textile centres like Ghent and Sint-Niklaas, the port city of Antwerp and some Walloon industrial centres had strong Orangeist factions.

There was more to the counterrevolutionary movement than just self-interest. Cultural and ideological issues also played a role. Reunionism was a pipe dream of the Walloon Francophiles. King William's attempts to shackle the Church had won the admiration of many anti-clericals. They rightly feared the Catholics would become the new nation's prime beneficiaries and this was enough of a reason to stay loyal to William. The court's nobility – core of the metropolitan fashionable court scene – also remained faithful to the old dynasty and some noblemen even actively joined the resistance. In short, the counterrevolutionaries belonged to the upper crust of society, primarily the high industrial and commercial bourgeoisie, not the lower or middle classes. Because of its social structure, the movement was mainly limited to the larger cities.

The contra-revolutionaries did not get involved in parliamentary action since many of them did not want to collaborate with the new regime out of principle, and as such did not participate in national politics. The new electoral laws also made it difficult since the victors of 1830 had made electoral taxes much higher in the cities than in the countryside, giving the countryside voters, who could easily be swayed by the patriotic clergy, dominance over the city voters. The counterrevolutionaries were thus forced to look for less orthodox political strategies and soon, plans for revolt and even a coup materialised.

The Reunionists gave up all hope as soon as Leopold became king, and abandoned the fight. Some made their peace with the Belgian state while others remained loyal in their opposition and joined the Orangeists, who remained a disruptive political force up to 1840. The publication of party newspapers aptly illustrated the Orangeists' sense of organisation. The Dutch king's cabinet exercised a certain supervisory role, and in Brussels a central committee was established, with local centres of Orangeist resistance in several cities organising Orangeist resistance. Their actions in Ghent and Antwerp in 1831 caused considerable controversy and when Orangeists bought the royal Dutch stud farm in 1834, Belgian patriots took their complaints into the streets. The last Orangeist conspiracy was uncovered in 1840.

The Orangeist party never wanted to be part of the Belgium's national power structure, nor did it gather a massive following among the lower classes, necessary for a successful counter-revolution. As such it was doomed. The situation was different in some cities, and from those regional bases, it vainly tried to obstruct the regime. In a number of large cities, the Orangeists won a clear majority during the October 1830 municipal elections. They held on to this local power between 1831 and 1839, and even managed to extend their share of the vote. Ghent was a case in point. But an Orangeist decline was inevitable. King William's 1839 signing of the treaty of the XXIV Articles was the fatal blow, after which the Orangeists reinforced Belgium's liberal wing. It was a logical move since they shared the liberals' economic vision and anti-clericalism.

From that moment onwards, the internal consolidation of the Belgian state was definitive, also in the cities. From then on, other internal controversies would dominate domestic politics.

Domestic Post-Revolutionary Politics

It is very difficult to give a balanced overview of the domestic policy of the successive governments and parliamentary majorities over the first 15 post-revolutionary years. Often the military and diplomatic issues and the suppression of the Orangeist movement disturb a clear image of the political balance of power. Moreover, clearly delineated political parties with a well-defined programme were nonexistent in the period between 1831 and 1845, as were representatives and government officials toeing the party line. Aspiring parliamentarians either had to help create their electoral organisation or depend on existing organisations. As a result, legislators did not have a precise political label. More than a sketch of the broad ideological lines in the political evolution cannot be given here.

The composition of parliament broadly resembled the political structure of the National Congress. Up to mid-1836 and briefly again in 1838-1839, the Catholic and liberal Unionist factions dominated parliament. The more progressive members of the factions wanted domestic policy to keep as much as possible to the radical revolutionary principles and they defended the democratic commitments of 1830. The moderate Unionists, who were in the majority, wanted law and order to prevail first and foremost. The king's role in domestic policy was a controversial issue. The progressives denounced Leopold's ever-increasing claims on power while the moderates counted themselves lucky to have an authoritative monarch.

The social and economic background of the legislators was important with a view to an analysis of the different aspects of political decision-making. The majority of parliamentarians still wanted to safeguard the interests of the landowners and the Church. In the Senate, they held a near monopoly. In the Chamber of Representatives, the landowners and representatives of domestic industry outnumbered the new industrial bourgeoisie; but the intellectual bourgeoisie – lawyers, doctors, civil servants and magistrates – were important newcomers. Yet the inclusion of many government functionaries in parliament was usually an extra support for the government majority.

An overwhelming parliamentary majority did not object to the increasing role of the Catholic Church and religion in society. The radical anti-clericals were a minority with little or no influence, and, from about 1834, the Catholic majority could count on the king as an important ally. And even if their political interests were not always identical, the Church, landowners and the monarch formed a powerful coalition.

The Catholic political faction, led by the Church hierarchy, and several (mainly aristocratic) landowners backed laws in Parliament that favoured the expansion of the Catholic religion and morals. In their eventual goals, they were as such very much in line with Rome. They did differ, though, as far as tactics and strategy were concerned. The Belgian Church had accepted a constitution with liberal principles and was an active participant in the parliamentary regime. The Vatican stuck to Ultramontanism, bent on centralising authority around the Catholic clergy, led by an ancien régime monarch who reigned by the grace of God. Yet for opportunist reasons, a tacit agreement had been reached concerning the position of the Belgian Church: Rome turned a blind eye to the bishops getting the most from the constitution and the elected parliament.

The Church was able to capitalise on developments because its religious authority allowed it to set out a policy for its obedient flock. For the Catholic electorate, politics became a religious duty, especially during elections. The Church became a well-oiled political machine that made sure the Catholic electorate voted for the right candidates. Its permanent, hierarchical structure turned the lower clergy into electoral agents, with the high clergy setting out guidelines. The Catholic landed gentry usually provided an additional boost during the electoral campaigns since their position of power in the rural countryside allowed them to influence the voting of many a voter who was dependent on them. And the rural voter was important in Belgium's early elections since the electoral system favoured the countryside over the city. Small wonder that parliament was very friendly towards the Catholic movement initially.

It would be wrong to assume, however, that the Catholic political establishment was monolithic at the time. The bishops tried to dominate the whole movement from the top. This was not to the liking of the younger, lower clergy, who had fought the absolutism of William prior to and during the 1830 revolution. They favoured an extension of political freedom keeping central power in check, advocated local decentralisation and some even had a touch of republicanism about them. Since they represented, and often came from, the lower social classes, they wanted to give those classes a bigger say in the political process. Their influence depended on the political power of their flock. The aspirations of the lower clergy in favour of a democratic regime and against the conservative Catholic powers (aristocracy and higher clergy) were completely in line with this.

Also among supporters of Rome there were Catholics who did not agree with the majority policy supporting the bishops. They were suspicious of the State, since it had constrained the Church before. As such they came out in favour of maintaining and strengthening federalism, with its throwbacks to the ancien régime. Their loyalty to the freedoms and customs of local communities has to be viewed in this context. It was clear that the Church hierarchy could not accept its authority being challenged from within its own ranks and from 1831 to 1839 it fought to suppress internal dissent. The bishops were able to count on the full support of the aristocrat leaders and on the 1832 *Mirari Vos* encyclical, which condemned democratic reform.

But also the aristocrats and other Catholic lay groups sought more autonomy and an independent power structure where the episcopate was kept at arm's length. Catholic parliamentarians were very much like other legislators when it came to consolidating their political position. They built a dense local network of influential clergymen and dignitaries and pursued contacts with high-level government Catholics. Once they were minister, governor or envoy, they were even able to enlist government officials in their electoral campaigns. In short, the Church could not ignore their demands for real participation in government, or even prevent them from relegating the clergy to the background. This struggle laid the foundations of the later struggle between proponents of a Church-led Catholic party and the more liberal-minded Catholics.

The Vatican ran its own Belgian policy, trying to get rid of the liberal rulers and replace them with Ultramontanes as soon as possible. It was in the Vatican's interest to have conservative Catholic representatives in parliament instead of the vocal Catholic democrats, who had gained a seat thanks to the help from the lower clergy. When the pope considered progress too slow, he effectively supported Leopold I, who also wanted to eliminate the democrats and increase the Catholic-conservative majority. This conflict within the Catholic movement came to the fore during the 1837-1839 elections and the conservatives, who had been joined by the bishops, prevailed.

Leopold's position in this partnership stood out. Even though he had gained the throne as a result of revolution, his education, ideas and entourage remained very much ancien régime. He despised the constitution because of all its limits on royal executive power. His mission was to increase his power, and he often tried to use the letter of the constitution for his purposes while disregarding the spirit of Belgium's founding fathers. Some constitutional articles served Leopold particularly well, notably those on the command of the armed forces, the declaration of war and the signing of treaties, the appointment and dismissal of ministers and the article on royal immunity. The incessant attempts to increase his executive powers were most evident in his foreign and military policy, and in his efforts to control ministries and make ministers subservient. To make sure he would be able to control government ministers, Leopold wanted to prevent the development of well-organised party structures supporting them. In order to free himself from the constitutional restraints, he aligned himself with the Catholic conservative bloc. The king would protect the interests of the Church and, in return, the Catholics would back his attempts to extend his own prerogatives. In practice, this meant that he encouraged the bishops to only allow hard-core monarchist Catholics to gain a seat in parliament; those would then help him in his quest for more power.

The clerical powers were not about to yield control of the Catholic movement easily, though, not even to the king. They had fought royal interference before the revolution and they were not about to be pushed into a second-class role again. It was also a known fact that Leopold favoured so-called unionist cabinets to extend his power. The king wanted centre-right governments with ministers he could appoint himself, largely independent of parliament. A centre-right coalition implied that moderate liberals would have to be part of the team and would have to be able to count on the support of the Catholic-royal alliance. To lure the bishops to his cause, Leopold obtained the support of the papal envoy in 1837, testimony to the excellent relations he had, as an ancient régime monarch, with the Vatican.

During the early years, parliament faithfully mirrored the balance of power between the different political blocs; the same was true for the government. Generally, it can be said that the coalition was fairly well catered for at government level, which had not been the case during the first three years after the revolution, when the question of independence still needed international recognition, and apart from Catholics, also liberals were necessary in order to solve the problems of international policy. So the De Muelenaere government included Unionist liberals and, as of October 1832, the cabinet even had a majority of moderate liberals (Lebeau, Rogier, Goblet). However, as soon as it became clear that Lebeau was not able to persuade the majority of the need to extend royal powers, Leopold I sought the support of the Catholics and put the conservative Catholic aristocrat de Theux in charge of the cabinet in 1834; the government firmly remained in a Catholic grip up to 1840. After the patriotic unrest of 1838-1839 had subsided, it increasingly became clear to the liberals they no longer needed the union with the Catholics and some started dreaming of a non-unionist, fully liberal government.

Yet neither the king nor the Catholic majority were prepared to give up a system favourable to them. The all-liberal 1840-1841 government of Charles Rogier and Lebeau, then, was nothing but an interlude, one that Leopold and the Catholics used to show that an anti-clerical cabinet was still unrealistic. The distrust of the Senate was another element ensuring that this liberal government only stayed in office for one year; they were replaced by the moderate liberal centrist Nothomb, who was willing to make concessions to the monarch and the political right, a policy that allowed his government to last until 1845. After the brief interlude of the Van de Weyer cabinet, which just continued Nothomb's policies, de Theux returned to power in 1846-1847. By that time, the composition of parliament had changed to such an extent, to the advantage of the liberals, that another unionist centre-right cabinet was out of the question and Leopold grudgingly had to accept an all-liberal government based on a parliamentary majority.

For well over a dozen years, the Church, landowners and the monarch had done their best to safeguard their interest. The next section describes the results of their ambitions.

The Promotion of Catholic Interests

Several examples can be given of the policy of power of the Catholic majority and the governments based on this majority. They were usually successful in safeguarding and expanding their interests during the early years; the liberal opposition, backed by moderate liberals in the different governments, could do little more than slow that process in an attempt to take the sting out of Catholic policies. Catholic laws again and again spawned anti-clerical opposition; we will only mention the most marked examples.

The 1831 electoral law, favouring the Catholic countryside, has been mentioned above. The electoral law had blunted Orangeist opposition in the cities, but also formed the basis for the Catholics' majority and as such became the opposition's prime battleground. The lower electoral tax in the countryside allowed the clergy to use its moral authority to the fullest and impose its political will on the many small but enfranchised farmers. The result was that city voters were outstripped by rural voters in nearly every electoral college. The 1831 law undeniably protected the Catholics' hold on power and kept many anti-clerical townspeople from positions of power.

Education also brought the liberal opposition to the political frontline. in order to understand Catholic policy, the well-know basic principles have to be recognised: in the framework of its proselytism, which claimed to possess the absolute truth, the Church wanted religion to become the foundation of education again, as it had been before the French revolution. Teachers and books had to proclaim the same Catholic convictions. The principle of neutrality was rejected as a denial of Catholicism. A Catholic monopoly on education was the only possible starting point, implying not only that Catholics had to maintain an education system themselves, but also that public education, too, had to be controlled as much as possible by the clergy. After the secular policies of William, against which the Church had rebelled, it expected the earlier monopoly to be reinstated through the freedom of education in the constitution. They used the constitutional provision to expand their own educational network, and their political majority to bring public education back into the Catholic fold. Most cities and communes put up little resistance, either because they were controlled by Catholic councils, or because religious morality still ruled and made sure a school could not survive without the support of the local priest. It allowed the clergy to directly control primary schools in several cities and communes.

The 1842 law on primary education was no obstacle for Catholic aims, either. It acknowledged the inseparability of morals and religion. It underscored the clergy's factual supervisory role, subsidised private education and allowed every city or commune to establish its own Catholic school. The liberals secured one concession – city councils had to appoint teachers. This provision allowed municipalities under liberal control to start up non-confessional primary schools.

The Catholic strategy also worked in the secondary school system, where alliances with city authorities ensured that the clergy remained largely in charge. When Sylvain Van de Weyer tried to push through a more liberal policy concerning secondary education in 1846, he met with fierce Catholic resistance and was out of office after only seven months. In the meantime, Catholics had achieved a virtual monopoly on the training of teachers, and the Catholics also enjoyed a comfortable position at university level. Parliament allowed the state universities of Ghent and Liège to survive, at the request of the liberals, but Leuven was abolished as a state university, and turned into a Catholic institution. Moreover, Catholic professors were over-represented in Belgium's central examination board. The 1841 attempt to grant the Catholic University of Leuven (KUL) corporate status failed, however, because of the overwhelming liberal opposition against the Nothomb ministry. Successive governments made sure stamp duties were kept as high as possible to collar the anti-clerical press; government aid gave the church the means to keep culture, including literature and theatre, under its social control; local authorities were forced to fund religious infrastructure.

All of these initiatives have to be seen in the same context. The so-called reactionary law of 1842, which was aimed at safeguarding and reinforcing Catholic power in the cities by means of a break-up of the electorate, was viewed by the liberal opposition as the best example of the clerical politics of power. The liberal opposition could not prevent the law from passing, since it had the backing of both the monarch and the Catholics.

Social-Economic Policy

There are no detailed studies as yet on the economic policies of the successive administrations. The scarce data available point in the direction of the continuing strength of the political power of the landowners. This should not be surprising, as it would take until 1850 before industry made its decisive breakthrough in Belgium. Agriculture was still the determining factor for the general economic climate. When harvests failed, as during the 1845-1847 farm crisis, the poor would still end up on the brink of starvation. The lack of supplies made sure prices went through the roof, and in rural Flanders, the combination with the rapid decline of the cottage industries led straight to starvation. The countryside in Belgium, and especially in Flanders, was dotted with small farms, where intensive work on small patches was the norm. The few landowners reaped huge profits by dividing up the available land and allowing a surplus of aspiring tenant farmers to drive up the lease rates.

The excessively expensive rates forced the farmers to take on additional jobs in order to survive. It created Flanders' domestic linen industry and nail production became a prime cottage industry around Liège and in Hainaut. Affluent merchants brokered between the exploited domestic workers and the buyers. The Flemish domestic linen industry fell into a sharp decline between 1830 and 1845: it could not compete with the mechanically produced cloth from the already partly industrialised sector. Yet this was not new: the domestic textile industry had already been in crisis long before 1830 before its definitive collapse, which resulted in a change in the economic balance of power. During the crisis, the number of workers who could no longer survive in agriculture exploded, and the rural exodus toward the industrial and commercial centres intensified, not only strengthening the numbers of the industrial proletariat, but also increasing the number of paupers in the cities.

For the landowners, on the other hand, the evolution was very profitable. Lease rates for farm tenants were extremely high; grain prices yielded big profits; the value of land increased, as did the demand for land for investment purposes. It did their wealth, reputation and authority a world of good and they used their majority position in parliament and government to safeguard their interests. The policy on grain prices was a case in point. Under pressure of circumstances in the wake of the revolution, the provisional government had kept grain prices low, liberalised trade and banned export and transit. All this went against the interests of the landowners, who called for agricultural protectionism and high import duties. The landowners got what they wanted in 1834 when a sliding scale system was introduced: the landowners were allowed to set an average price that would provide a normal profit margin. As long as the price did not sink below the financial limit, trade was unrestricted. Once corn prices went under the limit, the sliding scale system came into effect and import duties increased relative to the size of the fall, while export and transit remained unrestricted. The law was backed by a large majority in parliament, proving again that the interests of landowners far outstripped those of the industrialists and merchants, who wanted as much free trade as possible. The law was temporarily suspended during the 1845 farm crisis in an attempt to stave off famine, but at the same time, parliament made sure the lease rates for tenant farmers remained high. The crisis in the linen industry during the early 1840s also showed the power of landowners when their interests were at stake. They refused to accept a reduction in the price for flax, the raw material, and they rejected any attempts to reduce their profit margin.

Even if the conservative forces still dominated the nation's institutions, the industrial, commercial and financial powers were already preparing to transform Belgium into one of the most important industrial nations on the European continent, with the biggest per capita production rate. Blast furnaces, cokes and steam engines revolutionised the metal sector and the Watt engine drastically changed the coal industry. Combined with the increased output, these new techniques can be said to have been a real revolution. Such drastic innovation and investment was a heavy drain on the finances of the mostly modest family-run companies, which did not always have the necessary financial reserves. Concentration of capital and the creation of new management structures solved these problems. The limited company or corporation pried open the closed management structure of old firms, remove small owners and bring Belgium's heavy industry under the control of a small group of investors. Around 1845, holding companies already controlled close to 50 % of coal production.

Société Générale was a prime player in this process. Since its foundation in 1822, the company provided credit for the coal and steel industry and during the 1830-1834 economic regression, it starting taking direct stakes in companies. The crisis put several major firms in financial trouble and Société Générale decided to move beyond providing short-term credit and created investment companies. Around 1840, this 'mixed bank' controlled vital sectors of the textile and heavy industry and the foundation of its industrial empire was already well under way. Another financial institution, the Banque de Belgique, tried in vain to break the monopoly of the

Orangeist-tainted competitor, but this did not prevent the fortunes of the financial and industrial powerhouses becoming intimately intertwined from the 1830s onwards.

The transformation of the industrial and financial sectors held inevitable repercussions for the rest of the economy. The domestic market was soon found insufficiently solid financially in order to provide enough profits, and the industrialists had to start looking abroad for new markets. Foreign trade quickly expanded and Belgium's road, rail and waterway infrastructure had to be urgently improved. The industrial centres needed efficient transport facilities between them, but also towards the foreign markets. The two banks invested heavily in the construction of roads and canals.

It was obvious that private capital in each of these industrial sectors would benefit from a positive government attitude. In 1830, Belgium had largely copied economic rules from the Napoleonic period. The key player in the industrialisation process, the Société Générale, was certainly denied the goodwill that later governments and parliaments would give it. Minister de Theux, for instance, was a typical representative of the conservative landowners and a proponent of traditional systems of production. He even disliked financial capitalism. He ran an obstructionist policy whenever and wherever he could. Investment companies faced an uphill battle to obtain government approval and there was even a personal conflict with the bankers de Meeûs and Coghen. Even in 1842, the bank failed to get more than provisional parliamentary approval for its statutes.

There was hardly any evidence of a successful capitalist involvement in government politics, in spite of King Leopold attempts to help. He was not blind to the bright future the new industries had in stock for Belgium and realised a long-term alliance with industry offered great prospects. But in the period between 1831 and 1847 this proved impossible as yet in a country economically and politically dominated by agricultural interest groups. These groups, moreover, enjoyed the support of the Church, whose ancient régime philosophy made it suspicious of the new investment forms.

This did not mean, however, that there had not been any successful attempts to use the state in the process of industrialisation led by the banks. The measures the provisional government took to protect industry remained in place, and the state paid for the dense rail network, designed by Rogier in 1833-1834, which gave Belgium's industry a modern infrastructure and brought foreign markets to its doorstep. The government also subsidised road and canal construction. So even if the economic symbiosis of conservatives and liberals was still some way ahead, they had already been able to find some common ground.

When it came to foreign trade policy, it was obvious that free-market politics had not seen a breakthrough yet. Belgium was still trying to conquer its own place in protectionist Europe. Several fledgling industries wanted to shield themselves from foreign competition and successfully sought protectionist measures. Others wanted limited free trade, seeking bilateral agreements with as many countries as possible based on the principle of trade reciprocity. This tentative free-market policy was applied with great care, though: at first, only nations with non-competitive industries were invited to sign such agreements. After the Treaty of the XXIV Articles forced Belgium into a policy of neutrality, successive governments treaded carefully before joining custom unions. It closed limited trade agreements with France and the German free trade association in 1844-1845. The Zollverein treaty was an attempt to open up the German market for Belgium's metal industry. The law stipulating that fees had to be paid for ships sailing up the Scheldt, which according to the Treaty of the XXIV Articles had to pay tolls to the Netherlands, also proved that liberal economic policies were gradually gaining ground.

When it came to determining an overall trade policy, however, protectionism reigned supreme. The 1844 law on differential levies discouraged imports and was a victory for the proponents of a Belgian fleet, who wanted to use the levy system to protect trade in Flanders' maritime regions. The industrial regions in Wallonia, where canals and rivers were an economic lifeline, opposed the law and the issue became one of the many occasions when economic policies clashed with regional interests. There was a tug of war between the different regions and sectors that was sometimes settled to the advantage of one interest group, and then of another.

There was little or no discussion about any social policy. In the next chapter, we will discuss the attitude of the affluent class towards the social problem. Here, we can suffice by pointing out that the government barely intervened when industrial capitalism turned the working class into proletarian paupers. It counted on charitable organisations to control the poor masses. The boards of coal mines and factories were given total freedom to dominate and exploit huge groups of workers. The prohibition of coalition, inscribed in law, together with repressive forces of the government guaranteed ample support should workers try to resist.

The Role of King Leopold I

Leopold was undeniably a major factor in consolidating Belgium's independence. It has been mentioned earlier why he was an acceptable compromise figure: his marriage to the daughter of the French king and the close family relations with Britain's Queen Victoria further improved his standing, which he continuously managed to strengthen through shrewd matchmaking on behalf of his relatives. His position allowed Leopold to dominate Belgian foreign policy and largely keep it out of the hands of parliament. It started a tradition that Leopold's successors have always tried to continue.

When it came to domestic policy, Leopold wanted to foster good relations with unionist governments in an attempt to expand his own powers and to create sufficient goodwill toward the financial sector. Despite his alliance with the conservative Catholics, Leopold was often spurned by the de Theux government. The ratification of the municipal law and the feud between the government and the Société Générale were ample proof that Leopold failed to have everything his way. The king found a better friend in the government of moderate liberal Jean-Baptiste Nothomb.

After barely two years on the throne Leopold started to work out the tactics to strengthen his authority. The municipal bill, put to the Chamber as early as 1834, tried to expand the authority of the central powers in the municipalities and was also aimed at increasing the control of the monarch and government over parliamentary elections. The bill specified that the king would appoint and dismiss mayors and aldermen. Since these officials would become very much dependent upon the government, it was expected they would sap the opposition's strength at the ballot box. It was clear that the king, who had been forced to accept a Constitution that gave him little room for manoeuvre, was trying to get compensations through the law on the set-up of municipalities and provinces. The National Congress had indeed left it to parliament to draw up these laws, without interfering itself.

The Lebeau-Rogier government could not get the bill through parliament, forcing the monarch to turn to the Catholic majority. The clergy was unwilling, however, to throw its full weight behind Leopold. This explains why, during the 1834-1836 period, the bishops were reluctant to eliminate the democratic low clergy, which had joined republican democrats in opposing Leopold's ambitions. Leopold was hopeful the de Theux ministry would give him a triumph but after three years of heated debate during 92 parliamentary sessions, a compromise text was the best the monarch could get – the mayor and aldermen would be appointed by the king but only from the elected members of the municipal council. This meant that Leopold's hold over municipal politics was to remain limited.

Six years later, Nothomb would give the king much of what he desired. Nothomb's 1842 bill included the provision that Leopold could also appoint mayors from outside the city councils. Leopold and Nothomb were obviously counting on support from the right to get the bill approved. In order to secure this support, they linked the bill to a new law on electoral districts aimed at securing the Catholic majority in the cities. The 1842 law, which was repealed in 1847, greatly increased the king's prerogatives in the municipalities.

The king was initially also denied any promising results when it came to his support for the Société Générale. The new nation drew strength from the development of industry and the creation and expansion of companies. Leopold was convinced the financial sector deserved a reward for services rendered. Personally, he had benefited, too, which was another reason for his goodwill towards the world of high finance. Building on his excellent contacts within the Société Générale, his private wealth was steadily increasing.

But the Catholic landowners, patriots and democrats did not share his views. They felt that Société Générale was still tainted by its Orangeist past and they rightly suspected that it wanted to monopolise industrial policy. Their differences came to a head in 1836 when Leopold wanted to appoint Meeûs and Coghen, directors of the bank, to the position of Minister of State. At some stage, it would have allowed the directors to take part in ministerial meetings, where they could have influenced government policy. There was angry protest from several sides and the conservative de Theux government took an intransigent position. Leopold was forced to abandon his hopes, but he had made his intentions clear. He wanted to offset the Catholics' political dominance by bringing in the banking directors, leaving the monarch in the position of referee. Such a position would have increased his powers in the cabinet. Again Nothomb yielded where de Theux had been obstinate. No purposeful research has been conducted, but the say of bankers at government level certainly appears to have been much greater under Nothomb.

In conclusion, it can be said that Leopold I tried to expand his constitutional role as much as possible – though not always successfully –

and diminish that of parliament. A definition of the then form of government would have to point out that the balance of the nation's policies tended more towards the monarchy than towards parliament. Over a third of parliamentary seats were held by appointed officials, increasing the king's sway over the political institutions.

The Liberal Anti-Clerical Opposition

The Catholics, landowners, traders and the king dominated politics. It was bound to invite increasing opposition at some time or other. Opponents could even be found among the members of the high bourgeoisie. For obvious economic reasons, industrialists, bankers, some merchants and ship-owners could not accept the concept of a society dominated by agricultural interests and domestic industries. And insofar as they were not already part of the Orangeist opposition, they started to act against conservative policies. The middle class also started opposing a regime that had pushed aside the democratic ideals of the revolution and denied them a political say.

Opponents came from all walks of life, but they had one thing in common: the Church was the enemy. The proponents of economic free trade inevitably clashed with conservative Catholics, since the Church still based its earthly powers on landownership and the cottage industries. Democrats and the backers of a more secular society also clashed with religious interests. And the bourgeois quest for independence of the individual could not be reconciled with the authority of the Church. These citizens could not tolerate any religious control over politics, in spite of the fact that many of them were practicing Catholics themselves, who agreed that religion was the best way to subdue social unrest. They also wanted to get away from the meddling of the Church on social, non-religious issues. It should also be mentioned here that there were a few landowners among this last group, namely the buyers of confiscated Church property, who had traditionally taken an anti-clerical stance ever since the French and Dutch regimes.

It would take years before all these different groups formed a united front. The Orangeist bourgeoisie, as mentioned before, had its own reasons to oppose the creation of a new nation without an alliance with anti-clerical Belgian nationalists being on the cards initially. The intellectual, anti-clerical democrats tried to find allies in the working class and they actively backed meetings organised by the proletarian resistance, even if they refused to back their aspirations for a democratic order with revolutionary action. Instead they wanted a parliamentary reform movement which brought them closer to an anti-clerical citizens' party.

When unionism began to lose its *raison d'être* around 1840, the three groups started to approach each other. The Orangeists tried to join up with the anti-clerical movement and they reinforced the liberal movement, with whom they shared ideals on a secular society and a free-trade economy. The social issue remained a great divider. The social conservatives held a sizeable majority and the group included eminent leader figures (Lebeau, Devaux, Frère-Orban, Verhaegen, etc.). There was no desire for social reform within this group, and they did not want to see their power lessened by allowing the lower classes any participation.

A left wing began to emerge, however, demanding a gradual expansion of the electorate and measures to ease the dire plight of the working class; they were driven partly by humanitarian, partly by rational considerations. A guiding principle was the realisation that a suppressed proletariat held too many dangers for society. The progressive rhetoric could not hide a hint of paternalism and the quest for a more just society usually got stuck in theoretical analysis. When thoughts had to be turned into action, many turned to the right wing instead. Yet the anti-clerical movement counted some among its members who were not against radicals joining the opposition. It was slowly being turned into a party between 1839 and 1842.

Early on, a lack of organisation denied the liberal anti-clerical opposition any electoral successes. Its first organised initiative came in 1834, when it countered the establishment of the Catholic University of Leuven with the creation of their own Université Libre in Brussels. A party structure slowly took hold as of 1836, but more noticeably from 1839 onwards, and within five years local electoral organisations were set up in the most important cities. These soon developed into real party divisions. The swift transformation from a loose association of opposition groups into a real political party was completed in 1846 when the Liberal Congress met in Brussels to agree on a binding, national party program.

The speed and efficiency with which these diverse groups were turned into a tightly structured party was a combination of several factors. The liberals had skilled leaders and organisers within their ranks, who were not afraid to engage in open conflict. Figures like Verhaegen in Brussels, and his numerous alter egos in the other cities were essential in this process and they all had one thing in common – they knew how to mobilise the disgruntled but inert liberal electorate and lead prospective voters right into their local party offices.

The support of the Masonic lodges was also instrumental. Freemasonry became a political tool, especially in Brussels, around 1836-1837. Under the French and Dutch regimes, the lodges had already been hotbeds of anti-clerical opposition. When the Belgian bishops condemned freemasonry again in 1838, they actually gave the signal for the total identification between freemasonry and anti-clericalism, and as such turned the lodges into an electoral machine at the service of the liberals. The electoral organisation L'Alliance, for instance, founded in Brussels, became the basis for local party organisations in cities without lodges. By 1842, most cities had liberal electoral associations. It was also L'Alliance that provided a coordinated structure four years later. Because freemasonry became politicised, the liberals were able to use its organisational platform to set up a full party structure in very little time.

The liberal party structure also profited from the alliance with the anti-clerical Orangeists. The first coalitions were set up as early as 1836 and as of 1839, they became commonplace in most cities. The democrats joined the opposition party in 1841 and further swelled the ranks of the liberals. The democrats knew full well they were a minority representing mostly disenfranchised citizens and tried to build a position of power within the citizens' party. Their main aim was to organised grass-root support to build up their position within the party. Many radical youngsters joined the electoral associations, where they were tireless workers within the propaganda machine, contributing to the efficiency of the associations. The expansion of the party press went hand in hand with the increase of electoral committees. Every liberal-minded city and region had its own party paper, which turned out to be an essential electoral tool to influence the urban electorate by means of effective campaigns. The Catholic party press was no match and the liberals were able to maintain this strategic advantage for a long time. In short, the anti-clerical opposition had set up a political party structure, aimed at the urban electorate, which was quickly poised for electoral success.

In view of the stipulations of the electoral law and the fact that most anti-clerical voters were to be found in the cities, the liberals clinched their first electoral successes exactly there. After a few years, some cities even had liberal majorities and one-party municipal executives. The liberals wanted to use these majorities to strengthen their opposition but since the municipal councils packed little effective power, they were little more than protest forums or pressure groups. They demonstrated their potential political strength with some spectacular actions though. The liberals organised mass petitions against the electoral law, against the 1841 fall of the first liberal government of Lebeau, against plans to grant the Catholic University of Leuven corporate status, against the 1842 electoral district law and the primary school law. Each time, the petitions were backed by press campaigns, but in the end, they had little effect, since the liberals were too far removed from the centres of power.

That changed in 1845, when parliamentary elections proved to be the political breakthrough the liberals needed. It was not massive enough to get King Leopold to give up his preferred centre-right cabinets. But when the liberals celebrated another famous electoral victory two years later, there was no denying them. The de Theux government lost its grip on power and the conservatives were finally forced to negotiate with the Liberals. Over ten years of opposition came to an end for the Liberals and the industrial bourgeoisie was on the verge of entering its political prime.

Early Socialism

There was no organised mass working class resistance during Belgium's early years (1831-1847), when antidemocratic and conservative forces ruled. The early socialist movement was built around groups of middle class intellectuals and craftsmen who wanted to wrestle free from the grip of the regime. Together, the two groups made up the core of what could be called the early socialist movement.

The members of the former group are not unknown. Some of them had been active on the left fringes of the bourgeois anti-clerical party and most of them had been involved in the revolution and the opposition. The results of the revolution had disheartened many, but during the 1830s they were replaced by a new crop of young, idealistic democrats from Brussels university circles and from the reformist middle class in industrial cities like Ghent, Liège and Verviers. They founded democratic associations and their own press, breathing new life into the radical movement. They started attacking conservative governments with relentless zeal, inversely proportionate to their success. To expand their political base, they linked up with the lower middle class, which already was a recruiting ground for the liberals, and with the working class resistance. They offered financial support, helped organise opposition, wrote propaganda articles in their newspapers and were stump speakers at rallies.

As such, they infused the movement with ideas characteristic for the intellectualistic early socialism. Their ideology was a complex mix of numerous influences, both their own and foreign. They were not only under the spell of Saint-Simon, the founder of French socialism who attacked the concept of private property and social exploitation and proposed a kind of collectivism as an alternative, but also adopted the egalitarian principles of French revolutionary G. Babeuf and his Italian disciple Ph. Buonarroti. The utopian socialism of Ch. Fourier was added to the mix as well. This French ideologue wanted to divide humanity in phalanxes that individuals would join, working on a voluntary basis for the common good. Few knew about Marxism. Overall, then, they should be characterised as radical progressive reformists rather than systematic revolutionaries who wanted to change the world. Most wanted to hold on to the core principle of liberalism – property – even though the concentration of wealth in the hands of society's upper crust was condemned and the Enlightenment's principle of equality was the central theme. Their vision of a welfare state and the recognition of the right to work should undo social injustice. The citizen had to be drawn to the cause of early socialists with reason and rhetoric, not violence.

During the 1830s and 1840s, the political actions of the working class were directly linked with these intellectual early socialists, yet the working class resistance did have its own characteristics. It should be stressed once more that it had not originated in the industrial and factory proletariat but among craftsmen. This chasm is not easily explained. The few data available about this emerging industrial proletariat allow the following hypothesis: the intensive industrialisation of the first half of the 19th century initially drew its manpower from the unemployed and the destitute. Since they were dependent upon the (few) social services the state provided, they could be turned into a meek workforce. The early industrialists thus used what Marx called 'relative overpopulation'. This workforce without schooling and without a sense of class, still to be taught the labour discipline of industrial capitalism, was unable to organise any class-conscious, collective resistance. It was the first generation of an uprooted class, which started to expand the factory proletariat and mutual competition around 1840, as a result of the decline of the cottage industry and the agrarian overpopulation. Such a situation did little for the development of class consciousness. It was too much to expect from these rootless people who had migrated from an agrarian or pre-industrial society into the urban industrial environment, a total transformation for them.

The craftsmen found themselves in a different position. They could build on the corporate traditions of the guilds. The legal ban on setting up unions or coalitions to demand wage increases had affected their structural strength, but the craftsmen countered the law by creating special funds for social welfare and pensions, which effectively replaced the role of the guilds. The bourgeoisie's great fear for the unskilled proletariat, best illustrated by the strict appliance of the anti-coalition law, left the factory workers without a proper organisation to defend their rights. Craftsmen were allowed some sense of organisation, as the funds proved, because they were seen as far less threatening, and much closer to their own class. This meant that opposition in these circles could rely on existing organisational structures. The craftsmen were trained, specialised, and many of them were literate. This helps explain why they were impressed by the reform theories of the radicals. Their resistance was strengthened further by the decline of the cottage industry and the rise of the mechanical industries.

Jacob Kats was the key resistance leader during the 1834-1840 period. This weaver had been a primary school teacher during the years of the United Kingdom of the Netherlands and he used his rhetorical and writing talents to captivate his working class audience. He soon became their political mouthpiece. Folk theatre was Kats' initial means to try and start the fight for emancipation. The monologues in his plays had raised the consciousness of his audience, and were soon replaced by rallies and discussions in which the workers were active participants. The success of his meetings, at first only held in Brussels, spread to other Flemish cities from mid-1837. A meeting in Ghent, the textile centre which was going through an industrial crisis in 1839 (affecting the factory proletariat directly), even turned into an uprising. The army had to be called in to suppress the so-called 'cotton revolt', to which the entire democratic movement had contributed.

When Kats and other leaders were imprisoned, others took over and experimented with new ideas. Starting in 1843, people's associations were set up, first in Brussels and then in other Flemish cities. These people's associations had more radical ideas, though, and where Kats had always preached caution and renounced the use of violence, the new leadership was ready for more forceful action. The most striking expression of this new stance was seen in April 1846, when the economic crisis in Flanders led the people's associations to call for a mass march on Brussels. The so-called hunger march on Brussels, aimed at pressuring the government into taking action, turned into a huge fiasco. The march was announced three or four days in advance and the police had ample time to take measures against the protest action.

Even though this period saw attempts to organise workers' resistance, it is obvious that the resistance was far from widespread enough to worry the established powers.

The All-Liberal Government of Rogier and Frère-Orban (1847) and the Revolutionary Events of 1848

It has been pointed out before that King Leopold had always been intent on making any government subservient to his ambitions and that he strongly opposed the concept of political parties. Up to 1847, he had always been able to appoint servile, politically mixed governments. So it was a bitter disappointment for him when after Liberal Party's election victory he was forced to accept a strong one-party cabinet headed by Rogier, a man he personally disliked. Moreover, this government was intent on realising the 1846 liberal party programme. The halcyon days of Unionist governments at the service of the king were clearly over.

The Liberal program included several anti-clerical policies, especially a controversial one on education. The liberals wanted to end the clerical grip on education. The state would use its constitutional rights to give public schools the means to compete with their Catholic counterparts. The clergy's control over public education had to be abolished since it interfered with the constitutional freedom of speech and opinion. The Liberals also wanted to get rid of the 'reactionary' 1842 electoral district and municipal laws. The democratic wing within the party had made sure a lower electoral tax was part of the government programme. Despite the objections of the social-conservative wing, the proposal was to bring the tax down to its constitutional minimum. The programme even included some vague intentions about improving the plight of the working class, another concession towards the radicals. But the government had barely been sworn in, let alone started to put the programme into practice, when it had to face the revolutionary events of 1848; it reacted quite adequately.

The Parisian revolution broke out in February 1848 and panic soon spread to all of Europe's bourgeois and conservative regimes. The fires of revolution fanned out to Vienna, Rome, Berlin, Naples and other big cities, and Belgium at first also appeared to be a likely target. A number of the preconditions seemed to be present, at least. The activities of the people's associations were mentioned earlier, and even though the 1846 hunger march on Brussels had been a failure, it had shown that the movement had a good following among craftsmen. The intellectual democrats were also very active and the support of the disenfranchised petty bourgeoisie had boosted their position within the Liberal Party. The Liberal Congress had already been forced to accept some of their demands and in the Brussels Alliance, the progressive wing was so strong that it caused a split within the local party structure. These democrats also had close relations with the leaders of the working class resistance and set up contacts with exiled German socialists and democrats active in Brussels around 1845, including Karl Marx and Friedrich Engels. In November 1847, all these groups decided to cooperate and they founded the '*Association Démocratique*' – the Democratic Association, with representatives of all the subgroups of the democratic movement at that time. So by 1848, the democrats had a structural organisation that could take charge of a possible revolution and they had active branches in the capital and several provincial cities.

The February revolution in Paris, which abolished the monarchy and founded a leftist republic, still took the Belgian democrats by surprise. Hard-line revolutionary ideas were hardly characteristic of them, after all. The intellectuals and some working class leaders shied back from violence and few wanted to follow the example of the Parisian revolt. But the French revolution itself made their minds up for them. A group of fiercely republican, exiled Belgians formed a 'Belgian legion' to liberate the nation. Belgian revolutionaries had to create disorder wherever they could to prepare for the invasion of the legion. Revolution would surely follow and a democratic republic would be established.

That was counting without Belgium's state forces. The so-called legion that entered Belgium at the border commune of Risquons-Tout soon was a legion no more. The revolt in Belgium was little more than a few scuffles in cities. There were a number of riots in Brussels, but the police soon had the troublemakers under control. Ghent knew more trouble, especially because of the involvement of workers. But there too, the revolt turned into a republican defeat. The Belgian army easily controlled any attempt at revolt, be it in Flanders, Hainaut or on the French border. It became clear that the democratic movement had been unable to sway the proletarian masses, even during this crucial period, making the intervention of the security forces all the easier. A smart government policy took care of the rest.

The social-conservative rulers had anticipated that the winds of revolution would in all probability also batter Belgium. Despite their ideological differences, the Liberals and Catholics closed ranks and, under a Liberal government, they prepared to break any revolutionary resistance. Neighbourhood militias were reinstated in many cities to protect the bourgeoisie's property. The army prepared for war and Prime Minister Rogier imposed special economic measures, including a supplementary tax and a government loan to avoid a shutdown of industry and dangerous mass unemployment.

The government also approved a series of semi-democratic reforms that went further than the Liberal program in an attempt to rob the radicals of any support at the low end of the middle class. The electoral tax was brought to the constitutional minimum in the entire country, just about doubling the urban electorate. It was a clever move, since the idea of broadening the electoral base was the only issue that united the disenfranchised petty bourgeoisie and the democrats. Meeting this demand weakened the radicals and lost them part of their support group. In another concession, the government abolished the levy on newspapers, which improved the integration of the new electorate. The Liberal cabinet also ruled that anyone who held public office could no longer be a legislator, yet another of the democratic demands. The many civil servants and magistrates who had occupied the benches of the Chamber and the Senate until then had always been the mainstay of conservative policy. On top of all those measures, Rogier also abolished the conservative 1842 laws. Overall, this progressive policy pleased many a moderate progressive and lured them away from the democratic movement. In the end, only a hard core of revolutionaries was left and they were unable to initiate and lead the resistance by themselves. The existing order was kept in place because of this lack of impetus in the democratic movement and because of the feeling of goodwill created by the government in those circles of the urban middle class that until then had always been denied a say in politics as a result of the high electoral tax.

For the democrats, 1848 turned into a disaster. Their support, on the rise before 1848, dwindled to a minimum. The petty bourgeoisie turned its back on them; he social-progressive anti-clericals were scared off by the republican and revolutionary ideals; the events of 1848 themselves proved that the ideals of the democrats lacked in appeal and could not mobilise the working classes. The radical minority soon lost the little power it held and the movement only survived for a few months beyond February 1848.

The Liberal Party emerged victorious. The government was strengthened and was enjoyed the confidence of the whole parliament. The solidarity among the social-conservative forces was also tightened. The new elections that were called – made necessary because of the new electoral tax rates – were dominated by the battle between conservatives and democratic republicans. The result was that the Liberal Party made substantial gains, strengthening the Rogier-Frère-Orban government after 1848. Moreover, it had proved the soundness of the parliamentary regime and secured the monarchy, which even swayed King Leopold. The conservative European powers looked on in admiration. Gone were the last question marks whether Belgium belonged among the established nations of Europe. In other words, the consolidation of the Belgian state was completed.

Freedom of Language, Gallicisation and the Resistance of Language Lovers

Even though the language problem was hardly the centre of interest before 1850, a short overview of language policy is appropriate here.

The early years held few clues that Belgium would later be dominated by the divisive Dutch-French language issue. The ruling classes in Flanders, Brussels and Wallonia all spoke French. In Flanders, Dutch was spoken only by the disenfranchised. French had become the preferred language of the ruling classes in Flanders during the 18th-century Austrian period and the French rule had obviously reinforced this. French as a language of culture and social interaction became a status symbol and a sure way to adopt the social and cultural airs of the aristocracy, high bourgeoisie and intelligentsia. For the Flemish bourgeoisie and upper middle class it was a vehicle for social promotion. Flanders' native language was pushed down the social ladder to the majority of the population – lower middle class, farmers and workers. During the Dutch interlude, King William was unable to reverse the decline of Dutch in the upper classes and his language policy was firmly opposed in the South, in Brussels, and even in some frenchified Flemish circles. Belgian revolutionaries used the language issue to canvas support against the Dutch.

It was a *fait accompli* that French would become the ruling language in the fledgling nation, keeping in mind the social background of the leading circles. It took the new rulers only a few months to start pushing through measures that effectively turned French into the sole official language, also in Flanders, even though constitutionally there was a freedom of language. The revolutionaries argued that Dutch, as spoken in Flanders, was a mere dialect while French, as an established language of culture, was superior and thus deserved its pre-eminent position. A bilingual status would endanger Belgium's unity. Dutch would continue to be tolerated as part of Flemish regionalism and particularism, and the francophone rulers were also prepared to show their goodwill towards writers who wanted to use Dutch as a standard language. Any further concessions were out of the question. Throughout Belgium, including Flanders, the state would only employ speakers of French.

Brussels, Belgium's political and financial centre, was instrumental in spreading the francophone spirit. Ahead of the revolution, as an unofficial capital, Brussels had already been a major administrative centre with a lot more speakers of French than the other cities of Flemish Brabant. The Dutch King William had been unable to counter the trend, and Brussels showed a very distinctive language situation in 1830. French was more prevalent in the capital than elsewhere in Flanders and the seeds of bilingualism were already present. After 1830, a battalion of civil servants, especially in education and administration, made sure French would rule in the capital and also on the communal level elsewhere. The arrival of Walloons and foreign intellectuals (the liberal state was very attractive for intellectuals) further reinforced the trend.

The only systematic resistance against the language regime came from two groups of Flemish writers. Both of these groups were very involved in the issue of the language problem. Ghent was the centre of an academic, Flemish literary circle, which included Jan-Frans Willems. Most of them had started their literary career ahead of the revolution, in an environment beneficial to Dutch-language intellectuals. A group of writers from Antwerp, who were generally much younger, had never known such a advantageous situation. Hendrik Conscience and Theodoor Van Rijswijck belonged to Flanders' artistic, bohemian intelligentsia. The fact that these writers wrote in Dutch (philological studies and novels) turned them into founders of the Flemish movement. They made sure Dutch survived as a cultural language in Belgium at a time when successive governments sought the complete gallicisation of Flanders.

The writers had little or no political impact however, mainly because of their lowly social background. Most of them, even the academics, were autodidacts and the gallicised bourgeoisie looked down upon Flemish writers. It did not help that some of them had tentatively (and logically) backed the Orangeists. They could not possibly become an electoral force since most of their middle class supporters fell outside the financial voting criteria. Those who did make it to the ballot box had usually been gallicised along the way.

They could not and would not count on the working class either. The writers approached the Flemish language issue from a petty bourgeois angle and few made a link between the dire economic conditions in Flanders and the language question. For them, there was no connection between the social issue and the Flemish movement. During the 1848 revolt e.g., they backed the king. They also totally underestimated the Catholic anti-clerical polarisation gaining in importance during the 1840s, and continued to believe in a third, Flemish party to fight for their linguistic rights. But since the writers could count on little support beyond the Dutch-speaking petty bourgeoisie and middle class in a few cities, their party was bound to fail at the ballot box and as such was completely discounted by the major parties. Even their efforts to set up a partisan newspaper were doomed.

There was one constructive contribution to the Flemish Movement, however: the 1840 petition to demand that Dutch be used, alongside French, in Flemish schools, courthouses and administration. The action was a success, in part because it was backed by some Catholics and part of the lower clergy, among whom canon David, central figure of the traditionalist Flemish-minded in Leuven. The petition received ample press coverage and it put the Flemish demands in the public forum, ensuring a climate in a few regional elections that made certain demands admissible. In Antwerp and East Flanders, the provincial councils approved the use of Dutch alongside French in provincial administration. But the first generation of 'flamingants' had little else to show for their efforts.

Early on, the Flemish movement was remarkably moderate in nature. It respected the Belgian institutions and took care not to criticise the new state. It relied on peaceful means (brochures, petitions, leaflets) to get the attention of the government and then politely requested intervention. Their demands were far from extreme in the context of the time, and they left an important role for French in Flanders. When the francophone ruling classes retorted with outright rejections, it fanned the fires of a much more radical flamingantism. It was clear that the language issue had the potential to become a serious political conflict in its own right. The social-political relations were about to change thoroughly in the second half of the 19th century, allowing the Flemish movement to earn its place in the political arena.

Chapter II

The Triumph of Liberalism (ca. 1850-1884)

The revolt of 1848 had failed to fundamentally change Belgian politics. If anything, the existing form of government had drawn strength from the crisis. The strategy of the Liberal government did, however, ensure that new sections of the population entered into the political forum. It would take much of the 1850s and 1860s to absorb them into the existing party structures, via different political channels.

After 1848, there was no stopping industrial capitalism, on both economic and social levels. Political liberalism followed in its wake. It would dominate Belgian politics for almost three decades and it took some time for Belgium's political structure to adapt. The 1852 election victory was not impressive enough to force king Leopold into appointing a second consecutive one-party Liberal government. After the 1848 revolutions, the right was on the rise through much of Europe, and the economic slump of the 1850s reinforced the trend, allowing the king to use this rightist climate. The unionist Liberal Henri de Brouckère (1852-1855) and the Catholic centrist politician De Decker (1855-1857) both led governments that much resembled the unionist cabinets of the early years. They turned much of the 1850s into a transitional period.

That all changed in 1857 when the Liberal Party won 70 out of 108 seats in parliamentary elections. Two years later, they also had a majority in the senate. The triumph of political liberalism would continue until 1884. Rogier and Frère-Orban jointly led a Liberal government until 1867 and Frère-Orban headed a second liberal cabinet until 1870. Even during the Catholic intermezzo from 1870 until 1878, the governments of Jules d'Anethan and Jules Malou barely deviated from the social and economic course laid down by the Frère-Orban and Rogier cabinets. Economic liberalism and the political principles of capitalism became the anchors of society, and once the bourgeoisie had laid down the political fundaments of the capitalist system, the Catholics and anti-clericals became bitter enemies again and there would even be a kind of ideological civil war during the 1879-1884 liberal government of Frère-Orban and Van Humbeeck.

Economic and Social Changes

The most fundamental changes were to be seen on an economic level. Belgium became a major player on the world market and was able to compete with the greatest industrial giants. The textile industry increased production between 300 and 800 %. Ghent's 1873 cotton exports were three and a half times as high as in 1845. Verviers' wool-washing industry used seven times as much raw material in 1870 as three decades earlier. New industrial sectors, including the linen, shoe and clothing industry, were mechanised in record time.

Heavy industry thrived because of the heavy demand for machines and train and tram rails. Mechanisation processes were refined, and production boomed. The output of the coal industry increased eightfold between 1830 and 1880. The figures for cast iron were even more staggering: an increase of 1400 % between 1850 and 1870. The Cockerill company made Belgium the main producer of machines and railway engines. Vielle Montagne became a major player in the zinc industry and Belgium produced a quarter of the world's glass. The arms production facilities around Liège were among Europe's biggest. By the end of the 1860s, mass production of cheap bessemer steel and soda production began to flourish. In the most important industries, Belgium could claim the biggest per capita production of the continent. The feverish industrial expansion was export-driven and cheap labour gave Belgium an important competitive edge on the international markets, also outside Europe.

Dividends of up to 40 % were not unheard of and the select group of investment capitalists who had already created their industrial empire ahead of 1850 earned amazing profits. Between 1850 and 1872 the value of Société Générale's stock and investment portfolio rose to 77.2 million francs, compared to 11.6 million francs for the Banque de Belgique. New, rival captains of industry entered the field and fought each other tooth and nail and only the strongest, smartest and boldest survived, founding new empires. Belgium's industrial class created a long list of heroes – Victor Tesch and Gustave Boëll (steel), Eduard Empain (tram company), Evence Coppée (coal), Ernest Solvay (soda), E. Otlet and S. Philippart (railways), and Andre Langrand-Dumonceau (insurance), all of them models for the new generation of industrial and financial capitalists, who would often establish new Belgian holdings. Small family firms and individual capitalists were forced to give way to bigger companies in the increasing trend for concentration of capital. This trend was fuelled by the massive breakthrough of stocks in limited companies as a prime investment.

Despite strong fluctuations in the markets, influenced by wars in Europe (Crimean War, Italian and German unification), it was generally fairly easy to find buyers for the increasing production. Until 1873, there was even a long industrial expansion, only interrupted by a few brief but serious slumps. The 1871-1873 period provided one last boom. The United States was going west and needed all the steel it could get for its rail network. The economy went into a slump afterwards, creating an industrial crisis that would last into the 1890s, also in other countries.

By that time, industry had already eclipsed farming as the driving force of the economy. Agriculture accounted for half the gross national product in 1846 before sagging to 39 % in 1866 and 29 % in 1880. It did not stop the landowners from cashing in on the economic boom, though. Agricultural prices hit their peak in between 1866 and 1878, and especially wheat reaped great profits. But imports, among others from the United States, started to swamp the domestic market and created a farm crisis that would hit the sector hard in the final quarter of the century.

Small, marginal farmers were still living in very difficult circumstances. Many were reduced to seasonal labour on big farms, factory work or stints in the underpaid cottage industry to earn the major part of their income. The rural depopulation continued and the migrating masses settled in the cities and industrial centres, sometimes doubling the population. The highest concentrations were found in Liège and Hainaut. The population increase in and around Charleroi and the Centre region was 4.5 to 5.5 times the national average.

The definitive breakthrough of industrial capitalism obviously also had its effect on other social levels. Huge fortunes were made and the increase of personal property was striking. From 1861 to 1873, the patent taxes that industrial companies had to pay rose by 52 %. Patent taxes on holding companies accounted for a quarter of the total and some 400 limited companies or corporations brought in as much profit as 20 % of all real estate income. As the industrial bourgeoisie amassed its newfound riches, it was welcomed into the highest circles of the nation.

The aristocratic landowners saw which way the new wind was blowing and many put their money in the banking, credit and insurance sectors. The landowners merged with the bourgeoisie, even at a social level. In the 1860s and 1870s, the Catholics sought to break the monopoly of the liberal bankers and created a universal, Catholic financial powerhouse. Capitalism had to be 'christened'.

The most remarkable figure in Belgium to eye the capital of Catholic conservatives, among whom there were many farmers and small owners, was the up-and-coming André Langrand-Dumonceau, founder of the Royale Belge. He built his financial empire on very shaky, some might say fraudulent, grounds. When it went bankrupt, several Catholic politicians, board members of Langrand-Dumonceaux' companies, were dragged down with it, making it one of the biggest financial scandals of this era – and financial catastrophe, corruption and fraud were hardly unusual at the time. Few made it to the top and competition was ruthless in a world dominated by stock speculation and a ceaseless drive for higher dividends and profits. The capitalist system was dominated by the very few at the top and it was next to impossible to move up the ladder from the lower social ranks.

Joining the middle class or the petty bourgeoisie was a more realistic aim. Their ranks swelled because industrial capitalism could not survive on cheap labour alone. It also needed a solid framework of professional specialists, including managerial staff, technicians, civil servants, trained clerks, teachers, doctors, lawyers, etc. The expanding cities boosted the retail trade while the increasing wealth of the high bourgeoisie created several specialised craft businesses and firms. There is not much information available yet about the precise economic and social expansion of the petty bourgeoisie and middle classes during this period. The following figures are characteristic, though, and indicative of this expansion: the intellectual professions flourished, and within the electoral corps, their representation grew far quicker than the average from 1864 onwards, clearly showing a significant increase in wealth. Research shows that in Ghent, 60 % of the new voters for the 1848 elections were craftsmen, innkeepers and retail traders. Almost 30 % were employees, civil servants, doctors and lawyers. Obviously, industrial capitalism was instrumental in creating and developing this heterogeneous 'helping' class. There was a sense of upward mobility and soon this growing class tried to turn its social dynamism into political action.

In stark contrast, the situation of the industrial proletariat could not be more different. Much of the working class had been uprooted from the rural areas and once the workers arrived in the city, they only added to the pool of cheap and willing labour. In the coal and metal industry, employment doubled in between 1830 and 1860. The steel industry's workforce quadrupled between 1846 and 1872. Both industries attracted the surrounding agrarian 'overpopulation' and, because of cheap rail transport, an eager labour force from further away, in Flanders. This surplus of unskilled labour led to sharp competition among the workers. When there was a slump in the demand for labour, a disastrous crisis for the working class followed. The workers became part of the machinery, as easily replaced as nuts and bolts, and forced to keep up with the pace of the wheels of industry. A worker was socially isolated and ostracised by the rest of society. Belgium quickly became a paradise for industrial moguls because the nation met two key preconditions for getting much richer much quicker – working hours were extremely long (between 12 and 14 hours) and pay was extremely low. Any economic crisis hit the worker rather than the employer and enormous fluctuations in pay, in tune with market conditions, always left the worker unsure whether he or she would be able to earn the bare necessities.

The number of women and children working increased steadily; even in the mines, they were put to work for, on average, a third of the normal pay. Unlimited, underpaid women and child labour obviously drove the pay level down even further, making it an absolutely necessary addition to the family income in order to escape hunger and misery. Even a 'well-to-do' labourer spent up to 85% of his income on elementary needs. The system of paying in kind and forcing the workers to spend their money in certain shops were well-established means of ensuring that part of the miserly pay flowed back into the coffers of the employer. The working class was crammed in grimy urban slums, in dank and smelly tenements where half of the families only had a single room that lacked the most elementary sanitary facilities. The working class was undernourished and life expectancy hovered around 45 years. An already high mortality rate was driven further upwards by industrial accidents and occupational diseases. This vast majority of the population, working in deplorable circumstances and unhealthy buildings, was economically and socially oppressed and exploited by industrial capitalism, driven by the bourgeoisie.

The domestic worker in the cottage industry was possibly in an even worse situation. The overwhelming majority worked in Flanders' towns and villages where they produced clothing, lace and leather. The old-fashioned domestic workers increasingly faced industrial competition and were forced to work ever longer hours for ever less money. They were also part of the fairly homogeneous working class, living on the edge of total poverty. Looking at the living standards of the working class over many centuries, it can be said that it had never sunk lower than during this phase of the industrial revolution.

The Liberal Party's Economic and Social Policies

This economic and social evolution led to a political change of course. The bourgeoisie became the one and only power, with an ideology to match supporting and justifying Liberalism's position of power. The thoughts and acts of the liberal citizen were ruled by an irresistible, optimistic belief in progress, the prime principle being the perfectibility of humankind. Industrial labour was its driving force, and individualism, autonomy and creativity were the guidelines. As such, there was, on the one hand, a unity of thought and action, and on the other hand the everyday practice of industrial, commercial, managerial activity, in which the final product was dependent on rational pragmatism. Rationalisation of bourgeoisie life was the consequence.

An absolute and unlimited right to property was deemed natural and had to justify the unquestionable claims to ownership. This philosophy of progress was based on extreme individualism, the recognition of the struggle-for-life principle and the survival of the fittest. This also justified cutthroat competition between individuals. Economic liberalism was turned into a scientific principle and economic success and the matching bourgeois values into virtues. These were part of a consistent liberal ideology, which also dominated the social climate. The classic liberal wage theory never took into account whether pay would cover the most essential needs of the worker. The relationship between capital and labour was the only norm, exclusively based on the laws of supply and demand. Labour was assessed on the basis of its usefulness only, just like any other economic value or product.

Obviously, the liberal bourgeoisie refused to take any responsibility for the increasing poverty of the working class. For them, it had nothing to do with the ruling power structure, or with the social-economic relations that they had created. This entailed a moral approach to social problems. By elevating economic success to the highest good, it became acceptable to consider the working class as morally, socially and culturally inferior. People without morals, inherently lazy and stupid deserved no better lot in life. The ideology only encouraged their shameless contempt for the working class and such considerations allowed the liberal bourgeoisie to physically split up society along class lines and make sure there would not be any contact between high and low society. But this social segregation policy also underscored the bourgeoisie's fundamental fear for the proletariat. Because of their sheer numbers, the workers always were a potential threat to law and order. To counter this, social control was tightened by means of repression or paternalism, both seemingly adequate measures.

In a sense, it did not really matter whether the ruling class was religious or church-going or not. Since capital had been christened and the bourgeoisie was the sole ruler, the Church aligned itself closely with this new wealthy class and counted on it for its financial security. The Church became a willing accomplice in prolonging the division of power between capital and labour. Religiousness was an asset for the worker; this was something on which almost everyone agreed – from hard-core Roman Catholics, over less committed members of the Church to the anti-clerical bourgeoisie. This should not be too surprising, with a view to the Church's social ideology at that time, as it can be seen in Belgian missionary projects. Wealth was seen as the result of such virtues as diligence and frugality. It was considered a sign of God's special blessing and elevated the rich to God's privileged class. Benevolent charity and alms were part of the obligations of this class. Poverty too was the work of nature and, hence, of God. Workers were told to subject themselves to God's will and suffer their lot, as the rewards of heaven were awaiting them. In the meantime, the worker was told to toil hard and provide as much as possible for the family. Such teachings did take a certain degree of neediness into account, and it was considered part of the spiritual harmony and interdependency between rich and poor. Against the background of this social philosophy, which relied heavily on charity, the conservative Catholic C. Woeste uttered the following characteristic words during a parliamentary debate on social policy: "Gentlemen, we need the poor. How can we fulfil our duty of charity otherwise?" In as many ways, the worker was told to respect property. The social hierarchy had to be respected since it was part of the natural order

God had imposed. Exploitation, including child labour, long hours and exhausting work, were all considered regrettable but unavoidable.

Just as much as there was a consensus on the suppression of the working class, all of the ruling classes agreed on the role of parliament and the state in the establishment of a free-market economy. The state was mainly restricted to regulating the economy and had to intervene when bourgeois interests came under threat. It also had to assist in the search for new markets, in creating a good trade and investment climate, in keeping the national currency healthy, and in providing an efficient transport network of roads, canals and railroads. It took a centralised system with an efficient bureaucracy to meet these challenges financially and technically. On the other hand, the state had to refrain from any action that could impede the development of capitalism. On social issues, it took a hands-off approach and never intervened on wage policies or labour conditions. The efficiency of the civil parliament, the judicial basis of which had already been laid down in 1831, was also measured with a view to the aforementioned principles. During debates, in which the economic interests of different bourgeois groups clashed, big business and the representatives of financial, industrial and commercial capitalism forged compromises to serve their common good. Employers' interests were defended through acceptance or rejection of bills. Securing these interests was often a very direct process since a great many captains of industry held a parliamentary mandate, apart from prominent defenders of liberal policy from the so-called 'helping' class (such as lawyers). In 1870, no less than five of the seven Société Générale directors held a parliamentary seat or a ministerial portfolio.

It mattered little whether a one-party Liberal government or a Liberal-Catholic coalition ruled since the economic interests of the bourgeoisie always came first. That was evident as soon as the first Liberal government of Rogier-Frère (1847-1852) took office. It was during the revolutionary months of 1848 that the government started putting its committed liberal economic program into practice. The big banks, especially Société Générale, were in trouble and the government wanted to lend a helping hand. Because of its policy to invest long-term in Belgium's industry, Société Générale could not cope when worried people wanted to withdraw their money during the political crisis. The government allowed the bank extra issuing possibilities and came to its aid. It also imposed a fixed exchange rate, which avoided a slump in the value of the franc. The creation of a national currency issuing house in 1850, the National Bank of Belgium, was a logical consequence of government policy. It allowed the conventional banks to fully focus on their industrial and commercial activities without being slowed down by currency-issuing distractions.

The government was also trying to get the economy back on its feet after the 1846-1849 slump. Rogier and Frère-Orban extended public works spending to jumpstart the economy. It was yet another illustration of the liberal state's regulatory role. The reactions of the establishment were strong, though, once the financial implications became clear. They proved that the bourgeois basis of parliament was not yet strong enough to unconditionally support liberal policy. To ensure the State's aid to capitalism, Frère-Orban wanted to tap a new source of income: inheritances. The landowners protested, causing a government crisis and forcing new Senate elections. Little was left of Frère-Orban's original plans when he settled for a 1 % inheritance tax. It was still too early to speak of an absolute liberal economic reign during the Frère-Orban years, but the success of his policies already contrasted sharply with the Liberals' political weakness prior to 1848.

Even if the 1852-1857 centre-right governments failed to turn back the political clock, they were able to slow the pace of liberal economic innovations. They did help tear down the walls of protectionism. From 1852 to 1856, the differential rights were further dismantled and bilateral deals with Britain, the Netherlands and France greatly reduced the burden of tolls and levies. The new liberal power elite would truly emerge in 1857, when Rogier and Frère-Orban led a one-party Liberal government and were able to turn the aspirations of the bourgeoisie into laws and government policy. The Catholic Liberals d'Anethan and Malou continued in the same vein from 1871 to 1878 and were more than equal to the task of promoting industrial liberalism. Frère-Orban then led another Liberal government until 1884.

Foreign trade was the key area for liberal policy. It has been pointed out before that Belgium's domestic market was too limited for the expansive industrial production, and that the signing of trade agreements was crucial. Free-trade principles were on the rise throughout industrial Europe, and so Belgium was able to sign toll agreements with its main trading partners: with France in 1861, Britain in 1862, the Zollverein and the Netherlands in 1863. The main drawback was that Belgium had little negotiating leverage as a small industrial nation. Bigger states with wider markets were able to invest more and work with larger quantities. In other words: the major European powers were able to use economic cooperation as a political negotiating chip.

Belgian foreign policy offered plenty of examples, among them the Franco-Belgian relations during the reign of Napoleon III. The emperor had dreams of annexing the kingdom to the north and using the Belgian economy was part of that plan. Britain made sure, however, that Belgium would not sign trade agreements that compromised its political independence. After Napoleon III failed in his attempt to annex the Grand Duchy of Luxembourg in 1867-1868, he tried to turn Belgium into France's economic satellite. With government backing, the French Compagnie de l'Est tried to buy the rail company of the Belgian province of Luxemburg. It would have given the French control over the transport network in Belgium's southern industrial belt. In the end, France backed off. It faced the threat of British opposition and was unwilling to risk a conflict with Belgium at a time when Franco-German relations were already extremely tense. But the incident proved that Belgium was only able to formulate its own foreign trade policy thanks to the game of balancing and counterbalancing the forces of international relations.

On the domestic economic front, protectionism was a thing of the past. Road tolls and municipal tolls on food were abolished in 1867. Four years earlier, with the financial aid of neighbouring nations, Belgium had been able to pay off the Dutch into relinquishing their right to levy shipping charges on the river Scheldt. Import duties were further reduced in 1858 and 1865. Successive governments set up a stable currency system and helped develop the Belgian credit sector with the creation of the *Gemeentekrediet-Crédit Communal* and the ASLK-CGER (General Savings and Annuity Fund) in 1865. But the major victory of economic liberalism was the reform of the Code of Commerce. With a series of laws between 1867 and 1872, the stock exchanges were fully de-regularised and an 1872 law lifted government control over corporations or limited companies. Such a company no longer needed government approval for its foundation. Expectations were that the mandatory publication of company bylaws, composition of the board and annual results would be sufficient to protect investors against fraud. Shares in the social capital were still to be declared on establishing the company, but only 5% of the amount needed to be actually deposited. In short, there was a fertile climate for the unbridled growth of limited companies in the industrial, commercial and financial sectors. But this stripped-down legislation played into the hands of swindlers who would often defraud unwitting investors.

The liberal principles also applied to the development of infrastructure and governments were more than willing to work hand in hand with private initiative. As soon as the state had constructed Belgium's core infrastructure and profits were about to be reaped in railway construction, it gave the private companies plenty of concessions to run the network. By 1870, three-quarters of the rail network had been taken over by private enterprise. The tariff war in the transit trade between public and private lines was always disadvantageous for state lines. Furthermore, the state took over railway lines operating at a loss and it bought up lines from companies that were in financial difficulties, such as the one owned by the reckless industrialist Philippart. At the state acquisition in 1873, the principle was that it should not affect the interests of other private companies. Such a government policy obviously had a negative impact on state finances and the national debt started to grow.

The social policies of the Liberal governments were also fully geared towards the wealthy industrialists and investors. Any right of the economically weak was ignored in this system. No-nonsense, non-intervention policies in the wage and price sectors were the order of the day. An 1878 parliamentary bill, seeking to set a minimum age for child labour and ease the conditions of women's labour, was rejected in the name of freedom. Over the years, the ruling classes had perfected their system of social control and the working class was held in a suffocating grip of restrictive laws. No measure was more effective than the so-called 'labour logbook'. It was provided by the municipal authorities and any employer could claim it on taking on a worker. Anyone who did not suffer the boss's whims lost his 'labour logbook' or was given a negative evaluation. In both cases, the consequences were disastrous. The 'labour logbook' turned out to be an ideal tool to stifle any individual revolt.

The Civil Code allowed the employers additional ways to suppress the workers. The notorious article 1781 simply stated that in case of wage disputes the employer would be taken at his word; the worker, on the other hand, had to provide hard evidence. On top of that, the employer chaired the special council that had to settle such disputes, and carried the deciding vote. There was a ban on setting up unions until 1866. In theory, the ban also applied to employers but they realised that a common approach to wages and working conditions was essential in controlling the labour market. The ban was replaced by article 310, which guaranteed freedom of labour and punished anything endangering this right to work or any form of intimidation. So, in theory at least, there was a right to strike in 1866. It made no difference in practice, however, since prosecution and conviction were ensured on other grounds from then on. The anti-strike tactics of the security forces also remained ruthless after 1866. To discourage any union activity, they seized strike funds and imprisoned their leaders. The state police and, if necessary, even the army were called in as soon as the great masses joined in protest action. Police brutality made sure that any attempt at labour resistance was smothered early on. Some strikers paid for resistance with their lives at shootings during strikes.

The Belgian liberal regime also provided a number of examples of social segregation policies, employed by the bourgeoisie both on private and government levels. They were complementary to keeping social control. Even though research into this has only just started, much can be derived from documents on housing and urbanisation policies, both by the government and by the private sector. Urbanisation projects had bourgeois interests at heart as a rule. The fearful bourgeois always had to be protected from the proletarian masses. Class differences became increasingly acute in the urban structure and real estate speculation drove the poor further into decrepit and crowded neighbourhoods, without any form of compensation. Urban improvement plans, which could be characterised as the battle of the bourgeoisie against the dangerous contamination by the paupers, victimised many workmen as well. The poor were forced from the tenements and driven into even worse urban ghettos, again without compensation, resulting in the spatial segregation of the economically weak and strong. At the same time, the bourgeoisie settled into leafy, residential areas far removed from the squalor of the poor. They built large boulevards that became urban segregation lines.

Language also was a great divider, as has been pointed out earlier, and the use of French reinforced social divisions and fostered segregation. According to statistics, the process of gallicisation did not increase spectacularly in either Brussels or Flanders; actually, there was a status quo in Brussels. In all probability, also this language situation can be seen as evidence of the civil segregation policy. The bourgeoisie had used French for years and, at a certain stage, it had no interest in further stimulating the use of the language among the lower classes. The high bourgeoisie limited such social linguistic promotion to the middle classes.

Cultural segregation, finally, added to the huge social gap and even leisure was class-ridden. Alcohol abuse was rife among the workers and although popular entertainment existed, there was no connection whatsoever with such bourgeois entertainment as opera, theatre and concerts, or the comforts of the private club. In other words, socio-economic inequality and segregation of classes pervaded all structures of society and every physical and mental aspect of daily life.

The Labour Movement

The widespread exploitation of the working class created totally different types resistance in comparison with early socialism. New groups and new leaders, new ideologies and new organisations came to the fore. The following evolution can be distilled from existing literature.

The misery industrial capitalism created and the economic crises spawned ever more anger and wild, uncoordinated resistance increased significantly. In 1861, some 15,000 Walloon workers went on strike; in 1862 they kept up a strike for one and a half weeks. But any action ran into the solid wall of the law and order apparatus. The army shot to kill during the repression of the protest actions and, in the end, hunger finished off any remaining resistance. Initially, there was no link between the protest groups, the urban crafts proletariat and the radical intellectuals of the 1840s. And even though the events of 1848 had decimated their ranks, a hard core of those intellectuals had persevered. From 1852, a French contingent of political exiles fleeing the reign of Napoleon III joined this group. At about the same time, the radical intellectuals lured several young Belgian university students (H. Denis, G. De Greef, E. Hins and C. De Paepe) to their meetings. They won the workers' respect and as new leaders, they started spreading the anarchist ideology of Proudhon. Future society would be based on a series on autonomous, interconnecting ‘communes’ that rejected any supervisory state structure, which was considered a part of bourgeois society. The ideology lacked collectivist notions and the working class had to free itself from capitalism by setting up production and consumer cooperatives and organisations of mutual support. Strikes to demand higher wages were condemned and considered useless since they only drove up prices.

Anti-capitalist craftsmen who wanted to mobilise the working class and set up strong labour organisations to promote socialism sought cooperation with the intellectuals. Some of them (N. Coulon, J. Pellering) even experimented with production cooperatives during the years 1849-1853. The experiments failed for lack of capital, reinforcing the conviction that the revolutionary energy of the labour force was better used for social revolt, and was wasted on setting up organisations. Others (e.g. D. Brismée) preferred to set up strong labour organisations that relied on internal cooperation to improve life in the short term.

Such a strategy gained more support than the revolutionary one. Workers joined professional organisations to demand better wages and help each other out. The mechanical spinners and weavers of Ghent each created their own union in 1857 and were not only the first to recruit among the factory proletariat, but also to dare go on strike to demand better conditions, while the craftsmen's associations generally respected the ban on strikes.

Politically conscious craftsmen and left-wing intellectuals started working together directly and organisationally. Because of the 1848 defeat and the centre-right governments in the 1850s, it was tough to set up an open and united political front. The resistance of the democrats was redirected and aimed at the Catholics. The issue of civil burials – indirectly politically important – became a rallying point. As a result of industrialisation, part of the working class was rejecting their religious beliefs. Someone working in industrialised, rationalised urban surroundings seemed to have fewer needs for religious activity, which was especially functional in an agricultural, rural society. Many workers could no longer live with a religion that preached the acceptance of misery. To make matters worse, the Church strongly identified itself with the oppressor. The Church's contempt for the worker was visible in the religious burial ceremony, which perpetuated social inequality in death, hence the demand for civil burials. The Church, and religion in general, were not only seen as an obstacle in the emancipation of the lower social classes but were also considered a capitalist tool to exploit the proletariat, preventing insight into just social relations.

All of this ensured that the Belgian labour movement was based on strident anti-clericalism and rationalism. The 1850s saw the emergence of the first associations of freethinkers, *L'Affranchissement* (1854) and *Les Solidaires* (1857), built on these principles. Their organisational role should not be underestimated. The groups recruited their members from craftsmen's associations and the lower middle class, which was living in social symbiosis with the former. In Brussels, the political discussion group *Le Peuple, association de la démocratie militante,* essentially an emanation of *Les Solidaires,* was founded in 1861 and became the cornerstone of the initial Belgian chapter of the First International.

The First International Working Men's Association (London, 1864) and its influence opened a new era in the Belgian labour movement. The foundation of the First International in Belgium was important for several reasons. First and foremost, it solidified the internal organisational structure of a permanent labour organisation. It also stimulated cooperation between intellectual study groups, professional labour organisations and the freethinkers. Organised resistance linked up, for the first time, with the uncoordinated resistance in industrial centres. Intellectual leaders like De Paepe, Hins, De Greef and Denis quickly realised that the greatest revolutionary potential could be found among the miners and factory proletariat, not among the dwindling groups of urban corporatist craftsmen. The leaders organised meetings, collected strike funds, sent representatives to strike meetings and their lawyers worked free of charge when strike leaders were taken to court.

Propaganda campaigns and the support for social revolt helped organise the labour movement. The Belgian members of the First International in London wanted to expand beyond Brussels and set up a regional network supervised by a central, national structure. By 1870, the First International had some 60,000 members in Belgium and had regional divisions in the most important industrial centres. The joining of existing professional workers' federations, health care associations, consumer cooperatives and the freethinkers accounted for much of the expansion. In Ghent, the unionised weavers and the labour federation *Vooruit* (Advance) joined in 1865 and laid the foundation of the city's dynamic socialist tradition; E. Moyson was the key figure there. The *Volksverbond* (People's Union), founded by F. Coenen among the craft proletariat, grouped Antwerp's labour action in 1867 and also joined the International; the *Volksverbond* also coordinated other existing activities. The International found strong backing in Liège province among the Verviers textile workers and in southern Belgium's industrial belt around Charleroi, and in the Centre and Borinage regions.

The first International did more than just develop the organisational structure of the Belgian labour movement. It also instilled class consciousness, helped in developing a strategy and promoted socialist ideology. Some Belgian former Proudhonists started backing Karl Marx and defending collectivist theories. Cesar De Paepe, the ideologist of Belgian socialism demanded the collectivisation of the nation's farmland, mines, ports, rail network, etc. The Proudhonists were still a majority, however, and anarchist ideology, as preached by Mikhail Bakunin, prevailed during the 1870s. Anarchism also propagated a system of independent basic cooperative cells, but unlike Marxism, did not call for central leadership. Marx first wanted a political battle to gain power and install a socialist society in which the means of production would be common property.

The Belgian branch of the First International went into decline as of 1872. Most members did not pay their fees, turning the International into a powerless bystander during strikes. Time and again, crises ruined the laboriously founded organisations; the labour movement had no tradition of long-term resistance. Their tactics – organise and strike only in case of a crisis – were ineffective and caused disappointment and mistrust. The organisational structure disintegrated during the economic crisis of 1873.

The bloody suppression of the 1871 Paris Commune and the split between anarchists and collectivists within the Central Council were cruel blows from which the First International never recovered, and the organisation slowly disintegrated during the 1870s. In Belgium too, the central structure collapsed and the movement was reduced to a number of local cells. The organisations of freethinkers played a fairly active role in keeping alive the little that was left.

During such desperate days of chaos and confusion – in the mid-1870s it was back to square one in some cities – social democracy seized the moment and started to fill the void. The reform movement made quick progress, especially in Flanders and the province of Brabant, and it started cooperating with the progressive wing of the Liberal Party. It would take until the 1880s and 1890s before this new socialism would dominate the labour movement, and as such, this phase in the Belgian labour movement will be treated in the next chapter.

Middle Class Social Progressiveness

Some bourgeois circles had an impact on the labour movement and a number of students and intellectuals formed an integral part of proletarian resistance. There was also some cooperation with social progressives. It was the result of a widespread political movement, active on several political levels during the 1860s, and best described as 'progressivism'.

The social changes within the petty bourgeoisie and middle class were the driving force behind the movement. The year 1848 had had a profound political impact on large parts of these social groups. A relatively large swath of the population, citizens in between the upper crust of society monopolising political power and the lower middle class, workers and the industrial proletariat, now held a numerical majority. The electorate in most cities had doubled and in some towns, two-thirds of the electorate were new voters. The time had come to mobilise this new political class. But as the constitutional borderline between voters and non-voters (electoral tax was 20 guilders, or 42 francs) was artificial, and hardly took into account the social class awareness of this middle class, there was room for expansion in the new protest movement, which also functioned outside the actual electorate, focusing on the lower levels of the middle classes. This disenfranchised class was seeking political recognition and there was only one way to get it – attack the ruling class. Young, smart and enterprising leaders rose from these layers of society and tried to turn social protest into political power.

It clearly was a comprehensive middle class protest movement, stressing the specific interests of the middle class in all sectors of society. On the one hand, this meant it was potentially a unitary movement that wanted to turn against the ruling powers; on the other hand this also implied that it was present at different political levels and took positions on existing conflicts: it had its own opinions on the powers of the monarch, state-church relations, language and social issues. These often clashed with government policy. In politics, the middle class was upwardly mobile and its political consciousness was evident in its social progressiveness, rationalism and pro-Flemish 'flamingantism'. Very outspoken in this social progressivism was that it was the key of a new movement which, though there were different factions with their own ideas on which aspects to stress, never lost sight of the overall goal and kept the ideological bond between the factions very tight.

Social progressivism developed a wide-ranging programme in the socio-economic sector. It did not question the fundamental principles of capitalism since private property and economic liberalism had allowed the middle class to thrive. They were even the most fervent backers of free trade, which was viewed as a way to undermine the privileges of the wealthy.

Another way to attack those privileges was the demand for a thorough tax reform, including the introduction of a progressive tax system dependent on wealth. Obviously, they also sought an extension of the right to vote. They refused to accept the concept that the upper crust of society automatically had to become its political elite too. They wanted their own class to become part of the political leadership. Through their education, they had intellectually joined the higher classes, and as such were ready to take up their place in the civil parliament. In view of their status as educated people they demanded voting rights based on education and rejected any electoral tax. It also explained their efforts to widen schooling and improve education.

On social politics, too, the ideas of the progressives clearly differed from conservative liberalism and they built bridges with the labour movement. Their motivation, however, was not always idealistic. Some progressives acted out of a sense of social justice to ease the plight of the working class. Others were more opportunistic and tried to use labour resistance to boost their own, petty bourgeois, ambitions. For the majority, socialism had to be kept at bay and the labour movement had to be controlled by a progressive bourgeois party. 'Peaceful progress' was the key principle in the social programme of the progressives. They claimed the worker was socially inferior because he was intellectually inferior. Democratic mandatory education had to do away with social injustice. As soon as the working class attained a higher cultural level and gained the respect of the bourgeoisie, it would be ready to become part of the political process. The progressives' demands for universal suffrage were thus always linked to the introduction of mandatory education.

Instead of class segregation, they backed integration which would ease the fears of the upper classes and avoid the workers turning into dangerous collectivists or anarchists. There were also purely humanitarian reasons to make sure that the working class became part and parcel of society. Political, social and cultural institutions had to become centres of reconciliation where civic virtues were taught. All those legal bans that only fuelled labour resistance had to be scrapped and the government had to abolish the most outrageous abuses. Women's and child labour had be strictly regulated, the notorious article 415 prohibiting coalition abandoned, the worker's logbook eliminated and cooperatives established. Those were the major principles of the social progressive philosophy.

Other demands of the progressives also flew in the face of the government and especially the monarchy. Leopold I died in 1865 and was succeeded by his son Leopold II. The change had no impact on foreign and military policy. Both monarchs considered the defence of Belgium's territory their main task. They thought the moral guarantee of the European powers to protect Belgium in exchange for neutrality woefully inadequate. Instead, the Belgian royals wanted an armed neutrality, backed by a strong defence. Rogier was among the many government officials backing the principle and the international situation of the 1860s argued in their favour. Europe's conservative power alliance had broken down in the wake of 1848 and it had upset the balance of power. It turned a small nation like Belgium into a soft target. The disappearance of small nations during the unification of Italy and Germany and Napoleon III's expansionist policy only added to the diplomatic unease. Royal and government circles also feared Belgium would be turned into a battleground in case of a Franco-German war.

So the king and government constantly pressured parliament into increasing the budget of the Ministry of War, expanding the army and building military fortifications. The progressive movement totally opposed those measures. It wanted to ease the tax burden and as such drastically reduce military expenses. The issue came to a head in Antwerp, where the government had planned to reinforce the ramparts. These ramparts, which would contain the expansion of the city, also threatened the local landowners' interests and they joined the protest of the progressives.

The progressive movement also contested the centralist principles of the king and government. They wanted far-reaching decentralisation and give more autonomy to the provinces and municipalities. Some progressives even wanted to turn Belgium into a republic to counter the authoritarian style of the monarchy. Indeed, Leopold II had picked up where his father had left off. The crown remained a conservative bulwark and showed its power whenever ministers had to be dismissed or appointed or whenever parliament had to be dissolved.

Without dismissing the important nuances within the group of progressives – on almost any point of action some were very moderate, while others took a much more radical view – it can be claimed that their demands were to be found in the programmes of the political associations founded by them over the years. The history of progressive organisations is a very complex one, which can hardly be discussed in full within the constraints of this book. The links between social progressivism and rationalism, between social progressivism and flamingantism and between social progressivism and the labour movement make it impossible to treat the movements separately. The general line of development sketched here is, as such, not limited to social progressivism, and will also incorporate the two other movements (rationalism and flamingantism).

Between 1848 and 1860, the movement was held back by a lack of political consciousness and organisational skills. Their petty bourgeois interests fell through the cracks of the classic conservative Catholic vs. anti-clerical liberal division. In many cities the progressive movement turned into a showdown of the Catholic and liberal lower middle and middle class against the ruling classes. Strong anti-militarist sentiments united these diverging forces in Antwerp and the Meeting Party was created in 1860. It won seats in municipal, provincial and national elections and three years later, it defeated the Rogier government. There were similar united progressive fronts in other cities, usually involving meetings in the propaganda campaigns.

Belgium's electoral system did not make life easy for these progressive groups. The political ground rules of the majority system favoured a two-party system and left little space for any third political group. Unless they won clear electoral majorities, they were forced into the role of pressure group within the two-party system. This was the choice of most of the progressives, without excluding common progressive actions for electoral purposes.

At the time, the anti-clerical Liberal Party seemed the naturalally of the pressure group since it also moved in urban anti-clerical circles and shared common ground on rationalist and liberal principles. At the same time though, some liberal Catholics groups, including *La Jeune Droite*, represented by such Catholic parliamentarians as A. Nothomb, J.B. Coosemans and, on occasion, J. Malou, also wanted to expand voting rights, if only to break the liberal hold on the cities by appealing to the masses that had remained Catholic. Within the Catholic 'legal country' they met the resistance of the entire social-conservative bloc of members of parliament, the court, the papal envoy and the bishops.

The progressives started to make headway from the mid-1860s onwards. They were very active at the Catholic congresses in Mechelen in 1863, 1864 and 1867. The Antwerp Meeting Party dumped its anti-clerical wing and evolved into an entirely Catholic party; during the 1864 government crisis, the Meeting Party became the focus of Belgian politics: the Catholic candidate prime minister A. Deschamps even tried to use the progressive movement for his own Catholic purposes, including some of its demands in the so-called 'Meeting Programme' of the government. As could be expected, the king rejected it. When the Catholic Jules d'Anethan ended 13 years of one-party liberal rule in 1870, he cunningly sidelined the leftist faction of his party by partly granting the main point of the platform of the *Association pour la réforme electorale*, founded in 1869. Lowering electoral taxes on a provincial and municipal level was seen as the fulfilment of the main aim of the progressive Catholics, after which the group began to disintegrate. Unity was restored in the liberal-Catholic camp, opening up the opportunity to fight the common battle for the expansion of economic liberalism and against ultramontanism and rationalism.

The progressives were successful in reorganising the Liberal Party in the cities (where anti-clericals held a comfortable position of power and could afford internal discussions), and by widening its appeal down the social ladder they brought electoral success and opened up the way for new ideas. During the 1860s and 1870s, each liberal city had a strong progressive wing and victories in municipal and provincial elections were precursors of a national breakthrough. The progressive liberals held their own National Congresses in an attempt to influence the Liberal Party as a whole. They took their party battle with conservative Liberals to extremes and they sometimes issued separate lists of candidates, or even appealed to non-liberal voters. Around 1870, they even dominated Belgian liberalism. The Liberal election defeat that year was widely blamed on the party divisions. The Catholics would remain in power for the next eight years. The power of the progressive wing did not diminish during those years spent in opposition, partly because the lowering of the municipal and provincial electoral taxes (down to respectively 10 and 20 francs) played into their hands. When the Liberals came back to power between 1878 and 1884 under governments led by Frère-Orban and J. Bara, the progressives were ready to resume their role as pressure group.

Practical results were hard to come by, however. Social-conservative liberalism was in power and neither the liberal progressive wing, nor the small group of Catholic progressives, could do much about it. Only a few laws took their social concerns into account as far as they did not compromise liberal fundamentals. They included the abolition of the coalition ban and the lowering of municipal electoral taxes in 1871, as mentioned before. For the rest, there was disappointment: during the Frère-

Orban-Bara government, they were unable to push through their demands on universal suffrage and social legislation, and had to be content with suffrage based on education (primary education diploma or certificate of competence) for the municipal elections in 1883. It made it easier for some of them to make the switch to social democracy.

The Liberal Freethinkers and Anti-Clericalism

Rationalism was the other way for the politically conscious middle class to express itself, and there was more room for that within the Liberal Party. Roughly the same progressive elements defended this second objective next to social progressivism. It is not unrealistic to see freethinking radicalism as a way for middle class intellectuals, including lawyers, professors and high-level civil servants, to establish their political credentials. A sizable group of conservative liberals did not mind a religion that ensured law and order, or the role it claimed in society. These ideologists ran behind the times, however, as it was evident that a society based on industrial capitalism needed a secular framework that relied on rationalism and scientific knowledge. So there was more than enough room within the Liberal Party for intellectuals who provided the foundation for a secular society. They served two political strategies: when the liberals were in power, the rationalist movement was used to divide the progressive front; when the Catholics ruled, the movement's anti-clericalism was an opposition weapon.

Rationalists based their ideas on a positivist philosophy: the unquestionable right of each person to freely discuss and judge each issue at hand, based on rational arguments and logical independent thoughts. Science was the only guide for truth and reality. All ideas based on rational thought had to be respected and tolerance was a key principle. Reason allowed humankind to set its ethical standards; rational action and thought would liberate man from moral control and authority. By arguing that social justice was a characteristic based on knowledge, they put themselves in line with the socially-oriented positivist movement and they linked up with the social-progressive program.

The early liberal generations had aimed their attacks at the Church by decrying its far-reaching impact on society, but now there were widely heard opinions that conservative, authoritarian Catholicism, with its absolutist claims on the truth, threatened the development of citizens, progress in society and the emancipation of the lower classes. Religion, defined as the relation between a worshipper and a supernatural, sacred being that had to be venerated, was simply rejected. Catholicism was replaced by deism and, in some cases, atheism. Science, notably Darwin's theories of evolution, stripped Catholicism of its (materially inaccurate) dogmatic and supernatural arguments. The liberal freethinkers condemned the Church's extreme wealth, its centuries-old authoritarianism and its stifling hold on society. In short, the freethinkers provided the ideological basis for the secularisation of society and the relationship between state and Church. It was the moral authority the citizens needed to distance themselves from the Church and develop their own political strength.

The freethinkers provided social alternatives and this partly explained their success. The issue of civil burials was a case in point. An official cemetery had the legal status of a sacred place that fell under the authority of the Church. It was the last show of contempt for any non-religious citizen when his burial in a graveyard was denied on the grounds that it would desecrate the site. So there were ample reasons for the non-churchgoing citizen to concentrate on actions to introduce a civil burial service, legally restrict the Catholic claims and, at first, link up with a similar action organised by the labour movement.

By the end of the 1850s, the liberal freethinkers were able to exploit the anti-clerical discontent the conservative Unionist governments of De Brouckère and De Decker had created, and they founded a militant action group. The educational issue had a big impact. Rogiers Liberal government had put the educational program of the Liberal Congress into practice in 1850. It centred on secondary education since most of the electorate had had its schooling there and since an efficient network of secondary schools would surely help the liberal cause. The law distinguished between two kinds of institutions for secondary education, all of them single-sex boys' schools. Ten 'Royal Athenaeums' and fifty public secondary schools would come under direct state control. Apart from those, the authorities backed or subsidised municipal and provincial schools. These included a great many Episcopal colleges. The law also clearly stated that education in public institutions had to be neutral and that any control by the Church was excluded. The clergy was invited to teach religion but had no authority when it came to other courses. It sparked heated discussions in parliament and the Catholics organised petitions. The coordinated protest actions could not prevent parliament from approving the law, however.

The breach between government and Church was repaired under the centrist De Brouckère government. The Antwerp Convention of 1854 originally was nothing more than a deal to settle a local school conflict. But the government decided to use it as a blueprint for other municipal schools. It enjoyed the support of the bishops and as such guaranteed the cooperation of the clergy in implementing the law on secondary education, as it put the clergy back in control in a great many schools, ensuring that all teachers would be Catholic. There is no need to stress that anti-clerical elements were far from pleased with this 'convention' policy, which led to the dismissal of many liberal teachers. This had been the case before, with the approval of the Faider bill (1852), which restricted the anti-Napoleonic (and as such anti-clerical) press in Belgium and showed the government's goodwill towards the rightist Second Empire in France.

The Catholic government of De Decker was faced with a political row centring on two professors of Ghent state university who had expressed dissenting opinions on Catholic principles. The bishops attacked the state universities and the Free University of Brussels, only adding to the anti-clerical climate that reached fever pitch in 1857. The so-called monastic law increased control of the Church over charity. The virulent reaction, including violent street protests, of an anti-clerical front which united dogmatic and progressive liberals and the working class forced De Decker to resign. The Liberals emerged victors in the subsequent election and would remain in power for the next thirteen years.

By the end of the 1850s, the rise of Ultramontanism would further polarise Belgian politics. Its authoritarian streak and provocative demonstrations only added to the anti-clerical resistance of the freethinkers, with the Liberal Party serving as a fertile breeding ground. Before they were properly organised, these progressive, rationalist citizens associated themselves with labour movement organisations, but in 1863, they founded the freethinkers' association *La Libre Pensée* in Brussels. It soon spread to other liberal cities as well. The liberal press, liberal cultural organisations such as student unions (among them *'t Zal Wel Gaan* in Ghent), universities, literary circles and Masonic lodges – they all spread the freethinkers' ideas and joined the battle for civil burials. The freethinkers were also frequently the provocateurs behind protest against Catholic demonstrations. Within the Liberal Party, they helped set up the social progressive pressure group and made sure it had a heavy anti-clerical character.

One can claim that these rationalist associations were directly responsible for the Liberal Party's anti-clerical slant. They prepared the legal basis for many a bill or proposal to turn Belgium into a more secular society. With Paul Janson, Emile Feron and others, they even had parliamentary representatives who had a direct impact on decision-making.

The freethinkers stimulated anti-clerical policy: from 1859 onwards, new municipal burial grounds were no longer allowed to be consecrated; there was an ongoing battle for government control over the administration of Church assets; in 1865, Leuven University lost its effective monopoly on grants and scholarships. Slowly but surely, the liberal governments were eating away at the traditional burden that the Church had placed on the state. In 1879, primary schools were secularised. One year later, Belgium broke diplomatic relations with the Vatican. The clergy was given less of the religious services budget. All this only went to prove that the influence of the liberal anti-clerical wing had even increased under the 1878-1884 liberal Frère-Bara government. Little wonder that the Catholic backlash was severe, and led by Ultramontanism.

Ultramontanism versus Liberalism

The impact of Ultramontanism from 1857 to 1881 cannot be fully understood unless it is put in the context of the emergence of the modern, secular, anti-clerical state. It was mentioned earlier that this Catholic variant of anti-liberal traditionalism demanded a dominant role for religion and the Church in society. The Church, according to them, had the right to intervene directly in political life in an attempt to lead its sinful flock towards truth and spiritual salvation. As such, the Church was put above the state.

Early on, the Church had willingly accepted the constitutional monarchy, the parliamentary regime and its political freedoms. The early governments had indeed been instrumental in consolidating a Christian society. It had been the case prior to 1847 and during the De Brouckère and the De Decker governments of 1852 to 1857. The Liberal government of Rogier changed the political complexion and his law on secondary education had been a first warning sign: the parliamentary regime was no longer able to guarantee the Church's prerogatives. The resistance against the monastic law and the long liberal anti-clerical reign took away the last illusions. The secular measures of the liberals were seen as direct attacks on the traditional rights of the Church. The Ultramontane principles became more entrenched and the rejection of liberalism and its political institutions ever more extreme.

The Church was looking for other ways to regain full control of its flock. The bishops made extra efforts to make sure parochial life thrived. The distribution of the lectures of St. Vincent de Paul, the activities of the Saint Francis Xavier congregation and others, mass organisations and manifestations (pilgrimages, processions) were all in aid of the Church's efforts to keep both the 'legal' and 'actual' nations within its realm. Faith was manifested without restraint, and liberal ideas were aggressively attacked; it was stressed time and again that the Church had to be the centre of public life. The Vatican orchestrated the whole operation. In Rome, the pope himself was in the midst of a brutal battle to hold on to his earthly powers and he called on the help of all European Catholics (the so-called Roman Question). The Vatican turned ever more dogmatic and authoritarian. It approved controversial dogmas – notably on papal infallibility and on the immaculate conception – new miracles and new saints' days and holidays. The Ultramontane movement, trying to safeguard a confessional society, was fully in line with the Vatican and turned into a much more potent anti-liberal weapon than most of the Catholic legislators.

Several aspects of these liberal-Catholic parliamentary leaders have been discussed earlier, among others their wish to be as politically independent as possible, free from stringent episcopal control and from a confessional party in the context of which they could be called to account by non-voters. They wanted to respect religious-philosophical neutrality on the condition that the state left the Church enough room to organise religious life. They held bourgeois liberal views on the economy and social policy and they accepted the foundations of the parliamentary regime. Their role in the progressive but marginal 'young right' during the 1860s has also been pointed out. During the Mechelen congresses they had openly declared their liberal principles, among others through the Frenchman Montalembert, giving expression to their acceptance of constitutional freedoms. When the *Quanta Cura* encyclical (1864) rejected the modern political freedoms in the strongest possible terms, the Belgian liberal Catholics simply rejected the Vatican's call.

On an organisational level, the congresses mentioned above had a stimulating effect. From 1865 onwards, the constitutional and conservative electoral colleges, which had their roots in the post-revolutionary period, slowly started to form one national federation. Together with the federation of Catholic Circles (1868), which was an association of non-political Catholic groups, it formed the structural backbone of the future Catholic party. The Catholic Circles became more politicised and after one decade, the two merged in 1878 to form the Federation of Catholic Circles and Conservative Associations. The Catholic legislators, however, were not easily swayed and stuck to their political autonomy, weakening the Federation's central command. They also failed to cover up the deep divisions that separated the liberal Catholics, who were largely backed by the press, and the Ultramontane wing.

When the Catholic liberals came to power in 1870, it was clear that economic-liberal aims were their priority and that they were very moderate when it came to state-Church relations. They accepted the authority of the clergy on purely religious issues, but politically they acted as individualistic citizens. The Catholics wanted parliament and government to create conditions that would allow their religion to thrive, but the state was not to pressurise non-Catholics and deny them their freedom of thought. It was, in short, a realistic Catholic compromise policy in a society where the autonomous citizen was all-important. The governments of d'Anethan and de Theux-Malou did not abolish the controversial laws of their secular predecessors. The government of d'Anethan wanted a compromise solution on the issue of civil burials, based on the individual consecration of graves. It would take two decades, until 1891, before such a solution was finally accepted.

The Ultramontanes considered this kind of liberal-Catholic compromise sheer cowardice and treason. In combination with the anti-papal thinking among freethinkers in the 1870s as a reaction to the show of power by the Church, this led to the Ultramontane propaganda machine going into overdrive, which in its turn was part of the reason for the anti-clerical electoral victory in 1878.

Even though the Ultramontanes had been active before 1860, their fighting spirit became particularly intense around 1870. By then, the bishops had the backing of a new generation of leaders. The aristocratic landowners started to feel ill at ease in an increasingly liberal society and several of them actively joined the Ultramontanes. Some among the first generation of bourgeois nouveaux riches also joined the movement; they sought out the Church, hoping it would provide some form of social control. Ultramontanism even lured some members of the middle class who also yearned for an ancien régime led by the Church and the aristocracy. Their grassroots support, obviously, did not come from the 'legal country' with the right to vote, but from the lower classes where the Catholic congregations and non-political organisations had a big impact. It quickly turned into a crusade against liberalism. The spectacular, massive demonstrations of faithful believers, which were always Catholic political manifestations, were a much-used weapon in the struggle. The anti-clerical counter-demonstrations brought the conflict onto the streets of many Belgian cities during the 1870s.

Which alternative type of society did the Ultamontanes propose, then? They reproached liberal Catholicism for not respecting the fundamental principles of Catholicism, i.e. the Church leading and controlling all sectors of life and society. The liberal state and the Belgian constitution refused to recognise this and the most radical of the Ultramontanes wanted to establish a Catholic state, politically under the direct control of the pope. In Belgium itself, the papal authority would be represented by a religious party, led by the bishops and a militant Church, with an ancien-régime monarch as ally. Their political and social ideal was a medieval class structure. Parliament would have to be replaced by a system of class representation. This political philosophy was traditionalist and corporatist. The majority of the Ultramontanes, including the bishops, held more moderate views. They did not reject the current regime and wanted to achieve Catholic supremacy working from within the ruling constitutional framework. That did not stop them from insisting on reversing some constitutional articles.

On the level of social policy, they differed little from the liberal Catholics as both wanted to prevent any resistance from the working class. The Ultramontanes tried to build grassroots support by organising employers' charity, the importance of which is not to be underestimated. In 1867, the Federation of Belgian Catholic Workers' Associations emerged by grouping all Catholic charitable works for the workers. The Ultramontane wing tried to use the Federation to spread conservative corporatism through the establishment of guilds. A class hierarchy where charity and solidarity united everyone would serve two purposes: counter liberal individualism and prevent any attempt of the working class to organise. The Ultramontane vision of corporatism was patronising: it established the upper classes at the top of the pyramidal structure. The social elite would have the responsibility for the well-being of the working class.

The Ultramontanes never grew into more than a small minority within the conservative movement, but their enthusiasm and fervour belied this. The intensity of their actions, from small groups and publications even increased after 1870. The arch-conservative Pope Pius IX, the papal envoys and bishops such as Gravez (Namur) and Montpellier (Liège) openly backed the writings and actions of the Ultramontane ideologue Charles Périn; this Leuven professor provided the ideological framework for such issues as the incompatibility of liberalism and Catholicism, the restoration of the Catholic state and the principle of paternalist corporatism.

However, capitalism and the parliamentary regime had already firmly taken root and were not to be denied by the ideas of Ultramontanism. A new pope was chosen in 1878; Leo XIII wanted to adapt Catholicism and the Church to the economic, social and political realities of his time, a process he considered inevitable. In 1878 he told the Belgian Catholics to recognise the constitution and around 1881, Ultramontanism had lost much of its lustre, even though it did leave its traces in political life. Liberal Catholicism had eventually prevailed, but the 'school war', which would break out in 1879 as a reaction to the bill on primary education, allowed Ultramontanism to leave its mark on the liberal state, which all Catholics had to accept as the only way of realising a Catholic society.

The School War (1879-1884): pivotal point in the clerical vs. anti-clerical conflict

The government reverted to militant anti-clericalism during the years 1878-1884, when the Liberal team of Frère-Van Humbeeck put an end to the Catholic interlude. The 1842 law on primary education, inspired by the Catholics, was an obvious target and Van Humbeeck lost little time before he tabled a parliamentary bill in 1879 to abolish the 1842 Nothomb law. Only in the large, liberal urban centres had city councils been able to rid municipal education of its denominational character, but in rural areas and smaller cities, official education had remained under the firm control of the clergy. The Van Humbeeck law tried to undermine the Church's strategic position by imposing the need for recognised diplomas for teachers, bringing schoolbooks and programmes under state control and stripping Catholicism of its status as the basis of education. From then on, parents would have to request religious courses outside the normal curriculum; municipalities had to have at least one neutral school and were no longer allowed to found or subsidise private schools. The 1881 law on secondary education was very much in the same vein: it gave the government the possibility to establish new secondary schools whenever it wanted (12 athenaeums, 46 secondary schools for boys and 50 for girls) in order to guarantee parents a freedom of choice for their children, in competition with Catholic education.

For the Church, it turned into an 'us against them' situation and the entire Catholic camp reacted as one against the Van Humbeeck bill. Representing the high clergy, archbishop Deschamps took charge of the resistance movement. Fire-and-brimstone sermons from the pulpits, demonstrations and public meetings mobilised the faithful and a petition on the issue gathered over 300,000 signatures. The action was endorsed by Catholic politicians and high civil servants (provincial governors, area commissioners, mayors). The government made a concession at first – teachers were requested to use the 'moral and Christian principles characteristic of all religions' as their guideline.

Measures subsequently taken against rebellious civil servants and clergy led to a veritable ideological civil war. Religious pressure was widespread, even though most liberal Catholics did not think it politic. They were afraid – rightfully so, as it happened – that moderate citizens would move away from the Church. The bishops did not let up, however. Public school personnel, parents of public school pupils – in short, everyone who backed public education – was no longer deemed worthy to receive communion. All those families were in effect excommunicated. In Catholic Flanders, where the influence of the Church was all-pervasive, public schools did not stand a chance, especially since the clergy, with the financial backing of the aristocracy, high bourgeoisie and countless citizens, made an extra effort to establish new primary schools. It turned into an anti-liberal tide. When diplomatic relations between the Belgian liberal government and the Vatican were broken, it was as a consequence of this ideological civil war.

The financial impact of the government's educational policy necessitated higher taxation, which did not make the liberals any more popular either, especially with the petty bourgeoisie and the middle class, who deserted the liberal cause. The 1884 election victory for the Catholics was in part due to this.

The impact of this school war was huge. As far as the number of pupils was concerned, it was a clear victory for the Church: the private Catholic network had 80 % of all pupils. For many liberal families it meant the end of religious practice. The liberal and petty bourgeoisie took to anti-clerical habits, passed down to the next generations.

The sheer political impact was not to be neglected either. The Catholic camp united around a common goal. It brought liberal Catholics and Ultramontanes closer together in the National Union for the Restoration of Grievances (1883). More than ever, bishops and clergy were leaders on the political level. It also fulfilled the Ultramontane dream of a truly Catholic Party led by the Church. An organised confessional Catholic Party was established in 1888 from the fusion of the Union and the Federation, and its binding programme was set up without the input of the parliamentary right wing. And even though the contrast between the liberal Catholic right and the Ultramontanes did not cease to exist, it would ensure the basis for a Catholic rule, which was keen for revenge immediately after 1884, and would remain in power until the First World War.

The School War left the Liberal Party in disarray. Even though the progressive wing had seen its anti-clerical aims realised, the militancy of the progressive anti-clerical wing and its almost obsessive drive to fight the Church had monopolised too much of the party's energy, and as such the social progressive wing had been unable to push through the electoral reforms which would have allowed it to expand. A division between the social-conservative and social-progressive liberals became inevitable and the latter were drawn to the labour movement. The dogmatic wing took one good look at the 1884 election results and rejected militant anti-clericalism. Forty years of liberal domination had come to a definitive end. Secular liberalism had its limits and the School War had proven that it was tolerated only as long as it did not impede Catholic fundamentals in vital social sectors, notably education. Granted, the liberals had been able to rid the state of the Church's overpowering interference, something successive Catholic governments would be unable to undo, but they had also come head-to-head with the power of the Belgian Catholic Church, which was not about to yield its centuries-old authority. The divide between clerical and anti-clerical Belgium could no longer be bridged.

The school war was not the only cause of the shift in balance. The 1884 election was also a harbinger of new conflicts that would dominate the second half of the 1880s. The Catholic party had not only succeeded in mobilising die-hard Catholics and disgruntled moderates, but in its traditional role of defender of agricultural interests it had also taken the complaints of the crisis-stricken rural electorate to heart. The 1884 election proved to be the political breakthrough of the farmer. The Catholic victory can also be explained by the formation of alliances with the conservative liberals since both groups were united in their fear for socialism and radicalism. The change in power of 1884 thus not only concluded an era, but also rang in a new phase in political evolution.

Petty Bourgeois Flamingantism

The slow march towards Flemish emancipation turned into the third conflict zone of Belgian politics. And here too, the progressive wing of the middle class was instrumental in bringing the issue to the fore. Without reservation, flamingantism can be considered the third channel for power-conscious middle-class citizens to enter the political fray. The leaders of this group often belonged to, and at the same time appealed to, the social classes that had not yet been gallicised. They were starting to be sensitive to the social frustrations resulting from the language barrier (e.g. the appointment of Walloon civil servants in Flanders) and wished to use Dutch as a language of culture in education, literature, theatre and in cultural associations. The slow but steady move towards democratisation noticeable in all of these sectors only reinforced this flamingantism.

For the new generation of politicians, this was new and fertile ground that could yield rich crops for themselves and the established parties. Moreover, this Dutch-speaking middle group came to mean something on an electoral level after 1848. The parties had to keep the interests of the electorate into account, and as part of the movement of small urban and middle class citizens, the Flemish Movement began to get some political influence. In particular in cities such as Antwerp and Ghent, the increase in Flemish-minded voters carried electoral implications after 1848.

The Flemish Movement always kept very close to its origins. Its leaders and supporters were part of the petty bourgeoisie at best and their moderate demands did not reach beyond demanding guarantees for a bilingual Flanders. Their social demands were little more than carefully progressive. Apart from a few exceptions (e.g. E. Moyson in Ghent), the labour movement and the Flemish emancipation movement did not join forces. The political development of the Flemish Movement and the social progressives was strikingly alike. At first, flamingantism was the catalyst in the unification of the Catholic and liberal progressives. Then it helped develop distinct wings within the established parties. During the 1850s and the beginning of the 1860s, the majority of flamingants rejected the Catholic vs. anti-clerical divide that ran through Belgian politics. They did think the contrast was relevant, yet they did see the sense in cooperating with different opposition groups at a local and regional level.

By the mid-1850s, flamingantism thrived on its anti-government stance. When the Catholic Pierre De Decker came to power in 1855, his Flemish sympathies moved him to set up a commission to investigate the language issue. Leading Flemish partisans cooperated with the Commission, which reported to the government and proposed political solutions. The fall of the De Decker government ensured, however, that nothing was effectively done.

De Decker was succeeded by the Liberal coalition of Charles Rogier, who had little time for and even less interest in the Flemish demands. He reacted negatively to the report and published a counter-report, stressing the political need to hold on to a monolingual francophone nation. A language law on notary acts never materialised; an amendment to allow Dutch during university entry exams was rejected; the influx of Walloon civil servants in Flanders and the government's accommodating attitude towards the annexionist French empire of Napoleon III only reinforced the flamingants' anti-establishment feelings. It pushed them further into the opposition camp, right alongside the anti-dogmatic and progressive factions.

The results of their actions were most obvious and strongest in Antwerp. The city's middle class had remained overwhelmingly Dutch-speaking and they enthusiastically backed the language demands of the flamingants; moreover, the anti-militaristic and decentralisation demands coincided with those of the Meeting Party, in which the flamingant *Nederduitse Bond* was undoubtedly the driving force. But even though the movement had a few real chances in Antwerp, it was exactly there that it fell apart around 1868, the victim of the increasing Catholic vs. anti-clerical rift. There was no way the Flemish Movement could get around the political consequences of Belgium's two-party system and it was forced to adapt.

Both the Catholic and Liberal parties opened up their ranks to the most promising and dynamic elements of the Flemish movement. They attracted the pro-Flemish vote and provided the ideological arguments that further fanned the linguistic fires. Their integration into the different parties was not all that smooth though. The defenders of the Flemish cause raised quite a few eyebrows in the francophone upper-echelons of the parties, but as the political battle between the Liberals and Catholics intensified and the difference in votes grew ever narrower, the pressure group was able to increase its political influence.

In the Flemish wing of the Liberal Party, people like J. Vuylsteke and J. De Geyter were key figures. Their ideological theories inseparably intertwined liberalism and flamingantism. They claimed the Church and clergy were responsible for the intellectual inferiority of the Flemish people. Based on that core principle, they waged open war on the Church and wanted to emancipate Flanders through secular education. Student unions such as *'t Zal Wel Gaan* (Ghent) and *Scild en Vriend* (Brussels), cultural associations such as the *Willemsfonds,* and press organisations had to raise grassroots support and establish municipal Liberal Flemish Federations between 1864 and 1875 in Antwerp, Ghent, Bruges and Brussels. It was instrumental in getting Flemish candidates on liberal election lists.

Much the same could be seen in the Catholic Party, where flamingantism was also claimed as a natural ally. The local language and religion were two inseparable issues that constituted the essence of the Flemish people. The leading Antwerp publicist A. Snieders thought so, as did, in Catholic West Flanders, Albrecht Rodenbach (who claimed a leadership role with his *Blauwvoet* movement), and the Catholic Meeting Party supporters. An Ultramontane element was never far away since it was always looking for traditional, stabilising factors, which a local language, steeped in a pure past, surely was. As a result, the nationalist popular movement had a lot of Ultramontane support. The Catholic flamingants could not match the popularity of their liberal counterparts, however. Political flamingantism was an overwhelmingly urban movement, and the Liberals still ruled the cities.

The result was that the flamingants were now divided by conventional party lines. Yet there were still unsuccessful attempts at continuing the 1840s tradition of cooperation across party boundaries. But even the cultural and library associations, which had wanted to stay neutral, eventually fell prey to polarisation. The liberal *Willemsfonds* had its Catholic counterpart in the *Davidsfonds* as of 1875. Flamingant organisations, such as the Flemish Association (Brussels) and De *Nederduitse Bond* (Antwerp) also met that fork in the political road and had to make a choice.

A Flemish umbrella organisation proved to be an unrealistic political aim and, in practice, coordination was limited to crisis moments, when the masses beyond the electorate needed to be mobilised. Successful joint action in favour of Coecke and Goethals, two Flemings who had been sentenced to death in an exclusively francophone trial, was a case in point.

The political pressure of the Flemish movement yielded some results and the first legislators with Flemish or flamingant sympathies entered the different representative bodies: De Baets, Heremans, De Vigne, De Maere and Vuylsteke in Ghent, Van Beers, Gerrits, Coremans, De Geyter, Van Rijswijck and De Laet in Antwerp, and Vanderkindere and Buls in Brussels (the latter two, however, got their mandates thanks to their progressivism rather than any flamingantism). The government could no longer disregard the Flemish vote, and language demands could be raised with some chance of success in the opposition; they were tabled as important for the party interest to the French-speaking party colleagues. Three language laws were passed. The use of Dutch in criminal law was approved in 1873 and five years later Dutch was introduced in Flemish administration. In 1883, public secondary education had to teach some courses in Dutch. Those were tactical concessions more than anything else and they certainly did not stop the gallicisation of Flanders. Northern Belgium was far from being an officially bilingual region, since the laws were rarely put into practice.

The Flemish Movement suffered the fate of most political movements of the time: it would take until the late 1880s and early 1890s before real change became evident. By then, the social political situation had changed, allowing the Flemish movement to gain momentum and change course.

Chapter III
The Expansion of Democracy (1885-1918)

In history, periods of relative socio-economical and political stability, gradual change and sudden transformation randomly follow one another. Around the turn of the century, the pace of social and economic change suddenly picked up, affecting all sectors of society and the population at large. The expansion of democracy over that period was one of the most fundamental political transformations in Belgian history. It created the basis of Belgian society as we know it and the developments one century ago still determine politics to this day.

The working class joined the political system and forced drastic changes in what used to be an exclusively bourgeois regime. However, it did not affect the fundamentals of the liberal nation, and economic liberalism and its political twin, parliamentary democracy, survived relatively unscathed. The expansion of parliamentary democracy was the result of two opposing forces at work. The working class had come of age and shed its inhibitions and it demanded political power to improve its lot in life. The ruling classes wanted to safeguard capitalism from social revolt and saw a steady, supervised integration of the working class into the political process as the safest option. This conflict and process of adaptation were central events around the turn of the century, and as such also in this chapter.

Social and Economic Democratisation

There is no way to understand the determination of the workers in their struggle for emancipation or the way in which the bourgeois rulers adapted the liberal state to the new circumstances without taking into account the changes in the then economic and social climate. The 1873-1874 depression of the capitalist economy lingered on into the 1880s. Belgium lost much of its access to foreign markets because several European nations reverted to protectionism to stave off the economic crisis. It left Belgian industry struggling and only the wealthiest companies were able to survive. This also encouraged a tendency for concentration.

From about 1895 onwards, the economy started to recover, in spite of a few short and sharp crises. Annual growth of Belgium's industrial production grew to 3.5 %, trade flourished again and industry went through a second industrial revolution. The new revolution was marked by the mechanisation of the chemical and nonferrous industries, the introduction of new sources of energy and their application in the gas and electrical engines. The emergence of petroleum pushed coal into a long and slow decline. The metal industry expanded anew and the electrical installations allowed for a breathtaking increase in output.

Capitalism imposed the quest for sustained or ever bigger profits, forcing industry to cast its nets for new markets ever wider. To escape the protectionism of its European competitors and search for more profitable markets, Belgian captains of industry went looking beyond Western Europe. Industrial leaders showed exemplary activity in this drive for new markets and the large profits associated with them. Around 1895, Cockerill expanded in central Russia and even into China, followed by other metal companies. The Empain industrial group built tram networks in China, South America, Central Africa and Egypt (Heliopolis). The Otlet group deployed its activities in the same sector and the same regions. Solvay was already strong in both Eastern and Western Europe when it expanded in Russia and North America. In 1899, Belgian investments in Russia totalled 300 million francs.

Colonialism and imperialism were vital allies in the expansion of capitalism in the pre-war period; they created new markets and provided new raw materials. Leopold II made sure Belgian investors poured their money into the Congo, which even before 1914 had all the unmistakable signs of growing into a strong economic colonial empire. Société Générale would dominate this colonial economy. The unavoidable arms race started around the turn of the century and the Belgian steel, metal and arms sectors profited. The economy was booming, exploitation results were good, entrepreneurs were buoyant, speculators feverishly sought fresh profits and corporations increased from 147 in 1880 to 2249 in 1901. During this period, careless investors soon paid the price, however. Massive fraud, notably through the creation of bogus companies, as well as petty financial crime, cost them dearly.

The international explosive industrial growth gave centre stage to the moguls of capitalism, who took charge of the major financial empires and slowly but surely turned the concept of 'monopoly capitalism' into reality. The crisis and the rationalisations that had followed, had forced the petty bourgeoisie and upper middle class out, to be replaced by big business. Most independent 'empires' of individual capitalist competitors were no match for the powerful financial holdings that could face up to foreign competition. Cartels and trusts became an economic factor and competition on the international market was impeded by price fixing, agreements on the purchase of raw materials and the centralisation of trade.

Yet there is no doubt that Belgium already had its share of dominant financial groups. The steel empire of Victor Tesch spilled beyond Belgium's borders into the Grand Duchy of Luxembourg and Saarland before it was turned into the Arbed industrial powerhouse in 1911. Empain created and controlled his own holding and became an international giant in the tram business before moving into the electricity sector with the ACEC company in 1904. Cockerill was Belgium's steel and metal giant with an annual turnover of 55 million francs, paying dividends of 20 to 30 %. It counted 11 subdivisions, was horizontally and vertically integrated and had factories all over Europe. Control of the international soda market, and to a lesser extent of coal and cokes production, earned the Solvay group respect far beyond its borders. Mergers and takeovers in the glass industry left the crystal company Val-Saint-Lambert with 19 million francs in annual turnover. None could compete with the overall scope of Société Générale, which added coal and metal companies from Hainaut to its impressive holding, and also showed interest in other economic sectors. The Banque de Bruxelles holding expanded into Wallonia's industrial belt, entered the electricity sector and aligned itself with the Coppée and Warocqué groups.

A select few people, commanders of the economy, ran the Belgian economy at the turn of the century. They were Belgium's oligarchy, the 'haute finance', the 'upper ten'. Whatever they might be called, they stood at the absolute top of the social pyramid, and their income could equal that of a thousand of their workers. They purposefully sealed themselves off from almost any other layer of the bourgeoisie, among others by trying to marry into the aristocracy.

As so often, the worker was left behind with little to show for all the increase in productivity and economic good times. The overwhelming majority of the proletariat remained enclosed in a very vulnerable economic and social situation. Wages remained very low. Women's and child labour still was an everyday reality. In those sectors that made giant profits, wages were sometimes higher. The second industrial revolution required better technical skills and wages rose with the level of schooling, leaving the ordinary workers as replaceable assets in the production of semi-finished products. Those with technical skills formed a 'worker's aristocracy'. This upper crust of the working class was able to live in symbiosis with the petty bourgeois backers of the labour movement. For them, the worst was over.

It is generally accepted that exactly this limited and relative improvement in certain sectors influenced the increasing militancy of the proletariat in this period. The small improvement in living standards only served to highlight the intolerable social abuses. Dissatisfaction with the present situation grew and led to massive protest and demands for political participation and better protection of the weak by the government.

No doubt there is a dialectic relation between these demands and the consideration of them by the then ruling classes. Those rulers with a good grasp of reality saw that is was possible to reconcile these wishes with the interests of the liberal nation. By increasing the standard of living and thus increasing the size of the domestic market, the government could find new room for economic expansion. Solvay was one of the first to see the advantages of turning the working class and lower middle class into consumers. This vision implied, however, that the members of these social groups adopted the material values and patterns of consumption of bourgeois society, or at least got acquainted with them. In short, they had to be integrated in a petty bourgeois society.

The electorate and parliament were the channels for the progressive integration of these classes on a political level. The fact was unavoidable, though, that the traditional workings of the liberal state would be seriously complicated by the integration of the working class into the system. The relations between the state and capitalism had changed to the extent that the political expansion did not endanger any liberal fundamentals. Internationalised capitalism had become so powerful and independent on the international stage that it no longer depended on the national state. Belgium itself depended almost as much on the patronage of its economic juggernauts. As long as economic liberalism remained the cornerstone of the state and as long as the government could be counted on to develop new foreign markets, some financial and industrial powers were willing to be flexible and cooperative during the expansion of democracy. If the labour movement accepted the same core principles, nothing stood in the way of negotiations.

The objective evolution sketched above obviously only emerges when viewed from a distance. For anyone living through the period, confronted with the daily dynamics of this dialectical process, dramatic at times, this progressive adaptation of the political climate to the new economic and social realities was an extremely turbulent period.

The Labour Movement Moves into the Social-Democratic Camp

The years around 1900 established the labour movement as a force to be reckoned with. For the first time in its existence, it set the political agenda and was able to push through fundamental change in political life. The militant workers formed a well-organised mass movement. After years of uncoordinated protests, it now organised strong strike actions and aggressive, massive street demonstrations. Throughout the country, the working class joined en masse. All of a sudden, the bourgeoisie found that traditional weapons would no longer keep the militant forces of the working class at bay.

The incredible transformation took place within the context of a transitional phase, during which the labour movement bridged the gap between the 'two types of socialism' – its revolutionary and social-democratic wings. The division went back to the First International, and even after the demise of the First International, the rift had remained. On one side, the revolutionary group totally rejected the ruling regime and wanted to foment revolt and organise revolutionary strikes to take power and impose radical changes. They saw an enemy in anyone who tried to keep them from violent revolt. They were agitators during general strikes, not only to effectively scare the bourgeoisie, but also to force a direct confrontation that would eventually turn into revolution.

Those who wanted to work within the established system also reinforced their position. Many had rejected the idea of a violent socialist revolution after the failure of the Paris Commune. Instead, they sought progressive reforms within the liberal democratic regime. The working class had to achieve its goals through political emancipation, not revolutionary violence. They saw a socialist parliamentary majority as a realistic aim and everything – labour resistance, the trade union battle – had to be subservient to this overall goal.

The establishment of social democracy would take careful organisation. Every idea that lived among the workers had to be channelled towards economic, social and political groups. The reformist strategy was built around the establishment of a labour party and universal suffrage in an attempt to seize power, undo social injustice and win the class struggle. The general, political strike was part of that reformist model – it was an extra-parliamentary and legal way to gain political power. Many hopes were pinned on parliament and a helping hand from the progressive section of the Liberal Party was more than welcome for the social-democratic ideal. The two even agreed on electoral alliances with the bourgeois left, which looked favourably on the working class for well-known reasons. The logical consequence of this – participation in a government coalition with a bourgeois party – laid bare sharp differences within the labour movement. This 'ministerialism' was never accepted as a social-democratic principle but rather as a tactical weapon, a means to an end in the first step towards political power.

In analysing the most essential concepts of the labour movement, it is clear that a new ideology was developing within the movement, which showed some common ground with the progressive bourgeoisie – capital and labour could be reconciled in this reformist model. The aggression of the proletariat had to be gently turned into a non-violent wait-and-see attitude that fitted within the limits of the political system. The grand socialist vision was put on hold to prepare for the integration of the working class in society as such. Only the ideals remained radical and revolutionary – the hope that progressive transformations would be able to subvert bourgeois democracy, paving the way for a socialist and collectivist society.

The Belgian labour movement did not yet show a clear distinction between both strategies during the 1880s. In practice, both tendencies were present at the same time, both integrated and parallel to each other. Revolutionary anarchists in Liège and Verviers and the radical Hainaut movement led by A. Defuisseaux were the main agitators in the biggest and most violent strike wave ever to sweep across industrial Wallonia. It started in March 1886 in Liège's metal sector and quickly expanded to the three Hainaut industrial areas. Violence and destruction, including the demolition of a glass factory, unleashed the traditional repressive measures: the army intervened and killed dozens, ten in the town of Roux alone. Hundreds of workers were condemned in court and several leaders were prosecuted. But the battle-hardened Hainaut workers of the Defuisseaux movement were not impressed and in May 1887 they organised a second wave of strikes. This time, the general revolutionary strike also had the political aim to secure universal suffrage. Neither in Liège, nor in the rest of industrial Belgium, however, did it have the same effect. This strike was symptomatic for the revolutionary climate among the workers in the heavy industry in Wallonia.

The reformist camp could also claim its first successes during those years. Reformist leaders started creating the precursors of the socialist party in cities with a strong labour tradition. L. Bertrand, a marble cutter, had centralised the political activities of several Brussels' unions in the Chamber of Labour in 1878, the basis for the Brabant Socialist Party. A similar tendency for political unification was seen in Ghent, and Eduard Anseele had an even easier job mobilising the textile workers in Ghent. The local chapter of the First International helped create the Flemish Socialist Party in 1877. Socialist leaders took the initiative to centralise all those forces in 1885 with the creation of the *Belgische Werkliedenpartij* – Belgian Workers' Party. Workers who had gone to primary school or had passed an electoral exam were allowed to vote in municipal elections (starting in 1887). The breakthrough had opened the door to the establishment of political workers' associations and electoral alliances with the liberal progressives in several cities. Cooperation with this bourgeois left also took place in the framework of the *Ligue de la Réforme Electorale*.

During the strikes of 1886-1887, the social-democratic wing clearly made its abhorrence of violence known. For fear of disappearing, the newly formed BWP, and with it the cooperative and health care organisations, came out against the strikes and even expelled Defuisseaux. In reaction, he immediately founded the more radical *Parti Socialiste Républicain* (1887) mainly based on a strong Walloon-Hainaut grassroots support, started a militant propaganda and unleashed the local strikes of 1887. The failure of the second strike exposed the organisational weakness of the Walloon labour movement. And when the '*Procès du Grand Complot*' (the Great Conspiracy Trial) proved that Defuisseaux' party was infested with stool pigeons and state security agents, a wide socialist solidarity closed the strike leader and his Walloon followers into the warm BWP embrace again. The 1890 Oath in St. Gilles Park sealed a compromise between revolutionaries and reformists pledging to cooperate during a general strike for universal suffrage. It completed the reunification of the Belgian labour movement and was a decisive victory for the social-democratic camp.

How can this fundamental evolution be explained? Why the revolutionary reflexes in Wallonia and the reformist stance in Flanders and Brabant? Rather than in a difference in national identity, the cause is to be found in economic and social factors: a comparison in working conditions easily explains the difference. Going on the presupposition that there is a causal link between the revolutionary and radical character of the labour movement on the one hand, and the intensity of class consciousness among the Walloon working class on the other hand, several specific factors point to a higher social and political consciousness among the Walloon working class than up north. It was not just a working class with numerical weight (some 500,000 labourers), but they were working almost exclusively in the expansive heavy industry. Their wages were heavily influenced by price fluctuations, and as a result expectations could easily be frustrated during crises. The workers were under constant pressure from anonymous shareholders-owners. They were emotionally unattached to their company, and unfettered by any organisational structure. The situation in Wallonia, much more so than in Flanders, was a recipe for wild and violent strikes that threatened the ruling classes. The bourgeoisie reacted just as violently, only increasing class consciousness. There was also a sheer physical explanation for the volatile mood. The working class was housed in cramped conditions near mines and blast furnaces, leaving no place for a sense of moderation. Anarchism and revolutionary rhetoric felt at home there.

Flanders offered a different picture and a population with much less social consciousness. Textile was rural Flanders' only industrial sector with a deep-rooted tradition. Textile centres turned Ghent and Aalst into the sole major industrial cities. Industrial growth was far from expansive. Moreover, textile was the worst-paid sector, partly because of the surplus of cheap labour. Each successive agricultural crisis kept adding to the labour force. These numerous newcomers, uprooted from their agricultural surroundings, and still under the spell of the authoritarian village structure, where baron and priest ruled, were not the right social group for radical revolutionary action; neither were the large group of commuters. The Flemish and Brabant labour movement recruited most of its membership not from among the proletariat but from among the craftsmen. Their lives were intertwined with the lower middle class. They had a strong sense of belonging and took pride in their profession, their intellectual development and schooling. As a result, they were much more susceptible to the idea of non-violent, careful reform, even more so in their attachment to urban craft- based organisations with a corporatist ancient régime tradition. They were a natural match for the social-democratic cause. Cooperatives had already proved their value and the hope was that political organisation would perpetuate progress. The structural organisation of the party called for a labour bureaucracy that was to take care of the management of associations, giving priority to the survival of those organisations; the last thing these people wanted was a revolutionary distraction. They were part of this small corps of privileged workers, whose living conditions were slightly better and who found it easier to give up dreams of revolt and concentrate on legal emancipation instead.

Also in Belgium, the socialist reform movement achieved its goals through the bourgeois camp. The BWP and the progressive liberal group of Paul Janson were chips off the same block. There never was a clear dividing line between socialism and social-progressivism despite the fact that the collectivist ideology was a constant debating point. The intellectuals and leaders in both camps were on very good terms with one another. The organisational network covering both groups included professional, social and political organisations, and the link with labour organisations was laid alongside those. The reasons urging the progressive citizens to keep the labour movement in the grip of the 'enlightened' bourgeoisie have been mentioned earlier. On an ideological level, many of them held on to the principle of equality propagated by liberalism in its early days. Steadily the moderate, progressive-liberal reformist ideals became a key part of a strategy to promote class reconciliation, providing new political opportunities. They could use the militancy of the working class in their battle against the conservative ideology.

Bourgeois leaders had to defend the reformist interests of the working class in parliament. They made sure that socialists and social progressives grew ever closer together. They led the labour movement towards class reconciliation and tried to reconcile the liberal principles of individual freedom and free-market competition with the demands for state intervention in the social sector. Especially the freethinkers' associations were places where these leaders could meet, and they appear to have been instrumental in developing the reformist movement and putting it into practice. Both the progressive and socialist sides worked hard at this between 1880 and 1890.

The ideological play between liberal progressive, social-democratic and Marxist ideals was condensed into the BWP's 1894 Quaregnon programme.

The compromise text, written by E. Vandervelde, blended the most workable ideas in a coherent whole that appeased each wing and stopped internal opposition against reformism. Humanist social progressivism said the revolution had to take place first and foremost in each and everyone's mind. The Quaregnon text stressed non-violence and sought to meet such aims as universal suffrage, mandatory and free education and social legislation. Revolutionary zeal was sublimated into such theoretical principles as class struggle, the classless society, collectivism and the working class as the engine of the class struggle. Quaregnon was proof that the Belgian labour movement had turned into a reform movement. The promotion of democracy in the liberal state was the priority.

The Social-Democratic Programme

The systematic development of a big socialist 'pillar' within society was a spectacular achievement of social democracy. Work, social life and the intellectual expression of the working class were represented in one all-encompassing movement. It was the basis on which the political powers of the Belgian labour movement would build in the next years.

Consumer cooperatives held a key role in this development. The success of socialist bakeries during periods of crisis and inflated bread prices gave rise to the foundation and extension of a whole range of associations in several cities. It brought the workers into direct contact with the movement, supplied militant personnel and cash for propaganda and created a local core for socialist life to assume reality. *Le Progrès* in Jolimont (1886), *La Maison du Peuple* in Brussels (1884) and *Vooruit* in Ghent (1880) were prime examples of the strength of the organisational network. *Vooruit* took the lead under Eduard Anseele, a paternalistic socialist businessman who managed it as an almost capitalist cooperative. Just ahead of the Great War, it had its own textile factory, fleet, publicly traded stocks and it was in the process of setting up a bank.

Around these complexes, the socialist movement developed its own health programmes, pharmacies, insurance companies, cultural associations, theatre groups, choirs, brass bands, libraries, philosophical circles (freethinkers' associations), trade unions, printing presses, newspapers, etc. Trade union offices steadily expanded across the nation. Success soon spread beyond the socialist cradle in Ghent, first of all into Hainaut where the highly qualified glassblowers had united in the *Chevaliers du Travail* –

the Knights of Labour. Around the turn of the century, trade unionism had settled into many other cities (around metal, coal and wool workers and dockers) and the social umbrella organisation already counted some 125,000 members.

The massive impact of the BWP can only be understood if we consider its hold on this intricate and numerically strong organisational network. The numerous associations and groups were the prime recruiting ground for the socialist rank and file. It affected the BWP's institutional structure since the associations and groups, not the individuals, were members. Turning these cooperatives, health systems, associations and others into a political organisation was not easy. At the BWP's inception, trade unions made up only one-third of the member associations. In order to safeguard unity in such a diversified party, the leadership relied on centralisation and discipline, hierarchy and bureaucracy with authoritarian figures like Eduard Anseele and Emile Vandervelde at the top. The BWP would have to get its power from the authority of numbers.

The strength of the socialist group and the powers of the party went hand in hand. Knowing this, the Belgische Werkliedenpartij-Parti Ouvrier belge (BWP-POB) tried to establish new organisations in different sectors and centralised the many local associations. It increased its trade union activities to attract the Walloon industrial proletariat and it provided financial support and militant backing during strikes. These activities would have to back up the organisational measures – establishing federations for each branch of industry and subsequently allowing them to grow into national centres. The trade unions were professionally structured organisations that were not easy to cooperate with. The establishment of the Trade Union Commission in 1898 proved to be the solution. From then on, the socialist trade union movement expanded and became a strong pillar within the party. There were similar unification drives in the cooperative and insurance sector (*Prévoyance Sociale*, 1907), in the health service sector (National Association of Socialist Health Services, 1890), in the freethinkers' associations, etc. This evolution reinforced the grassroots support the BWP needed to do battle on the political front.

Parliament was the social-democratic key to paradise and there was only one way to get there: universal suffrage. The BWP started action in earnest in 1896 with its first street protest. Four years later, it managed to mobilise 70,000 to 80,000 people to back the same demand. After the Oath in St. Gilles Park, the left wing pressured the party leadership into organising a general strike for universal suffrage. Sixteen people were killed in Mons and 5 more in Antwerp – the result of the suppression of this massive political strike of 1893. But it did force the terrified bourgeoisie into concessions. In the end, a toned-down version of universal suffrage, which gave plural votes based on wealth, education and age (ensuring the bourgeoisie of a safe majority), was approved. It made sure the BWP entered into parliament, even though the numbers were still limited.

The Socialists wanted more and the battle for a 'one-man, one-vote' system continued. The Walloon rank and file was restless and demanded more decisive action, especially after the relative successes in the next elections. When it became apparent in 1902 that constitutional reform was again put on the back burner, the socialist camp in Hainaut had had enough. The subsequent strike was chaotic and ill-prepared. Six people died at the hands of the police force in Leuven, enough for the BWP leadership to call off the action. The dissatisfaction of the more radical undercurrents within the socialist movement and the fact that it became more and more apparent that the party was going nowhere, forced the party leadership to prepare new extra-parliamentary actions. The 1913 general strike was not going to be as disorganised as the 1902 edition. The party leadership had called on the workers to put savings aside and despite a massive participation, everything remained calm and peaceful. As soon as the Catholic government showed the first signs of caving in to the demands, the Socialist Party leadership called off the strike. It had received word that the king and government leader Charles de Brocqueville were willing to initiate constitutional reform, against the wishes of the political right. The Great War that was to break out one year later put everything on hold once more. The government had other concerns than a constitutional reform and the 1914-1918 conflict would have its own impact on the demands for a general suffrage for men.

The show of restraint of the Socialist Party's leadership was undeniably the result of the cooperation with the progressive liberals. Bourgeois intellectuals joined the BWP and the creation of a new independent progressive party made certain that reformists would take the upper hand from 1885 onwards. The Socialists joined an 1883 demonstration organised by the progressives to seek a reform of the electoral law. They even attended the progressive liberal Congress of 1887. The alliance was further strengthened when the progressives joined BWP actions for universal suffrage and set up joint electoral lists. When the dream of universal suffrage was reduced to a plural voting system, the progressives were hit hard and only had one way to reply – seek true universal suffrage. So even after 1894, cooperation remained useful for both sides since an electoral coalition was the only – theoretical – hope of pushing the Catholics out of government. This joint quest for political power remained just about the only reason to continue cooperation after 1900, with the 1912 elections as a concrete example. Thanks to proportional representation (1900) the Liberal Party had found a new stimulus, and under the leadership of P. Huysmans it steadily and consciously moved towards the centre, with its extreme left wing defecting to the socialists and the most conservative elements finding refuge with the Catholics. Not only did the liberals find the need for cooperation less and less pressing, also the socialists found it ever harder to stomach the concessions to keep the liberal progressives on board, especially since the 'one man-one vote' principle remained a dream.

So steadily, opposition within the BWP against the progressive liberal principles of class reconciliation, anti-collectivism and reformism grew louder. The opposition group, which revolved around such leaders as L. De Brouckère, H. De Man and others, had already opposed the BWP's 'ministerialism', and in 1891 (the Second International) protested against the adoption of the principle on tactical grounds. But the problem remained a theoretical one: Catholicism had such a comfortable hold on power that there was no chance at all of the BWP being invited to join the government. Moreover, the First World War would create a change in course as far as this particular reformist principle was concerned.

The Breakthrough of Christian Democracy

From 1885 onwards, the spectacular growth of the socialist labour movement was such that those in government could no longer disregard Belgium's social problems. Just like the liberals, the Catholic Party and clergy did their utmost to prevent violent, Marxist-inspired actions against the state. There was a real threat that the labour movement would become a formidable political force led by an anti-clerical and non-religious BWP. This development had to be stopped in order to recapture and re-christen the working class – that was the Catholic point of view. The progressive Catholics only had to look at the 1886 strike and other left-wing actions that caused bloodshed to realise that the social policy of non-intervention of the Catholic government was no longer tenable and that paternalistic religious charity would no longer do. Moreover, the expansion of the electorate made it vital for the Church to lure at least part of the proletariat back to its cause. If the Church wanted to keep control of the changing society, more adequate measures would have to be developed. The need for new social organisations was clear.

In view of the close relationship that had developed over the years between capital and Catholicism – the bourgeoisie backed conservative social action of the Catholics since the Church was seen as an ideal tool to keep social order – it was obvious that these social organisations would have to comply with a number of specific principles. The capitalist principles, especially the right to own property and the importance of the family were never questioned. Society's hierarchy, with a capitalist class at the top, was a key element, making the fight against class opposition and class hatred a logical consequence. Any antagonism between capitalism and labour had to be appeased in a spirit of Christian charity, with a view to strengthening the unity of the Christian community on a social level. In short, the labour movement to be created would mainly consist of instruments of reconciliation, preferably with a paternalistic character – i.e. controlled by the Catholic bourgeoisie. These mixed professional organisations in all economic sectors had to be the basis of a corporate society. Also parliament would have to be reorganised along these principles.

The Ultramontane corporatist views had a big impact and were designed to stop trade unionism in its track by means of a disguised paternalism and, again, charity. Only mixed unions, where employers and workers had to work in solidarity under the guidance of the employer, were accepted. Such unions were modelled on the concept of medieval guilds, when, so the story went, owners and labourers lived as one happy family in a benign religious spirit. These ideas were high on the agenda during the Liège congresses of 1886, 1887 and 1890 which were organised with the intent to re-christen the workers. The Catholic leaders Ch. Perin and especially J. Helleputte defended the ideas with conviction. But in spite of the creation of a few Catholic guilds in Flemish cities, the limited success of this corporatist movement could not be denied.

The factory workers scoffed at such ideas and the evolution in the socialist camp quickly made clear that it would take more to counter the socialist surge. Corporatism was abandoned around 1890 and, logically, led to a tentative move towards separate unions. With his 1891 encyclical *Rerum Novarum,* Pope Leo XIII played a fundamental role in the change.

Though he preferred a corporatist structure, the pope did accept the concept of workers-only unions, which would be able to organise more efficient anti-socialist action. Yet also these unions would have to remain loyal to basic capitalist principles, promote harmonious cooperation with the employers, seek peaceful solutions through negotiations in committees or other organisations, refrain from strikes and gladly accept any concession from higher up the social ladder. Guilds were turned into Christian unions in several cities, and leaders such as A. Pottier in Liège and A. Verhaegen in Ghent were the driving force behind these anti-socialist Catholic associations. Their actions went beyond the establishment of unions, as they tried to build a comprehensive labour movement, including health care and charity organisations, to rival the socialist one. In order not to antagonise small businesses, there was less activity in the cooperative sector, which fitted the strategy of the Catholic party of conquering that specific social group politically.

Support in huge numbers did not come naturally and the anti-socialist, Catholic labour movement never got close to the membership totals of the socialist labour movement during the early years. But some local priests and Catholic dignitaries persevered and by 1912, they were able to organise the anti-socialist national ACV-CSC union. Two years later it consisted of 28 centrals and 41 area associations, with a total of 65,000 members. The Catholic health care sector was also steadily expanded and centralised (National Central, 1906) from 1900 onwards. Local priests who had been steeped in the social ideology of the Church became the driving force of the organisations, especially after 1900. Within the parochial framework, the pastoral and social tasks merged.

But there was no way to win back the workers of Wallonia's heavy industry and Ghent's textile sector. The Catholics drew their membership from craftsmen and Flemish labour circles. Pre-war expansion was limited for the Christian labour movement, but there were good perspectives. Industrialisation in Catholic, agricultural Flanders, which started around the turn of the century, promised considerable possibilities for expansion for the Christian labour movement. The large numbers of Flemish rural labourers who would be employed by the factories, or would commute from their village to the industrial centres, became a prime target. They would be received by unions with a familiar Catholic spirit, in order to have their interests defended. The local village priest would make sure that the farm labourer who had been a member of the Catholic Farmers Union would be an industrial worker with a membership card of the Catholic labour union.

Just as the socialist labour movement relied on the BWP, the Christian social organisations were looking for a Christian-democratic political structure, which proved quite a bit more difficult. The priority of the Catholic Party and Church was to safeguard parliamentary and governmental domination. So it was essential that unity within the Catholic camp was kept, and that the authority of the clergy and the Catholic conservative bourgeoisie was not questioned at a time when the socialist BWP was making political inroads. Concessions that could threaten the unity and Catholic parliamentary majority, notably on the one-man one-vote principle, were out of the question. Catholic workers and their leaders had no autonomy during elections since it went against the principle of class solidarity and against the authority of the Church. As such, the development of autonomous, democratic forces within the conservative bourgeois Catholic Party was seriously limited.

The unscrupulous attack on the ideas of Father Daens, which came from anyone who was Catholic and conservative around the turn of the century, should be seen in this context. 'Daensism' was not a real labour movement. What it did do, was to channel the discontent that had grown, around 1890, among small Flemish farmers, seasonal workers, Catholic village teachers and clerks in the Aalst region and a number of East and West Flanders rural centres, about the hypocritical, conservative, francophone Catholic leaders. It offered an alternative for people who refused to turn to socialism because of its anti-clerical stance. It was a Christian, democratic and Flemish alternative.

Father Daens, a priest in Aalst, was the standard bearer of the movement and after the 1892 creation of the Christelijke Volkspartij (Christian People's Party) he was elected to parliament where he did not hesitate to support the left in demanding universal single suffrage and an improved social policy. Soon a mighty, well-coordinated coalition, including local bishop Stillemans, the arch-conservative parliamentarian Ch. Woeste, the Catholic Party and the monarch, whose power also relied on bourgeois Catholicism, opposed him. Even the pope intervened and barred Daens from saying mass. Under the unrelenting pressure of the Catholic establishment, Daens's support dwindled and so did the Christian democratic impact on the party. He broke away from the Church in 1898 and increasingly shifted towards the left. His alliance with socialism was more than the Vatican could take. Leo XIII condemned Daensism in 1905 and pushed the movement towards its final decline.

The same attempt to keep the entire Catholic camp under the political control of the bishops and bourgeoisie also showed in the hesitant stance and the actual impotence of the Christian-democratic wing. The *Anti-Socialistische Werkliedenbond* (The Anti-Socialist Workers Association), founded in 1890 by A. Verhaegen in Ghent, did not back demands for universal suffrage. The Catholic trade unions failed to join any protest actions to demand the expansion of the electorate. The *Volksbond* (People's Association, 1891), in which Helleputte exercised his corporatist influence, was just as moderate but called on the Catholic leadership for high representation on the electoral lists in an attempt to enter parliament that way.

The progressive Christian democratic wing (J. Renkin, H. Carton de Wiart) did not agree with this stance, and brought internal Catholic discord into the open. The Catholic leadership refrained from taking as tough a stance as against Daens. Helleputte was forced to resign, and Verhaegen, a compromise figure, was called upon to save the unity of the Volksbond. It would take until 1905 before the Christian-democrat movement would be able to force the conservative wing into making an important concession. Only then did the bishops recognise Christian democracy as an independent group within the Catholic movement, besides the conservative *Verbond der Katholieke Kringen en Conservatieve Verenigingen* (Association of Catholic Circles and Conservative Societies). They legitimised Christian-democratic demands for electoral candidates and an independent programme but only on the condition that no Catholic government could ever be toppled in favour of the opposition. The official recognition of Christian democracy as part of the Catholic class organisation was a fact.

This theoretical victory did not bring the Christian-democratic leaders any immediate practical increase in power. There was no breakthrough in parliament or government before 1900. The general plural voting system, combined with proportional representation around 1905 helped somewhat more. Overall, the parliamentary majority of the Catholic Party was steadily decreasing and it became clear that the conservative Catholics could no longer do without the support of the Catholic workers in some electoral districts. The Catholic hegemony was under threat and there was palpable fear that the Christian labour movement would either join the BWP or break away from the Catholic core. The time for compromise had come and the

Catholic leadership was forced into concessions. They succeeded in keeping Christian democracy underrepresented, but could not prevent it from growing into a political pressure group that would try to affect the government's social policy.

The Democratisation of Voting Rights and Social-Political Integration

The progressive liberals, social democrats and a number of progressive Catholics wanted to gain political power by extending electoral rights to all adult men. Universal suffrage was not only a main topic within all factions of the opposition, but also a point of discussion among the forward-looking bourgeoisie. The revolutionary events of 1886-7 could not be wiped that easily from the bourgeois collective memory, and massive socialist actions and strikes had also brought the realisation that suppression no longer sufficed to preserve the existing political order. Some conservative leaders realised how powerful the working class could become. They recognised that extra-parliamentary action could threaten the regime and that the time had come to neutralise the most explosive powers by offering limited concessions.

The role of minister Auguste Beernaert in between 1884-1894 was decisive. He was one of those prescient conservatives who saw that socialism needed to be contained and kept out of government. The political energy of the working class had to be redirected towards the traditional institutions of the liberal state, under the control of the bourgeoisie. The integration of this new political class had to be slowed down to make sure the newcomers would have time to absorb the traditions of the bourgeois institutions.

The changes in the electoral laws at the time confirmed this. Universal suffrage with plural voting rights was approved in 1893 by the Beernaert government as a concession following a demonstration in 1891 and the suppression of a strike in 1893 which claimed a number of lives. This compromise abolished the system of electoral taxation and granted every citizen the right to vote, yet still clearly gave the conservative forces an advantage. Heads of families living in a house for which a certain minimum tax was paid, owners of a property valued at over 2000 francs and holders of a higher education degree received one or two additional votes. As such, the 850,000 voters with one vote did not outweigh 1,240,000 votes of the wealthy and educated citizens. It was logical that the Catholic conservative majority stayed in power after the 1894 elections, with 68 % of the seats. The BWP was kept a long way from a majority, with only 28 out of 152 seats; the election turned into a disaster for the Liberals: the alliance with the Socialists, combined with the electoral system that awarded an absolute majority in two voting rounds, reduced its presence in the Chamber to only 13 %.

The municipal election rules also changed to universal suffrage with plural voting rights, and the bourgeoisie feared – not without reason – that a great many industrial centres would be turned into socialist bulwarks. As it was, an earlier relaxation of the electoral laws had already handed sixty-odd Walloon municipal councils to the BWP. The conservatives found it especially worrying that socialist mayors would head the local police forces. As such, the 1895 municipal electoral law was primarily aimed at reducing working class power. Again, tax payers and property owners were given additional votes while workers under the age of thirty were denied voting rights. Migrant labourers could not go to the polls either since voters had to live in one municipality for at least three years. The electoral law also functioned as a test-case for concessions to the corporatist Helleputte faction within the Christian democrats. In cities of over 20,000 people, a number of municipal council members would be appointed by employers and workers using a system of parity. This system again handicapped the numerically stronger working class in the urban centres. The Christian democratic left wing and the socialist movement resented this and again had a common cause.

Also after 1894-1895, the progressive liberals protested against the same measures that had stifled the progress of the BWP. They wanted to turn the disastrous results of the Liberal Party around and were hoping universal suffrage combined with proportional representation would prove to be the way. The liberal camp even threatened the Catholic government with the introduction of Liberal-Socialist coalition lists that could break the Catholic majority. The conservative Catholics wanted to avoid a social-democratic breakthrough at all cost, giving preference to a bourgeois-liberal increase in power, and decided to split up the alliance. The liberals were granted proportional representation but no universal suffrage. If the guarantees were sufficient to keep the Catholic monopoly in place, the government was prepared to make concessions. The Van de Peereboom proposal (1899) suggested so many conservative-Catholic guarantees that even the Christian democrats advised the author to tone it down.

The new De Smet-de Naeyer government eventually succeeded in dividing the socialist-liberal opposition. The centre liberals and even a number of progressive liberals backed the 1900 law that introduced proportional representation, but disconnected it from universal suffrage. Soon afterwards, the Liberal Party increased its presence in the Chamber to 21 %. The Catholics safeguarded their majority position, be it only with a 56 % share of the vote. They would have to take into account a strengthened Christian-democratic left wing from 1905 onwards. The separation between progressive liberals and socialists became evident. The Socialist Party was isolated during elections and in parliament. It had reached its limits within the electoral system with plural votes. The disappointing 1902 election proved that the right-wing strategy had worked: proportional representation coped with the BWP breakthrough and even managed to contain it. The Vandervelde-Janson bill concerning universal suffrage (1901) was disregarded and it would take until 1913 before the working class would make further parliamentary advances.

Whatever the debate on electoral reform, women were a non-factor. There were precious few calls to treat men and women equally. Feminists were a tiny minority, even among women. They were a select group from the intellectual bourgeoisie demanding full civil rights for women and the right to work, as an alternative for a dull life at home and, frequently, arranged marriage. The political right wing did not welcome them since the Church demanded the submission of women. But also among left-wing groups, calls for the vote for women were few and far between. The moral authority of priests and the Church over women of all walks of life was such that even the anti-clericals were not that enthusiastic to demand voting rights for women. The Socialist Party, too, was hesitant in practice. So Isabelle de Gamond and other feminists were given the opportunity to plead their cause, but could not count on any real support; granting women the right to vote was utter utopia ahead of the First World War.

In the meantime, the bourgeoisie had managed quite well to safeguard the power of the elite through legal adhesion of the masses. The bourgeois character of parliament had not changed that much since 1894. There were thirty-odd BWP parliamentarians, who wanted to adapt the system from within, but they were still too far removed from power and, in effect, they did not want to change the essence of the Belgian state. The majority of the social-democratic representatives were intellectual moderates and progressive liberals who had defected. At that time, Parliament was not about to lose all of its original, traditional functions, even though the first signs of a change in function were surfacing.

The capitalists no longer wanted to be dependent upon parliament and preferred to put immediate pressure on the government. They wanted to deal with the labour movement without parliamentary interference since the legislature was no longer the exclusive domain of the bourgeoisie. It was no coincidence that employers chose this time to set up their own pressure groups and that captains of industry left the halls of parliament. The legislature had to be reduced to a body to neutralise social energy and contain it in parliamentary action controlled by the bourgeoisie through the necessary legal concessions. The integration of the working class and social control of the labour movement had to be channelled towards the democratic institutions. The political process of democratisation at that time was based on those principles.

Little research has been conducted into the other channels for this integration and 'bourgeoisification' process and for political democratisation. A number of facts point to a large number of political, social, economic and cultural institutions and associations being created around the turn of the century with the apparent aim of bringing the new political classes in contact with each other and with the bourgeois ideology. As far as present research allows conclusions to be drawn, it seems to have been a slow integration process: every increase in wealth brought a tiny, select group of the upwardly mobile working class in contact with the lower reaches of the petty bourgeoisie, which became the social framework of reference *par excellence* for this group of workers.

The role of the Church in this process of socialisation has already been pointed out, and will later be discussed more in depth. But also the liberals displayed an interest in providing the workers with a 'framework'. Few data are available on the numerical strength of this movement, but it is a fact that, by the end of the century, a number of liberal workers' associations, cooperatives, health programmes and cultural associations had been founded. When working hours shortened, the extra time for leisure was monopolised by ideological institutions that promoted class reconciliation and integration, and purposefully targeted the masses. A number of sports, such as football and cycling, lost their strictly elitist character and became 'democratic'. The press no longer only served as a 'civil public' discussion platform but also became part of the process. The emergence of the mass media, be it with or without party links, but always defending the economic liberal system, was a typical phenomenon of this period.

It is no coincidence, either, that general mandatory education, seen as a guarantee for a moderating effect on extended voting rights, was put in place in the same period. The 1914 Poullet law brought mandatory education until the age of 14, and was voted in just before the First World War broke out. Improved schooling served several purposes. Children had to be prepared for the ever more sophisticated demands of industry, but primary education was also a good introduction into bourgeois society and created an ideal artificial pre-bourgeois environment for the developing child and the future voter.

Even some socialist associations played an indirect part in this process of socialisation. The first labour agreements with the employers did not serve any disintegrating function, but laid the foundations for the suppression of class warfare and the peaceful settlement of conflicts. The bureaucratic trade unions, health services and cooperatives were also part of this integration process, while some intellectual and cultural associations, notably the socialist freethinkers' union, provided the process with mental guidance. The state coordinated and controlled all those social integration efforts.

The governments of this period wanted to turn the workers into integral members of the liberal system, for instance by giving them the chance to gather a modest capital and become the owners of a modest home. The promotion of savings became part of the integration ideology and giving the workers the opportunity to accumulate possessions was an efficient way to promote love of labour, instil the virtue of thrift, foster acceptance of the value system of the petty bourgeoisie and oppose any social-political unrest. Especially in schools, the importance of teaching people to save was stressed. The ASLK/CGER was the government's financial instrument to achieve this. The bank had been founded in 1865 and had offices in every town. It targeted the small saver, from school children to workers and women, and helped finance the construction of modest homes. By 1913, 40 % of all Belgians had a savings account with ASLK/CGER and 70 % of its customers belonged to the working class. The Catholics and Socialists created their own savings banks and further promoted thrift among the working class.

State Intervention in the Social Sector

Following the social-democratic and liberal-progressive fight for the democratisation of Parliament, the acceptance of the principle of state intervention in the social sector was a major triumph for the left. Yet at the same time, 'enlightened capitalism' could also claim victory, since it was part of a strategy based on the principle that what was good for the worker, eventually would be good for the liberal state.

The first step was taken in 1886, when violent social revolt forced the Beernaert government to take a serious look at the social problems of the nation and a parliamentary labour committee was put to work. One year later, the government outlawed the system of paying workers in kind and in pubs. Joint industrial and labour councils were created the same year to counsel the government on disputes between employers and workers; they would later evolve into the so-called 'parity committees'. The government also took measures against public drunkenness and the dilapidation of working class housing. Labour law councils were reformed in 1889, with employers facing increasing working class representation. Legislation on women's and child labour as well as social housing was reformed in the same year. Industry could no longer employ children under the age of twelve and women under twenty-one were banned from working underground in mines. Twelve to sixteen-year-old boys and twelve to twenty-one-year-old girls were not allowed to work more than twelve hours a day.

After this first series of labour laws, Beernaert's much more conservative successors halted the process; it took until 1900 before the Christian democrats were able to re-ignite the process. As the left grew stronger in parliament, the legislative initiatives increased. Following the Royal Decree of 1891, the first law on old-age pensions was approved in 1900. The 1903 law on industrial accidents stipulated it was no longer up to the worker to prove his innocence. Mandatory Sunday rest was approved in 1905. After the Christian democrats forced the government of Paul de Smet de Naeyer to resign, more labour laws were approved when the Christian democrats Renkin and Helleputte were part of the Schollaert (1908-1911) and de Broqueville (1911-1918) governments. The maximum working hours per day for miners was brought down to nine. Two years later women's and child labour in coal mines was banned under the age of fourteen and a pension at age sixty was approved. The pension guarantee looked better than it actually was. Because of silicosis, or black lung disease, precious few miners enjoyed the privileges of retirement. The prospect of the 1911 election forced the Catholic governments into several concessions: night work for women was outlawed, child labour was further restricted and pensions for the military and civil servants were approved.

Ahead of the Great War, there were basically two categories of social legislation. One category regulated working conditions, including working hours, labour contracts, age limits, etc. Another tackled the more peripheral issues, including social security guarantees in case of illness, disability, old age and unemployment. Finally, both on national and local levels, new legislation and budgets greatly improved hygiene. Health councils and inspections, measures against epidemics and the bulldozing of slums were all part of a crusade against disease and the proletariat's threatening ghettos.

Which interpretations can be given for this policy of social intervention? First of all, the social laws were not very expensive for the government and in a time of economic expansion, could easily be carried by the wealthy. Moreover, the social intervention laws served a good purpose since it was aimed at containing the threat of proletarian revolt and disciplined labour organisations. Parliament understood that the working class was no longer prepared to accept the situation and that philanthropy and charity had had their day. The new concessions were granted out of sheer self-interest and the batch of social legislation around 1886-1889 underscored this. It was clear to all that the violent strikes of 1886 had broken the taboo. As the bourgeois fear subsided, so did the concessions. During the second phase between 1900 and 1911, the Catholic bourgeoisie simply wanted to hold on to power. The Christian democrats had to be appeased at that point, and they had to be given the political weapons to do battle with the Socialists.

Social legislation was adapted as much as possible to the needs of bourgeois society. Instead of class segregation, the time had come for integration and the working class had to be turned from a foe into an ally of the establishment. Striking abuses of power, and situations that directly affected the middle class, had to be eradicated and nothing was more symbolic than the razing of slums. Even though social and ethical concerns also played a role, it cannot be denied that there was the precondition that social considerations should not affect economic production. Several laws did little more than institutionalise already existing situations: public relief work for the poor, protection of society's weakest and abolishment of the most scandalous of abuses. There was concern that the labour force had to be turned into productive elements of society again. There was precious little interference in the employment and wage sectors, and no enforcement of a minimum income or a general limit on working hours. A maximum working week was only realised in 1909, and then only in the all-important energy sector, while reduction of women's and child labour met with the most stubborn resistance from conservative Catholics and liberals. On top of that, the social laws were rife with exemptions and easy to manipulate and thus effected little fundamental change. The infamous article 310 on the strike ban was not revoked, and severely hindered the struggle for better social conditions.

Overall, social legislation of the time was a half-hearted attempt to ease the plight of the workers and basically served the purpose of preserving the political order. Yet, for the liberal bourgeoisie, state intervention was a fundamental change. For the first time, two cornerstones of economic liberalism – absolute individualism and unbridled economic freedom – were under threat. The bourgeoisie fully understood though, that the intervention was all for the good of capitalism. Only the government was in a position to force competitors to make gradual improvements in the situation of the workers, and to limit unnecessary competition between companies. The government did not interfere directly in the labour market, though, leaving it up to the big cities to manage unemployment funds and job markets, where the local supply and demand were introduced in a spirit of reconciliation.

Catholic governments put their own mark on social legislation. They wanted to promote the moderate elements of the labour movement and create conditions favourable for the development of autonomous Catholic institutions, supporting the power of the Catholic Party. The principle of subsidiarity was thus institutionalised in the social sector. With the financial backing of the state, several social duties were delegated to private institutions. From 1900 onwards, Catholic governments started subsidising savings banks, health services and unemployment funds. The 1894 laws on social security had cleared the way, and stipulated that only recognised institutions meeting certain demands and conditions were eligible; as a result, this subsidy policy mainly benefited Catholic private initiative. It angered the radical liberals and socialists who insisted such controls impeded the emancipation of the working class.

Progressive liberals and social democrats wanted more direct state intervention in the social sector. Social legislation had been a key part of their programs for years; they saw it as common ground shared by those who did not accept that capitalism was allowed to make victims among the workers, and those who realised that Marxist rule and a classless society were not just around the corner. For them, the first social legislation was just a precursor to the 'welfare state' and proof that the worst was over for the proletariat. For the first time since the inception of industrial capitalism, a limited group of workers enjoyed minimal protection and could look forward to a better future, partly due to social democracy.

It would be a mistake to think that the Belgian state was evolving in a socialist direction, though. The limited measures left society very much capitalistic in nature. There was no direct state intervention in the economy and state enterprises were limited to communication, public transport and utility companies, managed by the municipalities. Several Belgian cities, including Brussels, were known for their 'gas, water and electricity socialism'. Some socialist ideologues considered this so-called 'municipalism' as a local application of their collectivist principles, but reality told a different story. Most of these utility companies needed lots of investment, yielded little profit and were extremely risk-prone. Private companies just did not want to touch this sector during the early stages. But as soon as the public utility companies turned a profit, interest surged and the governments concocted investment formulas that gave private firms a stake in such companies (mixed companies, so-called 'intercommunals').

The mutual symbiosis of state and society was mainly limited to the social sector and the liberal philosophy remained unchallenged on the purely economic level. When coal was discovered in the Kempen region, it was immediately evident that such riches could not belong to society at large, but to the rich landowners. Belgium's right wing was united in demanding it be turned into private property, without any state intervention. Belgium's fiscal system also remained a taboo area. The state mainly earned its income from indirect taxation and the big fortunes and high incomes were taxed very little. The fact that during this period, any limited democratic reform (income-based taxation) remained on the drawing table was proof that the conservatives still ruled.

The Battle for the Farmer's Vote

The democratic electoral changes forced the political parties to look for votes in almost every sector of society. The battle between socialists, liberals and Catholics for the favours of the working class was a case in point. The introduction of universal suffrage with multiple votes made it important to appeal to other voters, too. In spite of the fact that little research has been conducted, it may be reasonably assumed that a number of poor middle-class shopkeepers had earlier found a home in the labour movement, while the more successful traders had been won over by liberal and Catholic progressive movements; as such, the political battle for this social group was not very important.

Small farmers and agricultural labourers, on the other hand, still had to be won over by the political parties, and representing 21 % of the active population in 1890, they were worth fighting for, even though this group was in relative decline. They could easily push the political balance one way or another, especially in Flanders. The BWP and Daensists, but also the liberals, were the first to actively pursue this new electoral group and the Catholic Party was immediately worried it would lose traditional allies. Moreover, there was the threat that the dwindling rural population would become susceptible to demands for emancipation; this encouraged the Catholics to become highly active among the farmers. Church and religion had long been intimately intertwined with the farming community and the Catholic Party was a traditional defender of agricultural interests. For the Catholics, the farmer embodied Christian values, was the guardian of the faith and of morality, and a pillar of the Church. Because his property was so important to him, the farmer wanted law and order first and foremost. Farmers were the bulwark against socialism, materialism and individualism. Safeguarding the increasingly politically conscious farmer class became the prime objective of the Catholics. The creation of small farm properties was a key part of the Catholic strategy to counter socialist infiltration.

The long crisis in the farm sector that started during the 1870s reached its climax between 1885 and 1895. Prices collapsed, sometimes by as much as 40 % and investments dwindled since industry was much more profitable. By 1910, the share of farming in the gross national product had declined to between 15 and 20 %. The crisis changed the basics of Belgian farming. Small family plots, where intensive farming was the only option, survived the depression, as the living standards of the farmers were excessively low and the labour force consisted of non-paid family members. An evolution to small and mid-sized farms and the decline of massive land ownership had other reasons, too, such as the inheritance system. Two-thirds of the farms had no more than two to ten acres of arable land. A lack of cash and credit kept new technologies, like special fertilizers, out of reach, and exacerbated the crisis.

The social situation of these small Flemish farmers and labourers was miserable. In order to stay alive and pay the tenancy, farmers and their families led a life of endless toil, even more so than the industrial proletariat. Many emigrated to the United States, and over 200,000 went to Wallonia and France between 1890 and 1910. Thousands of seasonal labourers were exploited in Walloon and northern French farms, and many made the daily commute to the nearest industrial centres looking for supplementary income. Small farmers in Flanders, hard hit by the depression, lived a sad life of poverty.

The Catholic party did not protect these small farmers by acting against the high lease rates, nor did it call for a protectionist farming and grain policy since the economic-liberal Catholics on no account wanted to interfere with industry. Belgium had gone too far down the road of industrial expansion to start meddling with agricultural protectionism now. Up to 1894, the small farmer was a non-factor. When he became a political player, his problems, including the lease system, also came to the fore. The government guided Belgian farming, with the help of limited subsidies, towards profitable, labour-intensive choices (cattle farming and market gardening). Other initiatives to modernise and re-orientate farming included a regulated price policy, fiscal measures, agricultural education and new transport infrastructure.

Local initiatives adapted to the immediate needs and mentality of the small farmer complemented government action. During the Catholic Liège congresses, plans were made to improve the farmer's lot by creating paternalistic guilds, farmers' cooperatives and insurance funds, counting on the elite to provide the initial capital. When local priest J.F. Mellaerts of Heist-op-den-Berg founded the first guild to organise the joint purchase of advanced fertilizer in 1890, with the help of Helleputte and Schollaert, he actually laid the foundations for the creation of the Boerenbond (Farmers' Union). The dynamic Boerenbond thrived and would become one of Flanders' most powerful financial institutions. The Boerenbond guilds supervised the creation of sales and purchase cooperatives, dairy farms, insurance institutions and credit banks to boost the development of small farming properties, which had been very limited in Flanders up to then.

The Boerenbond quickly spread its roots deep in Flanders' fertile fields, even before the First World War. The parish system, with its priests leading the agricultural organisations, was instrumental in creating a solid Catholic farming class which felt at one with the Church. The Catholics had been unable to rally the labour movement behind their paternalistic principles, but in the guilds of the Boerenbond they were able to forge Christian solidarity among the landowners and tenant farmers, instil faith in the leading role of the upper classes and set out family, religion and property as the sacrosanct foundations of society.

Socialism could not get its voice heard in the farming villages. The impact of Daensism has not been clearly calculated yet, but with its verbal attacks on the big landowners and excessively high lease rates, and with its calls for state intervention in favour of small-scale farming, it was undoubtedly popular in the Flemish countryside. Unlike Daensism and Catholicism, the BWP defended collectivism, something that was staunchly opposed by most farmers. The farmer was totally devoted to his small plot of land. And in case he did not own property, acquiring his own land was his biggest ambition. The fear of collectivism was fanned by Catholic anti-socialist propaganda and the BWP, despite its virulent attacks on big landowners, did not stand a chance.

The BWP's anti-clericalism, even though it was toned down for electoral reasons, did not go down too well in rural communities either. Due to a lack of local militants – the Church's social control in the countryside prevented almost any contact – the socialists did not know the Flemish farmer and his mind-set well enough and, in spite of enormous campaign efforts, the BWP failed to get any political hold at all in Flemish villages – even in Wallonia they had little success in the countryside. The anti-clerical Liberals fared likewise.

Catholics vs. Freethinkers

The Catholics reigned supreme in the decades ahead of Great War. But the Catholic movement feared a return of anti-clerical governments, and it was also worried its electoral base would be undermined by increasing rationalisation and secularisation, so it showed great dynamism and activity. The bishops, clergy and politicians, in fact the entire Catholic bloc did its utmost to expand Catholic rule over every sector of society, and to widen its control over the state.

To protect its flock against increasing secularisation, the Catholic Party started building institutional ramparts. It promoted a policy of philosophical apartheid and Catholic ghettos, with a separate pillar integrating every part of society and adapted to social status, social needs, age and sex. The Catholic pillar encompassed everything from the Boerenbond farmers' union to associations for the self-employed, workers' associations, youth organisations, women's guilds and leisure groups. Together with the already established religious and charity organisations, they held a sizable part of the population hermetically sealed within the Catholic camp. The clergy, more than ever central to political activity, boosted the electoral campaigns and was able to build on the institutional framework of the Catholic pillar, which came under the firm control of the bishops and conservative bourgeoisie. National umbrella organisations were set up to coordinate policy and religious education. The Catholic Party, which after 1918 would be reformed as a class party, defended the political interests.

Big business had also joined the Catholic camp. The Catholic aristocracy and high bourgeoisie had steadily been turned into one upper class. The privileged, elitist position claimed by the establishment was reflected in the solid conservative principles characterising political Catholicism at the time.

The Catholics had been able to rule on their own for over 30 years, unencumbered by any need to forge compromises with the secular forces. The electoral majority system and the particular application of the proportional representation system assured the Catholics of a constant parliamentary majority, as did the fact that their policy had largely been aimed at rural interests. During this long period of monopoly power, they could shape political and public life and through the appointment of civil servants, they soon enjoyed a virtual hegemony over state institutions, the army and the judiciary. Liberal appointments were out of the question, and in the Catholic elite vision, it was unimaginable that any social democrat would get a position of trust.

Once in power, the Catholics promoted the principle of subsidiarity. They wanted to limit state interference as much as possible in an attempt to give Catholicism a free rein. The State had to fund, but have no control over, such important sectors as education, health and social welfare, housing and culture. Such a hands-off policy guaranteed the autonomy of Catholic organisations, granted them financial viability, gave them a large say in state policy and allowed the Catholic Party to gain strong social and electoral grounding. The Ultramontane principle of 'subsidised freedom' helped create Belgium's 'pillarised society' that would become the dominant system in the 20th century.

The Catholic show of force was all too clear in education. The 1879 anti-clerical school laws, the School War and the creation of the costly public school network had given the Catholics an appetite for revenge. From 1884 onwards, Catholic policy would focus on reinforcing Catholic private education with public funds and turn public education into a Catholic instrument. The Catholics had barely moved into their government offices in 1884 when they abolished the liberal school laws of Van Humbeeck. Every municipality was again allowed to fund Catholic primary schools and official degrees were no longer a necessity. In Catholic Flanders, this simply meant that almost all public schools were turned into Catholic institutions. Initial tolerance on mandatory religious education was inspired, among others, by Leopold II, and municipalities were given the choice of either making religious education mandatory in their schools, or to offer special classes for children that did not want to participate in religious courses. If there was no school providing religious classes in a certain municipality, the state had the obligation to provide them. These concessions were repealed under minister Schollaert 1885 when the Catholic realisation grew that religion was the ideal ideological weapon to keep the Socialists at bay. Any talk of choice and special classes was gone. In primary schools, religious education was mandatory but heads of family could ask for a special dispensation. In little time, the Catholics had turned back the clock to 1842, the year of the initial breakthrough of the Catholic education model. The 1895 law did lead to systematic campaigning by freethinkers' associations and anti-clerical municipal governments encouraged people to massively ask for dispensation of religious classes, leading to the factual neutralisation of public primary education in cities such as Brussels and Antwerp, and in industrial centres (especially in Hainaut).

When Mercier became archbishop, the Catholic congress of Mechelen (1909) demanded complete financial equality for Catholic schools. Private (so-called 'free') education had felt the need for increased subsidies as a result of the increasing competition of public schools in anti-clerical cities and areas. In this boom period of international political-religious battle there was no room for a pacification compromise on the School War, as some moderate Catholics would have liked. Instead, pope Pius X chose for a fully-Catholic restoration strategy, with a religious education offensive to match.

Catholic education received a further boost in 1911, when a government bill sought to increase funding for private primary schools by approving subsidies per student. It was another blow to the public school system which, unlike the Catholic schools, could not count on outside financing. Liberals and socialists jointly opposed the bill and were able to stop it at the committee stage, but the 1914 Poullet law on mandatory education finally granted the Catholics their wish: state subsidies for private schools were considerably increased. However, the law did grant the state control over educational programming and teachers had to have official degrees.

It will be obvious that the Catholic pillar was absolutely dominant. The Belgian nation and Catholic establishment seemed to be one and the same. Cardinal Mercier turned Belgian nationalism into an almost religious cult. The national basilica of Koekelberg (1905) would be built in order to symbolise that union.

In comparison, the freethinkers were in a completely different situation. On a political level, there was a gradual and almost complete collapse. There was a brief anti-clerical flare-up when the 1884 Van Humbeeck law on education was abolished; socialists, dogmatic and progressive liberals organised a huge demonstration in Brussels and the mayors of several big cities joined in a coalition to oppose the Catholic laws. Due to the massive influence of the clergy, the protest soon petered out to make way for increasing social-economical conflict within the freethinkers' camp; the polarisation overshadowed any joint anti-clerical stance. Factions split the movement, the anti-clerical leaders had no political impact and the social issue dominated everything. After 1900, anti-clericalism took another blow when the centre liberals and social democrats drifted further apart.

And just ahead of the war, the BWP dealt the freethinkers a political blow when it expelled their associations from the party. The associations had long been active within the BWP and they had helped foster the alliance between socialism, anti-clericalism and rationalism. The influence of progressive liberals and bourgeois intellectuals reinforced the trend. In theory, religion was a private matter, but the BWP had long been virulently anti-clerical. But the 1894 and 1900 elections made it painfully clear that their anti-Catholic stance severely limited any chances of growing in rural areas and in Catholic Flanders. Socialist parliamentarians were elected exclusively in Wallonia. The party started to weed out freethinkers' organisations and in 1913, banned them altogether.

Despite the demise of political anti-clericalism, the national freethinkers' federation, founded between 1880 and 1885, persevered. This group of progressive and social-democratic freethinkers organised protest actions every time Catholics tried to turn back the clock on controversial laws or boasted their unchallenged power. The federation organised a mass petition against the Catholic school laws and had plenty of proposals in store to check advancing Catholicism. Anti-clerical manifestations would accompany the fruitless attempts to break the Catholic majority through liberal-socialist cartels.

Their political impotence belied the continuing advance of rationalism and de-Christianisation. The trend had taken hold as a side-effect of Belgium's industrial revolution around 1850 and gathered pace during the so-called second industrial revolution, as could be seen in the expansion of the network of freethinkers' associations. The Socialist movement, expanding around the turn of the century, also made sure that, especially in Wallonia, workers turned their back on Catholicism. The liberals showed a similar increase in organisational activity. The decline in Church practice was not always based on sheer atheism, but more often on doubt, uncertainty, indifference and anti-clericalism. The result was an increase in civil burials and divorces and a decrease in Church weddings, baptisms and other Church practices. The Walloon industrial centres, Brussels and a few Flemish cities with leftist majorities took a lead in this.

Cultural Flamingantism

The fundamental social, economic and political changes also had their impact on the Flemish Movement. Flanders itself changed: industrialisation slowly expanded from southern Belgium into Flanders from 1880 onwards, and showed itself for the first time outside the traditional textile industry. During this second industrial revolution, Wallonia started to show some signs of wear and tear, especially in coal mining, and Wallonia's belligerent labour movement started to turn off investors. Big business started to look to Flanders instead and found a surplus of cheap and unschooled workers, kept docile by the clergy. The proximity of ports was an obvious bonus.

The Brussels and Walloon holding companies built non-ferrous and chemical factories in the Kempen region and along the Brussels-Vilvoorde-Willebroek-Boom axis. Shipyards were set up in Hoboken, Antwerp and the first cokes factories were built in Zeebrugge because of the overseas coal import through the port. The harbour in Antwerp went through a major expansion and in 1901 coal was discovered in Limburg. All new industrial investment in Flanders was created and controlled by Brussels and Walloon big business, further extending francophone domination over Flemish industry. Flanders provided cheap labour, but the industrialisation also increased the demand for skilled personnel (technicians, clerks, management).

While heavy industry remained francophone, medium and small businesses produced a new class of Flemish economic leaders, with Lieven Gevaert as a prime example. The Flemish employers created a strong autonomous structure in 1910, a precursor of the *Vlaams Economisch Verbond* (VEV, Flemish Economic Union) and they could count on the backing of the Catholic banking institutions, forerunners of the Kredietbank. They rejected the francophone industrial bourgeoisie and created a Flemish alternative based on the Catholic model of class reconciliation. And since they wanted the Belgian state to shift economic policy more towards Flanders, they demanded more Flemish rights, and as such opened up new opportunities for the Flemish Movement.

The social integration policy of the time also offered new opportunities for the Flemish Movement. Within such a concept, it was obvious that the bourgeoisie, administration and the people would have to learn to speak the same language. Universal suffrage with plural voting rights put most Flemings on the political map, forcing politicians to address them in Dutch during election campaigns. The Flemish wing of every political party gained in stature and expanded its political backing. With the exception of Brussels, where it was in a much further stage, a further gallicisation of Flanders was out of the question. The Flemish middle class was increasingly conscious of its language and culture and it realised that the promotion of Dutch in public institutions would open up the labour market for Flemish intellectuals. Flamingant worries served as an idealist sublimation of their struggle for concrete, professional interests. As the attitude changed, the membership of the flamingant movement rose, and consequently, sales of Dutch-language newspapers and interest in Flemish literature increased and pupils and students became much more militant.

The Flemish Movement became more powerful, self-conscious and forceful, yet it lacked a unified and organised party structure. Instead, pro-Flemish politicians were spread over the existing parties and tried to increase their clout with the help of external pressure groups. The Flemish movement remained prudent and petty bourgeois, and its initial demands were limited to a set of language laws that were in essence half-hearted attempts to promote Dutch in a bilingual Flanders. Some language laws were approved during the 1890-1899 period, regarding Dutch-language courses in state universities (1890), the use of Dutch in Brussels and Liège appeal courts (1891) and in military criminal justice (1899).

The language laws caused a lot of frustration because of their half-hearted content and deficient application. Such frustration, combined with socio-economic progress, provided an extra boost and an ideological and political innovation for the Flemish movement around 1895. University professors J. Mac Leod and A. Vermeylen, linguist M. Rooses and especially economist L. De Raet were at the heart of a new concept – 'cultural flamingantism'; also the Rodenbach tradition of the Catholic, bourgeois student movement joined them (Dosfel, Vliebergh). They provided solid analyses, proving that language discrimination was partly to blame for the material backwardness of the Flemish worker, clerk, farmer and shop-owner. They called for a fight based on elitist cultural individualism. The Flemings had to change themselves through self-development, into a cultural elite that would allow Flanders to grow and catch up intellectually and materially. The movement, stimulated by Flemish 'people power' had to produce an enterprising Flemish industrial and intellectual bourgeoisie that would eventually overshadow the francophone elite. In short, through an increased 'tribal consciousness' and elevation of the people by a cultural elite, Flemings could become the dominating force in Belgium. In order to achieve this goal, education was crucial: secondary, technical and university education had to become Dutch-speaking. The flamingants turned it into a fundamental issue. They wanted to rid Flanders of its francophone upper crust and, for the first time, opted for a monolingual Flanders. As it turned out, one issue would come to crystallise all their demands: Ghent State University had to be turned into a Dutch-speaking institution.

Faced with this combative movement, the Catholic Party reacted in familiar style. Flanders had to be kept under Catholic control. The high clergy was francophone, as was the Catholic high bourgeoisie, and they would back the party. Catholic flamingantism had to make sure, however, that in the expanded electoral system, the Catholic character of the Flemish was rid of foreign elements such as gallicisation, and safeguarded against socialist ideas. A few right-oriented Catholic-flamingant members of parliament continued the petty bourgeois Meeting tradition in the Chamber of Representatives. Catholic pressure groups were created to lure the pro-Flemish Catholic voter after 1894, and existing groups were activated (Vlaamse Katholieke Landsbond, Antwerp Nederduitse Bond) through alumni associations and organisations of shop-owners; they were never allowed a high status within the party, though. In the vein of traditionalism (language as a religious instrument for the preservation of a traditionalist cultural pattern), a number of priests and Catholic teachers were also promoting the Flemish-Catholic link. They received the full support of the Christian-democrat and farmers' organisations, which stressed certain Flemish demands in order to safeguard the maxim that Flanders and Catholicism were inseparably linked. The benevolent attitude of the new class of Flemish employers towards the Christian-democratic formula of cooperation and class organisation under the leadership of an enterprising elite, also led this group into backing an initially minimalist Flemish program; the Antwerp successor of Coremans, F. Van Cauwelaert, was a good example of this trend.

The Liberal Party experienced a process of democratisation after 1900 and turned towards the pro-Flemish petty bourgeoisie to recruit more members. Circulation of the Brussels newspaper *Het Laatste Nieuws* rose to 75,000 in 1912, underscoring the growth of liberal flamingantism. It had several legislators (among others L. Frank) in the House of Representatives and was politically well organised in electoral associations, which would merge into the Liberal People's Association in 1907 and the umbrella Liberal Flemish Association in 1913. The link between the liberal progressive wing and the flamingants remained – in Antwerp this Flemish-liberal movement held a strong position – but it no longer had strong proportions. The flamingants around the Ghent *Volksbelang*, for instance, chose to associate themselves with the centre-right wing of the party.

The socialist leaders sidestepped the Flemish issue and did not try to turn it into a political weapon; several reasons can be offered for this. The BWP backed the majority of the Second International in promoting the international dimension of the class struggle and opposing nationalist tendencies. According to socialist reasoning, the final victory of democracy would automatically solve all language issues. The Flemish movement played no essential part in the quest for universal suffrage, so the socialists could do without it. The Flemish issue did not fit in the socialist concept of the class struggle. Cultural flamingantism was elitist, many pro-Flemish parliamentarians were conservative, the electoral base of the BWP was in Wallonia, and anti-clericalism was overwhelming among the BWP leadership – more than enough reasons not to get involved. The pro-Flemish socialists may have been in an unenviable position, but many did act. The Antwerp branch, for instance, never hid its flamingant stance, while the group around Camille Huysmans saw Flemish emancipation as part of the battle for better wages and cultural enhancement. And since the Flemish demands were essentially democratic, the BWP always voted in favour of new language laws.

The new vigour of the Flemish movement and the beneficial political constellation showed during the parliamentary debate on the so-called 'equality law', which aimed to give legal status to the use of Dutch in parliament and in official publications. A bill to recognise Dutch as an official Belgian language was introduced in 1895 by De Vriendt and Coremans. At first, francophone opposition made sure that the Senate diluted the proposal, but united and unwavering extra-parliamentary Flemish protest made sure the law was also approved in the Senate in 1898.

The promotion of Dutch in Catholic secondary schools also became a controversial political issue. The francophone episcopate and the Catholic Party leadership strenuously opposed a proposal by Coremans in 1901 to extend the 1883 law on the use of Dutch in some courses in public schools to the private network as well. The Catholic establishment categorically rejected Dutch as a mandatory language of instruction and made sure the measure did not get through parliament. The bishops also dismissed a binding say of the government in private secondary education, as it was not subsidised. But the Catholic flamingants persisted and, backed by the Christian democrats, they tabled a compromise bill in 1910, which allowed the private network the choice between the public school system or a mandatory eight hours of Dutch classes a week. Parliament approved it and after years of open conflict, the Catholic flamingants emerged as victors.

Meanwhile, the culture-flamingants, in cooperation with flamingants from almost all political parties, had begun to focus on the battle over the francophone bulwark of *Rijksuniversiteit Gent* (RUG, Ghent State University). They wanted to turn the university into a monolingual Dutch-speaking institution. Professor Mac Leod led a First Higher Education

Commission that proposed a gradual linguistic transition, but he faced the argument that the university would lose too many students that way. Once the parliamentary battle over the use of Dutch in secondary schools was settled, all pro-Flemish forces focused their efforts on Ghent University; a Second Higher Education Commission was set up in 1908 under L. De Raet and M. Rooses, and the mass meetings it organised turned into an overwhelming success. The francophone backers of the university created *L'Union pour la défense de la langue française à l'Université de Gand*, their own union to defend French at the university. Soon, there was no political way around the issue anymore. A bill was introduced in 1911 but failed to get through parliament ahead of the war.

Other language laws underscored the increasing impact of the Flemish cause in all parties. In 1908, Dutch was approved as an official language in the Brabant high provincial court. The 1907 mining law even contained an article on language, and in 1909 a language law for the labour courts was voted. The 1914 law on mandatory education said that in primary schools, courses had to be taught in the mother tongue. It was not strictly applied in Brussels, since people were convinced one had to know French in the capital. Brussels' exceptional status made sure the city would become increasingly francophone, but it also included a perspective of bilingualism that the French-speakers resolutely rejected.

Unsurprisingly, the first resistance against a bilingual nation came from Brussels, and it was based on the fear that Walloon civil servants would lose jobs in Brussels and Flanders if Dutch was accepted as an official language. It also was an attack on the privileges and supremacy of the French language. Mandatory bilingualism in the public sector would turn into a monopoly position for the Flemings. Francophones were convinced they had the inalienable right to exclusively speak and know French without this being an impediment for a career in administration and other public sectors, and the right to an equal share of public functions. In other words, francophone civil servants, doctors and lawyers were afraid that the use of Dutch in public life in Flanders and the bilingual status of Brussels held serious threats for their careers. They could also count on the support of the national francophone bourgeoisie.

When the language laws were approved, anti-Flemish reactions came from some Walloon liberal intellectual circles; they even voiced federalist demands when it became increasingly clear that Catholic Flanders kept the conservatives in government, against the electoral wishes of leftist Wallonia.

Some socialists had similar objections. This Walloon movement opposed bilingualism and the mandatory knowledge of Dutch in the Walloon part of the country. It wanted to maintain the francophone sphere of influence in Flanders and Brussels and considered Flemish emancipation nothing but a dangerous attack on francophone power, which had prospered in Belgium since 1830, much to the satisfaction of the francophone population. In summary, immediately before the First World War the seeds of the three components of the linguistic problem were already present: a militant Flemish Movement, the inception of a Walloon federalist movement and the bilingual problem area of Brussels.

Colonialism and Militarism

During the latter part of the 19th century, Western Europe was facing overproduction and the capitalist quest for maximum profits took countries to regions where raw materials and cheap labour were plentiful. Belgium entered this battle for economic and political hegemony over colonial areas with gusto. Belgian colonialism was special since it was driven by the monarch himself. It was a personal initiative of Leopold II to investigate the economic potential of the Congo basin, and during the 1884-1885 international conference in Berlin, Europe's other colonial powers recognised Congo State as the personal possession of the king in return for free trade rights there. Leopold II set up a ruthless system of exploitation in the central African region. To maximise the export of rubber and ivory (the profits in 1901 were as high as 18 million francs), he enlisted local workers who had to slave away in inhuman conditions, under the supervision of local civil servants and under pressure of the most terrible repression (lethal penal expeditions, incarceration, beatings etc.). How many thousands of lives this exploitation cost the Congo is still an extremely controversial question regarding the Congo policy of Leopold II.

Apart from amassing his personal fortune, Leopold II also wanted to serve the interests of Belgium's capitalist class. The monarch had already been successful in urging holding companies to invest in China and the Middle East. Now he wanted them to be an integral part of his Congo policy. Trade concessions for British and U.S. companies were redirected towards interested Belgian investors. The Empain group, Société Générale and a number of Antwerp bankers started to monopolise the colonial activities. Union Minière was founded in 1906 to manage the Katanga mines. During the pre-war period, Belgium steadily created its colonial bourgeoisie which would do its utmost to keep the Congo in Belgium's sphere of influence.

During a period when economic pressure groups had a major impact on foreign policy, it should come as no surprise that the government backed Leopold's Congo initiative. The king had an authoritarian style, much like his father, and he used his authority as constitutional monarch to the full to get government backing. Some ministers and parties tried to oppose this, and in the Congo affair both factions were reflected. At first, the king could count on minister Auguste Beernaert. The Belgian state participated in the creation of a Congo railway system, it granted the monarch subsidies in 1887 and 1889 and agreed on a new 25-million-franc colonial loan in 1890. New credit facilities were approved in 1895, although this time conditions included that the Congo would be turned over to the Belgian state if the king failed to repay his debt.

It started to dawn on Belgian leading circles that Congo would be better off as an independent Congo state in the hands of the Belgian state. The British Casement Report, the Inquiry Commission, the Congo Reform Association and other international criticism exposed Leopold's ruthless colonial policy. Belgium's economic interest groups added their weight to the debate because they feared all of Congo might soon be lost for them. Even the Socialist BWP, which had initially created an anti-Congo movement, now wanted to annex the colony on humanitarian grounds; among others, Vandervelde backed this demand. The annexation negotiations were held under the Schollaert cabinet. In the end, Leopold II was willing to surrender sovereignty over the area, but wanted to hold on to a large 'crown property' to continue his work on such prestigious projects as the Tervuren Museum and the Cinquantenaire Park. Socialists, Liberals and Christian democrats could not accept such a state within the state and Leopold II had to abandon plans for a personal fiefdom in the heart of Africa. Parliament approved the law to turn Congo into a Belgian colony in 1908, and this Colonial Charter laid down the basic principles of colonial organisation, transferring most of the authority over the region to the Minister of Colonies. The local Governor-General had little authority. Parliament and the political parties took little interest in colonial issues at first.

The king also took military issues to heart. Together with prominent representatives from court circles, the high financial circles, the army command and a number of right-wing politicians, Leopold II was part of a movement to expand the army, enter into military alliances to safeguard Belgium's territory and even claim strategic frontiers like the Rhine and Scheldt rivers. The king exercised strong pressure on his government to approve more military spending, the creation of new fortresses and the replacement of the system of drawing lots by personal military conscription. The anti-militarist liberal and Catholic progressives had already tried to obstruct Leopold II's military ambitions during the 1860s and 1870s. The socialists had objections against the unjust lottery system which allowed the wealthy to buy out of military service. It was a terrible blow for many in the countryside when the lottery condemned them to several years of service away from their familiar surroundings. The BWP also turned aggressively anti-militarist after the army had taken part in bloodbaths to suppress strikes. Starting in 1887, The socialist *Jonge Wacht* (Young Guard) youth organisation set up anti-militarist actions to explain to working class soldiers the repressive character of the army and win them over for the Socialist cause.

The joint opposition of socialists, progressive liberals, Christian democrats and Daensists was able to hinder the policy of the militarist coalition, but it could not stop them from going ahead with their plans. New fortresses were built in the Meuse valley and a new line of military defence was set up around Antwerp; the latter project was a compromise to come out of the so-called 'forts question' (1905). It proved a lot more difficult to change the conscription system. The conservative bourgeoisie – acting out of self-interest – did not want to cooperate even though some of them claimed that after the 1886 strikes they could no longer trust an army with working class recruits. This group saw personal conscription as a means to exert better control. The fact that also the clergy benefited from the old system meant that there was no unanimous stance from the Church hierarchy concerning the abolition of the lottery system. It was only shortly before the death of Leopold II in 1909 that Parliament accepted limited personal conscription for one son per family. Because of the threat of war, it was abolished, and replaced by general personal conscription in 1913.

The threat of war was very real in many other ways. The arms race intensified around 1900 and even speeded up further as the war drew closer. This increased the international influence of Cockerill's ammunition factories. In Belgium and just about everywhere else in Europe, right-wing nationalism was on the rise.

The Impact of the First World War on Domestic Policy

The German army invaded in August 1914 and forced the Belgian troops to entrench behind the Yser river. From then on, patriotism was no longer limited to the militarist, conservative groups. The Socialist leaders aligned themselves with the De Broqueville government, backed the mobilisation and became part of the national solidarity movement. Their patriotism, which was an inherent part of the BWP's reformist and revisionist policy, swept away the mistrust of the conservatives. This show of class cooperation proved that Belgian socialism viewed itself as an integral part of the regime, and wanted to act in the same vein. Opposition against this imperialist war was minimal and certainly not enough to prevent Emile Vandervelde from being appointed Minister of State in 1914. Two years later, he would join the Belgian government which had found a home in non-occupied Le Havre in October 1914. Liberal Paul Hymans also joined the government, completing the 'sacred union'. Catholics, Liberals and Socialists cooperated in the National Committee for Aid and Food Supply that was created in occupied Belgium under the patronage of Société Générale and Solvay. The Committee tried to solve the problems of supply and unemployment. In absence of the king, Cardinal Mercier took the role of guardian of the peace and national unity.

Albert I, the new king, found that the monarch, in times of war, was relieved of the constitutional responsibility towards his ministers, and that he, as head of the army, should personally take command of the troops. At first, the king, army command, the government and leading patriots all agreed on one essential point: Germany was not going to be allowed come out of this war a strengthened nation. Any compromise peace agreement would be rejected. In 1917, the internationalist socialists met in Stockholm and called for a pacifist policy of negotiations aimed at ending the unprecedented slaughter of the working class. This created untold division within the BWP; Camille Huysmans could not get his party to the negotiating table and the BWP stuck to the government line until the end. Apparently, Albert started to look favourably on Huysmans' initiative and it is widely known that he was willing to personally negotiate a compromise peace deal with Germany. But the talks failed time and again because of Germany's territorial claims on parts of Belgium and other demands. By negotiating with the enemy, Albert went against the majority of the government and clashed with the allied partners. However, just like his son after him, the king was convinced that his war powers exceeded the normal constitutional limits.

The flamingants did not participate in the general Belgian spirit of patriotism. They had long been distrustful of the government as far as the application of the language laws was concerned, and the German occupation offered unexpected opportunities. Some pro-Flemish activists in occupied Belgium and a number of Flemings who had fled to the Netherlands wanted to use the occupation to push through their demands. The Germans went along, happy to create friction within the Belgian camp. With their '*Flamenpolitik*', which included the separation of Walloon and Flemish prisoners of war, they took advantage of the activists' willingness to collaborate. Most of these activists, among them relatively many freethinkers, apart from Catholics, sought a federalist solution for a Belgium independent from Germany. The separatist wing, which wanted to create an independent Flemish nation, was the most energetic. With German approval, it created the Raad van Vlaanderen (Flemish Council) in February 1917, a kind of advisory parliament that first declared the administrative separation of Flanders, and full Flemish independence in early 1918. The Germans wanted to control all of Belgium, though, and dissolved the Council. Collaboration with the enemy had yielded some results, though. Ghent university had become Dutch-speaking; but many professors, including a number of pro-Flemish academics, resigned and the new university was not successful. When the armistice was signed, it was clear to the activists that they had chosen the wrong strategy. Even the hope for a compromise peace, which would have been to the advantage of the activists, had proved to be nothing but a dream.

Flemish intellectuals like A. De Beuckelaere, F. De Pillecyn and H. Borginon, mainly members or former members of the Catholic student organisation, had joined the army in 1914, either as volunteers or as conscripts, and sought out one another once the frontlines had stabilised. They were appalled by the language conditions in the armed forces. Too often uneducated Flemish boys from the lowly agricultural or working class were commanded by francophone officers who did not even speak a word of Dutch. When the soldiers demanded better language rights, it was considered disobeying military discipline: the law on the use of Dutch in the army had been voted through parliament before 1914, but would only be applicable from 1917 onwards. The Flemish intellectuals created the illegal

Front Movement in 1917. It infiltrated all army units and organised several troop demonstrations.

The protest movement included an ambitious political program. It demanded a monolingual Flanders, a division of the armed forces into Flemish and Walloon regiments and Flemish autonomy. The army command tried to intervene and took action against many of them. The movement was illegal and its program extreme, and some Front members were in contact with collaborating activists. Moreover, they wanted a negotiated peace, increasing their tendency to desert. Worst of all for francophone patriotic Belgians was the Front Movement's action just ahead of the armistice. When the army needed the Front soldiers to stave off a final German attack, it was served warning that the Fronters would not pick up their arms unless a list of Flemish demands was met. It did not come to negotiations and the end of the war turned their action into an empty threat. Just like the Activists, the Fronters had made a serious miscalculation.

Fortunately for the Flemish movement, most of its members had not collaborated. Those who did not want to subordinate Flemish demands to German imperialism included A. Vermeylen, L. Franck, F. Van Cauwelaert, C. Huysmans and P. Fredericq. Especially the three ‘crowing roosters’ (Huysmans, Franck and Van Cauwelaert) had been so active within the party structures that the francophone patriotic establishment was unable to condemn the Flemish movement as a whole. A wholesale rift within the Flemish Movement was thus avoided. The efforts of these flamingants made sure that the Flemish demands survived the war and could end up on the negotiating table again.

The Activists and Fronters did have a direct impact on the evolution of post-war flamingantism, however. The Fronters continued to mobilise the common soldier, reinforcing the democratic foundation of the Flemish Movement. The demands for a monolingual, federal and autonomous Flanders had been made, once and for all. While the Flemish Movement had been a nationalist movement *sui generis* before 1914, the war had given it a nationalist tradition on which it would continue to build.

The war also had a direct impact on the labour movement. When called upon, the BWP had proved it had accepted capitalist society and it now insisted that its cooperation be rewarded with political equality. Since conservative mistrust had disappeared, no one was left to stop a further integration of the labour movement in society. After the war, the political field was left to those (first of all the enterprising, economic leaders) who sought an increasing integration of the workforce in the industrial-capitalist society in a spirit of cooperation with the national economy.

Chapter IV
From the Great War to the Great Depression

The three main areas of tension were already established well before the war. From previous chapters, we know that they are the following: (1) the social divide had turned into a battle between pressure groups and parties seeking to increase their parliamentary representation and decision-making powers; (2) the clerical vs. anti-clerical divide, highlighted in the rivalry between public, neutral education and private, Catholic institutions; (3) the language question, marked by the relation between Flanders, Wallonia and Brussels, which before the war had not grown into the communal rifts they would become. The introduction of universal single male suffrage changed the complexion of each of the three conflict areas, as will be explained in the following sections

The Beginning of the Era of Universal Single Suffrage and the New Political and Social Relations

The war had changed the political balance of power to the extent that the Catholic bishops were no longer able to control society through their wide and dense network of social, cultural and political organisations. After the introduction of the universal single male suffrage, the Catholics realised that absolute majorities were out of the question and that coalitions with anti-Catholic or a-religious conservative parties had to be considered.

The need for coalition governments increased the influence of political parties. The parties had to further reinforce the construction of the ideological pillars. Another new development was the emergence of small, often one-issue parties, including pro-Flemish, radical labour and extreme right-wing parties that made for a vocal addition to parliament. The new patchwork of parties made it increasingly difficult to set and execute a coherent government program. Negotiations between party leaders became the order of the day. The chairman of the cabinet was given the title of 'prime minister'.

The coalition governments and their inherent instability opened the door for Albert I and Leopold III to exert influence on policymaking. They argued that statesmen should not act as the representatives of their parties. The royals tried to get them to restrain their political parties each time the interests of the nation or the monarchy were deemed to be at stake. Yet the 'system of Loppem', stimulated by Albert, which will be discussed later, did test the parliamentary regime, especially during the 1930s depression. However, it may be stated that the monarchy, apart from the three main factors mentioned above, was the fourth determining element until the middle of the 20th century.

Immediately after the war, the BWP and the Christian labour movement (which after the application of universal single male suffrage was to get more influence) won major concessions but the Socialists were quickly swept aside, especially after the failed experiment of the 1925-1926 Poullet-Vandervelde government. It would take until 1935 before the Socialists made a return. Even though it could hardly be considered a revolutionary party anymore, the BWP would retain its 'evil' image in the eyes of the petty bourgeoisie and Flanders' rural and small-town proletariat, and would continue to do so until the Second World War. And once the conservative Liberals no longer had to fear Catholic absolute majorities, they happily ostracised the Socialists. A specific anti-clerical coalition was not urgent since the School War remained in the background, and would only briefly come to life in 1932.

The social and economic problems dominated the post-war years. The whole 1919-1940 period was characterised by fluctuating prices and profits, and frequent crises combined with massive unemployment, especially during the depression of the 1930s. The Great Depression not only threatened the capitalist economy, but parliamentary democracy as well. The Belgian economy had been slow in adapting to the new economic situation. It still relied too heavily on coal, iron, textile and semi-finished products, all of which were difficult to market during the depression, mainly because of increasing protectionism on foreign markets.

There was no way of getting around the language issue, even though the Flemish demands, specifically the calls for a Dutch-speaking university in Ghent, were consciously ignored. For Belgium's francophone bourgeoisie and intellectuals, winning the war had been a victory of Latin civilisation over the Germanic hordes. The experiment with the Von Bissing University in Ghent during the war and the hunt for Flemish activists had only strengthened the belief that unitary Belgium was best served by far-reaching gallicisation. The economic development of Flanders and the depression of the thirties would ensure, however, that federalist solutions to the language problem would become a topic of discussion before the Second World War.

The second industrial revolution had been kind to Flanders. Ghent, Zeebrugge, Vilvoorde, Willebroek, the Kempen etc. had become economic growth areas. Thanks to the relations with the Congo, among others, the service sector (especially the harbour in Antwerp) attracted all types of industries. Walloon and Brussels holding companies, notably the Société Générale, founded a number of big companies, but also several independent Flemish entrepreneurs built successful businesses. The contribution of Flemish investors should not be forgotten, but there was no Flemish university to train Dutch-speaking engineers and secondary technical education was still trying to get off the ground. The Catholics, led by the bishops, had tried to develop this sector of secondary education and have it subsidised, but had clashed with the freethinkers, who had realised the political importance of schooling skilled labourers.

Despite the overall economic downturn in the interbellum, Flemish industry continued to develop after 1918. Labour was still relatively cheap and lured investors to the north. Domestic labourers and small farmers found jobs in textile and other industries. The Limburg coal mines, where exploitation only started after the war, also helped ease unemployment. Flemish commuters identified strongly with their village and kept their faith while the Walloon urban proletariat had already lost it after the first industrial revolution. Christian labour unions made sure that class warfare was kept to a minimum. Flemish socialism was limited to the cities and failed to get a grip on the rural poor that had flocked to the city looking for industrial work in between 1919 and 1930.

Among the Dutch-speaking captains of industry that L. de Raet had so longed for, Lieven Gevaert, a pro-Flemish Catholic and co-founder of the *Vlaams Economisch Verbond* (Flemish Economic Union, 1916), and Zwevegem wire producer Leon Bekaert, who defended a unitary Belgium, were two prime examples. The VEV grouped merchants and owners of Flanders' small and medium-size businesses and came to symbolise the fledgling, overwhelmingly Catholic Flemish bourgeoisie.

Flanders' birth rate far outreached that of Brussels and Wallonia and by 1939, despite sizable emigration, half of the Belgians were Flemish, not including those in Brussels. Flanders' part in industrial employment rose from 31 to almost 39 % in between 1919 and 1937, while Wallonia's dropped from 51.4 to 41.1 %. It would take until the 1960s before Flanders would become the most industrialised region of Belgium. In 1935, the overwhelming majority of the 350,000 unemployed were Flemish.

Despite making major strides forward, Flanders still lagged behind and even the steady economic shift north between 1919 and 1940 did not have a fundamental impact on the social and economic structure. But the pro-Flemish middle class, including many intellectuals and owners of small and medium-sized businesses showed signs of impatience and politics had to take that into account.

The Loppem Agreements (11 November 1918) and Their Political Fallout

The wartime government of Le Havre had turned into a 'sacred union' when Socialists and Liberals joined the coalition. Immediately after the 11 November 1918 armistice signing, King Albert summoned several prominent economic and political figures to his Loppem headquarters on the outskirts of Bruges. He chose not to invite right-wing conservatives because he knew it was highly unlikely that the old-fashioned Catholic right wing would be willing to make democratic concessions. After three decades of monopoly rule, the monarch knew that the concept of a new relationship would be lost on them. Instead, Albert had realised there was a need for radical change if democracy, the unity of the country and the monarchy were to survive. The 1917 Russian revolution and left-wing revolutionary action in central and Eastern Europe had shown the need for 'enlightened conservatism' that Albert shared with several important businessmen and capitalists. First and foremost, universal single male suffrage was approved in 1919, even ahead of the necessary constitutional reform.

The king and the royal court wanted to extend the sacred union with the Socialist Party to contain the threat of social revolt. Barely ten days after the armistice signing, Belgium had a new government led by Catholic L. Delacroix, the so-called Loppem government, which consisted of six Catholics, three Liberals and three Socialists. Delacroix, a confidant of Archbishop Mercier's, had the profile of a consensus man. Charles Woeste and the rest of the old right wing was angered that a new government had been agreed on even before the king made a triumphant return to the capital and parliament was reconvened. Universal single suffrage was deemed unconstitutional, and rightly so. Three 'sacred union' governments succeeded one another, two led by Delacroix, who was backed by investor Emile Franqui of Société Générale, and one, in 1921, by Edmond Carton de Wiart. In his inauguration speech on 28 November 1918, L. Delacroix promised universal single suffrage, but hardly mentioned the prospect for a Dutch-speaking university or the abolition of the infamous Article 310 of the penal code, which stipulated heavy penalties for obstructing those willing to work during a strike. It was in stark contrast with King Albert's address, which had taken up both issues.

The old right wing called the events in Loppem, where the king, a number of representatives of economic and financial interest groups and politicians such as liberal P.-E. Janson and socialist Anseele and a few independent Catholics such as Jaspar had met, a 'coup de force'. The Catholics wanted more concessions on private education to compensate for universal single suffrage and grand coalition governments and the liberals and socialists accepted this. For years to come, and much to the displeasure of Albert, the right-wing nationalists claimed that the king had capitulated to the socialist and Flemish politicians and that the creation of the Loppem government had presented the country with a *fait accompli*. Especially the inclusion of socialists caused deep mistrust, despite their patriotic attitude during the war. The party had also distanced itself from its republican past.

Loppem necessitated a system of coalition governments since no single political party was strong enough to impose its political program. There was a need for compromise and pacification, and party leaders became key players in the political debate. Political decision-making was turned over to a new elite. Steadily, and especially after the Second World War, party chairmen would decide on political issues, above and beyond parliament and government, turning so-called 'particracy' into an ugly word. Especially the extreme right wing resisted such a political system. At least, it was thought that the 'damage' created by universal single suffrage had to be contained as much as possible. Also Flemish-oriented movements within and outside the Catholic world were seen as a threat. The anti-Flemish Cardinal Mercier, a number of francophone right-wing Liberals and war veterans claimed the Loppem agreements were nothing more than the total capitulation of the nation's leading classes. The anti-Loppem movement was totally anti-democratic and would become a cornerstone of Brussels and francophone fascism.

After the first constitutional revision of 1893, Belgium completed a second one on 7 February 1921. The Senate was reformed and consisted of those who were directly voted into the legislature, provincial senators and co-opted senators. Women's voting rights completed Belgium's truly universal suffrage at a municipal level but a breakthrough at provincial and national level would only come after the Second World War. Liberal and socialist opposition was to blame for the further delay. The Catholics demanded voting rights for men and women over 25 in an attempt to safeguard their majority. The King, socialists and liberals stuck to 21, and for men only. The offer by the socialists of implementing the right to vote for women immediately on a municipal level brought the right wing to this compromise. There was a fear that voting rights for women would boost the right. Resistance was strong from Cardinal Mercier, who had not been consulted in 1920 and 1921; he had to be restrained not to protest openly against plans to grant universal suffrage at age 21.

The single vote brought about fundamental changes in the electoral balance between the parties. (For the distribution of seats in the Chamber of Representatives, cf. appendix). The Catholics would not win an absolute majority at any stage in between the two wars, even if the votes of the Catholic Party supported by Mechelen are added to those of mostly Church-oriented but not necessarily clerical Flemish nationalists and, starting in 1936, the Rexists. Even though the Flemish Christian union wing can certainly not be put on a level with the conservatives, the percentage of all social and economic conservatives – the defenders of the capitalist free-market economy, but not necessarily of class solidarity – stuck close to the 60 % mark, dipping to a low of 57 % in 1925 and a high of 62.5 % in 1939. The working class parties fluctuated between 35.1 % in 1921 and almost 43 % in 1925, and between just over 38 % in 1929 and less than 36 % in 1939. Overall, there was a great sense of stability, with the exception of the extraordinary years ahead of the Second World War, when the majority of the Catholics was briefly broken.

But there were huge differences between the regions, and that would soon be translated into linguistic-communal difficulties that would come to dominate politics. In Flanders, the Catholics – combined with other clerical parties – had an absolute majority, in stark contrast with the results in Brussels and Wallonia, which had a longer industrial tradition. In francophone areas, the Catholic conservatives were strong only in the rural areas. Ahead of 1936, the Catholic Union won in between 44.5 and almost 50 % of all votes in Flanders. In comparison, the BWP (and the numerically negligible communists) scored in between 25 and 30 %. In Wallonia, the conservative forces, including the liberals, remained far below the 50 % mark for most of the time (45 % in 1925). The elections of 1921 and 1939 were exceptions. In the Brussels region, the Catholic Union won in between 27 and 37 %, with the 1936 polls a notable exception. Compared to the rest of the nation, the liberals were relatively strong in the capital, and peaked at 25 % there.

Up to 1936, the election results made for a stable Chamber of Representatives. Before 1932, the traditional parties won over 90 % of the seats. With the exception of 1925 and 1936, the Catholic Union was the biggest group. In 1925, the Socialists held an equal number of seats and in 1936, the Catholic Union came second to the Socialists largely because of the rise of Flemish nationalist parties and the extreme right-wing Rex party.

The electoral results, a consequence of universal single suffrage, forced the political parties into coalition governments. From then on, every single government was the result of long and sometimes tortuous negotiations between the three traditional parties. The political elite often had to settle for an unstable compromise. Three-party coalitions of 'national union' were only agreed on in times of crisis, as was the case in the wake of the First World War and between 1935 and 1939, when the economic crisis dominated. There was not a single coalition government of Liberals and Socialists between the two wars since their differences on socio-economic, financial and military issues were just too big. The liberals were part of almost all governments, with the 1925 Catholic-Socialist coalition of Poullet-Vandervelde and a short period in 1939 as the only exceptions. In Wallonia and Brussels, the right wing of the Catholic Party was strong enough to make sure that Socialist-Catholic coalitions were limited to the short-lived experiment of Poullet-Vandervelde, which lasted all of eleven months. There was little government stability, with eighteen coalitions in just twenty-one years. Despite the numerous internal crises, the continuity of authority of the governments was stronger than appears at first sight.

In the wake of elections or a government crisis, the king consulted with political leaders and other prominent figures before appointing a politician to broker a new coalition. The political mediator had to tread carefully and take the shifting power structure of each party into account: Flemings versus Walloons versus Brussels citizens, the city versus the countryside and, more specifically for the Catholic Party, conservatives versus progressives. The liberals and Catholics often granted their party leaders precious little room for manoeuvre, making for arduous government talks. Apart from negotiating with the parliamentary factions, the mediator also had to take into account the interests of extra-parliamentary groups, i.e. the parties and lobbyists. In 1918, the first successful go-between was named prime minister. After the Great War, the role of the party leaders increased considerably, but even they often had to take their lead from the leading ministers, who enjoyed the trust of the king. In practice, the parliamentary leaders of the party also played a major role in the party itself and in the different organisations that made up the ideological pillars.

Governments rarely waited for a vote of no-confidence before resigning. They usually did not fall because they were put in a minority position in parliament. When they had to push through unpopular social-economic measures, they requested special powers from parliament to be able to act without too much interference.

The monarchs were not too keen on granting the parties and the parliamentary groups a large say during coalition talks and on government policy, since it restricted their own executive authority.

King Albert and His Governments

Albert I, and later his son Leopold III, were able to use the constitution to their advantage to influence the formation of governments, their composition and largely also their programmes. But the ministers themselves still had the final say. They were accountable to their respective parties, which they controlled to a higher or lesser degree. They had to cover for the actions of a monarch who, according to the constitution, was not responsible. As head of the executive branch, Albert often presided over cabinet meetings and was often part of decision-making. It was only after 1925 that he became a less frequent visitor during ministerial meetings. The king needed approval of at least one member of the government for any public declaration or publication of a letter to a minister.

The king did not like it at all that, on important issues, the ministers failed to consult him before drawing up plans with parties and pressure groups. In 1929 and again in 1931, he refused to accept the resignation of the Catholic-Liberal Jaspar government, first over a dispute concerning the

Dutch-speaking university and two years later over language use in administration. In 1931, Albert gave the prime minister and the anti-Flemish liberals a piece of his mind, since the government had not even deemed it necessary to await the result of the parliamentary debate before offering its resignation. In 1932, Albert was, subtly, instrumental in bringing down the Renkin government, which was under pressure because of Belgium's bad budgetary situation. He addressed a letter to the prime minister and asked that it be read out in parliament. Renkin preferred to resign instead.

In this case, Albert was able to rely on the constitution, which stipulates that the monarch appoints and dismisses ministers, but only with ministerial approval. At the royal court, the king had, and still has, personal advisors, a secretary and members of a royal and military cabinet. The monarch also consulted numerous prominent figures from the clergy, political and cultural circles, and, especially, influential industrialists and bankers. The latter had to supervise the reconstruction of Belgium's industry, which had been destroyed by the occupying Germans. It was a priority, together with the maintenance of a strong currency and healthy state finances. On top of that, Germany had to be forced into meeting its war reparation commitments. As part of foreign policy, defence had to be strengthened and military service had to be reformed. All this increased the control of the financial institutions over government policy. Another priority centred on the Flemish minimum programme and the demands for a Dutch-speaking university in Ghent. There was no urgency since both the Catholic and liberal parties faced internal divisions on that issue. It would take until the end of the 1920s before the linguistic problem would threaten the monarchy and government again.

It was often said that Emile Franqui of the Société Générale was the most powerful man of Belgium, that he was able to make or break governments. He heartily recommended Société Générale's Gerard Cooreman and Delacroix as government leaders immediately before and after the war. Several other prominent Catholic and Liberal politicians were also linked with the world of business. The Empain group was represented by G.Theunis (who also represented Société Générale) and C. Gutt and the Banque de Bruxelles group had M.-L. Gerard, who was Albert's first private secretary. For the king and for the wealthy, such men were a comforting thought and a reassurance that Belgium's economic and financial policies were in good hands. They often also made profits in the Congo. Together with Union Minière and other businesses, the Société Générale determined Congo policy, which was hardly ever discussed in Parliament. Even after Albert's death, Emile Francqui continued to play a vital role and he was involved in the negotiations that led to the so-called bankers' government, with Georges Theunis as government broker.

King Albert I had a sense of *Realpolitik* and he realised that in this complicated parliamentary democracy he had a thankless task. He was able to call on people that complied with his political vision and kept others out of government. Catholic Charles de Broqueville fell out of royal favour at the end of the war, but it hardly stopped Albert from calling on his political talents afterwards. De Broqueville's secretary had been able to prove, backed by legal arguments, that the king still needed the support of a minister, even in times of war. But de Broqueville had been a trusted and respected ally since 1911 and Albert insisted he became interior minister during the first Delacroix government in November 1918. Together with the Catholic Jaspar, who was a friend of Franqui's, de Broqueville had to persuade the traditionalist right wing of the Catholic Party that elections with universal single suffrage could take place even ahead of a constitutional revision.

In 1926, the king again called on de Broqueville, this time to become defence minister in the Jaspar government. Albert wanted him to persuade the socialists and Flemish Christian democrats to accept a compromise on the length of military service, somewhere in between the six months they demanded and the ten months that the king and the government wanted. The king called on de Broqueville one last time in 1932; as prime minister with special powers, he had to push through drastic austerity measures to counter the economic crisis. It soon proved an impossible mission for the 72-year-old.

The royal court also called on others. The liberal P. Huysmans was put on Foreign Affairs and his party colleague Albert Devèze was a defence minister who had to keep the Liberal Party in line. A. Carton de Wiart and J. Jaspar had to make sure the Catholic Party remained a united bloc since the king was worried that the Flemish problem, the military service issue and the conservative-progressive divide would tear the party apart. The royal cabinet and several prominent liberal and conservative Catholic politicians made sure the press followed the government line closely.

The spirit of the post-war 'sacred union' soon evaporated. When it became clear there would be no revolution, when the revision of the constitution was completed under the Theunis government and when the socialists had obtained the social legislation they had long sought, there was no more reason to stick together. Starting in 1921, Albert wanted to rid the government of 'the extreme-left', namely the socialists (who sat in parliament to the left of the anti-clerical leftist liberals) and he tried to keep Christian-democratic backers of the Flemish minimum program out of parliament. Among the latter, the king targeted F. Van Cauwelaert, calling him a 'démagogue clérical et collectiviste' in his letters. Van Cauwelaert had embarked on the so-called 'mystic marriage' with pro-Flemish socialist C. Huysmans in Antwerp's city council and Albert saw this as a precursor of a split in the Catholic Party. Together with Cardinal Mercier he wanted to avoid this at all cost and he called on the pro-Flemish but conservative A. Van de Vyvere to mediate. He had to safeguard Catholic political unity and stave off an anti-militarist alliance. Albert needed the support for his military project and in return he was willing to make a few promises on a Dutch-language university and the use of Dutch in the army. But those elements were under the authority of parliament, where mainly the Walloon, Brussels and a few francophile liberals refused to budge. The monarch needed the liberals but was increasingly irritated by the rabid anti-Flemish Devèze, whom he saw as a threat to the unity of the kingdom. War veterans from Wallonia and Brussels and Belgian patriots, who were infiltrated by an extreme right-wing element, organised impassioned demonstrations and put the king in a difficult position just before his death in 1934. He received a petition to oppose the reintegration of 70-odd civil servants who had been dismissed after the war for their unpatriotic pro-Flemish behaviour. The Flemish ministers threatened to resign if the demonstrators got their way. Albert sidestepped the issue by promising to put it to an ad-hoc committee. Before the relative breakthrough of Rex (and L. Degrelle) a few years later, most war veterans and right-wing Belgian patriots looked up to the 'knight-king' and considered him a natural ally. And even though they were disappointed, they stood by him. Albert was popular, had a lot of moral authority and he had a sizable influence on politics, even beyond the traditional areas of defence and foreign policy, which were largely considered a royal prerogative since Leopold I.

The end of Albert's reign was also affected by the Great Depression, which followed in the wake of Belgium's centennial celebrations of 1930. Despite the availability of special executive powers, the 1932-1934 government of de Broqueville-Theunis had been unable to do anything about the crisis and its catastrophic unemployment rate, due to the orthodox and old-fashioned monetary policy. The Great Depression hit the working class, small farmers and middle class with full force. The governments pursued a deflationary policy marked by cheap exports because of low wages and cheap imports because of a strong currency. Oddly enough, the depression – the biggest the country and the entire capitalist world had ever seen – was not at the centre of the 1932 elections. Instead the education issue resurfaced. The BWP and the liberals, after their party congresses, wanted to scrap subsidies for private schools. The Catholics, encouraged by a pastoral letter, turned it into an election issue and they gained three seats, significantly, at the expense of the mainly church-going Flemish nationalists.

The Political Parties

The Catholic Party had been led by representatives of the paternalistic *Katholieke Verenigingen en Kringen* (Catholic Federation of Associations and Circles) and was embodied by arch-conservative Charles Woeste. With the prospect of universal single suffrage, the party was forced to make drastic and quick changes after the war, despite opposition from prominent members. The labour movement demanded better places on the electoral lists, especially in Flanders. Before the creation of the *Algemeen Christelijk Werkersverbond* (ACW, General Christian Workers' Association), new Christian democrat organisations were founded ahead of the 1919 elections, anticipating the new electoral system. They no longer wanted to cooperate with the old-fashioned *Volksbond* (People's Union) and instead they wanted to become an independent order within a reformed Catholic Party. Before 1914, the Catholic Party was little more than a loose cluster of groups. The Christian labour movement and the *Katholiek Vlaams Verbond* (Catholic Flemish Union) won ten of the 52 Flemish seats in the Chamber during the 1919 elections. Their leader, and founder of the ACW, founded the parliamentary group of the so-called democrats. The labour associations were ready to take their place in a reformed and clearly structured party, much to the dislike of the conservative elites. The Belgian Catholic Union was created on 14 September 1921. The official Dutch name was *Katholiek Verbond van België*.

The Union consisted of four different orders:

(1) The old conservative *Fédération des Associations et des Cercles* (Federations of Associations and Circles) consisted of the bourgeoisie and aristocracy, which had a sizable representation in Brussels and Wallonia, but also in Flanders, much to the delight of Cardinal Mercier. The Federation had lost its monopoly control over the party but remained the major force during election campaigns, especially in Wallonia and Brussels.

(2) The powerful *Boerenbond* (Farmers' Union) lived by the motto 'Religion, Family, Property' and was pro-Flemish. A weak Walloon counterpart, the *Alliance Agricole,* was created in 1930.

(3) The *Algemeen Christen-Democratisch Verbond* (General Christian-Democrat Union), founded in 1920, was a confederation of the trade union (ACV), health care organisation (*Landsbond der Christelijke Mutualiteiten*), cooperatives (*Verbond van Coöperaties*), women's guilds, etc. It involved some 700,000 people. In 1921 the name was changed to *Algemeen Christelijk Werkersverbond* (ACW). It included several moderate pro-Flemish leaders, notably H. Heyman and P. Poullet. Its Walloon counterpart, the *Ligue Nationale des Travailleurs Chrétiens,* renamed *Mouvement Ouvrier Chretien* (MOC) in 1945, was a lot weaker and at first had to be led by the ACW.

(4) The *Christelijke Landsbond van de Belgische Middenstand* (The Christian Belgian Middle Class Federation) was the weakest link. It was founded in 1919 by a priest and counted some 25,000 members. The reason for its weakness was the fact that the middle class proved an individualistic group with a heterogeneous social structure. They were also a prime target group for the liberal competition and they preferred to ally themselves with the elite rather than with the democrats.

The general council of the *Katholieke Unie* consisted of 6 members of each of the four orders, among who a limited committee was elected, under a rotating chairmanship. The Flemish democrats were unhappy with the way in which the Federation of Associations and Circles continued to dominate the electoral campaigns. There was no real central leadership and no leader. The Catholic Union did not have a modern infrastructure and lacked centralised financing. The Christian mass organisations felt neglected, and to make matters worse, the antagonism between the pro-Flemish and francophone wings showed no signs of abating.

Already under pressure from socialism, liberalism and atheism, the high clergy was worried about party unity. Religion remained the major link between the different orders and the common defence of private education cemented this union. The francophone right wing of the party used the School War to keep the Christian labour movement out of the grasp of the Socialists. The Central Office of Catholic Education became the most important episcopal pressure group to enforce some discipline in the Catholic camp. When the School War briefly flared up in 1931-1932, the Central Bureau took control. The bishops had no qualms about taking partisan stands during election campaigns and they made sure encroaching de-Christianisation had no political impact on the Catholic Party ahead of World War II.

The party would be seen as an anchor of security, a place where traditional values of property (however small) and family (with the women safely at home) still prevailed. The Catholic Union's programme itself, in 1921, was elevated above and beyond the orders and focused on the defence of private education, family, property, free enterprise, national unity, the monarchy, an austerity policy, reconciling labour and capital by the improvement of social legislation. All these issues were held together by religious doctrine and the, often convoluted, papal encyclicals. The Catholic Union was overwhelmingly democratic and pro-Flemish in Flanders, and conservative in Wallonia.

The conservative Catholics had trouble adapting to the democratic changes in society. At first they tried to apply universal single suffrage in a way that would benefit them – impose high age limits, give an additional vote for the heads of family and immediately apply women's voting rights, which was, in a sense, a democratic move. Then, dignitaries set up their own national-Catholic electoral lists and sometimes even drew a third of the Union's votes. They opposed the system of different orders within the party and the Flemish minimal program of Van Cauwelaert and his *Katholieke Vlaamse Landsbond*.

An influential minority among the conservative Catholics rekindled counterrevolutionary traditionalism. They accused the Christian democrats of being promoters of class warfare, condemned the economic liberalism of the conservatives and took pride in being reactionary. Encouraged by part of the high clergy (e.g. Mgr. L. Picard), they put themselves above the party. Charles Maurras and his *Action Française* was a shining example, and like the French reactionary, they criticised parliamentary democracy and yearned for a hierarchical society based on law and order. The movement was centred in and around Leuven University and its francophone student associations. It was tolerated by Cardinal Mercier and supported by the pre-

and post-war Catholic annexionists. Some right-wing Liberals also dreamed of such a '*parti de l'ordre*' to counter socialism, Christian democracy and flamingantism. It called for an anti-democratic nationalism and a corporatist society led by a strong monarch. In 1925, P. Nothomb called Mussolini '*un soldat de la Chrétienté*' against socialists, communists and trade unionists. Cardinal Mercier was also firmly against any involvement of the Christian trade unions in the class struggle. They had to limit themselves to moral improvement, otherwise they would betray the spirit of the *Rerum Novarum* encyclical. The *Katholieke Actie* (Catholic Action) movement (cf. infra) in fact reinforced the influence of the higher classes in the Catholic Party.

The chairman of the Catholic Federation of Associations and Circles, Paul Segers, fell under the spell of the fascist francophone bourgeois circles and wanted to reform parliament based on a semi-corporatist system. It would have blunted the sharper edges of universal single suffrage. Even though Segers opposed a Mussolini-style dictatorship, his program was adopted in 1936 by the fascist Rex party of L. Degrelle. The leader of Rex nevertheless accused Segers of collusion, forcing Segers out of the Catholic Party.

The Catholic Party's ultra-conservative wing (e.g. pre-war paternalist P. Crokaert) wanted to restore pre-war traditions within the party and attacked the ACW, LTNC and KAJ-JOC. The traditionalist clergy considered these right-wing groups a-political and entirely Catholic. They were only truly shocked when many bourgeois and petty-bourgeois Catholics flocked to the Rex party, which had developed out of Catholic Action groups, and to the extreme right-wing Flemish nationalist VNV. In Wallonia and Brussels, they were drawn to the *Association Catholique de la Jeunesse* (ACTE), which kept itself officially out of politics but was trying to discredit KAJ-JOC and Christian trade unions. One young man, L. Degrelle felt right at home and was in charge of the *Christus Rex* publications, which were backed by the clergy. It would take years before the Catholics realised the inherent danger in this. By that time Degrelle was well on his way to create a dissident, disgraceful and eventually clearly fascist party that would threaten Catholic unity.

In Catholic Flanders, many among the lower clergy were trying to give the associations of workers, farmers and the self-employed a Flemish character. The solidarity between the orders was not linked to any fascist ideology, as was the case in the francophone right wing (which had not yet been completely taken out in Flanders).

The Socialist Party and its ministers had fully cooperated with the allied cause during the Great War. The Socialist leader E. Vandervelde approved of the Russian February 1917 revolution led by Lenin but later condemned the October revolution by Lenin and the Bolsheviks because it sought a separate peace with Germany. Ahead of the 1919 elections in Antwerp, M. Terwagne, but especially a few Hainaut Socialists, including Jules Destrée, joined up with the hyper-nationalist Pierre Nothomb.

Anti-German sentiments were so strong after the Great War that during the first socialist congresses only the party's left wing was willing to consider sharing a table with German social democrats to prepare for the reestablishment of the Second International. It did not really seem to matter to the BWP that part of the German social democrats had not betrayed the International and that a soldiers' uprising and a socialist revolt in Germany, bloodily suppressed, had opened the way to end the war. It seemed only the Antwerp Socialists tried to counter this groundswell of chauvinism during the party congress. The Brussels leftist group of J. Jacquemotte also held out its hand to the German social democrats.

Many had criticised C. Huysmans because, as secretary of the Second International he had attended the 1917 meeting in Stockholm, which was also attended by Germans. The conference's aim had been to find a way to end the monstrous massacre the Great War had become. King Albert was not among Huysmans' critics. After the war, the so-called 'man from Stockholm' was still not welcome in his party.

Despite left-wing opposition against socialist integration into the bourgeois system, the socialist congresses of 1918-1920 found a large majority backing continued government participation, which was expected to lead to important social improvements. As expected, universal single suffrage allowed the BWP to score the biggest gains. Under the guidance of Vandervelde, the BWP proved to be a tight-knit party with good parliamentary discipline immediately after the war, something that was lacking amongst the liberals and Catholics. Even though the party was a confederation of cooperatives, unions, health care organisations and workers' associations, it was led by the general council and the party bureau. The rank and file became BWP member by joining a union, cooperative, etc. Trade union leaders, some of whom were also in parliament, dominated the party. The trade union leaders were pragmatists and they were geared towards short-term achievements. Their membership numbers and financial clout often were decisive during party congresses. The General Council included representatives of the trade organisations affiliated with the BWP, the district organisations (federations), the cooperatives, the socialist health care organisations, the centre for workers' education, the youth central, the women's organisations, etc. The Bureau of the council took care of the day-to-day running of the party. Unlike the Catholics and liberals, the annual socialist congress gave the ministers a strict mandate, which limited their room for manoeuvre. King Leopold III did not appreciate that even though he appointed the ministers, their hands were tied by the party in this show of particracy.

The most important demands of the Socialists were met during the first post-war years (universal single suffrage and a number of immediate demands) and the Socialists realised that an absolute parliamentary majority for their party was out of the question. The BWP was very much a workers' party and since the increase in manual labourers slowed down, the number of peasants declined, and the tertiary sector was developing rapidly, the party had reached the limits of its expansion. By the end of 1921, the biggest strikes were over, the bourgeoisie no longer feared a world revolution and the inclusion of socialists in government became optional. The BWP failed to expand its program to attract other segments of society, e.g. small shop owners or service industry employees.

The party shied away from immediate confrontation during a period when a new political and social attitude called for a climate of negotiations and restraint. After spending some years in government during and just after the war, the BWP kept the airs of a governing party even in opposition, patiently biding its time. The many organisations of the socialist pillar were now firmly rooted in capitalist society, and the party did not want to endanger this. In industrial Wallonia it already ruled countless municipalities and its political appointee system had earned it a faithful electorate. Scores of people found work in cooperatives or other socialist institutions. Such party faithful were not going to criticise their leaders.

Socialist rituals included militant songs and rousing rhetoric, all predicting the inevitable collapse of the unjust capitalist system. Socialists formed one big family, spanning everything from a political party over sometimes impressive event halls (*Vooruit* in Ghent) to brass bands, theatre groups, gymnast groups, 'red' football teams, nature lovers' groups, holiday centres for all ages, freethinkers' associations etc. Intellectuals and skilled workers who wanted something more than the conformist search for reforms within the bourgeois system, formed a sometimes vocal minority. Some prominent figures like E. Vandervelde and L. de Brouckere remained faithful to the Marxist interpretations of society. They knew where the boundary was that a socialist was not allowed to cross ideologically and ethically. The aging Vandervelde had to live the day that, of all people, the first Socialist prime minister, Paul-Henri Spaak, disregarded his objections (and those of a turbulent congress) and approved trade relations with the fascist rebels in Spain (the Burgos affair, cf. infra). The leadership of the party was certainly no more reformist than the majority of its members, who were sensitive to social recognition.

Eduard Anseele also disregarded internal criticism to expand his socialist empire and integrate it into the capitalist market economy. But his many companies fell victim to the Great Depression. The bankruptcy of the *Bank van de Arbeid* (Labour Bank) dealt a severe blow to this kind of reformism. A number of small investors were hurt and the right wing, including Degrelle, jumped on the opportunity to attack political-financial collusion. The episode hurt the trust in the workings of parliamentary democracy.

The BWP finally joined the government again in 1935 and it would become a rock of stability. The party leadership could do without any spontaneous action from the socialist rank and file, such as the wildcat Borinage strikes of 1932 or even the successful general strike of 1936. The party leadership certainly did not encourage such a release of social anger, but was not beyond exploiting it for opportunistic reasons. It used the 1936 strike to push through far-reaching social and institutional measures. At the same time the BWP was trying to persuade others that the Socialists were no allies of the Communists, whatever the right-wing conservative press might write.

It has been explained before why the party had not benefited as much from the second industrial revolution as the Christian organisations in Flanders. The Socialist Party was an overwhelming force in industrial Wallonia but found the going very tough in Flanders. Even though it counted some pro-Flemish militants in its ranks, the party preferred to stress international proletarian solidarity rather than the language issue, especially in its youth movement. Since many pro-Flemish laws were seen as social advancement as well, the BWP backed them when it came to a parliamentary vote. Within the party, they sought to reconcile the two language factions. Unlike the liberals and Catholics, the socialists never had to deal with an influential pro-francophone bourgeois or aristocratic elite within their ranks. Any educational or other activities were obviously conducted in Dutch. Huysmans and H. De Man approached the issue from a neo-Marxist angle arguing for a nationalism based on equality, not domination.

The Communist Party was made up of two groups in 1921 – the Brussels *Jeune Garde Socialiste* (Young Socialist Guard) of the painter W. Van Overstraeten, which was part of the Communists Third International, and the organisation of J. Jacquemotte, national secretary of the syndicate of clerks, and publisher of the weekly *L'exploité*; Jacquemotte had left the BWP to found his party. Apart from Van Overstraeten's leftist movement, a number of small communist groups had formed inside and outside the BWP in several Flemish cities since 1917, among others from the Socialist Young Guard. In contrast with the BWP leadership, which wanted to continue the war until victory was gained, and did not support any peace talks, the small groups had been pacifist and anti-parliamentarian since 1917, democratically Flemish-oriented in a leftist, even slightly anarchist way; they admired the 1917 Russian revolution and the German soldiers' and workers' uprising (Spartacus). A prime example is the activist J. Van Extergem, who joined the communist party after a long prison sentence, and would die in a German concentration camp.

In 1921, several small Flemish and Walloon Communist groups joined Van Overstraeten's anti-parliamentarian movement. Jacquemotte's group *Les Amis de l'Exploité* was a splinter group within the BWP which opposed the party's reformist ministerialism and sympathised with the Russian revolution; it protested against any concessions the party had to make to participate in any government. The Antwerp BWP federation took a similar stand. At first, it did not approve of Lenis's methods to gain power (in contrast with the socialist newspaper *Le Peuple*, which totally condemned the Bolshevist uprising) and insisted that the BWP rejoin the Second International and sit down with the German socialists. But as a split with the BWP became more and more inevitable, Jacquemotte increasingly started leaning towards the Russian October revolution. After he split with the BWP he joined the Third International, after a merger with the Van Overstraeten group.

The new Communist Party stuck to the Third International in the sense that it sought parliamentary representation. Most of the BWP's left wing, however, refused to jump ship to the Communists. The Communist Party, hurt by ideological disputes over parliamentary or direct action, remained largely insignificant until the crisis of the 1930s. In 1928, the Bolshevik Comintern called for war against the social-democratic traitors, who were called social fascists, and demanded that communist cells be set up in companies. The 'old party' chose instead for Trotsky, who had called for a permanent revolution and against socialism in one country. The Trotskyites founded the Fourth International in 1928 and had a sizable share of the Communist vote in Hainaut.

The Liberal Party won its grassroots support among the middle class with little sympathy for the Church and among freethinker intellectuals. The liberal national council and party bureau were controlled by ministers, former ministers, parliamentarians and former parliamentarians. The leadership was in the hands of a small elite which ruled the party with little interference from the party's lower echelons. Since the Catholic Union operated in pretty much the same way until 1936, the two were natural political allies. The Liberals were part of government coalitions almost throughout the period between the wars, with the short-lived 1925-1926 (Poullet-Vandervelde) and 1939 (Pierlot I) Catholic-Socialist cabinets the only two exceptions. They always ruled with the Catholics, and the Socialists sometimes made it three-party coalitions. Their almost continuous government participation stood in stark contrast with the electoral losses (not just in number of votes, but even more so in number of seats) caused by universal single suffrage. The Liberal Party, which was much stronger in Wallonia and Brussels than in Flanders, won an average of 16 %. It did not have a well-defined programme and fed off voter dissatisfaction with other parties (on economic or Flemish questions) during electoral campaigns. The liberals had not developed an intricate and efficient pillar system, but this was partly compensated by the strong and popular liberal press.

After the war, the balance shifted steadily from political-religious issues to the social-economic problems, the language and military service issues. The School War came to the fore briefly during the 1932 campaign after the Liberal Congress (under pressure from the powerful *Ligue de l'Enseignement*, which the socialist teachers' union had joined) had called for the dismantling of subsidies for Catholic private education. It would have effectively put an end to the 1919 compromise that granted such subsidies in exchange for the single vote system. The anti-clerical convictions of the party elite were not as strong anymore and the freethinkers, even with the support of the freemasons, were too weak to rally the left wing of parliament behind their views on school subsidies and a neutral public education system. The pragmatics within the BWP also wanted to avoid a confrontation with the Catholics over the issue, even though they stuck to the conviction that the public school system remained a way to undermine the hegemony of the Catholic party and Church.

Leaders, especially the authoritarian Devèze, wanted the liberals to be a 'law and order' party, anti-socialist and anti-Bolshevik. The 1921 electoral campaign was a direct attack on the BWP's internationalist pacifism and against collectivism, which was portrayed as a threat to individual freedom.

Many among the party faithful leaned more to the left than the leading politicians who in fact led the party: Hymans, Devèze, P.E. Janson and, in Brussels, the anti-Flemish mayor A. Max. The liberals had had their own social organisations since the end of the 19th century, including the *Help U Zelve* (Help Yourself) cooperative, health care organisations and even a liberal workers' union that sought a harmonious relationship between labour and capitalism. These associations were controlled by the bourgeoisie and they made sure the social organisations could not really participate in party decision-making after the First World War. Their representatives were kept well down the electoral lists. Little wonder a number of progressive liberals quit the party after the war and joined the BWP. The 1930 creation of a liberal trade union umbrella organisation had little impact. It defended the free-market economy, opposed the class struggle and nationalisations. On the other hand, it also demanded more social security, economic and social democracy and opposed unbridled *laisser faire*.

A new wind started blowing through the party at the end of the 1920s; a new generation of ambitious young men began to gain influence, notably R. Motz, who had a strong position in the Liberal Young Guard and had the support of pro-Flemish and socially-oriented movements (*Liberaal Vlaams Verbond*, founded in 1913, and the independent *Willemsfonds*, which also counted pro-Flemish socialists among its members). The authoritarian party leadership was criticised, as was the excessive economic and political power of monopolistic financial capitalism; even the notion of government subsidies during times of crisis was not rejected outright, as long as it did not interfere with the laws of supply and demand.

On a national level, the Liberal Party opposed the concept of a Dutch-speaking university in Ghent and, in 1920, made its government participation conditional on the maintenance of the francophone university. Three years later, it only grudgingly accepted the Nolf compromise, which outlined the creation of a bilingual university. In between 1929 and 1932 the Liberals withdrew from government or threatened to do so at least three times over parliamentary bills on a Flemish university or the mono-linguistic administrative status of Dutch in Flanders and French in Wallonia. It wanted compensations for the francophone minority in Flanders, even at a time when the party's wallingants had already accepted the concept of a monolingual Flanders.

The more democratic and pro-Flemish wing had little impact on party policy up to the end of the 1930s – A. Vanderpoorten became minister in 1939. Yet the *Vlaams Liberaal Verbond* and *Willemsfonds*, influenced by J. Hoste jr. of the *Het Laatste Nieuws* newspaper, cooperated to temper the power of extremely bourgeois and in Flanders often pro-French associations. As a minimalist, Hoste had chosen the side of Van Cauwelaert (cf. infra).

Pressure Groups, Employers' and Labour Organisations, Social Dialogue and Social Legislation

Many pressure groups tried to lobby public opinion and the political parties on economic, financial, communal, ideological levels. Some had their representatives in parliament and even in government. The employers and labour pressure groups were among the most important and had a major impact on social consultations, the creation of joint committees, collective bargaining agreements and the creation of extensive social legislation. The balance of power between the employers and labour organisations helped determine the position of parliament and government on the social issues.

Unemployment was rampant during the First World War. The Germans had removed a large part of Belgium's industrial infrastructure and much of the working class was reduced to living off handouts from the National Committee for Aid and Food Supply, which operated under the patronage of the U.S. Commission for Relief in Belgium. E. Francqui of the Société Générale was chairman of the Committee and together with a small group of Société Générale investors, and without government or party interference, he organised the distribution of aid to a majority of Belgians. As of 1917, Société Générale governor Jean Jadot and representatives of the Solvay Institute started preparing blueprints for the post-war reconstruction of the nation. The government took their advice to heart in 1919 and relied heavily on their plans. So, in effect, Belgium's big industrial and financial groups were largely responsible for leading the nation through the difficult early post-war years, supported by the socialists. The period could have been marked by revolt and riots, but the government moved quickly to meet some key political and social demands. It approved the eight-hour workday and universal single suffrage, index-linked wages and introduced a progressive income tax system. The right considered the latter a direct collectivist attack on property.

Unemployment peaked at one million in 1918 and an economic crisis hit again in 1920 after a short-lived recovery in 1919. Eighteen months after the armistice, industrial production stood at only 85 % of 1913 levels. Wages had not been adapted to take the devaluation of the franc into account. And the Liège and Borinage working class went back on strike, with some 290,000 industrial workers involved in protest actions during 1920.

Money for the reconstruction of the nation was supposed to come from the German restitution payments. To kick-start the reconstruction effort, the National Bank created the *Nationale Maatschappij voor Krediet aan de Nijverheid* (NMKN, National Society for Credit to Industry), and up to 1924 it did little else than refund war damage. For the authorities, the NMKN and the *Algemene Spaar- en Lijfrentekas* (ASLK, General Savings and Annuity Fund) would only later become means to interfere in the economy.

The war and the first post-war years were marked by a spate of mergers in industry and banking. The Société Générale strengthened its control over other smaller banks, by either acquiring them or through partnership agreements. It bought up the famed *Fabrique Nationale d'Armes de Guerre* (FN) arms maker, the *Cockerill* and *Providence* metal works, the *Ateliers de Constructions Electriques de Charleroi* (ACEC) electricity company and the Carbochimie chemical company. In 1928, it took over the important Banque d'Outre-Mer. The other big holding companies did not stand by idly. The Empain group (Chemicals, ACEC, blast furnaces, etc.), Solvay (chemicals, glass, textile, blast furnaces), Boël (coal and metal works) and Banque de Bruxelles-Coppée all ventured into new directions. Some cooperated with each other, or with Société Générale and Banque de Bruxelles, for instance to create the chemical group *Union Chimique Belge* (UCB). Overall, they stuck to the core industries, the ports and colonial interests.

It was obvious that industry and big business also wanted a political stake. They were represented in almost every government, and often held key positions, especially at the finance ministry. They were trusted by the bond and stock markets. It was during the Great Depression that the middle class merchants started criticising this 'hyper-capitalism' that threatened small and medium-size businesses.

Employers had been organised in a pressure group since 1885. After the First World War, the *Comité Central Industriel* (CCI), precursor of the *Verbond der Belgische Ondernemingen* (VBO, Federation of Belgian Companies) defended their interests at a national level, and would become the most important employers' pressure group. In Flanders, the Vlaams Handelsverbond (Flemish Trade Federation, 1908) developed into the *Vlaams Economisch Verbond* (VEV, Flemish Economic Federation) in 1926, and it would become the mouthpiece of a young pro-Flemish bourgeoisie. The Catholic *Kredietbank*, which developed out of the *Boerenbond*, would later assume that role.

The Flemish ACVW promoted class reconciliation within the Christian social doctrine. The Flemish industrialist and 'social employer' L. Bekaert was a central figure in this Flemish pressure group around 1930, while the Walloon counterpart, the *Association des Patrons et Ingénieurs Catholiques* (APIC) was more focused on the region's heavy industry.

Trade unionism also boomed during the 1920s. On 24 May 1921, the government finally abolished the much-feared Article 310 of the penal code and lifted the suffocating constraints on the right to strike; this move had been announced by the king and the government since 1918.

Even after the 1866 repeal of the ban on union associations, heavy fines and prison sentences remained for setting up picket lines and uttering threats or insults, or anything that could be interpreted as such by a judge. Ahead of the war, few workers belonged to trade unions – in 1910, only 7 % of the workforce was unionised; at that time, they were concentrated in certain sectors. Some 50,000 of the 120,000 unionised workers belonged to the Catholic union. By 1920, the socialist union already had 700,000 members, while ACV, the Catholic union, only had 160,000. The number of members in the socialist *Syndicale Commissie* hovered around 550,000. By 1939, the socialist union (renamed *Belgisch Vakverbond*, BVV, Belgian Union, in 1937) had 540,000 members compared to 340,000 for the Catholic one. In 1930, 35 % of the workforce was unionised and the highest concentrations could be found among manual labourers in big companies and civil servants. Few employees of small and medium-size businesses joined a union.

The reason for the expansion of Belgian trade unionism could be found in the situation during the war when the government allowed unions to pay out unemployment benefits, a strategy that brought in a lot of new members. Until shortly before the Second World War, workers could enrol with a fund, mostly run by his union; the worker would contribute a relatively small sum. The government created a National Crisis Fund in 1920 on which the unemployed could rely in case the union coffers ran dry. Such crisis fund support was also paid out through the unions, and sometimes, there was an additional payment by municipalities and provinces. Non-union workers had to take care of themselves. Many miners in Limburg were not unionised and had to rely on municipal relief for the poor in times of crisis. Unemployment benefits were not considered an automatic right and covered the bare necessities only.

Since they were allowed to manage benefit payments, unions gradually became part of the system – and they became increasingly bureaucratic institutions, as did cooperatives and health care institutions. Already in the immediate post-war years, union leaders opposed strikes and were frustrated when they could not prevent wildcat strikes. J. Wauters, the Socialist minister for Industry, Labour and Provisions, applied the necessary pressure to persuade employers and unions into cooperating within joint committees. As of 1919, such committees in several big companies were able to clinch collective bargaining agreements that included minimum wages and index-linked pay. Joint committees and collective bargaining agreements proved to be effective methods to prevent social action. Many backed such social pacts and a number of regional and sector-based collective bargaining agreements were concluded in between the two wars. Union leaders were prepared to drop demands for an immediate rise in purchasing power in favour of security for large groups of employees, and thus tried to soften the impact of market mechanisms. The collective bargaining agreements were hardly ever nationwide, or for more than one sector. The movement slowed after 1922 when the employers started to organise themselves again after the frightening post-war years.

The retail price index was far from perfect, open to manipulation and only a rough approximation of the cost of living. When it dipped, wages had to follow, forcing unions into action to make sure spending power would increase. An economic upturn in the second half of the 1920s pushed wage scales higher. During the Great Depression, when workers were literally lining up to get a job, employers felt they were in a strong enough position to question index-linked wages. In practice, wages dropped in the weakest economic sectors while the strongest sectors did not submit to the index link, but sometimes increased wages in real terms.

In spite of increasing advertising, the era of mass consumption had not arrived yet. Productivity increases, without which wages cannot rise in real terms, were limited to such new sectors as the automobile and electronics industries, where workers were already enjoying the so-called English five-day week. Union leaders did not go on the offensive, looking for pay increases beyond the index increases and they stuck to a careful, non-threatening reformist policy.

After the war, the Socialist union started centralising its structure and union representatives often turned into the mouthpiece of the central leadership instead of the spokesmen of the union members. The union leadership counted on them to prevent wildcat strikes. The Communists often provoked those, either actively supporting or creating labour protest, before setting up action committees with other dissidents. By 1924, the union leadership had had enough and expelled them from the leading echelons of union power. The union itself became an integral part of the BWP.

At a political level, the union was more conservative than the party. In between 1929 and 1932, a majority of socialist parliamentarians also held leading positions within the unions, cooperatives and health care organisations. Nationalisation of the means of production was still seen as the main goal but strike action was no longer considered the best means. Steadily the union was drawn into the capitalist fold and became an integral part of the control mechanism of economic life. In fact, its impact was limited. In the General Council of the BWP, Union leaders were the biggest backers of Socialist participation in government. Unions and cooperatives were primarily concerned with the stability of the Belgian currency and the control of inflation. Rampant inflation would have driven the labour organisations and their savings banks to ruin. During the Great Depression, unions just stood by, patiently waiting to see whether the economy would collapse. It took until 1937 for the younger generation to change tack; at the foundation of the BVV, they started talking about real worker control, joint management and the nationalisation of core industries and credit institutions. It would take until after the Second World War before demands for anti-capitalist reforms were carefully formulated.

Within the Catholic camp, the ACW General Christian Workers Union was created in 1921. The umbrella organisation grouped Catholic unions, cooperatives, health care organisations, women's guilds and youth groups. The ACW did (and does) not have individual members; it grew into the most important part of the so-called Catholic pillar. The conservative Catholics rejected a structured organisation or orders as they feared it would go on to develop an independent policy, but the Church and party elites were very effective in controlling the Catholic workers. After a difficult start, the ACV Catholic union accepted its role within the ACW, an organisation that was not solely intent on defending workers' rights. Its health care organisations and cooperatives were also open to small shop owners, non-active people, etc.

The ACW (from 1945 also MOC, *Mouvement Ouvrier Chrétien,* in Wallonia) and ACV never had as much impact on Catholic party politics as its socialist counterpart had on the BWP. The ACW's first goal was to contain the socialist, anti-clerical influence. Like other Christian organisations, it had an army of priests to back its cause. The ACV union spread its gospel in Catholic schools, in grassroots organisations, women's and youth groups and gradually, it won over the Flemish industrial proletariat. It was especially successful in Flanders: many Flemish workers were commuters, and lived in comforting small villages, where they used to be, as small farmers, under the moral authority of the clergy and Catholic dignitaries. Their dream remained to own a little house in their own village. While the Walloon industrial proletariat continued a tradition of class struggle, the Flemish worker remained a thrifty saver.

The Church and especially the Catholic bourgeoisie found it extremely hard to adapt to the new realities after the First World War and meet the demands of the Christian workers. They did not like the new political system of enlarged representation of the different orders, despite the fact that it was based on the principle of class reconciliation. The Christian unions and even the *Katholieke Arbeidersjeugd* (KAJ, Catholic Workers' Youth, JOC in Wallonia) youth organisation, founded by the priest J. Cardijn in 1924, faced deep mistrust.

The strategy of the bishops complied with the Vatican guidelines of Pius XI, who created the Catholic Action programme in 1922. The grand project called for a greater participation of lay people in religious activity. As of 1925, the annual Christ the King Day had to celebrate the mystical union between the faithful and Christ. Society had to be christened, or re-christened, through the missionary zeal of lay people under the guidance of the pope and the bishops, to protect it against atheism, socialism and liberalism. But the goals of the Catholic Action were open to interpretation. The ACV, the ACW and even the KAJ youth organisation (which pledged, after insistence of Cardijn, to steer clear of politics) were not on the same wavelength as the bishops, who sought to keep all Catholic groups under tight control, including the *Katholieke Vlaamse Studentenbeweging* (Catholic Flemish Student Movement), which from the end of the 1920s was replaced by the *Katholieke Studenten Actie* (Catholic Student Action). The latter did not at all line up with the aims of the Catholic Action programme, and was far less militantly pro-Flemish. Thanks to Cardijn, and in spite of the mistrust of the bourgeoisie, the KAJ succeeded in being recognised by Pius XI as a perfect form of Catholic Action. The ACW would have preferred its own youth movement; it entered into educational work, among others at the *Sociale Hogeschool* (Social Polytechnic) in Heverlee, where future leaders of the different Christian labour organisations were trained. ACV, ACW, and up to a point also Cardijn went against Catholic hierarchy and insisted that Catholic Action should mainly be aimed at social conditions. But papal and pastoral instructions tried to rein them in.

ACW and ACV became ever more militant, so that in the 1930s the socialist union often felt the need to cooperate with the Christian organisations, much to the outrage of the right-wing. But the more it became clear the Socialist union was not the radical organisation it was made out to be, the more the two unions started cooperating to achieve their common goals.

The ACV interpreted religious social doctrine in terms of class reconciliation through negotiations, social agreements, and, eventually, joint management. The union based its belief on the 19th-century *Rerum Novarum* encyclical and Pope Pius XI's 1931 *Quadragesimo Anno*. Together with the ACW, the union defended traditional family values, backed child support for large families, disapproved of married women who worked outside their homes and defended financial support for women who stayed at home.

The labour movement and post-war conditions were instrumental in expanding and improving social legislation. The working week was set at a maximum of 48 hours (eight hours a day); article 310, which severely restricted the right to strike, was abolished and the state subsidised the Crisis Fund. Apart from those realisations, a special mention should be made of the law of 10 December, 1924, which institutionalised pensions for workers. The pensions were funded by holding back part of the wage package, a contribution from employers and state subsidies. Reality was not as rosy. Often workers did not meet their contribution commitments because of unemployment or because of employers who neglected to do the necessary. A great many elderly had to make do with an insignificant pension or even none at all. Medical insurance was optional and most of the workers joined the health care program of their ideological pillar. The system of unemployment benefit has been described earlier. The improvements in social legislation slowed for a long time after the 1920-1921 crisis and would pick up again only after the general strike of 1936. In between, laws were voted in 1927 on insurance against occupational illnesses and in 1930 on child support and the extension of industrial accident insurance.

The Flemish Movement and the Language Laws

After the armistice, Belgian patriotism was on a high and wanted to turn back the linguistic clock. But soon, the Flemish issue would return with a vengeance and dominate political life. Universal single suffrage had expanded the Flemish electorate and for the first time and the establishment of a Flemish nationalist party became a realistic possibility.

The leaders of the Front movement had already written an open letter to king Albert on 11 July 1917, demanding a royal promise to institute language equality in administration, the armed forces and higher education immediately after the war. They also insisted that the members of the *Raad van Vlaanderen* and the founders of the Ghent Von Bissing university would not be prosecuted. Finally, they demanded an autonomous Flanders in a federal Belgium and based their arguments on U.S. president Wilson's theory on the right to self-determination of people. Thus, the basis of the post-war Flemish Front was laid in 1917. All federalist movements, especially the so-called maximalists, were later inspired by this fundamental position. At first, the wartime stand of some Flemings at the front, and especially within the occupied territories, created a wave of anti-flamingantism and Flemish public opinion turned against these activists.

Many Flemish war veterans, however, joined the *Verbond der Vlaamse Oudstrijders* (VOS), a veterans' movement that would have an important role in the creation of a new party, the *Vlaams Front* or *Frontpartij* (Flemish

Front Party). The pacifist movement soon counted tens of thousands of members and in 1920, it organised its first Yser pilgrimage in remembrance of the fallen Flemish soldiers. The first such meeting came after the desecration of tombs bearing the inscription AVV-VVK – All for Flanders, Flanders for Christ. The ceremony in Diksmuide turned into an annual mass meeting to push Flemish nationalist demands. From 1930, when the Yser Tower was inaugurated, right-wing Flemish nationalism started to gain more and more influence. In and after 1930 (centenary of Belgian independence), the anti-Belgian streak became ever more virulent. The VOS demanded a general amnesty and insisted that Ghent University be turned into a Dutch-speaking institution. The secret 1920 Franco-Belgian military agreement (cf. infra) met nothing but opposition.

The continuing democratisation, especially the universal single male suffrage, also had an impact on the Flemish movement. The influence of the pro-francophone upper classes within Flanders and the Catholic Party waned. The activists turned 'cultural flamingantism', which had not been anti-Belgian before 1914, into an anti-Belgian movement for political autonomy. The electoral impact of the Front Party was limited, so it had to rely on the pro-Flemish minimalist faction, led by Van Cauwelaert, in the Catholic Party and, to a lesser extent, on the BWP. Only the Antwerp BWP federation backed a Flemish minimalist program. The Catholic camp especially was willing to reintegrate the activists, even though they included a number of freethinkers. The disillusionment within the pro-Flemish wing was such that it turned into an anti-Belgian attitude, and gradually into disgust for a parliamentary system that refused to fully take the Flemish demands into account. Party politics, shedding Flemish demands for short-term gains, also contributed to the movement's slow slide towards right-wing, anti-Belgian and anti-democratic nationalism. It won support from the Flemish middle class and petty bourgeoisie and soon one thought dominated the Flemish movement – the Belgian state had to be destroyed to achieve Flemish autonomy or create a Great 'Dietsland' together with the Netherlands.

The Catholic Van Cauwelaert, backed by Brussels liberal Hoste and, up to a point, the socialist Huysmans defended the so-called minimum program. It wanted to make Flemish public life completely Dutch-speaking – from administration to the judiciary, the armed forces and education. The so-called maximalists attacked this strategy as insufficient, even though the mid-term implications were significant. A linguistic division in education and the armed forced had to lead to a linguistic split in the central administration and to a change in the structure of the unitary state. And even though an important 1921 law called for administrative monolingualism in the two regions, parliament continued to resist the move for seven more years.

Social pressure on Flemings to speak French was big in the Brussels region but most Dutch-speaking citizens of the capital were not flamingant. They rarely voted for specifically pro-Flemish electoral candidates. Municipal councils promoted the use of French in schools. The Flemish Catholics were primarily worried about party unity in the capital and did not dare take a clear stand on the issue in 1921. Steadily, the situation became irreversible. Three Flemish towns were officially added to the Brussels agglomeration in 1921 (bringing the total to sixteen) and while Flanders became more and more Dutch-speaking, Brussels became more francophone.

In 1920, 58.7 % of the agglomeration said it was francophone or francophone-bilingual. In 1930, that was 62.7 %, and by 1947, the figure stood at 70.6 %. In 1939, only 19 % of children went to Dutch-speaking schools. The negative pedagogical implications were ignored. The Brussels Flemings were not convinced their own language and culture was all that important. The Flemish Movement took it upon itself to protect these people against themselves.

The October 1920 Liberal Party congress refused to accept that Flemish administration and the judiciary had to be monolingual Dutch-speaking. They also rejected the mandatory bilingualism of civil servants, even in the capital. The prominent Liberal leaders wanted to keep Ghent University a 'torch of French culture'. The pro-Flemish liberals, united in the *Liberaal Vlaams Verbond* (LVV, Liberal Flemish Union), hardly dared raise their voice for fear of being called activists or 'krauts'. Francophone influence in the Liberal party remained strong until after the Second World War, backed by trade, banking and the courts, and by such papers as *La Flandre Libérale* in Ghent and *Le Matin* in Antwerp.

Pressured by Camille Huysmans and most of the Antwerp federation, many Flemish socialists were willing to consider the linguistic demands as long as they would not lead to a break-up with the Walloon wing. In the old socialist bulwark of Ghent, there was less enthusiasm; Anseele preferred to focus efforts on the development of cooperatives within the capitalist state, industries and such institutions as the Labour Bank instead of spending too much energy on turning companies or Ghent University into Dutch-language institutions.

The maximalists were in the Front Party, which had been able to win five seats in the 1919 election. Activist demands ranged from simple federalism over the abolishment of the Belgian state to the integration of Flanders in the Netherlands. The original aim of the Front Party was autonomy for Flanders and its policy was anti-militaristic. In 1922, the party turned anti-Belgian but not anti-democratic under the influence of the activists. At first, the movement that launched the slogan 'Never again war' attracted socialist and communist sympathizers and artists, including the Antwerp writer Paul van Ostaijen. All kinds of socialist and humanist do-gooders, expressionists and avant-gardists who had backed the idea of a compromise peace during the war, found a home in the Front Party, or even in the tiny *Communistische Partij-Vlaamse Federatie* (Communist Party-Flemish Federation). The remnants of the Daensism movement also joined. The party paper *De Schelde* (with the freethinker H. Vos as editor) was progressive in many ways. When a left-wing progressive student was killed by police during a 1920 pro-Flemish demonstration in Antwerp, it caused outrage. It was characteristic of the time that this H. Van Den Reeck, and others within and on the fringes of the *Vlaams Front*, took an extreme-left and marginal stance. As the Front Party failed to make further political inroads, its right wing took over under the leadership of Joris Van Severen.

Maximalists and minimalists, in the meantime, did cooperate to demand an amnesty. Because the governments were so slow in addressing the Flemish demands, the population started lending a more sympathetic ear to the activists' arguments. In 1928, the imprisoned activist August Borms won a large majority of votes in local elections even though he was ineligible to take office, beating a liberal candidate. The francophone patriots saw it as a bad omen and started to worry about the unity of the country. The most intelligent realised it was necessary to address the language issues. It would allow the pro-Flemish Belgian unionists to realise their minimum programme. Huysmans and Walloon J. Destrée agreed in 1929 on a *Compromis des Belges*, which rejected the split-up of the nation but nevertheless recommended monolingual regions. The document was signed by 27 members of parliament. The Flemings had made an important concession in the document since administrative bilingualism had to be assured in Flemish towns if enough people asked for it. In any case, linguistic minorities in Flanders would get guaranteed protection. The

Borms controversy had turned the Flemish demands into a key political issue and after the May 1929 elections, Catholic Prime Minister Henri Jaspar made a commitment to solve the issue. From then onwards, the government took the initiative.

The Flemish demand for higher education dated back to long before the First World War. Even though King Albert had made certain promises about a Dutch-language university in Ghent in 1918, the idea met stiff resistance from liberal ministers and Catholic francophone conservatives. The Flemish minimalists and socialists exerted enough pressure, though, to make sure that a bilingual university was reluctantly accepted in 1923. At the 'Nolf University', named after the legislator who tabled the bill, Dutch-language students had to take one-third of their classes in French and vice versa. The system satisfied no one. Proposals for a full Dutch-language university resurfaced in 1929 and, once the Liberals were offered guarantees on francophone primary and secondary education in Flanders, they gave in. The law was finally approved on 5 April 1930.

Later that year, the government also banned the Ghent professors from teaching at the *Ecole des Hautes Etudes* in Ghent, which had been set up as a francophone reaction. The liberal ministers wanted to resign but the king refused to accept their resignation. Every time the Flemish movement made an inch of progress, the francophone war veterans and other Belgian patriotic movements tried to counter, often with anti-Flemish and anti-democratic arguments. A number of officers from the armed forces who opposed a split along regional lines and mandatory bilingualism in command posts, were members of, or influenced by, the *Légion Nationale*, which was founded in 1922 by P. Hoornaert. The movement found its inspiration in Italy's fascism, which also recruited its members among the war veterans; Germany and France saw similar evolutions.

King Albert was ever more convinced the language issue was an increasing threat to Belgian unity. During the war, the king had already shown more willingness than many of his ministers to consider some 'reasonable' concessions. He considered the Dutch language equal to French, German and English and he thought it a pity the language did not get more respect from Belgium's ruling classes. He was also counting on a great many Flemings voluntarily remaining bilingual and thus safeguarding the unity of his kingdom.

To a lesser extend, the king could also consider radical wallingantism as a threat to national unity. The *Ligue d'Action Wallonne* of G. Thone (with alongside him a number of liberals like A. Buisseret and J. Rey and socialists F. Dehousse and G. Truffaut) was a group of francophiles who wanted to integrate Wallonia into France. It did not prevent some of the movement's leading members from becoming Belgian ministers after the Second World War.

The application of some of the language laws left much to be desired, as the 1921 law that forced civil servants to know the language of the region proved in Brussels. Around 1930, the Walloons had accepted the concept of monolingual regions, but obviously with a bilingual administration in Brussels. The 1932 language laws confirmed this principle of language uniformity in the regions; they were hardly applied in Brussels, or cleverly bypassed. The Walloons were against bilingualism and they dropped the cause of the minority of francophones in Flanders. Monolingual Dutch-speaking education in Flanders steadily undermined the francophone bourgeois minority in Flanders, in spite of the mainly francophone Catholic institutions and the so-called transmutation classes. In Brussels and its surrounding municipalities, gallicisation was unstoppable, as they were free to choose the language of their internal administration.

More language laws improved the Flemish position further, among others concerning the use of Dutch in Flemish courts. A 1938 law stipulated that every army recruit had to be instructed in his mother tongue. There were numerous violations of the law however, especially in the Brussels region. Flemish activist F. Grammens started painting over the monolingual French street signs in Brussels, and his controversial tactics sometimes yielded result. When he continued such action during the war in occupied Brussels, the Germans were not amused and he harmed the Flemish cause more than he helped it.

Foreign Policy up to 1936: the end of imposed neutrality

The influence of the king on foreign policy had traditionally been sizable. During the war Albert rightly stuck to the view of the violation of neutrality. As supreme commander of the Belgian forces he had been able to stay on Belgian soil behind the front line of the Yser, when the government had retreated into France, to Sainte-Adresse near Le Havre, in order to fight a mainly defensive battle. Albert was convinced the Belgian constitution restricted his responsibilities to defending the national territory and he refused to formally join the allied war effort that sought the total destruction of the enemy. Britain and France only guaranteed Belgian neutrality. When it came to protecting the interests of the Belgian Congo, he almost mistrusted France and Britain as much as he did Germany. He refused to believe this war was about 'justice and civilisation' and he refused to send his soldiers to their deaths on the other front lines. The king would wait until the eve of the final attack on German positions in 1918 to put his men under allied command. Just a few months earlier, Albert would have happily agreed to a compromise peace restoring Belgium's old borders. His informal steps to sound out the enemy alarmed the French and British governments. But without their backing, Albert would not have agreed to a separate peace, not even if the Germans had made acceptable proposals.

During the negotiations preceding the Treaty of Versailles, Belgian diplomats sought territorial expansion and exceedingly high restitution payments. Belgium was reminded of its limited contribution to the allied cause but the government and public opinion remained convinced that the violation of Belgium's neutrality deserved hefty compensation payments.

King Albert I, and his son Leopold III after him, were convinced that Belgium should continue to be an essential piece in the continental balance of power because of its central location and history. Leopold was of the same mind with his father on most other issues, too, yet Albert and Leopold have been judged differently by history. Albert was the 'king-knight', the victor in a war he despised. Leopold III turned out to be a loser for accepting defeat in a war that was later won.

During the war, the first calls were made to end Belgium's neutrality once Germany had been defeated. F. Neuray and his right-wing Catholic paper *Le XXième Siècle* lobbied hard and even obtained the support of de Broqueville, who had led Belgium's wartime government. The group also won the backing of a number of Liberals and Walloon Socialists. Belgium had to join the war aims of the allied nations and shed its neutrality after the war to become an integral member of any peace conference. The 1839 neutrality treaty had to be replaced by a Franco-British guarantee pact. Nationalist hotheads like Neuray and P. Nothomb were already dreaming about territorial expansion into the Netherlands, which would have to surrender Zeeland Flanders, Maastricht and Dutch Limburg. They also set their designs on Luxembourg, which had been lost to Belgium in 1839. King Albert could agree on the latter idea only. These ultranationalists made their voice heard within the government and created stirred trouble. Because of this nationalist agitation, de Broqueville had to hand over his foreign affairs portfolio to Paul Hymans in 1917; Hymans was the co-founder of the Belgian policy of independence, which at first had been strongly French-oriented. It was only in 1936 that Belgium would openly distance itself from this vision.

The negotiations at Versailles (12 January – 6 May 1919) did not really take the Belgian demands into account. Hymans and Vandervelde had entered a long list of requests – the end of mandatory neutrality, the territorial acquisition of the Grand Duchy of Luxembourg, Maastricht and Dutch Limburg from the Netherlands and Moresnet, Eupen and Malmédy from Germany. In Africa, it wanted to expand its colonial reach at Germany's expense. It wanted a better deal with the Netherlands on the River Scheldt and the Ghent-Terneuzen canal. It also wanted hefty German restitution payments. France, however, also had designs on the Grand Duchy and the Netherlands was in no mood to hand over territory.

In the end, the Treaty of Versailles gave Belgium Eupen, Malmédy and Moresnet and the mandate over Rwanda and Burundi in central Africa. Its mandatory neutrality was revoked. Germany also had to pay 2.5 billion goldmarks in restitution which, compared to France, was a relatively high amount. From now on, foreign policy would no longer be shackled by the constraints of neutrality, a *'politique des mains libres'*. The territorial ambitions had hardly been met, much to the disappointment of the nationalists.

The grand coalition led by Delacroix signed a Franco-Belgian military agreement on 7 September 1920. It was a purely defensive agreement that guaranteed military assistance only in the case of a non-provoked attack from Germany. The agreement was linked to the Luxembourg issue since both France and Belgium sought the closest of relationships with the Grand Duchy. After Luxembourg left the Deutsche Zollverein, a majority in Luxembourg wanted close economic relations with France. France did not push for a Luxembourg referendum in return for the military agreement with Belgium. France attached more value to its relations with Belgium after a U.S-British agreement to contain Germany fell through. For the French government it was self-evident that Belgium was part of its sphere of influence. Little wonder the agreement enraged the pro-Flemish circles. Germany also had to be forced to meet its restitution commitments and had to be prevented from becoming a military power again. Some Belgians wanted a joint Belgian-Dutch defence of Dutch Limburg while others sought to include Britain in the Franco-Belgian military agreement, but

Britain did not want this. Belgium was expected to field an army with the same proportional strength as France, which implied an extension of military service. In the light of the regret about Britain's refusal to be involved in the agreement, Belgium tried to reduce the political impact of the Franco-Belgian agreement by limiting it to technical contacts and talks between the chiefs of staff. The agreement also included a technical military deal that had to remain secret. Both countries also registered a fairly innocent text with the League of Nations, proof that a regional alliance had been set up. It stipulated that the agreement, which was purely defensive, covered only the time span of the occupation of Germany's Rhineland.

In early 1923, the military agreement was already causing problems, as France single-handedly occupied the industrial Ruhr region to enforce reparation payments. The Belgian government was pressured into following this initiative, even though it was not technically bound to do so by the bilateral military agreement. The brutal occupation was internationally condemned. Military service was extended despite severe socialist and Christian-democrat criticism. The latter gave way after obtaining concessions on the establishment of a Dutch-language university in Ghent. The Ruhr adventure quickly turned into failure. German inflation skyrocketed and the Franco-Belgian intrusion was successfully countered by mass strikes. The Belgian government and the king had been wary of the fact that France might want to use the occupation to establish an independent Rhineland. France needed the Ruhr cokes to turn its Lorraine iron ore into steel and the Belgian steel barons were dreaming of a 'Franco-Belgian industrial empire', which would also include the Grand Duchy. The realisation of this old French ambition would have left Belgium half surrounded, and even more under French influence.

Belgium and France shook hands on a bilateral trade agreement in 1923 but the Belgian legislature rejected it in early 1924. Many considered it a bad deal and the BWP also condemned French aggression in the Ruhr, along with all leftist parties in Western Europe. When the Flemish Catholic 'minimalists' and the Front party also raised objections, the government of G. Theunis was outvoted and offered to resign. However, the king refused to accept the resignation. In elections in April 1925, the BWP got the biggest increase in votes, and the Christian-democrat-socialist government Poullet-Vandervelde was formed, which aligned its foreign policy with the League of Nations. The Dawes plan reduced German reparation payments and called for an end to the Ruhr occupation. Belgium was granted a disappointingly small share of the payments, greatly exceeded by the American claims. The 1925 Locarno Pact guaranteed the demilitarisation of the Rhineland and improved international relations. The Rhine Pact, which was part of the Locarno agreement, guaranteed the Belgo-German borders as specified by the Treaty of Versailles. All disputes would be settled by arbitration. The Rhine Pact was important to Belgium since the Belgo-German borders were now guaranteed by Britain and Italy. Belgium was now both a guaranteed nation and also a guarantor itself. Both international agreements cemented Belgium's foreign policy in an international system of collective security and allowed Belgium to ease its military dependence on France, even though the 1920 military agreement was not annulled.

The United States and France were the driving force behind the 1928 international Briand-Kellogg Pact, an addition to the pact of the League of Nations, which renounced the use of war and made a commitment to settle international disputes by peaceful means. From 1930 onwards, Hymans had to seek ways to reduce the Franco-Belgian military agreement to a bare minimum. Paris did not want to budge on the issue and was convinced the deal was still useful despite the new international agreements. It was certain that the bilateral agreement would allow French forces, in case of a direct German threat, to enter Belgium without a special permission from the Belgian government. Art. 16 of the League of Nations also recognised this right of passage. By 1935, Hymans, and Belgian foreign policy in general, still had not been able to rid Belgium of its specific military commitments towards France. It proved a propaganda windfall for the anti-French and anti-Belgian Flemish nationalists.

The Dutch did not like the way Belgium was shedding its mandatory neutrality. Since the Netherlands stuck by its own neutrality, Belgium no longer insisted on a bilateral military agreement to protect Limburg from a German invasion. After 1925, both sides agreed to change a few clauses in the 1839 Treaty of the XXIV Articles, including some advantageous provisos concerning the Scheldt and other rivers. The Dutch legislators, however, did not approve this 'impossible agreement' before the war. They did not like to see Antwerp being turned into a war port with access to the sea. What would happen to the Dutch neutrality then? There were also economic conflicts involved. It was expected that the Dutch would allow the creation of a canal from Antwerp to the Rhine estuary and share in the costs. Rotterdam, Amsterdam and their dockers protested. Flemish nationalists spread rumours that the secret military Franco-Belgian agreement might involve an occupation of Dutch Limburg in case of a conflict with Germany. Belgium's wish to annex parts of the Netherlands was still fresh in Dutch minds. Conflicts of interest in connection with the Scheldt estuary, changes in the regime of river estuaries in general, the Meuse flow rate, etc. would stay on the agenda for a long time.

Chapter V
From the Great Depression to the Second World War

The Great Depression and its social aftermath put a sudden end to the relative euphoria of the late twenties, bringing several old grudges back to the surface, and reinforcing the discontent of part of the bourgeoisie with the democratic system after the introduction of universal single suffrage. It was a time of political polarisation both on the right and left, and within the traditional parties. Corporatist and 'New Order' tendencies affected even the labour movement. The 1936 elections turned the political conventions upside down and ended a period of relative stability under conservative Catholic-Liberal governments. The extreme left-wing Communist Party and the extreme right-wing Rex and VNV stretched the limits of the brittle parliamentary democracy. The pillars of the Flemish movement, Flanders' middle class and petty bourgeoisie, fell under the spell of the rabid right-wing anti-Bolshevik ideology at a time when a more imminent danger was developing in Nazi-Germany. The Socialist Party and its union abandoned the practice of class struggle and joined the Christian labour movement in seeking reconciliation between capital and labour. The Second World War would accelerate the establishment of 'neo-corporatism', a compromise system that was based on partnership negotiations and increased social welfare.

The Short Rule of Leopold III (1934-1940): the executive in a fragile parliamentary democracy

The early days of Leopold III's reign coincided with the establishment of a new generation of politicians. The new king held his inaugural speech in both main languages, a sign that something fundamental had changed in Belgium. The young king was also touched by the worst excesses of social inequality and, unlike his father, was suspicious of big business, something which was in line with the 'right-wing revolution' ideology; it was a sign of the times. Unlike Albert, Leopold ruled in years of continual economic depression, social and nationalist unrest and increasing threat of war. He could never match the prestige of his almost mythical 'king-knight' father. He was impatient and rubbed some governments the wrong way; his personal foreign policy caused tension. He often called ministers to account and sometimes lectured them in statements that were made public. Yet the young king had personality and most political leaders and a majority of Belgians were impressed. Many saw in him a strong leader in uncertain times, somebody elevated above obscure party politics. After the landmark 1936 elections and the political breakthrough of Rex and VNV, Leopold was forced to reign with unstable three-party coalitions of Catholics, Socialists and Liberals. The Catholic Party, which had lost many votes to Rex and VNV, was also ravaged by internal strife. Its bourgeoisie clashed with labour and its pro-Flemish wing with the francophones. The king detested 'particracy' but that did not stop Leopold exerting a great deal of influence on eight successive governments.

The head of the executive became visibly more active. The king and his cabinet staff at the palace made sure he respected the formal constitutional constraints and their traditional interpretations, but those did not stand in the way of treating his ministers as politicians who were his to fire and appoint. A number of conflicts were the result. Leopold loathed any interference from party bureaus or congresses which, especially in the case of the socialists, set strict conditions on who could become minister and what the government programme should look like.

Leopold also had to face increasing street unrest from certain pressure groups. During tumultuous street demonstrations, the Brussels and Walloon liberals joined right-wing patriotic war veterans and officers protesting the latest language laws. The laws included a more equitable balance in administration and the armed forces, and the controversial reintroduction of teachers and civil servants who had been convicted for anti-Belgian activism during the Great War. The pro-Flemish Catholic parliamentarians were at first stunned by the electoral success of Rex and VNV, which had eroded the Catholic grassroots electorate. From then on, the Christian-democrat 'minimum' language demands of Van Cauwelaert were considered insufficient and any more concessions that benefited francophones were out of the question.

The king, commander-in-chief of the armed forces, became a target of demeaning criticism in demonstrations by war veterans and was unfavourably compared with his revered 'knight-king' father. Surely, Albert would never have pardoned activist traitors, the argument went. The increasing polarisation between Belgian patriots and Flemish nationalists caused several government crises and was a threat to national unity. More so than his father, Leopold was worried about the francophone refusal to consider the legitimate non-separatist demands of the Flemish movement.

It would be the choices made by Leopold III during the Eighteen-Day Campaign in May 1940 and his attitude during the first years of his imprisonment that would later give rise to the 'Royal Question'.

The Political System During the Great Depression

The October 1929 stock market crash on Wall Street sparked the Great Depression and the economic crisis hit Belgium during the second half of 1930. It turned into the worst depression of the capitalist era and its effects were still felt on the eve of the Second World War. The political consequences were huge. In Germany, the collapse of the economy was instrumental in Hitler's rise to power.

Ahead of the Second World War, Belgium remained a low-wage country. It specialised in semi-finished products that required few skilled labourers. Flanders often provided the unskilled labour in Walloon mines and sugar refineries at a time when Limburg coal mines already sent foreign workers into the pits. The Walloon-Brussels holding companies invested little in the innovative economic sectors such as metal construction; it was bound to have disastrous consequences. Between 1923 and 1929, the production index rose from 100 to 140 before dropping back to 108 during the second half of 1930. Industrial activity in 1934 stood at 67 % of 1929 levels. Despite a temporary recovery, there was a further deep slump in 1938. The Great Depression went hand in hand with unprecedented levels of unemployment. 'Overproduction' caused a dramatic collapse of prices and investments. Numerous companies went bankrupt and the petty bourgeoisie suffered. Total spending power of wage-earners decreased considerably in the 1930s. Belgium's Catholic and liberal business leaders and politicians were long convinced that this crisis too, would soon blow over and refused to interfere in the laws of supply and demand. All hopes were pinned on a deflationary policy that would bring relief: low prices and, above all, low wages, would promote exports. Since other countries embraced the same policy or devalued their currencies, it had little effect.

The state had to cut wages of civil servants and teachers, make additional savings on welfare, etc. Deflation led to cuts in wages, pensions and unemployment benefits and would generate a wave of strikes in Wallonia in 1932. The miners had seen their nominal wages cut by 35 %.

In spite of a concentration move in industry and banking (in 1926-1930 there had already been an important merger of banking and industrial capital), the crisis also hit the big, supposedly strong, companies, and several were threatened with bankruptcy. When a new generation of politicians and economists came into office in the three-party Van Zeeland government in 1935, the policy changed: the currency was devalued, state intervention and public work projects were resumed and the battle against unemployment became a priority.

In 1932, two people were killed during wildcat strikes that were actively supported by Communist militants in the Borinage region. The BWP and the socialist union were not at all pleased. When the economic recovery became apparent in 1936, labour unrest followed: a general strike began in the Antwerp port on 2 June 1936 and quickly spread to other sectors throughout the country. It led to the convocation of a National Labour Conference, which was clearly based on a similar initiative by the French Popular Front. Other such conferences would follow in 1939 and 1940, and the tradition was continued after the Second World War. The workers had a sense that better times were coming after the crisis and they thought they had every right to demand an improvement in their working conditions. Yet the unions were hesitant and initially did not support strike action. Delegations from labour unions and employers met under the chairmanship of Prime Minister Paul Van Zeeland. The meeting set minimum wages and agreed on six mandatory and paid holidays. Child support was increased and union freedom guaranteed. The principle of the forty-hour workweek was not accepted, except in a few hard and dangerous sectors. Because of a lack of productivity and tough foreign competition, Van Zeeland considered it economically irresponsible to force companies to reduce hours from forty-eight to forty without loss of pay. The National Labour Conference was a decisive step in the move towards negotiations between labour, employers and the government. Despite the economic crisis and a right-wing authoritarian counteroffensive, the Christian and socialist unions had been able to reach an honourable compromise without having to make too many concessions. Their militancy and the political influence of the Christian labour movement within the Catholic Party had paid off.

The year 1936 proved crucial in other respects, too. A few months ahead of the general strike, the elections had given extremist parties a parliamentary breakthrough. On the right, Rex clinched 21 seats, and VNV doubled its number of seats to 16. On the left, the Communists secured 9 seats, gaining 6. And despite the addition of 15 seats in the Chamber, the Catholic Union and the BWP lost respectively 16 and 3 seats. One thing was clear – it was impossible to rule without the socialists and especially the Catholic conservatives were very worried after this political earthquake. Also the Catholic hierarchy was concerned about the 'impotence' of the divided Catholics. The realisation grew that the Catholic Party was in bad need of reform and even had to be federalised in an attempt to regain the Catholic voters that had been lost to Rex and the VNV. To achieve that, the power of the ACW within the party had to be broken and the Flemish legislators had to be granted more linguistic concessions. The anti-democratic tendencies were not limited to Rex and VNV alone. The right wing of the Catholic Party and, to a much lesser extent, the liberals and socialists also fell prey to the phenomenon.

The Spanish Civil War further polarised public opinion. Only the socialists, communists and a small group of ULB liberal intellectuals backed the legal, Spanish republican government against General Franco's fascist rebels, who were backed by Germany and Italy. The republicans had to make do with much less support from the Soviet Union, but it was enough to make the Belgian Catholic and liberal bourgeoisie worry about the communist impact on the civil war. When things turned ugly for the Spanish Catholic church, mainly because of destruction and persecution (more by anarchists than by socialists or communists), the Belgian conservative forces retorted with virulent anti-communism. The BWP meanwhile had to hold off grassroots pressure to forge a Popular Front coalition with the still weak Communist Party. The Christian-democratic trade union and the ACW, who were part of the coalition government and essential partners during social negotiations, had no respect whatsoever for those 'godless' Spanish republicans. The KPB (Communist Party) won little respect and was accused of taking all its orders from Moscow and Stalin's Communist International. In 1936, Stalin started executing and eliminating all his opponents, the original revolutionaries. Yet the left-wing democrats were much more worried about the aggressive Nazi-Germany. Only a few realised that the Spanish Civil War was a precursor to the Second World War. The overwhelming majority was convinced that Belgium's foreign policy would be able to keep the nation out of a new European conflict.

On the domestic front, government instability was unprecedented. Opposition was strong when the government reverted to deflationary measures to counter the new economic crisis in 1938. The language issue, epitomised by battles over cultural federalism and amnesty, only added to the government's troubles. Belgium had six governments within four years, including a Catholic-Socialist coalition that lasted all of seven days in February 1939. Apart from this so-called ‘Mardi Gras’ government and the slightly longer-lived 1939 Poullet II Catholic-Liberal coalition, all governments were grand three-party coalitions. The Socialist Party considered it a major political victory when Paul-Henri Spaak became Belgium's first socialist Prime Minister. His government lasted only nine months and steered a very conservative course. The continuing instability only reinforced those who dreamt of an authoritarian government. Issues such as mandatory unemployment insurance would keep surfacing in government programmes, but would always remain unresolved.

Amnesty turned into one of the most divisive issues. It brought protesters into the streets and governments to their knees. The wallingant liberal Justice Minister F. Bovesse resigned from the second Van Zeeland government in April 1937 because his party opposed a bill that granted activists from the Great War amnesty, yet he had signed the bill himself. Afterwards, Belgian patriotic war veterans took to the streets where they clashed with pro-Flemish war veterans. The controversial bill became law later that year when all socialist legislators, most (especially Flemish) Catholics and some pro-Flemish liberals voted in favour. In 1938 later the amnesty issue brought down another government. A certain Dr. A. Martens, who had been sentenced to death for his involvement in the Great War before he won amnesty, became a member of the Royal Flemish Academy of Medicine. Again, street protest broke out and the government of Paul-Henri Spaak fell, following a conflict between the king and his ministers. The government had announced the membership of Martens before Leopold had signed the decree, thus putting the monarchy in an embarrassing situation. The king was outraged at being faced with a *fait accompli*, and being forced to ‘cover for’ the government. The next Socialist-Catholic government lasted exactly one week. The king dissolved parliament before the government had formally offered to resign. It was a typical move for

Leopold III, and the government obliged under protest. Leopold had seized the opportunity to summon the ministers to the palace where he, exceptionally, chaired the cabinet. The monarch vented his dissatisfaction with the workings of the Executive and with party interference. On 2 April 1939, election day, Dr. Martens voluntarily resigned. The whole Martens episode frustrated the Flemish parties, but after the amnesty protests in 1937, Leopold's popularity was on the rise again among the Walloon and Brussels patriots.

Leopold III was looking to reinforce the executive powers, and especially the monarchy, as soon as he became king. Albert I had unexpectedly died in an accident on 17 February 1934. In the last pre-war years, he fought governments that did not even await a vote in parliament before resigning. Governing 'without party interference' became a success formula and even defenders of democracy like Paul Van Zeeland called for law and order and supported the concept of a strong monarchy. Barely recovered from the shock of the 1936 elections, Van Zeeland set up a special study centre for state reform, which published its findings in 1937. Its conclusions included a recommendation to strictly abide by the constitutional article 65: "The King appoints and dismisses ministers." It also called on the parties not to restrict the king by vetoing certain persons. Only for really important questions should governments clearly ask for a vote of confidence. The traditional parties had lost some credibility during the 1930s since they had been unable to contain the rise of extremist parties, unable to provide stable government and unable to stave off an economic crisis. In 1938, Leopold III let it be known to the politicians and the public at large that according to the Constitution, he, and he alone, appointed ministers. He prohibited government mediators from meeting with the parties before forming coalitions and he made it very clear that ministers did not serve their party or region, but the executive. Since the traditional political parties and parliament were going through rough times, there was little objection to giving Leopold more political initiative. The results, however, were very limited.

The federalist view gained strength after 1935. In Flanders, the VNV, the bourgeois pro-Flemish wing of the Catholic Party and such Catholic pressure groups as the *Davidsfonds* gained influence. In Wallonia, some socialist and liberal intellectuals and politicians started to feel really threatened by the Flemish Movement. Belgium had been good to Wallonia so far and the Walloon Catholics, fearing an anti-clerical Wallonia, were defenders of a united Belgium. L'abbé Mahieu, who set up a Walloon nationalist party – with little success – was the proverbial exception to the rule. Starting in 1938, the Walloon socialist congresses backed federalism that went beyond culture and language. They started to worry about Wallonia's demographic shortfall and the steady decline of heavy industry.

The Study Centre for State Reform also concluded that each linguistic region needed cultural autonomy, a logical consequence of the 1932 law on administrative monolingualism, which at that time had already worried Walloon civil servants in Flanders. Now, the Study Centre proposed to split up the education ministry and to create separate cultural councils. The Dutch-language and francophone cultural councils were inaugurated on 7 February 1938 and had to advise the authorities on fine arts, literature and science. There was not much advising to be done ahead of the Second World War and it would take until the Royal Question and the School War were settled before federalism became a political issue again.

After the 1936 elections, the time had come for the pro-Flemish faction in the BWP to raise its voice. At its first congress in 1937, it called for cultural autonomy but against a federal state. Leaders like C. Huysmans, A. Vermeylen, H. De Man and H. Vos stressed the need for Flanders to catch up economically with the help of an interventionist policy, as did a few younger leading figures. The social aspect, which did not have to be contradictory to the national aspect, also prevailed at a grand celebration of the Battle of the Spurs in Kortrijk in 1939, with even Spaak and a few Walloons attending. The communists had gone one step further in 1937. A small Flemish Communist Party had been founded under the influence of ex-activist J. Van Extergem; it asked for Flanders' right to self-determination and a Flemish Popular Front. The francophone liberals remained the strongest unitarists, resisting any division of the education ministry. For them, it was worth a government crisis two weeks ahead of the German invasion.

Consensus vs. Social Conflict: the road to an initially corporatist social pact

In times of economic depression, bourgeois elites and the labour movement all tend to focus their attention on the state – the distributor of the nation's wealth and the keeper of law and order. The bourgeoisie was far from homogeneous. The industrial and holding capitalists sometimes appeared ready to strike compromises with the labour movement. They were a strong force in government and backed the kind of bourgeois democracy it helped create in 1918. The labour movement's reformist leaders wanted the state to be a neutral mediator between labour and capital. Just ahead of, and especially during the occupation, both sides would be able to secretly lay the foundations for the collective bargaining model and the welfare state. The labour movement turned out to be one of the staunchest defenders of bourgeois parliamentary democracy, and that was only an apparent contradiction. Socialist and Christian unions proved strong enough to turn the old visions of right-wing corporatism into a system of balanced negotiations. The war even accelerated that process. The class struggle ideology and the grand designs to take power had become the programme of a small militant minority. In fact any new step in social negotiations had to be laboriously forced from reluctant employees. The petty bourgeoisie and middle class – either patriotic or pro-Flemish – and the intellectuals they created were open to the conservative revolution. They counted themselves among a natural elite and rejected democracy as 'the absolute lie of equality' and degenerate intellectualism. They were looking for a totalitarian state and a Leader, a State as form, with the people and the nation (and then the race) as content. The ideology was called national-solidarism ahead of the war and national-socialism during the German occupation.

During the depression of the 1930s, the employers and competing unions put the funding of the unemployment benefits at the centre of political attention. During 1934 and 1935, the employers attacked social security as an artificial impediment in the labour market that endangered the government's deflationary policy. The three-party grand coalition of Van Zeeland changed course in 1935 and the government also consulted the labour movement on decisions, especially during the discussion on mandatory unemployment insurance. The employers wanted to cut out the unions as the institutions that took care of the payments. The ACV Christian union protested heavily since it realised it stood to lose its hold over the workers. The socialist union, however, favoured an automatic deduction from wages to fund the mandatory insurance. The 1936 compromise, phrased by H. Fuss (appointed Royal Commissioner for Unemployment in 1936), called for an automatic deduction but allowed the unions to keep a merely formal role as an institution that paid out the allowances. The ACV resisted automatic deduction, saying the union funds should remain at the core of the system; the employers rejected this. The bill inspired by Fuss did not get through parliament. It also stipulated a contribution by the employers. Yet the 1938-1939 Spaak government was able to force employers to pay a special unemployment contribution of 200 million francs. Because of the war, no new bill was put before parliament, even though a blueprint was already on the table. Unions and employers would continue to work secretly on this during the war and it would become the basis of the 1944 social pact.

Within the BWP, the old Marxist theories and leaders like E. Vandervelde were on the way out, making room for a new generation headed by H. De Man. The transition left the Socialist Party looking for direction. The 1931 BWP congress approved an economic crisis plan that failed to meet the demands of the party's left wing. These left-wing circles set up a pressure group around the magazine *Action Socialiste*. The Socialist Anti-War League was pacifist and for a time also anti-capitalist. After the failure of the 1932 strikes in the Borinage, the Communist Party started calling for committees for a united front in factories, independent from the unions that they thought weak. These committees had to prepare for a general strike. It proved a smart move on the part of the communists and in 1936, they would triple their number of seats in parliament. The Socialist Young Guard and the *Action Socialiste*, where a young Paul-Henri Spaak was an eloquent agitator, all wanted to use the general strike to establish a socialist society. Most of the *Action Socialiste* would abandon these ideals in 1934 to back the non-revolutionary Labour Plan of De Man, a non-Marxist minimum programme offering a progressive alternative in a BWP that had lost direction in opposition.

The Labour Plan called for a planned interventionist economy, boosted by inflationary policies. Unemployment had to be solved by means of a government policy aimed at full employment, along the lines of Keynesian theories, measures taken in Germany and the New Deal policy of the democratic president Roosevelt in the United States. The Plan De Man went beyond that. It called for nationalisation of the energy and banking sectors. The state had to become the guardian of financial institutions. All this would give the government the means to regulate and stimulate the economy. The party faithful at the 1933 Socialist Christmas congress hardly knew what hit them.

De Man, who had gone from deputy chairman to chairman of the BWP in 1939, sought solutions within the nation-state – '*socialisme national*'. The class struggle was not a war between the proletariat and the bourgeoisie, but instead a battle between investment capitalism and its victims – workers, farmers, small shop owners and clerks. The proletarian conscience was in fact an inferiority complex and it was the task of the socialist intellectuals to change this and provide guidance – hence the meaningful title of the magazine *Leiding* – to create a new culture to replace bourgeois hegemony. The socialists had to abandon their revolutionary terminology since all it did was hide a passive attitude concerning the collapse of the capitalist system. Class solidarity was primordial and De Man wanted to create a neo-corporatist union to join white and blue-collar workers. Corporatism had to be based on negotiations, including joint committees. It was a system that was already backed by the Christian ACV union and many influential socialist union leaders. De Man also knew how to use his non-conformist personality to appeal to the younger generation, in spite of the resistance of the old party leaders, who objected to De Man's and Spaak's authoritarian socialism.

De Man found it hard to spread his influence beyond the BWP. On the Catholic side, the ACW and the clergy wanted to keep the Church's flock within one party, even though De Man's solidarity and corporatist principles could be reconciled up to a point with the Catholic vision. Apart from the Catholic bourgeoisie, which still abhorred the very mention of intervention economics, the party also had a few young, mainly Flemish economists like G. Eyskens who backed the planned Keynesian economy to compensate for the excesses of unbridled capitalism.

De Man's Labour Plan hardly got off the ground, even when its spiritual father himself was Public Works and Employment Minister in 1935. De Man blamed his failure on resistance within his own party and the outright hostility of capitalism. The OREC (National Service for Economic Recovery), founded in 1935 by the first Van Zeeland cabinet, based itself on the Labour Plan when it prescribed royal decrees to force companies to limit production and force them to merge or close when continued competition was deemed harmful. Joint committees and collective bargaining agreements had to become commonplace. The OREC found its enemy in Finance Minister M.-L. Gérard, the arch-conservative representative of investment capitalists. He made sure the National Service became superfluous. The calls to reform the banking sector had little effect; the creation of the Banking Commission in 1935 was the only breakthrough. The bankers themselves wanted to rationalise and clean up their sector following the many bankruptcies during the long economic crisis and agreed to a voluntary code of good behaviour. Also the earlier banking law of 22 August 1934, which had forced 'mixed banks' to split up into ordinary deposit banks and holdings (or long-term investment banks) was a move that the bankers welcomed. Even when De Man became the first-ever socialist Finance Minister in 1936, he remained incapable of pushing through the principles of a planned economy. He ended up disappointed in the political party system and a parliament elected by universal suffrage, and an authoritarian state became ever more appealing to him. De Man wanted to see a stronger executive and his popularity within the party diminished quickly as his calls for an 'authoritarian democracy' increased. He did win the trust and friendship of Leopold III, whose voluntary neutrality or independence policy De Man supported.

De Man remained in close contact with the king during the German invasion (the so-called Eighteen-Day Campaign) and afterwards and on 28 June 1940 he proclaimed the dissolution of the BWP, even though he had no authority to do so. He called on the socialists to rally around the monarch in a single party and be part of a national revival, in cooperation with other 'live forces' of the nation. The Union of Manual and Intellectual Labourers became a unified trade union that was created with the active support of the German occupier; it was a failure. As a staunch monarchist and Belgian patriot, he became the odd man out in the collaboration movement. Increasingly isolated, he fled to Switzerland. His wartime past came to overshadow his contributions to the future collective bargaining economy. The socialists, who helped to secretly realise the post-war social pact, were indeed co-creators of the model.

The 1931 papal encyclical *Quadragesimo Anno* reinvigorated the corporatist ideology. The extreme right saw the papal call as an important argument to replace parliamentary democracy with a corporative legislature with representatives from the different professions, all joined in a spirit of class reconciliation. There would be no proportional representation but employers and labour would be each other's equal in a system of state corporatism resembling fascist Italy's. The Christian labour movement disapproved of the class struggle but not of strikes if other means failed, and saw in *Quadragesimo Anno* little more than an invitation to improve consultations and negotiations with employers. No fewer than five bills were tabled during the 1930s yet none came to fruition ahead of the German invasion. But they, too, were an important step on the long road towards the post-war collective bargaining economy.

During the Great Depression, part of the employers turned their backs on so-called hyper-capitalism. The state and government were kept under the thumb of banks and holding companies. From 1932 onwards, the Catholic ACV and ACW turned against liberal individualism and called for a planned economy with co-management of wage-earners. Others, among them authoritative provosts, wanted to bestow corporate personality on unions and employers' organisations. Collective bargaining agreements needed to include a peace clause with mandatory sanctions. A legislative bill from Christian democrat H. Heyman in 1934 incorporated much of this but did not include representation of corporatist political interests. The socialist union could not accept the corporate personality and concluded that the bill was too respectful of private property. The proposal never got beyond the consultation stage.

The Catholic organisation of Flemish employers had different corporatist views on the economy. In 1933, the employers still had not accepted the king's Loppem agreements, the de-facto recognition of the right to strike and the principle of unemployment benefits. The organisation, in contrast with its francophone counterpart (APIC), mostly represented medium-sized and small employers, and wanted corporatist measures to reduce competition and a single union for employees. After Belgium's capitulation in May 1940, an LVACVW representative brandished a corporatist manifesto – not rejected by the high clergy – that did not fit into the plans of the German *Militärverwaltung*. The occupier wanted social peace first and foremost, and as such did not see the intentions of the large Belgian employers' association (CCI) to drastically cut wages as opportune. In 1933 already, a Flemish Catholic employers' group had argued that social legislation should be based on corporate agreements, not on parliamentary initiatives. Employees should not be allowed to interfere in economic issues and the powers of the unions had to be drastically curtailed. The francophone APIC wanted corporate personality for the unions, but did not insist on the single union or judicial prohibition of strikes. It understood that political corporatism was unattainable in a region with such a strong and militant industrial proletariat. But during the Great Depression, Flemish and francophone employers alike wanted to return to a pre-First World War system of social relations. To achieve this, labour organisations had to be weakened, creating a new battleground between employers and unions. Labour groups were against any economic management structure that would weaken state intervention. The Catholic ACV union, too, dreaded the establishment of a corporatist parliament that would imperil the political say of the workers.

Once the worst of the recession was over, around 1935-1936, the government began to get involved in economic management structures. The socialist union preferred negotiations to strikes and when the Socialist Party was finally allowed into government again, it wanted to prove itself a loyal ally. The union men of De Man's generation put all their hope in government participation. Key union rights, specifically the right to strike, would remain untouchable, but under De Man's guidance, resistance against a legal framework for social consultations weakened. Some thought it would even increase the powers of the unions since it would give them the right to enforce the application of social legislation. Questions were asked whether the state could not become a neutral third partner in the social consultations between employers and labour instead of being an instrument of the bourgeoisie. In 1937, the BWP refused to take further part in the debates of the Study Centre for State Reform whenever it came to social issues since it felt that Catholic employers were just trying to weaken union powers. But the socialists changed their attitude when the bill of Catholic Economics Minister P. Heymans was tabled. The bill mustered a large enough consensus – it was also accepted at a congress of the BVV (the new name of the socialist union) – but failed to make it through the legislative process because of the tense international situation in 1939. The Heymans bill had met certain socialist demands: the choice for corporate personality was left open; joint committees had to be established in every sector of trade and industry; in collective bargaining agreements, a special deposit had to be created and in case a judge ruled against either side in a dispute, the deposit would be transferred to the aggrieved party; industries had to set up professional councils to give parliament and government advice on their sector. The advisory bodies were to be grouped in an economic Council. The organisations would not be run on the basis of equality since employers were better represented than unions. The state would no longer have the right of initiative. Everything remained in the conditional, though, since the bill never became law.

The Marxist wing of the BWP unsuccessfully objected to any kind of intra-company cooperation between workers and employers since it was convinced that the unions, which they still considered as a political battle force, should integrate no further in bourgeois society. That spirit would live on during the occupation with the communist-inspired *Comité de Lutte*

Syndicale and the *Mouvement Syndical Unifié* of A. Renard. Overall, though, it was the pragmatic wing that would gain the upper hand after the liberation and build on the pre-war foundations. There were continued covert efforts to develop this social pact that would become a cornerstone of post-war politics. There no longer was any mention of deposit or criminal liability. In general, the neo-corporatist compromise had little in common with the blueprints for a new Belgium designed by several right-wing Catholics. The plan of these conservative patriots fell in line with the pre-war 'new order' ideas: a strong executive power with the king at its head and parliament houses with a corporatist character.

The Right-Wing Movements in a Divided Catholic World

The tumultuous year 1936, with its strikes, shock election and the Spanish Civil War, sharpened Belgium's contradictions. It further polarised the political right and left, also within the Catholic Party. The general strike, which was backed by the Christian union, and the ominous threat of a left-wing Popular Front shocked the Catholic – and liberal – bourgeoisie. The old elites still had not fully digested the breakthrough of universal suffrage, and the concept of class reconciliation had not sunk in. It was the reason why corporatism wanted a strike ban and why judicial liability for unions sounded so appealing to them. They went looking for a right-wing anti-socialist majority in Belgium. Even though a left-wing Popular Front did not materialise in Belgium, the right wing started building a Christian counterpart in Flanders. It pre-empted any cooperation between Catholic flamingants and the left. The Catholic Party fared badly in the 1936 elections, and the defeat may have reinforced the federalist movement within the Flemish wing of the party, but it also undermined trust in democracy in that part of the population that was not involved with the working-class world. The ACV and ACW rejected the right-wing cooperation between Catholics and fascist Flemish nationalists of VNV and Verdinaso. Like the socialists, they were looking for the expansion of social consultations with employers and the government. The ACW was specifically worried about the 1937 cooperation agreement between Rex and VNV and the call of the Catholic paper *De Standaard* for a merger of the Catholic world around a platform that strongly resembled the Rex programme: sharp criticism of political parties, ill-disguised sympathy for

Italian and German fascism, strident anti-Marxism and support for far-reaching corporatism.

Fascism was already strengthening its hold on large parts of the continent and in Belgium, Catholic circles were willing to embrace the 'new order' ideology. Many Flemish organisations, including the VOS, VEV, *Vlaams-nationaal Zangverbond* (Flemish National Singing Association) and even the cultural *Davidsfonds* were apparently in favour of Flemish concentration. Many were disillusioned by the slow pace of language reform despite the strong Flemish Catholic representation in the Chamber of Representatives. Frustrated, an important part of Flanders' more or less intellectually developed youth sought refuge in radical Flemish nationalist circles. Anti-Belgian sentiments turned into anti-democratic sentiments and a host of political-financial scandals were cleverly exploited by Rex and a number of right-wing Catholic papers. *De Standaard* publisher G. Sap savagely attacked Van Cauwelaert, who lost much of his authority as a result. He had been involved in the 1934 financial problems of the *Bank-Unie*. Also the bankruptcy of the *Algemene Bankvereniging*, a spin-off from the savings and credit funds of the *Boerenbond* rocked the Catholic world. It cost the Catholic Party more than one vote from Flemish peasants and tenant farmers who had been hit by the banking crisis. They moved further right to the *Vlaams Nationaal Verbond* (VNV, Flemish National Federation) which backed the demonstrations and the milk delivery strikes of the new *Boerenfrontsyndicaat* (Farmers Front union).

The Catholic Action and student federations campaigned against degenerate liberalism, socialism, bolshevism and already against Jewish investment capitalism.

The high clergy was worried about the political impotence of the divided Catholics which, among many other things, could harm the interests of its education network. Yet it did not want to yield to a unified front that would move towards the extreme-right and potential anti-Belgian VNV fascism, and away from the Catholic character of all its organisations. In Germany, the Church had already had to submit to the heathen totalitarian state, to 'brown bolshevism'. So when Rex forced local elections in Brussels in 1937, Cardinal Van Roey made a stand against Degrelle and publicly backed P. Van Zeeland, prime minister of the ruling three-party coalition. At the time, the large majority of the people still rejected anti-Belgian and anti-democratic views that had been adopted by the Flemish nationalists. So did the socialist and Christian labour organisations, in spite of the fairly widespread Catholic-Flemish consciousness in the latter. The socialists were a minority in Flanders and they did not want to antagonise their Walloon comrades with a right-wing nationalist federalism. The same applied on the Catholic side, where the Flemish ACW did not want to abandon the LNTC in a mainly left-wing Wallonia. It only exposed the deepening rift between the workers on the one side and the nationalist petty bourgeoisie and middle class on the other.

The crushing defeat in the 1936 elections led to a reform of the Catholic Party. The extreme right wing only gained a limited foothold, despite the references to corporatism and the 1931 *Quadragesimo Anno* encyclical. Especially the *Katholieke Vlaamse Landsbond* (Catholic Flemish Country Union), which was no longer led by F. Van Cauwelaert, had been trying to obtain a regional split within the party. In an attempt to break the power of the *Federatie van de Kringen* once and for all, it demanded far-reaching autonomy for the Catholic Party in Flanders. But Van Caewelaert, the ACW and the *Boerenbond* did not want to push things to extremes and did not go beyond demanding a decentralisation of the party. By creating the *Katholieke Vlaamse Volkspartij* (KVV, Catholic Flemish People's Party) and the *Parti Catholique Social*, which together formed the Catholic Bloc, the structure of the different orders within the party was seriously weakened. The *Federatie van de Kringen* did not survive the development and the ACW and the *Boerenbond* preferred regional organisations that would not undo national unity. They were even willing to put aside their autonomous political activities if the party demanded it but they insisted on representation in the political bodies, and a say in issuing electoral lists and setting up the party programme. Even if the different orders shed their powers within the party, the Catholic Bloc would in practice remain a structure of different orders – as the later CVP, building on the 1936-37 reform in 1945 would prove. The numerical predominance of the workers and farmers was instrumental in this. In Wallonia and Brussels, the situation was different. The *Fédération des Associations et des Cercles* even wanted to include Rex in a Catholic francophone bloc in an attempt to recover some of the votes the party had lost there. Its wishes fell far short of reality, though, especially since the high clergy objected. In Flanders, the remains of the *Federatie van de Kringen* was replaced by the *Algemeen Katholiek Vlaams Burgersverbond* (General Flemish Catholic Citizens' Association), in order to create a Flemish and conservative counterweight to the other 'recognised' but no longer 'composite' orders.

In its programme, based on the values of family and company and on the ethical concept of personalism, the party stressed it was non-confessional even though references were made to the Christian foundation of society. After the war, the new Flemish Catholic party, the CVP, would do the same in its 1945 Christmas programme. In practice, the influence of the bishops remained just as strong. They led the Catholic Action and expanded its initiatives to include adults. The educational action was taken away from the ACW, which in practice did manage to keep a great deal of influence. The most important change was that the renewed Catholic party finally created a strong central structure, with a discipline that even extended into the KVV Chamber and Senate factions. The political power of the different orders within the party shifted to a limited directorate with a chairman. Change was not immediate, though, since the party stuck to old traditions when it came to the last coalition negotiations ahead of the war.

The pro-Flemish bourgeoisie in Flanders had long demanded reform and many of them had come under the spell of corporatist and authoritarian movements. They wanted to restore unity and make sure the party would bounce back after the disastrous 1936 election result. During the reform talks that same year, members of the Flemish party board called on S. De Clercq, the leader of the VNV, to open negotiations concerning the creation of a Christian Flemish Party. The KVV negotiators aligned themselves with the right-wing corporatist group of the *Nieuw Vlaanderen* (New Flanders) magazine, which included V. Leemans and the young G. Eyskens. It sought to concentrate 'all vigorous popular forces [...] on an unequivocal, Flemish nationalist platform'. By the end of the year there even was an agreement in principle between the KVV and VNV moderates. De Clercq, though, was convinced that the KVV just wanted to recover from its election losses. The ACW group also opposed any deal and towards the end of 1936 the bishops publicly opposed anyone who backed the principles of an authoritarian state. They also rejected a radical federalist programme that threatened the unity of the kingdom and thus the privileged position of the Church.

In the end it became clear that the VNV had no intention to sacrifice its independence. For the VNV, the deal with the Catholics would have been a minimal agreement in principle, and the radicals knew such a cooperation deal would have held back the party's political breakthrough. The tentative programme included equal treatment of public and private education, scrapping the concept of federalism, the rejection of state corporatism, the maintenance of parliamentary democracy and union rights. Even though the overall cooperation idea was quickly buried, it did not stop the creation of joint electoral lists for municipal elections. Some Catholic conservatives (mainly the *Algemeen Katholiek Vlaams Burgersverbond*, which had only recently been part of the KVV) were bent on this municipal cooperation and during the first months of the German occupation it would draw a number of party Catholics into the vortex of collaboration.

Ahead of the war, the 'new order' movement was much stronger within the Catholic network than in liberal or socialist circles, in spite of the later evolution of De Man. It hardly affected the overwhelming majority of industrial workers and farmers.

Belgian and Flemish Fascism Before and During the Second World War

The *Vlaams Nationaal Verbond* (VNV, Flemish National Federation) was created in October 1933 and the extreme right-wing groups attracted the predominantly pro-Flemish and Catholic lower-rank civil servants, retail traders, employees, some farmers and rural industrial workers who had been badly hurt by the crisis. It was just about the same social group that had propelled Hitler to power in Germany. The flamingant Front Party in Antwerp did not want to join at first. The transition was confusing and a number of social-progressive freethinkers (among them H. Vos, editor of *De Schelde*) opted out. But by 1936, the VNV had already clinched 16 seats in the 202-seat Chamber, twice more than the Front Party four years earlier. The VNV stagnated afterwards. The party was led by S. De Clercq, a Catholic teacher and former front soldier. He had become involved in the language debate in and around the linguistic border town of Enghien-Edingen in Hainaut. He was an enthusiastic organiser rather than a charismatic leader or ideologue. De Clercq was influenced by West-Flemish radicals like R. Tollenaere and more pragmatic figures like H. Borginon, G. Romsée and, more specifically, historian and ideologue H. Elias, who had already built a case for an organic and democratic corporatist state in 1933-34. Under Elias' concept of democracy, political parties would have to disappear, starting with the 'State-Catholic' party (and with it Van Cauwelaert). The Socialist party would collapse 'in the face of national syndicalism'. In an independent Flanders, Greater Netherlands or Dietsland, a government would have to rule by decree. Even ahead of the war, this 'organic democracy' pretty much equalled totalitarian fascism. Within the party, he did have to take into account the moderates who still expected something from the workings of parliament, and who supported the principle of leadership. Whenever De Clercq hesitated between his radical or pragmatic advisers, which was often, his fervent anti-Belgian, pro Greater Netherlands conviction carried the day. The pluralistic and democratic Flemish-national wing within the VNV was soon overwhelmed by an increasingly totalitarian-fascist group, with its leader, its cult, its uniforms, drums and flags.

Aggressive, revolutionary language of nationalist, Catholic youth groups dominated. Priests and other mentors preached the incendiary language of anti-Belgian, anti-freethinkers, anti-liberal, anti-socialist intolerance. Once the agreement in principle with the Flemish Catholic party had been cancelled, De Clercq was banking on the final breakthrough of his party at the cost of the Catholics. It did not happen, largely because of his rabid anti-Belgian stance. His dreams of a Greater Netherlands (with the Delta symbol, for *Diets*) and pro-German sympathies put off much of the pro-Flemish electorate. After stagnation set in, it became clear that a new war would offer the only opportunity to seize power. When the Germans swept across Belgium in 1940, there was no hesitation whatsoever to start collaborating and profess a devotion for national socialism.

Since 1934, Germany had been seen as a natural ally to counter France and francophony. De Clercq received financial backing from the German *Propagandaministerium* for the *De Schelde* paper (succeeded by *Volk en Staat* in 1936) and unbeknownst to the rest of the party, he cooperated with the German *Abwehr*, the secret service of the *Wehrmacht*. During the occupation, he publicly took pride in the fact that he had helped the *Abwehr* in setting up a sabotage network within the Belgian army. He tried to impress the German military authorities in Belgium – the *Militärverwaltung* – in an attempt to be recognised as the sole leader of a national-socialist Flanders. Going against the wishes of Elias and war veteran Borginon, the VNV party paper *Volk en Staat*, and even more so the magazine *Strijd* turned virulently anti-Semitic even ahead of the war. Jews, freemasons and Marxists were all depicted as degenerate rabble. Already in 1936, there was talk about an 'international assembly of freeloaders in a world suffering under the trash of Jewish science' and 'other races that stand in the way of Flemings and need to be unmasked'. Few readers complained, and even when the invective was toned down a little just ahead of the war, it came back with a vengeance during the occupation, when Jews were already threatened with physical extermination. But also the francophone right-wing papers were full of anti-Semitic articles ahead of the war. It also inspired the patriotic National Legion, years before some of its members would die in concentration camps.

De Clercq, bent on amassing as much power as possible, dreamt of creating a united Flemish party during the first months of the occupation, but the German *Militärverwaltung* told the VNV to refrain from making calls to create a Greater Netherlands. Propaganda had to be limited to issues concerning Flanders and Belgium as long as Hitler was pondering the political future of Belgium and the Netherlands.

During the occupation, the VNV used the backing of the *Militärverwaltung* to secure key positions for its party members and a number of opportunists who joined the party in 1940-1941 in the hope of obtaining a post. Even the VNV moderates, who later on did not dissociate themselves from their leader, or did so at a very late stage, were able to take over city halls, or become provincial governors. Others even became administrative secretaries-general. The royal court considered Romsée's appointment a lesser evil since he positioned himself at the court as an anti-separatist.

The VNV soon faced fierce competition. The political *Algemene Vlaamse SS* (General Flemish SS) had been able to win over the cultural *Deutsch-Flämische Arbeitsgemeinschaft*, better known as *DeVlag*. Both groups had fewer members than the VNV, but against the wishes of the *Militärverwaltung*, they were backed by H. Himmler, SS Reichsführer and head of the Gestapo. For DeVlag leader Jef Van de Wiele, Dutch was a German dialect and the Flemish and the Dutch belonged to the German race. Flanders was to become part of the German Reich, a Reichsgau. Hitler thought along similar lines: Flanders should never be able to win a significant autonomy. Many in the Algemene Vlaamse SS and DeVlag had no Flemish nationalist background and they did not mind the a-Christian, even anti-Christian views of Nazism. In contrast, the VNV insisted on an independent Flanders in the New Europe. Flanders, possibly a Greater Netherlands, had to stick to its language and its cultural and religious identity. The Algemene Vlaamse SS considered this pure provincialism that could not be reconciled with its own 'German and Continental' views. In the conflict between the *Militärverwaltung*, which backed the VNV, and Himmler, the Algemene Vlaamse SS and DeVlag came out against De Clercq, whom they depicted as a 'stupid clerical', not a true national socialist. In a bidding contest for German political favours, the VNV had already committed itself totally to national socialism and even created a national socialist youth organisation, the *Nationaal-Socialistische Jeugd in Vlaanderen* (NSJV, National-Socialist Youth in Flanders). DeVlag responded in 1943, when it helped set up a Flemish wing of the Hitler Youth.

The *Militärverwaltung* wanted law and order and considered the VNV Flanders' best party to guarantee this. De Clercq offered military collaboration with Germany already ahead of the German invasion of Russia in June 1941. The VNV wanted to pre-empt any Algemene Vlaamse SS move to do likewise and started recruiting volunteers for the *Waffen-SS*. It was the price the VNV had to pay to align itself with the Germans and be able to be recognised as the sole national socialist party in Flanders. Military collaboration was far from smooth though. The Flemish Legion of volunteers was sent to the eastern front in 1943 and simply incorporated into the German SS units, practically without Flemish officers or Flemish chaplains (Mechelen would not provide them). The situation caused friction within the VNV and resistance against further recruiting. De Clercq died in 1942 and the more moderate VNV leaders selected Elias as the new leader. Germany's chances for an overall victory were already dwindling fast but the VNV still reconfirmed its faith in Hitler and National Socialism. The party also continued to search for autonomy for Flanders or a Greater Netherlands as part of 'Germanic solidarity'. The battle between Himmler and the *Militärverwaltung*, and between the VNV and the Algemene Vlaamse SS-DeVlag continued unabatedly. Because of growing resistance, Elias was forced to momentarily suspend the VNV recruitment of volunteers for the *Waffen-SS*. By that time Elias and most others realised that the creation of a Greater Netherlands did not fit in with the plans of the SS or Hitler. But Elias continued to insist on blind obedience. He had this almost surreal hope that Germany and the allied nations would sign a compromise peace and that the VNV would be allowed to keep law and order during a transitional period.

Another reason for irritation was that Rex leader L. Degrelle mobilised his whole party for the SS in 1943 and proclaimed all Walloons true Germans. Little wonder Hitler and Himmler liked Degrelle better than De Clercq, Elias and the entire VNV. On the eastern front, Degrelle and his *SS-Sturmbrigade Wallonia* were part of relatively successful withdrawal operations, something Degrelle would not let go unnoticed in Berlin. Degrelle wanted to be *gauleiter* of a district that would cover more than just Wallonia and incorporate the old Burgundy territories. Hitler had no such plans. The Nazi leadership tended toward a *Flamenpolitik* that reduced Wallonia to a potential colonial territory. Degrelle's *Sturmbrigade* attracted some 8,000 Walloons, citizens of Brussels and even a few Flemings. Degrelle's troops had the Belgian tricolour emblazoned on their uniform. In their fight against Bolshevism, they were able to call on Belgian officers released after 1940. The troops were commanded in French, compared to German for the Flemish *SS Sturmbrigade Langemarck.* In all, some 12,000 Flemings went to the eastern front.

The VNV was able to claim many key positions during the occupation, even beyond administration and police. With the backing of the *Militärverwaltung,* the VNV was well represented in the Organisation Todt, which built a defensive wall on the Atlantic coast, the *Kriegsmarine,* industrial security forces and the national socialist transport organisation NSKK. The *Dietse Militie-Zwarte Brigade* (Diets Militia-Black Brigade) was a security force for collaborators which had to become the core of a future Flemish army. During the war, it ensured the protection of key collaborators, who after 1942 increasingly became the target of resistance groups. Retaliation was ruthless and DeVlag-Algemene Vlaamse SS and its actions stood out. They killed Société Générale governor Alexandre Galopin and their 1944 raid in the Hageland around Leuven left a trail of death and destruction. Countless people were deported to concentration camps. When the allies entered Belgium in September 1944, many political, military and police collaborators fled to Germany, where they set up an attempt at a government in exile, continuing the struggle against Belgium and the allied forces. Some, including Elias, who had already been put under house arrest, refused to accept the now total dominance of the SS. After the liberation, the Belgian people turned both against the VNV and DeVlag-Algemene Vlaamse SS. The 'blacks' – named after the colour of their uniforms – were hated by the population at large for their persecution of resistance fighters and especially for their backing of the deportation of people who refused to work for the occupier.

A small minority of right-wing Flemish nationalists, who had been largely isolated from the popular masses both socially and ideologically, discredited the Flemish movement until well into the 1950s and slowed the development of a federalist Belgium. While Walloon collaboration had clear totalitarian and fascist roots, extreme right-wing Flemish nationalism had been a pernicious aberration of the democratic demand for Flemish emancipation. The anti-Belgian attitude, lack of progress on the Flemish issue and effects of the economic crisis did not fully explain the attitude of part of the Catholic petty bourgeoisie and intellectuals. Many volunteers who fought on the eastern front said they were drawn to collaboration by the virulent anti-liberal and anti-Bolshevik propaganda of the Catholic Action. They said they heard the siren call of the fanatical priest-poet Cyriel Verschaeve and went out to defend Germanic and Catholic Flanders against the Asian Bolshevik hordes. Democratic Flemings were hardly impressed by these arguments. The SS denigrated a Christian faith with Jewish origins. Despite the compromises of Pope Pius XII, there was just no way the systematic elimination of Jews, Slavs and gypsies could be legitimised. On top of that, the Church – even though it had followed a policy of the 'lesser evil' – had never encouraged collaboration and sometimes used barely concealed terms to condemn it. Collaborators in uniform were not allowed to set foot in church, even during funerals. During the occupation, the cardinal was able to defend the interests of the Church and the lay organisations it controlled. Collaborators were not allowed in the Catholic University of Leuven. And when the Church flexed its muscle, the *Militärverwaltung* had to concede ground more than once. Only near the end of the war did the Church encourage resistance, but it condemned armed retaliation against collaborators.

Perhaps the most typical example of the 'right-wing revolution' ahead of the war was the *Verbond van Dietse Nationaal Solidaristen* (Verdinaso, Association of Diets National Solidarists) founded by poet and former activist W. Moens and led by former front soldier J. Van Severen (1894-1940). The leader was a visionary personality who had been influenced by Maurras and by French and Latin right-wing culture in general. Van Severen distanced himself from what he considered romantic, sloppy flamingantism and he fascinated a number of young intellectuals and farmers. And after rejecting an anti-Belgian stance in 1934, he even attracted a few members of the francophone high bourgeoisie and aristocracy, who also provided financial support. Van Severen claimed a conservative revolution had to be led by an ascetic and disciplined elite. His corporatist views called on wide-ranging solidarity between the different orders. A Greater Netherlander in origin, he cast his territorial net wider in 1934 and wanted to include Wallonia and northern France to reflect the historical Burgundian Low Countries of Charlemange. Verdinaso earned the scorn of the VNV when it started using the Belgian flag again. Degrelle, on the other hand, rejected the name *Etat thiois*, but adopted the Burgundian flag (St. Andrew's Cross) as a symbol. A stylish militia, organised along paramilitary lines, gathered in camps. Despite his pro-Belgian sympathies, Van Severen was arrested when Germany invaded in May 1940. He was put on one of the infamous ghost trains to France in the company of elements posing a threat to the state, such as communists, a few German agents, Jews and anti-fascists fleeing Germany. He was turned over to the French authorities along with a few thousand others and on 20 May, in Abbeville, shot and killed by drunken French soldiers under the command of officers who did not even know who their victims were. The executions shocked Flanders and were immediately exploited by the German and Flemish nationalist propaganda. It is not even sure that the aristocratic Van Severen, who preferred Mussolini to Hitler, would have collaborated with the Germans. Some of his followers did, but Verdinaso as such died with its leader. Many preferred to stay on the sidelines during the war and some even joined the resistance, but without abandoning their right-wing revolutionary ideals.

The most important has already been said about L. Degrelle, the young and eloquent 'chief' of Rex and his origins in the Catholic Action. The ambitious and adventurous Degrelle was much more an opportunist than an ideologue. His campaign against the political-financial scandals – prepared by the right-wing Catholic P. Crokaert, also an enemy of 'hyper-capitalism', starting in 1932 – was a huge success in times of crisis and, out of the blue, Rex won 21 of 202 seats in the 1936 elections. His slogan '100 % Catholic' had paid off. Degrelle decided to take his chances and in October that year he organised a demonstration in Brussels with the backing of war veterans, soldiers and state police officers that could have ended in a putsch. One year later, Cardinal Van Roey opposed Rex when Degrelle forced early local elections in the capital. The party largely collapsed and ended up with a mere four seats in 1939. The deal between Rex and the VNV also distanced many war veterans and Catholic right-wing patriots. They preferred an authoritarian regime with the king as the only leader and their war memories fuelled anti-German feelings. It spawned a right-wing monarchist resistance during the war. It was typical that demagogue Degrelle told his *SS Sturmbrigade Wallonia* that the king backed their cause even though Leopold and Cardinal Van Roey had rejected his calls for Belgicist collaboration. His scandal sheet *Le Pays Réel* relied on subsidies from Italy and, to a lesser extent, from Germany. Representatives from Belgian financial holdings also paid up. Degrelle involved Rex in the activities of the political SS and succeeded in ingratiating himself with

Hitler. In the final months of the war Degrelle's militia committed horrific crimes during retaliation raids, killing, amongst others, the freemason and former liberal minister Bovesse.

Belgian and Walloon collaboration had been totally fascist from the outset. In Wallonia, there was no resentment whatsoever towards Belgium. Even though the military collaboration in southern Belgium was of the same magnitude as in Flanders, the Walloon version was much less willing to be at the service of the occupier. Unlike Flanders, Wallonia had never had an amnesty movement for collaborators. Yet, it did have extreme right-wing, fascist groups run on military discipline. In a pre-war tradition, they were backed by extreme right-wing figures from the bourgeois and aristocratic wing of the *Parti Socialiste Chrétien* (PSC), the francophone Catholic party. They no longer wanted to suffer the domination of the left and the Socialist Party in Wallonia and also wanted to counter the influence of the MOC in the Catholic hierarchy. They wanted the king, the Church, the army and police to restore the traditional old order.

The End of the Collective Security System: the policy of independence and the Second World War

Several key events augured the end of Europe's collective security system: Adolf Hitler seized power in 1933; Germany withdrew from the Geneva disarmament conference and left the League of Nations; Mussolini proposed, without any useful outcome, a four-nation pact between the United Kingdom, France, Germany and Italy in order to keep the peace in Europe. And when Nazi Germany cancelled the Locarno treaty on 7 March 1936 and put an end to the demilitarisation of the Rhineland, the future started looking ominously bleak. German troops again stood at the borders. Belgium was veering towards a policy of unconditional diplomatic independence. The developments of the 1930s had brought the message home that it was of no use for a small nation to become the willing and powerless pawn of the major powers France and the U.K. In conservative circles and at the royal court it became clear that the 1920 military agreement with France had to be reviewed as soon as possible. France had closed a mutual assistance agreement with the Soviet Union in case of a German attack. France's Popular Front was mistrusted. It was feared the Front would come to the aid of the Spanish government in its war against the German and Italian-backed rebels. Even at the end of Albert's reign, the monarchy was convinced Belgium had to regain a sense of international diplomatic independence. King Albert I and king Leopold III tried to keep defence minister Devèze – who on this point tended to be at odds with his party colleague P. Heymans – from building fortifications on the German border to safeguard Wallonia from destruction while French reinforcements were on the way. France, however, insisted on its right of passage. Walloon public opinion backed defence minister Devèze while Flemish pacifists and nationalists and Christian democrats campaigned under the slogan 'Cut loose from France'. It proved a huge success during the Yser pilgrimages. As a condition for agreeing to an increase in the army budget and an extension of conscription (both resulting from the new obligations), their parties demanded that the secret agreement with France be ended. Berlin knew ahead of Paris that Belgium was going to become neutral again. Socialist Foreign Affairs Minister Paul-Henri Spaak proclaimed Belgium's new independence policy in July 1936. King Leopold III, the driving force behind the diplomatic development, confirmed this in a speech to an exceptional cabinet meeting, highlighting the 'policy of free hands'. French public opinion was shocked as it had long looked upon Belgium as a natural and friendly ally. It came at a time when France was brokering a new European security pact to replace Locarno. Belgium joined without much enthusiasm.

Belgium used its 'free hands' to close bilateral deals, specifically with neighbouring countries. Britain and France reluctantly agreed in 1937 to guarantee the inviolability of neutral Belgium's territory, accepted that Belgium was no longer a guarantor itself, and in a joint declaration, both nations promised assistance in case Belgium was attacked. Germany obviously applauded Belgium's voluntary neutrality. Flanders welcomed it while Wallonia accepted it grudgingly. Rex and the VNV were all smiles.

Despite Belgium's change of heart, France remained convinced that consultations between the French and Belgian chiefs of staff would continue. Leopold III made sure that such contacts were kept to a minimum. Spaak and several top diplomats meanwhile tried to soothe frayed nerves in Paris and London, arguing that, in any case, Belgium's geographical position would automatically draw it into any European conflict. It was more than Leopold could stand. In a personal initiative, he reprimanded the Belgian ambassador in Paris for being too accommodating towards the French. Leopold feared it would give the impression Belgium was not serious about its neutrality.

In fact, Belgium was creating an illusion and its neutrality certainly did not reinforce the resilience of Western democracy. Socialists like Vandervelde and Louis de Brouckère were suspicious. It was a tough time for the government, because of the Spanish Civil War. It split Belgian public opinion down the middle. Belgium officially abided by the League of Nations' non-intervention policy even though Germany and Italy clearly violated it. But the government could not prevent volunteers from joining the international brigades fighting fascism in Spain. Spaak outraged many socialist militants by establishing economic relations with Franco's nationalist Spain in 1938, ahead of the end of the civil war. Spaak was backed by the Catholics and liberals. The financial groups wanted to safeguard their economic interests in Spain. In the face of a seething BWP congress, Spaak was able to push through his 'realistic' policy. E. Vandervelde, one of the fiercest opponents of the so-called Burgos policy, died in December 1938.

Germany invaded Czechoslovakia in March 1939 and one month later, Berlin renounced a treaty with Poland. It closed a non-aggression pact with the Soviet Union in August of that year. On the same day, Leopold III made a futile appeal on behalf of the Oslo group (the later Benelux countries and the Scandinavian nations) to maintain world peace. From September 1939 onwards (the 'phoney war'), the Belgian army was on a war footing, but the country desperately stuck to its independence policy. Leopold wanted Belgium to see through its independent policy to the bitter end. He wanted to dramatically increase the already enforced censorship of the press but failed to convince the government.

In the winter of 1939-1940, a piece of incredible luck threw the German invasion plans into the lap of the Belgian chiefs of staff, bringing yet more indications that Hitler was just waiting for the right moment to invade, yet Leopold and his military advisor R. Van Overstraeten clung to the policy of absolute neutrality. Belgium even refused entry to the French and British forces (the guarantors) in April 1940 in spite of the agreement asking the two nations for protection in case of an aggression on Belgium. Moreover, much to the incomprehension of Walloon public opinion, it even sent two Belgian divisions to the French border.

On 10 May 1940, the population and a hastily summoned parliament – without the King's presence – were pleased to find their earlier allies again. A few hours later, in a radio address, Leopold III announced that he was, following the example of Albert I in 1914, taking command of the armed forces in defence of 'our territories'. He considered it his royal prerogative, a move that needed no government approval. During the Eighteen-Day Campaign, Prime Minister Pierlot wanted the government to bear the constitutional responsibility of military policy. Barring that, he wanted at least to be informed of developments. Was the king, after all, not head of state?

When defeat seemed inevitable on 25 May, the king and his government entered a dramatic confrontation in Wijnendale. Leopold refused to leave Belgian territory together with his government to continue the war at the side of those who had guaranteed the nation's neutrality. The monarch rejected the advice of his ministers and, from then on, his actions were no longer 'covered' by the government. Leopold was convinced he had completed his duties by defending Belgian territory for all he was worth. He preferred to remain among his people as a prisoner of war rather than join his government in London, as the Dutch Queen Wilhelmina had done.

The ministers refused to resign and rejected a request by telephone to approve the king's actions. Leopold needed such an approval to be able to negotiate on the conditions of Belgium's capitulation, the demobilisation of the troops, etc. However, Hitler imposed an unconditional surrender. The ministers had unjustly feared that the king would abuse a government approval by negotiating a separate peace with Germany and form a new government during the occupation. Leopold, however, had written a letter to the British King George VI, promising him he would do nothing that would harm the allied cause. He said he did not want to 'desert' his people and wanted to watch over them during the occupation.

The government in exile, at that moment still in France, judged that the monarch, a prisoner of war, was unable to govern and assumed sovereignty. It joined the allied cause in London from October 1941 onwards and in fact governed against its own king, who remained loyal to neutrality in an occupied nation.

France considered Belgium's capitulation and Leopold's surrender nothing short of treason. Paris was looking for a scapegoat because its own defeat was imminent. The hundreds of thousands of Belgian refugees were not really welcomed in France. Suspicion turned into occasional hostility. The situation pushed the government and parliament towards breaking relations with the monarch. It became official during a meeting in Limoges on 31 May 1940. Following the French government, they openly condemned his actions in quite offensive terms. After the French were defeated, some

Belgian ministers openly questioned whether it was, perhaps, not better to return home. They contacted the king, and even the German government, but were turned down by both. In these uncertain times nobody could predict if and how long Britain, the other guarantor, would hold out. Ministers Gutt and A. De Vleeschauwer moved to London, and it took several months and much hesitation before Pierlot and Spaak joined them. Britain recognised them as the legitimate Belgian government once they were there. In the meantime, Minister De Vleeshouwer had made sure that the Congo would be at the full disposal of the allies. Without breaking with the king, as some politicians who had left for London earlier, among others Huysmans, wanted to do, he kept the colony for Belgium and at the service of the allied war effort (raw materials and soldiers against Italy in East Africa)

In Belgium itself, public opinion by and large backed the king. He had avoided a bloodbath and had chosen to remain among his imprisoned soldiers, albeit within the confines of his royal Laeken palace, and surrounded by his *entourage*. The crushing defeat was blamed on a deficient government and parliament and on the political instability of the past years, which in its turn was blamed on the party system. The censored newspapers profusely lauded the king and attacked the 'Limogeard' government. They called on all Belgians to rally around the monarch and heed his call to go back to work and save the country from ruin. The Germans gave a good impression; they were orderly and helpful during the repatriation of Belgian refugees. Little was said about the slaughter in the village of Vinkt, where more than eighty elderly people, widows and children were killed the day before the capitulation. The tide began to turn during the early autumn of 1940, when food provisions turned out to be scarce and when it became obvious the war was not about to be won by Germany – Britain bravely continued to fight.

It contrasted sharply with the summer months. A German victory seemed certain and Belgium would have to make sure it won its rightful place in a 'new Europe'. H. De Man kept in close contact with the royal court and decided to dissolve the BWP. He wanted to create a unified trade union but failed to keep it together. Most of the pre-war union leaders left the *Unie van Hand- en Geestesarbeiders* (Blue and White-Collar Workers' Union) shortly after they had grudgingly joined it. Strikes were supposed to be illegal but it soon became obvious that workers who did put down their tools, especially in Wallonia, won bigger wages and food provisions than De

Man's unionists. In May 1941 the 'strike of the 100,000' broke out in the Liège region, inspired by the Communists.

On 15 May 1940, the Pierlot government had put the fate of Belgians in the hands of a consortium of bankers, including Société Générale governor Alexandre Galopin, M.-L. Gérard of the Banque de Bruxelles and F. Collin of the Kredietbank. It faced huge unemployment lines. The German *Militärverwaltung* wanted the Belgian industry to support the German war effort as much as possible and insisted on law and order. It was even indignant when it found out how much the wages had been cut when industries resumed production.

A number of magistrates and high-bourgeois Catholic and liberal politicians sought contact with extreme right-wing elements to push their point that Belgium needed a sort of royal 'directorate' to safeguard independence as much as possible. Several extreme right-wing 'patriotic' collaborators backed such plans and were encouraged by members of Leopold III's court. Leopold himself maintained that his status as prisoner of war did not allow him to make political statements. Leopold was taking all possibilities into account, and at that time, most indicators still pointed towards a German victory. Belgium had to get the most out of the situation and the king certainly did not condemn certain forms of collaboration. Leopold himself and court officials had good relations with several patriotic collaborators and their newspapers (but no federalists or separatists).

In October 1940, the government in London called on all able-bodied Belgians outside the occupied territory to serve in the army and placed all diplomats under its authority. This countered Leopold's neutrality plans and his forced inactivity and lack of contact with his own people made him ever more impatient. He considered the world war a kind of revolution and he realised things would never be the same afterwards. The king wanted to give Belgium as independent a status as possible in a continent dominated by Germany. Court officials, people from Leopold's wider entourage and leaders of the Christian labour movement were working on a corporatist charter during the 'wondrous summer' and autumn of 1940. Also leaders of the Christian labour movement, who were in contact with the cardinal, participated in this. Prominent legal scholars and advisors designed a blueprint for a new constitution based on a reinforcement of the royal powers and a corporatist parliament. The fate of ministers would be determined by the king and the backing of parliament was no longer a necessity. The Nation would not hold all power any more, but there was room for a royal referendum. Even though the king would still be covered by a ministerial signature, he would be able to use a veto. The whole construction was aimed at ending the interference of political parties and the constitutional plans were based on Latin-fascist models. Leopold could not prevent the governor of the mineral-rich Belgian-Congo from bringing the colony in the allied camp. Congo's colonial army was used against the Italian possessions in East Africa even though Belgium was not at war with Italy. The Italian crown prince was even married to Leopold's sister. Contrary to De Vleeschauwer, the king had wanted to keep the Congo neutral, and, as such, open to Nazi Germany as far as raw materials were concerned. Leopold lost the colony on the eve of his meeting with Hitler in Berchtesgaden on 19 November and was forced to face the Fuhrer without this vital negotiating tool, reducing his leverage to get a good deal for Belgium. The king's hands were tied as long as it remained unclear what Hitler wanted to do with Belgium, and as long as no peace treaty was signed. Marie-José, the king's sister and crown princess of Italy, asked for a meeting between Hitler and her brother and Leopold was hoping Germany would recognise Belgian independence. The Fuhrer would have none of it and, in retrospect, Leopold III and Belgium were lucky. As a kind of bait, the king offered the creation of an economic council that would become a link between Belgium and the occupying force. But when it came to his plans for the small kingdom, Hitler kept everybody guessing. Other sources show that Hitler wanted to turn at least Flanders into a *Reichsgau* of his empire. His *Flamenpolitik* pointed in that direction and it was in evidence when non-commissioned Flemish prisoners of war were released while Walloon POWs remained in jail. During his Berchtesgaden meeting, Leopold III made a case for the release of Walloon prisoners too, but to no avail. The king put himself on the political sidelines after the meeting and continued to ignore the London government. He ignored any attempts at reconciliation and did not encourage the resistance movement. He did write a letter to Hitler, on 3 November 1942, to protest against the use of Belgian forced labour in Germany. Queen Elizabeth approached the *Militärverwaltung* to make a case for a few Belgian Jews. But there was never any public protest.

With hindsight, Leopold's actions may appear peculiar, but during the first years of the war such an attitude was commonplace among the establishment. It was part of a right-wing ideology that even appealed to socially committed intellectuals. Leopold III obstinately stuck to his convictions, and those of his entourage. He continued to hope, until the early months of 1944, for a negotiated compromise peace settlement, which would hold the best chances for an independent Belgium. He expected the *Wehrmacht* to put and end to the excesses of Nazism and his main fear was the Soviet army would win a total victory, helped by the short-sightedness of British and American political leaders.

Leopold wrote a kind of political will on 25 January 1944, a few months before he was deported to Austria (early June) and stuck to his position that he had been right to stay among his people while so many others had deserted. Anticipating the future after the liberation, he saw 'the necessity of political reform that would do away with the party regime'. He considered the liberators as potential new occupiers against whom he had to protect Belgian independence. He claimed that not a single minister from the Pierlot government should be allowed to hold public office as long as they had not regretted their errors and 'fully and solemnly made amends'. The king was talking about a government that by its mere existence had made sure that Belgium would emerge as a victor from the war, in spite of the 1940 capitulation. It had even contributed to the victory by means of its colony. It was clear that Leopold had no, or precious few, regrets. The king also lashed out at what he saw as selfish liberalism and the scandalous divide between rich and poor. He called for a social system based on Christian charity and human dignity, joint social committees (probably in a corporatist framework), a guided economy and full equality between Flemings and Walloons. He remained convinced that parliamentary democracy and the party system would be unable to overcome the problems.

Only a privileged few knew about the king's actions and his political ideas during the occupation, and the one event that was public knowledge was badly received. Leopold remarried in September 1941 with the Flemish commoner Lilian Baels. Especially Brussels and Wallonia were shocked. Leopold's first wife Astrid had been very popular before she was killed in a 1935 road accident. When the announcement of his remarriage was read in the nation's churches, countless officers and francophone soldiers were still suffering in German POW camps. The civil marriage a few months later was not approved by a minister, a move that was unconstitutional. This argument would be used after the war to prevent the return of the king.

Especially the freethinkers and the progressive part of the population opposed the return of the king after the liberation since he had not abandoned his authoritarian visions (cf. chapter VI). Others failed to see what exactly Leopold had done wrong to deserve such a fate. They included the many that had shown sympathies for a 'new order' in 1940, others who had patiently sat out the war, people who feared Bolshevism more than Nazism, all the committed or pragmatic collaborators, and those who had practised a policy of the 'lesser evil'. The majority of those who backed the king were Flemish and Catholic. Those on the left of the political spectrum, and the freethinkers of the centre, saw a threat to democracy in the return of the king. They were more numerous in Brussels and Wallonia than in Flanders. It was the main reason why the Royal Question threatened the unity of the nation after 1945.

Occupation, Collaboration and the Resistance Movement

Belgium and part of northern France lived under a German military authority – the *Militärverwaltung* – from June 1940 to July 1944. It is only during the final months of the occupation that Hitler installed a *Zivilverwaltung* headed by an SS official. The *Militärverwaltung* did not directly depend on the national socialist party and it resisted the pushy interference from the SS as much as possible. Its task was to put Belgium's economic and human potential at the service of the German war effort. It insisted on law and order to achieve this and the *Militärverwaltung* tried to cooperate with existing institutions as much as possible. The military authority even tried to keep radical, unpopular collaborators from Rex, DeVlag and the Algemene SS-Vlaanderen away from these institutions in an attempt to keep cooperation as smooth as possible.

In absence of the ministers, the day-to-day running of the nation came down to the secretaries-general of the ministries ('a delegation of power in wartime' following a law of 10 May 1940). They had to cooperate with the *Militärverwaltung* and needed its approval. As the war progressed, it became increasingly difficult to respect the Belgian constitution, especially when it came to law and order and the anti-Jewish measures. In Antwerp, the police helped to trace and arrest Jews. The 1942 order to send Belgian workers to Germany also posed problems. Before the measure, many unemployed workers had gone to Germany 'voluntarily' since wages were higher and social services better. Hitler had not undermined most of the material achievements of the labour movement. The Belgian franc had been devalued against the Reichsmark, after wages and prices had been frozen. Pay was allowed to rise slightly afterwards but it did not improve spending power since it was necessary to turn to the black market for some things.

Several secretaries-general resigned. Others stuck to a containment strategy, a 'policy of the lesser evil' and held on to their position to prevent SS or military protégées from taking over. But soon, the *Militärverwaltung* was able to impose some of its candidates, including V. Leemans and G. Romsée of the VNV at the interior secretariat-general (with authority over the police). Some collaborated publicly. Romsée was given a severe sentence after the war, as was G. Schuind, the justice secretary-general who had been an SS candidate. He was forced to resign in 1943 when he refused to cooperate further with the occupier's law and order authorities. Others desperately tried to find a middle ground somewhere between the constitution, the German occupier and an increasingly hostile population. They were the target of sharp criticism from the underground press and the government in London. The food shortage was a huge problem, and sometimes led to strikes. E. De Winter, who was responsible for food provisions attempted to force farmers to make their supplies available and at the same time combat the black market, where even the Germans went to stock up on goods.

Companies knew well enough that article 115 of the penal code prohibited selling goods to the enemy. On the other hand, there was incredible unemployment and the likelihood that the occupier could take coercive measures like the withdrawal of the means of production and the deportation of workers. The necessity to feed a population, in a country in desperate need of grain for bread, potatoes, etc. was also primordial. The doctrine of Société Générale governor Galopin centred on rejecting any arms production and the refusal to seek profits from the bartering trade, offering Belgian products in return for food imports. Germany owed Belgium an enormous amount of money after the war which, when the Cold War became a reality, was never claimed. The Belgian government had already distanced itself from the Galopin doctrine in 1942. To get around article 115, the concept of 'emergency situation' was invoked, but it was only in 1945 that a decree toned down article 115, which allowed for a more clement assessment of possible economic crimes during the war. The occupiers had instituted 'goods centrals' (1940, distribution of raw materials between companies) and 'groups' (1941, employers' institutions, with mandatory membership, following the '*Führerprinzip*'). Unlike trade unions, the employers' organisations were tolerated during the occupation and they used these economic decrees of the occupier to boost their political clout. They were able to clandestinely use it during negotiations for the post-war 'social pact' (cf. infra). It was especially the Société Générale, with its interests in the Walloon mines and metal industry, which put itself in an impossible position by maintaining a policy of low prices and, especially, low wages. After the liberation, more realistic employers' organisations were able to persuade trade unions to boost productivity in return for joint negotiations and other neo-corporatist concessions. The course of the war speeded up a process that had already been in the works before 1940 (cf. supra).

The decision to join the resistance depended on more than one element; in many cases, the choice of the group was rooted in ideology and political convictions or sensibilities. The intense dislike of Germany, which had invaded Belgium for the second time and the dogged resistance of Britain soon swung the mood around from passive resignation to enthusiastic patriotism. Left-wing resistance built on several years of anti-fascist action. The union 'battle committees' and the unitary union of A. Renard were certainly inspired by this. It was no coincidence that the armed Partisans of the Independence Front included many survivors of the Spanish Civil War's international brigades. Jewish Communist refugees from Central and Eastern Europe started attacks on collaborators as early as 1941, and even attacked German soldiers for a short time; but strict repression always followed their actions. Belgium's right-wing resistance relied on a network of organisations of war veterans and released military officials. They were convinced their resistance was in line with the king's convictions. They shared his dissatisfaction with parliamentary democracy at first, but they softened their stance as the war wore on. Near the end of the war, they not only condemned the Germans and their collaborators but National Socialism as well.

For several reasons, the government in London was not exactly well-loved by the resistance and the population at large when the country was liberated. The liberation and the triumph of democracy – it was, after all, Britain and the USA who had proved their superiority and mettle – created great expectations, but the pre-war indecisiveness could not be allowed to return. People were counting on a new generation of leaders who had spent the war in Belgium. The old familiar faces only brought back memories of the miserable 1930s and the debacle of 1940 (cf. chapter VI). Many conservatives were hoping a quick return of the king would change things for the better. Some papers even claimed Leopold had been 'the first among the resistance fighters'. The resistance movement was not split up along political party lines. Many members from the different political parties had been involved in different secret intelligence services, the clandestine press, the organisation of escape routes for allied paratroopers and other resistance activities. The suffering was intense. Many were killed. Others were tortured or ended up in concentration camps.

The communists got involved in the resistance movement in early 1941, a few months ahead of the German invasion of the Soviet Union. The 1939 non-aggression pact between the Soviet Union had left the Belgian communists in limbo when Germany invaded. But as of March 1941, they started working on the creation of a sort of Popular Front for Belgian independence – the *Onafhankelijkheidsfront* (OF, Independence Front). The leadership of the Front included, apart from communists, also socialists, liberals and even some Catholics. Mass arrests in 1943 and the reinforcement of less ideologically committed patriots made sure the Front largely slipped out of the Communist Party's grasp near the end of the war. The OF prepared a national rebellion in 1944, led by liberation committees, but this was not to the liking of the government in London, which provided relatively less support in the form of arms and money for the OF anyway. The swift progress of the Allied armies and the return of the Belgian government prevented the OF from claiming the role of national liberator.

The strong showing of the Front was partly responsible, however, for the inclusion of the Communist Party in several governments just after the war. The Communist Party, which had become increasingly patriotic during the war, also won its only big election victory, taking 23 out of 202 seats, in the first post-war election of 1946. The Belgian Communists realised that the Soviet Union, now licking its wounds, was primarily concerned with consolidating its power in Eastern and Central Europe. Political bickering and infighting was responsible for the decline of the OF. It did take a leading role in opposing the return of Leopold III.

The *Witte Brigade* (after the liberation known as *Witte Brigade-Fidelio*) was an offshoot of the liberal youth movement in Flanders, but the resistance movement also attracted people of different political backgrounds. It was very active in Antwerp, also in the armed resistance. The *Nationale Koninklijke Beweging* (NKB, National Royal Movement) was primarily Flemish and originally a right-wing Catholic organisation that rejected the restoration of parliamentary democracy, although that was little known among its membership, which even included some socialist workers. Because it backed Leopold, the NKB received no support from the government in London, even though it paid a high toll in lives. The *Leger van België* (Army of Belgium), which later became the *Geheime Leger* (Secret Army), was also a royalist resistance movement and included many military officers who refused to accept the 1940 defeat. It first contacted the British, not the Belgian government, which mistrusted its royalism and its initial preference for a military-authoritarian regime. Only after the Germans arrested several leaders of the Secret Army did the London government improve relations and send arms. The Secret Army was responsible for several sabotage and purely military actions on the eve of the liberation. Group-G was the expert in sabotage, though. This Group-G was founded by members of the *Cercle du Libre Examen* of Brussels University and had already proved its mettle during the years of the Spanish Civil War. It acted on orders of the Allies and was responsible for a series of efficient and spectacular sabotage attacks. Group-G disbanded itself after the liberation and never sought political power, in contrast with the other resistance groups (with the exception of Witte Brigade-Fidelio), which recruited many new members during and after the liberation.

The resistance groups did not really have a durable impact on post-war political developments. They were important as pressure groups to defend the moral and material interests of the resistance fighters and their families. They also opposed any leniency for collaborators and rejected amnesty out of hand. They were split on the Royal Question with the right backing a return of Leopold III and the left opposing it. The strengthened Belgian patriotism, with few exceptions, opposed any plans for federalism, and this did have a political impact, as will be explained later.

Chapter VI
Restoration and Renewal (1944-1950)

It cannot be denied that the occupation between 1940 and 1944 released forces of which the political elite that took power on the liberation of the country, was the emanation. It was a force to be reckoned with. Democracy was on the rise, patriotism was on a high and a drive for renewal dominated the political agenda and implied that the anti-democratic past few years were definitely over. But the need to reconstruct and reinforce Belgium's shattered political institutions was even stronger than any reform movement. The political system had been based on economic liberalism, expanded parliamentary democracy and the emergence of a social negotiation policy. Post-war policy between 1944 and 1950 was bent on destroying the movements that had attacked these political cornerstones during the war. Communism had to be contained and Belgium's political landscape had to be brought in line with the economic and ideological demands of the U.S.-led Western alliance. A policy of repression and political cleansing had to take care of the extreme right. This process of restoration was completed by 1950. By that time, most of the groups that had helped set the policy had also gone through organisational renewal and the political system had started functioning differently. Overall, change was moderate. The war had created one huge new political issue, though – The Royal Question. It would give the Catholic Party an absolute majority in the Chamber and the situation would dominate much of the 1950s.

The Balance of Power During the Liberation Period

The occupation had had one major impact on post-war politics – the left expanded its powers. The breakthrough of the KPB (Communist Party) was an unmistakable sign and it came in the wake of its wartime activities. During the liberation it was able to come to the aid of the allies with a disciplined partisan army. The liberation of Belgium only took a few days, and the communists helped eliminate enemy troops, guard prisoners of war and seize arms at a time when the Belgian government troops still needed to regroup and be rearmed. The KPB won much prestige and sympathy because of its role in the OF, its coordinating activities as a minority in the resistance movement and the many communist lives that were lost during the actions against the occupier. For obvious opportunist reasons, the ranks of the resistance groups swelled just ahead of the September liberation, and it was also reflected in the increasing membership of the KPB. The victories of the Soviet army, which indirectly reflected well on the communist regime of the Soviet Union, only reinforced this. The communists were able to largely fill the void left by the dismantling of the socialist trade unions during the war. Their clandestine activities and their resistance against forced labour in Germany also paid dividends.

The communist leadership knew the time was ripe to reinforce the party's political position. On the one hand, the KPB had to compete with the socialists, as it also recruited its members and support group among workers and office clerks. On the other hand, it needed those same socialists to set up a comprehensive left-wing front. Its moderate language indicated the party was intent on luring part of the socialist electorate further to the left. The KPB backed the post-war economic production policy and did not plan any frontal attack on the capitalist power structures that had been restored after the liberation. And even though it was republican, the party did not insist on scrapping the monarchy. The socialists had a problem: the communists' strong grassroots support and their tactical moderation made it impossible to launch an unconditional attack on them. And the socialists, too, saw the possibilities of a joint left-wing coalition. The conservative parties and the Allied supreme command had to overcome their fear of communism and take Belgium's political reality into account. They wanted to neutralise the influence of the KPB by integrating it in government coalitions; that was the preferred strategy to contain them.

The socialists found it difficult to regain their political footing after the war. The actions of H. De Man, the wait-and-see attitude of some leaders during 1940 and 1941, the collapse of the union movement and the decline of socialist cooperatives and health care organisations had affected the party; at the same time, the communists were eating into the left wing of the socialist electoral base. The party was also internally divided: the 'London group' of pre-war politicians that had fled the nation and joined the government in exile had little in common with a younger, more radical group that had been illegally active in occupied Belgium and had risked life and limb in the resistance movement. It created problems when the two were rejoined after the liberation. The input of the 'illegals' was the most important since they had been working systematically on party structure during the occupation and they were instrumental in preparing the socialists for government immediately after the liberation. Pragmatic leaders like A. Van Acker, L. Major, E. Anseele jr. and A. Spinoy came to power and formed a tight bloc.

The 'London group' did not nearly have the same cohesion. They were ideologically split and there was mutual mistrust between the socialists in government and the members of parliament. The lack of permanent contact with their party colleagues in occupied Belgium reduced their say in preparing post-war policy. The party effectively lived in two worlds and the 'Londoners' could hardly start lecturing those who had worked under the German occupier to resurrect the party. Moreover, the London plans did not always prove to be quite adequate. However, it did not stop both sides from agreeing on the common goal of post-war policy. The restoration of parliamentary democracy was a priority for both since there was a fear that the right would want to create a conservative regime built around the king. Such plans did indeed exist in certain military circles. The socialists also insisted on stiff sentences against collaborators. They did not favour abrupt social economic reforms but preferred a state-run economy and the expansion of a coherent and mandatory system of social security for all workers. Most of these demands had already been raised by the BWP ahead of the war.

The party needed to win over the left-wing union movement if it wanted to beat the communists in the battle for the hearts and votes of the working class and if it wanted to have a key role in the reconstruction of the nation. Communist committees, anarcho-unionism and the drive for unified trade unions stood in the way of an immediate socialist takeover. The radical wing represented some 40 % of total union membership and it forced the socialist leadership to reform the old BVV union into the *Algemeen Belgisch Vakverbond* (ABVV, General Belgian Union), a much looser and more leftist organisation than the pre-war union.

The divisions within the party itself were overcome more easily, in a spirit of compromise. The party's bureau, which ran the day-to-day affairs, was equally split between the Londoners and the 'illegals'. Party chiefs like P.-H. Spaak and C. Huysmans were able to return from Britain and retain their position. But in the group of 'illegals', 80 % was new: the war had thinned the ranks of the socialist leadership, creating room for renewal. The two groups combined gave the party a double legitimacy and experience. The new balance between Flanders, Brussels and Wallonia illustrated the socialists' firm intention to produce a united, centrally-led party. The communist unionists pressured the BWP into accepting individual membership, but the party continued to keep its links with the other socialist pillar organisations. The party also changed its name, from BWP to *Parti Socialiste Belge-Belgische Socialistische Partij* (PSB-BSP, Belgian Socialist Party), in an attempt to show it was resuming political life with a clean slate. But its policies, programme and ideology had changed little as the party pragmatically moved into a moderate social-democratic direction. The PSB-BSP was willing to be a loyal partner in restoring pre-war society and in return it obtained key political posts, a comprehensive social security system and a certain degree of state control over the economy.

The spirit of a united anti-fascist and patriotic battle against the occupiers remained the inspiration, also after the liberation, for some progressive Catholic intellectuals and trade union militants from Wallonia and Brussels to tear down the pre-war pillarised labour world and create a moderate unitary party and trade union beyond the ideological borders. The Walloon Christian labour movement had been more radical. Unlike its Flemish counterpart, it had been confronted much more directly with the powerful employers and had been unable to rely on a strong middle class and agricultural groups as buffer organisations. Contacts with the socialists and the left-wing resistance groups only reinforced the opposition of these progressives against the patronising attitude of a conservative Catholic Party and the conservative bishops. Their hopes of creating a wide political front were shattered soon after the liberation when it became clear the PSB-BSP leadership was unwilling to risk the wrath of its left wing by pushing the party structure and ideology towards the centre. The Christian workers also opposed the membership of communists in the ABVV and both sides drifted apart.

When a deal with the socialists proved impossible, the leaders of this progressive Catholic movement decided to set up their own organisation in time for the first post-war elections. Local initiatives in early 1945 eventually led to the *Union Démocratique Belge* (UDB, Belgian Democratic Union), which held its first congress in June 1945. Being asked to be part of the government in July 1945 gave the UDB some political impact, but it was always evident that its lack of finances, flimsy party structure and the absence of easily recognisable candidates would cost the party at the ballot box. The bishops reduced the UDB's prospects even further when they barred the Catholic flock from joining the party's electoral lists. The UDB ended up with 2 % of the vote in 1946. It was proof that the Church and the Catholic Party leadership would not accept any division of the Catholics or any political obstruction to the restoration of the pre-war power structure.

Indeed, the Catholic world did not emerge from the war a homogeneous bloc. Apart from active resistance fighters, it had also had its share of supporters of the 'new order'. The Church had taken a cautious attitude towards the Germans during the war, and its backing of authoritarian corporatism and anti-Soviet stance entailed that the Catholic movement had not rejected any form of cooperation with the occupier out of hand. The goal of this opportunism was to keep the core Catholic institutions, including schools and youth organisations, within its grasp. The conservative heavyweights of the pre-war party kept in contact during the war and, around figures like L. Moyersoen, had reformulated their authoritarian demands. The post-war structure had to be based on a strong executive branch with extensive royal powers at the expense of parliament. Their desires also included the abolishment of universal suffrage, the creation of a corporatist Senate and restrictions on electoral eligibility. Traditional Belgian nationalism, with all its criticism on parliamentary democracy, was not dead and buried. It was still recruiting new backers among Catholic dignitaries, industrialists, military officers and the clergy.

However, the spirit of the liberation hardly created the ideal climate for the realisation of these demands. Times were better for the Catholic labour movement since the UDB forced the Catholic Party to be more open to democratic ideals. To contain the left-wing surge, it was advisable to take some progressive ideas on board. Moreover, a certain renewal at management level was taking place in the ACW, allowing the young generation to take charge of the expansion of regional and local structures. Within the party there was a movement to leave the conservative constraints of the old class party behind, insist on more political say for the Christian workers and demand a more equal spread of wealth and income. The ACW led such a renewal and it paid off in more legislative seats.

The August 1945 founding congress of the *Christelijke Volkspartij-Parti Social Chrétien* (CVP-PSC, Christian People's Party) and the subsequent Christmas programme where sprinkled with such terms as renewal, reorganisation, rejuvenation, unity and progressivism. A new generation of

Catholic politicians, including T. Lefèvre, R. Van Elslande, P. Harmel, R. Houben and J. De Saeger emerged and would continue to dominate the post-war CVP for years to come. The authoritarian ideas were mostly rejected and linguistic differences were pushed aside to preserve party unity and create a coherent political platform. The moderate A. De Schrijver was elected chairman.

The structure, programme and ideology of the new party proved that this renewal was a mainly formal matter, however. The party charter claimed the party was no longer based on a class structure but on individual membership, but in reality the party carefully controlled its organisational structure on central, regional and local levels, making sure that all social and economic groups were proportionally represented. In practice, the class structure was thus retained. The party did become much more the basis of the whole Catholic 'pillar'. It combined and layered the forces of the different Catholic classes more efficiently. A vague personalism, borrowed from the French philosophers J. Maritain and E. Mounier, replaced the former solidarism. In order to appeal to as wide a public from the political centre as possible – a move that often irritated the high clergy – the party shed its confessional character, opening itself up to anyone who accepted Christianity as the foundation of Western civilisation. At first, the bishops did not take the party's newfound independence too seriously and still tried to impose their will. But they also realised it was essential to have a strong united centre party to defend a Catholic-inspired society against anti-clerical attacks.

Some of the reforms were not altogether progressive. The extension of voting rights to include women certainly met the demands of the feminists but was in the first place aimed at widening the electoral base since politicians knew all too well that primarily women attended church services. Granting a second vote to the head of a family underscored similar party concerns. The reduction of the powers of parliament could hardly be called a democratic demand. The party's social and economic programme showed few signs of renewal. The CVP stuck to capitalism (be it with certain reforms of a 'personalist' sense) and strongly rejected any Marxist ideas. It granted the state a regulatory role to create the right conditions for private initiative and called for legal and mandatory consultation between everyone involved in the production process. Its main goal remained class reconciliation and social peace. The 'Third Way' in between capitalism and Marxist collectivism was limited to the expansion of pre-war social legislation, the suppression of the most obvious capitalist abuses and a better distribution of the available goods. Property and family remained the cornerstones of society. Overall, the Catholic party's renewal was limited to the emergence of a moderate reform movement that limited the domination of the paternalist right wing.

Some of the socio-economic ideas also appealed to a group of 'enlightened' employers. Some business leaders wanted to cling to their full authority while others refused to reject corporatism as it had functioned during the war. But the enlightened group, especially in the metal sector, wanted to improve cooperation between capital and labour. Pragmatism also pointed them into this direction. The war had been particularly hard on the working class and social revolt was still possible. The left was also in a good position to criticise the wartime production policies of the Belgian employers. It was a badly kept secret that Belgian companies had produced semi-military goods for the Germans during the war. Business in general was scared that the left, and the communists, would force a breakthrough. It was most likely that business started funding the OF near the end of the war and helped a number of union members in an attempt to counter this. The willingness to make economic and social concessions should be seen in the same light. Whatever the motivation, it did produce results. The wartime contacts between representatives of the employers and a number of socialists and Christian democrats led to a 'social pact' immediately after the liberation. The employers won guaranteed social peace in return for a comprehensive social security system to be set up by the state. The key economic management issues – the authority of the employer and the profit principle – survived unscathed.

The different employers' federations had cooperated closely during the war, and the relative importance of the group in favour of negotiation ensured that, once Belgium was liberated, the employers adapted their organisational structure. The reform of the CCI into the *Verbond der Belgische Nijverheid* (VBN, Union of Belgian Industry) took place in early 1946 and consolidated the wish for a unified structure and better representation. It allowed the employers to speak with one voice in their relations with the trade unions and the government as the pace of collective negotiations increased.

The moderate reform movement swept through much of Belgium after the liberation, but the government in exile came back from London with less enthusiasm for reform. Its right wing was overrepresented (Spaak was the only socialist) and the Flemish wing underrepresented. Its authoritarian streak had already outraged Belgian parliamentarians in London, and it had not shown much interest for the leftist forces that might grow into an alternative power on liberation. There had been a few attempts at contact, but those had not done anything to change the government's conservative image. Many resistance fighters were sceptical and had no intention of throwing themselves at its feet. Instead of a triumphant welcome, the return of the government on 8 September 1944 was marked by criticism, mistrust and a lack of respect.

But the allies considered the Pierlot government a stable authority. The SHAEF (Supreme Headquarters of the Allied Expeditionary Forces) and the British supreme commander Erskine – Belgium lay within the British sphere of influence during liberation – were decisive in handing over the government's former privileges. The government in London was considered the only legitimate authority and it had actively participated in the Allied victory by retaining control over key sectors during the war. The Allies saw in Pierlot a bulwark against any leftist surge. But after a few months, the Allied supreme command had to recognise that the government's power base was far too small, that the lack of an electoral mandate affected its authority and that it no longer represented the new balance of power.

Leopold III, too, seemed not to have noticed the winds of change. For the left-wing resistance, Leopold incarnated the evil of collaboration. The resistance groups had been indignant that the monarch had refused to be freed from his Laeken palace. They also feared that, upon his return, Leopold would establish a conservative regime and exempt from prosecution specific forms of collaboration. His political testament showed that he did not at all react to the liberation by the Allied forces in the same way as the majority of the population: he never showed any gratitude towards the resistance and did not mention punishment of collaboration. He called the Allied victors the 'occupying forces'. His cool reaction, showing little solidarity with the allies, obviously resulted in bitter comments from Churchill and others beside him who knew the contents of the document in September 1944. The political testament of Leopold III showed his unwillingness to forget about the 1940 rift: he expected the ministers to publicly admit guilt before taking up any political responsibility. Obviously, the members of the Pierlot government found it difficult to stomach this political stance.

Despite all the trouble in September 1944, just about nobody questioned the concept of the monarchy itself. When parliament reconvened – obviously without the members of VNV and Rex – one of the first things it did was appoint Prince Karel, Leopold's brother who had had contacts with the resistance, as prince-regent. The Pierlot government was expanded near the end of September to include two KPB members, one representative from the resistance and socialists and liberals who had stayed in occupied Belgium. It was a clear strategy to adapt the political power structure to the new post-war situation. The resignation of the transitional government on 7 February 1945 following a dispute over food distribution and price policy led to a second phase of political change. By that time, even the SHAEF was hoping for a more effective left-wing policy that would be able to contain the communist surge. The socialists sensed it was their opportunity to take charge.

A. Van Acker, who had risen to national fame for his work on the social security system, became prime minister of a four-party coalition of Socialists, Catholics, Liberals and Communists. It did not last long, since the Catholics walked out in early August 1945, choosing to lay down government responsibility in order to regroup. Van Acker replaced them with more liberals and two UDB members until the February 1946 elections.

It took eighteen months before the first post-war elections were organised, for several reasons. The socialists and communists had an electoral interest in waiting for the return of prisoners from German concentration camps and for the sentencing of collaborators. Half of all the rulings to scrap civil rights were decided on before the elections. It was not the most careful job in the world though, since half of them had to be repealed later. Anti-communists circles hoped that the delaying of elections would weaken the KPB since it would give other parties sufficient time to reorganise themselves. Electoral opportunism also pushed Van Acker to postpone the introduction of women's voting rights for fear it would have profited the Catholic Party. Women would have to wait until 1949 for their first chance to vote.

The results of the elections were hardly surprising. We have already discussed the total defeat of the UDB; socialists, with 34 %, and communists, with 11.3 %, fell short of a left-wing majority. The Catholic CVP won 42 % in the Chamber and stranded within one seat of a majority in the Senate; apparently it was fully revitalised after its voluntary exile in opposition. Its centre program appealed to the electorate and the party also profited from the disappearance of pre-war extreme right-wing parties. Compared to the last pre-war elections, the BSP gained five seats; the communists managed to increase their total number of seats by fourteen. In contrast, the liberals had been slow to reorganise their party structure and lost sixteen seats.

A left-wing majority coalition was out of the question and an attempt at forming a socialist minority government failed. Instead Van Acker set up a government of seven socialists, four communists, six liberals and two experts. Again the government proved unstable and collapsed in July 1946. C. Huysmans emerged from long and difficult coalition talks as the new prime minister and continued with the same coalition for another seven months. By then, the political climate had changed to such an extent that the CVP was willing to work with the socialists. In the meantime, the successive governments had been dealing with the socio-economic reconstruction of the nation and the two thorniest issues to emerge from the war – collaboration and the Royal Question.

Economic Reconstruction and Social Cooperation

The reconstruction of Belgium's economy was very speedy compared to several other West European nations. It went hand in hand with the restoration of Belgium's liberal economic policy in several stages.

Once the country was liberated, the government in exile wanted the swiftest transition possible to the familiar pre-war free-market economy. It was immediately confronted with the imbalance between the remaining financial resources and the supply of goods and services. During the war, the combination of exceedingly high prices and totally insufficient wages had created an intolerable situation for the overwhelming majority of the population. The government wanted to push through both price reductions and wage increases as soon as possible. Finance Minister Camille Gutt prepared for a thorough currency overhaul to prevent hyperinflation once food rationing was abolished. All accounts were blocked in October 1944 and the old bills and coins were no longer valid on the market. Every individual could only change a small part of his money into new bills and was forced to dump the rest into special, temporarily blocked accounts and convert it into currency reorganisation loans. Gutt wanted to reduce circulation and hoped it would result in similar reductions of prices on the black market. Wage increases needed to be limited in order not to hamper price reduction. The September 1944 National Labour Conference limited wage increases to just 40 % compared to 1940 levels.

There was social compensation though. The left linked the economic recovery to the creation of a general social security system even though conservative circles opposed this as an irresponsible expenditure. The social security system was a key part of a compromise social pact that had been set up during the war by employers and the labour movement. The left wing of the socialist union and large parts of the Christian labour movement were not too enthusiastic about the pact though. Van Acker did his utmost in government and parliament to push the plan through. At the end of December 1944 a start was made on the legislation involved and on 16 January 1945, the *Rijksdienst voor Maatschappelijke Zekerheid* (National Service for Social Security) was founded. Several parts of the pact did appeal to the working class. It guaranteed every worker an income in case of unemployment, illness, disability or old age. The right to work was the official point of departure of the whole pact. The state recognised it had to guarantee a minimum income. The freedoms of union representation had been abolished during the war and the employers now provided legal guarantees 'not to hinder the labour organisations'. Joint committee negotiations on wages and working conditions became mandatory by law.

Despite the opposition of conservative and Catholic employers, many business leaders saw the advantages of such a social pact. The idea was not totally new since some aspects had already been discussed ahead of the war. The 1944 pact was a comprehensive core compromise that rationalised the pre-war legislation. The cost of the social concessions was compensated by increasing productivity. It countered the impoverishment of the working class and increased its spending power. The power of the employers remained intact since the principle that 'good management of a company was the basis of the nation's prosperity' survived. The terms of the pact also laid out that the workers 'recognised the legal authority of the employer' and that they would 'work dutifully'. Strikes were a threat to stability, so they systematically had to become subject to negotiations. Strike action became institutionalised and the individual right to strike that circumvented the trade unions was curtailed. Social tensions had to be eased in a spirit of solidarity.

That was still too much to ask for in 1945. Social relations were tense, all the more because government policy failed for the most part. It turned out to be incredibly difficult to keep prices under control by putting limits on the currency circulation. Van Acker's new coalition changed course. Gutt's measures were cast aside and a large part of the savings that had been temporarily blocked were released onto the market. The government itself now took initiatives in the pricing sector. It set maximum prices and caps on profit margins for essential products. Other products were subject to set maximum 'normal prices', under the control of the courts. The government subsidised certain products and it made sure that the worldwide increase in agricultural prices did not result in exceptional price rises. Subsidies were also used to control retail prices and price reductions were announced for certain products. The government's far-reaching pricing policy was also coupled to a wage freeze in several sectors. It is difficult to confirm at this stage whether all these measures had the desired effect, but it is beyond doubt that government policy prevented post-war Belgium from the kind of spiralling inflation that crippled France.

The government also tackled the question of industrial production. Any recovery was dependent on the availability of energy and the government spared no effort to increase coal production. Coalminers were granted special social benefits and German prisoners of war were forced to work in the mines. They were later replaced by Italian immigrants and displaced persons. Additional coal imports guaranteed sufficient energy provisions. All these measures had a positive impact on industrial production and most sectors had already reached or moved past pre-war levels in 1948.

This 'led' economy, as it undeniably was, did not clash with the interests of big business. The power of the industrial owners remained intact. Communists and socialists could call for all the nationalisation they wanted – the arms industry, the energy sector and banking – but, in contrast with France, they had no success in Belgium. Government subsidies to industry, especially the coal sector, did not involve stringent controls and were aimed at compensating the losses resulting from the price freeze.

Van Acker relied on governmental decrees to push through the pricing and production policy. A decree of 12 April 1945 allowed 'civil mobilisation' in the energy and transport sector, which came down to an effective strike ban. When a price hike of 30 % in the energy sector was approved while wages were not adapted, protests led to a strike in early 1948, resulting in civil mobilisation and the dismissal of many workers. The strike was a climax in the political battle between communists and social democrats, won by the latter. After the communists withdrew from the government in 1947, a new coalition had come to power. Social democrats and Catholics now cooperated under P.-H. Spaak, with G. Eyskens as Finance Minister. Eyskens embodied the modern economic policy of the new CVP. The state became an economic coordinator of the planned economy on the condition that it guaranteed social peace and promoted class reconciliation. The Catholics did not fundamentally oppose the socialist demands for a bigger government say in the economy, nor did they oppose the further development of social policy.

The government compromise included the commitment to end the strict economic policy of the previous government and restore economic liberalism in the pricing sector. The Spaak government also wanted to gradually put an end to state interference: barring a few exceptions, rationing was lifted and the free-market principle was restored as much as possible. Supermarkets slowly started spreading across the nation. The abolishment of the system of maximum prices and subsidies was next on the agenda. Government interference increased, however, in the financial sector, especially in the National Bank. The range of activities of the NMKM bank, the national industrial credit company, was also extended.

The Spaak government did not neglect the social aspect of the economy. The classes had to be brought closer together and a social law created company and sector-based joint committees. Work councils in big companies had to be consulted whenever economic issues with a social impact were tackled. Results were not immediately obvious since most of the work councils were still very much in an experimental phase and the few that worked with any efficiency had little influence on economic policy. The government's social housing policy was much more efficient. Bonuses were accorded to builders or buyers of small houses. Other measures in the private home building industry further boosted construction and staved off the danger of a housing shortage.

There are several indications that the Spaak government laid the foundations for the socio-economic policy of the 1950s and 1960s. The state claimed a coordinating role in the further development of capitalism and was focused on keeping the social peace. As we will see, this economic policy of restoration and renewal was greatly facilitated by the effects of the U.S. aid programme that also benefited Belgium to a large extent.

The Elimination of the Extreme Left and the Extreme Right

After the liberation, it was time to settle accounts with the authoritarian and fascist forces that had collaborated during the occupation. The return to the pre-war parliamentary democracy system was a priority. It would be unjustified, though, to view the repression exclusively in this light. Which other motives did play is difficult to pinpoint at this stage. The subject is still topical in present-day politics, and the literature on the subject is undeniably influenced by this. The lack of really objective research means that there are still a number of blind spots in our knowledge of the period.

The resistance movement was the obvious driving force behind the punishment of collaborators. It was more than understandable that people who had lost family or friends, or who were themselves victims of imprisonment, terror, deportation or concentration camps, demanded justice. It was further reinforced when the horrors of the camps, the extermination of Jews and other minority groups, the torture and 'medical experiments' became public knowledge. More and more people felt that punishment was necessary. Renewed Belgian patriotism resulted in a purge of the collaborationist forces that had threatened the nation. It is also plausible that there was a movement within the left that wanted to use the purge to eliminate anti-labour forces. So, the government as well as all sectors of the organised resistance were actively preparing a purge as soon as the Allied forces entered Belgium. Resistance groups compiled lists, gathered evidence for legal charges and even started locking up people. The government put the decisions it took in London into effect as quickly as possible.

The insistence on severe punishment was tempered by practical and specific considerations in some political circles. Repression should have no adverse effect on social and economic reconstruction –many agreed on that. The role of the king and his court during the war also softened the stance of many royalists. A group within the Flemish right wing showed moderation considering their ideological links with those who had cooperated with the Germans intellectually or on pro-Flemish grounds. The latter two categories were well-represented within the Catholic Party.

Little is known about popular repression during the liberation or after the return of political prisoners from concentration camps. It included lynching, looting and arson. Statistics on the more formal types of justice show a few main tendencies. Unlike other countries, Belgium did not have special courts to judge collaboration; instead, military courts dealt with penal offences against the security of the nation. The military court primarily focused on possession of arms, economic collaboration and severe cases of assistance to the enemy. The auditors-general dealt with political collaboration. The judgment of collaborators was left to military courts after bad experiences in the wake of the First World War. There also was an urge to proceed swiftly: the population needed a signal that effective measures were being taken to guarantee law and order. The military court system was expanded and by February 1946 it included 21 courts-martial and by 1947, 134 criminal divisions. The extensive powers of the auditors-general later came under criticism.

There was no denying the system worked speedily. Some 50,000 people were arrested and 37,000 detained in September 1944 alone. By the end of the year, 2,000 cases had been dealt with. After June 1945, there was a second wave of arrests with the return of pro-German Belgians from the defeated Germany. The number of charges was remarkably high. Some 350,000 files led to around 53,000 convictions; 84 % were classified without further action. The lion's share of sentences concerned the possession of arms. Members of German military groups, police and paramilitary organisations accounted for 60 % of the cases. Political and intellectual collaboration led to another 27 % of convictions. Those condemned had held administrative or executive positions in parties and organisations with a national-socialist programme or in pro-German political institutions. Treason leading to arrest and worse accounted for another 8 % of convictions. Since the defendants were also accused of extending the war by cooperating with the enemy, the state also claimed damages, which resulted in the confiscation of property of collaborators.

The decree of 19 September 1945 set the wheels of a purge in motion. Military auditors investigated the war past of suspects and were looking for signs of unpatriotic actions. Whoever appeared on the list could be deprived of their civil and political rights, including the right to vote. Some 405,000 files were compiled, leading to about 90,000 court cases. The membership of a party or organisation that had come to the aid of the enemy accounted for some 70 % of convictions. Suspect civil servants were sucked into an administrative purge. Mayors had the means to punish collaborators by refusing them an attestation of their civil rights. The different measures pushed collaborators from the key positions they had held in administration and political institutions during the occupation.

Evidence has since laid bare irregularities in the process: similar offences led to disparate sentences. Punishment was at its harshest immediately after the liberation and after the return of concentration camp survivors. In all, 1,202 people were sentenced to death and 242 of them were actually executed. The majority of them had had a leading role in murderous terrorist operations or raids. The leaders of collaborating parties suffered the same fate. Some of them were sentenced in absentia since they had fled to right-wing authoritarian countries like Spain and military regimes in South America. There also was a great divergence in the length of prison sentences. At first, the average sentence was seven years' imprisonment, while political leaders received stiffer sentences. Many clemency measures were approved as of the end of 1946, and by 1950, the number of detainees had dropped to 2,500. Collaborators were usually set free after serving one-third of their prison sentence. Statistics show that the military auditors interpreted their brief in widely different ways. In each region, the variation appears to have been quite disparate.

The political consequences of the repression, centring on economic collaboration and the Flemish-Walloon contrast, turned into a web of controversy. The left accused the government and the judiciary that they were too moderate and did not dare take on the collaboration of big business while coming down hard on small companies. Legislation was a lot more flexible after the Second World War than it was in the wake of the First World War. The concept of economic collaboration was given a restricted interpretation and a detailed list was made up of the kinds of trade with the occupier that could be considered punishable offences. Implicitly, it was recognised that suspects would escape a sentence if it was clear that the company had to trade with the occupying forces to ensure continued employment or food provisions and if it was clear that the suspect had not collaborated for personal gain. It was also assumed that the government in London had approved this so-called Galopin doctrine. Companies that had not cooperated beyond this 'policy of the lesser evil' would face no punishment. It is not unreasonable to claim that this served the interests of big business. There was a consensus within successive governments on the restoration of economic liberalism and the reconstruction of the economy so it could be surmised there was a willingness to protect the big companies. This did not mean, however, that all major economic collaborators got off scot-free, or that only small companies were prosecuted. Recent studies have shown that repression mainly hit medium-sized businesses, merchandise traders, building contractors and all those who had sought personal gain.

Debate is still raging in literature whether the pro-German Flemings were treated fairly. One group of authors claims there was no anti-flamingant repression and that the courts instead treated them even-handedly. They base their conclusions on statistics showing that the number of death sentences, executions and life sentences was higher in Wallonia and that Flemish long-term prison sentences did not outnumber the Walloon cases. A geographical spread of the convictions shows that the total numbers in some Flemish districts were as low as in certain Walloon regions.

Pro-Flemish authors claim that the anti-flamingant forces abused the repression in an attempt to destroy the Flemish Movement. Judges from gallicised circles failed to fully grasp the political and often idealistic motives for collaboration. These authors say it took no more than a pro-Flemish past to become a target. Backers of the Catholic Party said the predominantly francophone left-wing resistance just wanted to settle accounts with Catholic Flanders. The authors use overall population figures and sentencing statistics to show there was indeed an imbalance at Flanders' expense – 0.73 % of the population in Flanders, compared to 0.52 in Wallonia and 0.56 in Brussels. The number of light sentences also appears to have been higher in Flanders: 14,115 against 8,013. As long as the files are not open to everyone, however, the exact correlations are difficult to gauge. But since the Flemish VNV had a much more popular base than the francophone Rex and since membership of these and similar groups were a punishable offence, it is obvious that the sanctioning for political and ideological collaboration was much higher in Flanders. So it is not a far-fetched claim to accuse some politicians of trying to use the repression to hurt the Flemish Movement as a whole.

The history of the amnesty movement has not been the subject of much in-depth research. It is clear, though, that the amnesty movement tried to systematically falsify the history of the repression. The group sought a complete remit and based its arguments on the poverty the collaborators and their families had to live in, the harsh conditions in the internment camps and the political nature of the Flemish collaboration. They claim that there was no crime involved, and as such no guilt. They remain convinced that truth was on the side of their grandparents, their parents and themselves. It goes without saying that committed democrats show little understanding for these arguments.

The return to traditional parliamentary democracy also had to deal with the breakthrough of the extreme left, c.q. the Communist Party. Anti-communism was part of the anti-democratic bias of right-wing nationalism. Its representatives could be found in key echelons of power, including the industrial and financial elite, the army leadership and the Church. The socialists, too, wanted to regain their pre-war political advantage, so the KPB faced enemies from across the political spectrum.

The first assault on the Communist Party's position of power came with the disarmament of the resistance. The Pierlot government, backed by British Supreme Commander Erskine wanted to demobilise and disarm resistance groups as soon as the national police force was armed again. They considered the situation a powder keg and thought it far too risky to integrate the left-wing resistance movement into the armed forces. At first, miners and transport workers were drafted to boost the economic reconstruction. In October 1944 the female members of the resistance movement were discharged and the communist partisans were removed. One month later, the whole partisan army had to be demobilised. The resistance groups protested vehemently against the measures since the Germans were not completely overcome yet. The KPB ministers resigned and helped organise protest meetings and demonstrations. During the mass demonstration of 25 November 1944, there was even an exchange of gunfire between armed partisans and the state police, but nobody was killed. The decommissioning of arms was briefly interrupted, but in the light of a lack of funds and supply, the complete disarmament of the partisans resumed a bit later.

The political right, however, used the events to discredit the KPB. The communists were intent on putting their stamp on government policy and participation in the ruling coalition sapped their political power. The 1945 Van Acker government made sure the communists were able to take few political initiatives yet forced them to show solidarity with the moderate policies. It gave the socialists sufficient time to start recovering much of the non-Catholic working class. The 1946 election results did nothing to change this strategy and the four communist ministers in the new coalitions were no real threat to the economic restoration policy.

The international tension of 1947 and 1948 further precipitated the decline of communist power. The United States wanted to contain communism and the Marshall Plan and the Cold War were testimony to that. The CIA and U.S. interest groups actively supported the anti-communism of the socialists. The Soviet Union's undemocratic conduct in Eastern Europe also was a blow to the communists here. Much like in France and Italy around the same time, the KPB left government for good in March 1947.

The communists also lost their foothold within the socialist ABVV trade union. The right wing, led by L. Major, thrived in the chilly climate of the Cold War and tried to push out the communist union members. It wanted to become part of the Western bloc and restore links with the BSP. The February 1948 strike against a wage freeze in the energy sector was a turning point, as the communists turned it into a protest against the Marshall Plan. Between 1948 and 1950, KPB militants were carefully weeded out of the trade union's higher echelons. The trade union was ready again to align itself with the BSP and in 1950, the Joint Action coordinating body was created, incorporating the different socialist organisations and practically restoring the socialist pillar to its former glory. Electoral results rose to pre-war levels. Cooperatives, health care programs, youth and women's organisations regained much of their old membership. The union was predominately socialist again and a strong unitary party defended the political interests of social democracy. By that time, accounts with the communists were pretty much settled.

Apart from the demise of the KPB in post-war Belgium, it is worth mentioning how the government treated the resistance movement as a whole. Patriotic action was politically and legally recognised and measures were taken to acknowledge the fate of political prisoners and those who were taken to Germany to work there. Following pressure from the Catholic Party, the Jewish survivors of the Holocaust were not recognised as political prisoners. The overwhelming majority of Jews who had been deported from Belgium and survived the genocide did not even receive damages, as they did not have the Belgian nationality.

The Royal Question

The opponents and proponents of Leopold III have already been mentioned. Those who had hoped for and contributed to an Allied victory were in the anti-royalist camp. For them, Leopold was the symbol of collaboration and a gutless wait-and-see policy. The camp included members from the London government and the Communist, Socialist and Liberal pillars. They had a long list of grievances: they criticised the pre-war policy of neutrality, the king's preference for a strong executive power, the conflict with the government in 1940, his visit to Hitler in Berchtesgaden, the frequent and close contacts of his entourage with collaborating circles, his marriage to Lilian Baels, his felicitations to Hitler, the deportation of the royal family ahead of the liberation, the fact that the king had not publicly condemned the persecution of Jews and the forced labour deportations, and his refusal to back the resistance.

Leopold's proponents included almost the whole Catholic camp and just about everything to the right of the CVP; a few Catholic 'Londoners' and Walloon progressive Catholics were the exceptions. Many wanted to justify their own war actions by defending the king. Most of them appreciated that Leopold had prevented Belgium from being turned into a bloody battleground in May 1940. They were also convinced that the monarch's cautious approach was responsible for the relatively sedate mild occupation regime. All those who had taken a wait-and-see approach during the war, collaborators who were counting on clemency and even the part of the resistance that backed the king's conservative and nationalist viewpoints, were hoping for a return of Leopold III. For arch-conservative Belgium, the monarchy was an essential institution to set up an authoritarian nation. Several extreme backers of the royalist camp who sought an unconditional return of Leopold found an important friend in Catholic minister A. De Vleeshauwer.

The Pierlot and Van Acker governments had done their utmost to keep the issue off the agenda, but there was no avoiding it in April and May 1945 when the communists demanded that Leopold abdicate. The BSP bureau backed a similar call on 10 June 1945 and the socialist trade union also came out against a return of the king. Socialist Prime Minister Van Acker left for Leopold's temporary residence in Strobl, Austria, to negotiate his return. Leopold had to publicly praise the Allied forces, his entourage had to be purged and he had to renew his commitment to parliamentary democracy. At first, an agreement remained out of reach. After Van Acker's return from Strobl, the split over the monarchy deepened and when negotiations resumed in June, the king's commitment to meet the conditions was no longer sufficient for an agreement. The government no longer wanted to take the responsibility for a royal return and offered to resign. Leopold III did not succeed in replacing the government, and decided against returning before a referendum on the Royal Question had been held. He moved to Prégny in Switzerland instead.

A fervent press campaign, especially in *Le Soir* and *Le Peuple*, set the tone. It resulted in a bitter and impassioned parliamentary debate, dominated by P.-H. Spaak. The CVP backed the king and insisted on a referendum. Its proposal was rejected and the Chamber and Senate decided that it was up to parliament alone to rule whether king Leopold III was still able to reign. The Catholics left the government after the vote.

The historian J. Pirenne, who was close to the king, took on the defence of the monarch. His 1946 white paper, which was not made public, included the argument that not the king but the government had made a mistake in 1940. Pirenne said that the king had fully respected the constitution and that he had strictly maintained a neutral position. A commission studied the Pirenne paper and published a report the next year which had little impact on the entrenched opinions. There was a temporary lull in the political storm when the KPB left government and Spaak forged a Socialist-Catholic coalition that let the hottest political issue cool off a bit.

The results of the 1947 census called for an expansion of parliament and forced new elections. The CVP focused its entire campaign on a call for the return of the king. The election results of 26 June 1949 marked the demise of the communists, who lost thirteen seats, and a slight decline for the socialists. The liberals won a dozen seats and the Catholics increased their representation from 92 to 105 seats in the 212-seat Chamber and won a majority in the Senate. There was no way around them when the new coalition had to be formed and they insisted on the organisation of a referendum, which the king also wanted.

It took a long and painful crisis before the liberals finally agreed to become the minority partner in the centre-right government of Eyskens. The date of a consultative referendum was set for 12 March 1950. A majority of 57.6 % voted in favour of a return, but the regional differences were extreme: while Flanders backed the king with 72 % of the vote, Brussels and Wallonia massively voted against a return of the king. The liberals did not really want to be part of government if the king were to return in these circumstances. The king also recognised the problem and did not want to ignore socialist Wallonia. He proposed a compromise – he would temporarily abdicate in favour of his eldest son Baudouin and return only when the situation had calmed down. It would take the three traditional parties to agree on that, but the socialists insisted on more conditions, including the demand that the king would have to remain abroad during the transitional period. The CVP insisted on an unconditional return. The protocol of 15 April 1950 did not provide a solution.

It took new elections and the CVP did even better this time, winning the absolute majority with 108 seats out of 212. The one-party Catholic government led by Duvieusart immediately started preparing the unconditional return of the king, and set it for 22 July 1950. But the socialist trade union and a leftist action committee was preparing resistance. The Walloon industrial belt went on strike on July 6 and on July 26 the transport sector joined the protest action. There were plans to bring the whole steel industry to a standstill and a march on Brussels was being prepared for early August. There were calls for the creation of a Walloon republic and when state police shot and killed four people in Grace Berleur, the smell of revolution was in the air.

Pressured by outside events, the government and the king started negotiating again on 31 July. The extremists among the royal advisors wanted the creation of a strong government that would be willing to confront the resistance movement. A majority of CVP ministers were not prepared to do this and the Duvieusart government threatened to resign. Eventually the king offered to abdicate in favour of his son Baudouin. A dramatic epilogue ended the Royal Question: the chairman of the KPB, J. Lahaut was said to have called out 'Vive la République' – 'Long live the republic' – during Baudouin's swearing in ceremony. One week later he was shot dead in his home in Seraing. The murder was never completely solved. Leopold III fully relinquished the throne on 16 July 1951 when his son Baudouin reached majority age.

Analysing the events, several hypotheses can be formulated. One could question the BSP motives, considering their intense rivalry with the communists at the time. It was useful for the party to focus all attention on the issue and stick to an uncompromising line. Its grassroots support vehemently opposed Leopold and on top of that, such a policy took the winds out of the communist sails during the vitals years of 1945 and 1946. After that, the Royal Question became the ideal rallying point for the anti-fascist forces, especially since the ultra-right-wing groups had unconditionally backed the king. During the election campaign, the monarch and the ultras became one and the same. In this way the BSP were able to gain an edge in their electoral battle with the CVP. When they took the lead of the anti-Leopold movement during the crisis period of 1950, the socialists also restored their domination over the labour movement.

There is also much support for the argument that the CVP used the Royal Question to advance its own political aims. At the time, it wanted to mobilise as many voters as possible in an attempt to win an absolute parliamentary majority and set up an all-Catholic government to settle the School War. By choosing the call for a referendum and a return of the king as its election platform, party unity was undeniably restored. The left was temporarily overcome and it made the Catholic Party a haven for all those who had collaborated with or had shown sympathies for the German occupiers, and saw this political stance symbolised in the figure of the king. The bishops also used it to safeguard their position and presented the Royal Question as a holy war of Catholicism against godless liberalism, socialism and especially communism. It was a theme that touched believers and church-goers and as such reinforced the unity of the Catholic pillar. The withdrawal of the Catholics from the Van Acker government in 1945 could be seen as part of that strategy. Once the social security bill had been voted, all efforts went into securing an absolute majority. The 1946 election result showed that the Catholic Party had inherited a lot of Rex and VNV votes and that prospects were good to win a full majority later. It made its 1947 government participation conditional on amnesty measures in an attempt to win over the pro-Flemish right wing, which already showed results in the 1949 elections. The elections had brought an absolute majority tantalisingly close and the result of the royal referendum made it almost a foregone conclusion. It can hardly be a coincidence that the subsequent crisis resulted in new elections and a CVP victory. It is plausible to assume that the climax of the Royal Question in April-June 1950 was part of that strategy. After the creation of the all-Catholic Duvieusart government, the king proposed the creation of a grand coalition and apparently, the Catholic hierarchy did not like the idea. This hypothesis makes it plausible that the protocol of 15 April 1950 met with CVP resistance. The choice of the Catholic government to back the principle of abdication on 1 July 1950 was certainly linked to the fear of the moderates of the destabilising effect of army interference, a potential civil war and the break-up of Belgium. But it also had to do with the fear of the CVP that it would be no longer possible to rule on its own after such a traumatic conflict.

Other observers point to the obstinacy of the king himself and his views on the monarchy and executive power. Leopold did the left – and its fears of the royalist right and the restriction of the parliamentary regime – a big favour by refusing to justify his war actions and reacting coolly to the allied victors and the resistance. By vetoing the London government, he ruled out a compromise at first. His political testament was proof that the king was convinced he had been right all along. His views on royal executive power also left precious little room for manoeuvre. He obstinately continued to stick to those ideas – as the white paper illustrated – and the problem escalated into the 1950 crisis and his forced abdication. His consultation of General Van Overstraeten immediately on his return in 1950, and his belated attempt to replace the Duvieusart government during the night of July 31, 1950, and replace it with a core cabinet of prominent non-political party figures were the last illustrations of his political vision. His views on the monarchy were also reflected in his insistence on a referendum and his determination to have the referendum result observed by a government of national union. This referendum strategy made it possible to deny the parties a direct say in the question of his return and to call on important sectors of the population who backed the monarchy. The strategy backfired since it went against Catholic policy and reinforced left-wing opposition.

In the end, Leopold chose to safeguard the monarchy and his dynasty instead of endangering the unity of the nation. This last chapter in Leopold's saga is one of the few things on which the key players have had no fundamental differences of opinion. The concept of the constitutional monarchy and the Saxe-Coburg dynasty were never in question. Prince Karel, Leopold's brother, had been regent since the liberation and his constitutional stance restored confidence in the monarchy. During the crisis of 1949-1950 he used his influence and actively searched for a solution that could bridge the left-right divide.

The hard-line Leopold supporters were bitter and disappointed and turned their wrath against the CVP. Since the Catholic politicians had succumbed to pressure, they were now traitors. The right wing within the party wanted to settle accounts with the moderates and the left wing. To keep the issue from escalating, an investigative commission was set up and some moderates were temporarily sidelined. It is beyond doubt that the abdication caused a crisis within the CVP. It lost some of its trustworthiness and at the 1954 elections there were still some Catholic breakaway lists. The Catholics were able to restore the unity of the party around the School War. Based on new studies, some authors claim that Lahaut's murder was part of a reactionary plan of Leopoldist ultras. It was meant to be a provocation to increase tension even further, giving the establishment of an authoritarian regime another chance. It failed because the communists did not fall for the provocation and since there was no more room for anti-democratic forces within the Belgian political climate.

Integration into the Western Bloc

Post-war renewal was specifically evident in foreign affairs. Belgium shed its neutrality policy during and immediately after the war and became a country that had an important role in the creation and stabilisation of Western Europe within the U.S. sphere of influence.

The origins of the change are predominantly to be found in the war itself. The conflict between Leopold and the government can essentially be reduced to the question whether Belgium should join France and Britain in opposing Germany. The king did not want to; the government did. In exile, the government tried to cooperate as closely as possible with Britain and rejected any concept of neutrality out of hand. The traditional ties with France and the Netherlands were reinforced, and when the United States joined the war, the government in exile had little trouble in befriending them, too. The Pierlot government was fully committed to the Allied cause and invested all its energy in the war effort to unconditionally defeat the Axis powers. In this cause, it was even willing to cede part of Belgium's sovereignty. So overall, the main goal of the government in exile was to boost cooperation with the Allied powers.

The Belgian government hoped that the founding of the United Nations would be able to keep peace and promote collective security and economic reconstruction. The Belgian government may not have been directly involved in the preparatory work to create the international organisation, but it did send a delegation to the Conference of San Francisco and became a member in 1945.

Close cooperation between the Belgian government and the Western world gained a new, important impetus after the liberation. From about 1946-1947, there was increasing fear among proponents of the Western liberal system that Soviet Communism would threaten the very basis of the European capitalist model. Communist coups were considered a possibility in many West European nations, including Belgium. There was grave danger in the economic crisis and social unrest. The United States had every interest in keeping the Western world out of the grip of the Soviet Union and communism. One way to deal with this was to get the West European economies back on their feet as quickly as possible. Washington had to reconvert its war economy into a peace economy and to boost U.S. employment and expand foreign markets, the U.S. administration started an economic aid policy. Modest at first, it turned into the massive Marshall Plan aid programme in 1947, named after the Foreign Secretary G. Marshall. West European nations, suffering from great material losses and a shortage of cash, were all too happy to accept the U.S. offer. They bought cheap goods and equipment in the dollar zone. They also obtained credit to engage in large-scale reconstruction. In order to distribute and budget this American help, a special body was founded, the Organisation for European Economic Co-operation (OEEC); many countries joined this new organisation.

Belgium was enthusiastic about the Marshall Plan. Industrialists and investors immediately saw the potential of a quick economic recovery, especially since Belgium's production and export capacity had not suffered as badly as some other European nations'. The socialists and their union were also duly impressed by the opportunities offered by the American aid programme in their quest for economic recovery. The government gladly accepted the invitation to negotiate Belgian participation in the U.S. plan and even took initiatives in searching for solutions for certain technical questions. Parliament overwhelmingly approved membership of the OEEC, ensuring that Belgium obtained hundreds of millions of dollars in reconstruction aid; only the communist factions opposed the plan.

The Soviet Union obviously protested against the U.S. strategy of economic aid, which led to the division of Europe into two blocs, with the U.S. gaining the leadership over Western Europe. The Marshall Plan, in other words, ushered in the Cold War and led to the withdrawal of the communists from West European governments. By accepting the U.S. aid, Belgium de facto chose to belong to the Western camp.

These developments increased the mistrust between East and West and the fundamental divide became ever more apparent. The year 1948 was marked by the communist coup in Prague and the Soviet resistance against the independent policy of Yugoslav leader Tito. The most significant event, however, was the Soviet blockade of Berlin, which prompted the Western airlift to fly in provisions.

Because the United Nations could not break the stalemate of the Cold War, West European nations tried to set up regional security arrangements in an atmosphere of growing polarisation. There was a growing sense that precautionary measures had to be taken against the Soviet Union. London took the initiative and in 1948, a regional organisation to build a common defence was set up between Britain, France and the Benelux countries. It was a move the United States heartily applauded.

Belgium played an important role in the creation of this Brussels Treaty. As a small country that had been invaded twice in less than thirty years, Belgium was in need of military and diplomatic guarantees in case the United Nations failed. The Pierlot government in exile had already made it clear during the war itself that Belgium wanted to be part of a regional security organisation. But as long as the KPB was part of the government, such an initiative could not get off the ground. When the Cold War gradually intensified, the government was able to come forward as a true proponent of such an organisation. It did not only agree to the British proposals, but actively contributed to the realisation of the Brussels Treaty, which was ratified by parliament without any problems.

Belgium continued to be just as positive when, in the wake of the Brussels Treaty, negotiations were expanded to include Canada and the United States. It eventually led to the creation of the North Atlantic Treaty Organisation on 4 April 1949. The military and political alliance was partly created after independent attempts to set up a European defence system failed to gather pace, mainly because of internal strife and the fear for a resurgence of German militarism. Twelve nations, including Belgium, joined NATO and thus put the fate of Western Europe in American hands, since the United States, as the strongest ally, took on a predominating role. The Pax Americana was established in Europe.

Belgium's post-war foreign policy was strongly influenced by the events of the war. Belgium sought to be part of many more political and military alliances than it did after the First World War. The kingdom sacrificed a great deal of its national constitutional sovereignty and any hint of neutral or independent policy was suppressed.

Belgium made itself politically, economically and military subservient to the United States and as such was fundamentally integrated in American policy. An important part of foreign policy escaped the control of the government and parliament. Belgium's security policy was entirely decided by the Western alliance. Military and foreign policy became part of the U.S. strategy and the government also backed the United States within the

United Nations. It was a one-sided policy that put Belgium firmly within the U.S. sphere of influence, also in its relations with the communist world.

Also on this topic, not all factors explaining this remarkable evolution are known as yet; as such, this introduction has to limit itself to hypotheses. It can be said that the Royal Question played an important role in this process of transformation. The conflict between king and government made sure that for the first time since independence a government was able to set foreign policy without royal interference. Regent Karel preferred to stay on the foreign policy sidelines, and the London government was able to continue its own policy without worrying about the head of state. The post-war parliament was overwhelmed by the newly created international dimension of foreign policy and it gave the government and the foreign affairs minister unprecedented freedom to chart Belgium's international course.

Socialist P.-H. Spaak was a committed proponent of Western unity and a faithful defender of British and U.S. interests. As Minister of Foreign Affairs, Spaak showed himself to be a most eloquent defender of the Western bloc; he was already personally involved in the creation of this Western political bloc during his war years in London and in 1946 he chaired the first general assembly of the United Nations. He was also offered the chairmanship of the Marshall Plan's OEEC. It was Spaak who had drafted the first plans for a tightly-woven West European military cooperation. He also made sure that within NATO, Belgium would become one of the most faithful U.S. allies in Europe. Obviously, the important role he played on the international stage reflected on his position as Belgian Minister of Foreign Affairs.

But it was not only his international reputation that earned him this respect; the Belgian establishment also strongly backed him. Big business and the financial world also supported the pro-U.S. stance, while Spaak was still able to rely on the backing of the major part of his own party and an important part of the political right; a number of prominent union leaders could also agree with his foreign policies. At first, he had to take KPB opposition into account but as the power of the communists waned, Belgium was able to become an unconditional participant in the Pax Americana.

Chapter VII
Conflict and Conflict Management in the Religious-Philosophical Sphere

The Catholics and freethinkers had been at loggerheads since the creation of Belgium, fighting over the role of the Church and religion in society. That battle entered another crucial phase during the 1950s. Wide layers of society were being integrated in the social political system through the cultural sector, which became a key ideological battleground. Secondary education and leisure directly and massively became part of the democratisation of society. The Catholics wanted to hold on to their organisational and ideological control of the process while the freethinkers wanted a neutral state to take charge. The majority position won by the CVP in the 1950 elections further polarised the conflict, setting the stage for the second School War. The 1959 compromise that ended the conflict largely met the Catholic demands but also recognised a number of interests of the freethinkers' movement and further institutionalised the pillarisation of Belgian society. The most important rule to pacify both sides was the application of proportional representation of the political and ideological forces in whatever conflict zone under discussion. Because of its numerical strength, the Catholic pillar was able to hold on to its control of education and the socio-cultural sector in Flanders. In southern Belgium, the freethinkers were the dominant force. The advent of the secular society, as was the case in much of Europe starting with the 'golden sixties', did not really affect the political power of the Catholic, Socialist and Liberal pillars. But it did introduce far-reaching ideological pluralism at the basis, which was apparent within the party structure. It reduced the impact of the clerical-anticlerical conflict zone. The abortion and euthanasia issues and their liberalising solution at the turn of the century proved that the Catholic vision was no longer predominant in Flanders or in Belgium.

The School War and School Pact (1950-1959)

In order to understand the impasse developing between Catholics and non-Catholics between 1950 and 1958 concerning the issue of education, it may be useful to recap the different viewpoints. In their quest to build a Christian society, the Catholics had always insisted on the fact that religion should dominate education. Neutrality was seen as the opposite, and thus rejected. The Catholics preferred to create their own private schools, opposed neutral public education where possible and tried to control it when it did start to flourish. Plentiful state subsidies needed to safeguard the existence and domination of the Catholic educational network. The freethinkers defended the opposite point of view: because of the constitutional freedom of speech, the state had to make sure there were enough publicly funded schools with neutral education, open to everyone. Subsidies for private education allowed the state to supervise the use of funding and to restrict competition with public education. Ever since independence in 1830, the Catholics had set the tone for educational policy. At the level of primary schools there was almost no neutral education available outside a few big cities with non-Catholic municipal governments. But even at the level of secondary and technical education, the creation of public schools depended on the consent of government and parliament, and since the Catholics had been in government almost throughout the 1884-1950 period, the expansion of public schools had been minimal. The absence of an organic law meant that the state had not been able to open a technical school before 1937 while the number of public secondary schools remained low. The expansion of public secondary education was even capped up to 1934, after which the limits were dropped. Private Catholic education had been able to expand as much as it wanted and private primary schools were granted the necessary subsidies.

The post-war situation gave a new twist to the debate. After 1945, industry, trade and the service sector needed better qualified and better trained workers. It put the spotlight on secondary education. It no longer was a monopoly of the bourgeoisie and since the schools had to welcome the great masses, secondary education became a political instrument. The baby boom after the war also made clear secondary education would only gain in importance. The left wanted to broaden its recruitment base by expanding public education. They hoped democratic technical and secondary schools would become a bulwark against further Catholic domination. The socialist education ministers between 1945 and 1947 tried to set a policy to lift the restrictions and allow the state to set up new initiatives to promote free public education at all levels.

School fees had been of secondary importance as long as the pupils came from bourgeois families. But now that also the less wealthy were to be welcomed massively, funding became an essential element in Catholic secondary education. The majority of secondary schools (53.5 %) were still in Catholic hands before 1950 but there was a fear that the school fees and salary cuts of teachers would become a heavy burden in the upcoming battle with public education. In the course of the 1930s, the limitations on the expansion of public secondary education had been formally lifted. The post-war CVP-PSC wanted to limit the growth potential of public education and reinforce the Christian foundation of the existing public schools through the introduction of Catholic teachers. At the same time, funding for private education had to be increased. The clergy still defined this policy as a religious battle, with the interests of the Church at stake. The CVP-PSC, however, sought their arguments in the constitutional principles of freedom and equality. Catholic parents had to have the right to send their children to subsidised private schools.

In this crucial battle, the Catholics could count on an extremely strong and cohesive pillar. Created in between the two wars, it was in full expansion after World War II. The clergy and the Church hierarchy were the core of the pillar, and from that position they were able to control the other organisations and grant religious legitimacy. The Church relied on its parishes, bishoprics, schools and charities to spread the word. This basic layer was reinforced by many cultural lay organisations with a strong religious-philosophical identity, such as youth and women's organisations and general educational groups. The next layer consisted of the cultural and socio-economic organisations like the *Davidsfonds*, the Christian labour movement and the *Boerenbond* and employers' organisations. The cornerstone of the entire edifice was the party itself, providing unity and cohesion on a political level. The moral authority of the bishops gave the pillar a strong ideological cohesion and ensured votes for CVP-PSC became a matter of conscience. The Catholic pillar was a cradle-to-grave organisation. The institutions were closely intertwined and memberships overlapped, leading Catholics by the hand throughout their lives. Catholic education was a key link in the long chain.

The Catholic demand to expand state subsidies was already part of the CVP-PSC 1945 Christmas programme. The party set the funding of private technical education as a precondition to participation in the 1947 Spaak government. The first education crisis hit the government in April 1948 but was solved by increasing the subsidies for private technical education while the first steps were taken to put religion and non-confessional social studies on an equal footing; the right to state initiative in education was politically recognised. The CVP-PSC congress of 1948, however, stated clearly that all private schools had to be subsidised and in the election campaigns of 1949 and 1950, the education issue was second only to the Royal Question. Education was an issue that always mobilised voters and this consideration was certainly part of the Catholic strategy to obtain a majority. After the Catholics won their parliamentary majority, P. Harmel of the PSC became education minister from 1950 to 1954.

The Catholic education policy made its first impact in June 1950, when Harmel doubled the subsidies for private secondary education, allowing wages to rise and tuition fees to go down. Teachers without a proper degree were in a majority in private education, but the government decreed that once they had seven years' experience they would be paid as much as teachers with a degree. The organic laws of 1952 and 1953 linked state subsidies to the number of pupils at the different Catholic levels. A legal basis for the creation of public technical schools was provided, but it was restricted by a number of conditions. Since the municipality or province had to approve new schools, it was nearly impossible to expand the public technical network in Catholic Flanders. Joint committees had to approve new state initiatives and make recommendations on the educational programmes. Graduates from private education were given extensive possibilities to teach in public schools but the bishops forced them to send their own children to Catholic schools.

The freethinkers obviously considered the Harmel laws a declaration of war. They did not contest the principle of subsidies but their size; they also demanded more stringent controls on the use of the funds. They considered it a Catholic plot to keep public education a poor second in the schooling system, and the establishment of the right of control by the Catholics over constitutional state initiatives concerning education only served to strengthen this view.

Even if they wanted to react strongly, the freethinkers were in a much weaker position than the Catholics on the political battleground. They lacked organisational unity and the occupation had had a negative impact on their militant associations. They were spread over different pillars – the socialist, liberal and communist ones – that competed against one another on the socio-economic level. They each had their own unions, their own health programmes and hospitals, their own credit institutions, their own youth and women's associations and their own cultural societies. The socialists had a strong and cohesive pillar, with more loyal grassroots support; the liberal pillar looked somewhat shakier but still kept its grassroots support together. On education, the liberals were more elitist than the socialists and the party political divisions reduced the freethinkers' education policy to a minimum programme. It was aimed at overturning the Catholic laws that were obstructing the division between Church and state and at defending the development of the secular society. The party political differences made for a hardly cohesive political force.

The first task of the divergent anti-clerical groups was to join forces and organise resistance against Catholic dominance. Several associations played and active role, among them the *Ligue de l'Enseignement*, humanist organisations and education unions: the socialist ACOD (*Algemene Centrale der Openbare Diensten* – General Central of Public Services), the *Vereniging van Socialistisch Onderwijspersoneel* (Association of Socialist Education Personnel), the *Algemeen Verbond ter Bevordering van het Officieel Onderwijs* (General Association for the Promotion of Official Education), the *Liberaal Vlaams Verbond* (Liberal Flemish Association) and the liberal education union. The freemasons also took a stand, but their authority had taken a serious blow since the 19th century. Membership had dwindled to a few thousand and it covered the entire political spectrum, from Marxists to liberals, from deists to atheists, from Jews to Protestants. They did not belong to the core of the freethinkers and when they did take part in the debate, it was more on questions of a more general humanist nature. Their role in the School War was limited compared to that of the freethinkers. Soon after the war, the modern humanists argued in favour of a separate level for the non-religious part of the population and they set up associations to achieve that goal. Neutral education was their unconditional demand, and they mobilised their associations to that goal.

The anticlerical groups organised demonstrations and set up other protest actions. But they concentrated most of their efforts on the 1954 election campaign. It paid off since the socialist and liberals made enough gains to undo the Catholic majority in parliament: the CVP-PSC lost thirteen seats in the Chamber and five in the Senate. Socialist A. Van Acker brokered a Liberal-Socialist coalition that would remain in power until the 1958 elections.

Education minister L. Collard immediately went to work to undo the Catholic education laws. The joint commissions were abolished, the number of graduates decreased, and in public schools the choice between classes of religion or non-confessional moral studies was fully guaranteed, both in Belgium and in the colony. The state was also given the right to set up autonomous public primary schools. Private school subsidies were not questioned as such and the level of salaries was not affected, but the subsidies were made dependent on a number of criteria. Wages were paid out directly to teachers, making sure private schools could not use those funds for other purposes. The profession of teacher was protected and degrees became mandatory. Scores of private school teachers without degrees – only 6 % of 2,688 priests teaching in schools had a proper degree – could no longer claim full financial equality. Small schools had to be restructured, a move that would hit Catholic secondary schools since 43 % of them had fewer than 100 students.

Especially these last restrictions and the fact that state initiatives could be widely extended, enraged the Catholics, and new measures only made it worse. Some 110 interim-teachers with a Catholic degree were dismissed and the budget for private education was cut. It was considered a provocation and the whole Catholic pillar was mobilised in a campaign against the government. T. Lefèvre was the leader of the *Nationaal Comité voor Vrijheid en Democratie* (National Committee for Freedom and Democracy), a group that included CVP-PSC leaders and leading figures from the Catholic pillar organisations. Frequent protests by the bishops resulted in a School and Family Fund. It became a mass protest movement that used all legislative and non-parliamentary means at its disposal. Twice between March and July 1955, tens of thousands of demonstrators took to the streets. Most of the demonstrators came from Flanders, were parish churches flew a black flag. Over two million people signed a petition. School strikes, non-cooperation in official events, and boycotts of state savings accounts and suspected 'freethinkers' products' only added more pressure. After the law was voted through parliament, the Catholic mobilisation weakened. It was the main campaign issue for the 1958 elections, though, and it gave the Catholics a resounding victory as they surged from 95 to 104 seats in the Chamber, but it was not enough for a majority government. G.

Eyskens was allowed to lead a minority government, only on the condition that the CVP-PSC would work on a compromise solution for the protracted education issue.

At last, all political parties were showing the political will to end the School War. The Catholics realised they lacked the majority to restore the Harmel laws. The left wing of the BSP-PSB no longer wanted to cooperate with the liberals, and union circles were beginning to show signs of more extreme views. These factions had gained importance because of the 1958 electoral defeat. The liberals wanted to rule with the Catholics but could not do so unless they buried the School War hatchet. A special procedure was set up to solve the problem. The party leaders pushed the pressure groups and legislators aside and set up a joint education committee to negotiate in a spirit of compromise. It resulted in the School Pact of 6 November 1958. It covered a twelve-year period and set up a permanent School Pact commission that would manage the system. Parliament ratified the Pact on 29 May 1959; party discipline obviously played a key role in the vote.

The compromise was based on the principle of parental choice – they had to be able to send their children to a school of their ideological choice within a reasonable distance from their home. It meant that public education was allowed to expand its network while new state subsidies would make sure private, Catholic education was free of charge. Wages and management funds would be guaranteed by the state leaving only the maintenance and construction costs of the school buildings in private hands. The neutral character of public schools was guaranteed by a staff of teachers, two thirds of whom had to have a public school degree, and there had to be a mandatory choice between courses in religion and non-confessional social studies. Criteria on pupil enrolment, school programmes and degrees were also laid down by law, and soon gave the Catholics a considerable edge. The effect was a qualitative improvement of teaching, and thanks to the efficient coordinating role of the *Nationaal Secretariaat van het Katholiek Onderwijs* (NSKO, National Secretariat of Catholic Education) the Catholic education system got the structural backbone it had lacked before. The CVP-PSC was able to use the School Pact to maintain and even expand the domination of Catholic schools. Enrolment in higher secondary education was a case in point: over the period of the School Pact, its number of pupils rose from 59.9 to 63.7 %. At the end of the period, in 1972, 66.7 % of Flemish pupils was attending a Catholic school, and 17.6 % a public school; in the francophone part of the country, the ratio was 42.4 % in the public schools and 20.9 % in the Catholic schools.

Pluralism, Secularisation and 'Socio-Cultural Catholicism'

The School Pact had a far-reaching effect on the political system. Polarisation and escalation were by and large a thing of the past. Instead of the ruthless quest for a parliamentary majority came consultation and the principle of proportional representation. The rules to solve conflict through negotiations had been laid down and they were also used to solve cultural and philosophical issues. The rights of ideological groups were institutionalised and the attribution of subsidies reflected their numerical strength, reinforcing the powers of the pillars. It largely neutralised the Catholic-anticlerical conflict but liberated that energy for other political struggles. It brought the social-economic and language issues to the fore. The religious-philosophical factor did not disappear altogether, but gradually left the political scene.

The changes within the Liberal Party were a good example of this trend. It had been foundering since the war and its electoral percentage rarely went into double digits. But now that the school pact was signed, the liberals were ready to start a renewal of the party. At the urgent request of their chairman, O. Vanaudenhoven, the party tempered its anti-clericalism, opened up its ranks to Catholics and primarily focused its efforts again on the defence of economic liberalism and anti-collectivism. The party changed its name in 1961 to become the *Partij voor Vrijheid en Vooruitgang-Parti de la Liberté et du Progrès* (PVV-PLP, Party for Freedom and Progress). The change worked well; at the next elections (1965) they were able to attract the Catholic liberals and increase their share of the vote to 20 %. By 1968, half of its electorate consisted of practicing Catholics; this severely weakened the position of the freethinkers in the party. The change of direction was emphasised further when the 'neo-liberals' of Guy Verhofstadt swept to power in the Flemish PVV. They opened up their ranks further to include Catholics and Flemish nationalists.

The Liberal change left it up to the Socialist Party to defend the anticlerical interests and the position of public education. But the socialists, too, opened up their ranks to left-leaning Christians. During the Catholic-Socialist government of Spaak-Lefèvre (1961-1965), both trade unions cooperated and defended joint positions. On 1 May 1969, Socialist Party chairman L. Collard appealed to left-wing Christians to breach the pillar structure and join the workers' forces. It largely fell on deaf ears within the Christian labour movement. In Wallonia, a left-wing labour front spanning the religious divide stood a better chance, though it created constant strife within the Catholic *Mouvement Ouvrier Chrétien* (MOC). In Flanders the issue was kept alive by intellectuals who were left on the fringes of the party and the labour movement, among them the editors of *De Nieuwe Maand* (1971). When the BSP-PSB split along linguistic lines in 1978, the Flemish SP rekindled the idea, as they were looking for an expansion of their electorate. The socialists were not only targeting the Catholic ACW, but also all Christian progressives. Party membership was no longer automatically linked to membership of other branches of the *Gemeenschappelijke Actie* (Joint Action), and in 1982, the Flemish socialists opened up their electoral lists to non-party members. The socialists also tried to attract the environmental and peace groups, and the politically homeless from the Catholic pillar.

The process of pacification on the philosophical level also paved the way for the simmering language tensions to lead to the creation of several parties, including the Flemish *Volksunie*, the francophone *Front des Francophones* and the *Rassemblement Wallon*, all of them more or less pluralist in character.A few environmental parties also emerged. Especially *Agalev*, with its origins in Christian circles, quickly opposed the whole Belgian pillarised political structure and wanted a renewal and expansion of democracy, defending philosophical tolerance.

The political developments pushed the militant freethinkers' movement ever more to the edge of the party structures and into humanist associations. The activities of these humanist associations expanded because of the School Pact, the newfound status of non-confessional moral studies, support for the associations and guaranteed use of the media. But most of the non-religious sections of society did not really want independent structures, forcing the humanist associations to recruit primarily among intellectual groups within education, administration and the socio-cultural sector. Since subsidies were based on proportional representation, such a situation meant fairly limited funding. Yet this was not reflected in a lack of organisational activities. In Flanders, the *Humanistisch Verbond* (Humanist Union) was founded in 1951; the 1971 *Unie van Vrijzinnige Verenigingen* (Union of Freethinkers' Associations) umbrella organisation helped organise local action and alternative activities for the non-religious section of society. It included humanist help in hospitals and prisons. Cultural activities stressing the development of young people and the use of the media were also set up. There was a similar development in francophone Belgium, where rationalist and humanist organisations joined under the *Centre d'Action Laique* (CAL) umbrella organisation with a fairly complex federal structure. In 1980, parliament approved funds for the *Centrale Vrijzinnige Raad* (Central Freethinkers' Council), consisting of UVV, and CAL and the secular society was granted constitutional recognition in 1993. Under the Socialist-Liberal-Green Verhofstadt government (without the Christian democrats) the 2002 law on the structuring and subsidising of organised freethinkers' philosophy was voted. In each province, a non-confessional society was recognised, with Brussels getting two. Each of these twelve societies was granted staff and housing. Additional centres can be founded locally, with the funding coming from the provinces and the Brussels' Capital Region. It allowed the freethinkers' movement to be institutionalised within the existing pillarised system. There was no longer a strict call for a division between Church and state and instead room was made for a juxtaposition of religious philosophical groups based on tolerance. The Socialist-Liberal-Green government did again open up the discussion on the mixing of public and religious ceremonies (e.g. the *Te Deum*).

From the mid-1960s onwards, the secular movement quickly affected the Catholic pillar. Progress in society was based on rational technology and was evident in increasing automation, increased productivity and higher wages, turning large parts of the population into prime consumers. Tolerance and the anti-authoritarian mentality turned against Catholic authority and religious duties. Mass media, the opening up of rural society, increased women's labour, the commercial leisure industry and the creation of Third World and environmental action groups all eroded organised Catholicism.

Encroaching secularism also hit at the heart of the Catholic pillar. Ever more priests and monks left and the traditional stream of vocations turned to a trickle. More obvious even was the speedy decrease in attendance for religious services. In twenty years, the rate of faithful churchgoers dwindled to a mere 14 % of the population. The Church's moral rules on marriage were ignored by a majority of Catholics. Yet it did not affect state subsidies since the Church received funds based on the people living in their parish, not on the number of churchgoers. The core of Catholicism was also undermined from within the pillar. Because of an increasing reliance on lay teachers, ideological divergence spread within Catholic education. Structured religion also lost out in the health and social care sector, for the same reasons. This tendency was even more striking in the unions. The success of the pluralist parties, even among churchgoing Catholics, showed how Church hierarchy had lost its grip. During the 1960s and 1970s, the Catholic pillar increasingly consisted of members whose direct link with religion was severely weakened. The regular churchgoers steadily became a minority, and 'seasonal Catholics' and irregular churchgoers the majority.

Paradoxically, the decrease in church practice had no negative impact on the membership of the pillar organisations. On the contrary, membership totals increased in the trade union, education and cultural sectors, especially in Flanders. Religion-sociologists have explained this seeming contradiction by developing the concept of 'socio-cultural Catholicity' which became a surrogate for the slumping Catholic religion as such. People maintained their own specific climate of life and thought, in which the traditional Christian values could be given a place, as a result of a long process of socialisation in a world dominated by the Church. Those Christian values were equated with the values of Western society and humanity as such. The Catholic identity, which the pillar guaranteed, thus gave its members a sense of moral and social superiority. It turned into the Catholic pillar's most efficient protection. The pillar also drew its strength from its role in the functioning of the state. The Catholic sense of class cooperation, solidarity between capital and labour and its preference for free-market policies all served the ruling socio-economic model. Increased employment within the pillar and party political appointments made a great many families dependent upon the system and the pillar became an engine for social promotion. Further centralisation and permanent structural coordination between the different organisations of the pillar, combined with cohesion on the political level, contributed to the success of this 'social-cultural Catholicity'.

The strength of the pillar gave discordant opinions no chance. Calls for an independent Christian labour movement went nowhere. In the early 1980s, some Flemish progressive-Christian circles considered the desirability of a new autonomous party, or even a pluralistic workers' party together with the socialists, but both options never made it beyond a minority idea. Only a few jumped ship to the SP, and the majority remained loyal to the CVP. When the Catholic trade union set a more radical course under its new chairman Willy Peirens, it reinforced unity within the Christian labour movement. The situation in Wallonia was different since the socialist union was a lot stronger there; the ties with the PSC were broken there. The foundation of *Solidarité et Participation* in 1982 saw to that. But SeP never meant anything as a party. The merger with the PS did happen, in the nineties.

In conclusion of this section, something needs to be said about the recognition of Islam in Belgium. As a result of immigration, this religion started to show itself to a much greater extent since the 1960s. From the beginning, Muslims concentrated on establishing their own institutions (religious spaces with their own imams) in order to secure the continuity of their religion. In 1974, the Islam was put on an equal level with the other recognised religions. This mainly had its effect in education, and was hardly felt in other sectors, mainly because of the fear of advancing fundamentalism – a spectre that was raised after 9/11 and fully exploited by the extreme right – but also because of the diversity within Islam, which hampers the establishment of a generally recognised umbrella organisation. In 1998, a representative body of the Islamic religion was first elected. The council chosen in 2005 has to make suggestions concerning mosques and imams in local communities. The financial authorities, especially in Flanders, make a priority of transparency in this respect.

The Federalisation of Education and Culture

The strong position of the Catholic pillar allowed the CVP to play a primordial role on the religious-philosophical level during the 1970s and, as the linguistic dispute flared, it was increasingly unwilling to make concessions to the ideological minorities in Wallonia. Anti-clericalism was on the rise south of the linguistic border and in Flanders, the Catholics became ever more conceited. Because of its numerical strength, the CVP-PSC was an indispensable partner in government, causing a real CVP-trauma among the anti-clericals. Especially in Flanders, freethinkers felt repressed as a minority.

Freethinkers referred to the education and cultural policies of the CVP as prime examples of the Catholic power. There were few changes as far as objectives were concerned; the Catholics just insisted on more subsidies and rationalisation of the public education system. They considered it a legitimate demand since parents increasingly sent their children to private

Catholic schools. They wanted a coherent Christian education in a uniform ideological climate. The concept of pluralist schools had been a short-lived idea, and only in Christian left-wing circles. The CVP wanted funds for student transport, extra personnel and extra-curricular activities. They wanted priests and other religious teachers to be paid as much as their lay counterparts and insisted on subsidies for construction and maintenance costs without property rights being affected. In November 1970, the CVP made it clear it wanted a review of the School Pact. A special commission, speaking for the NSKO, was established, and in every successive government crisis between 1971 and 1973, the CVP raised the same demands. In July 1973, it was rewarded with a reform package in return for backing the Catholic-Socialist coalition of monolingual francophone socialist E. Leburton. The Catholics won most of their financial demands. Pay scales were adapted and a fund, providing long-term and low interest loans, was created to build and renovate schools. In compensation, public schools would be able to extend the rate of their own alumni in their staff to three quarters.

At the same time, progress had been made on the federalisation of cultural issues, a longstanding demand of the Flemish movement. The 1970 constitutional reform created two culture councils and gave them decision-making powers on a series of cultural issues. Naturally, the CVP dominated the Flemish Cultural Council and, backed by the Flemish nationalist *Volksunie* (VU), tried to federalise education as much as possible. The anti-clericals realised this would put public education under threat and opposed the concept. The francophone PSC Catholics rejected the idea, too, since they wanted to protect Catholic private education in anti-clerical Wallonia. In the end, the issues that had already been dealt with in the School Pact were not federalised.

The creation of the Culture Pact should be seen in the same light. The chairman of the liberal *Willemsfonds,* A. Verhulst, took the initiative in 1973 with its proposal to extend the School Pact into the cultural field. By 1974, the bill had become a decree. The protection and rights of ideological and philosophical minorities were guaranteed on the basis of proportionality, safeguarding the rights of freethinkers in Flanders and Catholics in Wallonia. The *Vaste Nationale Cultuurpactcommissie* (Permanent National Culture Pact Committee) was created to oversee the application of the pact. But the CVP's political power made sure that Catholic cultural dominance in Flanders was prolonged and that CVP ministers had authority over the issue until 1981. The Committee did not work efficiently in the 1970s, either. When federalisation was extended to new cultural and individual issues in 1980, the Flemish lobby of freethinkers wanted to expand the Culture Pact to include these issues as well. But the CVP resisted any such attempt and the status quo was maintained.

The 1981 Catholic-Liberal coalition of W. Martens returned the Flemish education portfolio to the CVP after 22 years of socialist-liberal management of public education. The reign of Minister Coens was marked by a constant search for a 'level playing field' for both the francophone and Flemish communities and for both public and subsidised private education. The state was barred from giving its own educational system preferential treatment and in consequence the Catholic schools were given an additional 5,700 new jobs. The austerity measures of the time also had a big impact on education. School construction funds and operational subsidies were restricted, staffing ratios tightened and personnel costs drastically cut. The austerity policy went hand in hand with an overhaul of the educational programme to meet the economic realities of the 1980s. This rationalisation, reorganisation and cost-cutting hit francophone education hardest; in Flanders, public education suffered most. It left the Flemish state school system traumatised – in just seven years it lost 18 % of its personnel and 13 % of its pupils. It meant the end of the School Pact Commission since all the measures were approved by special decree, disregarding the concept of consensus decision-making.

The public school sector's confidence had been badly shaken and it put its last hope in a demand for an Autonomous Council, which would not directly fall under the authority of the minister nor be affected by fickle political trends. The PVV and SP also wanted such protection to be guaranteed in the constitution and made it a precondition before education could be fully federalised, as the CVP and VU wanted. The PSC opposed such a move, though, since it would put Walloon Catholic education at the mercy of the socialists. Negotiations on the issue could only start once the PSC had been given financial guarantees on the survival of francophone Catholic education. Following a broad agreement between the CVP, PVV, SP and VU, the *Autonome Raad voor het Gemeenschapsonderwijs* (ARGO, Autonomous Council for Public Education) was created in 1988 in Flanders. In francophone Belgium, the management of public education was handed over to the minister of the French Community.

During the coalition talks in 1988, much attention was given to rewriting article 17 of the Constitution. The educational freedom of choice for parents was now guaranteed in the constitution as well as the right of the community to organise its own education and the right to organise education along religious-philosophical lines. The freedom of choice in public education between religion and non-confessional moral studies was confirmed. The duty to subsidise private education was also embedded in law. The principle of equality was qualified, though: the law and the decree could take into account 'objective differences, among which the specific characteristics of each organising power, justifying special treatment'. The *Arbitragehof* (Court of Arbitration) was given the power to annul any law or decree that countered this freedom of education.

So even when the Flemish education ministry came back into the hands of the socialists with minister L. Van den Bossche, austerity measures and the equation of both educational networks continued and were extended to higher education as well. Public schools continued to lose jobs while employment in the private, Catholic network kept increasing. Austerity measures were just as bad in francophone Belgium, even though cuts were more evenly balanced between both networks. The French Community was not given much leeway under the funding laws, making the consequences dramatic for the personnel. Francophone teachers went on strike for months at a time and took their protests onto the streets more than once during the first half of the 1990s.

Meanwhile in Flanders, the ARGO tried to reinvigorate public education. Local councils of teachers, parents, pupils and local socio-economic circles had to work out a strategy of expansion and overcome the malaise through efficient school management and innovative personnel statutes. These local councils have a degree of financial co-responsibility and have some control over hiring and promotions. Arguing that the bodies of public education have to reflect all tendencies in society, the Catholics gained a blocking minority within the Central Council and also a Catholic government commissioner. Operational subsidies for private education were now granted along the same principles, and they also got substantial extra subsidies. Under the Catholic-Liberal-Green government school groups were established in public education, and cooperation within and between the different networks was encouraged. ARGO now guarded investments and large-scale infrastructural works. Municipal and provincial schools were encouraged to become open schools and also offer non-confessional moral studies. Until 1988, the evolution of university education ran a more or less parallel course on both sides of the linguistic border. Both in Flanders and in Wallonia, the democratisation of higher education involved diversification of the universities, caused by regional interests and philosophical factors. Flanders had two big universities (*Katholieke Universiteit Leuven* and *Rijksuniversiteit Gent*), two medium-sized ones (*Vrije Universiteit Brussel* and the pluralist *Universiteit Antwerpen*) and three 'incomplete' ones (Catholic faculties in Kortrijk, *Katholieke Universiteit Brussel* and the pluralist *Limburgs Universitair Centrum*). On the francophone side, the *Université catholique de Louvain, Université Libre de Bruxelles* and *Université de Liège* were all similar in size; apart from these, there were also three 'incomplete' universities (a Catholic and a state institution in Mons and Catholic faculties in Namur and Brussels). After the federalisation of education, also universities had split up and gone their own ways. It was clearly shown again how far they had grown apart when the Bologna restructuring emerged in 1999 – through the introduction of the Bachelor-Master structure and cooperation between universities and other institutes of higher education a harmonisation of European higher education was the ultimate goal. In the francophone part of Belgium, the cooperation was brought about between universities at PhD level. In Flanders, associations were founded between a university and one or more polytechnics; among others, one big Catholic association was established. The programmes are or will be recognised by a special accreditation body in cooperation with the Netherlands.

Moral Themes as Political Issues

As in most Western democracies during the 1970s, moral issues gained the political high ground in Belgium too. Family planning, contraceptives, abortion, single motherhood, children out of wedlock, homosexuality, alternative forms of co-habitation, euthanasia and the like were all themes that flew straight in the face of Catholic views on life and death, procreation and sexuality, the ideal of the family with marriage as a central concept, and motherhood as the only and ultimate life-fulfilling aim of women.

The increasing secularisation set the tone for this evolution. People increasingly controlled material, physical, psychological and social aspects of reality and started to act according to their views, knowledge, planning and techniques rather than according to their religion. Principles organising life and giving sense to it, were being detached from religion and Church. The right to self-determination and the total autonomy of the mind became essential elements of anyone's individual rights. It was the breakthrough of the secular society and it affected progressive Christians too. Humanism's rationalist ideology spread through much of society and people felt attracted to the principles of individual responsibility, autonomous decision-making and freedom of thought. The time had finally come to profess that non-believers have different ideas about life and death than Christians, and that there should be room for their points of view in a pluralistic society.

The feminist movement had an important role to play in this process. The fight for the emancipation of women was being fought in the wake of the development of the consumer society, the increase in women's labour, better education for women, the dominant small, open family group and new family values where women were the equal of men and where motherhood no longer was the be-all and end-all. *Marie Mineur, Dolle Mina* (Mad Mina) and other feminist groups raised the awareness of women and let their voices be heard within parties and pillar organisations to demand equal pay for equal work and other rights. The effect of their efficient actions was soon felt: the legal position of women improved, they were given more professional opportunities, marriage was given a less central position, and countless inequalities between the sexes made it onto the political agenda. The political emancipation process was further galvanised with the institutionalisation of the feminist movement within advisory councils and ministries.

Abortion legislation became the key topic for the feminist movement and the secular forces during the 1970s. The issue was loaded with symbolism for both proponents and opponents. For Catholicism, abortion should be part of criminal law. The bishops maintained that women could only find complete self-fulfilment in motherhood. Life had to be respected from the moment of conception, and this general principle made any other claims illegal. The *Pro Vita* lobby was the most radical proponent of the Catholic view. The PSC and CVP backed the position of the bishops. Those who sought a liberalisation of abortion demanded that women be given the right to self-determination in case of an unwanted pregnancy. On top of that, illegal abortions were often extremely dangerous. A number of progressive Christians also backed abortion legislation and called it more in line with social reality.

In 1971, socialist senator W. Calewaert and two liberal senators proposed a bill, calling for a partial liberalisation of the abortion law, stirring up much reaction. The pro-abortion forces were fully released two years later when Dr. Peers, a socially engaged doctor in Namur was arrested and put on remand, accused of performing abortions. It brought the issue fully into the open and many proponents made their first public stand in favour of liberalisation. A long period of stagnation followed. The *Nationale Commissie voor Ethische Problemen* (National Committee for Ethical Issues) was set up in 1974 but made precious little progress over the next two years. No government took any initiative and the issue was left to parliament. Several more bills from socialist and liberal legislators were put forward, but the CVP-PSC was able to maintain its veto.

In reality, however, much had changed by the end of the 1970s. Abortions in hospitals became common practice and the judiciary rarely intervened. Around 1981 public prosecutors wanted to force the government and parliament into action and started to prosecute again. A pro-abortion lobby group used the trials to mobilise public opinion. A majority of the population considered the penal law outdated and in 1986 liberals and socialists both backed the abortion bill of Lallemand-Michielsen. The FDF and environmentalists added their votes to create an ad-hoc majority in the Senate. During the government coalition talks of 1988, the socialists made sure initiatives in the Chamber would be taken soon. From then on it all went very quickly. The Catholics tried in vain to stave off the inevitable; the CVP refused any dialogue, but the bill was also approved by the Chamber in March 1990.

King Baudouin let it be known that he considered the law unacceptable and that his conscience would not allow him to sign it. His convictions were steeped in traditional Catholicism and the backers of the abortion law considered it a slap in the face since parliament had already approved it. The king could count on sympathy among the population but in political circles his stand was very controversial. The king had allowed his private conviction to prevail over his executive duties. None of the coalition partners were willing to risk a government crisis over this, though, so in the end, a constitutional construction offered a way out. The king was declared ‘incapable to govern’ and his prerogatives were temporarily given to a united council of Ministers, which signed the law instead. Afterwards, parliament reinstated king Baudouin. The unlikely scenario was defended on the ground that parliament had the ultimate authority over the interpretation of the constitution. The king's refusal to sign the abortion law created a new debate on the role of the monarchy.

The abortion issue had other political consequences too and left the CVP nursing a severe trauma. The Catholic parties forced their socialist coalition partners to refrain from taking any initiative on ethical issues that could threaten the coalition. They also realised that militant Catholicism did not have a political majority anymore. The party would have to become more tolerant if it wanted to remain a broad centre party. The CVP-PSC became more progressive during the 1990s – up to a point; the Christian profile in both parties was still very strong. When a CVP chairman went through a divorce, he had to step aside. The forces of renewal within the PSC did not have an easy time during elections of a new chair. And even if Church and religion, more than ever before, are outside the everyday world of the numerous users of the organisations of the Catholic pillar, giving these institutions the status of powerful financial concerns, one should not forget the 'socio-cultural Catholicity' that the management of these organisations tries to maintain. Undeniably, though, resistance against the secularised approach of ethical, sexual and family problems has greatly diminished in the course of the 1990s and after the turn of the century.

In the meantime, homosexuals and lesbians had been fighting a long battle for equal rights since the 1970s. Several interest groups came into being, among them *Belgian Lesbian and Gay Pride*, which made the movement visible on the city streets. Apart from them, there were other so-called 'holebi' (homosexuals, lesbians, bi-sexuals) organisations that militantly created awareness in the general population and in the political world, which was starting to open up to their demands. Especially the socialists and environmentalists supported this movement.

All these developments provided the governments under the liberal Verhofstadt (in 1999 and 2003) with a wide basis to tackle ethically sensitive legislation. The fact that these governments did not include the Christian democrats demands some explanation. After long years in opposition, the liberals, and in particular the VLD (*Vlaamse Liberalen en Democraten* – Flemish Liberals and Democrats) felt the urge to take charge themselves and realise social renewal. The 1999 elections were important – no fewer than seven parliaments had to be elected – and the campaign was dominated by a dioxin crisis in the food sector (cf. infra). The biggest government party, i.e. the Christian democrats, paid the price, while the environmentalists scored a huge election victory. The liberals became the largest political formation, and Verhofstadt set up a coalition with socialists and greens; in 2003 the coalition would be limited to liberals and socialists, with the greens losing out. In the 1999 coalition agreement, the ethical issues received the necessary attention: on the basis of everyone's individual conscience and conviction, parliament was to take its full responsibility on all ethical issues – without having to take into consideration Christian-democratic protests.

The concrete realisations of the Liberal-Socialist(-Green) governments were to be found in four areas: marriage and family, drugs policy, bio-ethics and euthanasia. After having reached an agreement in advance on the reduction of inheritance taxes and the recognition of official co-habitation, protecting the house and shared possessions, the status of marriage and co-habitation was legally put on the same level. The interests of divorced partners who were suffering under non-payment of alimony were also secured: they could now turn to a fund and payment of advances. After the Netherlands, Belgium became the second country to open up marriage to homosexual and lesbian couples, in 2003. In the same year, adoption legislation was simplified and brought up to date. Unmarried heterosexual couples now have the right to adopt children after living together for three years.

The 1921 criminal law on drugs use had been adapted and tightened in 1975, when government policy was still very repressive. Two decades later, the attitude towards soft drugs had become much more tolerant, and the issue was approached not only from the legal angle, but also from a human and recreational perspective. Especially progressives and environmentalists were asking to have the law brought in line with the new situation. Yet a compromise was slow in the making; individual use of small quantities by adults was allowed, but trade in soft drugs remained illegal. The new law contained a few terms that were very difficult to practically implement, though, and later revisions tried to rectify that.

Technological advances in biological sciences gave rise to a committee that would provide advice on the ethical, legal and social applications in biology, medicine and health care; especially the Christian democrats felt the need for this. In 1996, the *Raadgevend Comité voor Bio-Ethiek* (Advisory Committee for Bio-Ethics) was founded, composed on a pluralistic basis. Number one on the committee's agenda was euthanasia. It was prohibited by law to 'purposefully perform actions ending the life of someone requesting it', but doctors were not obliged to continue 'senseless' medical treatment, which effectively meant that ending someone's life as a side-effect of treatment for pain was legally acceptable, and applied frequently. Nobody wanted a repetition of the way in which the abortion law had been introduced, but also in this case, there was no initial agreement. The cardinal, Christian democrats, believers and many doctors rejected any form of euthanasia, and proposed palliative treatment as an alternative. These opponents were able to stop any legal settlement for a number of years. In the meantime, proponents had organised themselves: as early as the 1980s, freethinkers had established associations defending the right of a dignified death. They argued that a preceding declaration of the person involved should make euthanasia possible. Others wanted to go even further and allow euthanasia without a written declaration. Proponents preferred not to enter into discussion with the Christian democrats in parliament, and after numerous discussions among the majority parties in the Liberal-Socialist-Green coalition a compromise text was agreed upon in the spring of 2002. Euthanasia would remain illegal, but conditions were established that could allow a doctor to declare an emergency. The moral basis of the law was the right of the individual to decide on his or her own life and death. The proposal also specifies when euthanasia is not illegal, and lays down procedures and measures to make sure the utmost care is taken.

The *Raadgevend Comité voor Bio-Ethiek* had also started thorough and long discussions concerning embryos *in vitro*. In 2003, a law laid down the conditions for research on embryos; therapeutic cloning for reproduction is not allowed, unless it is used for the prevention of hereditary disorders.

It will be clear from this overview that the Liberal-Socialist(-Green) governments have made good use of their parliamentary majorities in order to make Belgium one of the most progressive European countries on a political-ethical level.

Chapter VIII
Economic and Social Policy Since the 1950s

During the 1950s and 1960s, capitalism was driven by mass production and mass consumption of standardised goods. Class relations needed a complete change to make the system work. The state counted on the labour movement to integrate the workforce into the economic process and there was a constant search to find ways to reduce class conflict and turn it into social conflict. A good example was the attempt to link pay rises to increases in productivity. The Keynesian state system did more than just provide a network for social consultation. It also increasingly took on the reproduction of the social labourer – turned into a social security state – and developed a series of methods to contribute (more or less directly) to reproduction of production means, investments and the like. Post-war growth was also marked by an increasing vulnerability of the competitive system – the more capital invested, the more labour productivity increased, the more the cost of equipment and raw materials rose, the more the decline in the rate of profit became evident.

It took a long time before the Keynesian principles took hold in Belgium. A movement within the power elite wanted to slow its development and the lack of discipline within the labour movement further delayed the process. The general strikes of 1950 and 1960-1961 were telling examples. The policy of economic expansion and contractual class relations only began to show some effect, albeit short-term, during the 1960s. The circle of prosperity was broken as soon as the policy of full employment – a price paid by the capital in order to institutionalise and bind the mass organisations of the labour movement to the state – led to a reduction of available reserve labour. It unleashed a fight over the spoils of profit. The system of mass production was affected to its core between 1969 and 1974. On the factory floor, the labour movement made new demands to reap the rewards of society's progress and turned to new, radical actions to counter the 'Fordist' principles of labour organisation put forward by international big business.

Increasing labour resistance soon spread to all sectors of society and augured in a long recession. The system of higher wages for higher productivity was destabilised and the subsequent restructuring was countered by ideas that opposed the principle of a decrease in profits. For the state, the crisis turned into one of the Keynesian model itself and paved the way for neo-liberal de-regularisation, which, in fact, is an authoritarian type of social state regulation.

Neo-liberalism thrived during and after the recession of 1981 and 1982 and, without a doubt, made the government's economic policy more effective. The neo-liberal economic recovery policy during the 1980s was instrumental in restoring profits and generating growth. But it did not reduce the ranks of the unemployed and growth itself did not reach the high levels of the 1960s. It was a short-lived expansion that could not rescind the negative trend set by the crisis of the 1970s. The system soon faced its shortcomings even though the fall of the Soviet Union and East-European regimes between 1989 and 1991 allowed neo-liberalism to catch its second breath. Growth suffered a decline within the G-7 nations as of 1989-1990 and Belgium slid into a new recession which reached its climax in 1993. From 1994 onwards, a new recovery set in, which culminated in a relatively good economic climate between 1997 and 2001 – the period of the ICT boom in Europe. In 2001, the year of the international dot.com crash, this optimistic climate quickly changed into low growth figures reflecting the general recessive trend of the period, in spite of the relatively good results of the Belgian economy in 2004. The renewed profit rate crisis in the new millennium – a crisis which crops up again and again in a 'new economy', built around the new paradigm of economic development and specialised in IT – gave rise to a new political-economic cycle of neo-liberalism. After a socially corrected neo-liberalism that grew out of the aggressive neo-liberalism of the early eighties, a new edition of an aggressive neo-liberalism developed, focusing on competitiveness and labour costs and absorbing the social components of the previous cycle in a competitive national liberalism that manifested itself in many shapes and at many levels. This new neo-liberal cycle found it difficult to develop in Belgium as the unique government coalitions lining up from 1999 onwards were exactly the result of, or an attempt at an answer to, a legitimacy crisis of the effectiveness of a neo-liberal economic policy. At the same time, a new edition of a Belgian anomaly concerning economic performance emerged during this new neo-liberal cycle, the beginning of which coincided with the dot.com crash.

Employment in the traditional industrial sectors, which in Belgium were dismantled faster than anywhere else, could not be replaced (or insufficiently so) by high-tech or service-sector jobs. This new version of the Belgian anomaly should be seen from the position taken up by Belgium, as a logistical space, within the process of globalisation. This implies it should also be interpreted with a view to the way in which internationalisation of capital is reproduced on the many domestic levels (federal, regional, community,...), the functioning of which cannot possibly be understood in isolation from the many lines linking them with the European supranational level.

The Organisation of Economic Expansion

Belgium's economic policy had failed to catch the wave of renewal during the 1950s and remained very traditional compared to the neighbouring countries. Up to 1958, innovation mainly centred on the codification and institutionalising of social consultations and the increasing interference of the state in the welfare system. It included the organisation of the social security system, education, etc. There were hardly any attempts to develop an economic policy directly centred on investments. A balanced budget was the government's chief concern. There was no active expansion policy to renovate Belgium's badly ageing industrial infrastructure. The slowdown in industrial development was also caused by tradition-bound capitalists. The holding companies continued to dominate industry and largely limited investments to the economic core sectors of coal, iron, steel, cement, glass and heavy metals. There was no focus on the dynamic sector of durable consumer goods. The decelerating growth of the economy was aimed at the export sector rather than at the development of the domestic market. State policy was deflationary and insufficiently targeted towards the creation of increased domestic demand. The 1960s brought change. The Belgian economy was restructured and the state played an increasing role in the financing of capital. The discrepancy between the new standards of mass consumption and the outdated production structure slowly disappeared. Social welfare was further extended and became part of the economic expansion policy. The expansion of consumption and demand was seen as a must for the long-term regulation of capital accumulation. At the same time new methods were developed to manage and control class opposition. The collective bargaining system, the social pacification policy, co-management principles and the like were all fine-tuned. State intervention facilitated the introduction of foreign capital in the growth markets and boosted economic activity. At the same time it also reconfirmed the marginal character of the Belgian economy, which was increasingly dependent on international trade and the health of the global economy.

Belgium tried out several methods to boost growth in the 1950s. Most centred on the financing of investments – the approval of state guarantees for loans by productive capital, fiscal exemptions for companies, and so-called interest subsidies (at first only given to public credit institutions, later also to banks). The subsidies allowed for the approval of low-interest loans and were aimed at easing the financial burdens on the accumulation of and profits from industrial capital. The mechanisms were approved in so-called 'expansion laws'. The process started tentatively during the first 1954-1958 Socialist-Liberal government of A. van Acker. It was only during the 1958-1961 period that the process was intensified. The 1958-1959 recession had been particularly painful in the coal and textile industries and laid bare a crisis of capital accumulation. It called for a more systematic long-term economic expansion policy. The 1959 expansion laws tried to counter the stagnation of the Belgian economy of the 1950s and anticipated the economic boom of the 1960s.

The political conflicts and processes leading to the main economic legislation in the 1950s and early 1960s have been insufficiently analysed for us to gain full insight into the class-strategic context within which this Belgian policy of expansion developed. Nevertheless, it is possible to distinguish the main tendencies of shifts in political power leading to important new economic policies. These innovations roughly reflected a change in the balance of power: traditional holding capitalism waned while 'modernist' capitalism, driven by multinationals, surged. The labour movement turned towards radicalism again, as the 1959 Borinage miners' strike and the 1960-1961 general strike clearly illustrated. They led to a switch in political alliances. During the second half of the 1950s and especially during the 1958-1959 crisis, traditional holding capitalism faced severe criticism. It was held responsible for the inability of Belgium's economy to accommodate technological advances and put them to good use. The criticism went hand in hand with changes in Belgium's social-political fabric.

The socialist trade union movement took the lead in criticising Belgium's monopoly capitalism. The ABVV-FGTB largely blamed the decline of the Belgian economy on the conservative investment policies of such big business icons as Société Générale, Brufina-Cofinindus, Solvay-Boël-Janssen, Empain, Evence Coppée, Sofina and Petrofina. They had blocked the flow of capital towards new industrial activities. To counter this negative trend, the 1954 and 1956 special congresses of the ABVV-FGTB developed a programme of sweeping structural reforms. It even had shades of the 1933 Labour Plan. It wanted to break the power of the holdings as financial constructions and institute reform measures, including control over holdings and nationalisation of the energy sector. The programme opened new long-term perspectives for the socialist labour movement, but it also had a downside. Internal strife between the left and right wings of the ABVV-FGTB bureaucracy increased and both sides fought over the means that had to be used to achieve the goals of the programme. The right wing of General Secretary L. Major stuck to the parliamentary calendar and refused to back widespread propaganda in favour of the structural reforms. The backers of Liège union leader A. Renard demanded the application of the reform programme hoping it would allow the working class to reach a new level, beyond the daily, immediate and elementary social strife. It put into question who should lead the economy. In reality, the 'Renardists' were in an ambivalent position. On the one hand, their strategy was in line with the concept of compromise inherent in the 1944 Social Pact and backed the creation of a new wages-labour relationship based on those principles. They also wanted to make effective use of the collective bargaining system to push through reform. Yet on the other hand, it gave important parts of the working class the possibility to use labour action and to mobilise themselves for protests. The Renardist strategy far from excluded that direct labour action would be the most productive way to push through reform.

The BSP adopted the key elements of the socialist trade union program during its 1959 extraordinary congress and the structural reforms became the official program of the *Socialistische Gemeenschappelijke Actie* (Socialist Common Action). It pushed the party towards the left, which was hardly surprising since it was in opposition against the Catholic-Liberal Eyskens government (1958-1961). The periodicals *La Gauche* (established in 1956) and *Links* (established in 1958) became the bulwarks of the party's left wing. The 1960 *Operatie Waarheid* (Operation Truth) propaganda campaign brought the structural reform programme to the grassroots level, especially the Walloon workers.

The Catholic unions went through a similar phase, although they could not match the socialists for radicalism. The central theme of the Flemish ACV-ACW focused on the responsibility the Belgian holdings bore for the lack of industrialisation in northern Belgium. The ACV was turning more radical in its defence of Flemish demands. It wanted employment to favour the region hit by structural unemployment, demanding a new industrialisation under the motto 'work in one's own region'. Catholic trade unionism was able to join the interests of the Flemish working class with the demand for a further industrialisation of Flanders with the help of foreign capital.

The ACV-ACW position echoed flamingant criticism of francophone unitary holding capitalism. The demand for an active regional economic policy became part and parcel of the Flemish movement programme as it attacked Belgium's unitary power structure. The movement further demanded a clear language frontier, cultural autonomy and a Dutchification of the work floor in Flanders. A new bourgeois elite, raised outside of the traditional circles of holding capitalism came to the fore and formed the core of an ideological bloc demanding the industrialisation of Flanders and the promotion of Flemish white-collar workers and civil servants within a predominantly francophone state apparatus. These modern capitalists found a friend in the Catholic Party, which was predominant in Flanders. During the 1958 election year, it proposed its *Sleutelplan* (Key Plan), which was based on Keynesian principles and alternative welfare economics to boost growth. This Key Plan appealed to different classes – promising a 'purposeful and dynamic, regional and balanced market policy – and represented the interests of the Flemish bourgeoisie as those of a comprehensive social movement.

The political strategies led to two developments. The official economic policy changed in the 1958-1960 period and the socialist labour movement, buoyed by its structural reform programme, became more radical. It was a radicalism that was further encouraged by the establishment of the Catholic welfare plan. It culminated in the social upheaval of the winter of 1960-1961.

A Catholic minority government took office following elections in the crisis year 1958 and put an end to the School War, turning education into a technical social-economic issue. It became part of an equal opportunity policy seeking an increase in labour productivity. The next government, a Catholic-Liberal coalition led by Gaston Eyskens, centred attention on economic growth and started adapting the state system to the needs of the neo-capitalist expansion policy. It was able to count on progressive financial groups, including Kredietbank, Paribas and Lambert. They pushed the government towards a broad reconversion policy. Eyskens introduced a series of general economic expansion measures and also established fifteen development regions to meet the economic challenges and counter the social protests in certain Belgian regions. The development regions were prime areas for foreign investment and also met the employment demands of the Catholic trade union. A *Bureau voor Economische Programmatie* (BEP, Office for Economic Programming) was created in October 1959 to make proposals and predictions about midterm economic and social developments. The office had to help companies to anticipate general economic trends. It had to apply the instructions of the *Nationaal Comité voor Economische Expansie* (NCEE, National Committee for Economic Expansion), a body created in 1960 that consisted of representatives of the government, employers and unions. The NCEE was meant to set out the general goals of economic policy (investments, employment, prices and wages). It soon became the key instrument to analyse government policy. But any willingness to pursue economic expansion was countered by the deepening financial crisis. It increased national debt and made the government dependent upon short-term credit from the Belgian banking institutions.

The General Strike of 1960-1961

Industrial capitalism, represented by the *Verbond van de Belgische Nijverheid* (VBN, Union of Belgian Industry), helped pressure the Eyskens government into approving measures to bring the nation's budget back under control. The infamous '*Eenheidswet*' (unitary law) – for economic expansion, social progress and financial recovery – called for a sizable increase in indirect taxation and a decrease in social spending (November 1960). It set off massive protests. During the winter of 1960-1961 it turned into one of the most serious class confrontations in Belgium's social history.

The start was spontaneous enough. The socialist public sector union ACOD (*Algemene Centrale der Openbare Diensten*) started off with a strike of government personnel on 20 December 1960 and immediately drew tens of thousands of Walloon private sector workers into the action. It plunged the country into crisis for a full five weeks. Some 700,000 strikers opposed the government and many spilled out onto the streets for mass demonstrations on an almost daily basis. Over 300 demonstrations marked the tumultuous times. The most important public institutions were completely paralysed for weeks on end and some strikers' units turned into semi-autonomous strike committees that tried to organise the social life of their backers. There were signs of pre-revolutionary tension in Wallonia. Walloon socialist mayors professed solidarity with the strikers and refused to execute the orders of the central government. Barricades throughout the Borinage Walloon industrial belt isolated many places. The government used sheer violence and ideology to turn the situation around. Powerful moral voices, like Cardinal Van Roey, condemned the strike movement and even called it criminal. In a sense, it legitimised the threat to use violence against the strikers. From the start, violent repression had been part of the government scenario. Over 18,000 state policemen had been mobilised to dismantle strike pickets and guard key areas. The army reinforced the state police forces. Up to 15,000 troops guarded industrial buildings, bridges and tunnels, train stations and post offices. The strikers matched the increase in violence of the security forces. In Wallonia, army troops had to wade through caltrops, trees, concrete blocks, car and crane wrecks to advance. Streets were dug up. Liège saw the worst fighting on 6 January 1961. In all, 75 people were injured during seven hours of street battles. Two injured strikers died a few days later. The following weekend sabotage increased in the provinces of Liège and Hainaut and especially in the Borinage. A train was derailed and there were attacks on bridges and high-voltage lines. Some 3,000 Belgian troops were brought in from Germany to protect rail and electricity infrastructure. On 9 January, the security forces started arresting strikers manning the pickets to prevent any attempt at revolt. Some 2,000 strikers were arrested and about half were sentenced to one month or more in prison.

The strike laid bare the different labour approaches of Flanders and Wallonia. South of the linguistic border, the strike quickly spread to all sectors of social life and the Liège steel workers used it to boost the structural reform programme of the socialist FGTB union. The Walloon workers were also threatened by the decline of Wallonia's industry, including the closure of coal mines. They wanted fundamental reform and demanded that the financial holding companies be stripped of economic decision-making powers. In Flanders, the whole of the ACV union backed the CVP while the socialist ABVV union and BSP party had failed to properly prepare the general strike. The general strike was never officially recognised by the ABVV national leadership, and it only reinforced the regional divide. For lack of national leadership, A. Renard founded a regional Walloon Socialist organisation committee on 23 December 1960 to organise the strike in southern Belgium.

The last phase of the strike was instrumental in several developments that would dominate political life over the following years. The Walloon strike leaders linked the socialist union programme of structural reforms to demands for Walloon autonomy and the elimination of the Belgian unitary state. The Walloon socialists had realised that the national balance of power would suffocate their social experiment. This federalist tendency caused an open rift within the socialist trade union after the strike. A discussion whether the socialist union should stay a national institution or be split up into federalist wings figured high; there was also the question of the laws on public order (1962-1963). Strike leader A. Renard also took up the leadership of the 1961 *Mouvement Populaire Wallon*. This pressure group called for federalism and structural reform.

In Flanders, the socialist union and party agreed on a memorandum (15 January 1961) that could make the Unitary Law palatable. It included a toned-down version of the structural reform programme and cleared the way for the 1961-1965 Catholic-Socialist coalition of T. Lefèvre and P.-H. Spaak, which was based on a policy of economic consensus.

Economic Policy in the 1960s

The Lefèvre-Spaak coalition was a compromise government that confirmed the economic and political changes since 1958. CVP and BSP agreed to pursue a dynamic policy of economic growth aimed at an intensified industrialisation of the country. It was the kind of government coalition that characterised the economic and social policy of the 1960s and it was the start of quasi-permanent participation of social democracy in government. It helped create a reformist technocracy. The BSP party reformed along the lines of 'modern socialism', becoming a technocratic party with increased political patronage and 'depolitisation' of its grassroots support. The Lefèvre-Spaak government introduced economic and political innovations and fine-tuned the social security system. Medical social security reform in 1964 caused a serious backlash and doctors went on strike. But in general, the government was backed by a comprehensive electoral base, primarily the Flemish bourgeoisie and labour movement.

The centre-left government further expanded the institutional framework for an active economic government policy, creating the *Nationale Investeringsmaatschappij* (NIM, National Investment Company) in 1962. The company, funded by the state, big business and the industrial sector, had to counterbalance the deficiencies of the Belgian financial structures and boost mid-sized enterprises. During the second part of the 1960s and 1970s, its reach was even increased and it became a sort of public holding that held minority stakes in different companies. But despite its growing investment portfolio, its impact remained marginal. In spite of the new trend within the industrial and financial bourgeoisie, the NIM remained controversial, in spite of its merely supplementary role in accumulation.

The funding of Belgium's economic expansion necessitated fiscal reform in an attempt to cut budget deficits. Based on the Unitary Law, the government approved a series of measures in 1962. They included the introduction of joint family tax returns and a system of automatic deduction of taxes that streamlined tax collection.

The introduction of the Belgian economy into the neo-capitalist growth model went hand in hand with the restructuring of non-competitive sectors. The coalmining sector and the textile, shoe and leather industries caused the most serious problems. The government decided to continue the closure of primarily Walloon coalmines and decided that only mines with a guaranteed market would be allowed to continue production. For the implementation of this programme, the *Kolendirectorium* (Coal Directory) was set up in November 1961; it inherited the functions of the former *Nationale Raad van de Steenkolenmijnen* (National Council of Coalmines), an advisory and research body. The situation at some condemned mines turned ugly and turned into outright revolt at Limburg's Zwartberg in 1966. The army and police used violence to end the uprising; they shot and killed two miners. The unrest in the Limburg coal mines only made the conversion of the whole sector inevitable. The 1966-1968 Catholic-Liberal government of Paul Vanden Boeynants and Willy De Clercq temporarily took over from the centre-left coalition during this period of recession. It could count on the support of the conservative capitalists yet did not go against the general trend to boost investments with state support.

At first, the economic expansion policy produced dazzling results. The 1960s showed an impressive development of the nation's productive capacity. An annual growth of 5 % exceeded all expectations. The Belgian situation, however, was part of an overall international surge in economic fortunes. The European Economic Community was founded in the same period. It was not as if the government took effective charge of the economy; it did not go beyond advising big business on financial strategies. It further underlined the regional imbalance in industrial development.

State subsidies came to the aid of domestic holdings that wanted to modernise the steel industry in Wallonia and the multinationals that wanted to expand the chemical and electronic sectors in Flanders. The age-old industrial strategy was quite literally turned upside down and this time northern Flanders surged while southern Wallonia went into decline. The Walloon labour movement turned defensive and became convinced it was discriminated against. Walloon resistance against the 1962 creation of the Sidmar steel plant in Zelzate on the Ghent-Terneuzen canal was a case in point. Flanders welcomed the U.S. capital injection with open arms and the Flemish bourgeoisie were the first to profit. With the support of a new, intellectual middle class, it quickly became a dominant player in the establishment of Flemish economic supremacy. The movement was led by the *Vlaams Economisch Verbond* (VEV, Flemish Economic Union), which transformed itself from a group of flamingant business leaders into an association of all Flemish-based enterprises.

The Development of the Collective Bargaining System

The rough outlines of the collective bargaining structure were already visible during the interbellum but the framework was institutionalised only after the Second World War. A system of social consultation between employers and workers was created step-by-step. This consultative system developed outside of the traditional constitutional structures and was not part of the conventional system of decision-making. In practice, the neo-corporative system quickly gained in importance and became an essential factor in the containment of class friction. The collective bargaining structures became an important means to stabilise relations within wage labour. Social consultations were intensified during the 1950s and collective bargaining agreements turned into common practice in all sectors. Instead of strikes and confrontation, both sides increasingly preferred to sit down to discuss such issues as wage increases and cuts in working time.

The general strike of 1960-1961 made sure that the sixties became the heydays of social consultations. The system may have been launched during the first post-war years but it had lost much of its lustre by the winter of 1960. An overwhelming majority of the working class no longer expected the consultative bodies to solve their labour problems, so it was looking for a direct confrontation with the government and capitalism. After the strike, the social consultative bodies were reinforced and a great many sector-based collective bargaining agreements were reached. Helped along by the economic boom, bilateral and trilateral negotiations had an immediate impact on the labour movement. The negotiations yielded a number of important social gains for the working class and it showed in the decrease of strikes during the 1960s. At the same time, though, the right to strike came under siege. The 1963 and other laws wanted to prevent a recurrence of the violent 1960-1961 strike after the *Verbond van Belgische Ondernemers* (VBO, Federation of Belgian Enterprises) had insisted on a reinforcement of the security forces. When the law was voted in parliament, left-wing and Walloon legislators protested sharply against what they saw as an infraction against the most elementary trade union and working class rights. The BSP-PSB management was facing a radical left wing within the party and during the 1964 'Irreconcilable Congress' the editors of the *La Gauche* party paper were removed from the party.

It was tough to separate neo-capitalism from the intensified social consultations. Economic growth and the increased costs of investments made sure that a long-term vision became essential, with careful planning of costs and wages. At an economic level, such planning had to remain indicative, but at a social level it had to be directive. Not only did social conflict need to be solved around the bargaining table, any solution also needed to make room for technological innovations. The 1954 Joint Declaration on Productivity by employers and the labour movement, which was discussed again in 1959, had to be seen in that light. The trade unions were willing to link an increase in wages to an increase in productivity and thus became co-responsible for the modernisation and reorganisation of under-performing enterprises. It also allowed the employers to plan the development of wages. Strikes were reduced to a last-resort weapon or as a way to exert pressure during negotiations. The first inter-sector agreement on social programming was reached on 11 May 1960. The employers recognised the fact that the workers had a right to material advancement while the unions accepted that better conditions could only be achieved in stages, respecting the hierarchical decision-making chain. The general strike of 1960-1961 proved that these principles were not immediately accepted by the working class itself, but gradually such social programming would become a cornerstone of Belgium's neo-capitalist system.

The social consultation system created an almost inextricable tangle of some 150 different bodies that often overlapped or made each other redundant. In order to clarify this institutional machinery, we have tried to summarise the many bodies in the following scheme. This scheme is highly representative for the negotiations of the sixties and seventies, but in spite of the crisis, deregulation and state reform of the eighties and nineties, it still reflects the current system fairly accurately. The rules for consultation and negotiation underwent major revisions after 1982, but the institutional infrastructure is still standing today. In laying out this scheme a structure according to levels and domains was followed. The distinction between bilateral or trilateral (with the government as the third party) bodies proved less relevant. Essentially, the government is always present, either as a legitimising body or as the receiver of the advice. A division according to authority – regulating and/ or advisory – was also used, but it was extremely difficult to accurately delineate these types of authority, and to correctly assess the real weight of the bodies in question. As has been pointed out earlier, the system worked in somewhat of a political void. It was not imbedded in the constitution and turned into a parallel decision-making system. It was ruled by cyclical factors and dependent upon informal and obscure communication structures between the different decision-making circuits. Moreover, negotiation is spread over a huge number of bodies, split (both in typically Belgian fashion and 'Fordist' fashion) between social and economic matters. In spite of this fundamental process of differentiation, it is possible to detect a number of tendencies and indicate the most important bodies.

The influence of the negotiation bodies is undoubtedly most noticeable on the 'social' level. The advice the consultative bodies agreed on was often binding and the social sector-based agreements imposed mandatory measures. The latter is especially the result of the law of 5 December 1968, legally linking the position of the collective bargaining agreements with the committees and granting them a disciplinary function in reaching and keeping social peace. Almost all collective bargaining agreements promised union members special perks if social peace was kept throughout the time span of the deal. The 1968 law imposed a 'peace duty' and allowed the authorities to supervise the agreement, giving the government a legal base for the use of security forces during obvious conflicts between the classes.

A national social negotiations body worth mentioning is the *Sociale en Economische Conferentie* (Social and Economic Conference), successor to the *Nationale Arbeidsconferentie* (National Labour Conference) which was first convened during the general strike of 1936. In times of important social or economic problems, this Conference brings together the responsible ministers and the so-called 'social partners'. The organisation proved its use during a series of spontaneous strikes during the 1970s and during the imposition of the economic austerity program of the 1980s.

Unlike the social consultation institutions, the economic consultative bodies were mostly limited to an advisory role. The decision-making powers of the collective enterprise council were limited to such social issues as holidays, working hours and hiring and firing criteria. Also company councils and the economic bodies advising government institutions on a national level have the same limited advisory role. An exception should be made for the *Nationaal Comité voor Economische Expansie* (NCEE), which has been mentioned before. This body was composed of the 'three partners', but only fulfilled an important role during the 1960s; it was able to seriously undermine the powers of the *Centrale Raad voor het Bedrijfsleven* (CRB, Central Council for the Business Community) and to obtain real decision-making authority, in contrast with most other economic bodies. In spite of the absence of organic or functional ties, a practicable distribution of work was reached fairly soon in working out the economic government policy in the sixties. Preliminary discussions of social and economic problems took place within the *Nationale Arbeidsraad* (National Labour Council) and the CRB. Their advice was then passed on to the NCEE, which in a limited number of meetings per year fairly quickly formulated a definitive version of the points of view.

A special mention should be made of the *Gewestelijke Economische Raden* (GERs, Regional Economic Councils) and *Gewestelijke Ontwikkelingsmaatschappijen* (GOMs, Regional Development Companies) which were created in a 1970 law to organise and plan economic decentralisation. The law in question established a *Planbureau* (Planning Bureau) to replace the *Bureau voor Economische Programmatie* (Bureau for Economic Programming); this Planbureau was given three levels of management: general, sector-based and regional. The regional management's task was to work out a plan for the regional economic development in cooperation with the GERs and GOMs. The (three) GERs had a complex composition; the agreement was that union representatives would take up a quarter of the positions, employers' representatives another quarter, and members of parliament and of provincial councils the rest, according to the principle of proportional representation.

The councils of public financial institutions (NBB, ASLK, NMKN, NIM etc.) have the authority to administer internal matters of the institutions and have an external advisory and controlling role. They gained importance during the 1960s when the state expanded its interests in investment policies. These councils tackle such important issues as fiscal and monetary policy, interest rates and the credit markets, and their advice is usually acted upon. The composition of these councils reflects post-war financial policy – the state's intervention role was consultative and did not impose controls on private investments. Few union representatives have a place on these councils and representatives of government ministers and private financial institutions dominate proceedings.

The Resurgence of Labour Resistance and the New Social Movements (1968-1973)

One of the key consequences of the social consultation and collective bargaining policy was the steady integration of the trade union structure into organised capitalism. The demands of union leaders were predetermined by the social consultation policies that fully respected the established balance of power. The union leaders came face to face with a series of inherent conflicts of interest – one moment they were supposed to defend the general interest of the nation, the next the interests of the poor, etc. It had a big impact on the unions themselves. The union bureaucracy became an institution in itself, removed from its grassroots labour support. Fundamental labour issues were sublimated into technical questions and the growing rift manifested itself in between 1969 and 1974.

The integration of union branches in the institutionalised negotiation structure was countered by a series of spontaneous labour actions openly questioning the social peace principle. According to the protesters, the integration policy had a counterpart in the system of mass production, of which the labouring class formed a valuable element. Increasing tension on the work floor eroded the policy of social integration. Some labour disputes could no longer be solved by the host of social containment institutions and suddenly, a seemingly innocuous problem could cause a major labour conflict overnight. The low levels of unemployment worked in favour of social labour resistance since the well of willing substitute labour had almost run dry. At the end of the 1950s, almost 10 % of the workforce, some 200,000 workers, was unemployed. Half a decade later, that army of unemployed had been more than halved; the average number of full-time unemployed stood at a mere 60,000. Keeping a strategic reserve intact became an integral part of economic policy, hence the use of an immigrant labour force as a competitive factor on the labour market. New immigrants from the Mediterranean shores were allowed in during the 1960s and by the early 1970s, Belgium's immigrant population had swelled to 720,000, or 7 % of the total population. Some 220,000 of them, the active workers, made up 7.2 % of the active population. At first, it failed to have the full desired effect. The 1967 recession pushed up unemployment and by 1968 the ranks of the unemployed had shot up to over 140,000, including some 100,000 fully unemployed. Within the working class, tensions rose between the native Belgians, mostly skilled labour, and the new arrivals. The government had to put a temporary halt to such immigration and even sent some immigrants back. But the parallel labour market had also created new centres of opposition. The working conditions of the immigrants – high tempo, high risk of accidents and low pay – were at the root of many protest actions.

At first, the increased tension on the work floor was evident in latent labour resistance – absenteeism, frequent turnover of personnel, increasing sick leave, theft and sabotage. From about 1968 (Ford strike) and especially from the end of 1969, the resistance gathered in strength, especially since a decline in unemployment to the 100,000-level worked in favour of the working class. During 1970 and 1971, the *Nationaal Instituut voor de Statistiek* (National Statistical Institute) counted more strike days in just two years (2,672,458) than over the whole 1961-1969 period (2,365,280). For the entire 1970-1973 period, 698 conflicts and 3,892,271 strike days were logged.

This renewed resistance had five characteristics. First of all, most of the strikes were spontaneous actions like the 1970 Limburg coalmine strike, wildcat strikes in the metal (Citroen-Vorst, Vieille Montagne-Balen, Boel-Temse) and chemical industry (Michelin-Sint-Pieters-Leeuw, Chemie Tessenderlo) and the 1973 Antwerp port strike. Secondly, the strikes were driven by unskilled labour and the lowest-income section of the working class, mainly immigrants, women and youngsters. It was the group that had most to fear from technological innovation and discriminatory measures within society. The crisis was most evident in industries with a high percentage of immigrant labour, including Ford-Genk, Citroen-Vorst,

Michelin and the Limburg coalmines. The role of the immigrant labour force also created tension within the labour front since it was sometimes difficult for the unskilled labourer to make his demands heard within the trade union structure (consisting of people with higher qualifications).

A third factor was the use of new tactics and protest actions. Go-slow strikes, sit-ins and the strategic occupation of plants turned the battle of trade union demands into a contest that centred on the organisation of production. They were an immediate attack on the industrial authoritarian hierarchy: board members were taken hostage, offices were occupied and foremen were the target of protest actions. Demonstrations and solidarity actions took the demands into the streets. A fourth characteristic was the qualitative nature of the demands. Even though pay increases were an integral part of a demand package, the workers also sought to reorganise factory work and institute controls on production. A last characteristic centres on geography. The revival in labour resistance started in Flanders, partly because of the decline of Flemish unemployment during the 1960s; another factor was the increasing 'Fordisation' of new companies in Flanders. The ageing Walloon trade union bastions of ACEC-Charleroi, Cockerill and others were long demoralised after taking tough blows during the general strike of 1960-1961 and joined the new wave of labour resistance only much later.

Overall, labour relations suffered a serious setback. The show of dissent on the shop floor touched the core of Belgium's social pacification policy. It refused to let labour strife be reduced to a mere Keynesian variable and expressed a longing for more labour autonomy. It coincided with an increase in tension throughout society during the late 1960s as student, Third World, urban, environmental and women's movements all made their big moves onto the political scene. They had little in common with labour resistance and were rooted in the fast-developing intellectual middle class, such as radicalised segments of the middle layers of the hierarchy of social institutions or highly qualified intellectual workers in ideological organisations (education, Church, etc.).

Around the end of the 1960s and early 1970s, these new movements thrived on a youthful basis. The student movement first really made a name for itself in 1966 during the *Leuven Vlaams* (Leuven Flemish) action to turn Leuven University into a monolingual institution. The linguistic protest movement originated at Leuven University but, at its zenith, encompassed much of Flemish student life. The anti-nuclear activists brought 15,000 demonstrators onto the streets in 1966. The *Leuven Vlaams* actions turned into a confrontation with the traditional authority of the bishops and the university institution and also took an anti-capitalist turn. The protest caused the collapse of the Catholic-Liberal coalition government of P. Vanden Boeynants and W. De Clercq. Student action was not limited to Leuven. At Brussels University, a broad democratic protest front was opened in 1968 and protest spread to Ghent the next year. At the same time, radical Catholic Flemish student circles galvanised the Third World movement, centring attention on Vietnam and Angola (and other Portuguese colonies). Student protest came to a head in 1972-1973 when 170,000 students took to the streets to demonstrate against the 'Plan VDB'. Defence Minister P. Vanden Boeynants had proposed to progressively change Belgium's armed forces into a professional army with an increased operational capacity, a new defence concept and the creation of an integrated command structure, joining state police, the armed forces, and the interior, public works, transport and economic affairs ministries. The state police also had to create a backup armed force. The students specifically protested, however, against the gradual abolition of postponements of military service. For weeks, Belgium was hit by strikes, demonstrations and occupations.

At first, the state, big business, captains of industry and the traditional institutions tried to contain the reinvigorated labour forces and the new social movements by criminalising them, by being excessively aggressive and by calling for an even stronger police response. The new social movements had a very complex relationship with the capitalist system. On the one hand, they were an expression of the crisis within the system. On the other hand, they were instrumental in dismantling and renewing the archaic cultural superstructure of the same system. Only a tiny part of those movements aligned itself with the working class and sought anti-capitalist solutions. The new social movements were partly rooted in the ambiguous modernism of the 1960s. This modernism was carried by a strong Catholic technocratic section and developed primarily in Flanders. It was based on a hybrid project that combined old values and innovations. It also created untenable tension between the developments in mass production and mass consumption on the one hand and the ascetic authoritarian base of the cultural sector on the other. Starting with the second half of the 1970s, the new social movements increasingly questioned the principle of reproduction in the welfare state. The ecological and anti-nuclear movement questioned the reproduction of mankind. Urban, health and transport action groups challenged the reproduction of the social habitat outside work. Women's and youth groups questioned the reproduction of subjectivity. But often the movements remained ambivalent. In their criticism of society, many fell back on an adapted and sublimated version of early-capitalist ideology. Norms were based on citizen's participation, self-development, small-scale development, nature versus urban structure, alternative energies and technologies, etc.

The reaction to the spontaneous labour resistance was just as complex. Grassroots pressure forced the trade union leadership to adapt its programme. An extraordinary ABVV-FGTB congress in January 1971, initiated by, among others, G. Debunne, who had succeeded L. Major as general secretary in 1968, changed the socialist union's structural reform programme by adding the demand for workers' controls. The Catholic ACV promoted the concept of workers' autonomy. It turned out to be a long-term option that could only be gradually realised through workforce participation in enterprises. Such adaptations were aimed at restoring the legitimacy of trade union bureaucracy. Underlining that same principle, trade unions were found increasingly willing to recognise strikes. Almost 90 % of strikes during the 1970s started out as wildcat actions. The unions also tried to restore their authority by taking the demands of strikers into the consultative bodies, which also reinforced the position of the unions within these institutions. The latter was a condition for the unions to keep fulfilling their integrative function.

The strikes between 1969 and 1973 created a momentary expansion of social consultations, usually involving the government too. Apart from the numerous meetings of the *Nationaal Comité voor Economische Expansie* and the activation of new bodies for planning and economic decentralisation as a result of the law of 15 July 1970, a socio-economic conference was held in February-March 1970 as a result of the violent Limburg coalmine revolt. It touched upon such social themes as guaranteed monthly wages, a pension increase, income tax and the inclusion of review clauses in collective bargaining agreements. There was also discussion on improved work floor democracy. At a 1972-1973 Employment Conference – the improvement of the economic climate had slightly reduced the high unemployment ratio of 1968, but unemployment was still higher than in the mid-sixties – financial holdings and trade unions shared the same stage and for the first time, the unions demanded controls on those holdings. But, both at the 1970 and 1972-1973 meetings, big business and the holding companies refused to budge or make concessions on structural reforms. And even the few concessions employers had made on the informative and consultative powers of enterprise councils remained difficult to enforce.

The employers preferred to grant workers pay increases and hoped it would ease labour tensions. Instead, the move further derailed the precarious situation and never came close to restoring an 'economic balance'. The essence of Keynesian pacification was to link an increase in wages to an increase in productivity. Real wages increased by 110 % in the 1960-1973 period while the increase of production per man-hour resulted in the average cost of consumer goods falling by 57 %. In effect, the decrease of the value of labour was immediately proportionate to the reduction of work time by 11 %. The mid-1970s marked a clear break in the wages-production linkage and a widening gap between the rise of wages and the increase in productivity became evident. Wages in the manufacturing industry rose by 44.35 % in the 1970-1975 period while production increased by 31 %. Between 1974 and 1975, productivity stopped rising, and was reduced in real terms. In the entire manufacturing sector, between 1972 and 1975, the value reduction per consumer item by 16 % (as a result of the increase of productivity) was not more important than the increase (by 16 %) of real-term wages; as such, the fall in value of labour (by 3 %) was less than the reduction of work time (10 %). The surplus value, which had started to decline during the late 1960s went into a fall half a decade later. From then on, capitalism was unable to win the class struggle without a slowdown in growth, a significant increase in unemployment and a fall in real wages. The crisis of the pacification mechanisms that started during the late 1960s did more than augur the economic crisis of the second half of the 1970s. In a sense, it caused the economic crisis. As long as the wage demands could not be brought in line with production increases, capitalism was convinced there was no other option than imposing material sanctions on the working class.

The Crisis of Crisis Management (1974-1981)

The 1974-1975 global crisis affected all highly developed capitalist nations alike, but local variables stood out. In Belgium, the crisis affected a series of long-term characteristics and the traditional structure of the Belgian economy.

The decline had much to do with the role of multinationals here. Transnational capital was part of a shifting global movement and was not necessarily in Belgium to stay. The 1970 economic expansion legislation allowed the government to use extra subsidies in an attempt to keep high-technology multinationals here. But as soon as the balance of power shifted in favour of the working class, multinationals either cut their investments or used their investments to cut the overall wage cost.

In one year, from 1974 to 1975, multinationals and mixed local-foreign companies reduced their planned investments by 60 %. This withdrawal of multinational investment mobilised part of the working class. The threat of closure or the effective closure of multinationals contributed to the phenomenon of company occupations in the second half of the 1970s. A number of examples are worth mentioning: numerous work stoppages, strikes and occupations in several branches (Charleroi, Ghent, Ruisbroek) of ACEC, where employment was being cut by the multinational Westinghouse (5,000 jobs were lost in the first half of the seventies); actions against cutbacks in the Belgian branches of Siemens, in which female workers played an active role; the drawn-out battle concerning the cuts in Fabelta (synthetic fibres); the struggle of textile workers against the restructuring, starting in 1975, of the clothing manufacturing industry (Macintosh-Zolder, 1975; Eisden 1976); strikes and occupations in the paper industry, especially in 1975-1976 (Intermills branches); experiments in self-production and self-management at Prestige-Tessenderlo (December 1975 – June 1976) and jeans producer Salik in Quaregnon (August 1978 and August 1979); the anti-capitalist dynamism in the Gilly branch (1975-1981) stirred up by the closure of Glaverbel (glass); the lengthy occupation of the petroleum refinery RBP (September 1978 – September 1979); the occupation of TV-construction company Sylvania-Tienen (1980); the actions at Monsanto-Gent (silicon) in 1980; the battle at Ford and Volvo and concerning the closure of Citroën-Vorst and British Leyland in Seneffe (1980-1981); the occupation in 1980 of Gregg-Europe (train undercarriages) in Lot in the hard-hit Zenne region; actions against job cuts in the Belgian Philips branches (1980-1981), etc.

All this labour opposition only worsened the crisis of the Keynesian subsidy mechanisms. It undermined the alliance between the multinationals and the Belgian state. The increased mobility of the multinationals exposed a weakened industrial structure, made more evident by a slowdown in the world economy. Competition in the traditional sectors of steel and semi-manufactured products increased. The effectiveness of the economic expansion policy waned quickly and eventually became part of the dismantlement policy. On the other hand, labour resistance against the relocation of multinationals forced the state to increase its financial interventions. It turned some of the factory occupations into hot political issues. Union action to protest against the loss of jobs at the ACEC electronics company led to the approval, in 1976, of the so-called 'Herman plan', which advised a temporary pact between the NIM, the Société Générale and the electricity holdings; this in turn led to a sharp increase of government orders for ACEC goods. In the battle around Fabelta, an agreement was reached between multinational AKZO and the state in 1976: the state took a majority participation through NIM, leaving AKZO the control over the company's sales. The occupation of the Prestige factory in Tessenderlo led to the approval of the principle that the state could take over the management of companies (loss-making or not) that faced a temporary closure. Following the crisis in the paper industry, the Walloon regional government created the Financière Intermills public holding. These reductions in production, however, were to the benefit of the mother companies of the multinationals, and the increasing state intervention had little or no effect on employment.

The crisis of the Keynesian subsidy system widened the gap between what the state was expected to do and what the state could do, considering the staggering costs. Pressure to increase intervention and expand employment in public institutions added to budget expenditures. Government spending accounted for 34 % of GNP in 1960, 42.7 % in 1973 and 50 % in 1976. To make matter worse, massive unemployment was a big drain on income. It created a severe budget crisis, marked by huge deficits. As of the mid-1970s it would have a fundamental impact on all political issues.

The financial crisis also exacerbated the economic rift between Flanders and Wallonia. The crisis had different characteristics north and south of the linguistic border and it showed in the nature of government subsidies. There was a public perception of 'selective help' for Flanders and 'generous aid' for Wallonia. It also affected the political balance of power. Factory floor occupations, for instance, were a mainly francophone phenomenon: 90 % of them took place in Wallonia. It was an indication that new regional power centres were emerging: the strong development of a Walloon federalist consciousness primarily boosted by the labour movement and the coming of age of a Flemish neo-liberal bourgeoisie. The latter tried to achieve further integration in the decision-making mechanisms of the unitary state, among others in order to avoid a Walloon workers' federalism.

The central goal and the chief mechanism for the restructuring of Belgium's economy was the restoration of the rate of profit. Displacement of capital to regions with a higher value increase rate was one means to attain this restoration of the rate of profit, but not the only one. The restructuring of production was increasingly complemented by increasing pressure to contain wages. Curbs on inflation became a key element of the national austerity policy. Economic policy made a clean break with the Keynesian paradigm of the unemployment-inflation relationship – higher inflation meant less unemployment, less inflation stood for higher unemployment. Industrial production slumped by 8.62 % in 1975 compared to 1974, full unemployment shot up by 69.37 % and the consumer price index rose by 12.77 %. The dysfunction was partly caused by the policy to boost demand by increasing credit creation. It reaped monetarist opposition. The backers of monetarism wanted to rein in inflation by containing wages and reducing consumption to cut back imports and improve the balance of payments. They wanted to turn it into a central economic theme.

The 1974-1977 Catholic-Liberal government of L. Tindemans issued the first austerity measures. The government wanted to start with a clean economic slate and broke with the policy of outgoing Walloon socialist Prime Minister E. Leburton (January 1973 – January 1974) who had tried to get a foothold in the oil sector with the IBRAMCO state company. The first Tindemans government built its policy around two necessities – further regionalisation and open warfare on rampant inflation and budget deficits. It pushed through a plethora of economic restructuring and austerity measures in 1976, constituting a major attack on the working class; there was an impressive series of 'recovery laws' (March 1976, December 1976), 'programme laws' (end of 1975 – beginning of 1976), 'austerity programmes', consumer index manipulations (1976), and reform plans for social security.

It was bound to result in a clash; resistance started almost at the same time as the restructuring measures. Workdays lost to strikes increased by 47 % in 1976 compared to the previous year. Factory occupations shot up and by the end of 1975 the labour movement started targeting the government. A first important development was the opposition against government plans to make the university system and scientific research more profitable. Apart from the mass demonstrations and occupations of certain university buildings, the movement was notable because it fostered cooperation between the student movement and part of the trade union world. Another important moment took a mere 60 minutes but the one-hour warning strike close to Christmas 1975 marked the first time the socialist ABVV union joined forces with the Catholic ACV to set up a common trade union front. The socialist union, driven by left-wing leader G. Debunne, followed it up with a national demonstration on 13 March 1976. The socialist union leadership backed grassroots dissent with an offensive strategy.

When it became clear that the government's austerity policy was no passing fancy and when it started affecting an ever bigger part of the population, opposition increased. The relations between the socialist union leadership and its grassroots support became more complex. Starting in the summer of 1976 (mobilisations in Wallonia against the manipulation of the consumer index), but especially in February 1977, when Tindemans proposed his government's new, large-scale austerity plan (the so-called Egmont plan), union leaders came under increasing pressure to set up a comprehensive counteroffensive. Resistance spread and work stoppages and other labour action targeting the government increased. The cries for a general strike grew even stronger in Catholic union circles. Grassroots pressure was instrumental in creating a joint trade union front. Two days before parliament was to start discussing the Egmont plan, the union front announced its complex action plan, including a series of 24-hour strikes in different provinces spread over five successive Fridays and national strikes in selected public sectors spread over three weeks. The reform of the welfare state threatened to undermine consultation councils, the social security network and other union achievements. It forced the union bureaucracies to go into opposition and prepare for action. The Friday strikes were a success with workers massively answering the call. It was an indication of the balance of power. The attacks on the working class put labour resistance on the defensive at first. But when the government policies turned ugly, the labour movement turned radical and went on the offensive. When unemployment ballooned from 163,000 in 1974 to 370,000 in 1977, the workers blamed the government. When economic policy attacked such sacred labour achievements as the automatic linkage of wages to the consumer index, the workers were ready for a fight. The working class set the demand for a 36-hour workweek with neither loss of pay nor an increase in production. The union leaders, however, were not of one mind, despite the united front. The Flemish Catholic ACV just wanted to exert pressure on the Tindemans government, while the Socialist ABVV-FGTB and the Walloon Catholic CSC wanted to bring the government down. But the unions wanted to keep a joint approach to safeguard their position in the consultation structure of the Keynesian state.

Faced with a strong working class and a strong trade union system, the government chose in 1977 to return to a system of negotiations with the labour movement. It coincided with the return of the socialists in government and the 1977-1981 period was marked by a series of attempt to regenerate parts of a Keynesian policy. Reducing unemployment was the key target of the government and a series of measures were approved to get people back to work. The 1978 Spitaels Plan created temporary, extra jobs in the public sector, the establishment of a *Bijzonder Tijdelijk Kader* (BTK, Exceptional Temporary Staff) and was also aimed at putting the unemployed back to work in the private sector. It also spread the system of early retirement. In May 1980 (under the Martens III government), a plan was added to boost part-time labour (flexible working hours, career breaks, etc.). This policy, obviously, was not at crossed purposes with the process dismantling employment in industry – there was a loss of 20 % in manufacturing industry between 1974 and 1980 – or the further increase in unemployment. It did allow the government to take more unemployed out of official statistics (168,906 people were taken off the lists in 1980). Such measures cost money, though – 32.7 billion francs in 1979 and 42.7 billion francs in 1981 – and added to the financial crisis; they came on top of the government share in unemployment benefit (76 billion francs in 1981). The state had to borrow ever more money on the domestic and international markets.

The restructuring efforts of the Catholic-Socialist governments sought to stimulate industrial renewal. A 1977 plan of Economics Minister Willy Claes was the result of exhaustive negotiations between government, employers and unions. The plan was based on self-financing by companies linked to changes in the tax system, specialisation through diversification to boost innovative technologies, the expansion of exports and an increase of public holdings. The creation of the 1978 *Fonds voor Industriële Vernieuwing* (Fund for Industrial Renewal) was a direct consequence of the Claes plan and intervened in industrial reconversion projects or in the renewal of production systems. The creation of separate public investment companies in Flanders and Wallonia (GIMs) further spurred institutional regionalism. The central government remained responsible for five national industrial sectors – coal, steel, textile, glass and shipbuilding. Some of these sectors were the subject of separate arrangements. Claes' 1978 Steel Plan acted on a request from big business itself to help push through a thorough restructuring of the sector, which included mergers and shifts in share ownership. The state won limited majorities on the boards of several steel giants, even though it left the leading positions to the big financial groups. A Textile Plan wanted to increase market share, lower production costs and clean up the financial structure of the sector in an attempt to save jobs. It did not include direct state participation in the sector but it did provide no-interest loans; the *Nationale Maatschappij voor Herstructurering van de Textiel en de Confectie* (National Company for the Restructuring of Textile Manufacturing) was established.

1982: the Breakthrough of Neo-Liberalism

The 1977-1978 new industrial policy of the centre-left was a quintessential reflection of the internal contradictions of Belgium's economic policy. The industrial strategy was still top-heavy with policy options and state reformist growth utopias that had dominated economic policy since 1959 – checks on the powers of 'parasitic' big business, support for 'dynamic' industrial capitalism during the expansion of state initiative, the manager vs. the banker, public power vs. private power, etc. In short, the technocrats of this so-called new industrial policy implicitly believed that all it would take was mere corrections to restore the potential for the growth conditions of the 1960s (including industrial initiative and guiding subsidies by the state). But the crisis was one of the Keynesian mechanisms themselves, i.e. the type of counter-tendencies set up by the state in the sixties to fight the decreasing profit rates. It was why the centre-left coalition was unable to provide the creative spark for industrial reform. The *Fonds voor Industriële Vernieuwing*, for instance, was reduced to taking care of the financial difficulties of struggling companies and did not generate innovative, high-tech industrial activities. What it did do was worsen the budget crisis.

Obviously, it does not suffice to describe the type of economic policy of the end of the seventies merely in terms of goals and failures. It is advisable, if not methodologically necessary, to take the capital's point of view and to ask about the effects of this type of economic policy on the evolution of profit rates. The most important conclusion concerning the 1974-1981 period was that the changes in economic policy were unable to bring industrial reform to a successful end and create the right conditions for growth. The crisis drastically changed the labour market's balance of power. In 1980, full unemployment had risen to 321,895 and total unemployment (including unemployed not receiving benefits, part-time unemployed and those absorbed into temporary state-subsidised functions) stood at 618,115. The wage scale evolution showed, however, that such changes in the power structure hardly affected consumer spending power. Overall, real wages of workers (in industry, trade and the service sector) rose by 3.9 % between 1974 and 1980. Spending power of the wage total of 'workers' started to fall from 1974 onwards, though; between 1974 and 1980, it decreased by 13.2 %. The real wage total of all wage earners (labourers, clerks, civil servants, miners), on the other hand, continued to rise slightly. Even if consumer spending power of wage-earners dipped 0.7 % in 1975 compared to 1974, it rose again by 6.14 % between 1975 and 1980. Real wages of the industrial workers though, shrunk badly, meaning that the swift dismantling of industrial employment starting in 1974 had a real impact on the relationship between wages and profits. The workers emerged as losers.

The restoration of the average profit rate encountered two more roadblocks. Increased employment in the non-industrial sector turned out to have contradictory consequences. On the one hand, from a traditional Keynesian contra-cyclical perspective, it countered the effect of industrial dismantling on global real wages, even though it failed to ease massive unemployment. On the other hand, additional employment slowed down production growth and negatively affected the surplus value. It also raised pleas for a restrictive wage policy and cuts in state expenditure. Additional employment increased the importance of the merchandise service sector, which was characterised by low production growth (average yearly growth of productivity, between 1974 and 1980, was 4.9 % in industry, 0.6 % in the private sector and 2.2 % in total). Also the sector of state administration, the development of which put pressure on the surplus value available for accumulation, was increasingly important. There was a second, more vital factor that held back a decrease in total real wages and real hourly wages: the automatic link between wages and the consumer price index. At first, the economic crisis was unable to break labour resistance and the attacks on the wage-index link resulted in united, but only partially controlled militant action, and had to be (temporarily) abandoned.

Because of the sustained slowdown in production growth, the government's social and economic pressure on the workers was not strong enough to help restore profit. The political industrial goals of the 1977-1981 centre-left government, including the development of high-technology industries, remained elusive.

The partial reinstatement of the social consultation structures did not bring back profits and only reinforced the employers' tendency towards a neo-liberal confrontation strategy. But the same factors that fed neo-liberalism also slowed its breakthrough. Labour resistance put checks on the austerity measures and limited the options of union leaders within the policy of class cooperation, which had been revived in 1977. Massive unemployment put the working class ever more on the defensive but did not affect its willingness to strike. ACV figures showed that between 1977 and 1981, the level of annual factory strikes hovered between 252 and 379. And from early 1979 onwards, labour resistance started to centralise its actions again. The austerity measures forced the unions to rely on cross-sector mobilisation. Both major unions held an action day in Wallonia on 29 March 1979, which included a 24-hour strike and a demonstration of 60,000 workers in Namur. In Flanders the ABVV socialist union took the initiative for a number of important cross-sector events: some 8000 ABVV representatives met at the Heizel in Brussels on 7 April 1979; there were national ABVV demonstrations on 7 December 1979 (with some ACV branches and delegations participating) and on 24 January 1981 (about 100,000 protesters).

A second factor that held back the breakthrough of neo-liberalism was the ideological climate. The crisis of the Keynesian system and state caused a problematic reform of the ruling ideology. The deep economic, political and ideological crisis limited the impact of alternative ideologies. Yet the crisis also fostered the creation and growth of new ideological counter-movements, including the anti-nuclear, environmental, peace and consumer movements, collective consumption movements, independent committees of the unemployed and anti-fascist and anti-racism demonstrations. It also provided a new lease of life for movements that had countered the ideological crisis in school and family during the late 1960s, including the women's movement.

The power of the working class and the labour movement impeded the imposition of a stringent recovery policy. And with the reinforcements of the new social movements, it also had a negative impact on the development of a coherent alternative civil project. The Keynesian practices, even though they were in crisis, continued to have a practical use. They blunted the sharp edges of class confrontation and continued to coordinate the different interests of the social partners. So, even though anything Keynesian was quickly losing credibility, the principles remained strong enough to slow down the development of neo-liberalism. The Catholic circles, for instance, were not easily swayed by the new right-wing ideology. Tendencies within employers' circles and the petty bourgeoisie pushed the Flemish Catholic CVP party in the direction of neo-liberalism but there were fears that such an ideology, combined with the crisis and a Catholic radical labour wing, would create a rift within the CVP-ACW group. Catholic populism could not go down the neo-liberal road too far and made sure the CVP held on to some elements of Keynesianism.

Because the traditional parties were slow to reorganise their ideological concept, it was left to the extreme right wing at first to launch the biggest attacks on the welfare state. The francophone CEPIC (*Centre Politique des Indépendants et Cadres Chrétiens*) was created in 1972, operated in the margins of the Catholic PSC and had connections with extreme right-wing groups like the *Front de la Jeunesse* and *Nouvel Europe Magazine*. It specifically targeted the trade unions and called for the restoration of private initiative and the profit principle. The 1978 UDRT-RAD (*Union Démocratique pour le Respect du Travail – Respect voor Arbeid en Democratie*) was an independent political party that defended the interests of the taxpayer. Typically, these groups were linked to the old elite or the old middle class of small shop owners and small and medium-size enterprises. They thus represented social segments that had been largely unaffected by the modernism of the 1960s. It made their role in the establishment of neo-liberalism very important, but it was always to be a mere supporting role. The old liberal middle class was to be the chief recruiting ground and ideological base of neo-liberalism. The anti-monopoly principles of the small producers and shop owners were not necessarily a stumbling block for the offensive of monopoly capitalism. Instead it was a pole of attraction and since its proponents also opposed the labour movement and the welfare state, it helped bring the real enemy in sight, from the point of view of monopoly capital. The trouble was, though, that this old middle class liberalism was itself unable to develop a forward-looking civil project.

Monopoly capitalism had to look elsewhere for a long-term strategy. The vanguard of a new intellectual middle class came into focus. The prime recruits worked in the economy, law and political science departments of Belgium's universities, within the youth departments of the CVP and PVV (cf. the *Radicaal Manifest* of the PVV youth branch in 1980) and in such media institutions as *Trends, Financieel Economische Tijd* and *Intermediair*. Neo-liberalism was being extensively studied in discreet employers' clubs like *Enterprise et Société*, and brought into the open by some of the nation's leading employers. Especially the Flemish bourgeois VEV became a prime defender of neo-liberalism (cf. the VEV *Roodboek* publication on state intervention of 1980).

A heavy dose of neo-liberalism was imported from the United States when the 'second oil shock' and the 1980-1982 crisis hit home. Slowly it began to dominate the bourgeois strategy and made major inroads into the traditional parties – especially the PVV and PRL, but also the CVP and PSC.

The neo-liberal program was an answer to, and the very opposite of, Keynesian ideology. Neo-liberalism reconfirmed the concept of the individual capitalist who claims competition and demand are objective facts, making government subsidies and interference not only unnecessary but also harmful. However, a clear difference had to be made between the way neo-liberalism presented itself within the constraints of the ideological battle and the way it defended bourgeois interest in a series of economic-political debates. The neo-liberal 'end of the welfare state' credo turned into the reform of the welfare state. The parts of the system that had come to embody labour achievements and in which the reformist labour movement held important positions were reorganised. The neo-liberal thesis of supply-side economics also has to be put in a Belgian context. The new economic policy did not run counter to a policy of demand stimulation. Instead it sought a thorough reform of demand: an extension of demand from capital income instead of wages.

Belgian neo-liberalism had its breakthrough around the end of 1981 and 1982. A first indication was the development of spending power. Starting in 1982, real hourly wages began to take a dive and the development was specifically hard on the working class, which lost 24.2 % of its spending power between 1980 and 1984. Overall spending power decreased by 17.7 % over the same period. A second indication was to be found in the changing relationship between real wages and labour productivity. The offensive of big business against the spending power of its wage-earners paid of in 1982 when the relationship was turned around in favour of labour productivity. The evolution of profits is a third indication. As labour income fell, profits soared from 1982 onwards. Retained profits after taxes and distribution of dividends rose from less than 20 billion francs (€ 500 million) in 1980 to 230 billion francs (€ 5.75 billion) in 1987 (169 billion francs in 1980 currency), while dividends rose from 60 billion francs (€ 1.5 billion) to 196 billion francs (€ 4.85 billion) (143 billion francs in 1980 currency) over the same period.

The financial strategies were a fourth indication. Income redistribution was turned to the advantage of income from surplus value, reinforcing monetary and investment capitalism. Especially the high interest rates and the continuing budget deficits were a boon for the financial sector. Income from loans (interests) rose from 285 billion francs (€ 7 billion) in 1980 to 545 billion francs (€ 13.5 billion) in 1987 (401 billion francs disregarding inflation). Simultaneously, there was a trend to turn loans into high-risk capital, partly because the state intervened by favouring high risk capital. It did so by reducing the taxes on productive investment. The Cooreman-De Clercq decree made it possible that, under certain conditions, the purchase of new stock became tax deductible. The enterprise-friendly tax climate also made it possible for holdings to increase capital and restructure their activities. Société Générale, a prime beneficiary of the Cooreman-De Clercq system (of the 300 billion in increases in stock capital, this group accounted for 20 %), withdrew itself from the traditional steel and glass industries and increased investments in the non-ferrous, banking, insurance, electricity and diamond sectors. It won a foothold in the telecommunications and electronics industries and increased its alliances with foreign holdings and multinationals.

The evolution of government spending was a fifth indication. The share of state expenditure in GNP rose from 50 % in 1976 to 60 % in 1981. In 1982, it started a slow downward trend of about 1 % per year and had come down to 52 % in 1989. The turnaround was the direct result of the government's disciplined budget-savings policy, which in its turn was linked to the policy of reducing pre-taxation on surplus value.

A sixth indication was the political make-up of the government. The Catholic-Socialist coalition was replaced by a Catholic-Liberal alliance in 1981, setting the stage for the political breakthrough of neo-liberalism. It should be noted that the neo-liberal policy was not limited to the liberal parties (PVV, which would later become VLD, and PRL) and Catholic employers alone. The change in political alliances should be seen as a way to subdue the socialist labour resistance which the PS and SP yet had to shake off.

The last, and most important, indicator was the evolution of surplus value. Even if it remained under the levels of the 1960s, it did rise significantly during the mid-1980s when compared to 1970s and early 1980s levels. The recovery of the surplus value was the foundation for the restoration of profits and the reorganisation of the activities of financial capitalism.

The Neo-Liberal Labour Policy (1982-1987)

Incessant wage cuts to benefit profits summarised the 1982-1987 economic recovery policy of the centre-right governments led by Christian Democrat W. Martens (his fifth and sixth cabinets). The share of wages in the nation's overall income structure was significantly reduced. Between 1980 and 1987, income from wages declined from 68.3 % to 59.1 % while income from capital, including loans, rent and dividends, together with retained profits for companies, rose from 15.1 % to 24.4 %. This income re-distribution dearly cost the wage-earner. It was the result not only of slumping employment but also of the temporary decoupling of the wage-consumer index link at several stages during the 1982-1986 period; for instance, in 1984, 1985 and 1986, one indexation per year was simply ignored. At the same time, indirect wages were also under attack; specifically, unemployment benefits suffered: the automatic index linking of benefits was abolished, a system of means testing was introduced, some benefits were cut or even abolished completely, etc. The most vulnerable, the long-term unemployed, were increasingly pushed into poverty. The extremely harsh winter of 1984-1985 brought the message home. One out of every 500 people was unable to pay the electricity bill and candlelight caused fires killing and injuring several people. Some municipalities opened soup kitchens.

The neo-liberal economic offensive went hand-in-hand with efforts to reinforce the state. The authoritarian streak was well illustrated by the fifth and sixth governments of Wilfried Martens, which repeatedly won approval from parliament to rule by decree. The move to boost executive power was not only evident in the constraints put on the legislature. It also manifested itself in the tendency to ignore social consultations or to avoid contractual settlements. The changes of 1981-1982 marked the transition from negotiated austerity measures to imposed austerity measures. The systematic interference of the Martens V and VI centre-right coalitions showed an executive moving away from the rules of the Social Pact and towards new, so-called trilateral social negotiations.

The combination of increasing labour deregularisation and a reinforcement of state interference became evident in the further dismantling of union rights and in the security forces' extension. The decline of union power and the breakdown of the system of wage negotiations implied that the judicial system backed the strategy of the employers against trade union militants. Between 1980 and 1988, over 600 union representatives were fired. The 1982-1987 reform on the social security sector was also increasingly being complemented with repressive measures. In an attempt to reduce the burden of social security expenditures, such as unemployment benefits, new selective conditions were created. The concept of family e.g. was rewarded and used as a criterion for the level of unemployment benefits. At the same time controls on the social security system increased.

The traditional police institutions were reinforced and also qualitatively strengthened. Important measures came in the wake of the dramatic events of 1984 and 1985, when terror spread by the so-called '*Bende van Nijvel*' (Nijvel Gang / Mad killers of Brabant) reached its zenith. A gang went on a ruthless killing spree and the human cost of their robberies in no way compared to the often pitiful loot. Often they based their actions on information from the state police or the army and their attacks were carried out with military precision; there were suspicions that some of the investigators may have been accessories. There were indications of an institutional twilight zone that had gone off the rails, a 'parallel state', a product of the dissuasion logic of the post-war state, composed of special police groups and extreme right-wing paramilitary groups linked to old, marginalised elites from middle-class PSC circles. At the same time, new measures were taken to develop a preventive control strategy aimed at containing social conflicts. They were legitimised by the bomb attacks of the urban guerrilla group *Cellules Communistes Combattantes* (CCC) and included a further reinforcement of the state police with a bigger budget, better equipment and training, more manpower and more authority. The state police and army also became more intertwined (in November-December 1985, paratroopers were deployed to restore order), cooperation with the other police forces was improved and new specialised intervention units (POSA units) were created. More cooperation at top levels was made possible between the most important police services, e.g. the *Anti-*

terroristische Gemengde Group (Anti-Terrorist Mixed Group) and the *College ter Bestrijding van het Terrorism* (Board for the Fight against Terrorism).The Chamber adopted the European Treaty to combat Terrorism on 22 May 1985. But the highlight of the security policy was the so-called 'Super Plan Gol'. It was put before parliament in 1986 and covered the issues of wiretapping, use of firearms by the police, special security companies, arms and ammunition, security in justice buildings, and municipal police.

The redistribution of income to the advantage of capital with a management technology that strengthened the more repressive aspects of state policy in its different aspects (restructuring of the social negotiation and social security state, limitation of state aid to national sectors, cutbacks in subsidies for public transport and for state companies, tendency to privatisation of parts of the state structure formerly organised as collective consumer areas, etc.) constituted the hard core of the implementation of the neo-liberal project between 1981 and 1987. However, it is only possible to understand the real impact of this combination in relation with the gradual development of a new, flexible accumulation scheme: no more standardised, uniform mass production, but custom-made products with a short delivery term, borne by flexibility both of the machine infrastructure (implementation of new technologies, especially IT and robotics) and the workforce. In other words: neo-liberalism also created the conditions for an in-depth revision of all elements determining income ratio (forms of labour organisation and technological production procedures, working hours and working rhythm, conditions of appointment).

The reorganisation of the labour process entailed the introduction of more working hour flexibility. Starting in 1983, the so-called 'Hansenne experiments' allowed for exceptional exemptions of labour law practices. But the exceptions steadily became the rule. A 1987 decree, the CAO 42 (Collective Bargaining Agreement 42) covering the whole private sector, with the exception of distribution, broke the ban on Sunday and official holiday work and the prohibition on night work for women. It also allowed the normal eight-hour working day to be exceptionally extended to twelve hours a day and fifty hours a week. Neo-liberal labour policy further polarised the labour market with all kinds of new 'flexible labour contracts', temporary contracts (work for a specific period), acquaintance contracts (young people working a limited number of hours for a specific period), 'small-time' contracts (the employee works less than a third of normal hours, at fixed or flexible times), 'call-up' contracts (the employer can call on the workers between an minimum and maximum number of hours per week), part-time, faze-in/out contracts) etc.

The breakthrough of the principle of flexibility symbolised the change in the social balance of power. Together with the introduction of new technologies and new principles of labour organisation came an increase in work intensity. It boosted surplus production and further restored profits. The success of the flexibility principle directly touches upon the development of labour resistance during the 1980s. One of the key factors in the breakthrough of the neo-liberal labour policy was the decline, starting in 1982, of trade union opposition at company level. The 1980-1982 recession achieved what the 1974-1975 recession had failed to do, i.e. subdue resistance. The 1974-1975 recession had accelerated the erosion of the full-employment policy and whipped up trade union militancy that had been built up between 1968 and 1973. The 1980-1982 recession worsened the depressed employment situation and multiplied closures and layoffs in the bastions and key sectors of the economy and it took the heart out of trade union resistance. Figures compiled by the research service of the ACV concerning strikes show the extent of the crisis: company strikes dropped from 316 in 1980, 252 in 1981, 167 in 1982, and 131 in 1983 to 107 in 1984. The neo-liberal offensive timed its breakthrough to coincide with factory closures and mass layoffs. There was no mechanical link, though, between the massive unemployment – downfall of the labour struggle at company level – and the breakthrough and subsequent implementation of neo-liberalism. Labour factors like union strategy, programmes and organisation of the labour movement also played their part. The leadership of the labour movement was instilled with the traditional values of class cooperation policy and union leadership wanted to maintain or restore the social consultation mechanisms. It left them with a jumbled policy of partly accepting certain austerity measures in the hope of holding on to their bureaucratic privileges within the social consultation structure. Instead they weakened the capacity to protest the worsening situation. So labour resistance at company level was not only affected by massive unemployment but also by union policy to cooperate with the economic restructuring, which meant more layoffs, and the austerity measures, which meant lower wages and cuts in other benefits.

The internal contradictions within the trade union strategy affected the labour movement during the 1982-1986 period. The decline in company strikes, however, did not mean that the whole working class had grown despondent. Important sector and cross-sector mobilisation took place in 1982: fight against manipulation of the consumer index; a demonstration of Walloon steel workers in Brussels in March 1982 that turned into a violent confrontation with the security forces; youth and women's resistance against the crisis. A general public sector strike and widespread protests dominated the September days of 1983. In April 1984 and the spring of 1986 there were actions against the Saint Anna Plan, eventually leading to a demonstration against new austerity measures on 31 May, in which some 200,000 marched in Brussels. The actions were not reinforced by an offensive union strategy, however. The ACV leadership largely backed the measures of the Martens V and VI governments, while the ABVV leadership steadily moved from a rejection in principle of the austerity measures to a partial acceptance of the policy in an attempt to safeguard earlier achievements.

Post-reformism, Competitiveness and Participating Management (1988-1992)

The ABVV demonstration of 31 May 1986 put an end to defensive, reformist opposition against the neo-liberal labour policy. It also was an important step in the adjustment of social democratic parties to post-reformist capitalism, i.e. a capitalism that no longer reproduces using social reform. The gradual acceptance of this new reality by the socialist union leadership during the 1982-1987 period coincided with the 'opposition' discourse of the Walloon PS and Flemish SP, which was notable for its moderation and its circumvention of mass resistance. The socialists rejoined the government in 1988 and it did not entail the classic mechanism of recognition and integration of mass demands. Instead, it proved the hegemonic powers of neo-liberalism.

The shift in coalition to a centre-left government, with the liberals in opposition, at first (1988-beginning of the 1990s) coincided with a temporary halt in the decline of wages in the nation's income structure and it could be linked to an increase in employment, which in its turn was a result of the recovery of the growth rate initiated by the policy of income redistribution, at the expense of wage labour. The demand for labour in private companies rose by more than 7 % between 1986 and 1991: the number of positions offered by companies rose from 2,278,000 in 1986 to 2,441,000 in 1991.

The pause was, as such, only partly caused by the change in coalition. The ACW-MOC Catholic labour movement had been instrumental in pushing through the switch, pointing out the dangers that continued centre-right austerity measures would pose for Christian-democratic and social-democratic institutions. They pointed out tensions between the basis and leadership, the loss of legitimacy of the mass apparatus of the organised labour movement, etc. At most, one could say that the 1988-1992 period brought a temporary halt to the expansion of austerity measures and budget cuts. The centre-right policy of the past was not questioned as such. The increase of wages in the national income scales in no way prefigured a return to the situation of the late 1970s. The trade union strategy to recover wage losses became the issue of sector-based collective bargaining agreements starting in late 1986, but the Catholic-socialist coalition put this in the framework of a consolidation of neo-liberal achievements on the issue of income from wages.

On the other hand, the consolidation of neo-liberal parameters could not be limited to converting past savings efforts into non-repayable sacrifices. A certain long-term vision was also necessary: clear rules and regulations needed to keep the future under control. Securing the state framework of wage costs led to the law on safeguarding the nation's competitiveness (6 January 1989). The law was mainly the work of the technocratic circle around socialist Economics Minister W. Claes, who was also deputy prime minister.

The goal and point of departure of the law – securing or recovering Belgian competitiveness – were based on a fairly complex mechanism with as its hard arguments the evolution indicators or evaluation criteria of competitiveness: export results (gain or loss of market shares of the *Belgisch-Luxemburgse Economische Unie* in comparison with the performance of five of Belgium's most important European trade partners), wage costs (wage costs per man-work unit in the private sector compared to the weighted average of Belgium's seven most important trade partners), financial costs (among others the evolution of short-term, mid-term and long-term interest rates in Belgium compared to the evolution in the seven most important trade partners), energy costs (price evolution per energy product and per consumer category in comparison with the evolution of the cost of each of these energy vectors in the five most important European trade partners) and the 'structural determinants' (among others the evolution of gross accumulation of companies and of research and development expenditure in comparison with the evolution in the five most important European trade partners). These criteria correspond with a set of instruments pinpointing the actors of the evaluation and their qualifications, and obviously the effective effects potentially generated by the evaluation. The normal evaluation procedure consists in a yearly report on competitiveness submitted by the *Centrale Raad voor het Bedrijfsleven* (Central Council for the Business Community) to government and parliament. The government then convenes the social partners to assess the results and sets up a new collective bargaining agreement in which Belgium's competitive problems are dealt with. If the government considers that the efforts of the social partners are insufficient it can, with the backing of parliament, take temporary measures to address the situation itself. The government can also take such measures when faced with extraordinary conditions abroad, such as a drastic change in exchange rates, which could quickly affect Belgium's competitive position. The initiative for this exceptional procedure, however, is exclusively in the hands of the government.

For several years, the government had had the authority to intervene directly in the wage structure if it rose above the average of the main trading partners. Those measures included devaluation, the temporary decoupling of the wages-consumer index link, wage cuts in sectors in difficulty, etc. The combined effect of the loss of employment, the increase in flexibility and government interference in the wage structure put Belgian competitiveness in a prime position by 1987-1988. And the law of 6 January 1987 wanted to perpetuate that position. It instituted permanent and preventive controls to stabilise or improve Belgium's competitive situation.

The law on international competitiveness summarised the neo-liberal revolution of the 1980s. The old Keynesian regime had offered the perspective of the continuing improvement of the 'material and moral well-being of the workers', on the condition that wages kept pace with productivity. The Fordist unilateral compromise sought a balance between the growth in productivity and real wages, (which was never officially codified), or in other words between workers' conduct/mass demand and relative surplus value production. The competitiveness compromise promoted a decrease in the price of labour and approved the decoupling of wages and productivity to the advantage of a development scheme that – even though it retains the growth of productivity as a central driving mechanism – institutionally eliminates labour productivity (decoupling wage costs from the goods produced) and reduces workers' conduct (in its bureaucratic form) to a variable of a national competitiveness barometer.

At the same time, there was, in the settlement of (wage) competitiveness, the beginning of a crisis of the effectiveness of the neo-liberal political economy. The law of 6 January 1989 answered an act that was, at first sight, highly contradictory. The scale of (mass) unemployment, mainly dependent on the increase in production capacity (shortening work time per unit produced), remained at a fairly high level at the end of the eighties. (Official) unemployment fell by almost 30 % between 1984 and 1989, but over 9 % of the active population was unemployed in 1989: 384,000 excluding older unemployed, early retirements, unemployed struck off the register, part-time unemployed, etc. If the criterion of (non-)performed working hours is used, respectively the total of all full-time unemployed and all part-time unemployed, the result is over one million men and women somehow confronted with unemployment at the end of the eighties and the beginning of the nineties. The effect of the recovery of the rate of growth on the rise in employment was weak to say the least. Moreover, the growth rate itself was well below the level of the 1960-1973 period. Industrial production, for example, not including the construction sector, increased by 18.63 % between 1983 and 1989, compared to a 34.42 % increase between 1960 and 1966, and a 39.75 % rise between 1967 and 1973. The regulation of wage competitiveness did not compensate for this recessive tendency, however. In fact, it strengthened the negative effects of mass unemployment on the evolution of consumer demand; in other words, it encouraged the chronic crisis of surplus value realisation.

The contradiction is to be found in a sharpening of the conflicting elements of the late-capitalist – third – technological revolution. This revolution fully broke through in the 1980s in the shape of half-automation and miniaturisation, in particular in the strong growth of so-called 'immaterial' production forces – new information technologies developed at the expense of chemical and electrical technologies. The spectacular recovery of competitiveness after 1982 can also be seen as the effect of a big increase in productivity, as a result of new, more specialised and flexible, decentralised labour processes and forms of labour organisation. The latter was no longer held back by an institutional desire for a dialectic of productivity and wages. The cycle of wage competitiveness largely coincides with the evolution of the surplus value rate: Belgian 'wage costs per product unit' – a formula that in contrast with the dominant criterion within the institutional competitiveness machinery ('wage costs per employer') does take into account the evolution of productivity – rose considerably in the seventies in comparison with the twenty most important countries, and then fell spectacularly from 1981-1982 onwards. At the same time, the New Technological System with its high productivity potential considerably increases the percentage of capital invested in 'dead' capital. On the one hand, mass consumer demand at the end of the eighties remained too weak in order to maintain a growth rate recovery; on the other hand, the new accumulation conditions (investment costs) generated an interest rate that was too low, and necessitated a policy of demand restriction. On the one hand, the new technologies represent an enormous potential of liberation: they are, to a large extent, an answer to the crisis of industrial labour (anti-Taylorist resistance, refusal of Fordist labour, etc.) in the late sixties and early seventies, and come down to a progressive reduction of the total of socially necessary work time. On the other hand, they generate an enormous labour surplus – their introduction and development went hand in hand with the end of the policy of reducing work time – and reinforce continuing social regression.

Having reached its ideological peak, neo-liberalism was thus forced to partly reduce the fledgling recovery, c.q. mass consumer demand. The saving efforts of the masses were not allowed to bring in a new economic spring for everyone.

The New Technological System, in other words, presupposes an almost permanent disorganisation. It generates a regulation of demand supported by a third demand, in between the profits and the wages: the consumption of the rich. This can only partly counteract the crisis of marketing opportunities, which, as a result of the relative reduction of global wage mass, encumbers the realisation of continuously increasing surplus value.

In order to control this disorganisation, neo-liberalism calls on a series of basic principles of social power technology of the post-war plan state. The neo-liberal revolution indeed only means a partial break with Keynesian political economy. The policy of supply and the no longer strictly linear or finalistic, but open forms of planning, grafted onto new soft technologies, are accompanied by a selective, hard policy of demand and of old, further refined planning techniques intended to keep the evolution of social relations controllable and predictable. This new regime can clearly be traced in the Belgian regulation of wage competitiveness. The law of 6 January 1989 has the threatening and safeguarding of competitiveness as its central themes. It is completely imbued with the 'bunker' ideology which was so characteristic of the prevention logic of the post-war plan state: it transforms the least hint of an overly strong rise in labour cost (in comparison with competitors) into a latent, constant threat.

It also inserts itself into the further development of a system of population-regulation power technologies referring to the necessary continuity – the continued existence – of its own population ('people', 'nation', 'region', 'community'). Competitiveness introduced an element of war. Instead of the classic liberal paradigm based on competition between many individual and distinct capitalists, this new neo-liberal measure on wage competitiveness smacked of nationalist competition. It was our 'own' economy against 'the German', 'the British', 'the Spanish',... economies. It encased the competitive forces of the companies into those of their nations. Looking at the system from that angle, it referred to the old Christian model of the enterprise society in the sense that the system fostered participatory management, with quality control as the main perspective. National competitiveness implied a national mobilisation of companies, a sort of cooperative of inter-linked companies that was responsible for the quality of its products. Moreover, the tendency to disorganisation implied in the New Technological System was also – and particularly – active at the company level. The high cost of investments led to an extension of equipment and production time. The time Belgium's industrial production capacity was used rose to 77 hours a week at the end of the 1980s and 70 % of Belgium's industry relied on shift work. It called for flexible and just-in-time labour systems, which generated new contradictions at the level of work organisation. Product demand was increasingly individualised, calling for production without stocks, goods that could be quickly manufactured and meet individual consumer demand. This new configuration of production held high risks, both on the supply and the demand side. Production without stocks made the system vulnerable to labour resistance. Work interruptions that affected one link, soon spread disorder throughout the chain. The 1990 half-day strikes at the Ford car plant in Genk were a case in point. Attempts to build the flexible factory as a consensual area were based on the very brittle structure of the production process. The Fordist factory after the war was built on cooperation between government, employers and unions and dominated the economic-social relations until the early 1970s. Post-Fordism undermined the dominance of the worker in the mass production chain and deconstructed the factory concept since it shed labour and contracted out work and services. It caused the further dismantling of the old core industries. It partly eroded direct labour controls on the production process, integrated autonomous action, and made the production process and the workforce more flexible. It also increased individual participation, enhanced political-economic knowledge acquisition and easily disrupted teamwork. Some old Fordist-Keynesian labour technologies had to be dusted off again to turn the factory floor into an area where a sense of solidarity still ruled. The new strategy of participatory management was not immediately able to reduce the impact of the new technologies. The first applications of the new labour organisation were mostly based on the Japanese model and especially centred on quality control, and they were usually unsuccessful. General Motors, FN, Glaverbel and Caterpillar were among the first to start using the new strategies. At the end of the 1980s, a second offensive of co-management further undermined the old Taylorist system of labour organisation. Integral quality control, a strategy that relied on competent, skilled labour, totally transformed the production methods. But a key condition for all this was a positive attitude of union representatives. The Catholic union for one was willing to put new ways of 'union association' into practice. An extraordinary congress of the ABVV-FGTB union condemned 'the totalitarian enterprise culture' at a time when the Flemish ABVV (FLIG) was already calling for sensible application of the principle of participatory management. The ABVV was driven by technological optimism that saw technology as a motor for growth. General Motors in Antwerp set off on the road of co-management in 1989-1990. Both Flanders and Wallonia set up projects to boost co-management, sometimes with union participation. In Flanders, the *Sociaal Economische Raden* (Socio-economic Councils), the *Reconversiemaatschappijen* (Reconversion Societies) and the *Stichting Technologie Vlaanderen* (Technology Foundation Flanders) are worth mentioning. In Wallonia, several sectors saw the establishment of a *Concertation stratégique* in early 1988. In Liège (Groupe Japon) and in Charleroi (CAAEC), eighty ABBV and ACV leaders participated in new institutions of co-management from the late eighties onwards.

Racism and the 'New Social Issue'

At the same time, both the regulation of wage competitiveness and participatory management were continued with a new racist approach. Racism not only affected the world of ideas ('mistaken representation', 'prejudice', 'ignorance' concerning 'others', etc.). It was also a technology of power and a split-up of labour based on bio-politics. Racism deploys counter-tendencies against processes of destabilisation, decomposition and deconstruction. It introduces a attitude of war with the survival of the 'own kind' – differentiated from the threat of 'strangers' – a stake. The breakthrough of new racism during the 1980s was partly caused by the contradictions in the regulation of the third demand, or the disorganisation created by the new technological system. The quantitative dismantling of the mass demand regime corresponded with a consumer regime based on better, new technology goods and the exclusion of many from that system. The tension between the need to maintain certain conditions for growth and the need for ever higher surplus production boosted the value of the goods: more quality, faster distribution of a wider array of goods, stress on design, culture and individual taste, etc. This increase was by nature targeted at a limited number of target groups. The new regime, clearly traceable in the post-modernist big city – the shifts in the Brussels' social or spatial structure are good examples – also corresponded with transformations in the production structure. It was the result of a thorough transformation of the working class. The growth of the high-tech industries coincided with the creation of parallel circuits of absolute surplus production, with a decrease in employment in the 'secondary' industrial sector and growth in the 'tertiary' service sector. Post-Fordism split up the working class in a relatively small core of stable labour, a broad, segmented periphery of unstable labour, a differentiated army of unemployed and a new underclass of poor.

The so-called new racism was the result of this production and consumption structure. The exclusion of many from the production and consumption structure caused a thorough reorganisation of the working class that went well beyond the factory floor and into the realm of society as such: collective consumerism, the urban aspect, organisation of accommodation, etc. The new racism acted against potential resistance and rationalised the new divisions in society. It represented a new tribalism that set people against people, culture against culture, region against region, community against community, city against city, neighbourhood against neighbourhood, etc. It was based on a system of seclusion, exclusion and confinement. An immigration stop was put into effect as of 1974 and residence permits were also curtailed. An example is article 18bis added to the 'foreigners' law' of 15 December 1980 through the Gol law of 28 June 1984. During the early nineties, measures were taken to keep refugees out, with an increasing number of so-called '*sans papiers*' – people without legal papers – forced into illegality. In general, the policy of seclusion, always based on planning acts of separation and division of spaces and populations, produced a series of simple binary differentiations: 'in' vs. 'out'; 'indigenous' vs. 'immigrant'; 'normal' vs. 'abnormal'; etc. A series of Belgian political and social rights were kept out of reach of foreigners. Voting rights for immigrants, an issue that had been open for discussion, was no longer so after 1982. Police actions further illustrated this logic: seclusion of migrant youths and identity controls in closed-off neighbourhoods. This logic was also visible on the factory floor. Volkswagen in Forest stopped employing non-European Union citizens during the 1980s. It shed light on how seclusion became exclusion. The policy of exclusion added to the substitute labour force and banned many unemployed for good from the production structure. The immigration stop coincided with the transition to a policy that condemned a sizable part of the foreign labourers and their children to a labour reserve pool that was already being filled with part of the Belgian population. In other words, seclusion and exclusion are complementary, and intimately and complexly entwined. Exclusion can operate as a way of existence – or a result of – the policy of seclusion. Simultaneously, seclusion operates within the field constituted by exclusion. The spatial/ethnic dichotomy introduces a competitive model in the excluded group: it sets 'indigenous' against 'foreigner', segregates along the lines of 'ethnicity' and 'culture', teaches the 'indigenous' poor to seek the causes of poverty in the 'foreign' or politically helpless poor. Compared with old racism, this new strain was less determined by blood and biology and more by culture. As a phenomenon, it was more subtle and 'civilised' and fed off social science. It postulated the existence of invariable cultural differences and made them absolute; it claimed an unalienable right to be different or condemned xenophobia. It spread the dogma of fixed cultural differences and called for containment democracy that enclosed and detained parts of the population. It herded certain sectors of the population within their own cultural identity and within stable ethnic boundaries.

New racism's ability to dominate was limited, though, and it was unable to control the contradictions of the new production system. New racism could just have been a catalyst for a novel type of resistance. That was evident during the riots of migrant youths in May 1991 in the Brussels municipalities of Vorst, Sint-Gilles and Molenbeek. The spark that set off the incident was a routine police identity control. It was the first climax in a wild cycle of confrontation that had no connection with classic, reformist labour resistance. It showed the potential for conflict created by new urban subcultures within the periphery of the flexible economy. It showed the existence of a new, instable, multi-form subjectivity. The reaction to the racist police violence was an offensive return to an identity constituted by new racism and a destruction of the same identity. It openly challenged the mechanisms of seclusion, exclusion and integration: 'They want us to integrate, but we've already integrated'.

The effects and recruitment potential of this new racism should not be underestimated. The zone of extra-institutional micro behaviour was not only about migrant riots, destabilising behaviour, or behaviour that openly challenges the organisation of space and of the prevailing regime of fixed identities. In a way, this zone has a polar structure, with a fascist pole, too. A radical consequence of new racism was extreme right-wing populism embodied by the *Vlaams Blok* (Flemish Bloc) in Flanders and *Agir* and *Front National* in Wallonia. The *Vlaams Blok* extended the logic of new racism into the realm of deportation and expulsion based on the argument that culture can only truly develop within its own territory. It would give the Flemish people the possibility to restore their own identity and boost social and economic development.

Extreme right-wing grassroots support was established during the second half of the 1980s, coinciding with the momentary recovery of economic growth. The successive defeats of the labour movement during the 1980s and the resulting disorientation and crisis within the working class also profited the extreme right. It fed off the disintegration of the old socialist camp. The incursion of the extreme right into the socialist camp was an indication of a connection between the reformist and extreme right-wing ideologies. The populism of the extreme-right inserts the emancipation of parts of the traditional socialist basis of the reformist apparatus into a process of re-coding or reclamation of territory that is meant to restore the lost points of recognition. The transition created paranoid fascist yearnings – 'priority for our own people', 'security', 'cleanliness' etc. – became rallying cries of the extreme right and replaced the concept of the class struggle. They continue the state-reformist mega-story of yore, built around labour. The precondition of this story was the political passivity of the masses. The extreme right built on a political structure that had kept the working class from becoming truly autonomous within the capitalist system. The post-war socialists had held on to parts of their ideology but their integration into the Fordist system intertwined them closely with the state structure. One example is the population-controlling aspect of the existing socialist movement, which reserved prosperity for the 'own' masses; as such it interiorised the technology of (state) racism, and even contributed to it.

The extreme right was able to break through because the ideological conditions of the 1980s were favourable and because, by relying on a series of basic components of post-war planning ideology, it could turn the post-reformist change of the socialist movement into a racist direction.

The creation of extreme right-wing grassroots support also showed why it was able, with relative ease, to affect and be part of executive institutions, social organisations, the media, etc. The breakthrough of the extreme right was met with a mix of disgust and condemnation of racism on the one hand, and an understanding of the phenomenon and adaptation of policy on the other. The elections of 24 November 1991 turned into a huge victory for the Vlaams Blok in Flanders, and the gut reaction of the anti-racist movements was to mobilise its support in protest actions such as *Hand in Hand*, *Objectief*, and, to a lesser extent, *Charta*. A second type of reaction, which was also linked to the anti-racism movement, was evident in the explanations that were offered, *ad nauseam*, for the stunning election result. They emerged from a highly developed twilight zone between scientific (especially sociological) research and policy. Three opinions dominated. One showed how elements from the extreme right-wing campaign usurped an essence of truth and became a basis for interpretation. It linked the Blok's success with the 'immigrant problem', 'petty crime', 'increased safety concerns', 'spineless' government action against 'illegals'. Solutions were plentiful: refusal to grant non-EU foreigners certain rights, sustained migrant and integration policy, the restriction of asylum policies, tolerance education, speeding up of the judicial process, security contracts, etc. Other interpretations sought out the roots of the extreme right's success and brought the real problems (incorrectly presented by the extreme-right) to the surface – social exclusion, poverty, the erosion of the social structure, increased anomy, the problems of living together, etc. In this case, the extreme right became a catalyst for the further development of a 'new social issue'. Fairly classic for this interpretation is the (traditional Fordist) distinction between economy and society – in order to allow the social aspect to be delineated as an autonomous area within which specific (problem) groups can be defined. Relatively new was the establishment of 'new divisions': the social issue no longer coincided with the capital-labour conflict, the production and labour process were no longer the core issue and had to make way for the urban contradictions and divisions such as rich vs. poor neighbourhoods, areas with good and poor infrastructure, etc. At the same time, the immigration policy-insecurity link dominated the debates. It offered arguments for an appeal to improve integration and allowed the further unlocking of the problem of (in)security and so-called problem areas, which in its turn also raised questions as to whether certain immigrant sections could be integrated. A third series of interpretations stressed a direct link with the 1991 election results and defined extreme right-wing policies as 'anti-politics'. It wanted to bring citizens back into the fold of democratic institutions, pointed out the necessity to 'bridge the divide between citizen and politics', create a 'citizen's contract' and establish a '*cordon sanitaire*' to isolate the Blok. At the same time, this technique retained close links with the paradigm of exclusion, and as such with the topics of (in)security, migrants, (multi-)culturalism etc. It called for a 'new urban ideal' and a 'new citizenship'.

The extreme-right brought forward a series of political innovations that were closely linked to the establishment of a new Belgium. The core issues that the surge of the Blok laid bare fell under the authority of the regions and communities: employment, social housing, education, culture, environment, health care, care for the elderly, urban renovation, etc. It could also be said that the (political) healing of the 1991 trauma was mainly done on a regional or community level (except for the more repressive aspects such as security contracts). The division of Belgium into communities and regions was not only a matter of transfer of authority. The further development of communities and regions can also affect the design of new policies, especially in connection with certain areas defined by the transferred authorities. The asymmetrical development of the Belgian regions affected the process. Flanders was in the forefront of the development of new policies. This could be explained by the fact that the breakthrough of the extreme right was first and foremost a Flemish phenomenon. But the ideology of the Flemish Community, which is not necessarily in total contradiction with the Blok, also offered an explanation. Flanders had institutional authority over such issues as (health) care, and as such exclusion and marginalisation and put it relatively high on the political agenda. The asymmetric development was also evident in the regional statistics. Flanders and Wallonia spent about the same on education, local authorities, public works and transport. But Flanders spent more on urban planning and housing, the environment and especially welfare (50 % more in 1996). Wallonia spent more on its economy and employment. Brussels, because of its complex linguistic, institutional composition, was a special case. It hovered between the so-called Jacobean assimilation model (assimilation of individuals) and the so-called Anglo-Saxon integration model (attention for ethnic or cultural groups or minorities, self-organisation of the different groups, etc.). But during the 1990s, it increasingly started leaning towards the Flemish model that attaches great importance to cultural differences, to the welfare and health of its population and to the participation of the lower classes.

A clear example of social-political innovation was the policy to combat social exclusion – the lack of opportunities in life – a new strategy in the battle against poverty. It was not as if increasing poverty was only discovered during the early 1990s. The notion of 'new poverty' entered the political scene alongside neo-liberalism during the early 1980s. It showed that structural poverty spread to new and more layers of society (more people claiming benefits and a tendency to poverty of many families through increasing insolvency and fundamental changes in spending patterns) following years of government austerity measures. The spread of poverty became a political theme and called for distinct policy approaches. The Martens VI government of 1985-1987 had its own state secretary in charge of the fight against poverty. But it was only during the late 1980s that the political theme of poverty really hit home. In the Flemish Community, important steps in the development and orientation of a specific section within the fight against poverty were a Policy Paper on the Fight against Poverty (5 July 1989) and the *Fonds Van den Bossche* supporting municipal policy for vulnerable social groups. The next step was the approval of a decree by the Vlaamse Raad (Flemish Council) on 31 July 1990, establishing the *Vlaams Fonds voor de Integratie van Kansarmen* (VFIK, Flemish Fund for the Integration of the Underprivileged), also known as the *Fonds Lenssens*; between 1991 and 1998, it received a yearly budget to be divided among Flemish municipal councils and social services battling a 'concentration of poverty and problems with migration and unemployment'. The anti-social seclusion policy was not part of the social security system and assessed poverty from more than just the income angle. Social seclusion had more to do with 'wellbeing' than 'wealth'. It indicated that opportunities had not been equitably spread across society, creating 'out-groups'. It also implied that the policy to combat poverty should also be one to promote integration.

There were many links between the policy to combat social exclusion and migrant policy and this was underlined by the cultural and welfare component of Flemish populism. Migrant policy was, indeed, mainly a Flemish creation. From the late 1980s, the Flemish government produced a series of policy papers, projects and statements that linked ethnic cultural diversity with social exclusion.

Brussels proved to be the new institutional laboratory of social policy *par excellence*. With the development of the Brussels Capital Region (starting in 1989) and the approval of more funds and programs on 'new urban problems' came a labyrinthine system of organisations; they were carried by new political organisational principles (transversality, partnering, participation), by links between the macro-level (Region) and micro-level (associations, neighbourhoods, etc.), by new bodies with an expressly local mission, founded by the Region, by coordination enabling lines of communication between the links of the new institutional complex, etc.

Recession, Tentative Recovery and Budget Deficit (1991-1997)

The new social issue did have an impact and should not be underestimated. Themes like social exclusion, immigrants and safety became issues for the media, political parties and scientific research. They became part of the new social movements, especially that of the Greens. They were an active part of the expansion of the ecological theme in the socio-political direction. The *Sociaal Impulsfonds* (Social Impulse Fund, successor to the VFIK, *Vlaams Fonds voor Integratie van Kansarmen* – Flemish Fund for the Integration of the Underprivileged), launched with the slogan 'a political choice for the city', and especially active in Antwerp, was a clear illustration.

The effectiveness of the issue was limited, though, because of its lack of immediacy. There was a lack of representation because people spoke in place of, or for, the immigrants and those who were socially excluded. This weakness was caused by the inability of the new social politics to counter the permanent disorganisation of the New Technological System. The new social policy was designed to counter the further advance of neo-liberalism, but it had been forced to work within the constraints of neo-liberalism (wage competitiveness regulation, restriction of mass demand, weak employment intensity of the new technologies, etc.). It was, in other words, forced to agree with the systematic undermining of its own realisations. Its position within the economic system clarified this. The rather weak recovery of growth, employment and wages at the end of the eighties was too strong if this recovery was compared with the conditions needed within the framework of a rise of productivity and a stronger rise of investment, for the profit rate to be adequately high. Profits continued to rise but were burdened by the increase in wage costs, even though it was slight. Timid growth culminated in a new recession and crisis during the early 1990s. Unemployment shot up again and the pressure on indirect wages increased. The start of the establishment of the new social policy coincided with the transition from growth into a new recession, stunting its full development. It had the potential to restore control and legitimacy but, from the start, it was reduced to a series of symbolic gestures.

Following the government's Saint Michael agreement, social security issues (which had remained a federal matter) gained in importance. Together with the 1991-1993 recession and increased unemployment, the authority over social policy of the Flemish, Walloon and Brussels regions was kept within existing limits. The recession, as a mechanism to repair wage competitiveness, also affected the upgrading and search for alternative financing of the wage system.

The budget deficit and overall debt forced politicians to envisage several scenarios to reform social security. There were calls to federalise the system and split it up along linguistic lines. For the Vlaams Blok it was a logical consequence in its drive for Flemish nationhood, but others, too, were thinking aloud that a split might not be such a bad idea. Prime Minister Jean-Luc Dehaene wanted to develop a new, comprehensive Social Project. But this scenario further emphasised the paradoxical disposition of the years 1991-1993. The recession was countered with the old formulas of the post-war consultation economy and welfare state. But the recession was about the radical implementation of a policy of structural reform and the linkage between wages and competitiveness. As such, the first calls for a new comprehensive social compromise already carried the seeds of defeat within them.

It was part of an international regressive tendency – the rediscovery of the New Deal approach and Keynesianism, the German 'industrialism', putting the post-Fordist organisation principles in perspective and proposing new neo-corporatist settlements. The development was spawned by the first serious crisis of neo-liberalism and post-Fordism when the integration of new technologies had failed to deliver a new period of growth. The regression did not necessarily need to be dysfunctional. Plans to beat the recession amounted to a partial inversion of the policy to reduce labour costs. They stood little chance of success since the good old Fordist way found it hard to overturn the lack of growth. In a sense, the recession was the crisis of the flawed linkup between advanced neo-liberalism and old social planning policy. Mass unemployment and the break-up between wages and productivity undermined the effectiveness of the negotiations.

The failure of the new social pact was illustrated by the quirky economic trends of the summer and autumn of 1993. That summer King Baudouin died and was replaced by his brother, Albert II. The nation had shown a rare sense of unity in mourning the 'king with a social conscience', yet three months later the idea of a new 'economic and social consensus' was already a pipe dream. The idea had begun circulating at the end of July 1993 and was included in the speech by Albert II on 9 August, at the end of nine intense days of mourning. The new social pact fell apart in October and was replaced the Global Plan, which was based on an idea from the National Bank. By the end of the month, social protest had already started and it would culminate in the general 24-hour strike organised by a joint union front on 26 November.

The anti-Global Plan movement, however, was unable to stop structural reform in its tracks, and could not come up with viable alternatives. There was no way to turn back the clock to the days of the 1944 Social Pact or to 1936. The resistance against the plan shared a regressive (re)action pattern with the proposition for a new social pact. It was a half-current, half-asynchronous resistance demystifying the neo-liberal growth projections, but hardly founded in the recognition of (new) antagonisms within the new productive space. It relied on the retention, with new conditions, of old institutions and power mechanisms.

The recovery of growth after 1994 was not based on a new social compromise interiorising mass demands or needs in the cycle of capital, but instead on a new defeat of labour. Corrective measures to contain wage costs were approved in 1993 and included an effective wage stop, the introduction of the so-called health index and measures to lower social costs. It resulted in the stabilisation of wage costs per product unit, low inflation and increased company profitability.

At the same time, the intensification of post-reformism was intrinsically crisis-prone, and directly linked with the economic climate. The gradual elimination of runaway labour costs had relatively little annual growth of some 1 to 2 % to show for it. There were a series of mini-recessions and the situation offered little hope for a soft landing. The solution that was offered for the 1991-1993 crisis clashed with efforts to drive back the recessionary trend by expanding the potential for mass consumption. But the expansion of private consumption was not the only thing that remained limited after 1994. Company investment also refused to get off the ground again. The spectacular accumulation of money capitalism came at the expense of a devaluation of productive capital. It was the result of the specific contradictions within the post-Fordist, new technology system, which was marked by insufficient growth. Demand created by state expenditures was also under pressure. It was held back by a huge overall state debt, which was also at the heart of international coordination measures as part of the drive to create the single currency. National measures to improve the competitive edge were extended at a European Union level to protect Europe's economic position on the global stage. Progress towards the Economic and Monetary Union (EMU) and a further centralisation of capital at a European level implied further neo-liberal measures. The Maastricht Treaty, which was brokered during the recession of the early 1990s (it was concluded in December 1991 and came into effect in 1993), stressed continued economic austerity. The treaty set tough conditions to join EMU. Annual budget deficit was not allowed to exceed 3 % of Gross Domestic Product and overall debt could not be higher than 60 % of GDP. A 1996 Stability Pact was added to the system; it stipulated that annual budget deficits should never exceed 3 % of GDP anymore except in extraordinary, momentary circumstances. The Stability Pact reinforced controls. It envisaged a procedure against excessive deficits with a system of increased sanctions for euro-zone nations that fail to keep to the guidelines on tight budgetary discipline and refuse to heed the recommendations of the European Union Council to remedy the situation. In Belgium, the budgetary deficit decreased by 4.1 percentage points between 1993 and 1996. EC-estimates indicated Belgium as one of the six nations with a 1996 structural deficit not exceeding the 3 % norm. Also the (enormous) Belgian gross debt with relation to GDP was reduced, from 136.8 % in 1993 to 130 % in 1996.

The 'White' Crisis

The crisis-like deepening of post-reformism was not only visible in a special economic climate. In fact, it preferably took form outside the economy. A clear example was the tendency for economic-political issues and certain private economic mechanisms to evolve into political-financial or personal criminal affairs or scandals: the murder of PS politician André Cools, the Agusta affair, the Dassault affair, the 'stolen shares' at the cabinet of Alain Van der Biest, illegal party funding, the Delcroix affair, the shells contract, the environmental box order, the hormone dossier and the murder of vet Karel Van Noppen, the *Hoog Comité van Toezicht* (High Commission of Supervision), the wasted billions of Belgian development aid, Boel, the Super Club file, tax fraud files, product fraud, infringements of tax and banking legislation, KB-Lux, the Stuyck affair, car rackets, drug trade, fraudulent bankruptcies, accountancy swindles, etc. Especially the investigation into the murder of André Cools (18 July 1991), who had been mentor and master of the PS bureaucracy for years, and the Agusta affair (1995) – and the role played by SP and PS ministers and socialist party organisations in these affairs – deepened the crisis of political legitimacy in the mid-1990s. The stakes were high, as these affairs involved the role and function of certain government orders, the mechanism of party funding through government contractors, and particular aspects of the muddling of certain segments of the social-democratic bureaucracy after 1988; through structural economic reforms, it had become the domain of a half-private, half-public group of new managers.

The Dutroux case merits a more extensive treatment in the description of the deepening legitimacy crisis of the nineties. It generated a broad protest movement with an immense number of subdivisions. Its culmination in the *Witte Mars* (White March) of Sunday 20 October 1996 contained elements that could be traced to, for example, the peace movement of the eighties, the anti-racist movement, the royal mourning days of the summer of 1993, and the events of 1989 in Eastern Europe. Beyond the wave of shock and protest, this case was connected in many ways to the economic level, even though the driving force behind the popular protest was the moral indignation about monstrous sexual practices, about the bodies of the girls assaulted and murdered in the Dutroux cellars, and about an 'incomprehensible' formalistic legalism (the so-called 'spaghetti decree'). Initially, labour protest had a significant part in starting up a movement in the hours immediately after the judgement of the Court of Cassation on 15 October 1996; it decided to take the examining magistrate Connerotte off the case because he had attended a spaghetti dinner organised by the parents of the murdered children. The protest took the shape of spontaneous strikes, for instance at VW in Brussels. The explicit labour resistance against the judicial and police apparatus would quickly give way to a comprehensive consensual White Movement.

Some political scientists have interpreted the White March of 20 October 1996 as the emergence of the New Citizen, a character that could be written into the story of the rift between politics and everyday life, which started in the aftermath of the electoral breakthrough of the extreme-right on 24 November 1991. The White March could be explained as a post-modern event, an escape from 'pillarised' behaviour and, wider still, as a clear symptom of the further downfall of a political system that had relied on passive 'pillar' masses and pragmatic elites for far too long. It could not be denied that the White March was composed of an entire array of opinions and attitudes, but this plurality and especially a possible political differentiation of the protest were suppressed to the advantage of a moral homogeneity that was staged as a-political. The White March was based on the construction of a large (300,000) and silent superior super-ego clad in white. It reverted to a partly pre-liberal concept of the political space with a bottom-up principle (from the unanimous multitude cleansed of politics and corruption to the corrupt powers-that-be) based on the power of numbers, without the masses formulating any demands, without political discussion or tendencies and fractions – in short, without parties directly or indirectly based on social differentiations, social layers or classes. This almost religious character of the White March, and by extension of the White Movement, was also clearly noticeable in the way that the protest directly brought the economy into the discourse. Investigative journalists in particular focused on the existence of usually well-hidden parallel criminal economic circuits and overexploitation (such as the studios of the sex industry); these discoveries were effortlessly integrated into an old fascination for sexual transgression, founded on religious beliefs. The fantasies were usually about clandestine perverse behaviour of figures of power and authority, and a special place was reserved for commercial paedophile networks. In this respect, the White Movement was anything but post-modern. Not only the movement, but in particular the way it was reported on in the media was imbued with old hermeneutics, an ancient regime of truth, Christian in origin, recaptured in an empirical and positivist scientific model, in the crime novel, in journalism; above all, it was integrated into the police and judicial apparatus, relying as it does on an act of unveiling and revealing the truth, respectively true facts.

Because of the nature of the case and the way in which it was explored, the crisis of legitimacy spread and mingled with a mix of ethics, law, deontology, belief and disbelief and paranoia. A strong ethical discourse emerged, somewhat obscuring the sociological and political discourse. This ethical discourse, corresponding with a revival of the figure of the ethical intellectual, reflected a crisis of neo-liberalism, usually through a moral condemnation of the economy and from a semi-implicit communal framework of reference. The same dominance of the ethical, or rather secularised religious, discourse about the economic discourse, and the mix of morality and law, not only served to legitimise the resistance against the law, but also to claim a right to suspicion. Apart from the New Citizen, the notion of 'crisis of confidence' featured in the lexicon spread by the Dutroux case. On reflection, this notion was also able to feed the permanent suspicion that divided the nation for eight years, until the trial in the spring of 2004, in 'believers' and 'non-believers'. The (dis)belief concerned the existence of networks. From the private libidinous and criminal Dutroux economy, lines were drawn to other centres – of clients and employers – preferably to one major centre, itself a network of the powerful, from which the entire network could be closed and protected. In other words, the 'heart' of neo-liberalism – which was central in the mainly ethical criticism of neo-liberalism – was nothing but the dirty and corrupt hunger of sexually delinquent rulers. The question about networks, and eventually the one network, yielded an extensive and special para-literature, mostly based on testimonies about sexual abuse that were usually not connected with the Dutroux case in a strict judicial sense.

Also the Dutroux Commission, established by parliament on 24 October 1996 and presided over by M. Verwilghen (VLD) was confronted with the question about networks. In April 1997 the commission phrased a withering criticism about the way in which the police and the ministry had conducted the investigations into the girls' disappearances; on 6 May 1997, it resumed proceedings with the question as to whether Dutroux had been protected by high-ranking figures. This resulted in a second report on 16 April 1998, concluding that there had been no such protection, but that Dutroux had been able to exploit corruption, carelessness and professional incompetence. During the Dutroux trial, which only started on 1 March 2004, Dutroux himself, his lawyers, a number of the parents and their lawyers, and the lawyers of one of the survivors, claimed that Dutroux had been one element in a much bigger network and had acted on instructions, and that the responsibility for the girls' death was also shared by his accomplices. Yet it was Dutroux, on 17 June 2004, who was found guilty of abduction, rape and murder. The jury was also able to convict him in his capacity of head of a criminal gang, but the reality of the ultimate network could not be made believable in the face of the facts. Those facts pointed to the simple, macabre and disgusting conclusion that the psychopath had not brought his victims into a commercial circuit, and had not even taken any initiative to trade their bodies, as he had let them starve to death.

It must be clear that the emergence and subsequent development of the White Crisis in the autumn of 1996 can only be interpreted as social alchemy, from a mix of elements and circumstances. Equally clear is the fact that we cannot speak of a 'recovery' of political efficiency after 1996, as – strange though it may seem – the White Crisis exactly unfolded within a climate showing a strong increase in the efficiency of politics, or at least of the central government. Viewed from the question of governance – the search for sound government – the Dehaene II government (1995-1999) actually scored very high marks. The government produced positive effects as it fulfilled its main brief, i.e. reorganising state finances, thanks to effective and decisive measures. The positive prognosis of the European Commission concerning the reduction of Belgium's structural budget deficit (cf. supra) came after the deficit had been brought down to the imposed critical 3 % limit – actually in the period following the peak of the White Crisis (the so-called 'Dutroux period'). An unthinkable Belgium – the heart of Europe without euros – was avoided. In 1998, Belgium was at the head of the first group of eleven countries to adopt the European single currency. The Dehaene government was also able to give direction to the new complex Belgian state model, even though it was effected in a fairly traditional way. The coalition of Christian democrats and socialists relied on a north-south axis dominated by the respective strongest political families in the north and the south, balancing the relations between the different federal states (in which the same families made up the government coalitions, except for the Brussels Region) by a synthesising umbrella Belgian federal level.

Confronted by an indignant and furious Belgian crowd, which formed bottom-up during the White Crisis, this synthesising level served as a starting point for a rhetorical crisis that explicitly indicated the deficiencies of the 'old' government discourse, which had referred too much to budget figures or the economy as such. It contributed to the gradual emergence of a new political culture, the reduction of the old party-political and ideological oppositions (such as left vs. right) and the establishment of so-called 'unity thinking' (*pensée unique*). This rhetorical reorganisation also directly tied in with the White Crisis. It interiorised the mass indignation preferably in terms of security – the general problem of safety, the problem that especially the extreme-right placed high on the agenda – and allowed decisive steps to be taken in reforms leading to one of the most important reorganisations of the police and the judiciary in Belgian history. Apart from conclusions by a few expert commissions, especially those by the parliamentary commission Verwilghen (cf. supra) led to managerial interventions in the police and the judiciary. The translation of these conclusions into new legislation was realised in going back to the technique of Belgian compromise politics or to the pacification decision-making with the political parties in the leading roles. This translation was speeded up after a new climax in the Dutroux case; on 23 April 1998 the predictably unthinkable happened: Dutroux simply escaped in the court of Neufchâteau. This weird event confirmed the findings of the second report of the Verwilghen commission of 16 February 1998 (cf. supra) in two ways: it illustrated the sloppiness and incompetence of certain police services, but also showed that Dutroux could not rely on a well-organised network, as he was re-arrested four hours after his escape thanks to the vigilance of a gamekeeper. Both the Minister of the Interior and the Justice Minister offered their resignation on the day of the escape. Four days later the new Justice Minister appealed to all democratic parties to cooperate in the reform of the judiciary and the police in order to avoid 'the extreme-right parties being the only winners'. An immediate start was made to the so-called Octopus Consultation, with the participation of eight political parties (all government and opposition parties apart from the extreme-right), which led to the Octopus Agreement on 24 May 1998. This agreement laid the basis for a police and judiciary reform; it reinforced the police ('unitary police force') and its autonomy at the expense of both legislative and executive powers. Moreover, it was to the advantage of more centralisation within the judiciary, and it benefited in particular the role of the Public Prosecutor at the expense of that of the examining magistrate.

Legitimacy and Economy (1997-1998)

The increased effectiveness of the state in the 1995-1999 period was the synthesis of the effects of the reorganisation of the social balance of power between 1982 and 1993. The Dehaene II government fitted into a new cycle of Christian democrat-Socialist coalitions starting in 1988, which did not break with the neo-liberal economic policy but even enabled a substantial further development of this policy by the creation and use of a set of instruments that guaranteed a long-term stability or increase of the competitiveness of the Belgian economy. Dehaene II was based on the labour defeat of late 1993 – the unsuccessful fight against the global plan – that linked up with the long cycle of defensive resistance of the traditional labour movement between 1976 and 1986, only resulting in defeats in the 1982-1986 period. The successful reduction of the budget deficit can be seen as the synthesis of increased state effectiveness, as controlling public finances went hand in hand with controlling of the wages, obviously in the public sector – the budget left no room for manoeuvre for union demands or government personnel action – but also in the private sector, where normalisation of wages became the guiding principle.

The framework of wage evolution and, more in general, of collective labour relations in the entire private sector was fixed in the hugely important *Interprofessioneel Akkoord* (Cross-Sector Agreement), which was concluded at the end of 1998 by unions and employers' organisations for 1999 and 2000. The agreement was made possible thanks to a fairly classical pacification technique based on the old pillar logic. The two major unions, ACV and ABVV, working together in a bureaucratic united front, largely acted as extensions of the friendly coalition. As indicated earlier, the 1990s union battle was mainly driven by a regressive reaction concerning the preservation of the old system of social pacification. The new agreement meant an end to this regressive action without a complete break with the old institutionalised forms of conflict management. The change in the position of the cross-sector union leaderships amounted to an end to a specific form of union autonomy within a regulated social life – the Belgian historical-social consultation model relied on a combination of autonomous union struggle and far-reaching integration of this struggle in the capitalist system – and a definitive choice of modernisation and normalised conduct as means to continue to play a regulating role. The change was the most marked in the ABVV, whose cross-sector leadership abandoned a strategy of constructing contractual positions of power from the bulwarks of large-scale industries and switched to imposing guidelines on companies and centrals from a responsible and stabilising role within Belgium and Europe. The unions' seal of approval for the *Interprofessioneel Akkoord 1999-2000* did not only mean a partly implicit, partly explicit agreement with the principle that unemployment may be caused by high wages, but especially a very explicit union acceptance of the legal wage norm determining that wage costs must not rise above the average wage costs of Belgium's most important trade partners. The protection of the competitiveness of the Belgian economy in Europe, which had been pre-structured and dictated by and contributed to the protection of European competitiveness in the world, was as such continued in a trade union protection of the same competitiveness.

Another face of the increase of effectiveness was the permanent, at first sight crisis-like character of neo-liberal productive order in the shape of unrelenting restructuring and closure of (parts of) sectors and companies. The list of dismissals and company closures in the first few months of 1997, for instance, was impressive: Forges de Clabecq, Renault-Vilvoorde, RMT, Nova, Alcatel Bell, Belgacom, Caterpillar, Bekaert, Boël, Bombardier, Philips, NMBS, etc.

Two closures in particular made the headlines and grew into complex union and political files. Steel producer Forges de Clabecq in Walloon-Brabant had known a long history of reorganisations. At the end of the seventies, it still had a workforce of 6,000, in the early eighties 4,000 remained, and at the end of 1996 a mere 1,800 were left. In early January 1997 the Commercial Court in Nivelles declared the company bankrupt. The bankruptcy was mainly due to an EC intervention concerning the Walloon Region, whose subsidy policy was judged to be a distortion of competition. The struggle for the survival of Forges de Clabecq created long and complex conflicts, especially between the ABVV leadership (both the cross-sector leadership and that of the socialist metal central) and a militant delegation of workers; the former was trying to reach a normalisation of labour relations in that period, and that involved accepting the European construction.

The battle for Forges illustrated one of the shapes taken by the break with the classical social-democratic constructions. This break-up was characteristic for the deepening of the post-reformist character of the nineties and continued to spread, in part because social-democracy at that time dominated both the EC institutions (Commission and Parliament) and a large majority of national governments, or at least constituted an important mainstay of national coalitions, as was the case in Belgium. It could take the shape of a relentlessly growing influence of the extreme-right in the basis of socialist organisations, with a conscious borrowing of symbols that were historically linked with the socialist movement in particular and the labour movement in general. Vlaams Blok, for instance, increasingly started using symbols like May Day, labour, Daens, Moyson, etc. from the mid-nineties onwards.

The break with social democracy also opened up completely different avenues. The long fight in French-language education, for instance, confronted the PS state with its own programme and principles in the spring of 1996. The climax came on 1 May 1996, with socialist symbols being removed from PS palaces by union militants from the education and other sectors in Brussels, Liège and Charleroi. PS leaders were also denied the opportunity to speak.

Yet another consequence of the break with social democracy was the (temporary) rise of an explicitly authoritarian trade union grassroots resistance, clearly illustrated by the fight for the survival of Forges de Clabecq. This fight was driven by a Stalinist-type reaction pattern (unitary union and unitary party, voting by clapping, negation of the plurality of needs and demands, lengthy speeches by the leader, use of blackmail and violence as arguments, subjectivist denunciation of structures...) brought into play against both the destructive character (the closure of the factory) and the liberation potential of post-Fordism.

The deepening of the post-reformist character of the period was also clearly traceable in the death throes of the Renault plant in Vilvoorde between February and July 1997. The French car giant Renault (the French state was the major stockholder in 1997, with 47 %) turned into a European multinational. When the Belgian plant closed, it was developing global strategies: a new plant was being built in Curitiba (Brazil), another was planned in Moscow with a view to extending the East-European market, there were new projects in India and Malaysia, etc. The closing down of Renault-Vilvoorde presented Belgium – but up to a point also France – with a new, extremely difficult socio-economic dossier dramatically highlighting the problem of employment. At stake was not just a company in a traditional basic Belgian sector, but in an old Fordist sector *par excellence*, which at the same time often showed an exemplary usage of new technologies and labour organisation, and whose realisation of surplus value needed to be strictly tuned to a post-Fordist restructuring of demand. The closure of Renault-Vilvoorde, the most productive of all Renault factories, was in line with the recession of the early nineties, which the automobile sector had not yet overcome in the second half of the decade. It was, in other words, linked with the overcapacity on the European car market, or sharply expressed the recessive character of the recovery after 1993, or more in general of a 'third demand' regulation that implied an overly strong concentration of consumption demand in too small a group.

The closure scenario involved a clear breach of the customs of consultations and negotiations. Instead of a negotiated and phased decision process (along the old Fordist lines), the option of a brutal, unexpected and irreversible closure was taken; in no way were any rules respected. The decision to close the factory was preceded by a French government decision. On 27 February at 5 p.m., the secretary-general of Renault announced the closure of Renault Industrie Belgique (RIB) at the Hilton hotel in Brussels. A short special works council meeting also took place at 5 p.m., during which the personnel delegation was officially informed. As a result of the decision to close, 3,100 workers lost their jobs, and keeping into account the consequences for suppliers, dealers, shop owners and the NMBS (which took care of transport), about 4,000 families were affected. Very soon, Renault workers decided to use radical action: finished cars were impounded in the factory compound.

Renault's strategy of closure and profit also quickly resulted in a broad surge of moral indignation, which in the post-Dutroux period somehow linked up with aspects of the white protest of the autumn of 1996. In Belgium, and particularly in Flanders, a broad front of indignation emerged, involving unions, politicians (among them a few ministers), employers, public opinion, lawyers and bishops. In the factory itself, a long series of actions started (even though only part of the workforce actually participated). On 7 March a one-hour work stoppage in the Belgian automobile sector (at Ford in Genk, Volvo in Ghent, Opel in Antwerp and Volkswagen in Vorst) expanded into France, Spain and Slovenia. The first Euro-strike was a fact. On 11 March the fight again crossed the border into

France. The axis Vilvoorde-Paris was realised in the emergence of a European grassroots union movement. The first Euro-demonstration took place on that day, involving 10,000 workers, both Belgian, French and Spanish Renault personnel. The Euro-manifestation in Paris was the prelude to the European March for Work, which took place in Brussels on 16 March, with 10,000 participants. On 3 April, the Brussels Industrial Tribunal ruled that Renault had acted unlawfully by not consulting the works council, and on 4 April, a French industrial tribunal came to a similar conclusion: Renault had also failed to consult the European Works Council. The reaction of the Renault top was short and simple: a judicial ruling cannot undo economic reality.

The political discourse, and the government's (especially the Flemish government's) discourse, could hardly do anything but align itself with the indignation about the arrogance of capitalism. Yet the political condemnation could not go very far, as it had created its own logic through its involvement in the establishment of a European market: winning a competitive battle. The structure of this logic was not essentially different from the private profit logic. The closure of Renault-Vilvoorde again highlighted, though, that credibility could not be gained by remaining silent about the economy. Consequently, the rhetorical reorganisation was adapted towards a moral condemnation of specific private economic malpractice (failure to respect the rules, etc.), but specifically towards the use of a new rhetorical figure, the one of impotence. However, the (political) impotence concerning the economy was not in the first place expressed by the federal Prime Minister, but by the Flemish political world and in fact especially by authoritative figures of social democracy (such as EU commissioner Karel Van Miert). At a certain point, also the protesters were gripped by this impotence: after Renault had implied that it could hardly act upon the judicial rulings and that only the economic reality mattered, the unions changed their strategy towards obtaining a 'good social plan' to support the workers who had lost their jobs.

This change of course in trade union strategy – the agreements for 'good' social conditions were signed in July – not only meant that the fight was no longer about keeping the factory open, but also that the demand for a reduction in working hours was abandoned. The main union demand had been a redistribution of work through a 10 % reduction of working hours. It may sound strange, but one of the most important results for the entire Belgian union movement of the fight for Renault-Vilvoorde was the liquidation of the demand for a reduction of working hours. At the time, this demand was being revived. Yet it soon transpired that especially the cross-sector ABVV top was aligning its strategy for the fight against unemployment with the government's action plan, designed in line with the European Summit of Luxembourg (which did not mention any reduction of working hours).

Counter-Globalism

Capital can escape social imperatives because it can rely on the existence of diverging movements and speeds controlling diverging temporalities: the flexible nomadic time of cross-border flash capital (of which Renault is only a weak example) vs. sedentary classical historical time of social politics, based on the historical incorporation of workers' mass needs in the general production conditions. Moreover, the current period of worldwide restructuring and internationalisation has been characterised since the seventies by cross-border movement involving the complete cycle of capital, i.e. money, goods and production capital. This is in contrast with earlier periods, like the transition to monopoly capital (1870-1914), in which only trade and financial capital were internationalised. However, this far-reaching de-territorialisation of capital does not mean that the state is not playing any social or economic role anymore. One of the neo-liberal basic postulates is that macro-economic policy can in no way realise a long-term support of growth and employment; yet structural interventions towards more flexibility and de-regularisation of labour markets and freer circulation of goods and services (cf. e.g. the European 'Bolkestein' guidelines) imply a stronger state intervention. Terms such as 'Belgian', 'Flemish', 'Walloon', 'Brussels' or 'European economy' can indicate politically construed economic realities used by capital – the movements of which are beyond the concept of national borders – to continue its social existence. We can talk of a global market, and by extension also of a global information society, but these notions cannot indicate a macro-economic paradigm independent from political categories – the global market emerged with the fall of the Berlin Wall and the end of the Cold War – and from further realisation of judicial forms implied by a new world order. This new order is primarily embodied by relatively new, relatively old global power elite structures (G7, now G8, International Monetary Fund, World Trade Organisation, World Bank, etc.) whose meetings, conferences and summits became major events from the end of the nineties thanks to the resistance of an anti-globalisation movement of which most tendencies soon profiled themselves as counter-globalist.

Many have seen the beginning of a New International in the recent global resistance, even though in effect it was the foundation of an international network (or even several international networks) with a variable geography. This geography entailed a break with the old organisational principles of earlier Internationals, which had the closed large industry production system as a modelling precondition. Moreover the main feature of the new radicalism was that a take-over (through the conquest of command posts of the civil state or the destruction of the civil state) was no longer the central goal of the movement. The relatively new anti- or counter-global resistance coincided with the rise of the Mexican Zapatist national liberation army of subcommandante Marcos on 1 January 1994 in Chiapas; it featured an organisational theory based on decentralisation and autonomy. This liberation army appealed for direct action and the creation of local alternatives to global capitalism. Another potential, and largely symbolic, beginning occurred in Seattle, in the autumn of 1999. Seattle combines an old-European modernism on an urban level with a Californian high-tech modernity and has known a long tradition of social struggle. Many heterogeneous groups merged in a large manifestation, involving 50,000 marchers, against the World Trade Organisation. Seattle inspired a series of impressive city marches or manifestations, at first with tens of thousands, later with hundreds of thousands of demonstrators: Geneva, Okinawa, Davos, Seoul, Marseille, Millau, Prague, Montreal, Stockholm, Genoa, Brussels, Bangkok, Washington, Barcelona, Florence, Paris, Mumbai, etc. The demonstrations were composed of polymorphous and polysemic crowds, not a single mass but a plethora of people with multiform resistance that was simultaneously wider and narrower than labour resistance, featuring very global slogans: *Another World is Possible. Mobilise for Global Justice*! These slogans were read and interpreted in many ways by trade unionists, farmers, youngsters, feminists, nomadic intellectuals, post-autonomists, anarchists, zapatists, Trotskyites, neo-Guevarists, Mao-Stalinists, liberation Christians, animal activists and Naked Protesters & Nude Activists.

The manifestations took place in the margins of the summits of the global elites, but emerged onto the foreground especially because of a media activism that granted them a very high dissemination rate thanks to the use of the internet and the development of activist alternative sites – *don't hate the media, become the media.* In Seattle, in 1999, Indymedia (Independent Media Center) saw the light; during the manifestations, it boasted more hits than CNN. Indymedia grew into a worldwide network of 133 stations, a kind of democratic CNN site featuring news, articles, photos, video and audio on anti- and counter-globalist events and more in general on less covered aspects of worldwide capitalism. A Belgian branch of Indymedia was also set up, and its multilingual site evolved from a discussion platform for activists to a news site run by dozens of volunteers, bringing a remarkable amount of information about union life and working conditions. Indymedia.be shows clear traces of classic, paleo-marxist, c.q. Mao-Stalinist-inspired activism, allowing it to easily shift with the counter-globalist movement towards an anti-war stance after 2001. Indymedia.be is an illustration of how new rules of imperial order can be countered with old anti-imperialist and especially anti-American answers.

The counter-globalist multitudinal spectacle, both on the streets and in cyberspace, represents only one side of counter-globalism. World Social Forums took place in 2001, 2002, 2003 and 2005 in Porto Alegre and in 2004 in Mumbai, followed by European Social Forums in 2002, 2003, 2004 and 2005, and by a long series of other continental, national or local meetings or forums. These forums do not function in isolation from the activist level, which actually has a very strong influence in their organisation and in the announcement of the point of view; yet the forums are also the promotion instruments of a professional mobilisation layer, of relatively new but also relatively old mobilisation executives, such as NGO executives, who are realising an association of counter-globalism with the New Social Movements or with the game of pressure and lobbying starting from ethical frames of reference. At the same time, they are enabling a fallback on local, regional or national political decision-making cultures.

The way in which counter-globalism had begun to function within the Belgian context from the middle of the nineties onwards, is a fitting illustration. Starting with that period, there was also (maybe especially in Belgium) the rise of an ethical movement – 'Petrellism, after the leftist Christian Petrella (UCL, advisor in the European Commission) and a group inspired by him, the Lisbon Group (cf. the report *Limits to Competition*, 1995), which questioned the cult of competitiveness starting from the conclusion that the state has lost against the (world) market. This movement identified the United Nations and the new global enlightened elites (industrialists with a social value system, global intelligentsia, trade union elites,...) as counter-forces and especially connected with the bureaucratic elites of the middle ground, respectively of civil society, within which especially the NGOs gained in importance during the nineties.

NGOs may be found in several areas, such as Third World or environment, but in a country like Belgium they are mainly identified with a soft 'tier-mondialism', a contrast with the Third World – third-world labour vs. first-world capital – putting the binary schemes of the Cold War from the sixties into perspective without actually abandoning the binary vision of the world. This kind of binary thinking was gradually strengthened with the representation of the world using a centre vs. periphery and later a north vs. south philosophy. At the end of the 1990s, NGOs evolved into the serious and professional branches of anti- or counter-globalism, as they had the experts and in Belgium managed a considerable part of the funds for development aid. As has been indicated before, they put their mark on the statements of the global social forums, especially the closing statement of the Second World Social Forum in Porto Alegre in February 2002.

In Flanders, the increasing influence of the NGO world was reflected in the evolution of the *Nationaal Centrum voor Ontwikkelingssamenwerking* (NCOS, National Centre for Development Aid) into 11.11.11 – the umbrella organisation of the Flemish north-south movements. The 2002 name change effectively meant the hijacking by a pluralist umbrella of a name (11.11.11) of an initially Christian fundraising campaign driven by charity. This confirmed the power of a third-world movement, the most well-structured and organised of the New Social Movements, to function as a network movement. The Flemish third-world movement, which had always mainly been the preserve of classical, mainly Christian pillar organisations (but also, for instance, of school communities' development aid drives), grew into a network encompassing 375 committees of volunteers and 90 organisations in 2005. The committees are to be found at a municipal level, the perfect level for moral mobilisation and fundraising. Among the member organisations of 11.11.11 there are other umbrella organisations: third-world organisations in the stricter sense of the word, country committees, the three main trade unions, adult education organisations, youth organisations, research centres, political youth movements and peace movements.

The evolution and powerful spread of the 11.11.11 ideology in Flanders should mainly be interpreted as one of the symptoms of the evolution of a church-bound Catholicism towards a socio-cultural Christianity. This so-called 'de-pillarisation', which has left Christian guilt-induction techniques in perfect working order, is usually marked by a progressive character and can supply the infrastructural instruments for a community-based policy of general activation of social life.

The formation of networks emanating from the third-world movement is not limited to Flanders, however. Pacifying justice interventions around and starting from the north-south opposition also come from the *Centre National de Coopération au Dévelopment* (CNCD), which also organises *Opération 11.11.11* but which, in contrast with the NCOS, did not institutionally and formally evolve into an umbrella, even though it groups about a hundred organisations. In fact the CNCD is less a coordinator of NGOs, of independent organisations, than the organiser of a solidarity orchestra in which the musicians are the NGOs, the authorities (of the federal, regional, community and municipal levels), the unions and the universities; it also explicitly involves immigrants in its operations, and immigrant organisations in the promotion of international solidarity. The CNCD, in its structure and functioning, reflects the much bigger influence of the socialist camp within the French Community.

Even though third-world organisations cannot be directly linked to the Catholic pillar, either sociologically or historically, they do always go back to the role of religious organisations and show traces of the organisational implications of Christian moral theology, at least in as far as they take up a non-governmental position (obviously true for NGOs) or set themselves up, separate from the government, as representatives of those who cannot represent themselves and cannot be represented by the government. In other words, we can see a few characteristics of the functioning of a certain ideological complex that we met earlier in the rise of the migrant question and the anti-racist movement. Our hypothesis is that, in Belgium, the hold of the north-south ideology on counter-globalism, respectively the continuation of and the counteraction against anti-globalism by NGOs, should be interpreted as part of the connection that became possible in the second half of the nineties between the moral legitimacy crisis of neo-liberalism and counter-globalism. Counter-globalism can be understood from globalisation, but just as well from a moral legitimacy crisis of neo-liberalism that can be spread and intensified by the existing old ideological infrastructure operating from an old anti-liberal, anti-individualistic and especially anti-materialistic community view of the world. The CNCD, which like 11.11.11 supports the forums of Porte Alegre, aims to sensitise public opinion for a *changement de société*. 11.11.11 is very explicit in opposing the neo-liberal market philosophy, thinks that the present globalisation subjects almost all of society to the laws of the market, and especially condemns the lack of (good) guidance of the free market by the government. Oxfam, one of the most powerful NGOs within 11.11.11 and part of a global organisational structure, opposes 'neo-liberalism, the worldwide supremacy of capital and any form of imperialism'.

Similar criticism is found in relatively new organisations founded at the end of the nineties. A slightly more radical denunciation of neo-liberal globalisation, rhetorically almost a denunciation of the market as such, emerged with the foundation of Attac. This organisation was established, among others by Petrella, following an appeal in *Le Monde Diplomatique* in 1998, as a warning to 'speculators'. Attac-International stands for a democratic control of financial markets and their institutions and more or less came down to the foundation of committees for the introduction of the so-call Tobin tax – a 0.2 % taxation on speculative stock market transactions, which should avoid financial crises and especially fund development projects in the Third World. Attac saw a spectacular world-wide growth, and in Belgium took the form of Attac-Flanders, Attac-Wallonia and Attac-Brussels, plus many regional and local Attac committees. Attac-Flanders sees itself as an associative network for a tax on financial transactions and for a strengthening of civil society. Thanks to lobbying, the translation of the demand for the introduction of the Tobin tax into a bill (with sp.a fraction leader D. Van der Maelen as the driving force) and the approval of the proposal in the Chamber in the summer of 2004, Belgium became the first country in world to give official political legitimacy to the Tobin tax. However, Belgium opted to wait for the other Euro-countries before actually applying the tax. In the summer of 2004, it was thought that the tax might only become reality after another ten years.

Attac, 11.11.11 and the CNCD had an active part in the foundation of the *Sociaal Forum van België* (SFvB, Belgian Social Forum), which was launched after the second World Social Forum in Porto Alegre (February 2002). In 2004, the SFvB boasted almost 200 organisations among which, apart from the ones mentioned earlier, large umbrella pillar organisations, trade unions, international solidarity organisations, north-south organisations, third-world organisations, organisations for the cancellation of third-world debts, organisations against world hunger, research groups, local and global platforms against violence and exclusion in a globalising world, organisations for sustained development, organisations for ethical savings and investment, peace organisations, environmental organisations, consumer organisations and counter-consumption organisations, farmers' organisations, women's organisations, organisations against partner violence, family planning organisations, gender groups, gay movements, educational organisations, organisations fighting the exclusion of the unemployed, organisations for a basic income, employment initiatives, organisations fighting poverty, anti-racist movements, refugee organisations, collectives against the imprisonment and deportation of asylum seekers, organisations for inter-culturalisation and democratisation of the media, centres for language classes, independent publishers, Christian foundation groups, anarchistic or libertarian groups, etc.

Counter-globalisation brought the political economy of capitalism to the fore again, but at the same time the frames of reference of the composing organisations promoted a stronger orientation on a moral condemnation and rejection of the economy, seen as the summary of an individualist, egotist, inhuman neo-liberal market philosophy. The SFvB intends to broaden the movement from two central axes, both recurrent ingredients of the counter-lexicon: global to local (decisions taken at an international level have repercussions on everyday life) and local to global (citizens have an influence where they live, work, protest). These two axes are undeniably sociologically important; they codify a *realpolitik* integrating the counter-movement into existing networks, organisations or movements. The SFvB realises a merger of many (almost all) social movements with an impressive ecumenical movement, which threatens the heterogeneity and diversity so characteristic of the counter-movement. Yet at the same time the many different areas, institutionally defined by intervention and action, are safeguarded and consolidated through renewed legitimisation with relatively new references (globalisation, neo-liberal market, etc.). The SFvB should in the first place be seen as an easy-to-read map of positions taken and won, revealing that few really new organisations or movements are part of the counter-globalism movement in its institutionalised form. Relatively new are Attac, which resumes an old demonising of speculative capital, gender groups that re-introduce elements from the women's movement and the gay and lesbian movement in a policy of identity, and the collectives against imprisonment and deportation of asylum seekers, giving the movement formed around migration from the mid-seventies a new form. It is also striking that the SFvB succeeds in involving the old movements, especially the trade unions, in counter-globalism. Yet the relation between the union fight and counter-globalism is tense, even though from an international perspective the new radicalism cannot be separated from union developments. Moreover, it is remarkable that those unions agreeing with the goals of the SFvB are anything but the old industrial workers' centrals, but white-collar centrals or sectors from public services. A distinction also has to be made between the positions of ABVV and ACV: especially the ACV, and in particular the Flemish ACV, is active in the field of globalisation and links up delocalisation, international competition, low wages and exploitation in the Third World.

Globalisation and Wage Norms

The question of the relationship between the counter-globalism movement and the unions may be answered from the set-up and progress of a few large counter-globalisation and European demonstrations taking place in Belgium between 2001 and 2005, such as the union demonstration (13 December 2001) and the anti-globalist demonstration (14 December 2001) on the occasion of the (European) summit in Laken, the Euro-manifestation of trade unionists, counter-globalists and others on 19 March 2005 in Brussels. It may also be answered from a series of social dossiers, from Renault-Vilvoorde to DHL, from Philips-Hasselt to Ford-Genk. These dossiers represent a sometimes complex, sometimes utterly simple synthesis of the effects of so-called globalisation, of the tensions between profitability strategies, carried by a highly mobile capital, and a local logistical infrastructure, including the local worker. The movement of counter-globalism, as we have described it, is remarkably absent in these dossiers, which points to the existence of lines separating the old social resistance from the counter-globalist movement or to the fact that globalisation and resistance can produce widely diverging configurations.

A fitting illustration of the relation between globalisation and resistance and of the position of the different actors is the strike at car window manufacturer AGC (Asahi Glass Company) in Fleurus. This constituted one of the longest open conflicts (early December 2004 – mid-March 2005) between a multinational and the workers of a local branch. One third of the jobs were axed, but the remaining workers would be burdened with 80 to 85 % of production. New personnel would be hired, but on precarious contracts. The socialist union made it clear that the board wanted to get rid of a combative delegation and militant core. In this situation, the unions refused to accept the restructuring or immediate negotiations on a social plan. On the contrary: they immediately took the board hostage for 24 hours and then started a very drawn-out strike. The board used blackmail by letting it be known a number of times that the survival of the company was being put at risk by irresponsible union behaviour. Wages due to the personnel were not paid. The board especially ignored elementary procedures of the system of social consultation, choosing to go to court instead. A judicial ruling allowed damages to be imposed, and the police to be deployed to break the factory occupation. After more than one hundred strike days, an agreement was reached that did not stop the reorganisation, but at least held a small improvement for the workers, in that social counselling became part of the reorganisation plan.

In the case of the Renault affair, almost the entire political world condemned the closure strategy, which came down to a very public demonstration of impotence. The strikers at AGC, on the other hand, became almost completely isolated, not only because of the lack in weight of the few solidarity strikes and cross-sector demonstrations in Charleroi, and the complete lack of any action in other European branches of AGC, but mainly because the political authorities actively opposed it. Walloon First Minister Jean-Claude Van Cauwenberghe (PS) declared that globalisation could not be stopped by an AGC picket line and called the strike a black mark on Wallonia's image. This linking of the image of Wallonia with the AGC conflict should be seen against the background of the high economic-political content of the whole incident. The conflict at AGC clashed with the Contract for the Future that Elio Di Rupo, chairman of the PS, had had the Walloon trade unions and employers' organisations sign in 2004. The contract entailed a social pacification as a pre-condition for an economic policy aimed at attracting investment. It was within this framework that Di Rupo launched a regional warning committee uniting representatives of the political world, of the unions and of employers' organisations around a common pursuit of investment-friendly conditions. This committee weighed heavily on the course of the strike at AGC. It accepted the reorganisation plan of the board and supported it by engaging, from the very start of the conflict, in a rhetorical strategy aimed at safeguarding the remaining jobs. It had a decisive contribution in the evolution of the conflict towards an isolated struggle of a group of socialist union militants against a multinational company. Their fight against globalisation took place in complete isolation from the anti- or counter-globalist movement.

Viewed from the perspective of social and political resistance, globalisation can function within several different strategies and have several meanings. Globalisation may stand for radical delocalisation in which the initiative lies with the company management and social resistance – by definition only defensive – is tossed back and forth between the multiple means to obtain a social counselling plan: from social negotiation in combination with conflict to social negotiation without conflict. The closure of Philips-Hasselt at the end of 2002, after years of reorganisation, is an example of a so-called wild globalisation, referred to as wild capitalism in the ethical mainstream of anti- and/or counter-globalist literature. Philips-Hasselt employed 1415 people, part of whom were still on the redundancy lists of the previous reorganisation, with another small part (about 110) being offered employment opportunities in other Philips branches, such as Eindhoven and Leuven. Within the group, Philips-Hasselt was the specialist knowledge centre for anything involving optical reading and writing systems. With its closure, the production and development of new appliances moved to Hungary. One of the machines in Hasselt was transported to China. In early 2005 already, the work force in the East-European factory was halved; the Hungarian staff was only guaranteed two years of employment. When the curtain actually fell on the Hasselt branch, a series of political interventions began. The unions, however, soon opted to pursue a good social guidance plan to accompany the closure, and especially a sizeable severance package.

In the Philips-Hasselt closure, certain attitudes emerged in workers, clerks and management that could also be observed in other reorganisations and delocalisations, and that, up to a point, were already present in the Renault affair. Roughly, it involved differentiations occurring within the workforce during reorganisations, with the following results:

(1) a group of employees in their fifties or thereabouts, not homogeneous, wishing to leave the factory site as soon as possible, whose wishes encourage an orientation towards early retirement arrangements at the earliest possible opportunity;

(2) an equally disparate group of usually younger employees who seek a quick negotiation of an adequately high severance package and who have employment alternatives – or think they do – and as such also want to leave the company as soon as possible;

(3) a group of middle-aged employees, usually with fairly high seniority within the company, who do not want to be fired, stay motivated, usually have a strong bond with the company, identify with it and believe in its future. As such they are prepared to fight, also because opportunities elsewhere on the job market are limited or non-existent.

Reorganisations and delocalisations are usually linked with unfavourable economic perspectives and high wage costs. An accusing finger is often pointed at the extension of the European Union, which crates areas with low wage costs without the protection of external borders. A study of UNCTAD, the UN organisation for Trade and Development, published in June 2004, documented that 50 % of big European companies had plans for delocalisation (and those accounted for half of all big European companies) to another European country; 29 % would move to another West-European country, 22 % to a central-European country. Within a wider framework, globalisation is mentioned as a reason; in short, multinationals scour the world for the cheapest labour available. It is possible to find well-trained personnel anywhere, and compact machines can easily be sent anywhere, so the argument goes. Cheap alternatives are pointed out, like factories in Asia. According to the UNCTAD study, 37 % of EU companies that wanted to delocalise, planned to go to an Asian country. Especially the People's Republic of China quickly evolved into the new Eldorado of international capitalism in the beginning of the new millennium, as it offered a series of unprecedented conditions (Mao-Stalinist discipline among the workers, far-reaching judicial repression, etc.) for accumulation and profit.

It is exactly in the light of these descriptions that globalisation – on a European or world-wide level, or even at the level of the nation state – can start exercising a disciplining function. The description of delocalisation in terms of 'globalisation' immediately offers a recipe – reduction of wage costs – from a social reasoning that starts from the removal of the weakest link in the system (countering the reduction of employment, effectively creating more jobs). This description and diagnosis are ingredients of the political discourse by political parties, but especially by powerful politicians, the National Bank and the OECD (Organisation for Economic Co-operation and Development), the economic think-tank for a group of about thirty rich industrial countries that has regularly pointed out the deterioration of Belgian competitiveness, more in particular the rise of wage costs above the wage norm. The argument of wage cost is a political argument, and was a key part of the policy of liberal tax cuts, a structural theme of the Verhofstadt I (1999-2003) and Verhofstadt II (2003-2007) governments. High wage costs can be kept in line by – partially or completely – cutting the link between wages and consumer price index. It is an old technique that can be defended up to a point by individual employers in individual companies (in particular in reaching a company collective bargaining agreement) from the point of view of pressure to globalise or delocalise; within the present economic climate, however, it tends to promote a freeze of consumer spending power. This tendency is, in the first place, the result of conflict, respectively consultation, between employers' organisations acting offensively and trade unions acting very defensively. The political level, c.q. the government, is allowing the social partners to play the game as before, but could take the initiative if no national general social agreement can be reached. Thus the proposal for a cross-sector agreement for the private sector, laboriously drafted in the night of 17 January 2005 after many long, complex, exhausting and extensively media-covered sessions, was rejected on 7 February by the ABVV with a tiny majority, realising the expectations and ambitions of the 50,000 demonstrators on 21 December 2004, made up of participants from the three main unions. There was also strong opposition within the ACV (the LBC, a white-collar organisation, voted against) and within the liberal union. Within the VBO the draft proposal was the subject of severe criticism by powerful employers' organisations. The federal government, which pledged € 252 million of taxpayers' money (for overtime, shift work and tax cuts) to save the proposal, completely copied the agreement, saving it, but not the social pacification. Social consultation was delegated to the different sectors, leading to several actions from mid-March 2005 onwards, for instance in the food sector, metal industry, paper industry and security sector. In other sectors, consultation at least ground to a halt: the bank and insurance, building and distribution sectors, and in the national committee for 300,000 clerks from different sectors. The main stumbling block, directly resulting from the national agreement, was room for real wage increases.

Flexibility and Wage Cost

The realisation and implementation of the Cross-Sector Agreement for 2005-2006 need to be viewed in the context of an unusually sharp employer offensive starting in the summer of 2004, which in a first stage implied a wage cut in the form of an extension of work time. This demand matched offensives elsewhere in Europe, especially in Germany. The extension of work time was not only a question of a longer working week, but also a longer working career, especially in the form of arguments for the increase of the retirement age, a revision of early retirement schemes and a restriction of career breaks. Biting negative criticism on the Belgian social model came especially from the VBO and the *Unie van Zelfstandige Ondernemers* (UNIZO, Association of Independent Entrepreneurs) who joined the hard line of the *Vlaams Netwerk van Ondernemingen* (VOKA, Flemish Enterprises Network) – successor to the VEV – and of the *Verbond van Kristelijke Werkgevers en Kaderleden* (VKW, Union of Christian Employers and Managers). An important moment that almost grew into a test case was the proposal for the extension of the working week from 37 to 38 hours. Under pressure from the evolution in Germany, this was on the table at Siemens-Atea in Herentals at the end of June, and was accepted in early September.

But there were also moments of resistance, when similar proposals were dismissed out of hand (e.g. at the German metal company Marichal Ketin in Sclessin and at Volkswagen in Vorst). In other words, there was tension between the demands of the employers' organisations and work time – and more in general the company labour organisation policy – which in the autumn led to a change in the employers' offensive. The demand for a longer working week disappeared into the background. Central positions in the list of demands were reserved for overtime on a yearly basis and especially for the end-of-career problems (working longer). The extension of the professional career had been high on the agenda since March 2002, when the European Council, in the context of the Lisbon strategy, had argued in favour of an extension of careers by five years. At the very beginning of 2004, months ahead of the employers' offensive, federal ministers Vande Lanotte and Vandenbroucke (both of sp.a) pointed out that the employment ratio in Belgium was too low, and lined up with the Lisbon strategy. On 12 October 2004, at the start of the parliamentary year, Prime Minister Verhofstadt submitted proposals to keep the over-55s working. The end-of-career question was linked to the question of wage cost and placed high on the agenda besides a different technique of keeping wage costs down.

Indeed, apart from a freeze on direct real individual wages, wage cost can also be brought down by a reduction of the social wage mass, in the shape of a limitation of contributions to finance social security. This technique does at the same time create financial compensation operations, though. Company benefits at the level of social security can result in pressure to raise taxation, especially indirect taxation, especially as a reduction of the pressure of wage cost realised through a cutback in social contributions – as was the case under the Verhofstadt governments – can further endanger the funding of social security and increase the pressure on the system. Yet this pressure is not exclusively external; the intensity of pressure on the social wage system is determined to a great extent by a chronic financial crisis of the social security state reflecting the shifts of the distribution of total produced value in the eighties at the expense of wages, including social wages (so-called replacement income).

Within this framework, consolidated from the nineties onwards, the evolution of the classic question for social wage protection can soon turn problematic. Social security spending remains under pressure of a relatively high unemployment rate of around 12 % – a constant because (high) unemployment, ever since the mid-seventies, has been a crucial instrument of a factually counter-inflationary economic policy (*Non-Accelerating Inflation Rate of Unemployment*). To a large extent, this policy consolidates a neo-liberal policy of income redistribution, and enhances a chronic crisis of the socialised wage. In certain cities and regions, unemployment can quickly shoot upwards, as was the case in 2005 in Brussels, where rates were over 20 %, in certain areas of Brussels even up to 30 %, as compared to 18 % in Wallonia and about 8 % in Flanders. Unemployment can be particularly high for young people: in Genk, for instance, 30 % of young people do not have a job. Youth employment, for which relief strategies were developed in the 1980s and 1990s, among others the replacement of the over-fifties, remains an important effect of a post-Keynesian employment regulation in the new millennium.

Another factor weighing heavily on social security expenses are illness expenditures, which increase as inability to work due to long-term illness increases. The number of blue- and white-collar workers with long-term disability because of illness rose by 15 %, or 25,000 individuals, between 1999 and 2003. At the end of 2003, according to health insurance figures, 200,000 people were long-term disabled. According to VOKA, this group includes older employees who find refuge in health insurance benefits instead of ending up on the dole or taking early retirement. It is clear, in this respect, that there is a particular increase in psychological and psychosomatic illnesses – the large-scale use of benzodiazepines and especially anti-depressants are symptomatic. Another factor is that these illnesses are being diagnosed more often, and as such are being recognised by health insurance. Yet the most important factor is increasing work-related stress, which is clearly linked to labour productivity and labour intensity; when a critical line is crossed, these can easily shift from productivity to unproductivity. Many of these symptoms were recognised within union activities and could grow into action themes – especially the ABVV took this to heart – and become the subject of conditions in collective bargaining agreements. In any case, there is a sizeable group of people who simply cannot be kept in employment from a certain age onwards. Many in this group are just unable to work any longer, or simply do not want to.

Social security budget problems have been constructed within the employers' and politicians' discourse exactly from the context of the specific Belgian developments concerning the age of retirement, and by extension the burden of the ageing population. In Belgium, people work more hours per week and per year than in the neighbouring countries: 1542 hours per year per employee in 2003 compared to 1453 hours in Germany, 1431 in France and 1354 in the Netherlands. From the perspective of labour productivity and intensity, the average Belgian worker displays a very high degree of labour activity. Belgium is the front runner as far as shift work with continuous production is concerned. At least one fifth of the total work force works in shifts. The 24-hour economy, which has always been widespread in the service economy (hospitals, police service, etc.) has expanded into industry, especially in the chemical sector, but also in the energy and food sectors. At the same time, the difference between official and actual age of retirement, or between official and actual career time, is nowhere bigger than in Belgium in the industrialised world. The legal age of retirement in Belgium is 65 for men and 63 for women, but the actual average age of retirement is 58. A large majority of the over-60s has long stopped working and receives an unemployment or health benefit, or enjoys early retirement. This phenomenon is directly linked with the high productivity of Belgian industry (cf. infra), with many jobs disappearing, but also with the extremely high rate of labour activity. Assembly line work, shift work, night work but also increasing responsibility and life-long learning in the framework of the New Economy (cf. infra) grant the worker a very high degree of consumption, which usually means that people suffer from burn-out in their fifties. A study by Kelly Services, the largest employment agency in the world, published in June 2005, reveals that Belgian employees are among the least satisfied in Europe.

Employers detect the possibility of total employment in a long-term projection; from this projection, it is understandable that they propose immigration in order to keep the labour reserve up to the same level, in contrast with mainstream union and political opinion. During the summer of 2004, the summer of the employers' offensive, VOKA stated that Belgium should attract many more 'guest workers', in order to 'keep our labour market alive'. The representative of the Flemish business community launched an appeal to ease immigration laws, c.q. to selectively abolish the immigration stop introduced in the mid-seventies, stating that it was no longer up-to-date.

Within the same projection, the growing burden of the ageing population is referred to: people live increasingly longer lives – life expectancy is going towards 85 years – and as a result there are more and more elderly people, whereas the current retirement age was set when life expectancy was about 70 years. Moreover, the actual retirement age is far below the official retirement age. The rhetorically plausible argument of the ageing population actually refers to a phenomenon whose effects are not yet traceable in social expenditure. According to the report by the Research Committee on Population Ageing, published in mid-June 2005, the extra costs of an ageing society will rise to 3.6 % of GDP by 2030, but social security expenditure will stabilise by 2010.

Activation initiatives are being taken by employers, by Europe (especially within the Lisbon process), by the political world, by several social state structures and by the so-called middle ground. They are summarised in the notion of the active welfare state developed earlier (e.g. by Minister Frank Vandenbroucke in 2000). The active welfare state project is mainly based on dissolving the borders of education and training structures and life-long learning for the workforce; this is defended against the background of a transition to a knowledge-based economy, a notion which is also central in the European Lisbon process. The activation initiatives mainly combine work, education, training and cultural initiatives, but hardly stand for an old employment policy based on the creation of jobs, whether or not through the reduction of working hours. Indeed, the active welfare state is more in line with the new social question (cf. infra) or joins the battle against 'exclusion', or even the battle against the extreme-right from a sociologically constructed relation between democracy and (especially socio-cultural) group participation. In other words, this is a policy of inclusion.

Within sociology, but also within political sciences the activation offensive is taking the shape of the construction of a new fault line, a contrast between individualism and a sympathetic society. As such, Vandenbroucke contrasts his own utopian, but reasonable project with a Latin passionate approach, even with Petrellism, which formed the basis of, for instance, *Het Sienjaal* (1995), a radical-democratic project, or the so-called Project Coppieters-De Batselier, a Flemish, social, ecological and global project meant to break through old party border lines, and which was probably an element in the establishment of the political axis sp.a-Spirit.

Activation can take many shapes, and is integrated in many initiatives. We have mentioned life-long learning and training schemes. Life-long learning has become a key political-rhetorical theme, especially for the Flemish government, but is first and foremost developed on the factory floor, especially in the human resource and personal development sectors. Another form of activation comes from financial stimuli against the background of low benefits in Belgium; this is one of the few countries where social benefits do not follow increasing prosperity, and social benefits are lower than in the rest of Europe. Benefits are kept low in order to create a bigger difference with minimum wage and to stimulate people to work. Yet activation of the unemployed is mainly based on a combination of control (of the willingness to work), training and financial sanctions. Unemployment benefit (federal level) and the counselling and training obligation (regional level) are combined in contractual agreements, i.e. agreements in terms of rights and duties. Since 1 July 2004 any claimants must prove that they are making enough effort to find employment. This measure also applies to young people in unstable schemes or in part-time employment. The new measure was not an isolated phenomenon, but matched what was going on elsewhere in Europe in 2004, especially in Germany.

The new unemployment law is being implemented in different stages in Belgium: first the under-30s, then the under-40s, the under-50s and the over-50s. This means that the activation of the unemployed and the activation of older employees, respectively the elimination of the difference between official and actual retirement ages link up. This link between the two policies at first sight is based on a combination of a policy of deconstruction of the army of unemployed and a policy guaranteeing the maintenance of a reasonably supply of labour; yet in actual fact it comes down to a policy of lowering wage costs through a reduction of social expenditure, respectively social contributions.

On average, tax rates for income from work are 43 % in Belgium (the average European rate being 36 %) compared to a rate of 30 % for income from capital (income from firms, from personal effects and real estate, income from self-employment). Yet employers advise a lower tax rate for labour, against a background of a battle against high 'wage costs'. In June 2005, just ahead of a new budget control, the federal government followed the same line of thought by going towards a shift from taxation on work to taxation on consumption through a rise in VAT rates on consumer goods.

The New Economy

Belgium's place in the new world order can also be described by taking a bottom-up view, starting from the conditions for a new world order, i.e. from the downfall and diminishing sovereignty of the nation state, from the increasing impotence to shape national capitals.

The Belgian economy's distinguishing feature is that it is shaken by a fantastically high rate of internationalisation. Just a few data will illustrate this: in 2001, the year in which the boom of the second half of the nineties turned into a crisis, the Belgian-Luxembourg Economic Union was the most international economy after Ireland and Hong Kong. This internationalisation, however, is not being made by Belgian, Flemish, Walloon or Brussels enterprises, companies or groups. They are the result of reorganisations coinciding with cross-border take-overs, mergers and partnerships. A famous example is the Agfa group, which in 2004 took the decision to trade its profile of photo-chemical group for that of a digital imaging group (active in the graphic and medical markets); this implied the take-over of the German GWI (a supplier of medical IT systems) and resulted in a considerable downsizing of the workforce.

Another example is to be found in the energy sector: Electrabel is the biggest power producer in Belgium, dominating all the links in the chain of electricity, and the major player in the liberalisation of the electricity and gas market since 2003, yet it is a daughter of the French Suez group. Through Suez, it has strong ties with gas companies Distrigas and Fluxys, in which the interest of the oil group Shell (until June 2005 a British-Dutch group) was bought by Suez in September 2004.

Yet another example is the prestigious Janssen Pharmaceutica (established in 1953 as a Belgian company), which has been a profitable daughter of the American Johnson&Johnson since the 1960s; in 2003, the company made a profit of € 355 million. It employs about 4,400 mainly highly qualified personnel and is well-known for its research and innovation. The Belgian pharmaceutical sector, with 26,000 employees and 6,000 researchers a major contributor to the knowledge-based economy, has known a remarkable expansion in recent years. This could be explained by a strong demand for pharmaceutical drugs in Belgium, and with a series of strategic decisions enabling expansion, which implied increasing independence (following the example of Janssen Pharmaceutica) and a series of complex take-overs and agreements. UCB, a very hybrid group, became a purely pharmaceutical company with a strengthened research department, in which also bio-technology is strongly represented. In 2004, Solvay followed a similar strategy by putting all its pharmaceutical activities in a holding of the Luxembourg model, facilitating agreements with other parties, in the shape of take-overs, mergers or agreements for specific drugs. Solvay cooperated with the Swedish Lundbeck, entered into a partnership with BMS (Bristol Myers Squibb) and closed a deal with the Russian Petrovax/Pharm, all in 2004.

This remarkable year 2004, in which the world economy revived after a period of recession and showed the strongest growth since 1976, was characterised in Belgium by a number of take-overs in the ICT sector with important consequences for Belgian economic performance. Network security group Ubizen, a long-standing high-flyer on the Brussels stock exchange, was taken over by the American BeTRUSTed, after quite a few problems. Real Software was bought by the American Gore Technologies; top manager Theo Dilissen played a leading role in this take-over. He had become the new chairman of the board of telecom company Belgacom in October 2004, and in February 2004 had approved the prospectus for the stock market flotation of the company. The interest of the state fell to 50 % plus one share in the autumn, thanks to the sale of 19.1 million shares, netting the state € 539 million.

Concerning cross-border mergers, not to be confused with take-overs, the merger of financial institutions has to be mentioned, such as the large merger bank Société Générale, which is no longer a Belgian but a French-Belgian bank, Deutsche Bank and ABN AMRO. All these mergers are situated within the Euro-zone, enabling them to build a strong competitive position, shielding them from the American banking giants.

One of the most important mergers in recent years, with a large impact on the degree of internationalisation of the Belgian economy, is the worldwide beer group Inbev, the sixth most international company in the world, established in 2004 as a result of the merger of the Leuven brewery group Interbrew (which had already bought Canadian, British and German companies) and AmBev (Companhia de Bebidas das Américas), supported by a few Brazilian venture capitalists. Inbev also realised a number of takeovers in China; its headquarters are still in Leuven.

It is not sufficient, however, to view the degree of internationalisation purely in terms of shifts in capital, mergers, take-overs and institutional or strategic management decisions. Also investments should be taken into account. Belgium is one of the most successful countries in the world concerning the attraction of foreign investment, at least relative to its share in world trade. In 2003, Belgium drew € 23.7 billion in direct foreign investments, more than doubling the 2002 amount, in spite of 2003 being the third consecutive year of a worldwide decline in foreign investments. Belgium shared the 2003 top position with the Grand Duchy of Luxembourg. Foreign investments are a very important contributory factor for the high degree of internationalisation in Belgium, even though we should not lose sight of the fact that, in the same year, Belgian companies themselves invested € 30 billion abroad. This was over three times the amount of 2002, putting Belgium in fifth place, after the USA, Luxembourg, France and the UK, in the world ranking of countries with the biggest investments abroad.

The large scale of foreign investments and the high degree of internationalisation of the Belgian economy can be explained historically, namely as a consequence of the particular post-war Belgian evolution. This development emerged fully at the end of the 1950s and in particular during the general strike of 1960-1961. Roughly, it came down, for the entire period between 1944 and 1986, to the existence of Belgian cycles, both on an economic level, a political-economic level and the level of the labour movement; all of these diverged from what happened elsewhere in Europe and the world. This specific development was helped along in the fifties by a slow accumulation of capital and even a stagnation of Belgian capitalism. It followed the immediate post-war national reconstruction – or rather the absence of an innovative reconstruction – as the swift post-war recovery quickly faded along with the diminishing foreign demand for heavy equipment and was replaced with the deficiencies of an old-fashioned industrial structure uniquely focused on the classical basic sectors of the Belgian economy. In a qualitatively constant technical-economical structure, Belgian capitalism was unable to sufficiently develop the forces of production and to implement structural reforms. The structure of Belgian capitalism was buried after the failure of the big strike of 1960-1961 under the influx of foreign, multinational investment. This multi-nationalisation encountered certain boundaries from the mid-seventies onwards. Together with the deepening of the first post-war international recession, the multinational capital withdrew progressively from activities and sectors considered insufficiently profitable.

The exceptional productivity of the Belgian network, with the phenomenally productive chemical sector as its highlight, can be explained exactly from this movement, the consequence of a neo-liberal Darwinism. The reorganisation starting in the mid-seventies has laid down the foundations for a very high degree of automation and productivity founded on job cuts, respectively the closure of companies with a low productivity and profitability. Belgium's huge productivity – the highest in Europe after Norway, Luxembourg and France – results from a reduction of industrial employment that was faster than anywhere in the world. Between 1974 and 1985, 40,000 industrial jobs were lost each year. From 1985 onwards, this reduction of employment slowed down to an average of 10,000 jobs per year. In 2000, jobs in industry only accounted for 24 % of total employment. The old, classical, Belgian industrial paradigm, which had its roots in the first industrial revolution, had been comprehensively demolished. On Tuesday 26 April 2005, the last cast iron came out of Blast Furnace 6 of Cockerill in Seraing: the end of an era. In 2009, the last blast furnace of the region will close in Ougrée. The final close-down in Seraing was realised by steel group Arcelor, which in 2003 decided to concentrate the group's European production of warm-rolled steel in maritime branches, namely in Ghent (Sidmar) and Dunkirk (Sollac). But we can assume that not only employment in the steel sector, but industrial employment as a whole will see a further dramatic reduction, maybe down to just 10 % in 2025. In 2004, for instance, a good year for the Belgian economy, 20,000 jobs were lost in the processing industry. At the same time, a spectacular number of new jobs was being created in the service sector. Between 1985 and 2000, employment in the service industry rose by 400,000 jobs.

Yet the high-tech, IT or service activities developing in Belgium cannot compensate for the destruction of industrial employment. During the New Economy, in the period of the IT boom (1997-2001) and especially in the period starting with the dot.com crash that came after the boom (2001-2004), a new version of the Belgian development has emerged: Belgium appears in the New Economy first and foremost as the country where classical Fordist sectors, such as car assembly, remain an important element in the structure of economic performance, and are more important than the New Economy. The part of new technologies – c.q. companies producing new technologies – in the Belgian economy is relatively small, while also in Belgium the New Economic high-tech companies are extremely vulnerable (cf. the serious loss of jobs during the dot.com crash in 2001-2002 at Company, IBM, Alcatel-Antwerp, KPBQuest, Siemens Herentals and Huizingen, FCI Mechelen, Lernaut & Hauspie, Philips-Hasselt, etc.)

This development should mainly be viewed against the background of the world economic climate, which the Belgian climate can perfectly match in view of its high internationalisation. In 2004 the eighteen biggest Belgian companies listed in the BEL-20 stock index showed a total profit of € 11.7 billion (half of which went to the shareholders). That was 40 % more than in 2003, and was the result of clean-up operations but also of the 5 % world economic growth. Belgium, as a small, open economy, completely matched the international recovery and went against the Euro-zone tendency (where there was no sign of a revival yet) to double its growth to 2.7 %, even though this feat was also influenced by government expenditure and even by a fairly strange explosion of consumer spending at the end of the year.

At the same time, the place of Belgium in the New Economy cannot be disengaged from the importance that the new information and communication technologies gained during the 'roaring nineties' in the climate of the world economy. The New Economy stresses the possibilities offered by technological advances for the accumulation of knowledge and the increasing complexity of dealing with knowledge – the New Economy is a knowledge-based economy. It does not only involve a radical change of the object of labour, respectively the raw materials (immaterial symbols, codes, linguistic or mathematical symbols, competences and initiatives taking the place of nature), but also a profound change in the relation between labour means and labour force. The two are no longer separate, as the means of labour are integrated into the body, into the brain of the living production forces. The New Economy became the paradigm of the nineties, of the dissemination of a linguistic turn in the economy in the shape of images, algorithms, words and music continuously flashing all around the planet. The planetary dissemination of the new information and communication technologies, especially in the shape of world-wide, albeit planetary and socially unequally distributed networks (the 'digital gap') such as the internet, was matched by an extraordinary leap forward in the production of, respectively investments in, the sectors of information and communication infrastructure (telephony, digital television, multimedia, IT, computers, etc.). The implementation of ICT saw an enormous expansion from the nineties onwards, not only in ICT-producing companies and in the service economy, but also in the Fordist industrial sectors and even in the old primary sector thanks to an increasing computerisation of agriculture. This implementation also hugely increased thanks to a massive distribution of new communication media among the general public. At the end of 2004, the number of company internet connections in Belgium (where two out of three families owned a PC) had increased to 381,000 and the number of private connections to 1.65 million; 4.2 million people over fifteen (i.e. 49 % of the population) used the internet on a regular basis. This fantastic increase of the demand for and the supply and production of ICT went hand in hand with a very high rate of accumulation. The corresponding rise in productivity profits was not high enough, however, to compensate for the spectacular increase of the rate of accumulation and of investments. Starting in 1997, the year in which the ICT boom took off in Europe, the profit rate in the US started to fall to the rhythm of the success of the New Economy. In other words, the New Economy relies on an interaction between an undeniably new paradigm and the actuality of the profit rate crisis.

This combination of the New Economy and the sustained crisis of profit rates can explain a new (third) political-economic cycle of neo-liberalism. It is a new edition of aggressive neo-liberalism that revolves around wage costs and incorporates the social components of the previous cycle in a competitive communal national liberalism. The beginning of this cycle can be dated fairly precisely; it started in 2001 following the dot.com crash and was soon fuelled by the effects of 9/11. The destruction of the Twin Towers, the many casualties and the particularly anti-American, anti-Semitic aggression and lethal madness at its basis, synthesised the contradictions of the New Economy. The urge to destroy the New World, the symbols and citizens of America, the land of immigration and mobility, was based on a particular application of the network principles of the New Economy – the political economy of Al-Qaeda is a network economy – and on a mobilisation of a construed, pure, territorialised own nation to oppose the decadent nation. It allowed the latter, as an imperial power, to use and convert the aggression into a mobilisation of its own American nation, at the service of new military initiatives – first Afghanistan, then Iraq – and of the implementation of counter-tendencies against the crisis of the New Economy and the profit rate, even though the military conquest aspect of the offensive hardly matched the economic strategies of American global enterprise.

The third cycle of neo-liberalism in Belgium has been developing in a special, at first rather unclear way. The first Verhofstadt government, a unique coalition of liberals, social democrats and environmentalists, was able to take office in the summer of 1999 in part because of the effects of a special form of legitimacy crisis of neo-liberal economic policy (cf. supra), thanks to a moral crisis of neo-liberalism through the White Crisis, the role of which was taken over in the run-up to the 1999 elections by the so-called dioxin crisis, a new legitimacy crisis that was allowed to erupt over a case of contaminated food and the failure of food inspection. The government picked up where the second (social) cycle of neo-liberalism had left off, and worked with rather leftist answers to the legitimacy crisis. This was also helped along by the fact that the election results of 13 June 1999 especially expressed the crises, mutations or shifts of political representation of a more underlying nature: the crisis of the CVP as a broad, hegemonic, inter-class people's party, the infringement of the monopoly position of PS and SP on the left by (green) parties tied in with the New Social Movements, the take-over of the integration functions of the old CVP by new liberal parties, the end of the big political parties and of the big political families, etc. Especially as the CVP was no longer in the government, the summer of 1999 opened up perspectives for a liberal Belgium in which the dominant Christian mid-field could be forced back, and a new political citizens' democracy could emerge. It was certainly the start of a new style of government, breaking with the tradition of previous decades. It was, however, a strongly curtailed liberalism; the Verhofstadt government stood for globalisation, but a limited globalisation with strict limits (high walls, strict controls, secure units, deportations) to immigration. Another factor slowing down a new, hard neo-liberal cycle was the fact that the PS had retained a huge number of votes, allowing social democracy to remain as a central axis of the government coalition. Yet it was exactly from social democracy and from the sp.a that activation initiatives were launched, focusing on a stricter control on unemployment and on the end-of-career problem from 2004 onwards. As indicated earlier, the aim of these initiatives was finding techniques allowing a reduction of wage costs without major disruptions to the realisation of balanced budgets and the reduction of state debt.

The transition to a new neo-liberal cycle became more clearly visible from the summer of 2004 onwards, the summer of the employers' offensive; but the federal elections of 18 May 2003 were also an important moment. The election results consolidated and strengthened the role of the socialist parties and pushed the green parties back into the opposition. Against the background of the question of immigrants' voting rights, it allowed the advance of a very right-wing movement within the VLD. Components of this very heterogeneous rightist movement no longer preclude cooperation with the extreme-right *Vlaams Belang* (Flemish Interest), the former Vlaams Blok, or even favour the realisation of a new large right-wing ultra-neo-liberal formation including extreme-right movements.

general point of reference	**means** (c.q. institutions)			
	pacification at the different levels[1]	judicial-ideological representation		
		social		*economic*
		regulatory	advisory	regulatory
	company	works council	safety and health committee	
	sector	bilateral committees (collective bargaining agreement) 1 national bilateral committee and ca. 120 committees for (sub)sectors		
stability of social relations	*national*	national labour council management bodies of social security system	social and economic conference	
	regional			

[1] ↔ = class line

◇ = consultation in 'neo-corporatist' perspective

[1] Other important economic bodies at the national level: Council for Consumption, Control Committee for Electricity and Gas, Consultation Committee for Steel Policy, Belgian Service for Foreign Trade, Advisory Council for Coal Industry, Advisory Council for Energy, Commission for the Study of Problems in the Metalworking Industry, Special Commission for Distribution

	financial	
advisory	regulatory	advisory
works council		
company councils		
Central Council for the Business Community, National Committee for Economic Expansion, Index Commission, Commission for Price Regulation[1]	councils of public financial bodies (NBB, NIM, NMKN, ASLK,...)[2]	
GERs GOMs[3]	regional investment companies (GIMs)	

[2] NBB = National Bank of Belgium
NIM = National Investment Company
NMKN = National Society for Credit to Industry
ASLK = General Savings and Annuity Fund
Other important financial organs are: High Council for Finance, Banking Commission, Communal Credit of Belgium, National Institute for Credit to Agriculture, National Fund for Professional Credit, Central Bureau for Mortgages, Institute for Rediscounting and Warranting, Council for Public Credit Institutions, Belgian-Luxembourg Institute for Exchange, European Monetary Agreement

[3] GER = Regional Economic Council
GOM = Regional Economic Development Company

Chapter IX

Increasing Tension Between the Communities and the Creation of a Federalised Belgium

The quarrels between the Dutch- and French-speaking communities and their impact on the bilingual capital Brussels turned into the post-war conflict to dominate all others. The conflict was often fought in a very hostile atmosphere, caused big electoral upsets, spawned new parties, countless demonstrations and dramatic political crises. It often ended up bringing down governments. The language issue had already created much tension during the 1960s, but consumed enormous amounts of political energy during the 1970s and 1980s. The essence of Belgium was at stake: the survival of the 1830 unitary nation. The most diverging and conflicting interests came to the fore, turning the 1988 and 1993 constitutional reforms into an extremely complex issue. The kind of political movements making this conflict possible and the different stages in the process of federalisation will be treated in this chapter.

The Main Players: The Flemish and Walloon Movements

The Flemish Movement came out of the Second World War politically and morally discredited. Since Flemish nationalism had leaned too heavily on fascist ideology and Nazi collaboration, the movement was a sitting duck for francophone vilification. As part of the national post-war healing process, all centrifugal forces that had eroded the Belgian concept were condemned. So the political elite largely sidestepped the linguistic issue between 1944 and 1960 and focused its efforts on the reconstruction of the unitary state, the Royal Question and the School War. The Flemish movement had little success and the flamingants were politically isolated. Flemish nationalist groups disappeared and even their ideological soul mates within the traditional parties could not shake the stigma of war-time collaboration.

The Flemish federations of the unitary PSB-BSP Socialist Party were facing anti-flamingant wallingantism and things were not much better within the Liberal Party. Even the pro-Flemish Catholics had a difficult time. When the Catholic Party was reorganised in 1945, the unitary programme stressed that the rights of Flemings as well as Walloons had to be respected. The CVP-PSC had ambitions to win an overall parliamentary majority and could well use the votes of the old collaborationist VNV to succeed. So the electoral lists of 1949 included a number of flamingants who had been compromised by their war past. The CVP shied away, however, from a blanket embrace of such figures that would have given the party a strong flamingant label. Even though some attempts were made, it was still far too early for any regrouping of the Flemish nationalist forces. In 1949, the core remnants of the Flemish nationalists tried in vain to build an election programme around the theme of amnesty for collaboration, but the votes were pinched by the CVP. The Catholic *Volksunie* (VU, People's Union) was created in anticipation of the 1954 campaign but would have to wait for its political breakthrough until 1961, when it won five seats.

There were enough indications to claim that the linguistic laws in the post-war period were applied at the expense of the Flemings. The francophones were clearly trying to recapture ground lost. The aggressive stance of the Belgian French-speakers in a sense revived Flemish consciousness. The 1947 language census became a catalyst when it became clear Flanders would lose a number of municipalities on the linguistic frontier and around the capital to encroaching gallicisation. What made things worse was that the pro-Flemish wing was convinced that the census had not been taken objectively. Cultural associations took a lead in opposing the development: the liberal *Willemsfonds,* the Catholic *Davidsfonds* and, since 1945, the socialist *Vermeylenfonds.* The three joined forces in opposing the 1947 language count. The cultural associations were able to free the Flemish cause from its political straightjacket and focused attention on the neutral, cultural character of the movement. The leaders did not belong to the political elite and were untarnished by collaboration. The participation of a number of liberal and socialist literary and educational figures even introduced an element of war resistance into the movement. The development did mean something for the restoration of the Flemish movement but it would be incorrect to claim that the manifestations had any real results in the political world. Between 1944 and 1950, the Flemish Movement remained burdened by the war and it would take until the end of the 1950s before it could emerge from the margins of politics.

At the same time, however, demographic, economic and social changes were taking place that would fundamentally reinvigorate the Flemish Movement by the middle of the sixties. In contrast with Wallonia, the population in Flanders increased. By 1971, 56 % of the population lived in Flanders. And because the economic expansion laws granted 58 % of the subsidies to northern Belgium, the historic wealth gap slowly disappeared. The old pro-Flemish business leaders were reinforced by a fresh supply from the service sector. The growth of the latter, however, was heavily dependent on the multinationals setting up Flemish subsidiaries. The Flemish bourgeoisie stood up to be counted even though it was squeezed in between these foreign companies and the old, unitary, francophone bourgeoisie of the Belgian holdings, and it lacked a broad industrial basis. Moreover, a group of managers and technocrats used foreign and domestic monopoly positions to exert influence on decision-making. The economic development also provided employment and promotion to graduates from university, higher, technical and secondary education. The expansion of intellectual petty bourgeois circles, a traditional recruiting ground for flamingantism, was boosted by other factors, too. The first graduates from the fully Dutch-speaking educational cycle entered a service sector in full expansion. Social-cultural organisations were going through a democratisation process.

In business and in administration, the 1950s were marked by an increasing drive for the recognition of a fully-fledged Flemish elite. Backed by a growing service sector and middle class intellectual support, a new political elite emerged ready to challenge the unitary leaders. The new elite infiltrated into the parties and demanded that the political system would start reflecting the social changes and favour the Flemish elite. It based its demands on the numerical strength of the Flemish population and wanted this to be translated into a political majority. As its power increased, the new elite also introduced its immediate backers into the party bureaucracies and by the end of the 1960s the passing of the political torch to the new generation was there for all to see.

All Flemish organisations had gone through a similar change of guard and a process of increased consciousness. The three main cultural associations (Davidsfonds, Willemsfonds and Vermeylenfonds) were important foundations for the Flemish elite since they offered a link to the parties and their ideological pillars. They would keep this central function and also provided cross-party consultation at times. Organisations like the *Algemeen Nederlands Zangverbond* (General Dutch Singing Association), the Volksunie and the Yser pilgrimage committee had reclaimed their position within the Flemish movement and renewed and increased their support. Political pressure groups were also created. A hard core of ultra-right-wing nationalists set up the *Vlaamse Militanten Orde* (Flemish Militant Order) in 1949 and *Were Di* in 1962. The *Vlaamse Volksbeweging* (Flemish People's Movement), which was created in 1956, had a much wider democratic base, as did the 1958 *Vlaams Actie Comité voor Brussel en de Taalgrens* (Flemish Action Committee for Brussels and the Linguistic Border, which would later become the *Taal Aktie Komitee* (TAK, Language Action Committee). But as the elite forced a political breakthrough, the balance swung towards the parties.

A first indication was the reinvigoration of the Flemish nationalist and federalist-oriented Volksunie. As the heir to the pre-war VNV, it recruited mainly among the same circles of Catholic Flemings, petty bourgeoisie and the intellectual middle class. It had a right wing full of yearning for the old 'new order' days, a strong centre and even, by the end of the sixties, a social-progressive minority. The party's success increased from 1965 onwards as it took 20 seats in the Chamber, mostly at the cost of the CVP. It helped explain why the CVP-PSC was the first unitary party to be confronted with the creation of a Flemish autonomous wing. The national structures were already reduced to little more than a coordinating framework by 1969. The pillar organisations were dominated by this new Flemish class, which considered the CVP the most suitable political channel to defend the Flemish position. That opinion was shared by the Flemish financial elite, primarily the Kredietbank, and the *Vlaams Economisch Verbond.* The absorption of this new group in the top echelons of the Catholic pillar and party affected the prime position of the unitary right wing in the party. 'Neo-unitarists' reinforced that right wing in an attempt to use the numerical majority in Flanders in the strategy to win a national majority.

The pro-Flemish views of the CVP and Volksunie affected the other traditional parties as well. Traditional unitarism was long able to keep the upper hand within the BSP despite the flamingantism of the party's left wing. The socialist old guard feared being turned into a minority in Catholic Flanders and therefore preferred to take shelter under the wings of the strong Walloon socialists in a unitary nation. It was hard to make a swift career within the Socialist Party and the new Flemish elite were held back until the 1970s. They built up a Flemish identity, developed further within a Flemish context, and the party elders grudgingly followed in their wake. The initiative for a formal split of the party primarily came from the Walloon wing, though, and the francophone *Parti Socialiste* (PS) and the Flemish *Socialistische Partij* (SP) were created in 1978.

Unitarism was strongest in the Liberal Party. The party had long had a pro-Flemish group within its ranks but the party leadership did not welcome an independent Flemish position. Up to 1968, the PVV stuck by its unitary guns. But the political linguistic tensions made such a position untenable and by the mid-1970s, a split became unavoidable. From then on, the Flemish parties were able form a united linguistic front when and if required.

The new Flemish political elite were unanimous about one key issue: anything that referred to economic, social and political inferiority had to be eliminated. French language domination had to be eradicated and there was need for a distinct cultural and linguistic identity. Belgium's territorial principle, which had been created in 1932, was the starting point: the individual choice of language was rejected. All national public services had to be bilingual and the linguistic frontier had to be made permanent. There was a desire to control cultural issues, creating the demand for cultural decentralisation and autonomy.

There was much less consensus about Flanders' economic problems. The majority of them did attack the Belgian unitary principle to keep the different regions as far away as possible from meddling in economic policy. They demanded the continued industrialisation of Flanders to keep its population in work but agreed on little else. The more moderate political elite opposed the elimination of national economic solidarity: Wallonia was (and is) one of the most important trading partners of Flanders. The backers of economic decentralisation argued, however, that the economic interests of Flanders and Wallonia differed so much that the centrally-led economic policy was to the disadvantage of Flanders. Especially the Volksunie condemned the economic grant system and demanded autonomous regional taxation. And as the Flemish economy became ever more dynamic, the number of proponents of economic autonomy steadily grew.

The yearning for autonomy only increased during the 1980s and 1990s. The regionalisation of the country had created a political class that had to establish its Flemish credentials. Flanders was facing the fallout of successive recessions but was able to rely on the youthful vigour of its industry, foreign investments and SME traditions to escape relatively unscathed. It was able to adapt to the changing economic demands and created some regions that were among the most prosperous in Europe. The economic surge boosted self-esteem and self-awareness of the people involved and even led to occasional smugness and complacency in some. It was an ideal habitat for the development of an awareness of Flanders' nationhood. Increasingly, Wallonia was seen as a burden on economic expansion and steadily any feeling of solidarity with Wallonia waned in a number of Flemish circles. The breakthrough of the ethnocentric, authoritarian-populist and racist ideology of the extreme right in a number of Flemish cities during the nineties and the beginning of the 21st century only speeded up the process of radicalisation.

The development had far-reaching consequences for the Flemish Movement. Just like the VNV had done in the 1930s, the extreme right-wing Vlaams Blok turned Flemish nationalist ideology into a purely ethnic one in the 1990s, arguing that only a homogenous culture truly reflected the people. Pluralist society was condemned and separatism was promoted. The Vlaams Blok relied on this ideology to become the self-appointed mouthpiece of the Flemish Movement. Its ideas also made headway in such pressure groups as the *Davidsfonds, IJzerbedevaardcomité* (Yser Pilgrimage Committee) and the *Algemeen Nederlands Zangverbond*. The Volksunie, *Vermeylenfonds* and *Willemsfonds* turned their back on the wider front of the *Overlegcentrum van Vlaamse Verenigingen* (Consultation Centre of Flemish Associations), which had given the Flemish Movement such an impact in the 1960s and 1970s.

The traditional Flemish parties tried to counter the breakthrough of Vlaams Block by raising their Flemish profile, with the CVP taking the lead. The SP called for a socialist-environmentalist autonomous Flanders while the Liberal Party transformed itself into the VLD, a party with a strong Flemish profile. The Volksunie was held back by internal dissent and the election defeats at the hands of the Vlaams Blok. So it tried to improve its standing with a radical social and Flemish nationalism. The party split up, however, with the left-liberal wing founding *Spirit*, and the right-nationalist wing starting up the *Nieuw-Vlaamse Alliantie* (N-VA, New Flemish Alliance). A number of other top figures found refuge in the different traditional parties. Spirit entered into a cartel with the socialists and N-VA with the Christian-democrats. In each of these formations they continued the process of making Flanders more independent. In short, the last decade was marked by a comprehensive radicalisation of the Flemish pressure groups as well as the political parties.

The development of the Walloon movement was totally different. At first it was an anti-movement that found its *raison d'être* in countering the successes of the Flemish movement. It turned into the ideological home of political elites that rejected the existing political balance of power. Even though there were some Catholics among the Wallingants, it was primarily a movement joining anti-clerical and left-wing groups that felt their development was impeded by the Catholic conservative majority of Flanders. Its programme went beyond purely linguistic issues and the Walloon movement turned just about every political problem into a battle between the communities.

The post-war climate gave the Walloon movement an appetite for a good fight. The language laws of the 1930s and the resulting domination of Dutch in Flanders had been seen as an immediate threat to Walloon privileges. The contradiction between Catholic Flanders and anti-clerical Wallonia only reinforced the fear of a Belgium dominated by Flanders. Nazi collaboration of an important part of the Flemish movement only increased their dislike. In Wallonia's left-wing circles, the conviction grew that it was no longer possible to live together with the right-wing Flanders. The first Walloon Congress of October 1945 took a clear, separatist stand, rejecting a unitary Belgium and almost unanimously demanding an autonomous Wallonia. An overwhelming majority considered an annexation by France the preferable solution, even though it was clear to everyone that this was almost impossible.

The Walloon movement watched with growing concern how Flanders' numerical advance grew, the Flemish linguistic and cultural policy became increasingly important, and Flanders' economy boomed. The movement realised that the central government was selling Wallonia short, especially since Belgian big business had pulled out of the ageing core industries and invested little in the emerging sectors in the southern part of the country. The establishment of the Sidmar steel plant near Ghent in 1962 became a symbol of Wallonia's decline and Flanders' economic dominance. The Flemish population increased to the extent that seat distribution in parliament had to be adapted to reflect the new demographic situation, and the Walloon frustrations gained a political dimension. The fiercest criticism was not targeted at the holding capitalists who stopped investing in

Wallonia but instead at the Flemish bourgeoisie and political elite, who were suspected of wanting to take power at the expense of the Walloons.

By 1960, wallingantism had become a mass movement and it was backed by the Walloon wing of the socialist trade union, led by A. Renard. They wanted to make sure the Walloon worker would not become the victim of the political situation and wanted to push through anti-capitalist structural reforms to counter Wallonia's decline. The 1960-1961 winter strike was seen as proof that left-wing Wallonia was held back by unitary Belgium. The Walloon, especially the Liège, section of the FGTB gave rise to the *Mouvement Populaire Wallon* (MPW), which was strongly backed by the labour movement of the Walloon industrial belt. But the death of its charismatic leader Renard and socialist measures to prevent the repeat of the 1960-1961 explosion of labour violence had a negative impact on the MPW. It would take until the end of 1967 before the movement was strong enough again to exert pressure on the PSB, which opted for the MPW's federalist views during the Verviers congress.

By that time, the Christian labour movement had also seen the formation of a federalist wing. There were attempts during the 1965 and 1968 election campaigns to join all wallingant groups in a party that was as radical as the MPW. This *Rassemblement Wallon* (RW) was convincingly successful in the 1971 elections and became the second-biggest Walloon party. Its success was short-lived, though. Prominent leaders F. Perin and J. Gol defected to the Walloon liberal party, the PRLW, and the disappointing RW government participation cut its electoral following in half by 1977. The PS had raised its linguistic profile and reaped the rewards at the expense of the RW. The electoral success opened the eyes of the Walloon socialists. They sought to win a majority in Wallonia, and thus become an essential partner in the national government. It was a strategy that required the national break-up of the Socialist Party in two linguistic entities. By 1978, the divorce was a fact and the next elections were proof that the new *Parti Socialiste* had made the right move.

Economic reform was a priority for the Walloon movement – that much was clear from its motivation and social characteristics. It demanded that the central government opened its pockets to get the Walloon economy out of the doldrums. The movement counted on government initiatives and an advantageous grant system in a regionalised Belgium. State reform had to grant Wallonia a large measure of autonomy to have a shot at an economic revival. The demand for protective measures needed real political power to back it up. As such, the Walloon movement wanted to be the equal of Flanders at the national political level and traditionally demanded a veto right, the establishment of special parliamentary majority rules and parity between Flemings and Walloons at the national level. Cultural autonomy was far less important, even though it wanted to establish links with the francophones from the capital Brussels.

The burden of Wallonia's industrial past was especially hard to carry during the 1980s and 1990s. The dismantling of its heavy industry turned certain parts of the once-thriving industrial belt into the heaviest-hit in Europe. Limited public funds hampered reconversion in industrial sectors that were dependent on government orders. Technological traditions and entrepreneurial structures hardly stimulated the swift introduction of new technologies. The national financial solidarity mechanisms between north and south were of vital importance to Wallonia. The PS continued its wallingant strategy and developed nationalist groups within its party structure. The Walloon Region became its bulwark. Also the liberal party opted for measures that should stimulate an economic revival. However, the share of the Walloon Region in the GDP remained far below average, and unemployment hovered around a steady 20 %.

The Walloon parties considered the perceived radicalism of the Flemish parties, and particularly the Vlaams Blok's racist language, as aggressive nationalism and were humiliated by the triumphalism of politicians declaring the advent of a 'new' Flanders; all this was highlighted in the Walloon media. The social-political crisis hurt Wallonia's self-esteem. Protests and angry reactions followed and some radicals threatened to join France or create a '*Belgique du Sud*'.

The Third Conflict Area: Brussels

As the capital of a nation with two language communities, Brussels has been officially bilingual since 1932. In the post-war period however, gallicisation of the originally Flemish city continued unabated. French was considered a universal language and seen as an effective vehicle for social promotion. Dutch was still considered a backward language of the lower classes. Brussels' demographics made this characterisation easier: Flemish immigration into the capital primarily consisted of the working class while the Walloon influx was more intellectual. The Flemish newcomers spoke a dialect but their sketchy knowledge of French was enough to land them in the bilingual pool. Education, administration and business life was all part of an assimilation process that inexorably pushed the Flemings towards the French language. If the original generation became bilingual, the second generation often went one step further and became increasingly francophone. Especially the expansion of the service sector made sure that the pressure to speak French continued to weigh on all social classes within Brussels.

Outside Brussels, too, French kept spreading, from one suburb to the next outlying suburb and thus into Flemish Brabant. The 1947 language census, even though its result was disputed, showed that the municipalities of Ganshoren, Evere and Sint-Agatha-Berchem had reached the legal linguistic threshold to be annexed by the Brussels bilingual region. In between 1950 and 1965, the capital continued to expand and about a dozen municipalities were faced with the bilingual concept – a great opportunity for homeowners and local real estate agents but a dreadful situation for Flanders' language integrity. The Brussels francophones rejected the principle of territoriality and demanded language rights in education, administration and culture. They wanted to become part of the Brussels region, where francophones already held sway. They called for referendums to change the linguistic status of the Flemish municipalities in question.

At the same time, Brussels' francophone majority called for the application of democratic representation, granting the Dutch-speaking minority only a limited place in the leading political institutions and administration of the capital, and opening the way for a rejection of bilingualism. Continued gallicisation was necessary to expand the influence of the francophone elite in the capital. The francophone majority rejected any control on this process, arguing language freedom should not be obstructed. At first, the francophone elite was wary of federalism and decentralisation, as they were afraid of losing influence in a regionalised Belgium – Brussels thanked its central position to the unitary state – and of falling under the reign of Flanders in a two-part state. But as these principles gained momentum both in Flanders and Wallonia, they changed tack and started defending the concept of an expansive and autonomous Brussels region as the best way to retain francophone control of the capital and the nation.

The fallout from the war had a very negative impact on Brussels flamingantism, even more so than in Flanders. Flamingants had collaborated during the war and had tried to improve the position of the

Dutch language in the capital. A clear link between 'Flemish movement' and 'collaboration' had been the result. Brussels' tradition as a gallicised, anti-clerical city further reinforced anti-flamingantism. The Nazi's language policy in Brussels and the provocative actions of the Flemish language committee during the occupation increased the resistance against any post-war Flemish demand and affected the positions of Flemings in administration and education.

It took until the 1960s before a conscious Flemish minority became a social and political factor again. Dutch-speaking university graduates settled in Brussels, took up middle and upper management positions and reinforced the older generation of flamingant families. The social and cultural gap with Flemish locals who spoke dialect could not be bridged, though. Up to a quarter of the Brussels population was considered to be dialect-speaking Flemish, but based on votes for Dutch-language lists, it stood at 15 % in 1974 and rose to over 20 % in 1977. The CVP stood for half of that total and 30 % went to the Volksunie with the '*Rode Leeuwen*' (Red Lions) and '*Blauwe Leeuwen*' (Blue Lions) winning another 10 % each. All parties in the Brussels region had split into linguistic entities by that time and had their own programmes and demands. Traditionally, Flemish activities in Brussels had centred on the cultural associations, with the TAK playing an important role. Whatever party they belonged to, the Brussels flamingants were one cohesive bunch and were relatively effective in countering francophone dominance.

The Brussels flamingants had experienced professional discrimination first-hand in the capital, and were looking first and foremost for strict bilingualism of the capital and of all government institutions. They were representatives of a Flemish majority at a national level and demanded parity in all public and political institutions in the capital, as a compensation for the Flemish-Walloon parity on the national level. To counter continued gallicisation of the capital, they opted for the further development of Dutch-speaking education and cultural networks and insisted on an improvement of the Dutch language situation in education, health care and culture. And since they wanted to stay as closely aligned as possible with the Flemish national majority, the Brussels flamingants strongly rejected the proposal of making Brussels a third region. Economic decentralisation went against the interests of these Dutch-speakers, who sought to intensify contact with Flanders as much as possible while considering Brussels as a mere annex of the Dutch- and French-speaking communities. The political elite in Flanders backed them in principle. They also saw francophone domination over Brussels as a remnant of francophone domination over the whole nation. For them, it was inconceivable that a nation with a Dutch-speaking majority would not be guaranteed at least a bilingual capital.

Flemings and Brussels Dutch-speakers found a common cause in defending the Dutch language in the Flemish Brabant fringe around the capital. But the Flemish position was ambivalent. Many local merchants did not really mind the influx of often rich francophones. Others, though, conjured up visions of an 'oil slick' emanating from the capital and polluting Flanders.

Francophone Brussels started organising itself along political lines during the 1960s in reaction to the big Flemish demonstrations demanding better protection in the capital. A select group of intellectuals laid the foundations for the *Front démocratique des Francophones* (FDF) in 1965. It was an instant success and found widespread backing. In 1971, the FDF already won 28 % of votes in the Brussels region and three years later it was the biggest party in the capital, attracting over a third of the vote at the expense of PSB and PLP. Its followers primarily came from petty bourgeoisie circles. Its main goal was to perpetuate the existing social-political language situation. The imposition of an institutional language balance was seen as an injustice by many francophone civil servants and management and office personnel, as it would reduce their own prospects of promotion. The advancement of Dutch was considered by many francophones in Brussels as social and cultural regression. The FDF was also targeting popular discontent with the traditional parties, people who would back a new, pluralist party that took the interests of the francophones in Brussels to heart. The FDF was primarily a municipal policy party – led by a tiny group of prominent members encouraging a personal cult – that linked up with its base through municipal services and local organisations. It paid off since the FDF dominated city halls in several Brussels municipalities. Its local clout in the capital won the FDF a seat at the national negotiating table. Because of the francophone exodus from the capital, the FDF had to follow its electorate into the Flemish fringe and its main objective was to grant the francophone minority in the Flemish fringe a similar status as that of Flemings in the capital.

The relationship between the francophone Brussels elite and the Walloon movement was muddled. Even though there was a sizeable migration from southern Belgium, Brussels was never the cultural capital of Wallonia. Brussels did not nearly figure as large in the programme of the Walloon movement as it did for the Flemish Movement. Moreover, the Walloon movement fully realised that its demands stood a better chance in direct negotiations with Flanders without Brussels interference. The 1979-1980 alliance between the PS, PSC, RW and FDF represented only a strategic joining of forces. The FDF needed the support of Walloon federalism to boost its demands, while the RW, PS and PSC used the FDF to counterbalance the Flemish alliance. There was no real basis to support this political solidarity, however. Economic and political interests diverged too much to let the achievements of the francophone front reach beyond linguistic and cultural issues. The average FDF voter, after all, was in favour of a unitary state.

The political relations between the major actors in the capital started to change in the late 1980s. Brussels came under the spell of the European Union and further internationalisation. Mediterranean immigrants and their families, Eurocrats and other foreigners turned Brussels into a multicultural city, and as such the pressure of French as a lingua franca in no way diminished. The rising wealth of Flanders and the socio-economic deprivation of several municipalities surrounding central Brussels, with extremely high concentrations of non-Dutch-speaking inhabitants turned the capital into an unattractive place to live for Flemings, further cutting into the electoral stake of Brussels Flemings. Flemish culture in the capital thrived, palpable proof that Flanders continued to support Dutch-speaking initiatives in Brussels. But there was no denying that the creation of Brussels Capital Region as a third region in the Belgian constitutional framework created a rift between Brussels and Flanders.

Francophone Brussels used the multicultural development in the capital to reinforce its own position. The FDF became a victim of its own success. Since it had been able to put most of its programme into practice, there were fewer reasons to vote FDF. But it entered into an alliance with the PRL liberals, making sure Brussels would continue to be dominated by a strong francophile coalition. This strongly francophone Brussels obviously stubbornly resisted the strategy of the radical Flemish nationalists to regain the capital and the traditional Flemish parties continuing to defend Dutch-speaking interests in Brussels. The socialist PS concentrated its efforts on Wallonia, further weakening the alliance between Brussels and southern Belgium. The Brussels francophones continued to back their linguistic brethren in the Flemish fringe around the capital. Francophone, European and international Brussels had continued to expand, increasing the influx of non-Dutch speakers in Flemish Brabant. Flanders' territorial claim to keep these municipalities within its jurisdiction was slowly being accepted but the potential for political conflict remained, forcing the Flemish Movement to be vigilant.

Consequences of the Linguistic Legislation Strategy: drawing the linguistic border (1962), the language compromise of Val Duchesse (1963) and the Leuven Vlaams conflict (1968)

Trying to distinguish the outlines of the complex course of the linguistic conflicts, it is possible to claim that the sixties still reflected the traditional strategy of the Flemish Movement: looking for protective linguistic laws and trying to secure their proper application.

During the 1961-1965 Lefèvre-Spaak government, Flemish action primarily centred on the drawing of the linguistic border and the demarcation of bilingual Brussels. Two major protest marches on Brussels organised by the militant umbrella organisation *Vlaams Actiecomité voor Brussel en de Taalgrens* and the refusal of dozens of Flemish towns to cooperate with the controversial language census, forced the government to take action on the establishment of the linguistic border. The 1962 language law transferred the predominantly francophone and densely populated areas of Comines and Mouscron to Hainault while six villages in the Dutch-speaking Voeren region, some of which had francophone majorities and were economically oriented towards Liège, became part of the Flemish province of Limburg, in spite of vocal Walloon protest.

The Flemish wish to cordon off bilingual Brussels was granted. The capital was limited to 19 municipalities already part of it, surrounded by the Dutch-speaking district Halle-Vilvoorde. Public administration in Brussels had to be bilingual and personnel had to pass a language exam. Language parity at the managerial executive level had to be established within ten years and the recruitment of Dutch-speaking personnel in public administration was guaranteed. At the same time, the language use of Flemish parents sending their children to French-language schools became subject to a control system. A proposal of the prime minister to add another six municipalities with a strong francophone representation to Brussels met with fierce Flemish opposition and ended up a subject of compromise when the francophones living there were granted individual language facilities, including extensive administrative provisions and primary schools. The six held on to a Dutch-speaking status but became a separate district that belonged neither to Flanders nor to Brussels.

Since the 1963 language compromise brokered at Val Duchesse castle largely served Flemish interests, it was only logical that the Brussels francophones protested vehemently. It paved the way for the breakthrough of the FDF. The FDF surge seriously hurt the traditional parties in Brussels and the francophone parties raised the linguistic ante. The result was that the political positions hardened. The Brussels francophones had only one thing in mind: circumvent or at least minimise the 1963 language law. The strategy proved its value when the power of the Flemish vice-governor was weakened. The abolishment of language checks of the head of the family in 1970 was another indication. The francophone onslaught was also evident in the establishment of language parity in municipal councils and the continuing recruitment of francophone doctors and contract workers in social welfare hospitals. The question of the municipal administrative services in Schaarbeek finally illustrated the obvious political unwillingness to strictly apply the 1963 laws. The question took over three years to solve (1973-1976): all conceivable procedures and measures were invoked, and only when those were well and truly exhausted, could a magistrate, under police protection, ensure the application of the language law. Yet the entire incident was a measure by FDF mayor Nols that was utterly in contradiction with the stipulation of bilingual municipal services explicitly contained in the language law. It was one vivid illustration of how the 1962-1963 language laws continued to invite political controversy.

The university of Leuven, too, had become the scene of linguistic controversy, which dominated politics between 1966 and 1969. The bishops – trustees of the French-language university in Leuven – had announced the establishment of new institutions in Flemish Brabant, in the area between Brussels, Leuven and Wavre. The Flemish movement would have none of it and already had visions of a second francophone oil spill. Its defence was based on the recognition of the language frontier and the legal principle of the regional language being the official language. The Flemish students at Leuven took to the streets to protest against the plans of the bishops and a mass demonstration was held in Antwerp on 5 November 1967. CVP Member of Parliament Verroken tabled a counter-proposal and when the government showed little intention of transferring the *Université*

Catholique de Louvain (UCL) out of Flanders, the CVP ministers resigned, causing a government crisis. It meant the end of the unitary Catholic Party. The CVP and the PSC turned to the voters with different programmes. The 'Leuven Vlaams' issue had such an impact that all linguistically outspoken parties made major gains during the 1968 elections. The VU got twenty seats, the FDF five and RW seven. The Christian-Democrat-Socialist coalition led by Gaston Eyskens defused the tension and provided the UCL with enough funding to create a new campus in Walloon Brabant's Louvain-la-Neuve while the Flemish *Katholieke Universiteit Leuven* (KUL) remained in Leuven. The Dutch-speaking freethinkers demanded a fully fledged Dutch-language university in Brussels to counterbalance the *Université Libre de Bruxelles*. Following the financial efforts for Catholic university education, the ULB was split up, and the *Vrije Universiteit Brussel* created in 1969.

Because of the continuous quarrelling over the linguistic laws, both the Flemish and Walloon parties moved towards federalism. By the end of the 1960s, a separation of the cultural communities and the economic regions had become unavoidable. It would dominate the 1970s.

Federalism Gains Ground: the constitutional reforms of 1970 and 1980

Federalism first had a real political impact during the 1961-1965 government of Lefèvre-Spaak and the coalition cautiously started tackling the issue of constitutional reform in 1963. The traditional parties organised a round table starting from the results of the study centre Harmel (1958) and agreed in principle on regional and administrative decentralisation and cultural autonomy. Yet concrete results remained elusive. The 1965 elections brought a Liberal Party breakthrough and the coalition governments had a unitary slant and did not seek any constitutional reform. Cultural autonomy, however, continued to change the face of Flanders and Wallonia. In 1960, the unitary broadcast institute was split up in the Flemish *Belgische Radio en Televisie* (BRT, later changed to BRTN and then to VRT), and the *Radio et Télévision Belge* (RTB, later changed to RTBf). Separate culture departments were created in 1962 and the move was followed by a division in the culture ministry as such in 1966. Two years later, the unitary education ministry was split up as well.

The Leuven university crisis and the 1968 election results, marked by huge gains for linguistically outspoken parties, showed the defenders of unitarism that there was no way around constitutional reform. Prime Minister G. Eyskens used every trick in the political book and relied on the support of opposition parties to push through constitutional reform in 1970. The compromise called for the creation of two culture councils with limited decision-making powers – excluding, however, anything to do with the School Pact – and funded by the national authorities. The famous article 107 quater created three official regions, each with its own institutions and with economic decision-making powers. It established a system of stipends but denied the regions an independent fiscal system. Brussels was treated as a separate region with its own regional council. For personal culture and welfare issues, the region remained dependent upon Wallonia and Flanders. Wallonia was granted regional protection within the national legislature through the creation of an 'alarm bell' procedure. The vague language of the compromise text was very much open to interpretation and debate, however, which set off a political dispute that lasted throughout the 1970s. Neither the issues of authority or territory, nor the constitution of the new institutions were clearly described. Francophones were convinced that Brussels would be allowed to become a region much like Flanders and Wallonia while Flemings were just as convinced that Brussels would always remain a minor separate entity.

In parliament, each constitutional change had to obtain a two-thirds majority overall and a simple majority in each language group, forcing the federalists to count on a change in the electoral balance. When it did not happen immediately, constitutional reform was faced with a stalemate situation. The grand coalition of Leburton of 1973-1974 and the Catholic-Liberal-RW coalition of Tindemans of 1974-1977 failed to push through a definitive regionalisation. Developments were limited to the establishment of cultural councils in 1972, the split-up of several ministries and the creation of one Walloon and four Flemish *Gewestelijke Ontwikkelingsmaatschappijen* (GOMs, regional economic development companies) functioning alongside a number of advisory *Gewestelijke Economische Raden* (GERs, regional economic councils).

The Catholics scored big gains in the 1977 elections and Tindemans brokered a coalition government that included the strongest party of each of the three regions (CVP-FDF-PS) and the VU, and had a two-thirds majority in parliament. During the preliminary formation talks between the party chairmen, a solution was found. This 1977 Egmont pact to change the constitution, signed on 24 May, was further refined during negotiations at the Stuyvenberg castle. Even though the Egmont-Stuyvenberg plan allowed the national government and parliament to hold on to significant powers, it did grant the Dutch- and French-speaking communities their own councils with decision-making powers over cultural and personal welfare issues. Flanders, Wallonia and Brussels were each given regional councils with authority over territorial issues and separate regional governments. There was no language parity in the Brussels regional government. The francophones from the Brussels fringe in Flemish Brabant were allowed to vote in the capital and were granted their own community commission, much like the Dutch Culture Commission for the Brussels Flemings.

The last measures did not go down well with the radical Flemings, who considered them a denial of the bilingual status of the capital and yet another proof of encroaching gallicisation of Flemish Brabant. The creation of an anti-Egmont committee and protest demonstrations showed that the Flemish party chairmen had lost their radical Flemish grassroots support. But the neo-unitarists within the CVP also opposed the deal, be it for different reasons, forcing Tindemans to publicly announce his resignation during a Chamber session. The spirit of compromise that marked the Egmont pact cost the VU coalition partner dearly at the polls in 1978, as was to be expected. The extreme right wing deserted the party and created the Vlaams Blok. CVP chairman W. Martens formed a government of Catholics, Socialists and the FDF. Even though it had enough parliamentary seats for a constitutional reform, Martens also failed to get the Egmont agreements through the Senate, where a number of CVP legislators opposed the pact. A united francophone front further impeded constitutional reform, causing yet another stalemate.

Martens' third government, a classic grand coalition of the three major political families – due to the economic depression the linguistically-oriented parties lost ground at the next elections, while the liberals gained seats – finally succeeded where others had failed and parliament approved the government proposal in August 1980. Martens had to take the tenuous links between Wallonia and Brussels into account and broke up the overall agreement into separate chapters to improve the likelihood of compromise. His plan included three phases: the creation of regional governments; their separation from national government and the demarcation of their authorities by Parliament; and, in a final phase, a solution for Brussels.

Thus, from 1982 onwards, Belgium had, besides a national government and parliament, a Flemish Council, made up of the merger between the regional and community councils, with decision-making powers on culture, personal welfare and a number of territorial issues. The makeup of francophone Belgium was more complicated since the francophone Community Council, which included Brussels francophones, remained separate from the Walloon Regional Council. The legislators were not directly elected in this phase and reflected the national electoral balance of power. The Brussels executive remained part of the national government. The national state provided proportional stipends for the regions and communities with Flanders getting the biggest slice, reflecting the bigger population: a 55-45 edge from the language community pot and a 57.5-42.5 margin from the regional provisions. Promises were made to progressively grant more fiscal authority to the regions and communities.

The Martens-Gol government also settled the issue of the German-speaking Eastern Cantons. The constitutional revision of 1970 had set up a German Cultural Council and ten years later, the decision was made to have its members directly elected. In 1983, the authority of the Council was extended to include personal welfare issues. But when it came to strictly regional issues, the Eastern Cantons were considered part of Wallonia.

The 1985 elections set up the Catholic-Liberal government of Martens VI and, at the same time, the different councils were also renewed and new executives were created. In Flanders, Minister Geens ruled with a comfortable Catholic-Liberal majority while the national government partners also held a majority in the Walloon Region and the Francophone Community. Slowly but surely, Brussels became a full third region, especially when the executive was granted the income from inheritance tax, apart from a number of other powers taken from the conurbation council, which was still functioning in its old composition. The Arbitration Court was created in 1984 to rule on jurisdiction conflicts between the different regions, communities and the national government. It is made up of magistrates and former politicians from both language groups. The court's decisions are final.

Overall, the 1980 constitutional reform was only a hesitant step on the road to true federalism. The regions and communities might have their own institutions and their decrees might be equal to the national laws, but financial means remained very tight, a mere 7.3 % of Belgium's total budget. The national government collected taxes and controlled almost all resources. Moreover, the lines between the powers of the national government and those of the regions and communities were still fairly vague. But the regions and communities continued to seek more autonomy and were backed, partly out of economic self-interest, by the two biggest political parties: the CVP in Flanders and the PS in Wallonia.

Voeren and the Brussels Fringe: levers in the creation of the federalised state (1988)

The more the Catholic-Liberal coalitions of W. Martens tried to keep the linguistic issues off the political agenda in an attempt to concentrate on the economy, the more the issue of Voeren-Les Fourons seemed to reappear. Les Fourons became Voeren when it was transferred from Liège province to Limburg across the linguistic divide in 1962. Ever since, the region lived in a state of high political tension, all the more since the list *Retour à Liège*, led by J. Happart, an immigrant Walloon, won a municipal majority in local elections. Happart, who steadfastly refused to speak or prove he knew Dutch, was the candidate to become mayor. His attitude fitted the strategy of the francophone majority, which did not accept the 1962 decisions and wanted a bilingual Voeren. They argued that in a system of universal suffrage, mandatory knowledge of a language should not be a precondition to becoming mayor, and that instead, the will of the majority should be decisive. For the Flemings, the language frontier was inviolable. They claimed that the 1970 constitutional reform made it clear that the administrators of Flemish municipalities had to know Dutch, and as such a monolingual francophone mayor in Voeren was impossible. The question had implications far beyond the local level. Soon Happart became the symbol of Belgium's linguistic conflict for Walloons and Flemings alike. He became hugely popular in Wallonia, and the PS, seeking an overall majority in Wallonia, gave him a prominent spot on its electoral list; Happart was elected to the European Parliament.

Up to 1983, the government was able to control keep the issue more or less of minor importance relative to the economic recovery policy, but that year, there was no holding back Happart. The Martens government tried to transfer Voeren again, this time into Brabant, and grant it linguistic facilities like some other municipalities in the Brussels fringe. It unleashed a storm of Flemish protests and the idea was quickly dropped. SP representative M. Galle introduced a bill in the Flemish Council to make the knowledge of

Dutch mandatory for municipal administrators. FDF politician Lepaffe reacted with a proposal to guarantee a free choice of language. Meanwhile, the Council of State ruled that Happart's appointment was unconstitutional. The Court of Arbitration partly backed the ruling in 1986. It confirmed that the territorial principle as stipulated in the 1970 constitutional reform implied that the authorities in Flanders had to know Dutch but said it could not be imposed as an electoral condition. The Council of State reconsidered the issue and annulled Happart's appointment. The political climate within the government was increasingly tense and interior minister C.F. Nothomb resigned. In a last-ditch attempt to keep the linguistic peace the government concocted a formula that would allow Happart to become first alderman while some of his authority would be handed over to another alderman. The CVP rejected this and the Council of State called it unconstitutional.

Happart was not the only dark cloud on the linguistic horizon. In the six municipalities around Brussels where French-speakers enjoyed language facilities, francophones often won big electoral majorities, producing mayors and heads of the social welfare councils who did not speak Dutch. Here too, the francophones defended the right to use their own language. The Flemings claimed the language facilities applied only to the inhabitants of the municipalities concerned and not to the authorities. The Flemish view was backed by the Council of State. The annulment of the appointment of the Kraainem social welfare council chairman Capart made the headlines in 1987. The Council of State did not differentiate between elected officials and actual executive authorities, whereas the Court of Arbitration did. It stated that the language laws were only applicable to elected officials with actual executive powers (mayors, aldermen, heads of social welfare councils). The government tried to reach a compromise on the issue but faced the steadfast refusal of the PSC. The government was forced to resign in the fall of 1987, which led to a new phase in the conflict.

Even though socio-economic issues had an impact on the government crisis, it can be said that the 1987 government crisis was proof that the linguistic problem was still crying out loud for a constitutional solution. A transitional government prepared for constitutional reform and the coalition talks in the wake of the elections centred on continued federalisation, a settlement of the problems in and around the capital and on the cases of Happart and Capart.

The political context had thoroughly changed by the time the outstanding linguistic issues were settled in 1988. The socialists had shown an increasing appetite for government since 1985. At the same time, the Christian labour movement felt an increasing unease about the economic austerity policy and sought out its socialist partner for cooperation. The 1987 election result only reinforced this centre-left attraction. The CVP-PSC sank to a historic low. Combined with a loss for the liberal PRL and gains of the PS, it left the centre-right coalition parties with only a slight majority. The coalition talks would have to take into account the fact that the socialists had become the biggest political group. The CVP needed a long healing process to overcome this bitter election defeat and settle internal divisions, while the PS needed all its time to back down in the Happart case. Little wonder the government crisis turned into the longest that Belgium had ever known.

The prospect of a comprehensive constitutional revision combined with the immediate linguistic problems provided the political parties with a way out. The Happart impasse could be put in a wider institutional context opening the way for a constitutional bartering session involving social-economic, educational and ethical issues like abortion, all within one package. Because a government agreement was linked to a new constitutional step on the road to federalisation, any coalition deal had to have a two-thirds majority in parliament. CVP mediator Dehaene was eventually able to line up five parties (CVP, PSC, PS, SP and VU) that saw enough benefits in forming a government.

The five-party agreement was a victory for the federalists since a sizeable chunk of unitary powers was effectively transferred to the regions and communities, which won much more autonomy than what the 1980 constitutional reform had granted them. The economy, energy, public works, transport, employment, scientific research, the environment and environmental planning were the key sectors that were handed over to the regions while the communities controlled cultural and personal welfare issues, education and language. Devolution reached the stage where regions and communities were even allowed to sign treaties and create their own fiscal framework. The Senate would be adapted to the new federal structure, and directly-elected parliaments were promised, as was a federal state without residual jurisdiction.

The hot linguistic issues were also solved in a spirit of compromise where no one felt unduly hurt. On Voeren and the Brussels fringe, the Flemings were able to claim that the linguistic frontier and the language laws had been fully respected. The Flemish authorities were now in control of their Flemish municipalities without interference from the national government. In Flanders, they were able to dismiss any mayor or head of the social welfare council in case of language incompetence. It meant that Happart became a symbol of the past. The introduction of proportional representation and the imposition of consensus decisions within the aldermen's college in the controversial municipalities provided the Flemish minorities with real power. The francophone negotiators also had plenty to show for their work. The francophone language facilities around Brussels were made permanent. Council members and aldermen who knew no Dutch were now sacrosanct. Aldermen could be appointed through direct elections, in which case the election itself established an irrefutable assumption that they knew the language of the region. The establishment of an advisory college of provincial governors allowed the Walloon governors to exert pressure on Limburg in its handling of the Voeren issue. Citizens from Voeren were allowed to vote in Wallonia, in Verviers, for national and European elections.

The francophones scored a major victory in Brussels Capital Region, which was now fully recognised as a third region with its own elected council and executive. The fact that their edicts, in contrast with the decrees of other regions and communities, could be checked by the courts, diminishing the Brussels decision powers, was explained as a clever judicial trick. In return, the Flemings were granted a representation well beyond their demographic strength. With the exception of the president, there was full linguistic parity within the Brussels executive. The Flemings also held effective veto power since decisions in the councils needed a majority in each linguistic group, and the executive took decisions based on consensus and collegiality.

The francophones were also pleased with the funding measures. The needs of Wallonia were the starting point and national solidarity would continue to benefit Wallonia. Moreover, during a transitional period of ten years there were provisions for an overcompensation of solidarity that would only be gradually decreased. Only after that period would the solidarity mechanism fall back on the direct exchange between the development of Gross National Product and the revenues of the regions. The acceptance of the principle that the regions would share in the profits of GNP was seen by the Flemings as a victory: since Flanders was economically stronger, it would able to enjoy the fruits of its success. A similar transitional period was provided at the level of the communities. The Flemish majority would be realised by 2000.

Much like earlier constitutional reforms, the execution of the programme was spread over several stages. It allowed for supplementary political bartering and set a system of priorities, which made negotiations easier. The toughest decisions were pushed ahead, to a final negotiating phase.

Parliament started with the necessary reforms of the constitution in May 1988. In August, parliament approved the increase of executive and legislative powers of the regions and communities and endorsed the proportional representation in the Flemish executive, making it possible for SP and VU to enter this government. Parliament had also approved the law on language facilities on 9 August, not without problems. The government, however, ignored protests of both francophones and Flemings, and was backed up by Parliament.

The second phase started in the autumn of 1988 and tackled the contentious issue of Brussels. The powers of the Brussels agglomeration were transferred to the region and new Brussels institutions were created. Language groups and committees were created assuming the tasks of the former culture commissions; consultation and coordination bodies between both communities, charged with among others the regulation of the so-called 'bio-communal' issues were also appointed. Brussels Capital Region was granted the same powers and comparable financial backing as the two other regions.

Next, the fundamentals of a constitutional court were created. The judicial review rights of the Court of Arbitration were extended to include edicts. The Court was also given powers of annulment concerning the principles of equality, non-discrimination and freedom of education. Every individual or corporate body was now able to start annulment procedures, including citizens from the municipalities with linguistic francophone facilities, which meant another francophone demand was granted.

Finding a parliamentary special majority on the financing law took a great deal of time. Each department had to be scrutinised and tough decisions had to be made about which budgetary posts would be federalised. An extremely complex financial system was created granting regions and communities their own fiscal income (among others inheritance and registration rights) and taxation income (surcharges on parts of income tax, VAT and television license fees). They were also allowed to levy certain taxes themselves, lend money and draw on a national solidarity fund. The three laws of this second phase were all approved in January 1989.

In contrast with the technical details that characterised the first two phases of the agreement, the third and final part of the constitutional reform process was kept extremely vague. It was hardly surprising that this phase was very slow and difficult in the making. It directly touched upon the fundamentals of federalism and the negotiations dominated the political agenda between 1990 and 1993. The extreme right was enjoying its breakthrough and this affected the parties involved in the talks. The centre-left coalitions also knew that they could not neglect the social malaise, since the extreme right was feeding off it. At the same time, the government had to tighten its budgetary belt to meet the stringent conditions for participation in the European single currency. There were more than enough reasons to speed up negotiations and conclude this third phase.

The 1993 Saint Michael Agreement

The Flemish movement and parties had taken a more radical stance by 1991 and had opened a new offensive against the third phase of reform. They agreed on a joint minimum programme, including such demands as directly elected parliaments, more autonomy for the regions and communities and the adaptation to the federal structure of the national Chamber and Senate and the bilingual Brabant province.

Wallonia also toughened its stance. Any meddling from the national authorities or Flanders in Walloon matters faced immediate rejection. The 1991 fight over Wallonia's arms industry was indicative of the mood. The Flemish progressive parties wanted to set stringent criteria for arms exports but were stonewalled by the PS. The Walloon Socialists, long involved in the traditional arms industry around Liège, were even willing to risk a government crisis over the issue. It was an indication that they also wanted to take the next step towards further federalisation. A key part of any discussion was the insistence on national solidarity in the social security and health care sectors. They rejected Flemish claims that the financial north-south flow was unjust and refused to accept it as a basis for discussions.

It would take until early 1993 before the new phase in the pragmatic pacification process was finished. Parliamentary committees, working groups, a government crisis, a government agreement, dialogue between the communities – talks just seemed to drag on endlessly. It took the efforts of coalition broker and future prime minister Jean-Luc Dehaene to bring the process to a good end in 1993. The Saint Michael's agreement and the subsequent Saint Quinten's agreement again turned into a compromise with everyone – flamingants, wallingants and moderate federalists – showing willingness to cooperate.

The Flemish and Walloon proponents of more autonomy came away happy: regions and communities were allowed to sign international agreements on issues within their authority without much national interference. Environmental policy and much of scientific research was transferred to the regions. Notable exceptions, however, were health care and social security, in spite of continuing Flemish insistence. The federal institutional construction was as good as finished. The so-called 'double mandate' was abolished, and direct elections for the regional parliaments were approved. The Flemish Parliament had 118 members, including six from the Brussels Regional Council. The Walloon Council had 75 members. The Francophone Community Council was the exception and was indirectly composed of members of the Walloon Council and 19 francophone members of the Brussels Regional Council. The principle of territoriality was strictly applied, necessitating the division of the old electoral district Brussels-Halle-Vilvoorde, a longstanding Flemish demand. The bilingual Brabant province, covering areas of three regions and two communities, was abolished, and the provinces of Flemish Brabant and Walloon Brabant were created. The political powers over Brussels were transferred to the Brussels Capital Region and the community commissions. The governor and vice-governor still existed, but the latter no longer had jurisdiction over the communes with linguistic facilities. Flanders proved its emotional and political links with the capital by including a Brussels minister in the Flemish government.

The talks on reforming the national Senate also dragged on because of linguistic strife. The Flemings wished to see mainly the communities reflected in its composition, while the Walloons preferred the regions as a basis. A federal logic called for a scaled-down version of the legislature, but the senators made certain that did not happen. As a result the Senate offered a representation of the national state, the regions and the communities. The directly elected senators represented the federal state, the community senators were members of the community councils, which could entrust the authority to appoint those senators to the regional councils, and all of them together appointed the co-opted senators. The Chamber of Representatives was given a controlling function and was the final authority on legislative work, but the Senate was still more than just a meeting place of Belgium's federalised entities. It could still take legislative initiatives and serves as a body for legislative reflection.

The Flemish demand to be given final authority over decisions in the municipalities with linguistic facilities for francophones was not granted. The federal institutions even reinforced their role. A special committee, the *Vaste Commissie voor Taaltoezicht* (Permanent Committee for Linguistic Control) was able to check and enforce the application of the language regime and a deputy governor became language ombudsman. Legislators representing the francophones from the municipalities concerned were allowed to be part of the Francophone Community Council and the Walloon Regional Council, but only if it was the sole legislative office they held. The Flemings did not expect the latter measure to have a great effect.

The basic principles of the financing law escaped largely unscathed. The allocation of extra funding for the francophones was accelerated but the total was not increased. The francophones were able to solve the shortfall in their education budget themselves. They implemented drastic cut-backs, with heavy social consequences, while the financial intervention of the Region resulted in the Francophone Community having to cede powers to the Region and to the *Commission de la Culture Française*. It kept education under its own jurisdiction, but had to let go of all activities surrounding the schools. The *Cocof* thus gained decree powers.

Overall, it could be said that the Saint Michael agreement was another important step for the Flemish Movement in its march towards autonomy, from the point of view of the 1988-1989 decisions. The movement had gone through a drastic radicalisation process and the traditional parties had taken on the role of extra-parliamentary pressure groups. Both were instrumental in pushing through the fundamental federalisation phase. The Brussels francophones, Walloons and moderate federalists were able to slow the process but it was only to be expected that another Flemish offensive was to be launched soon.

Liberal-Socialist-Green and Liberal-Socialist Governments Continue the Devolution Process (1999-2005)

In spite of the pause planned after 1993 in order to implement the state reforms, the directly elected Flemish Parliament started to formulate new demands in 1996 already; the demands took the direction of confederalism. This radicalisation was not only due to the dynamism emanating from Parliament and government, but also to a growing self-assurance in wealthy Flanders, and to the pressure exerted by the surge of the extreme-nationalist Vlaams Blok. For three years, there were intense discussions leading to the 1999 Resolutions. (Con)federal Belgium was to consist of two states (Flanders and Francophone Belgium) and two areas (Brussels and German-language Belgium) with a lesser autonomy. The two states were to have an equal stake in their common capital in as far as interests beyond the city level were concerned. The autonomy of the states was to be extended as soon as possible, both on the level of powers and on the level of taxation. With a view to the connection between solidarity with the weaker Francophone Belgium and financial responsibility within the federal state, Flanders demanded that at least the flow of money would be divided anew, using objective criteria. Socialists and environmentalists insisted on federal grants for health care and social security, but the other parties wanted further devolution in those sectors as well. The lack of Flemish immigration and the strengthened position of French as a lingua franca did nothing to improve the minority position of Flemings in Brussels. As such, the Flemish Parliament wished to see a better protection in Brussels Capital Region and strengthened links with Flanders, especially with a view to the proposed transfer of the municipal law to the Region.

But the francophones, too, listed a number of demands in 1999. According to the agreements of 1988-1989 the law on funding had to be reviewed, and they especially wanted to see that applied to the education grant. Up to then, means had been allocated in the form of lump sums, and they were hoping that objective criteria would result in a more advantageous distribution. They were also prepared to talk about Brussels: they would also benefit from the extension of the claims of the Cocof and the VGC on the budget of the Brussels Region; moreover, they were prepared to look for solutions for the imminent danger that the thriving Vlaams Blok presented for the Brussels institutions.

The Liberal-Socialist-Green government of Prime Minister Verhofstadt (1999-2003) was not prepared to give priority to the communal problem, but it was forced to open the debate on funding. Because VU was necessary in Flanders to be able to form a Liberal-Socialist-Green government, the party was able to exert pressure to put other Flemish demands on the negotiating table as well. At the end of December 1999 there was a preliminary agreement about education funding; there were further discussions in the *Commissie voor Staatshervorming* (Costa, Commission for State Reform). These Costa-discussions took months, and as no headway was being made, the Prime Minister took control of the issue. This resulted in the Lambertmont Agreement of 2000. By taking foreign students into account in the distribution formula, and by enforcing a stricter control on the figures, a compromise was found for education. Starting in 2012, the community grants would also be adjusted to economic growth, and the additional education grant would also be distributed according to revenues from income tax. Fiscal powers of the regions were extended to include inheritance tax, property tax, registration, road and environmental taxes, donations and television license fees. Fiscal autonomy was now at 25 % of the national government's income. Apart from the regionalisation of municipal and province laws, the regions also got autonomy for agriculture, fishery, science policy and developmental aid. At the insistence of the francophones, however, health care and social security remained in the hands of the federal government.

In the spring of 2001, an agreement was reached on Brussels – the so-called Lombard Agreement. There were transfers from the region to the community commissions, and the Flemish position was strengthened. In the Regional Council the number of seats increased from 75 to 89, with 17 of the new seats going to Flemings, and in the VGC Council there were now five Flemish seats. In exchange for financial injections, the Brussels municipalities were encouraged to appoint a Flemish alderman or head of the social welfare council. In the police councils of five Brussels police zones established after the reform of the police service, a Dutch-language minimum representation was secured. From now on, the Brussels members of the Flemish Parliament were directly elected. A complex anti-Vlaams Blok construction was thought out; only one element proved constitutional: electoral lists of the same linguistic group could be linked before elections, and benefit from each other's surplus votes.

After the Lambertmont and Lombard agreements, the Prime Minister pleaded for a drastic reform of the Senate. This hybrid body did not sufficiently represent the components of the federal state, its composition was too similar to the Chamber's and also as far as jurisdiction was concerned, the Senate resembled the Chamber to too great an extent – that was the Prime Minister's criticism. The compromise reached in 2002 does indeed tighten the bonds with communities and regions: there is parity between Flemings and francophones, the Senate is composed indirectly by members of the regional and community councils and has five co-opted senators. Yet as far as its powers are concerned, little has been changed: the Senate holds on to its right to initiative and evocation. The Prime Minister's proposal to organise elections for the Chamber on a provincial instead of a constituency basis was also inscribed in the agreement. Popular politicians could now win their votes in much larger areas.

Brussels-Halle-Vilvoorde was the only constituency not included in the reform. The francophone parties did not want to sever the link between Brussels and the fringe, as the emigration of francophone and non-Dutch-speaking inhabitants of Brussels continued unabated, and those voters remained of the utmost importance for them. The Council of State rejected the system of imbalanced electoral colleges, keeping the old regulation for Brussels-Halle-Vilvoorde in place for the 2003 elections, in contrast with the rest of Belgium, where voting took place in provincial electoral districts. The Court of Arbitration then announced that the electoral district would have to be adapted by 2007. The mayors of Flemish municipalities in the fringe exerted pressure, and the Flemish government formed in 2004 incorporated the demand for a split 'without delay' in the coalition agreement. The proposals formulated by the Flemish parties in the meantime took into account the Flemings in Brussels, who would be politically endangered without the support of votes from Flemish-Brabant. The split-up of the electoral district is a federal matter, and the francophones have veto powers at that level; as such, negotiations with the francophones were necessary. The consultations of the spring of 2005 failed outright. Defending the status-quo, the francophones were in a comfortable position, and they raised the stakes under pressure of the FDF. The Flemish negotiators walked out under pressure of former VU members, who were now able to make their voices heard in different Flemish parties after they had either changed allegiance or formed cartels.

It might be useful at this point to give an overview of the linguistically-based problems halfway through the first decade of the 21st century, also because of the agreement to renegotiate the question during coalition talks in the future. The principle of territoriality remains high on the Flemish agenda. Starting from that federal logic, Brussels-Halle-Vilvoorde has to be split up both on an electoral and judicial level. Francophones and speakers of other foreign languages have to integrate in the province of Flemish-Brabant and respect the Dutch language and culture. The Flemish parties continue to object to the repetitive character of the linguistic facilities, which were rejected in the circulars by ministers Peeters and Martens. The Francophone Community cannot take any initiatives in municipalities with facilities. On the other hand, the francophones stand behind the principle of personality. French-speaking inhabitants of Brussels who move to the fringe, should be able to vote for Brussels candidates, and in the municipalities with facilities they should be able to receive support from the Francophone Community for personal welfare issues. Moreover, they fall under the definition of national minority as described by the Council of Europe. Flanders, in contrast, starts from the point of view that there are no language minorities in the Belgian model. The Brussels language laws are another bone of contention. Because of the increase in the numbers of contractual workers, the employment problems of immigrants and the shortcomings of Dutch-language teaching in francophone schools, the language stipulations cause problems for the Brussels authorities. A 'language courtesy agreement' was signed in 1998, confirming the requirement of bilingualism, but lowering the standards required for passing and promising adapted language exams. Proposals for a more in-depth revision of the language laws are on the table, but are usually viewed with scepticism by the Flemish.

It is to be expected that Flanders will again want to discuss the mechanisms of financial solidarity in the next round of negotiations, following the frustrating failure of the talks on Brussels-Halle-Vilvoorde. In short, the Belgian process of devolution is far from complete. In all probability, the future will see a new compromise to allow communities and regions to live together in the federal state.

Chapter X
Decolonisation, Relations with Zaïre-Congo and Foreign Affairs

International relations drastically changed after the Second World War. The United States established its dominance over the Western bloc, the European Community was created – on the one hand a link between the U.S. and Europe, and on the other hand the expression of an anti-American trend in certain fractions of European bourgeoisie – decolonisation and neo-colonisation continued all over the world: developments that had a fundamental impact on Belgian foreign affairs. The decolonisation of Belgian Congo was a first major problem and was followed by the neo-colonialist strategy of Belgian big business after Congo's independence in 1960. Belgium's incorporation in the U.S. military and economic policy of liberalisation of the world market was a second issue that affected foreign policy. The establishment of a European political framework and the role of Belgium within this construction also had a big impact.

From a historical perspective, the explicit tendency towards a dismantling of the Belgian constitutional national sovereignty has to be highlighted. After 1945, there was no longer any sign of a neutral or independent Belgian policy, as the number and nature of alliances went much further than after the First World War. Few countries pursued such a clear policy of military, economic and cultural agreements. No other country was willing to cede so much of its national independence to supra-national bodies. It is a policy that did change after the fall of the Berlin Wall, and certainly during the period of the second Gulf War, especially during the new war against Iraq (2003), when Belgium took a leading role in criticising the unilateral actions of the United States.

The Decolonisation of Belgian Congo (1960)

The Congolese independence movement was to have a serious impact on Belgian foreign affairs. The theme is of such complexity that only a few elements can be discussed here.

When the Bacongo were barred from meeting, the Abako party of Kasavubu provoked a bloody revolt in January 1959 in Leopoldville, to be renamed Kinshasa later. Abako demanded immediate independence, much like Patrice Lumumba and his *Mouvement National Congolais* (MNC) had done one year earlier. All of this happened under the CVP-Liberal government of Eyskens-Lilar (6 November 1958-1961).

Before the troubles, CVP minister M. Van Hemelrijck had already been working on a plan to reform the African institutions but it was a slow process since there was no political framework within Congo to fall back upon. Belgium had governed over the colony in an autocratic-paternalistic fashion that was much in the interest of the industrial and financial groups. But it left this vast nation utterly unprepared for independence. Belgium had gone little further than opening up secondary schools to the local population, a move that allowed some locals to move into the lower echelons of colonial administration. But overall, Belgium acted as if the colony would not be affected by the wave of independence that was sweeping through much of Asia and Africa. Higher education was kept out of reach of the indigenous population. Unlike neighbouring France, a huge colonial power, Belgium never thought of educating a new class of future administrators who could prepare the colony for independence. The sheer possibility of independence seemingly did not occur to many Belgians, and certainly not to Belgian colonists.

The 1959 revolt caught Belgium totally off guard and caused panic. In the Congo, many colonialists sabotaged Van Hemelrijck's government policy to start preparing the native population for independence within a reasonable timeframe. On 13 January 1959, King Baudouin promised the colony independence but did not set out a specific date. The monarch had made the radio announcement after consulting only a few government ministers. Van Hemelrijck was considered too progressive and was forced to resign, a move that the king did not regret. He was replaced by another CVP politician, A. De Schryver, who was seen as more realistic. The Congolese political parties, however, rejected the change.

But De Schrijver was forced to accelerate the policy of Van Hemelrijck, under pressure of circumstances. In January 1960, a Belgo-Congolese round table was held in Brussels, attended by eighty Congolese delegates. The date for independence was set for 30 June 1960. Kasavubu became president and Lumumba prime minister. The latter's party, the MNC, had come out of the elections in May 1960 the strongest party. The Congolese army, the former *Force publique*, started a mutiny on 5 July and the Belgian government decided to stage an armed intervention. The Congolese leaders considered this an act of aggression. Belgium started repatriating its colonists and the United Nations sent a blue-helmet force to the region.

The reintegration of the colonists in Belgian administration and economy and the issue of compensations caused a lot of discomfort, yet did not cause any important political problems, as was the case in France after the Algerian war; the Congo had never been a colony with an important white population. Yet the reintegration did add to the Belgian crisis of the summer and autumn of 1960. It also reinvigorated some right-wing 'Celtic Cross' groups, such as *MAC* or *Jeune Europe* (anti-Marxist yet also anti-American, anti-parliamentary, in favour of a unitary state and a strong royal authority, etc.) although they failed to have a lasting impact.

The Relations Between Belgium and Zaire

The relationship between Belgium and the republic of Congo, where many Belgians had held on to important economic interests, continued to be a major political headache. Congolese companies paid higher dividends than Belgian enterprises. Especially Katanga, with its capital Elisabethville (now Lubumbashi), was exceedingly rich. Through holding companies and affiliates, Société Générale controlled some 70 % of the colonial economy. The Union Minière multinational owned concessions in an area that was bigger than Belgium itself, and which the company more or less governed. The company was one of the world's largest producers of copper, zinc, cobalt, uranium and radium.

It was the reason why the Belgian government more or less openly started to back the separatist movement of M. Tshombe, who had declared the independence of a Katangese republic in 1960, a new state that could only survive thanks to Belgian support. Prime Minister Patrice Lumumba demanded the withdrawal of the Belgian army and the end of the Katangese secession. He asked for, and received, an intervention of the United

Nations. An international UN force was sent to the chaotic Congo. The intervention did not provide the solution that Lubumbashi had hoped for (the immediate re-establishment of his political authority in a unified country), but did cause the situation to stabilise.

Congo had sunk into a situation where several governments, based in different locations, contested each other's legality. Lumumba was killed on 17 January 1961 in Lubumbashi. Lumumba had been a controversial figure and enjoyed great popularity, never more so than on Congo's independence day when he lashed out at Belgian colonialism in the presence of King Baudouin. For the prime minister, Congo's independence was not a magnanimous gift from Belgium as the king had said, but the result of a long and ongoing struggle against colonialism. After his death, Lumumba was honoured in most of the world as a hero and victim of colonialism. Kasavubu and Mobutu, who controlled Kinshasa, had been involved in the kidnapping of Lumumba before he was handed over to the Katangese, who then went on to murder him. Lumumba was unjustly considered a Communist and was even blacklisted as such by the CIA. Lumumba insisted on Congo's unity and did not want to see it crumble apart into four provinces with little chance of survival. For a long time, there was great confusion around the circumstances of the murder of Lumumba. The question was raised as to whether the Belgian government was actually involved in the physical elimination of the first prime minister of the independent Congo. Forty years after the facts, the question even led to a highly charged debate in Belgium, eventually resulting in the establishment of a parliamentary investigating commission (2000-2001). The commission concluded that the Belgian government had shown little respect for the sovereignty of the Congo, and that some Belgian government members and other actors had a moral responsibility for the circumstances leading to the death of Lumumba. However, no direct evidence was found for any order by Belgian authorities (or individuals) for the assassination; it was clear, though, that they did nothing to prevent the physical elimination of Lumumba.

The actions of the U.N. blue helmets in Katanga were long hesitant. U.N. Secretary General Dag Hammarskjöld was killed in a plane crash in Rhodesia in 1961 when he was trying to intervene in the Congolese matter in an attempt to end Tshombe's secession.

After a few military U.N. operations, the Katangese independence was ended in early 1963. Belgium had stopped its unofficial support to the rebel province. The option of a 'reliable' Katanga next to a 'dangerous' central authority in Leopoldville no longer made any sense after the elimination of Lumumba. Up to 1965, popular revolt swept through the vast nation, especially in the east. The memory of Lumumba inspired the popular protests that turned against the excesses of the national army, the ANL, against the new bureaucratic caste and against soaring prices. Stanleyville, later Kisangani, was taken in 1964 and the People's Republic of Congo was created. In an attempt to turn the tide against the Lumumbist Simba (Lion) army of young peasants, Kasavubu called on Tshombe, who assembled an army of mercenaries, including old French OAS members, former Nazi SS troopers, South Africans, Rhodesians and Belgians. Yet the revolt spread to almost two-thirds of the nation. Tshombe called on the Belgian government to rescue western hostages in Stanleyville. Belgian paratroopers were dropped in and around the city by U.S. planes and the operation turned into a bloody affair.

The paratroopers were welcomed back as heroes in December 1964 and were addressed by the monarch. But the U.N. Security Council, backed by the Eastern Bloc and Third World nations, condemned the action as an example of unacceptable neo-colonial intervention even through P.-H. Spaak, in a rousing speech, stressed that the operation had been purely humanitarian. It took another year before Congo, with the help of mercenaries, was able to quash the revolt, which had claimed tens of thousands of victims.

At the end of 1965, the chief of the Congolese army, J.D. Mobutu, staged a coup; he toppled president Kasavubu and seized power. His neo-colonial regime enjoyed the full support of the United States, which had always condemned the Katanga secession. The U.S. administration had always maintained that a secessionist Katanga would leave the poorer Congolese regions an easy prey for communism. There was a distinct fear of Chinese communism taking root in the heart of Africa. Washington reasoned that Tshombe could not be the candidate of the West since he had been too accommodating towards the Belgian Congo lobby. On top of that Tshombe was unacceptable to the Congolese outside Katanga. Mobutu became president in 1966 and was the leader of a one-party nation. He was successful in attracting foreign investment, but the Belgian share steadily declined, partly scared off by Mobutu's threats. Large-scale projects like the Inga barrages, built with French and Belgian capital, were mainly meant for prestige purposes, as for the rest, the Mobutu regime was quickly heading for bankruptcy.

Mobutu set up a veritable dictatorship, with a unitary party (*Mouvement Polulaire de la Révolution*), fearsome political police forces and secret services and a ruthless repression (up to physical elimination) against all real or supposed opposition (politicians, military and church leaders, trade unionists, students, ordinary citizens). He pursued a seemingly nationalist policy aimed at restoring authentic Bantu values (*politique de l'authenticité*). In 1971, Congo was renamed Zaire, Christian names were replaced by African ones, etc. He was regularly on a collision course with Belgium, for instance when he nationalised the mining giant *Union Minière* and when, in 1973, he transferred all foreign companies to Zaireans loyal to the regime (*zaïrianisation*). These measures and other expressions of mismanagement led to an unparalleled deterioration of the economic and social situation of the country. The leaders emptied the nation's coffers while essential services were being neglected. Mobutu's regime was corrupt to the core and its wealthy leader invested his fortune abroad. He often travelled to Belgium in search of new loans and aid. He was host to Belgium's royal couple in 1970 and a decade after Lumumba's aggressive speech, it had the appearance of a reconciliation.

Apart from the United States and a few other countries, France also showed a great deal of interest in Zaire, much to the displeasure of the Belgian government and court. King Baudouin did his utmost to maintain close links with the former colony. Personal relations with the dictator remained close, despite the tension between the governments and harsh media criticism that often got under Mobutu's skin. But when the *Front de Libération National du Congo* (FLNC) invaded Katanga in 1977 and 1978, the Belgian government was in two minds. The FLNC was an opposition movement that, among others, wanted to take Kolwezi (for all its copper). It was already evident in March-April 1977 that Mobutu's army would not suffice to contain the situation, forcing Zaire to call on the United States, France's foreign legion, Belgium and especially reactionary Morocco. On the one hand, there was fear of a Soviet-Cuban victory, but on the other hand, there were serious doubts about the durability of the Mobutu regime. Mobutu, however, survived even the new onslaught of the FLNC in 1978, when there was hardly any resistance against their invasion. Eventually French paratroopers beat the hesitant Belgians to Kolwezi, where Europeans were threatened.

In the late 1970s, the Flemish Socialists took the lead in sharply criticising Mobutu's regime and its lack of respect for human rights in Zaire. The country was the recipient of an important part of the 0.3 % of BNP that Belgium spent on development aid, and continued to be a contentious issue that weighed on foreign and domestic policy all through the 1980s. Belgo-Zairean relations went through an important crisis in November 1988 when Prime Minister Martens made a series of proposals on debt relief. At a meeting in Toronto in June of that year, Zaire's creditor nations had agreed on a framework for debt realignment, and Martens went to Kinshasa with the offer to forgive 1 billion francs on a state-to-state loan total of 4.9 billion francs; forgive one-third of commercial debt in combination with a delay in payment and a Zairean commitment to repay debt interest. Mobutu reacted strongly in the hope a diplomatic incident would obtain him more concessions. In that case, Belgium would have to go beyond the Toronto framework and violate conditions of the International Monetary Fund. The situation led to a season of sanctions and threats. Sabena's rights to fly on Kinshasa were curtailed, development aid was suspended, Mobutu's Belgian castles were seized and old colonial and neo-colonial grudges surfaced again.

Ever since the bilateral Zaire agreements were signed in February 1990, the human rights theme became an integral part of bilateral relations. The Belgian policy of sanction threats if Zaire failed to meet democratic commitments was illustrated on 11 May 1990 when Foreign Minister Eyskens demanded a clarification concerning the murderous incidents on the university campus of Lubumbashi. It was also an indication of the ambivalence of Belgium, and the other Western powers, towards Zaire. Belgium temporarily froze development aid but maintained military cooperation. It meant a decrease in support for a corrupt regime that had created such a deep rift between the ruling clan and the population that the political conditions for further foreign investment had become nearly impossible. The change in Belgium's Zaire policy should be seen in this light. Belgium's industrial groups decreased their economic interest in the former colony and even Société Générale, which once controlled an economic empire there, jettisoned the remains of that empire during the 1980s. The economic interests of the big Belgian companies (not to be confused with the minor interests of Belgian entrepreneurs and shop owners still active in Zaire) were reduced to Sabena's quasi monopoly on flights between Belgium and Zaire, the banking activities of Belgolaise, which handled most of the Belgian-Zairean trade through its African network, and the textile and brewing interests of the Relecom group.

Mobutu's final fall in May 1997 was the result of both the military advance of L.D. Kabila's troops as well as the deep social, economic and political legitimacy crisis of Mobutu's dictatorship. In a very short time, Kabila succeeded in toppling Mobutu's regime, among others with the help of neighbouring Rwanda. The old (and ailing) dictator fled the country and would soon die in exile. By the time this happened, the former colony was no longer part of Belgium's economic or political preoccupations. Belgium made sure Zaire remained on the international diplomatic agenda in early 1997 but treaded extremely carefully. Belgian paratroopers were transported to two bases in neighbouring Congo-Brazzaville, poised for a humanitarian intervention or to protect nationals in Zaire. But in the end, no action was necessary.

The question was whether the new regime would also mean a new start for the country, which had been renamed Congo once more. Whoever had high hopes was soon disappointed: a civil war broke out in 1998, with the fighting parties being supported by troops of neighbouring countries. Once more, Congo was a deeply divided nation. Belgian diplomats made countless efforts to put an end to the bloody conflict, and the rivals were admonished to try to find a compromise. This more or less succeeded in 2003: the opposing parties agreed to form an interim government, promising democratic elections in the near future. Belgium resumed its official development aid and intervened regularly to safeguard the fragile truce.

Belgium and NATO

When Belgium became a founding member of NATO in 1949, this entailed a series of immediate military commitments concerning military stocks, including nuclear warheads, bases, arms investments and an extension of military conscription to two years. The KPB protested and demanded cuts in military expenditures and the abolition of both NATO and the Warsaw Pact. During the Van Houtte government (1951-1954), the BSP also started to insist on a reduction of military service and the CVP-PSC did the same when they were in opposition between 1954 and 1958.

Military spending decreased significantly after the (first) Cold War, from 5.5 % of GNP in 1952 to 3.9 % in 1956. At the time, opposition against NATO membership was also on the rise in the other parties. In the fifties already, the left wing of the BSP criticised Belgian foreign policy for being far too close to U.S. policy and demanded the recognition of the new communist countries and improved relations with the Eastern Bloc. Those relations did eventually improve but only after the United States took the lead. Like the other West European nations, Belgium took cover under the U.S. nuclear umbrella and became part of the military doctrine of mutually assured destruction. The fear of annihilation was such that the threshold to launch a first-strike offensive was just too high. Even if a war of the two superpowers had bypassed the Continent, Western Europe would nevertheless have stood little chance of surviving the catastrophe. The Western nations overwhelmingly let the United States take the lead. France was the exception and developed its independent '*force de frappe*'.

When the economy picked up during the 1966-1973 period, the European NATO allies started showing some signs of independence from the U.S., but Washington backed East-West détente too. The United States were embroiled in the hopeless Vietnam war, which disturbed the Pax Americana. In 1967, Belgian Foreign Minister P. Harmel issued a report that was backed by the other European allies and was also received fairly positively in the U.S. It demanded a bigger say for Europe in NATO affairs and addressed East-West security issues. Harmel wanted to create bilateral and multilateral relations across the Iron Curtain and prepare the foundations for a Europe-wide rapprochement. The foreign affairs minister of Poland was on the same wavelength as Harmel and wanted to promote lasting peace through a progressive demilitarisation of Central Europe. German Social-Democrat Chancellor W. Brandt developed his *Ostpolitik* in the hope that it could eventually lead to the reunification of Germany. The Prague Spring was a short-lived flirt of a communist nation with democratisation and it was brutally suppressed by Soviet troops in 1968. But even this unwelcome incident failed to stop the Harmel doctrine in its tracks. The overall goal remained to weaken, if not undo, the consequences of the 1945 Yalta agreement that split up Europe in superpower spheres of influence. The aim was to counter the political polarisation with détente and a partial disarmament in Europe. It was during this period of relative calm that Belgium accepted in 1966 to become host to NATO's headquarters in the Brussels suburb of Evere and the Alliance's military Supreme Headquarters Allied Powers Europe (SHAPE), in Casteau (Hainaut). French President Charles De Gaulle had asked NATO to move out of France in a show of military independence. France had its own nuclear arsenal but remained a NATO member, seemingly more in an associate, advisory capacity. The negative aspects included becoming a prime target in case of war but this was offset by the positive impact on the economy and a more elevated status for Belgium in the world at large. It also underlined Brussels' ambition to become the headquarters for several international organisations. In 1969, Harmel was the first Western diplomat to reopen East-West dialogue and he smoothed the way for the 1970 Soviet-German non-aggression pact. Harmel proved that a small country could have an important mediating role on the international stage.

In Harmel's wake, several Christian-democrat and even socialist foreign affairs ministers proved meek followers of the U.S leadership within NATO. One minister said in 1981 that Belgium had 'linked its fate to that of NATO to the bitter end'. Despite his European convictions and plans to improve intra-European cooperation, Foreign Affairs Minister Leo Tindemans also put himself in the Atlanticist camp. He failed to support the attempts to organise a European disarmament conference and backed, against the wishes of his own CVP party, the introduction of nuclear cruise missiles in Belgium.

This is not the place to exhaustively discuss the new armament strategies developing in the 1970s, related to technological advances in conventional weapons, rockets and missiles, chemical and biological warfare options, increasingly complex electronic communication systems, preparations for the extension of the arms race into space ('Star Wars') etc., nor to minutely spell out the SALT and START agreements and their unsettled status. It is worth mentioning, though, that during the 1970s, it dawned on some that a limited and relatively long nuclear war could be won. Such a war would include a combination of conventional and nuclear arms, including middle-range missiles, artillery with 'limited' nuclear components and nuclear landmines detonated behind enemy lines, and it could be fought in Europe. The European NATO allies were not intimately involved in the development of the strategy and were only partially informed. It took several years before Europe realised that the new strategy significantly lowered the nuclear threshold. The United States had become convinced that the principle of mutually assured destruction had become so absolute that it offered the enemy the tactical space to gradually extend its sphere of influence without risking nuclear Armageddon.

Initiatives for the installation of Pershing II and/or Cruise missiles with nuclear warheads on European soil took place in an atmosphere of renewed Cold War. The United States had shown weakness in Iran and Nicaragua and had failed to prevent the 1979 Soviet invasion of Afghanistan. Remilitarisation, the austerity measures and the overall economic crisis all added to the gloomy mood. It was during this period that the European allies were called on to accept Cruise and Pershing II missiles on their territory. But many of the European nations also saw the deployment as a bargaining chip to get the Soviets back to the disarmament negotiating table in Geneva. If the Soviets agreed to withdraw a number of SS-20 missiles, the West would also reduce its nuclear arsenal. There was talk of a 'zero option', but this was almost impossible to realise as the Soviets demanded that the French and British nuclear missiles also be included in the count. The NATO ministers, pressured by Washington, took a 'double track' decision in 1979 to deploy the Cruise and Pershing II missiles in a number of European countries if Moscow refused to withdraw part, or all, of its SS-20 missiles. The United States, which spent between a quarter and a third of its budget on the military, was hoping that the Soviet Union, faced with an increasing technological gap, would no longer be able to meet the challenges of the arms race. It would sap the economy to the extent that it would be forced to introduce liberal-capitalist changes.

From 1979 onwards, the United States repeatedly reminded its European allies of their duty of solidarity. The Dutch had failed to promise that year that they would allow missile deployment on their territory. Several other nations, especially the Scandinavian countries, had refused. Belgium apparently made a commitment in 1979 and even accepted a deployment calendar. Meanwhile, criticism on the dependence on the U.S. increased, especially since Washington was seen as the main culprit in the escalating arms race. Widespread resistance turned into the creation of the peace movement under the VAKA-CNAPD umbrella organisation in 1978, when the 'Disarm to Survive' demonstration against the neutron bomb was held. At the end of 1979, some 50,000 demonstrators protested against NATO's 'double track' decision. 25 October 1981 became a historic day when a quarter of a million people demonstrated in the capital to back the demands of the peace movement.

During the 1980s, the peace movement became a new political and ideological force in Belgian society and its massive demonstrations, which were held on an almost annual basis, put the political class under pressure.

Because of the peace movement, the Flemish SP became more radical and Catholic circles were faced with internal dissent. It was also instrumental in the growth and electoral breakthrough of the environmental parties Agalev in Flanders and Ecolo in francophone Belgium.

The peace movement probably also helped bring the Harmel doctrine back to the surface during the 1988-1991 period. Against Tindemans' Atlanticism, the Belgian government developed its own dynamism in the conciliation between East and West during those crucial years that were marked by the fall of the Berlin Wall and the collapse of East European communism. Belgium became a controversial ally during the 1990-1991 Gulf War. It showed extreme hesitance in using Mirage jet fighters to defend Turkey and refused to supply Britain with ammunition. It was a time when foreign policy was geared towards defence (in the hands of Minister Coëme and Chief of Staff Charlier), which in turn was centred on European issues. Alongside its NATO commitments, Belgium opted for a European defence structure and was part of negotiations with France and Germany to create a 'Eurocorps', a kind of embryonic European army.

After Willy Claes (who would later become Secretary General of NATO) became Foreign Affairs minister in 1992, Belgium tried to loosely integrate the Eurocorps into the NATO framework. Ever since the European Union's 1991 Treaty of Maastricht, defence was no longer the exclusive domain of NATO even though much work remained to be done before the EU could establish its 'Common Foreign and Security Policy'. Up to Maastricht, defence had been the domain of NATO, while the European Union had always been economically oriented.

Yet it is mostly against the background of a far-reaching integration of Belgium in the European construction that the critical, multilateral position of Belgium, c.q. the Verhofstadt government, in the period after 11 September 2001, characterised by new American military operations – first in Afghanistan, then in Iraq, where the Gulf War entered a new violent stage in 2003 – has to be interpreted. This integration in the European construction took the form of new initiatives, especially concerning the establishment of a European constitution and the compliance with the strict budget discipline in the framework of the European Stability Pact. Since 2001, Belgium's identity in international relations is intimately linked with the role of Brussels as the hard core of Europe – a Europe that is increasingly confident of its own competitiveness and that positions itself as an independent power. After a series of tensions and problems with Belgium, the American president admitted as much. The first stop on Bush's first overseas visit of his second term in late February 2005 was Brussels, the site of NATO headquarters, but first and foremost the centre of Europe and the capital of Belgium. But the relatively far-reaching 'multilateralism' – which was softened after Bush's visit – did not follow immediately from an independent European stance towards Washington and from an approach that aimed to be encompassing even on a European level. Belgian multilateralism follows the lead of the new world order, as it is judicially transcended by the United Nations, but which primarily answers economic processes of internationalisation based on capitals with a high circulation rate moving beyond the national borders, even though they increasingly and complexly rely on state structures and mechanisms for their translation into social existence. As discussed in the chapter on economic and social policy, the Belgian space is primarily a logistical space for international or multinational capital, which can be seen in the extremely high degree of internationalisation of the Belgian economy. In other words, Belgian foreign policy can also be seen as a consequence of processes of globalisation and of the special position occupied by Belgium within these processes. This can also explain the fairly strange convergence of positions taken by the Verhofstadt government in the run-up to the new war in Iraq at the beginning of 2003 and significant sectors of the new anti-war or peace movement which developed massively from the anti- or counter-globalism movement.

On closer inspection, then, Belgian foreign policy shows a fairly complex character. There is the multilateral tendency, which can be linked to the concept of an open Belgian logistic space; the latter is eminently suitable for the reproduction of international capital no longer dependent on the mechanisms of capital export of big imperialist powers, among others because it is internally fragmented. This multilateral tendency, which at certain moments is likely to culminate in 'anti-American' points of view, is simultaneously linked with a choice for a 'strong' and constitutionalised Europe, i.e. a national liberalism that transcends the 'old' European nation state borders to a certain extent, but that also 'lags behind' cross-border movements of international capital. Metaphorically speaking, this is about the tension between Brussels as European hard core and Brussels as a new global city.

Belgium and Europe

Western Europe has made great strides forward since the end of the Second World War, especially on the economic front. The Benelux economic union between Belgium, the Netherlands and Luxembourg, which had been conceived during the war in London, became a blueprint for West European integration (and eventually the Euro-zone). It was a customs union that coordinated economic, financial and social policy as well. The Common Market, which was later to turn into the European Union as we know it, decreased the impact of the Benelux construction, but the Benelux nations still packed more clout as a group than as three individual countries. Wallonia always remained suspicious about the Benelux since it feared the organisation would boost the standing of Dutch-speaking Flanders.

The European Coal and Steel Community was created in 1951 by France, West Germany, Italy and the Benelux countries and was an important and realistic point of departure for the establishment of the European Union. It created a common market for coal and steel realised the plan of Robert Schumann, a French-Alsace politician. Competition between the companies had to lead to industrial renewal in the sector and promote political integration in Western Europe. The United States actively supported the plan since they were proponents of French-German reconciliation and had funded Germany's industrial recovery through the Marshall Plan. A Luxembourg-based High Authority had to manage the international system and finance pit closures. In Belgium, some of Wallonia's loss-making coal mines were among the first victims.

The European Economic Community was created in 1957 through the Treaty of Rome and set up its headquarters in Brussels one year later. The EEC sought to gradually scrap custom duties and internal tariffs, create a common agricultural policy and set out joint industrial, regional, transport and development aid programs. Britain, Ireland and Denmark joined in 1972, Greece in 1981 while Portugal and Spain were added in 1986, in spite of protest by EEC farmers and specifically French winegrowers, who wanted to postpone Portuguese and Spanish membership as long as possible. Around two-thirds of the EEC budget was spent on aid and subsidies for the Common Agricultural Policy.

The crisis of the 1970s exposed many weaknesses in the system of European cooperation and currency speculation could not be avoided. Belgium was part of the so-called ‘currency snake’, a monetary system intended to limit fluctuations, and had to be bailed out by the German *Bundesbank* on more than one occasion when under attack from speculators. The situation made Belgium dependent on West Germany's thriving economy. In 1978, the system was extended to the EC. The ECU became a kind of umbrella accounting standard, used to determine the strength of national currencies in the framework of the European currency system. From 1979 onwards, the Belgian national bank had to intervene more than once when the franc threatened to slip against the ECU. A devaluation, which Belgium was able to avoid until 1982, might have boosted the export industry but it also made the import of oil and natural gas more expensive. Because it lacked sufficient income from taxation, the Belgian state was forced to lend money abroad against exorbitantly high rates, further increasing pressure on the franc. By 1981, foreign debt was so immense that it became difficult to obtain new loans.

The creation of the European Monetary System in 1979 freed the national currencies from the monetary 'snake' and they were floated freely again. Proposals were made to turn the ECU into an inter-European currency, comparable to the U.S. dollar. It was to boost Europe's monetary position and give European economic cooperation a concrete dimension. VAT was introduced in all EC member states. Agricultural policy was set by the Community's executive Commission and superseded national authority. It created near-constant tension between member states and the 'marathon' meetings of the agriculture ministers became legendary.

The creation of the internal market by the end of 1992 was at the heart of the 'Europe 1992' operation and marked the next step in the drive towards closer European unity. The increasing number of cross-border mergers and acquisitions brought the member states closer to a pan-European economy and put Europe in direct competition with the United States and Japan. The 'Europe 1992' operation had several consequences for Belgium. It improved the international status of Brussels (with the concurrent implications for residential space and the environment) but also highlighted the weakness of the Belgian economy. It was an important factor in the dismantling and restructuring of several sectors, companies and groups. It coincided with the loss of Belgium's main pillar of unitary holding bourgeoisie, i.e. the venerable Société Générale. The intimate historic ties between this empire and the kingdom disintegrated in 1988, when it became the object of a fierce battle for control between the Italian investor De Benedetti and the holding group Suez.

Together with the fall of the Berlin Wall and the unification of Germany (1989-1990), the operation 'Europe 1992' (which resulted, for instance, in the establishment the European 'open' internal market) paved the way for the creation of the Economic and Monetary Union, as set out in the 1991 Maastricht Treaty. The first phase of EMU involved an economic convergence programme that aimed to streamline national policies on inflation, budget deficit and currency stability. The programme set out to enable fixed monetary parities and a single currency. The convergence criteria to be fulfilled by every member state by 1996 were the following: inflation was not allowed to exceed the average of the three countries with the lowest levels by more than 1.5 % and long-term interest rates were not allowed to exceed the average of the top-three performing nations by more than 2 %; the overall budget deficit was to be 3 % or less of GDP; national debt was to remain within 60 % of GDP; the currency had to avoid devaluation for two years and remain within the 2.25 % fluctuation margin of the European Monetary System. The project of the single currency also implied the establishment of a Central European Bank, independent of the governments of the individual countries, with a board composed of representatives of the different central or national banks.

The ratification of the Maastricht treaty in Belgium, in itself politically not contentious, only encountered one problem: a first attempt at ratification failed in the Chamber of Representatives because there were too few members in attendance. The reaction of public opinion to the Maastricht Treaty was also lukewarm at best. In April 1992, four months after the landmark European Union summit in Maastricht agreed on the treaty, and three months ahead of its ratification (14 July 1992), 'Maastricht' only meant something for about half of the Belgian population.

Things have changed since, and the disinterest has gone. The Maastricht Treaty and EMU were important turning points. In the past, recessions always hit the credibility of the European institutions, but by sticking to the economic convergence criteria and strict budgetary standards, the European Union showed a way out. The Maastricht Treaty countered the 1990-1993 recession with the imposition of a concerted neo-liberal austerity programme (cf. Chapter VIII). Europe put its stamp on Belgian policy in 1993 when a hard-hitting economic austerity budget was approved. But the European Union also became a very visible player in the dismantling of uncompetitive industries. The European Commission punished subsidies that distorted competition (cf. the Forges de Clabecq dossier); it also meant the absence of a social policy (cf. the Renault-Vilvoorde dossier). In the first half of 1997, the concept of Europe was at the centre of social protest. A first European 'march for employment' was held in Brussels on 16 March 1997 and focused on the closure of the Renault-Vilvoorde plant.

The European Community, which turned into the European Union on 1 November 1993, remained first and foremost an economic actor on the national or internal political level. Yet Maastricht also offered the perspective for joint action on policing and judicial matters, foreign affairs and defence issues. At the level of justice and interior ministers, closer cooperation was evident during the establishment of Europol and in other police issues. Immigration and other problems linked to the 1985 Schengen agreement, voting rights for foreigners, labour conditions, security, health and equality issues were all affected by closer cooperation. A common foreign and security policy remained problematic. The main obstacles here may be linked to institutional concepts; this form of cooperation remains, after all, exclusively inter-governmental – in spite of the Maastricht Treaty, it is mainly worked out in the context of European Political Cooperation, and as such not binding. Another obstacle is the continuing rift between Atlanticists and proponents of a more independent European stance. It was no surprise that even in the case of agreement on a joint position, the member states talked in more than one voice.

The foreign policy problems were part and parcel of the limits of the European construction and inherent to its basic concepts. The limited success of a coordinated economic policy does not correspond with a common autonomous economic area. The convergence criteria, for example, do not reflect the existence of independent European capital, or of the establishment of coordination between the different national capitals. The European area guarantees conditions for competition at a European level – it reflects a crisis or reorganisation of the old nation states in the shape of a spatial re-defining of general production conditions – but is only of secondary importance for the action radius of capital. In short, Europe is a functional factor for capital movements, yet dependent upon the global economic developments. This leads to fairly paradoxical situations; a 'strong' Europe can quickly turn into an 'impotent' Europe. The examples of economic restructuring, reorganisation, closures and delocalisations in the chapter on social and economic policy clearly show this. Also the French social 'no' of 29 May 2005, followed by the Dutch social 'no' of 1 June 2005 to the European Constitutional Treaty can serve as examples. These rejections were prepared, to an important extent, in the run-up to and during the impressive Euro-demonstration of 19 March 2005 in Brussels, which was primarily a protest against the Bolkestein service directive (the regulation of free traffic of services in the EU). The rejections pushed the European construction headlong into a crisis of legitimacy – legitimacy of a process of constitutionalisation of a European neo-liberal space, of a process of codification that was in full development at the end of 2001, during the Laken Summit under Belgian EU presidency. The crisis showed in the onset of a Euro fall, even in a dispute of the legitimacy of the mere existence of the Euro, and in an impossible European long-term budget for 2007-2013. This crisis can be explained against the background of the failure of the Stability Pact mentioned earlier (common budget deficit and national debt standards, stabilisation of the Euro exchange rate) by national deviations. Belgium particularly questioned those deviations starting from a strong interiorization of the Lisbon strategy (cf. Chapter VIII on economic and social policy), which dated from 2000 and had as its main objective the establishment of Europe as the most competitive knowledge economy by 2010. This crisis can also be explained as a symptom of the true nature of Europe, which remains an administrative-bureaucratic construct to a large extent, even though it has contradictory consequences. As indicated, national governments can draw means from this construct – in the form of inflation and budgetary norms – which enable a home policy to converge, somewhat paradoxically, with a national policy of competitiveness – competing with other European countries – from which governments, employers and trade unions can draw legitimacy for a policy of reduction of wage costs. This implies that this construct is only powerful if it can rely on the 'old' nation states, whose governments are threatening to turn into carriers of a European neo-liberalism that itself does not have much of a legitimate state structure and that does not meet the main movements of capital, which primarily take place outside Europe. The result of this complex configuration is the further realisation of a European social movement which refuses the European neo-liberal bureaucratic construct, often from an anti- or counter-global position (e.g. from a resistance against delocalisation), but which because of this refusal of a national European liberalism almost inevitably seeks refuge in the 'own' nation state. This 'own' nation state can be the 'old' nation state, i.e. the historical, economic and social political framework within which the post-war New Deal (institutionalised social consultation, welfare state, etc.) developed, popular needs were recognised and integrated and the organisations of the 'old' labour movement formulated their projects for an alternative development. It can also be a relatively new nation state – under construction – which in the case of Belgium comes down to processes of regionalisation and devolution of communities on national-economic, ethnic or cultural grounds, corresponding to very contradictory processes of globalisation. Globalisation loses its abstract nature within the relatively new local, community or regional political levels giving their reaction in the form of resistance against globalisation.

Chapter XI
Mechanisms of Post-War and Present-Day Political Systems

There is a particularly rich literature on the political science of the post-war period, putting forward interesting hypotheses and discussing a wide range of subjects concerning the basic mechanisms of the political system. A summary of this literature is indicated here, certainly if it is confronted with the analyses of previous chapters; we can thus try to introduce a historical perspective.

Pacification Democracy

The theories of 'consociational democracy' or 'pacification democracy' have often been applied to the Belgian political system since the breakthrough of political sociology. Such a model of democracy confronts different subcultures; their conflicts, translated in specific and coherent organisational structures (pillars), have been so contentious, however, that the stability of the existing order is under constant threat. The democratic institutions have adapted themselves to the situation and political alternatives are constantly being sought to maintain the established balance of power. In such a system, political diversity coincides with political stability.

The system of 'pillarisation' – the network of associations and groups that constitute the core of an ideological family – runs through much of Belgian history over the past century. The three traditional pillars of Catholicism, socialism and liberalism have adapted themselves with remarkable efficiency to the shifting post-war developments. But even the smaller parties like the KPB and the linguistic parties VU and FDF quickly tried to create their own pillar structure to defend their interests. There was no way that they could match the influence of the traditional pillars, however, especially that of the Catholics. The pillars had (and still have) an impact on every possible aspect of Belgian society: banking, insurance, health care, education, the media, culture, etc. The structural relations within one pillar were of the utmost importance and the different organisations were closely intertwined, well beyond the financial level. They also provided one another with professional help, logistical support, information and prestige, and their claims and actions were geared to one another. Over the years, the pillars tightened their grip on politics. They infiltrated the legislative bodies, government administration and ministerial cabinets. They adapted government policy to the needs of the pillars, thus protecting themselves by pulling all important initiatives towards themselves. They turned themselves into oligopolies, with the Catholic pillar dominating Flanders and the socialist pillar reigning over Wallonia.

For a long time, the pillar principle had a positive impact on government stability, not only because every pillar wanted to feed off the state to maintain its position, but also because every individual was a member of more than one organisation within the same pillar. Overlapping membership made sure conflicts rarely ran out of control. Because the three major conflict areas – labour vs. capital, clerical vs. anti-clerical and Flemish vs. Walloon – ran right across the pillars and their membership, it reduced their intensity. It meant that potential enemies were confronted with one another within each pillar, a situation that led to more moderation. Since every individual was part of a pillar in which the three conflict areas coexisted, they were less likely to be carried away by a single issue and more likely to keep a sense of perspective. None of the fundamental tension areas could fully develop, resulting in mutual influence and moderation. It produced a mechanism of counterbalances which had a stabilising effect on politics. The School War also affected the social economic tension area while economic tensions had an impact on language strife.

Concerning the role of the elite in a pacification democracy, the Belgian example has also provided many angles. This political elite, with the task of defusing the tensions between the different pillars, creating contacts between the pillars and promoting peaceful compromise, does indeed function in all the conflict areas we have indicated. The elites hold key strategic positions within the pillars, and in the pillarised public institutions and government services, they are usually to be found in the top layers and the parties. To be effective behind the scenes, they needed plenty of room for manoeuvre, which made it essential to have the backing of their rank and file. It made the decision-making structure top heavy, which has led to political passivity among the electorate. This government by mutual consent has intensified contact between the different political elites and relations are based on mutual trust. It has produced a system in which moderation, pragmatism and realism were the key ingredients.

There are many examples in the political evolution of Belgium of how parliamentary democracy was adapted to fit the 'consociational model' of democracy. They have been pointed out in the overview of every conflict area. One of the main methods of easing and eliminating tension was to avoid one-party governments that imposed unilateral solutions. This has been very much the case in post-war Belgium. Since 1958, any solution to a political problem has taken the interests of the different pillars into account. Conflicts have been settled based on the principle of proportionality. Institutionalised negotiations made sure tension areas did not turn into open conflict. Pluralism and tolerance, two principles ideologically legitimising the existence of this model, were the preferred point of departure, taking into account the position of power of each pillar. Coalitions, compromises and pacts became the order of the day, creating extremely complex systems of negotiations and a staggering array of consultation and advisory councils. It turned into a system in which democratic parliamentary control was weakened. Policy issues were consciously reduced to technical questions. The complexity of the decisions and the competence of the experts and negotiators were of paramount importance. Discretion and the lack of a clear chain of responsibility led to the same result time and again: a political vagueness that widened the rift between the politicians and the electorate.

Without actually casting doubt on any of these claims concerning the Belgian pacification democracy, it should be pointed out that political science has mainly concentrated on two conflict areas, i.e. the religious-philosophical and the linguistic, and that the research material mainly came from the period between 1960 and 1975. The criticism on the results, and the additions that have been made in the meantime should not be omitted here. It was shown, for instance, that the negotiations on the socio-economic issue diverged from the classical pillar principle and developed a set of independent characteristics. It has to be put in the framework of a distinct negotiating structure, which includes specific consultation and advisory bodies, pacification techniques and its very own elite. Through the trade unions and the employers' organisations, a partial link was created with the religious-philosophical pillarisation. There was interdependence between the labour movement, which needed employment and social security protection, and employers, who had to rely on labour, consumers and social peace. The owners of the means of production could no longer unilaterally impose their conditions because of the trade unions and parties representing the workers. The 'neutral' state respected the balance of power and was the central coordinator between the social partners in an attempt to seek peaceful progress. Unlike the linguistic and the clerical vs. anti-clerical tension areas, the socio-economic one largely bypassed parliamentary democracy. Some controversies could be settled without any legislative interference, but parliament continued to have a role in other socio-economic areas. Because some legislators represented the social partners in parliament, the links between the two remained significant. But when the social partners sat down for negotiations, the cards were stacked in favour of the employers. The employers always had the initiative in economic life, had more means to defend their interests and a wider array of potential strategies. The unions were mostly on the defensive.

The recession proved that the pacification model was at its most effective during economic boom years. In case one issue could not be solved, there was always that little extra room for manoeuvre to solve the problem. There was an exchange of goods and services between the different conflict areas. A compromise could often be reached by expanding institutions and increasing appointments. Material concessions obtained ideological concessions. The social pact was based on the principle of increased productivity so as the pie got bigger there was always an extra slice to be divided. When the crisis hit, it was clear that the social pacification model was hurt by the decrease in profits. It forced fundamental changes in the 'consociational' model during the difficult 1980s. The system often stalled and the centre-right coalition, with its neo-liberal slant, tried to sidetrack the process. This was certainly the case in the socio-economic sector and in the religious-philosophical conflict zone. The Catholic-Socialist coalitions of the late 1980s pursued a different policy: the social consultation model became an integral part of government policy again and was more involved in the execution of the economic austerity measures.

Under the influence of an evolution in society, the pillar system has come under increasing criticism over recent years. The pillar mentality has disappeared in a large part of the younger generation. The soul of youngsters is no longer stirred by the religious-philosophical divide. The traces of a divided world have grown faint and the discrepancy between the dwindling number of practicing Catholics and the large impact of the Catholic pillar has grown starker. Society has turned increasingly competitive, pragmatic and individualistic since the 1980s and has eroded the pillar principle. The supporters of the smaller parties, like the VU, Ecolo and Agalev, were the biggest victims of pillarisation and started to fight the system. They were joined by the Flemish VLD neo-liberals of Verhofstadt. They argued that the pillars offered services that should be granted to all citizens. They were now denied a free choice since they had to pledge allegiance to one of the pillars. They said the alternatives were so limited that society as a whole suffered. Spurred on by developments, the traditional pillars went through a series of changes in their functions and contents. They played down their ideological profile, lost some of their impact on the media, found it more difficult to influence political pacification and saw the numbers of militants and members drop. Slowly but surely, they looked like being reduced to mere organisational networks. They did not just allow themselves to be driven from the positions of power, however. In spite of the severe criticism that even came from within the CVP, the pillar organisations closed ranks and continued to dominate political decision-making.

New Politics

The process of de-pillarisation sits in a framework of a much wider process of change and innovation. It is not only the religious-philosophical conflict area that loses influence to the benefit of a more pluralistic society; it is not only the classic pacification mechanisms that are weakened; instead, most basic mechanisms are undergoing change while new phenomena emerge. This is not a typically Belgian phenomenon; new political cultures are emerging all over Western Europe, mainly driven by the younger generations.

It has already been pointed out that the driving force behind the change is an extreme, competitive individualism that stresses individual freedoms and resists authority. The stress on material self-interest and on individuality not only leads to a colder society with less solidarity, but also to forms of exclusion and racist nationalism. The entire process causes a change in the relation between voters and politicians. The call for protection of the individual interests is ever louder, and the voter expects much from the government in this respect. The predominant idea is that politics should defend individual interests and solve the ensuing problems. The government is to fulfil this role as efficiently as possible and act according to the principles of current managerial philosophy and practice.

In analysing 'new politics', recent political and sociological literature tends to stress its populist characteristics. However, populism is a fairly broad notion that can be filled in gradually. Extreme-right populism, for instance, interprets the concept in a racist way, and positions it against the established elite whom they hold responsible for the current dissatisfaction. Popular sovereignty is the ultimate legitimate reference for political action. In other words, representative democracy is under attack. This is obviously not the case for parties that promote popular politics within the democratic model. They remain loyal to the principles of liberal democracy, do not engage in any discourse of exclusion and support an anti-racist philosophy, but they do use the popular themes, and adopt a popular tone of voice as well as a number of typically populist mobilisation strategies.

'The people vs. the elite' is, consequently, a frequently used theme in innovative politics. The people, the citizen as carriers of the popular will is what the populists try to embody. Tensions between the electorate and their representatives are undesirable and should be remedied. Intermediary organisations (pillar organisations, the 'middle ground') raise a screen between citizens and politics and as such should be relegated to the background. The silent majority, on the other hand, should be able to voice its opinions directly. Democracy presupposes, as much as possible, direct decision power in the hands of the voter: power to directly appoint representatives and leading politicians, hold referendums on all levels, pay attention to opinion polls – these are a few concrete examples of the highly praised direct democracy.

Politics should address the voter in a direct, plain, simple, clear, forceful way; complex, balanced analyses of intricate problems or procedures, or difficult and unpopular themes should preferably be kept off the agenda. Simple, obvious solutions for everyday problems, giving something to hold on to, definitely should be on it. Language and style should match this: polemics, conflict, exaggeration of detail are not avoided; emotionally charged points should definitely be made. In general, emotions are highlighted, along with morality and taking political responsibility. The question of personal responsibility of the politician is being asked, and politicians and political leaders are increasingly being judged on their character, background and private life. Relations between politicians and voters become more informal; charismatic, personalised leadership is highly appreciated.

Presentation, representation and perception are given a central position in the political message, which is obviously the result of the increased role of communication. Careful communication is a key concept in the new political culture; indeed, the complex subjects of our technocratic society should be handed down in simple terms, hence the need to employ communication and marketing professionals. The main route to the electorate is through the mass media, especially television. As will be shown later, this means that the media and political journalists have their influence in setting political priorities through agenda setting and priming techniques. They even have a leading role as far as presentation and representation are concerned, as they exert enormous influence on the way politics are depicted. Politicians are well aware of this, and adjust their conduct accordingly.

It is far from simple to distinguish the reasons behind these evolutions. In the previous chapters a number of factors were described that could set a context. It is obvious, for instance, that new politics interact with the hegemony of the strongly competitive market system and the process of accelerated economic globalisation, the new technological system, increased consumerism, commercialisation of the cultural sector and of the media in particular. We are in a transitional period threatening the economic interests of groups, generating unemployment and creating uncertainty, while all kinds of problems of adaptation to this complex, flexible, mobile and technocratic society emerge. The interaction of several government levels (federal, regional, European, international) only serves to increase the political complexity.

Policy itself is also a factor in the growth of social dissatisfaction. Cut-backs, clean-ups and rationalisation are operations affecting acquired rights and hampering negotiation mechanisms; as such, they cannot count on much support. It proves to be extremely difficult to reconcile neo-liberalism with new social politics. The fact that politics is losing its hold on economic and social developments and finds it difficult to keep its promises is something that cannot be hidden or justified, and in itself deepens social dissatisfaction. Moreover, increasingly large groups in society are enjoying better education, taking a more critical stance, expressing more doubts about the effects of policy, becoming more vocal, formulating their displeasure more clearly and taking a more independent position as voters. It is hardly easy for a politician to cope with this kind of voter.

In Belgium the process of renewal was further stimulated by the legitimacy crisis of the 1990s. The political scandals, and especially the Dutroux case, were important catalysts of dissatisfaction. The dioxin crisis of mid-1999 cleared the way for a totally new coalition – the first in fifty years without the Christian democrats – giving the new political forces an extra boost. In the new constellation, it was easier for those forces to break free, and from that moment onwards, the renewal really gained momentum. The old fault lines of the pacification democracy were pushed to the background and the shift even led political scientists to speak of a new fault line in the political system. To the left of the new fault line, there are the proponents of a tolerant, multicultural society with a strong democratic foundation; they support solidarity mechanisms and stress immaterial values. To the right there are the more selfish and ethnocentrically-motivated proponents of material values and authority. It is difficult to say whether this is really a new line of conflict, as the contrast is too diffuse and insufficiently institutionalised. The breakthrough of the extreme right points in the direction of the new line of conflict, but on the other hand, the popular appeal is also present in the parties to the left of and in the centre of the new axis. The following overview of recent evolutions of the different parts of the political system (parties, elections, Parliament, government, the judiciary and public opinion) will clearly show that also representative democracy is searching for a present-day translation of politics. Since the beginning of the nineties, the political class has spent increasing amounts of attention and energy on this operation.

Parties and Elections

One of the most remarkable consequences of the pacification model was the increasing power of the political parties, turning Belgium into a particracy. Internal strife within the pillars left it to the political parties to maintain unity. The parties became umbrella organisations that defended the interests of the substructures. It created a party-political pillarisation that encompassed all sectors of society. In the first place, it was the party elite that stabilised the system. Internal compromise on tension areas was reached in the party headquarters, as was conflict management between the pillars. The CVP, because of its heterogeneous background, was a master in such political strategy, and especially in the socio-economic field, it reflected the totality of the system. It allowed the CVP to play a central, dominant role in the pacification system. This sense of consultation and cooperation pushed the socialists into a reformist direction and they started to identify themselves with the state institutions in which they were represented. Maintaining and expanding their position of power became of paramount importance and often came at the cost of ideological integrity.

For all parties it was essential to control the composition of the electoral lists. As a rule of thumb, it was the party elite that decided who would be the party's backbenchers in parliament and since the top party echelons controlled campaign financing, the lists were strictly controlled. It became very much the exception for the preordained electoral composition to be changed. It meant that the party had control over the political careers of its representatives. The selection and control over political careers were powerful tools to instil party discipline. And discipline was needed each time the political elites needed to get a compromise through parliament. Any rebellious noises from backbenchers had to be stifled by the party's parliamentary group. The particracy was also evident in the fact that parties no longer left important issues to the parliamentarians, whose role was reduced to approving a compromise when asked to do so.

The dominant position of the parties was just as obvious when it came to the government: the formation of new governments also became the domain of the party leaders, who set binding agreements defining the coalition governments. The choice of prime minister, deputy prime ministers, ministers and secretaries of state were all subject to a careful balancing act between the parties. The erosion of government power was further evident in the control of the political parties over ministers, who almost became party representatives. In the discussion of difficult issues in government, the party chairmen interfered more than once and the pacification process was largely monopolised by the parties themselves.

It left the electorate with little effective power and all the political rules seemed ready-made to reduce the voters' impact even further. Decisions were so complex that they became impregnable. Political responsibility became impossible to pin down. The electoral programmes of the different parties increasingly looked alike. Little wonder the electorate became ever more indifferent. One of the conditions to make the pacification model work was a continued loyalty of the pillar's rank and file to the party. The political elite needed stable support and the reasoning was that membership of a pillar organisation equalled an electoral vote for the corresponding party.

But the increasing detachment between voter and pillar undermined that concept. While the older generation stuck to tradition and still voted along the politics of its pillar, the younger generation was much more individualistic and critical. The young were much more independent and mobile. People who have enjoyed higher education and who are better informed are not so easily led by a party. This allowed new parties to break through and make the political landscape much more heterogeneous. In order to mobilise and convince these independent, floating voters, new strategies and techniques were required, which the pacification model did not supply.

There were also other changes in the political system affecting the parties. Against the background of new politics, for instance, there was an in-depth discussion about election legislation: in order to 'bridge the gap with the citizen' the latter should be given a greater say. In 1995 the multiple preferential vote was introduced. Within the same list, more than one effective or reserve candidate could be voted for. For the 2000 Chamber and Senate elections, the weight of the simple vote for a party was halved. Voting rights for Belgians abroad were also eased. Electoral constituencies were considerably enlarged: for the Chamber of Representatives they went from district level to provincial level, and for the Senate even to the level of the entire Dutch-language or francophone area. An electoral threshold of 5 % was introduced. The fact that candidates mainly relied on television for their exposure was clearly a factor in this increase in scale. Previously, candidates seldom succeeded in getting elected outside the composition of the list set by the party, but in recent years, the number of preferential votes has increased considerably. More than 60 % of voters now vote for individual candidates. The introduction of personalisation and other modern marketing techniques in electoral campaigns is partially due to this evolution, often at the expense of the ideological level of the campaigns.

In the eighties, the (big) parties started to invest considerable amounts in expensive publicity and opinion polls in order to safeguard their position of power. The dwindling membership contributions obviously could not cover these expenses, and politically motivated gifts by companies were a legally accepted phenomenon. A direct link with government commissions should not be evident, but all government parties worked with a wide grey zone in the matter, and were not averse to taking risks. Shady and fraudulent practices were hardly exceptional. By the end of the eighties and the beginning of the nineties, the parties were confronted with a much stricter code of conduct set by Parliament. Italian clean-up operations, among others, took on an international character. Laws were introduced on party funding and open party accounts, and company gifts were made illegal. The commercialised media then proceeded to bring past political-financial scandals into the open. Real, but also alleged corruption caused much irritation in the period of austerity measures in the 1990s, and the political class was brought into disrepute. Files with elements of bribery led to the resignation of several (former) ministers (Coëme, Mathot and Spitaels in the PS; Claes and Vandenbroucke in the SP; Delcroix in the CVP). In the first half of the 1990s, the legitimacy of the political system was heavily criticised as a result of these scandals. As an indication that these kinds of practices were a thing of the past, the Liberal-Socialist-Green government tightened the controls on party funding even further.

During the latter part of the 1980s, the extreme right opened an attack on the traditional pillarised system. Many victims of social developments turned into willing recruits of the anti-democratic, ethnocentric, authoritarian and racist views of extreme right-wing groups. There were also other expressions of political powerlessness and resistance against the established power elite that had their influence on the electorate. Even though these trends had been noticeable before, they really emerged on election day 24 November 1991, which came to be known as 'Black Sunday'. The extreme right made an undeniable breakthrough and the traditional parties lost mostly on the centre-right of the political spectrum, with even the opposition liberal party failing to be seen as an alternative. The environmental parties made some gains, mainly to the left of the centre. The electoral shift was confirmed in the following years and caused fundamental changes in the political system. Up to 1991, Belgian politics had been marked by widespread stability, apart from the breakthrough of linguistically-oriented parties. The traditional parties would invariably win some 75 % of the vote. But the 1990s brought the biggest electoral shift since the Second World War and the number of floating voters rose significantly. These changes made for important reactions in the traditional parties.

The waves of immigration that had occurred since the sixties now began to have an electoral effect. Especially the right wing did not feel any inclination to grant non-naturalised immigrants the right to vote in municipal elections. Under pressure of the progressives and in the context of the introduction of the right to vote for EU citizens, naturalisation was made easier. Immigrants began to participate in elections as 'new Belgians'. In 2003-2004, all government parties except the VLD supported the municipal right to vote for immigrants. Within the party, the question caused heated discussion. In areas where new Belgians of foreign origin made up a considerable part of the electorate, the democratic parties took this into account in the composition of their lists of candidates. We will discuss the subject of the women's vote later, but it can already be pointed out that guarantees for a more equal representation given to women did result in a breakthrough of women in the parties and on the lists.

It is obvious that the parties developed new strategies to adapt to the changes in society. This began in 1992-1993 and really gained momentum in 1999 and especially with the introduction of the electoral threshold, which forced the smaller parties into action. The process has been fairly chaotic, and up to now has only resulted in a limited redistribution. The reforms have been top-down, and party chairmen have been the key figures, assisted by political marketing and advertising people. New names and logos were launched, programmes were rewritten and the party style modernised. In order to strengthen a party, it had to be opened up, the recruitment basis widened, and outside allies courted. The system of reserve candidates was reintroduced to satisfy the need for eligible positions. The media focused on individual defections of politicians, pushing the message of political redistribution into the background.

The renewal went hand in hand with a change of generations. Strong figures of the past became less prominent (Martens, Dehaene, Tobback, Maystadt, Moureaux, etc.) and more young candidates, more women and a number of new Belgians appeared on the lists. The intense personification and mediatisation of politics also resulted in parties looking for well-known television faces. Media celebrities began to appear on the lists and successfully presented themselves to the electorate in the enlarged constituencies. The most well-known politicians featured at the top of the electoral lists, and were replaced by reserve candidates if they were given a ministerial portfolio. It is a technique that offers opportunities for renewal and a broadening approach.

The old contradictions are steadily fading: Christian parties downplay their religious component, and the former anti-clerical parties more than ever welcome religious people with open arms. Consequently, there is not much room left for linguistically-motivated parties. In the regionalised

Belgian model, all parties have become regional parties defending the interests of their part of the country. The traditional parties have thus tried to take advantage of the disintegration of the language parties. The bigger parties have strengthened their position through redistribution and have integrated smaller groups. Both liberals and Christian democrats have looked for enlargement in the centre and have consequently improved their competitiveness. As a counterbalance for the centre-right, the left has tried to establish a strong progressive formation, with a fight breaking out between socialists and greens for a slice of this progressive cake. The socio-economic conflict has not really played a central role in this process of redistribution. Both the left and the right – albeit with obvious differences in approach – have viewed the process against the background of the synthesis between economic liberalism and social protection.

Because the extreme-right parties threaten fundamental democratic principles, the democratic parties have used the strategy of isolation. The so-called '*cordon sanitaire*' entails that they do not cooperate or make political arrangements with a party such as the Vlaams Belang. The conviction of the party for breaking the law on racism (2004) supports the position of the democratic parties in principle. In practice, the *cordon sanitaire* has created more conflict than anything else, especially in the right wing of the centre parties, and in particular in the liberal party. Opponents of the *cordon sanitaire* argue that the party can keep on presenting itself as the underdog as long as it is kept out of government, and as such can keep on growing. The forced cooperation between the democratic parties is also causing an unnecessary polarisation of the political system. In some Flemish municipalities the *cordon sanitaire* is also breached through informal coalitions and policy agreements.

How did these developments affect the different parties? The socialist parties were long able to count on the most faithful voters. Class consciousness of workers and employees still played an important role there. Despite a gradual decline (with the lowest point in the sixties), the socialists were able to largely withstand the electoral storms and they were little affected by the linguistic split into two different parties. The socialist decline was halted in 1981. Renewal and its federalist position produced results and by the end of the 1980s the PS-SP combination was Belgium's biggest political family again, for the first time since 1936. It was a lopsided victory that was primarily won by the PS, which had been able to successfully integrate both the left wing and the wallingants within its party structure. The Flemish SP wanted to force a breakthrough by opening its ranks to others but the strategy was not a success. The faithful socialist electorate, largely dependent on the public sector, made sure the PS survived as the strongest party in Wallonia when it was hit by a series of financial scandals and the murder of its former chairman A. Cools. And even though the SP was also accused of financial misconduct, its election results did not suffer in 1995. The extreme right did cut into socialist support by attracting trade union militants and voters in poor urban neighbourhoods, dipping below the 20 % mark. Both socialist parties had already shifted to the centre under the weight of neo-liberalism during the 1980s and in an attempt to beat the extreme right at its own game, the Socialists started stressing the theme of 'security'. In 1996, De Batselier took the initiative, on the Flemish side, for a new progressive front; he was explicitly looking at Agalev, the VU and the Christian trade union. The non-modernised SP did not have much appeal, however. An advertisement expert (P. Janssens) was headhunted to execute the new operation of renewal. Together with the popular Stevaert, they succeeded in rejuvenating the party and increasing its appeal to women and immigrants; they opened up the party to Christians through a priest-representative and attention for Catholic education. The SP was renamed *Sociaal Progressief Alternatief / SP Anders* (sp.a, Social Progressive Alternative / SP Differently). The new programme focused on a policy of equal opportunities, social redistribution through free education, transport and access to the media. The sp.a also became more Flemish and greener. By guaranteeing sufficient opportunities for Spirit representatives, they were able to form a cartel in 2000, eventually getting 23 % of the vote. The cooperation between socialists and environmentalists was more difficult. There were a few local cartels, but no regional one. In Francophone Belgium, Di Rupo embodied the renewal process. He was proficient in political marketing, relied on traditional leftist values and opened up the party, the lists and the cabinets to Christian democrats of the MOC, immigrants, women, the progressive middle ground and counter-globalists. Through government agreements with Ecolo, Di Rupo strengthened the party's green left wing. The *Ateliers du progrès* were open to anyone prepared to think about socialism while the party tentacles reached close to the population and the programme of social protection in a strong state helped to shield the party from the breakthrough of the extreme right. Election success followed: the modernised PS won the battle for leadership with the liberals with 40 % of the vote, making the socialist family the largest in Belgium again. Thanks to its strong position on all levels, the PS is the party of power *par excellence* at the beginning of the 21st century.

The Christian democrats and the liberals were subject to bigger electoral swings since they basically fought over the same middle class electorate. Even with a shifting electorate, the CVP-PSC's centre position always ensured a certain stability. In the early 1970s, polls pointed out that there was still a direct link between political affinities, church practice, the choice for a Catholic school and integration in the Catholic pillar. Since then, the ties have started unravelling and the importance of being a Catholic as a motivation to vote CVP-PSC has diminished. After the Christian democrats lost the overall majority they had held from 1950 to 1954, they fell back to an average of 36 % until 1978. Their strength in Flanders, where the CVP average stood at 47.5 % in between 1946 and 1978, turned the centre party into an essential negotiating partner. It was this role that gave the CVP such an important position within the government and pacification politics. The CVP suffered a severe setback in 1981 when it was reduced to a third of the votes in Flanders, losing many non-labour voters to the liberals. It failed to recover from the shock and on Black Sunday saw its score go below 30 %; by the end of the nineties, it was closer to 20 %. The smaller PSC experienced a similar downward trend. The party chairmen were forced onto the road of renewal if the Christian-democratic family was to keep its status as the biggest ideological centre party. The younger generations and the innovators thought that the resistance of the older generation remained too strong, and that the process of modernisation was not sufficiently fast and fundamental; as a result, there was a breakaway New Christian-Democratic faction within the CVP, led by J. Van Hecke. With Dehaene leaving after the dioxin crisis, the situation in the party became critical; chairman Declerck was not making sufficient progress, but after him Leterme gave a new impulse to the rejuvenation, feminisation and renewal process. The party opened up to non-believers to a greater extent than ever before, but hung on to the Christian predicate in its new name. The ties with the orders and the pillar elites did weaken, but the ACW was still supplying the majority of the representatives. The party radicalised on the Flemish level and embraced confederalism. This was stressed in the new name: *Christen-Democratisch en Vlaams* (CD&V, Christian-Democratic and Flemish). This facilitated a cartel with the Flemish nationalists from the former VU (now N-VA). The cartel became the biggest formation in Flanders in 2004, and brought the CD&V back into government. In Francophone Belgium, the process of modernisation was equally beset with problems. The old guard of the PSC (Nothomb) was also holding off renewal, which led to the removal of Deprez and his *Mouvement des citoyens pour le changement*. The change of guard of the generations did then take place under Milquet. Democratic humanism became the central tenet of the party, which presented itself as a fourth centre way besides liberalism, socialism and environmentalism. With the help of the PS, the *Centre Démocratique Humaniste* (cdH, the new name of the PSC) got back into the regional governments in 2004.

Overall, the Liberal Party was a stabilising factor since it often profited from defections of the Christian-democrat and socialist electorate. It tended to absorb shocks and as an intermediary party, it helped maintain the balance of power. It went through its roughest spell during the first decade after the Second World War, when its electoral results sank to historic lows. Its 1960 reorganisation proved to be a turning point and it happily fed off the decline of the CVP-PSC after that. Boosted by the climate of neo-liberalism, it became the one-but-largest party in 1981, only to suffer a considerable loss in 1985-1987. In 1992, Guy Verhofstadt transformed the PVV into the *Vlaamse Liberalen en Democraten* (VLD, Flemish Liberals and Democrats) in an attempt to break the centre-left hold on government. In his 'citizens' manifests' he promoted the VLD as the 'third way', offering an alternative between the traditional government parties and the emerging extreme right. He attracted newcomers from the conservative right and defectors from VU and SP. He had plans to change the pacification model and give it a conservative liberal slant. But a major breakthrough never happened and the VLD soon reverted back to a more traditional social policy. The situation was different in Francophone Belgium where PRL chairman Jean Gol wanted to set up a Liberal-Socialist coalition. But his strong grip on the party caused internal strife and a system of two co-chairmen failed. While the Socialist PS wanted to control the Walloon regional government, the PRL set up a cartel with the FDF to gain power in the Francophone Council. The interests of the francophones in Brussels and in the Flemish-Brabant fringe would be guarded by this federation from now on. Under the chairmanship of De Gucht there was a new attempt within the VLD to establish a broad popular party to take over the role of the CVP, with liberalism as the backbone and with attention for social problems and efficient government. Dissatisfied Christian democrats around Van Hecke were wooed, the progressive-liberal Vivant was integrated and individual ex-VU figures were tempted aboard. In the battle of competition with the Christian democrats, the formation of the Liberal-Socialist-Green government(s) in 1999 was of major importance for this VLD strategy. The coalition also forced the party, however, to take into account the programme of the socialists, which in turn led to friction with the liberal right wing. Conflicts concerning immigrant voting rights and the *cordon sanitaire* resulted in the split-off of factions (Beysen, Coveliers), and these internal conflicts also affected the 2004 election results negatively. On the francophone side, Chairman Michel envisaged a similar goal: offer a liberal alternative for the power politics of the PS. He enlarged the federation with the FDF to include the MCC of Deprez, and in 2002 reformed the federation into the *Mouvement Réformateur* (MR), a movement primarily taking *l'ère du citoyen* as the basic principle. This operation brought the MR roughly a quarter of the francophone vote, which was less than expected.

The language parties drastically changed the electoral balance during the 1970s and 1980s. The VU threatened the CVP in Flanders, the RW was a menace to the PS in Wallonia and the FDF eroded the position of the liberals, Christian democrats and socialists in Brussels. Most of the linguistic parties disappeared from the political scene as soon as their key demands were met. The VU initially was the exception to the rule. The RW and FDF fell back and many FDF politicians rejoined their old parties, a clear indication of the continuity and staying power of the traditional political families. The VU joined the government in 1980, backed subsequent constitutional reform and then paid the price in internal strife and bad election results. Both the CVP and VLD tried to lure parts of the VU electorate to their cause. In an attempt to survive, the father-son combination of Vic and Bert Anciaux rebuilt a slimmed-down party on two concepts: a shift towards the centre-left had to attract a younger electorate and a radical nationalist programme had to win voters from the Vlaams Blok. Anciaux jr. then concentrated on the left-liberal movements, tried to recruit in the electorate of the New Social Movements and also managed to get a few celebrities on board. The resulting *ID21* then agreed to an alliance with VU. The nationalist wing, led by Bourgeois, who campaigned for an independent Flanders (with Brussels as its capital) in Europe, fiercely protested against this development. As a result, the VU ceased to exist in 2001. Liberal-minded members joined the VLD; the Anciaux group formed *Spirit* (social, progressive, international, regionalist, integral-democratic, aimed at the future). Bourgeois was the central figure in the foundation of the *Nieuw-Vlaamse Alliantie* (N-VA), which set out a nationalist, centre-right course and was intended to be a democratic alternative for Vlaams Blok. Yet neither Spirit nor N-VA could make it independently. In Spirit, many a political career was at stake, and the cartel with sp.a was a solution, though not an ideologically simple one. Mutual respect was to be the key concept in the cartel. N-VA sought out CD&V in an attempt to survive in a system with an electoral threshold.

The environmental parties, too, tried to erode the power of the traditional parties. The green movement took great leaps forward during the late 1970s, but reached its electoral ceiling at around 10 % of the vote. The social strength of Flemish Agalev and Walloon Ecolo was based on the political activation of the 'soft sector' middle class, a highly educated middle-income group. Their electorate was relatively young and women were better represented than in other parties. The greens were unable to mobilise the backers of the emerging social movements and party membership was low compared to election results. They were well represented in big cities like Antwerp, Liège and Brussels but political progress was held back by internal difficulties: they did not succeed in mobilising the supporters of the different *Nieuwe Sociale Bewegingen* (NSB, New Social Movements); their membership numbers were and are low compared to the number of votes; there were disagreements between the green and red-green wings and over the professional development of the party. The proponents of a more professional approach prevailed and the environmental parties became the prime anti-extreme-right forces, getting involved in both municipal and regional government. The attempt to found a New Party starting from the White Committees, under the leadership of Marchal, father to one of Dutroux's victims, did not really involve any competition for the environmentalist parties. The movement did mainly recruit in the electorate of the New Social Movements, but it was organisationally too weak to score in elections. The leap ahead after the dioxin crisis in 1999 opened up the possibility of government participation for the greens. This did cause a few problems, however: immigrant voting rights – as we have mentioned earlier – were a thorny problem in the coalition, and a lack of government experience affected Agalev. In 2003, the party suffered a crippling defeat. It refused to give in to the lure of the sp.a from such a weakened position. The majority was adamant in its intention to spread a green total concept. The new name, *Groen!* (Green!), was chosen to strengthen this image, and a tentative recovery followed. In Francophone Belgium, the 1999 leap forward was even larger: Ecolo got 18 % of the vote.

Yet government participation was even more difficult for the party. Its ministers were given highly problematic dossiers (NMBS, DHL), and an extremely critical minority in the party actively opposed government participation. On the other hand, cooperation with the socialists did succeed here. The resulting *Convergences à gauche* concern social protection, sustainable development, transparent and participatory democracy and public guidance of the economy.

Belgium's traditional parties never really had to worry about a breakthrough of the radical left. After its early electoral successes in the wake of the war, the communists were gradually reduced to a marginal phenomenon and disappeared altogether from parliament in the 1980s. The Trotskyite *Socialistische Arbeiderspartij* (SAP, Socialist Workers Party) and the Maoist *Partij van de Arbeid* (PVDA, Labour Party – formerly called Amada) failed to score at the polls. The same held for the Walloon Christian Labour Party (SEP). After the Berlin Wall came down in 1989, the Flemish Communist Party reinvented itself as an open Marxist organisation and in Wallonia, the communists reinforced the Happart movement within the PS. Black Sunday also saw the emergence of a leftist-anarchist party in Flanders. Jean-Pierre Van Rossem, a stock exchange speculator who was charged with fraud, created a libertarian-anarchist party but was primarily a media creation. He was successful in a number of Flemish cities but soon faded after the elections. Prior to the 2003 elections, another experiment took place in the left wing in Flanders: the *Arabisch-Europese Liga* (Arab-European League) of Abou Jahjah and the Partij van de Arbeid prepared a joint list, under the name *Resist.* Leftist militants found it hard, however, to accept the fundamentalist Muslim discourse of Jahjah, and the list was unsuccessful.

Radical right-wing parties started out as marginal movements. To the right of the liberal party, the RAD-UDRT profiled itself as the anti-tax party and appealed to the disgruntled middle class, but it never won more than a few legislative seats. Some RAD members of parliament defected to the Vlaams Blok. The Blok initially wanted to be a pressure party for the VU and its calls for an autonomous Flanders won the party its own group of supporters. It attracted extreme right-wing groups like *Were Di*, VMO, and *Voorpost* and developed further as an authoritarian nationalist party that condemned the permissive society and backed traditional family morals. The Blok ideology tends towards the 'blood and soil' theories. The party stresses that 'race' and local character have to be protected against foreigners. Such talk was a hit during the 1988 Antwerp municipal election campaign and the Blok won a third of the votes, primarily in poor neighbourhoods and among unskilled workers and the unemployed. Antwerp 1988 was only a stepping stone to Black Sunday 1991 when it won 12 % of the vote in Flanders. The rise seemed unstoppable: in 2004, the party increased its share to 24 % in Flanders, and also made a breakthrough in smaller cities and towns. More young people, more men, more blue-collar workers, more less well-educated people, and especially many racist opponents of immigrants: that is the profile of their voters as it emerges from research. The *cordon sanitaire* keeps the party from government participation, and the laws on party funding, the negationism, racism and especially a conviction in court stimulated the Vlaams Blok to slightly adapt its programme and to change its name. The strategy of *Vlaams Belang* remains the same, however. It does not mince its extremist words for its supporters, but to the outside world it tries to profile itself as a party that is ready for government. Without distancing itself from the xenophobic main themes, it pushed aside its 70-point programme, attracted a few innovators and gratefully made use of the opportunities offered by the media to build a 'respectable' image, especially towards the opponents of the *cordon sanitaire* in the other parties. Francophone Belgium also saw a rise in the electoral scores of the Front National and other extreme-right formations, especially in the cities in deprived regions. In total, however, they only represented 5 % of the vote. The lack of strong leaders, the numerous internal conflicts, the rifts – e.g. the implosion of the Liège *Agir* in 1999 – the organisational weakness, the lack of efficient local structures and the fact that the extreme right has no access to the media are the factors explaining why the extreme right has not really managed to break through in Wallonia and francophone Brussels.

Changing Relations Between Government and Parliament

Belgium's pacification model also determined how parliament, government and administration operated. Things started changing at the end of the 1970s when the pillars began to lose their tight grip under the weight of increasing resistance. The New Social Movements and their ideas on participatory democracy touched the right chord, not only in the left-wing of the language parties and in the socialist parties, but also within the VLD. Even the government parties realised that more democracy was the right answer to the legitimacy crisis. During the late 1990s, 'new political culture' became the trendy catch-phrase and several measures to meet the popular demands were approved.

The changing post-war social relations left their mark on parliament and the democratisation of the electoral process became much more visible. It was not as if the Chamber was overrun by blue-collar workers, but through the education and social sectors and through the administration of pillar organisations, the children of workers made it into parliament, diluting its bourgeois character. The links between the parties and the socio-economic pillar organisations increased parliamentary representation of the working class to a great extent. Within the socialist party, their parliamentary representation rose from 16 to 18 % between 1946 and 1965 and it even doubled within the Christian-democratic party.

The legislature also became a more professional environment: being a parliamentarian became a profession and a career. Experts and study centres made the legislature more technocratic and less pillar-influenced, but also removed it further from the electorate. Backed by their party leadership, parliamentarians could count on a long career. Despite the breakthrough of a younger elite during the 1970s and again in the late 1990s, the social demographics of parliament remained fairly stable. Selection and recruitment was regional and it showed: parliament had a great many legislators who also held some municipal office. Their activities were geared towards their region, a necessity in order to maintain grassroots support. Another characteristic of the Belgian legislator was, and remains, a tendency to combine offices. The average for a parliamentarian stood at about 5.1 during the 1990s. The average is even higher in the big parties and covers a wide range of jobs in political institutions, at party headquarters, inter-communal institutions, the financial and commercial world, the media, professional organisations, education, law, pillar organisations, etc. The practice became a main target of the campaign for a 'new political culture'. The financial political scandals during the first half of the 1990s also led to a progressive weakening of the principle of parliamentary immunity. Since 1998, a go-ahead from Parliament is no longer necessary for a criminal investigation to be started.

For the first time in parliamentary history, the participation of women significantly increased. The introduction of women's voting rights took a long time to trickle down to the level of parliament. Between 1951 and 1961, only 3 % of legislators were women and it even sank further to 2 % between

1965 and 1971. Women's organisations and the parties paid little attention to the demands of feminist pressure groups. The second feminist wave brought some change during the early 1970s. The 1974 action 'Vote for Women' called on all women to use their individual votes to increase their numbers in parliament. A number of women's organisations backed the strategy and wanted to introduce some feminist demands in the party programmes. The radical *Verenigde Feministische Partij* (United Feminist Party) knew little success. The number of women in parliament doubled after the 1974 elections and rose to 6.6 %, a majority of them in Flanders. It rose further to 9 % in 1978, boosted by legislators from the CVP, FDF and Agalev. The socialists, VU and RW on the other hand had almost no women members of parliament. When the CVP and the FDF lost seats in the 1981 elections, the number of women in parliament almost dropped back to 1974 levels. Among the newly elected members of parliament, the percentage did not reach double digits and that was a low score compared to the neighbouring nations. The women's movement wanted to impose a change for the better and demanded the imposition of a quota system. The 1994 municipal elections turned out to be a first when one quarter of the electoral lists was reserved for women. The measure did affect the election results but women still stood less of a chance of being elected. In 1999, elections were first held under the law Smet-Tobback, stipulating a balanced composition of the lists. As the quota applied to the total list, and not the eligible positions, the increase was far from spectacular: from 18 % in 1995 to 22 % in 1999. Next, the obligation was introduced to put a woman in at least one of the first three positions on the list; in combination with the enlarged electoral districts allowing the parties more opportunities to target subgroups of the electorate, the total of the female representation in the Chamber increased to 35 %. The francophone parties were close to this average, and also the Flemish traditional parties showed a considerable increase, but the greens were still fare above the average.

Whatever the member of parliament's gender, they had to be an expert in the rendering of services. Politicians had privileged access to all services that were part of the nation's collective facilities through their dense network of pillar organisations and politicised government offices. It was their way to the hearts of the electorate. They became the go-between that linked the government institutions with the population. They handled thousands of cases, from building permits, over tax declarations to pensions, promotions in government service and telephone connections. A parliamentarian spent an average of twenty hours a month providing such services and it paid off when the voter went to the ballot box. There was a positive correlation between such services rendered and personal votes. It was an integral part of pacification democracy since the voter had to commit himself personally to the pillar or party. It also turned a potential collective problem into an individual one that demanded a pragmatic solution. The practice of such services rendered became a target of the 'new political culture' during the 1990s. This practice has considerably diminished, especially among the younger generation of politicians.

Since the powers of the government and parties increased it was only logical that those of parliament decreased. Parliamentarians were not in the best position to foster negotiations between the different pillars. Several issues were also taken out of their hands, dangerous discussions about problems possibly leading to confrontation between pillars were avoided and the legislators were reduced to ratifying the compromises brokered by their party elites. In short, the work of the government coalitions was to be protected as much as possible. The members of parliament for the ruling coalition partners had little to no room for manoeuvre. Legislative initiative primarily became a government prerogative. During the 1974 legislature, 88 % of laws were created through government initiative; the same rate applied for amendments of earlier laws. The few laws that were purely legislative initiatives were much slower in getting to the decree stage and their scope was limited. The voting pattern was almost always with the party, turning debates and votes into little more than a chore. Party discipline turned the vote on the annual budget into a formality. Political renewal during the 1990s wanted to restore the powers of parliament at the expense of particracy. It called for more parliamentary autonomy, legislative initiatives across party lines, ah-hoc majorities, the election of party chairmen independent of government coalitions, more powerful parliamentary groups and revaluation of committee work. The political climate of the 1990s made sure the issues made it onto the political agenda. To loosen the ties between government and parliament, ministers had to relinquish their parliamentary seat. The role of the legislature was also boosted when parliamentary inquiry commissions were used to investigate the political financial scandals and improve the credibility of the political system. The control on the way in which parliamentarians perform their tasks fits perfectly in this striving for credibility.

The composition of government coalitions was also affected by the pacification mechanism. Up to 1958, political strategy centred on winning unequivocal majorities. It was used by the left immediately after the liberation and by the Catholics from 1950 until 1954, only to be immediately countered by an anti-clerical alliance between 1954 and 1958. Things changed from then on with the introduction of the pacification model and the reliance on coalition negotiations. Centre-left coalitions, uniting Socialists and Catholics, were the most popular combination, alternated with centre-right (Catholic-Liberal) coalitions. From then on, anti-clerical government coalitions were no longer the order of the day. The language parties would never have affected the procedure, had there not been the need for majorities in each language group to reform the constitution. In 'normal' circumstances, their 20 % share of the vote could not have threatened the creation of traditional coalitions. The role of the political centre in the creation of government coalitions cannot be underestimated. The centre always had a choice, either to the right or to the left, and was the partner the others could not do without. The CVP-PSC had the strength and represented the social diversity needed to be a constant government partner. From 1958 onwards, it looked for coalition partners in socialist or liberal directions, or in both directions at the same time. It did not hesitate to use the language parties whenever this was strategically justified. The party supplied the prime minister on most occasions and they usually came from the strong Flemish wing: G. Eyskens, L. Tindemans, W. Martens and J.-L. Dehaene each dominated a political era. The socialists, liberals and francophone Christian democrats usually had to make do with the posts of deputy prime minister. The formation of the Liberal-Socialist-Green government in 1999 and the subsequent Liberal-Socialist government, both under G. Verhofstadt, represented a break with tradition. After more than forty years, there were no Christian democrats in power. It was a multi-coloured coalition in which the different parties were able to focus on themes important to them, under the guidance of communication specialists.

Even though a number of governments served the full four-year term, the average life of coalition governments between 1946 and 1971 stood at one year and eight months. It was much higher between 1950 and 1965, but during the 1970s, government life expectancy dipped to barely one year. Individual government members, on the other hand, had a higher life expectancy. Ministerial careers of five to eight years were not uncommon.

P.-W. Segers was in office for fifteen years and P.-H. Spaak for ten years. Also among more recent generations, some politicians can boast long government careers. The case of W. Martens has become almost proverbial, while J.-L. Dehaene dominated the 1990s, helped by the introduction of the concept of the 'full-term government'. This was introduced after the crisis of 24 November 1991 in order to safeguard government stability and to better fight the extreme-right threat. The number of government members increased steadily over the years, especially when state secretaries were added to the list. The successive constitutional reforms obviously boosted the number of government executives but there was an attempt to reverse the tendency in the wake of Black Sunday 1991. Even though there had been a few women in earlier governments, especially the Liberal-Socialist(-Green) governments increased their numbers, with the younger generation well-represented. These governments showed an overall generational change of the guard. New politics also made a ministerial post much less stable. The scandals and blunders (the escape of Dutroux, the death of an asylum seeker, etc.) only served to strengthen the calls for an increase in ministers' responsibility, certainly among well-informed voters and in the media. The fact that individual politicians were more than ever in the spotlight also stressed their individual responsibility. The debate was in full flow, and in six years' time it led to the dismissal of eighteen political heavyweights.

Since parliament was weakened in its decision-making powers over the years, government was consequently strengthened. Coalition agreements became strictly binding and extra-parliamentary work overseen by the government increased dramatically. The numerous round tables, social consultations, pacts, study groups and committee meetings were fitting illustrations of the phenomenon. The nature of legislative work followed suit and the government started ruling by decree, programme laws, crisis laws and special powers that all had a fundamental impact. They came as 'take-it-or-leave-it' packages, and were primarily used to reduce the role of parliament and strengthen the executive. The government ruled with unlimited powers for 33 months between 1981 and 1987. The efforts of the centre-left coalition during the 1990s to meet the Maastricht conditions for membership in the single currency changed little in the relations between the executive and legislative powers. In contrast with the disciplined compromise policy of the Catholic-Socialist governments, the Liberal-Socialist(-Green) cabinets encouraged a culture of debate. No more compromises off-camera, but on-camera, with the contrasts and contradictions on show in order to increase the clarity of decision-making. For ministers trying to apply this kind of strategy, it is essential that they can use the media effectively. But whenever it proved necessary, the coalition did not hesitate to revert to back-room politics behind closed doors (cf. Brussels-Halle-Vilvoorde).

The expansion of ministerial cabinets since the 1980s also tightened the grip of government on the civil service. The cabinets were an expression of particracy since they also used as nurseries for promising politicians, as waiting rooms for politicians temporarily out of a job, or as step-ups for promotions within administration. But they were also checkpoints for the parties to keep a close eye on their ministers. It was a public secret that they were sometimes part of an illegal circuit to fund the party coffers. Slowly but surely, they developed into parallel administrations that took away the major issues from the departments and protected the minister from his civil servants, much to the frustration of the latter. The cabinets were also a catalyst between politics and the lobby groups, representing both industrial interests and corporations vying for huge defence or public works contracts. The practice sometimes led to corruption and it took a major cleanup operation during the 1990s to impose new checks and controls. The 1991 coalition agreement also included a slimming-down of the cabinets.

The concentration of power in the political parties and the resulting pillarisation had long been a strong influence on the civil service. Appointments and promotions were subject to the principle of proportional representation and parallel recruitment procedures ensured that masses of civil servants were employed outside statutory regulations. The share of each party fluctuated according to the election outcome. The result was a totally politicised civil service in each and every sector: ministerial services, semi-governmental institutions, advisory and consultation councils, the media, cultural organisations, etc. This civil service pillarisation was well-organised and coordinated. Each party carefully kept lists and had ad-hoc committees that had to rule on candidacies. Political merits played a major role and top appointments and promotions were part of government negotiations. Parties were given a foothold in administration and thus protected themselves against electoral changes. It also ensured them of the loyalty of the civil servants, which was to the benefit of the pillar's strength. The system was particularly profitable for the CVP and the PS. The biggest parties in Flanders and Wallonia, and nearly constant government partners, they were able to claim most of the appointments and they had the candidate with the necessary experience for each and every opening. The downside of the system was that the indirect involvement of parties affected the professionalism and motivation of the civil servants. Protests against the system increased, obviously from the parties that had least to gain from the system.

The 'new political culture' also affected this debate. The principles of 'New Public Management' were introduced, and calls for a more efficiently and more rationally organised, more flexible and effective government were increasingly loud. A solid, transparent government, assessed on objective results, treating its citizens as consumers, was what was needed. Proper external communication needed to be set up. Policy planning, annual plans, progress reports, funding by grant, audits and consulting were the order to the day, and performance-related pay, based on competition assessment was being introduced. Top jobs were also opened up to external candidates. In Flanders, a campaign for Better Government was started up in 1996, and the federal level followed suit. Minister Van den Bossche launched the Copernicus Plan, which replaced ministerial departments with Federal Authority Services featuring policy councils and Programme Authority Services for temporary programmes. Top wages and appointments via private assessment agencies were the subject of much criticism. The new procedures for recruitment and assessment were seen by the trade unions as first signs of the undermining of the civil servant statute and the privatisation of government apparatus. The francophone socialists protested and had the Liberal-Socialist government repeal a number of measures. Because of the increase in the number of contractual workers, politicisation of the administration had certainly not come to an end.

Justice and Politics

The complex relationship between the legislative, executive and judicial powers and the population at large had long been problematic but experienced a full-blown crisis in the second half of the 1990s. This also resulted in fundamental reforms.

The problems were mainly structural in nature. Because of the constitutional separation of powers, magistrates had always demanded absolute independence. During the period of post-war repression they were given a considerable deal of social responsibility and this trend continued in a great number of socio-economic and ethical cases afterwards. A large number of measures, indeed, were backed by judicial provisions. The tendency for authoritative controls on the executive also became apparent in their treatment of the political-financial scandals. Because the judiciary dealt with ever more political cases, politics started showing a keen interest in the judiciary and applied the system of political patronage there too. Political interventions in the sector had been in evidence since the creation of the party system and were legitimised by the argument that law had to be a reflection of society as a whole. Religious-philosophical and ideological differences had to be reflected in the magistrates. The systematic application of the pacification mechanism further reinforced politicisation. The parties applied the proportional representation system to the magistrates just as much as they did to other sectors of society, and negotiated about their nominations. The Catholic and liberal groups, by tradition, had a big edge over the socialists. Politicians also approached courts and judicial officials as part of their 'services rendered' practice, which raised questions about the integrity and independence of the judges.

The magistrates had other problems to contend with, however. The justice system was also hit hard by years of austerity measures. The justice budget was cut back to the extent that it could no longer ensure a solid policy. Antiquated methods and bad conditions slowed down the legal machinery too much and seriously dented the image of the justice system. Increased work load and a ban on new personnel led to huge backlogs. Rich and powerful defendants were able to abuse the complex legal procedures, paralyse a case and obtain questionable judgments. Investigation and prosecution were affected by a lack of cooperation between different departments and internal competition within the different police forces. Even though the state police was demilitarised in 1990, it was still able to increase its policing powers afterwards. Public opinion rejected the judiciary as extremely conservative and inaccessible. This view was further reinforced by the lack of openness, occasional displays of disdain, a rigid internal hierarchy and a lack of internal controls. There was also increasing criticism from the political world. When the political-financial cases went to court, the judiciary was out to prove that top politicians did not enjoy any special privileges, and politicians such as Claes and Spitaels were severely dealt with.

The numerous dysfunctions undermined the confidence of the people in their legal system. Impotence and disinterest turned into a deep crisis of authority in 1996-1997, especially in critical and well-educated layers of the population. A succession of extremely emotional cases laid bare the shortcomings of the system and turned the justice and police systems into a target of stinging criticism: the police handling of the 1985 Heysel Stadium drama; the terror of the 'mad killers' of Brabant exposed links to state security, judicial police and the extreme right; the assassination of PS godfather A. Cools, with links to the Italian mafia; and the murder of veterinarian Van Noppen. All of these were important elements in the development of the crisis of legitimacy. The media played an important role in keeping the unsolved crimes on the political agenda.

All of this was nothing compared to the collective outrage that erupted in the summer of 1996, when the Dutroux child sex murder scandal broke. The decision of the Court of Cassation (which gave precedence to the principle of impartiality, even under these exceptional circumstances) and especially the escape of Dutroux only increased public anger. Public opinion was convinced Belgium's judiciary no longer represented or served the morals of the nation, and was incompetent as well. It led to a large-scale mobilisation.

King Albert II and Prime Minister Dehaene prevented the crisis from spilling over into something even worse and opened the way towards institutional consultations involving diverse sectors of society. An all-party parliamentary committee was created to investigate the dysfunctions and make proposals for drastic reform. Together with the government, it had to restore confidence in the nation's institutions. Despite party-political and linguistic tensions and corporatist reflexes from the judiciary, a number of fundamental reforms were approved to create a more humane and better-organised justice system.

Starting in 1998, laborious talks were held on different levels about the recommendations of the Committee, but the gravity of the matter encouraged the government parties to cooperate and to close the Octopus Agreement, which entailed the most important reorganisation since the foundation of Belgium. An integrated police service with a two-tier structure was created. The municipal police service, which can serve more than one municipality, was created by joining the municipal police force and the national police brigade of the local zone. It is responsible for administrative and judicial tasks at the local level. The federal police service integrated the judicial police, undercover police and the federal units of the national police force. In order to facilitate the integration, the same statutes, payment scales and training were stipulated for the entire police service. The establishment of the 196 police zones and the unitary police was started in 2000. Increased costs and differences in company culture did not make the task an easy one.

At the same time, the elimination of the problems in the magistracy was also on the political agenda. In reaction to the Dutroux case, victims were hence given the same rights as suspects, and the law on probation was tightened; it is no longer a ministerial matter, but is decided on by a committee. A uniform prosecution policy was ensured, drawn up by the college of Procurators-General, advised by the public prosecutor, together with the minister. The internal workings of the judiciary were modernised concerning work methods, organisation, company culture and contact with the public; more personnel was to be employed. The judiciary would be subject to external supervision: the High Council for Justice, composed of magistrates, lawyers, professors and experts, now decides on promotions and complaints.

As far as the fight against criminality is concerned – and we have seen that public opinion is enthralled by this – the government started drawing up plans in 1996 for a prevention policy and for the enlargement of the local police. The reform of the police and the judiciary also speeded up this policy. Certain forms of summary justice and alternative sentencing were introduced, along with security contracts and an enlargement of local police services. The latter were also brought closer to the public.

The Role of the Monarchy

The role of the king in the political system has always been shrouded in mystery and exposing the throne is still considered a grave political error. Only during periods of crisis does the monarchy offer a glimpse of its political role.

The Royal Question of 1940-1945 undoubtedly weakened the position of the monarchy. Leopold III had still had a major impact on politics, but the role of King Baudouin was much more limited. The increasing influence of political parties, lobby groups and governments further weakened the position of the monarchy. Increasing federalisation and government stability (the latter as a reaction to 'Black Sunday') only served to further diminish the scope of royal influence.

As years went by, the monarch's constitutional functions became almost purely ceremonial, including the dissolution of parliament and the signing of laws. Even though the constitution appoints the king as the third branch of legislative power, his real role is reduced to taking a pen and signing on the dotted line once parliament has approved a law. In the context of a parliamentary democracy, the king has to abide by the will of the sovereign people and his authority is always overseen by one or more ministers, a process that reduces him to a neutral actor. Even in the case of dismissing ministers, the prime minister has taken the place of the king. The ministers of the Regions and Communities are elected and confirmed by their parliaments and the king is no longer involved in activating decrees and edicts. The Saint Michael's agreement stipulated that the Chamber can reject a vote of confidence of the government and replace the prime minister, who has to be accepted by the king; also at this level, his power has been reduced.

Still, his influence continues to exist. Because of his decades of experience in Belgian politics, Baudouin knew how to move behind the scenes. There were many indications that the king had a considerable impact on coalition talks and the appointment of the prime minister and other ministers. His influence on the legislative work also continued to be felt. Diplomacy, foreign policy, the army, defence and justice – in all those areas the influence of Baudouin was clearly felt. His role in controlling the nation's centrifugal forces should also not be underestimated. In a nation with such a multitude of internal contradictions the king became a source of moderation and reconciliation, and this continued to give the royal house its standing. For long, Baudouin was an essential part in the preservation of unitary policy. Pressured by events, the monarchy has now yielded and backed unionist federalism, a system in which the king and the central powers still retain quite some room for manoeuvre. For unionists fighting a division of the nation, the monarchy is a strong symbol. Practicing Catholics, the elderly and housewives idolised Baudouin. He cared about society's underprivileged, promoted respect for human rights and his stand against racism and for increased solidarity won the monarchy much respect. This became clear when he died on 31 July 1993 and tens of thousands lined up to pay their respects.

The media helped create a myth, yet Baudouin did not touch the whole nation in the same way. Baudouin and Queen Fabiola were intimately involved in the Charismatic movement and increasingly stressed the religious aspects of the monarchy. This relatively new dominant Catholicism was on show during Baudouin's funeral and did not add to the popularity of the monarchy in anti-clerical, intellectual and socialist circles and among the New Social Movements.

Baudouin's refusal to sign the abortion legislation even caused a constitutional crisis. Against all executive customs, he stubbornly refused to sign a law that had been democratically voted, making it very clear he had fundamental objections. It undermined the symbolic function of the monarchy and harmed Baudouin's relations with the political elite. He publicly took a stand as a conservative Catholic against a democratic majority and as such openly revealed himself not to be above the political parties. It opened a new discussion on the monarchy. The most radical voices wanted the monarchy to be reduced to a purely ceremonial function. Others wanted a constitutional provision that laws would be enacted even if the king refused to sign them. There was no unanimity, however, and government ideas remained in the planning stage.

The announcement that Baudouin's brother Albert would succeed him came as a surprise since Albert's oldest son Philip had been quite openly groomed to take the throne. Baudouin also made sure in 1991 that his niece Astrid would be able to take the throne. Later it became clear that Baudouin had little faith in Albert's youngest son Laurent. During the crisis of the mid-1990s King Albert showed a strong social consciousness, rejecting extremism and backing a reinforcement of democracy. At the height of the Dutroux scandal he met with the parents of missing and murdered children and became a catalyst by criticising the justice system and demanding reform. The extremely difficult and exceptional circumstances of his actions prevented them from being seen as controversial; instead, they were interpreted in the context of the stabilising function of the monarchy in the Belgian political system. This function of stability helps explain why almost all political parties defend the monarchy.

Albert has remained popular and stories about an extramarital affair and an illegitimate daughter did nothing to dent this popularity. However, there are signs, apart from the growth of the republican Vlaams Blok/Belang, that the number of proponents of a ceremonial monarchy is on the increase. In 2002, the VLD congress voted in favour, and it was also referred to in the agreement between the PS and Ecolo. Opinion polls show that a large majority thinks the king is necessary, but also that indifference is increasing.

Media and Politics

Because of its powers of persuasion, Belgian politics has always been keenly interested in the media, and today more than ever before. Yet in the post-war period there has been a remarkable development in the relationship between the media and politics.

Initially, the tendency of pillarisation and politicisation were especially clear in the (printed) press. Most newspapers were very close to a pillar, party or trade union. Influential editorial writers made certain that the views of the party or pillar were convincingly communicated. Over the past few decades, however, financial groups have started to show interest in the printed press and have divided up the media landscape. In Flanders, the *Vlaamse Uitgeversmaatschappij* (VUM, Flemish Publishing Company) and the holdings it represents publish *De Standaard, Het Nieuwsblad* and *Het Volk*; de *Persgroep* (Press Group) owns *Het Laatste Nieuws, De Nieuwe Gazet* and *De Morgen* while the *Regionale Uitgeversmaatschappij* (Regional Publishing Company) publishes *Het Belang van Limburg* and *Gazet van Antwerpen*. Two publishers dominate the francophone press. *Rossel*, controlled by French media giant *Hersant* and the Hurbain family, owns *Le Soir* and *La Meuse*. The group *Vers L'Avenir*, controlled by the Namur bishopric and a few wealthy families, publishes *La Libre Belgique* and *La Dernière Heure*. All those papers have become more ideologically independent over the years but their link with the financial groups has not stopped them from continuing to seek ideological contacts with political movements or parties. The overwhelming majority of the papers represent the conservative Catholic and liberal views. For lack of financial means and wealthy customers, the socialist party press either disappeared (*Volksgazet* and *Le Peuple*) or was retargeted towards a more general public (*De Morgen*), loosening or severing the ties with the party. Smaller parties, such as the language and environmental parties, are not represented in the press or lack the support of a newspaper. Newspaper publishing has become a matter of business and business interests more often than not take precedence over quality of information, independence of reporting or social relevance of the message. Also in Belgium, concentrations of press associations have led to fewer voices, less diversity, less pluralism and, as such, less democracy.

The relations between broadcasting and the political world turned out totally differently. After the Second World War had proved the power of radio, the three traditional parties wanted to control the airwaves and backed the further development of a public network.

Broadcasting became a victim of pillarisation. Not only did the parties insist on being granted broadcasting time according to their electoral strength, they also had their representatives on the board and imposed an employment policy of proportional political representation. During political crises, there was often direct involvement from the party headquarters. Journalists were shackled by strict objectivity standards, which in their turn prevented outspoken critical opinions and promoted self-censorship among journalists.

The 1960 broadcasting law consolidated the situation rather than change it. With the breakthrough of television in the sixties, the same rules were simply imposed on the new medium. The Culture Pact more or less institutionalised the politicisation of the cultural sector. Party-political pillarisation and proportional representation always favoured the status quo, which was often reflected in the media contents. Even though the BRT-RTB was only split up along linguistic lines in 1977, both linguistic wings had been able to act autonomously on cultural issues since the 1960s. The Dutch and Francophone Culture Councils could then provide separate statutes for BRT and RTB. Based on the new situation, new broadcast authorities were created, and the pillars, parties, lobby groups and philosophical movements were granted broadcast time, allowing them to provide their own perspective on events.

The Flemish Catholics and liberals wanted to break the broadcast monopoly, however, partly because they thought the BRT was not neutral, partly because of ideological conflicts. When both parties entered the same government coalition in 1985, they saw the possibility of creating a competing news service. The abolition of a public monopoly fitted perfectly in the spirit of neo-liberalism and the idea of a private broadcast station funded by advertising slowly developed into a concrete project. The government announced the intention of breaking the BRT monopoly and creating opportunities for private initiatives. In Flanders, this led to the 1987 decree allowing the creation of one non-public station with the license to broadcast advertising. The *Vlaamse Televisiemaatschappij* (VTM, Flemish Television Company) was granted this license. And while other nations curtailed cross-ownership in order to prevent large media concentrations, Flanders imposed it: the majority of shares had to remain in the hands of Flemish newspapers and magazines. De *Persgroep* and *Roularta* held a majority of shares, but by the late 1990s, the Dutch media group VNU had taken control with two-thirds of the shares. A U.S.-Scandinavian media group broke VTM's monopoly in Flanders in 1995 and started up a second private network, VT4, under a British license. Since then, the number of commercial stations has increased further, and also thematic commercial stations have been set up. The Francophone Community had seen the advent of commercial television much earlier. The Luxembourg-based *Compagnie Luxembourgeoise de Télédiffusion*, backed by the financial groups Bruxelles-Lambert and Société Générale, had long ago established a foothold. It had founded, together with francophone newspaper publishers, the Belgian commercial television station RTL-TVI. Because of the 1988 law transferring authority on broadcast advertising to the communities, the two parts of the country have different regulations on the matter. In Flanders, public radio is allowed to broadcast commercial advertisements, but public television is not. The latter can, however, supplement its income with money from non-commercial advertising, co-productions and co-funding. The Francophone Community did allow the RTBf to broadcast commercial advertisements. In order to jointly protect the market from foreign competition, RTBf and RTL-TVI have closed a cooperation agreement.

Increased competition in the television broadcasting sector pushed the public stations into an uncomfortable position. In Flanders, the regional government tried to create a more competitive BRT. Between 1995 and 1997, the old leadership was replaced and a chief executive officer with business experience took over. Political influence was sharply cut back and the renamed *Vlaamse Radio en Televisie* (VRT, Flemish Radio and Television) was turned into a public corporation with a five-year management contract. In francophone Belgium, the RTBf was faced with similar problems. The ratings battle became tougher by the day and there were financial problems as well. A cooperation agreement with RTL-TVI was cancelled and one balanced-budget plan followed another. Structural reforms with a strong influence of regional interests were pushed through. On the francophone side too, the political class saw its influence reduced.

Media commercialisation changed electoral politics. The battle for the reader, listener and viewer, dictated by profit and the imperatives of the advertising world, was reduced to the lowest common denominator, creating a need for 'light', easily digested politics. Media discourse became much more noncommittal, and there was less room for extensive informative items; as such media content was depoliticised. Television turned politics into a personality showcase with plenty of entertainment thrown in. Tension, drama and competition took centre stage and in-depth, thorough political analysis disappeared. Political news has been forced off the front page by human interest, and political media content is becoming ever less distinctive.

Obviously, politicians show a great interest in a medium with such an impact on public opinion and television appeal has become a key requirement for most politicians. It allows television to play a central role in politics and it has actually become a competitor for parliament and government. This 'television democracy' has changed a number of things in the relationship between politicians and the public at large. Politicians have honed their media skills, relying on political marketing techniques. Government announcements have been turned into infomercials. 'Leaks' and targeted scoops have increasingly become part of a manipulated information service. Politicians have also adapted their language – they restrict themselves to catch phrases, veil their content with metaphors, and simplify complex problems. They feel the need to become performers. It also increases their dependence on journalists and it is clear that, both in relation with the printed press and the broadcast media, politicians have lost some of their power. Journalists are wielding a powerful political tool and they are very much aware of that.

Another phenomenon also emerged during the 1990s. Driven by higher ratings and sales, journalists claimed to be an ideal tool of participatory democracy and the ideal channel to question the institutions directly. An important part of the press acted as a sounding board for large parts of the public and tried to mobilise society. Enlarging collective emotions, playing popular themes (and prejudices), exchanging critical analyses for 'atmospheric' reports – they all became fixed items in this 'compassionate' journalistic rhetoric accompanying several political processes. Few denied afterwards that the media had been partly to blame for the anti-political climate, the rise of such media creations as Jean-Pierre Van Rossem, and the large media coverage of extreme-right themes.

This kind of journalism also emerged when a long series of real and alleged political financial scandals hit the nation during the 1990s. The coverage of King Baudouin's funeral was called 'media hysteria'. The media also had an important role to play in the missing children and Dutroux scandals and the subsequent White Movement. The very emotionally appealing style of reporting was turned into significant mobilisation. The insufficiently open attitude of the judiciary towards the press made it difficult to come to objective reporting, but it is obvious that the 'compassionate' character dominated this case. In short, an important part of the press was and is faced with a difficult choice between the dominance of commercial interests, which grants almost all power to public opinion, and the dignified exercise of its social control function with respect for the facts. Fortunately, a number of programmes and articles are living proof that some of the media are still able to be an essential link in the distribution of political information and the participation of citizens in the political debate.

In the breakthrough of the extreme right, the media encountered an additional problem. Initially, the strategy of isolation was also applied in Flanders. Vlaams Blok was ignored because the party undermined democracy and was openly racist. The media did not want to strengthen the party even further by giving it too much attention. As Vlaams Blok/Belang grew more important, however, the Flemish media changed to a strategy of confrontation. Movements with a certain impact cannot be ignored, and in this way, the party is denied the opportunity of using its position as the underdog, so the argument went. Yet coverage of the party needs to be critical and exposing. However, this attitude has grown weaker in recent years in most newspapers and broadcasting stations. Most of the time, the party is treated in much the same way as any other.

A Unique Kind of Federalism

In trying to distinguish a number of tendencies from the chronological story of linguistic strife, we are faced, first and foremost, with a few very general characteristics. The conflict was so divisive because it touched upon key aspects of the constitution. It involved fundamental changes in the division of power that affected much more than the language issue alone. Because constitutional reform required special parliamentary majorities, the linguistic conflict was dependent upon the electoral balance of any given day, providing the language parties with disproportionate power. The FDF was a case in point and the party used its power to turn Brussels into a political bone of contention. Negotiations were held between Dutch- and French-speaking parties that had already expressed differing opinions on other issues too. These demands often cut across the negotiations on a national level and complicated negotiations for a compromise. But the asymmetry in aims also had its advantages, since outside issues could be introduced in the linguistic bartering to round off a carefully crafted compromise. Economic, philosophical and ethical issues often became part of the bargaining mix, and more than once rescued the parties from an impasse. Such political acrobatics could not be used to the same extent on the issue of Brussels since demands are much more symmetrical there, which helps to explain the short-circuit situation. The importance of bargaining operations was also keenly felt in the failed negotiations on Brussels-Halle-Vilvoorde, as there was no balanced package of demands in 2005.

The language parties were never a natural mass movement, even though they won up to 20 % of the vote in the 1970s. The policy issues were created by a new political elite that broke through in the different parties and was able to mobilise the population. They put the linguistic issues on the agenda and built their career on it; through the establishment of new institutions, they opened perspectives for a lower elite. Opinion polls showed that the majority of the population did not feel very concerned by this linguistic squabbling, creating a rift between the politician and the public that was larger than the divide on other political issues. This situation gave the conflict its specific dimension and was evident during negotiations. The elites dominated the political consultations. Conflict management involved several groups at several levels – government negotiating teams, study groups, commissions, parliamentary groups, marathon meetings of party chairmen, discrete hearings and short public debates. But the link with grassroots support was a crucial element. For strategic and tactical reasons, there was a frequent need for the mobilisation of the rank and file. The marches on Brussels, the recurring riots in Voeren and the electoral shifts were telling examples. The link was tenuous at best, however. When the political elite wanted to push through the unpopular Egmont Pact, the cultural pillar organisations and party backbenchers refused to follow. Some sociologists have blamed the failure on the fact that the conflict area had not been properly institutionalised, allowing the pillars to withdraw their backing from the party elites. This changed once the dynamism of regionalisation was under way. The petty-bourgeois base of the Flemish Movement that was active in the cultural lobby groups was spread among the electorate of all Flemish parties. And since a strong link with the labour movement had already been established during the 1960s, this phenomenon of expansion was evident in southern Belgium well before it showed north of the linguistic border.

Negotiations always had to seek a consensus among the backers of a unitary nation, the neo-unitarists, the moderate federalists and the radical federalists. Each compromise had to meet some of the Flemish, Walloon, Brussels and centralist demands. Up to 1988, the solutions never went beyond what the unitarists and the moderate federalists deemed acceptable. Even the concessions of the 1961-1965 Lefèvre-Spaak government were aimed at shielding the unitary nation from extreme federalism. The 1970 constitutional reform also included elements that prevented the creation of autonomous, regional power centres. The Egmont Pact did not grant the institutions any more hold on regional policy and the August 1980 agreement, too, countered pure federalism. The interaction between continual compromise, shock reactions and the tendency towards pragmatic and directly attainable results created an extremely complex mix in which every party recognised some of its demands.

The year 1988 marked a fundamental step towards federalism. It saw a comprehensive and sweeping reform that was largely linked to the socio-economic problems. Because of the diverging socio-economic interests of Flanders and Wallonia, it became ever more difficult to pursue a coherent national policy. Reform also solved a number of thorny linguistic problems. The 1993 reform continued to build on this. Items that had made it to the de-federalisation agenda in the meantime were revived in 2000-2001, along with the question of funding. At this moment, this gives us a fairly good idea of the specific characteristics of Belgian federalism.

It is a well-established fact by now that federal Belgium is made up of several regions and communities, each with their own governments, parliaments and especially their own characteristics. The first obvious feature is the diverging economic development north and south of the linguistic border. Wallonia is still confronted with the restructuring problems of its old industrial sectors, and its high-tech industry is still relatively underdeveloped, even though the Walloon Region is trying to stimulate regional development through its investment policy (*Contract d'Avenir*, 2000; *d'Action*, 2005; *Plan Marshall*, 2006). On top of that, Wallonia's industry remains too dependent on state commissions. Short on cash, the Walloon governments have found it difficult to push through much needed modernisation. Flanders, on the other hand, is much better represented in the modern sectors and has boosted its economic programme through research and development. But since companies are largely controlled by multinationals – some 60 % of Flanders' industry is closely linked to foreign investors – Flemish economic intervention policy is limited by this dependence. The closing down of Renault was a poignant illustration. Social differences between the regions are an obvious result of this economic situation; unemployment figures have differed widely for years, with Wallonia showing double the rate of Flanders. Wallonia is heavily dependent on the solidarity mechanisms between the regions, which meets fierce resistance from the Flemish-nationalist corner. Flanders is also dependent on federal funding, but is loathe to contribute to the financial support of the federal state. Those problems are also a cause for Flemish dissatisfaction.

Federalism has also brought electoral and party-political contradictions to the fore. The central position of the Catholic party in Flanders finds its counterpart in the majority position of the socialists in Wallonia. Seen from the reverse angle, there is a socialist minority in Flanders and a Catholic minority in Wallonia. This political fissure is also evident in the structures and composition of the regional governments. The New Social Movements at first took better root in Flanders, as did the extreme right wing, making sure the 'new political rift' was and is much more visible north of the linguistic divide. Since the nineties, the differences have become ever greater. The breakthrough of Vlaams Blok/Belang had made the traditional parties bunch together even more as far as electoral strength is concerned, and because of the *cordon sanitaire*, they are also much more dependent on each other. In Wallonia, the contrasts between the parties remained bigger, both quantitatively and ideologically. Both parts of the country are also marked by an institutional asymmetry. In Flanders, region and community coincide, but they do not in Wallonia. The two also have different styles in coalition formation and ministerial departments. Yet diversity is an essential part of every federal nation. In the two parts of the country, different coalition governments have seen the light in recent years. The same goes for policy, for instance at the socio-economic level.

The differences are just as evident at the religious-philosophical level. The Catholic pillar obviously dominates Flanders and the freethinkers are certainly not a minority in Wallonia. The Catholic education network is predominant Flanders while there is largely a balance between the public and private school sectors in Wallonia. For its public education, Flanders has opted for an autonomous, pluralist management structure; in Wallonia, it remains in the hands of the government. A similar situation is found in health care too, with a more or less completely Catholic Flanders facing a much more secular Wallonia. The same divisions run through most of the religious-philosophical areas even though the process of de-pillarisation has started to partly blur the contrast.

The widest gap may be in the cultural sector. The creation of cultural autonomy during the 1960s has already produced starkly contrasting results. Flanders has reinforced its cooperation with the Netherlands in the areas of literature, media, the arts and education. Both also stand side by side when it comes to defending the Dutch language in a European context. Francophone Belgium had always been culturally drawn to France. The result is that Flanders and Wallonia have become two different worlds with their own cultures, and with ever less interest in each other.

The complexity of the new institutional framework clearly shows that Belgium's federalism is rather unique. An extremely complex political growth process, characterised by several hard-won and carefully balanced compromises, ensured the progressive erosion of the unitary state by regional institutions. An institutional maze, with a rich variety of institutions, usually without any symmetry, has been created, confusing all but the political insiders. At the heart of the federal system is the split-up into regions, which won autonomy on economic issues, and communities, which have authority over cultural and personal welfare issues. The regions are Flanders, Wallonia and Brussels Capital Region. The communities are Flanders, Francophone Belgium (Wallonia and Brussels) and German-speaking Belgium. Flanders decided on a fusion of region and community, a step that was not mirrored in Francophone Belgium; the German-speaking East Cantons are part of the Walloon Region.

Brussels' unique structure complicates things even further. For regional issues it has similar institutions to the two other regions. Brussels also has authority over its own local cultural and personal welfare issues. But for other community issues, powers have been delegated to the Flemish parliament and government on the one hand and to the French Community Council and executive on the other. Since the Brussels francophones are simultaneously part of the French Community Council and executive and part of the Brussels Region, they are in a better position to coordinate education, culture and the economy. The Walloons are not able to do that to the same extent and they would not be able to govern over the community without the Brussels francophones. It means Brussels has a certain control over Wallonia's community issues, while the opposite is not true. That is why some of the powers have been transferred to the Region and as such to the local Brussels cultural institutions. The relationship between region and community in Wallonia has grown closer at the expense of Brussels. The Flemings in Brussels have little power and little impact on the overall Flemish community. The fact that Flanders has chosen Brussels as its capital is a clear indication, however, of the importance that the capital of Europe holds for them. The specific functions of Brussels as national capital and international centre also entail institutional consequences and as a result, the national government continues to watch over urban development and transport.

The linguistic and cultural diversity of the federal nation (and partly of its constituent parts) is another characteristic of Belgian federalism. A federal nation with different cultures and languages is bound to be more complex. And it is a constant threat to unity, one that the federal republic of Germany, for instance, does not face, as all its constituent states share the same language. By leaving the linguistic territories as they were, the 1988 and 1993 constitutional revisions opted for clarity. Yet the cases of Voeren and the six Brussels municipalities with linguistic facilities cause very specific problems. Flanders continues to be faced with a large influx of non-Dutch speakers. The internationalisation of the Brussels outer suburbs reinforces the situation. The creation of the province of Flemish Brabant, which includes these municipalities, has allowed Flanders to adapt its policy to the changing situation, yet especially in municipalities with large non-Dutch speaking majorities, it continues to be difficult to find ways of living together, both politically and administratively. The difficulties in dividing the judicial and electoral Brussel-Halle-Vilvoorde district should be seen in the same context.

Belgian federalism can also be characterised as unionist since there is a strong political current resisting far-reaching autonomy of the regions and communities. Across the linguistic border and other political divides, its proponents often have strong links with the national government. Royal circles are obviously in favour. Especially in francophone political circles there have been calls to prevent a further undermining of the national institutions, for obvious reasons. It was most evident when talk turned to the financing of the different regions and communities. The national government still holds quite some autonomy over such funding. The fact that state debt is a federal matter also strengthens the power of the federal state. Opinion polls show that most people in Wallonia and Brussels, but also in Flanders, feel Belgian as well as an inhabitant of their own region. Yet a number of evolutions are clearly going in the direction of a weakening of the federal state. The proponents of federal power have not been able to prevent the regions and the communities from becoming a political actor on the international stage, for instance. The unionist tendency has so far held its own when it comes to the reform of the Senate. The upper house has not been reduced to an institution of the communities and regions but instead has held on to sizeable decision-making powers at a national level. Plans to turn it into a body that only represents communities and regions are becoming ever more concrete, however. The request by Flanders to devolve more powers – health care and social security are always mentioned – follows the same line of thought. The fact that there are no longer any national parties, but that each party is regional, and fights for the interests of its own region obviously only strengthens this tendency. The formation of different coalitions on regional or community levels and on the federal level entails that federal state power is no longer able to exert a strong influence on the regional and community governments. In short, the battle between the two tendencies is far from over, but all the indications are that devolution will continue to undermine unionism.

The unionist character of constitutional reform, finally, was also evident in the establishment of cooperative federalism during the 1988 revision. This agreement stresses the importance of consultation and cooperation between the regions, the communities and the central government. The laws on delegation of authority and distribution of funding both call for consultations at the executive level. The national government, the regions and the communities also have the possibility to sign cooperation agreements. Cooperation is even mandatory in cross-border sectors such as transport infrastructure. Any disputes are dealt with by a judicial college, and no appeal is possible after its verdict. Such cooperation agreements have already started up, but progress has been slow.

The least that could be said about Belgian federalism in conclusion is that the successive constitutional reforms of 1988 and 1993 have produced an original concept. The components differ greatly on economic, social, religious-philosophical, linguistic and cultural levels. The complexity and asymmetry of the institutions is confusing, especially when it comes to the Brussels political structures. The tension between unionists and autonomists has been responsible for a number of regulations that are quite unique, and will probably lead to more original solutions in the future.

Annexe I

Electoral Balance, 1847-1991

Composition of Chamber of Representatives and Senate in number of seats, 1847-1892					
	Chamber		Senate		
Year	Catholics	Liberals	Catholics	Liberals	Others
1847	53	55	32	20	2
1848	25	83	22	31	1
1850	39	69			
1851			27	27	
1852	51	57			
1854	54	54			
1855			31	23	
1856	63	54			
1857	38	70			
1859	47	69	27	31	
1861	50	66			
1863	57	59	25	33	
1864	52	64			
1866	52	70			
1867			29	33	
1868	50	72			
1870	61	61			
1870	72	52	34	27	1
1872	71	53			
1874	68	56	34	28	
1876	67	57			
1878	60	72	30	36	
1880	58	74			
1882	59	79	32	37	
1884	86	52			
1884			43	26	
1886	98	40			
1888	98	40	47	18	4
1890	94	44			
1892	92	60	46	30	

Source: J. Gilissen, *Le régime représentatif en Belgique depuis 1790*, Brussel, 1958, pp.188-189.

Composition of Chamber of Representatives in number of seats, 1894-1914				
Year	Catholics	Liberals	Socialists	Others
1894	104	20	28	
1896	111	13	28	
1898	112	13	27	
1900	86	34	31	1
1902	96	34	34	2
1904	93	42	29	2
1906	89	46	30	1
1908	87	43	35	1
1910	86	44	35	1
1912	101	44	39	2
1914	99	45	40	2

Source: J. Gilissen, *Le régime representatif,* p.190.

Composition of Chamber of Representatives in number of seats, 1919-1939							
Year	Cath.	Lib.	Soc.	Com.	Flemish Nationalists	Rex	Others	Total
1919	73	34	70	-	5	-	4	186
1921	80	33	68	-	4	-	1	186
1925	78	23	78	2	6	-	-	187
1929	76	28	70	1	11	-	1	187
1932	79	24	73	3	8	-	-	187
1936	63	23	70	9	16	21	-	202
1939	73	33	64	9	17	4	2	202

Composition of Chamber of Representatives in number of seats, 1946-1991

Year	CVP PSC	Lib.PVV PLP-PRL	(B)SP PS(B)	KP PC	FDF (RW) (PPW)	RW	VU	PLDP	Agalev Ecolo	RAD-UDRT	Vl. Blok	Others
1946	92	17	69	23								1
1949	105	29	66	12								
1950	108	20	77	7								
1954	95	25	86	4		1						1
1958	104	21	84	2		1						
1961	96	20	84	5		5						2
1965	77	48	64	6	3(1)	2(2)	12					
1968	69	47	59	5	12		20					
1971	67	34	61	5	24		21					
1974	72	30	59	4	22		22	3(3)				
		PRLW										
		PVV(4)						PL(5)				
1977	80	31	62	2	15		20	2				
1978	82	36	58	4	11	4	11	4	14	1		2
1981	61	52	61	2	8		20		4	3	1	
1985	65	46	67		3		16		9	1	1	
1987	62	48	72		3		16		9		2	
1991	57	46	63		3		10		17		12	4

(1) Front Démocratique des Francophones

(2) Front Wallon.

(3) In 1974: foundation in Brussels of the PLDP (*Parti Libéral Démocrate et Pluraliste de la Région Bruxelloise*).

(4) In 1977: the PRLW (*Parti de Réformes et de la Liberté en Wallonie*) is created in January 1977 by the merger of the PLP and the 'anti-collectivist' wing of the Rassemblement Wallon.

(5) PL: Brussels francophone liberal party. After the incorporation of the Brussels francophone liberals into the FDF, especially since 1971, the discord among Brussels liberal was considerable, with splits in the party, the foundation of new parties and defections from one party to the other.

Composition of the Different Directly Elected Representative Bodies in Federalised Belgium (1995-2004)

Composition of Chamber of Representatives in number of seats							
	CVP/CD&V PSC/cdH	PVV/VLD PRL PRL-FDF/ MR	SP/sp.a- Spirit	VU/VU-ID	Agalev Ecolo	Vl.Blok	Others
1995	41	39	41	5	11	11	2
1999	32	41	33	8	20	15	1
2003	28	50	48		4	18	2

Composition of the Flemish Council in number of seats, including Flemish representatives elected in the Brussels Region							
	CVP/CD&V- N-VA	VLD-Vivant	SP/sp.a- Spirit	Vl.Blok	VU/VU-ID	Agalev/ Groen!	UF*
1995	37	27	26	17	9	7	1
1999	28	27	19	20	11	12	1
2004	35	25	25	32		6	1

* = Union des Francophones

Composition of the Walloon Regional Council in number of seats					
	PS	PRL-FDF/MR	PSC/cdH	Ecolo	FN
1995	30	19	16	8	2
1999	25	21	14	14	1
2004	34	20	14	3	4

Composition of the Brussels Capital Council in seats														
	PRL- FDF/ MR	PRL	FDF- ERE	PS	PSC/ cdH	Ecolo	FN	CVP/ CD&V- N-VA	Vl.Blok	VLD- VU-O/ Vivant	SP/ sp.a- Spirit	VU	Agalev/ Groen!	Others
1989		15	12	18	9	8	2	4	1	2	2	1	1	
1995	28			17	7	7	6	3	2	2	2	1	0	
1999	27			13	6	14	2	3	4	2	2			2
2004	25			26	10	7	4	3	6	4	3		1	

	Composition of the Council of the German Community in seats							
	CSP-PSC	PFF/-MR	SP	Ecolo	PJU-PDB	PDB	SEP	Vivant
1986	10	5	3	1	5	5		
1990	8	5	4	4		4	1	
1995	10	5	4	3	3			
1999	9	6	4	3	3			
2004	8	5	5	2	3			2

Annexe II

Chronological Overview of Governments Since 1830

Provisional government

- L. De Potter, E. Vanderlinden d'Hoogvorst, Ch. Rogier, F. de Merode, A. Gendebien, S. Van de Weyer, A.E. Jolly, J. Vanderlinden, F. de Coppin, J. Nicolay: 26 September 1830 – 24 February 1831.

Governments under the Regency of K.L. Surlet de Chokier

- S. Van de Weyer, A. Gendebien, J.F. Thielemans: 26 February 1831 – 28 March 1831.
- J. Lebeau, E. de Sauvage: 28 March 1831 – 21 July 1831.

Governments under the monarchy

- F.A. de Muelenaere, J. Raikem, Ch. de Brouckère: 24 July 1831 – 20 October 1832.
  Unionist.
- J.A. Goblet, Ch. Rogier, J. Lebeau: 20 October 1832 – 4 August 1834.
  Unionist.
- B.T. de Theux: 4 August 1834 – 18 April 1840.
  Unionist.
- J. Lebeau, Ch. Rogier: 18 april 1840 – 13 April 1841.
  Uniformly liberal.
- J.B. Nothomb: 13 April 1841 – 30 July 1845.
  Unionist.
- S. Van de Weyer: 30 July 1845 – 31 March 1846.
  Unionist.
- B.T. de Theux, J. Malou: 31 March 1846 – 12 August 1847.
  Nearly uniformly Catholic.
- Ch. Rogier, W. Frère-Orban: 12 August 1847 – 31 October 1852.
  Uniformly liberal.
- H. de Brouckère: 31 October 1852 – 30 March 1855.
  Unionist.
- P. De Decker: 30 March 1855 – 9 November 1857.
  Unionist.

- W. Frère-Orban, Ch. Rogier, A. Vandenpeereboom: 9 November 1857 – 2 July 1870.
  Uniformly liberal.
- J. d'Anethan: 12 July 1870 – 7 December 1871.
  Uniformly Catholic.
- J. Malou: 7 December 1871 – 19 June 1878.
  Uniformly Catholic.
- W. Frère-Orban, J. Bara, P. Van Humbeeck: 19 June 1878 – 16 June 1884.
  Uniformly liberal.
- J. Malou: 16 June 1884 – 26 October 1884.
  Uniformly Catholic.
- A. Beernaert: 26 October 1884 – 26 March 1894.
  Uniformly Catholic.
- J. de Burlet: 26 March 1894 – 25 February 1896.
  Uniformly Catholic.
- P.J. de Smet de Naeyer: 25 February 1896 – 24 January 1899.
  Uniformly Catholic.
- E. Vandenpeerenboom: 24 January 1899 – 5 August 1899.
  Uniformly Catholic.
- P.J. de Smet de Naeyer: 5 August 1899 – 2 May 1907.
  Uniformly Catholic.
- J. de Trooz: 2 May 1907 – 9 January 1908.
  Uniformly Catholic.
- F. Schollaert: 9 January 1908 – 17 June 1911.
  Uniformly Catholic.
- Ch. de Broqueville: 17 June 1911 – 21 November 1918.
  Uniformly Catholic. During the war this government was expanded with liberals and socialists.
- L. Delacroix I (Kath.): 21 November 1918 – 17 November 1919.
  Catholic-Liberal-Socialist.
- L. Delacroix II (Kath.): 2 December 1919 – 3 November 1920.
  Catholic-Liberal-Socialist.
- H. Carton de Wiart (Kath.): 20 November 1920 – 20 November 1921.
  Catholic-Liberal-Socialist.
- G. Theunis I (Kath.): 16 December 1921 – 5 April 1925.
  Catholic-Liberal.
- A. Van de Vyvere (Kath.): 13-22 May 1925.
  Catholic.

- P. Poullet (Kath.), E. Vandervelde (BWP): 17 June 1925 – 8 May 1926. Catholic-Socialist.
- H. Jaspar I (Kath.): 20 May 1926 – 21 November 1927. Catholic-Liberal-Socialist.
- H. Jaspar II (Kath.): 22 November 1927 – 21 May 1931. Catholic-Liberal.
- J. Renkin (Kath.): 5 June 1931 – 18 October 1932. Catholic-Liberal.
- Ch. De Broqueville (Kath.): 22 October 1932 – 13 November 1934. Catholic-Liberal.
- G. Theunis II (Kath.): 20 November 1934 – 19 March 1935. Catholic-Liberal.
- P. Van Zeeland I (Kath.): 25 March 1935 – 26 May 1936. Catholic-Liberal-Socialist.
- P. Van Zeeland II (Kath.): 13 June 1936 – 25 October 1937. Catholic-Liberal-Socialist.
- P.-E. Janson (Lib.): 23 November 1937 – 13 May 1938. Catholic-Liberal-Socialist.
- P.-H. Spaak (BWP): 15 May 1938 – 9 February 1939. Catholic-Liberal-Socialist.
- H. Pierlot I (Kath.): 21 February 1939 – 27 February 1939. Catholic-Liberal.
- H. Pierlot II (Kath.): 18 April 1939 – 3 September 1939. Catholic-Liberal.
- H. Pierlot III (Kath.): 3 September 1939. Catholic-Liberal-Socialist.
- War ministry in London, H. Pierlot: 1940 – 1944. Catholic-Liberal-Socialist.
- H. Pierlot (Kath.): 27 September 1944 – 7 February 1945. Catholic-Liberal-Socialist-Communist.
- A. Van Acker I (Soc.): 12 February 1945 – 2 August 1945. Catholic-Liberal-Socialist-Communist.
- A. Van Acker II (Soc.): 2 August 1945 – 9 January 1946. Socialist-Liberal-Communist-UDB.
- P.-H. Spaak I (Soc.): 13 March 1946 – 19 March 1946. Socialist.
- A. Van Acker III (Soc.): 31 March 1946 – 10 July 1946. Socialist-Liberal-Communist.

- C. Huysmans (Soc.): 3 August 1946 – 12 March 1947.
  Socialist-Liberal-Communist.
- P.-H. Spaak II (Soc.): 20 March 1947 – 27 June 1949.
  Socialist-Catholic.
- G. Eyskens I (CVP): 11 August 1949 – 6 June 1950.
  Catholic-Liberal.
- J. Duvieusart (PSC): 8 June 1950 – 11 August 1950.
  Catholic.
- J. Pholien (PSC): 16 August 1950 – 9 January 1952.
  Catholic.
- J. Van Houtte (CVP): 15 January 1952 – 12 April 1954.
  Catholic.
- A. Van Acker IV (Soc.): 22 April 1954 – 2 June 1958.
  Socialist-Liberal.
- G. Eyskens II (CVP): 23 June 1958 – 6 November 1958.
  Catholic.
- G. Eyskens III (CVP), A. Lilar (Lib.): 6 November 1958 – 27 March 1961.
  Catholic-Liberal.
- Th. Lefèvre (CVP), P.H. Spaak (Soc.): 25 April 1961 – 24 May 1965.
  Catholic-Liberal.
- P. Harmel (PSC), A. Spinoy (Soc.): 28 July 1965 – 11 February 1966.
  Catholic-Socialist.
- P. Vanden Boeynants (PSC), W. De Clerq (PVV): 19 March 1966 – 7 February 1968.
  Catholic-Liberal.
- G. Eyskens (CVP), J. Merlot (Soc.) and, after his death on 22 January 1969, A. Cools (Soc.): 17 June 1968 – 8 November 1971.
  CVP-PSC-Socialist.
- G. Eyskens (CVP), A. Cools (PSB) II: 21 January 1972 – 22 November 1972.
  CVP-PSC-BSP-PSB.
- E. Leburton (PSB), L. Tindemans (CVP), W. De Clerq (PVV): 26 January 1973 – 19 January 1974.
  BSP-CVP-PSC-PVV-PLP.
- L. Tindemans I (CVP): 25 April 1974 – 18 April 1977.
  CVP-PSC-PVV-PLP; from 11 June 1974 CVP-PSC-PW-PLP (PRLW)-RW; after 4 March 1977 CVP-PSC-PVV-PRLW.

- L. Tindemans II (CVP), L. Hurez (PSB), P. Vanden Boeynants (pSC): 3 June 1977 – 13 October 1978.
  CVP-PSC-BSP-FDF-VU.
- Interim government until the General Election of 17 December 1978. P Vanden Boeynants (PSC) takes the place of L. Tindemans on 20 October. For the rest the government, which prepared the General Election, remained unchanged.
- W. Martens I (CVP), G. Spitaels (PS): 3 April 1979 – 24 January 1980.
  CVP-PSC-PS-SP-FDF. After the King had accepted the resignations of the FDF ministers, Martens could continue his government on 24 January 1980, after replacing the ministers. Yet generally, this cabinet would be referred to as a new government:
- W. Martens II (CVP), G. Spitaels (PS): 24 January 1980 – 2 April 1980.
  CVP-PSC-PS-SP.
- W. Martens III (CVP), G. Spitaels (PS), H. Vanderpoorten (PVV): 18 May 1980 – 7 October 1980.
  CVP-PSC-PS-SP-PVV-PRL.
- W. Martens IV (CVP), G. Spitaels (PS, replaced as Deputy Prime Minister on 26 February 1981 by G. Mathot, PS): 22 October 1980 – 1 April 1981.
  CVP-PSC-SP-PS.
- M. Eyskens (CVP), G. Mathot (PS): 6 April 1981 – 21 September 1981.
  CVP-PSC-SP-PS.
- W. Martens V (CVP), J. Gol (PRL), W. De Clerq (PVV), replaced in 1985 by F. Grootjans (PVV), Ch.-F. Nothomb (PSC): 17 December 1981 – 28 November 1985.
  CVP-PSC-PVV-PRL.
- W. Martens VI (CVP), J. Gol (PRL), Ch.-F. Nothomb (PSC), J.-L. Dehaene (CVP), G. Verhofstadt (PVV): 28 November 1985 – 21 October 1987.
  CVP-PSC-PVV-PRL.
- W. Martens VII (CVP), same deputy prime ministers as Martens VI: 21 October 1987 – 9 May 1988.
- W. Martens VIII (CVP), P. Moureaux (PS), W. Claes (SP), J.-L. Dehaene (CVP), M. Wathelet (PSC), H. Schiltz (VU): 9 May 1988 – 29 September 1991.
  CVP-PSC-PS-SP-VU.
- J.-L. Dehaene I (CVP), G. Coëme (PS), W. Claes (SP), M. Wathelet (PSC): 7 March 1992 – 23 June 1995.
  CVP-PSC-PS-SP.

- J.-L. Dehaene II (CVP), E. Di Rupo (PS), J. Vande Lanotte (SP), P. Maystadt (PSC), H. Van Rompuy (CVP): 23 June 1995 – 12 July 1999.
  CVP-PSC-PS-SP.
- Verhofstadt I (VLD), L. Onkelinx (PS), L. Michel (PRL), J. Vande Lanotte (SP), I. Durant (Ecolo), replaced by Y. Ylieff (PS): 12 July 1999 – 11 July 2003.
  VLD-PRL-PS-SP-Ecolo-Agalev.
- Verhofstadt II (VLD), L. Onkelinx (PS), L. Michel (MR), replaced by D. Reynders (MR), J. Vande Lanotte (sp.a), P. Dewael (VLD): 12 July 2003.
  VLD-MR-PS-sp.a-Spirit.

Flemish government

- L. Vanden Brande (First Minister CVP), L. Van den Bossche (Deputy First Minister SP): 1995 – 1999.
  CVP-SP.
- B. Somers (First Minister VLD), R. Landuyt (Deputy First Minister SP): 1999-2004.
  VLD-sp.a (formerly SP)-Agalev-Spirit (formerly VU or VU&ID).
- Y. Leterme (Deputy First Minister CD&V): 2004 – 2009.
  CD&V-VLD-sp.a-Spirit-N-VA.

Government of the Walloon Region

- R. Collignon (First Minister PS): 1995 – 1999.
  PS-PSC.
- E. Di Rupo, replaced by J.C. Van Cauwenberghe (First Minister PS), S. Kubla (PRL), J. Daras (Ecolo): 1999 – 2004.
  PS-MR-Ecolo.
- J.C. Van Cauwenberghe (First Minister PS), A. Antoine (Deputy First Minister CDH), M. Daerden (Deputy First Minister PS): 2004 – 2009.
  PS-CDH.

Government of Brussels Capital Region

- C. Picqué (First Minister PS): 1995 – 1999.
  PS-PRL-FDF-CVP-SP-VU.
- J. Simonet (First Minister PRL): 1999 – 2004.
  PRL-PS-FDF-CVP-VLD-SP.
- C. Picqué (First Minister PS): 2004 – 2009.
  PS-CDH-Ecolo-VLD-sp.a-CD&V.

Government of the Francophone Community

- L. Onkelinx (First Minister PS): 1995 – 1999.
  PS-PSC.
- H. Hasquin (First Minister PRL): 1999 – 2004.
  PS-PRL-Ecolo.
- M. Arena (First Minister PS), M.-D. Simonet (Deputy First Minister CDH), M. Daerden (Deputy First Minister PS): 2004 – 2009.
  PS-CDH.

Government of the German Community

- J. Maraite (First Minister PSC): 13 June 1995.
  PSC-SP.
- K.-H. Lambertz (First Minister SP): 1999 – 2004.
  SP-PFF-Ecolo.
- K.-H. Lambertz (First Minister SP): 2004 – 2009.
  SP-PFF-PJU-PDB.

Bibliography

As mentioned in the introduction, this bibliography does not claim to be exhaustive, but aims to provide orientation through an overview of a number of important and preferably recent works. For a full list of all available studies, we can refer to the retrospective and current bibliographies concerning the 19th and 20th centuries, among which the one in *Revue Belge de Philologie et d'Histoire Belge. Belgisch Tijdschrift voor Filologie en Geschiedenis* (RBPH-BTFG) is worth mentioning. Good but sadly outdated commented bibliographical overviews are to be found in the *Algemene Geschiedenis der Nederlanden* (vols. 13-15) and in the discontinued publication *Historical Research in the Low Countries* (Nederlands Historisch Genootschap, Utrecht). Slightly more recent is L.Genicot's (ed.) *Vingt Ans de recherche historique en Belgique (1969-1988)*, Brussels, 1990. Every part of the series mentioned below, *Nouvelle histoire de la Belgique contemporaine* (2005-2006), contains an extensive bibliography. Works with a political character published between 1945 and 2000 are mentioned in context in E. Witte, *Over bruggen en muren. Hedendaagse politieke geschiedenis en politieke wetenschappen in België* (Leuven, 2003). G. Vanthemsche et al are the editors of *De Tuin van Heden. Dertig jaar wetenschappelijke onderzoek over de hedendaagse Belgische samenleving* (Brussel, 2007).

General works and works on home policy of a certain period

A general overview of the different aspects of Belgian history is provided by *Algemene Geschiedenis der Nederlanden*, but also the chapters on Belgium in parts 9 to 12 of an older publication, which appeared between 1949 and 1958, are a treasure of reliable and useful information. The series *Nouvelle histoire de la Belgique contemporaine* (Editions Complexe, 2005-2006) contains nine chronologically defined parts : 1828-1847 (E. Witte), 1846-1878 (E. Gubin and J.P. Nandrin), 1878-1905 (G. Deneckere), 1906-1918 (M. Dumoulin), 1919-1938 (E. Gerard), 1939-1950 (M. Van den Wijngaert and V. Dujardin), 1950-1970 (V. Dujardin and M. Van den

Wijngaert), and Belgium and the Congo (G. Vanthemsche and J.L. Vellut). In recent years, several overviews of Belgian history have been published for a wide audience, among which M. Reynebeau's certainly deserves to be mentioned. An overview about Wallonia was published under the editorship of H. Hasquin: *La Wallonie. Le pays et les hommes. Histoire-économies-sociétés*, 2 vols., Brussels, 1976. In *Mijn land in de kering*, (Antwerp-Amsterdam, 1978), K. Van Isacker describes the social and political history of Flanders in the 19th century. Several volumes in the series *Twintig eeuwen Vlaanderen*, (Hasselt, 1972), are also devoted to the political situation in the 19th and 20th centuries. The same topic is discussed in E. Witte (ed.), *Geschiedenis van Vlaanderen*, Renaissance du Livre, Brussels, 1983 and in J.C.H. Blom and E. Lamberts, *Geschiedenis van de Nederlanden*, Rijswijk, 1993. Among the general works focusing on political aspects, there are the compendium of facts by T. Luyckx; the synthesis by E.H. Kossmann, *De Lage Landen, 1780-1980. Twee eeuwen Nederland en België*, Amsterdam-Brussels, 2007; X. Mabille, *Histoire politique de la Belgique*, Brussels, 1997 (revised edition in 2000); and H. Gaus, *Politieke en sociale evolutie van België*, part I, Leuven, 1992 (revised in 2001). Concerning the knowledge of political structures, we are indebted to specialists such as R. Aubert, J. Bartier, H. Balthazar, R. Dumoulin, H. Haag, A. Simon, J. Stengers, R. Van Eenoo, L. Wils, J. Willequet and many other younger historians, whose names do not all appear in the following summary list of recommended works and whose contributions appear in the quoted collective works and in many journals. G. Deneckere, *'Sire, het volk mort'*, with street protest as its topic, which was published in separate works divided into themes, sketches an image of political evolution between 1830 and 1940; for the 1890-1970 period, the same goes for *De gemeenteraadsverkiezingen en hun impact op de Belgische politiek* (Proceedings of the Gemeentekrediet colloquium, Brussels, 1994) and for *Natie en Democratie* (1890-1921). Belgian political history is also generally approached through the history of the Senate and the Chamber of Representatives between 1831 and the present. The former work, edited by V. Laureys et al. (Tielt, 1999), has a chronological structure; the latter, edited by E. Gerard et al. (Brussels, 2003), is structured thematically. Because of the disparity of contributions and of periods discussed, we may also mention the collections in honour of contemporary historians H. Balthazar, R. De Schryver, G. Kurgan, J. Lory, R. Van Eenoo, J. Stengers and L. Wills.

The list of works concentrating on a specific period in Belgian political evolution is still limited – apart from the nine-volume series mentioned earlier – to C.H. Hojer, *Le Régime parlementaire belge de 1918 à 1940*, Uppsala, 1946, Brussels, 1969 and *Histoire de la Belgique contemporaine 1914-1970*, Brussels, 1975.

As far as developments in the 19th century are concerned, we can refer to E. Witte, *Politieke machtsstrijd in en om de voornaamste Belgische steden, 1830-1848*, Brussels, 1973 and A. Cordewiener, *Organisations politiques et milieux de presse en régime censitaire. L'expérience liégoise de 1830 à 1848*, Paris, 1978.

On the occasion of the 150th anniversary of Belgium, a number of contributions about the 1830 revolution were published. The *Belgisch Tijdschrift voor Nieuwste Geschiedenis*, founded on the initiative of the late J. Dhondt devoted a thematic issue to the event; there was a Belgian-Dutch colloquium on the relations between the two countries (Ghent, 1981); A. Smits published a thorough revision of his book *Scheuring in de Nederlanden*, Kortrijk-Heule, 1983; and new elements can also be found in C.A. Tamse and E. Witte (ed.), *Staats- en natievorming in Willem I's koninkrijk (1815-1830)*, Brussels, 1992. In 1999, A. Smits published volumes 3 and 4 of his opus on 1830, while the 175th anniversary of the birth of Belgium stimulated the historical production about 1830 in 2005-2006. In the 1990s, the Belgian emergence as a nation was a topic getting a fair amount of attention. A number of articles on the subject appeared in *BTNG* and in 2004, a thematic issue (4) was published; *BEG* (Soma) did the same in 1997. On this topic, we should also mention K. Deprez and L. Vos, *Nationalisme in België, 1780-2000* (Antwerp, 1999), J. Stengers, *Les racines de la Belgique* (Brussels, 2000) and J. Stengers and E. Gubin, *Le grand siècle de la nationalité belge* (Brussels, 2002).

In 1984, a colloquium was held on the importance of the 1880s : E. Lamberts and J. Lory (ed.), *1884: un tournant politique en Belgique. De machtswisseling van 1884 in België*, Brussels, 1986.

In recent decades, the First World War has enjoyed renewed interest. S. De Schaepdrijver's work *De Groote Oorlog* (Amsterdam-Antwerp, 1999) was certainly a contributory factor, along with the articles published by this author. J. Horne and A. Kramer extensively described the German atrocities of 1914 (Yale, 2001).

As far as the interbellum and the Second World War are concerned, a clearer picture is gradually emerging, among others because of a number of contributions in the *Belgisch Tijdschrift voor Nieuwste Geschiedenis*. By way of example we will mention: H. Schoeters and D. Wallef, *Les collusions politico-financières en Belgique (1930-1940)*, VII, 1976; G. Vanthemsche, *De val van de regering Poullet-Vandervelde: een samenzwering der bankiers?*, IX, 1978; *L'élaboration de l'arrêté royal sur le contrôle bancaire 1935*, XI, 1980, 3; *De mislukking van een vernieuwde economische politiek in België vóór de Tweede Wereldoorlog; de OREC, Office de Redressement économique van 1935 tot 1938*, XIII, 1982, 1; L. Wils, *Bormsverkiezing en 'Compromis des Belges'. Het aandeel van de regerings- en oppositiepartijen in de taalwetgeving tussen beide wereldoorlogen*, IV, 1973, 34; and B. Henkens, *De vorming van de regering Van Zeeland (maart 1935)*, XXVI, 1996.

Also the *Belgisch Tijdschrift voor Filologie en Geschiedenis* has paid attention to this period; cf. e.g. R. De Groof and J. Tyssens, *De partiële pacificatie van de schoolkwestie in het politiek compromisproces na de Eerste Wereldoorlog, 1918-1919*, LXVI, 1988. Apart from this, a number of books were published dealing with this period: V. Janssens, *Burggraaf Aloys van de Vyvere*, Tielt, 1982; E. Verhoeven and F. Uytterhaegen, *De kreeft met de zwarte scharen. 50 jaar uiterst-rechts in België*, Ghent, 1981; L. Vos, *Bloei en ondergang van het AKVS*, Leuven, 1982; M.R. Tielemans, *La grande crise et le gouvernement des banquiers*, Brussels, 1980. Detailed information about Belgium's role in the Spanish Civil War can be found in a two-part theme issue of *BTNG*, XVIII, 1987, 1-2. D. Luyten published extensively on corporatism during the interbellum (Brussels, 1996). General overviews of this period can be found in: *De Jaren '30 in België. De massa in verleiding*, Brussels, ASLK, 1994.

More specific works about the problems of the Second World War are *Bijdragen tot de Geschiedenis van de Tweede Wereldoorlog* (1967-1995), and its successor *Bijdragen tot de Eigentijdse Geschiedenis. Cahiers du Temps Présent* (1996-), which contains, among others, numerous studies by A. De Jonghe on the occupation government and the conflicts in the context of the collaboration. M. Van den Wijngaert researched the policy of the secretaries-general during the occupation: *Het beleid van het comité van de secretarissen-generaal in België tijdens de Duitse bezetting, 1940-1944* (Brussels, 1975). Still an excellent introduction to the political situation during the Second World War is the work of J. Gerard-Libois and J. Gotovitch, *L'An 40. La Belgique occupée*, Brussels, 1971. More popularised works on the 'new order' were published by M. De Wilde (Antwerp, 1982) and W. De Bock, *De mooiste jaren van een generatie*, Berchem, 1982. Useful information on daily life during the Second World War is contained in the catalogue to the ASLK exhibition held in 1985. B. De Wever discussed the phenomenon of the Eastern Front soldiers (Tielt, 1984). M. Steinberg conducted extensive research into the different aspects of the Jewish question in Belgium (Brussels, 1983). R. Van Doorslaer and others discussed the same issue for the period between 1925 and 1942 (Brussels, 1994), and L. Saeren wrote about the history of the Antwerp Jews in the same period. (Tielt, 2000). G. Van den Berghe mainly discussed the holocaust and the prisoners in the concentration camps. P. Nefors analysed the role of the camp at Breendonk (Antwerp, 2004). S. Vanermen provided an overview of negationism (Brussels, 1996).

Apart from M. De Wilde, E. Verhoeyen and H. Van de Vijver's popularised overviews of the war years (Antwerp, 1973-1990), three excellent overviews have been published: E. Verhoeyen, *België bezet, 1940-1944*, Brussels, 1993 (with French translation); *België een maatschappij in crisis en oorlog. Belgique une société en crise, un pays en guerre*, proceedings of the colloquium 1990 (Brussels, 1992); and *België tijdens de Tweede Wereldoorlog*, edited by M. Van den Wijngaert (Antwerp, 2004). The proceedings of the colloquium on forced employment in Germany were also published (Brussels, 1992). D. Luyten studied corporatism during the war years (Brussels, 1997), while the 'politics of the lesser evil' were analysed from an economic point of view by M. Van den Wijngaert (Tielt, 1990), followed by the extensive work by P. Nefors (Leuven, 2000) and by A. Dantoing concerning the role of the Church (Brussels, 1991). *Entre la peste et le choléra* studies the attitude of Catholics during the occupation (edited by F. Maerten et al., Gerpinnes, 1999). M. Beyen analysed the attitude and production of historians during the Second World War in *Oorlog en Verleden* (Amsterdam, 2002). Many prominent 'new order' figures have had their biographies written by now; this is the case for S. De Clercq (by B. De Wever, Brussels, 1989), Gerard Romsée (by E. Raskin, Antwerp, 1995), R. Tollenaere (by P.-J. Verstraete, Kortrijk, 1996) and L. Degrelle (by M. Conway, Yale, 1993). Worth mentioning in connection with the punishment of collaboration are: L. Huyse and S. Dhondt, *Onverwerkt verleden. Collaboratie en repressie in België 1942-1952*, Leuven, 1991; D. Luyten, *Burgers boven elke verdenking. Vervolging van de economische collaboratie in België na de Tweede Wereldoorlog*, Brussels, 1996; F. Seberechts, *Ieder zijn zwarte. Verzet, collaboratie en repressie*, Brussels, 1994. Concerning the history of the resistance, F. Maerten's work on Hainaut (Mons, 1999) represented a breakthrough. The collaboration in Flanders was the topic of a collective work under the management of E. Corijn (Antwerp, 2002), while J. Gotovitch and C. Kesteloot also collected a number of studies on this topic (Brussels, 2002).

The study of the liberation and the post-war period has also been started: L. De Vos, *De bevrijding. Van Normandië tot de Ardennen*, Leuven, 1994. Aspects of Belgian politics are discussed in E. Witte, J.-C. Burgelman and P. Stouthuysen (ed.), *Tussen restauratie en vernieuwing. Aspecten van de Belgische naoorlogse politiek, 1944-1950*, Brussels, 1989, and in L. Huyse and K. Hoflack (ed.), *De democratie heruitgevonden. Oud en nieuw in politiek België 1944-1950*, Leuven, 1995. For information on the post-war period, the biography of C. Gutt by J.F. Crombois is also an important source (Gerpinnes, 2001). The same holds for P. Lagrou's studies on post-war patriotic memory (Cambridge, 2000).

Indispensable for the knowledge and better understanding of the workings of the Belgian political system of recent decades is the periodical *Res Publica*, published by the *Belgisch Instituut voor Wetenschap der Politiek* (Belgian Institute for Political Science). It systematically follows Belgian politics in its most diverse aspects, and for a number of years now, it has published a *Politiek Jaarboek* with overviews of the most important evolutions. A special mention should be made of thematic issues such as: *Belgium and Politics*, XV, 1973, 2; *Het Belgisch Parlement*, XXII, 1980, 1-2; *Particratie*, XXIII, 1981, 1; *Res Publica Belgica, 1970-1985*, XXX, 1988, 4. Equally indispensable for the study of the last thirty years – and not only for the political aspects but also for social and economic ones – is *Courrier hebdomadaire*, published since 1959 by the Centre de Recherche et d'Information Socio-politiques (CRISP), Brussels. The information provided in its issues is as objective as possible, and mostly vetted by competent contributors; cf. the catalogue for a full overview. Interesting contributions also appear in journals such as *La Revue Nouvelle, Contradictions, Vlaams Marxistisch Tijdschrift, Tijdschrift voor Sociologie, Politiek en Samenleving*, etc. Obviously a number of interesting political works have been published; we can only mention a few of the more important ones: L. Huyse, *Passiviteit, Pacificatie en Verzuiling in de Belgische politiek. Een sociologische studie*, Antwerp, 1970; *De gewapende vrede. De Belgische politiek na 1945*, Leuven, 1980; J. Meynaud, J. Ladrière and F. Perin, *La décision politique en Belgique. Le pouvoir et les groupes*, CRISP, Paris, 1965, to be complemented by J. Ladrière, *Le système politique belge, situation 1970*, 500me Courrier hebdomadaire du CRISP, Brussels, 1970, and by *Qui décide en Belgique? Mécanismes et facteurs de la décision politique,* in: *Dossiers du CRISP, 2,* 1969; W. Dewachter, *De wetgevende verkiezingen als proces van machtsverhouding in het Belgisch politiek bestel,* Antwerp, 1967; F. Debuyst, *La fonction parlementaire en Belgique: mécanismes d'accès et images,* CRISP, Brussels, 1966; P.-H. Claeys, *Groupes de pression en Belgique,* CRISP, Brussels, 1973 ; N. Delruelle, R. Evalenko and W. Fraeys, *Le comportement politique des électeurs belges. La rupture de 1965,* Brussels, 1970; F. Perin, *La démocratie enrayée. Essai sur le régime parlementaire belge de 1918 à 1958,* Brussels, 1960; R. De Smet, R. Evalenko and W. Fraeys, *Atlas des élections belges, 1919-1954,* 2 vols., Brussels, 1958; M. Swyngedouw, *De keuze van de kiezer,* Leuven, 1989; F. Delpérée, *Chroniques de crise, 1977-1982,* Brussels, 1983; J. Smits, *Democratie op straat. Een analyse van de betogingen in België,* Leuven, 1984; W. Dewachter, *Besluitvorming in politiek België,* Leuven, 1992; M. Swyngedouw et al. (ed.), *Kiezen is verliezen. Onderzoek naar de politieke opvattingen van Vlamingen,* Leuven, 1993; and B. Maddens, *Kiesgedrag en partijstrategie,* Leuven, 1994. On the Flemish side, M. Swyngedouw and J. Billiet systematically continue the research into party choice and political opinions for every election. On the francophone side, it is P. Frognier who conducts such research. W. Dewachter et al., *Het afscheid van het laatste dubbelparlement,* Leuven, 1997; L. Huyse, *De opmars van de calimero's. Over de verantwoordelijkheid in de politiek,* Leuven, 1999; S. Fierens, *Vijftig jaar volksvertegenwoordiging. De circulatie onder de Belgische parlementsleden, 1946-1995,* Brussel, 2000; W. Dewachter, *De mythe van de parlementaire democratie. Een Belgische analyse,* Leuven-Leusden, 2001; id., *Van oppositie tot elite.* Leuven-Leusden, 2003; C. De Vos and H. Gaus (ed.), *Schijn of scharnier. Politieke trendbreuken in de jaren negentig,* Ghent, 2004.

The role of bureaucracy, administration, political elites and the judiciary can be reconstructed with the help of the articles in the journals mentioned earlier, and with H. Van Hassel's *Het ministerieel kabinet,* Leuven, 1974; H. Cammaer, *Circulatietabel van de Belgische elite,* Leuven, 1977; A. Molitor, *L'administration de la Belgique,* Brussels, 1976; L. Huyse, *De kleur van het recht,* Leuven, 1989; L. Huysse and H. Sabbe, *De mensen van het recht,* Leuven, 1997. The historical context of the judiciary has also been given more attention in recent years, among others thanks to D. Heirbaut et al. (ed.), *Politieke en sociale geschiedenis van justitie in België van 1830 tot heden* (Bruges, 2004) and a thematic issue of *BTNG* (1998, 1-2).

The phenomenon of pillarisation was given wide attention between 1980 and 1995. The *BTNG* dedicated a thematic issue to the phenomenon (1982), and authors such as K. Dobbelaere, J. Billiet and L. Huyse also published on it. We will mention: J. Billiet (ed.), *Tussen bescherming en verovering. Sociologen en historici over zuilvorming,* Leuven, 1988; F. Demeyere (ed.), *Over pluralisme en democratie. Verzuiling en integratie in een multiculturele samenleving,* Brussels, 1993; H. Dumont, *Le pluralisme idéologique et l'autonomie culturelle en droit public Belge,* Brussels, 1996.

The legitimacy crisis that emerged as a result of the Dutroux case gave rise to a few interesting overviews, among which the one by C. Eliaerts (ed., Brussels, 1997); A. Tondeur, *L'affaire Dutroux. La Belgique malade de son système,* Brussels, 1997; N. Burnay et al., *La société indicible. La Belgique entre émotions, silences et paroles,* Brussels, 1997 ; M. Echardus (ed.), *Wantrouwen en onbehagen. Over vertrouwens- en legitimiteitscrisis,* Brussels, 1998.

Economic and financial history

We can still count the works of F. Baudhuin among the standard overviews of Belgian economic and financial history: *Histoire économique de la Belgique,* in: *Histoire de la Belgique contemporaine 1830-1914,* 3 vols., Brussels, 1928-1930; *Histoire économique de la Belgique 1914-1939,* 2 vols., Brussels, 1944; *L'économie sous l'occupation, 1940-1944,* Brussels, 1945; *Histoire économique de la Belgique, 1945-1955,* Brussels, 1958; *Belgique 1900-1960. Explication économique de notre temps,* Leuven, 1961; also the works of B.S. Chlepner, among which: *La Banque en Belgique,* Brussels, 1926; R. Demoulin, *Guillaume Ier et la transformation économique des Provinces belges, 1815-1830,* Liège, 1938; G. Jacquemyns, *Histoire de la crise économique des Flandres,* 1845-1850. In the meantime, a number of such overviews and monographs have been published, e.g.: B. Verhaegen, *Contribution à l'histoire économique des Flandres,* 2 vols., Leuven, 1961; H. Van der Wee, *De industriële revolutie in België,* in: *Historische aspecten van de economische groei,* Antwerp-Utrecht, 1972; P. Lebrun, M. Bruwier, J. Dhondt, G. Hansotte, *Essai sur la révolution industrielle en Belgique, 1770-1784,* Brussels, 1979; V. Janssens, *De Belgische frank. Anderhalve eeuw geschiedenis,* Antwerp, 1976; J. Delbeke, *Geld en bankkrediet in België, 1877-1983,* Brussels, 1988; G. De Clercq (ed.), *Ter beurze. Geschiedenis van de aandelenhandeling België, 1800-1990,* Bruges-Antwerp, 1994; P. Janssens, H. Verboven, A. Tiberghien, *Drie eeuwen Belgische belastingen,* Brussels, 1990;

A. Mommen, *The Belgian Economy in the 20th Century*, London, New York, 1994. For a general image of industrial development in the 19th and 20th centuries, cf. G.L. De Brabander and J. Gadisseur (ed.), L'Industrie en Belgique, 1780-1980, Brussels, 1981. M. Quevit tried to explain *Les causes du déclin wallon* (Brussels, 1978) from a historical perspective. Fiscal policy between 1914 and 1960, in its turn, was treated by A. Hardewijn (Brussels, 2003).

The works of B. Gille are still a necessity for information on the position of the banking house of the Rothschilds and the Société Générale in the 19th century. On this subject, J. Laureyssens also published interesting articles in *BTNG* (III, 1972, 1-2; VI, 1976, 3-4; XI, 1980, 1-2; XX, 1989, 1-2, 1992, 1-2); G. Kurgan-Van Hentenryk wrote a synthesis in: *Gouverner La Générale de Belgique*, Brussels-Paris, 1996. J. Lebrun analysed the banking and credit sector in Hainaut during the industrial revolution (Brussels, 1999). G. Jacquemyns dedicated five volumes to the 19th-century banker Langrand-Dumonceau (Brussels, 1960-1965). G. Kurgan-Van Hentenryk made an in-depth analysis of the activities of the 19th-century entrepreneur Philippart (Brussels, 1982). L. De Rijcke in his turn studied the activities of the Otlet family; M. Bruwier, N. Caulier-Mathy and J. Chapelle-Duliere also publish regularly on 19th-century industrial development. G. Kurgan-Van Hentenryk, S. Jaumain and V. Montens provided a useful *Dictionnaire des patrons en Belgique*, Brussels, 1996.

Apart from the articles by G. Vanthemsche that have already been mentioned, the following works about the interbellum should definitely be listed: H. Van der Wee and K. Tavernier, *De Nationale Bank van België en het monetaire gebeuren tussen twee wereldoorlogen*, Brussels, 1975 (a new version is in preparation); R.L. Hogg, *Structural Rigidities and Policy Inertia in Interwar Belgium*, Brussels, 1986; I. Cassiers, *Croissance, crise et régulation en économie ouverte. La Belgique entre les deux guerres*, Brussels, 1989. Concerning the economy during the Second World War the American J. Gillingham wrote a book that is controversial on certain points: *Geld maken in oorlogstijd. Economische collaboratie 1940-1945*, Ghent, 1979. E. Verhoeyen immersed himself in the Galopin-doctrine (*Bijdragen tot de Geschiedenis van de Tweede Wereldoorlog, 10*) and in the (economic) 'policy of the lesser evil' (Antwerp, 1990). We have already seen that M. Van den Wijngaert and P. Nefors followed in his footsteps. Rationing and food distribution under the German occupation were researched by A. Henau and M. Van den Wijngaert (Leuven, 1986).

With relation to the post-war and recent economic situation, we have used, among others: A. Devreker, *Welvaartsproblemen in Vlaanderen*, Antwerp, 1958; *La concentration économique* in: *Dossiers du CRISP*, 5, 1973; *Les groupes d'entreprises*, in: *Dossiers du CRISP*, 13, 1979; J. Bohets, *België en de multinationals*, Leuven, 1975; R. Michel, *Les investissements américains en Belgique*, CRISP, Brussels 1970; A. Lamfalussy, *Investment and Growth in Mature Economies. The Case of Belgium*, London, 1961; P. Joye, *Les trusts en Belgique*, Brussels, 1964; H. Daems, *The Holding Company and Corporate Control*, Leiden, 1978; P. Van Bellingen, *Meerwaarde en inkomensverdeling in België*, Antwerp, 1974; D. Vandenbulcke, *De buitenlandse ondernemingen in de Belgische industrie*, Ghent, 1971; J. Moden and J. Sloover, *Le patronat belge*, CRISP, Brussels, 1980; M. Dewaele, *Staal. Een monster zonder waarde?*, Antwerp, 1983; A. Mommen, *Een tunnel zonder einde. Het neoliberalisme van Martens V en VI*, Antwerp, 1987; Polekar, *Het laboratorium van de crisis*, Leuven, 1985; J. Gouverneur, *Kapitalisme vandaag*, Berchem, 1989; G. Quaden, *Politique économique*, Brussels, 1990; P. De Grauwe, *Onze schuld. Het ontstaan en de toekomst van werkloosheid en staatsschuld*, Tielt, 1994; J. Vuchelen, *De staatsschuld*, Leuven, 1993; B. Francq and D. Lapeyronnie, *Les deux morts de la Wallonie sidérurgique*, Brussels, 1990; *Rapport van de Club van Leuven. Vlaanderen op een kruispunt*, Tielt, 1990; H. Daems, *De paradox van het Belgische kapitalisme – Waarom bedrijven financieel goed scoren en toch strategisch slecht spelen*, Tielt, 1999; and R. Savage, *Economie belge 1953-2000. Ruptures et mutations*, Louvain-la-Neuve, 2005.

A number of important financial institutions have in recent years taken the initiative to have historically oriented monographs compiled by professional historians. A number of standard works were the result; they have proved very innovative for our knowledge of economic and financial policy. The most well-known examples are: *De Belgische spaarbanken. Geschiedenis, Recht, Economische functie en Instellingen*, Tielt, 1986; H. Van der Wee and M. Verbreyt, *Mensen maken geschiedenis. De Kredietbank en de Economische Opgang van Vlaanderen 1935-1985*, Tielt, 1985; id., *De Generale Bank. Een permanente uitdaging*, Tielt, 1997; R. Brion and J.-L. Moreau, *De Generale Maatschappij van België, 1822-1997*, Antwerp, 1998; E. Witte and R. De Preter (ed.), *Samen sparen. De geschiedenis van de spaarbank Codep en haar voorlopers*, Leuven, 1989; L. Van Molle, *Ieder voor allen. De Belgische Boerenbond, 1890-1990*, Leuven, 1990. For the sections relating to the latter subject, namely the history of agriculture, we also used information from the thematic issue that *BTNG* dedicated to this topic (1973, IV, 1-2), which features among others J. Craeybeckx, *De agrarische depressie van het einde der XIXde eeuw en de politieke strijd om de boeren*, 1973 and 1974. Meanwhile, the fundamental study by L. Van Molle, *Katholieken en landbouw. Landbouwpolitiek in België 1884-1914* (Leuven, 1989) has also been published.

Social history

Even though B.S. Chlepner, *Cent ans d'histoire sociale en Belgique* (Brussels, 1958) is completely out of date, it has not yet been replaced by anything else. A popularised introduction to the topic may be found in the reference work based mainly on leftist writings: *Wat zoudt ge zonder 't werkvolk zijn?*, 2 vols., Leuven, 1979-1981. C. Vandenbroeke paid attention to the social aspects of development in Flanders (Beveren, 1981). Several aspects of the social history of the 19th and 20th centuries are covered in: *Arbeid in veelvoud. Een huldeboek aangeboden aan Prof. Dr. J. Craeybeckx en Prof. Dr. E. Scholliers van de Vrije Universiteit Brussel*, Brussels, 1988.

As yet, our knowledge of social structures is mainly limited to the 19th century. Valuable contributions have been made by authors such as J. Hannes, J. Verhelst and J. De Belder in this respect. We are especially indebted to the studies of J. De Belder and those of C. Lis, who studied the process of proletarisation in 19th-century Belgium and especially in Antwerp. Most of their articles can be found in *BTNG* and in the Dutch *Tijdschrift voor Sociale Geschiedenis*. We also have to mention C. Lis, *Social Change and the Labouring Poor. Antwerp, 1770-1860*, New Haven 1986. Meanwhile, E. Vanhaute specialised in rural structures of the 19th century (*Heiboeren*, Brussels, 1992), while S. Jaumain and P. Heyrman wrote the history of the middle class. Jaumain concentrated on the period of the turn of the century (Brussels, 1995), and Heyrman covered the first half of the 20th century (Leuven, 1998).

A number of social themes have been the subject of scientific interest; plenty of data on the social conditions of the working class can be found in works on the labour movement, which we will come back to later. J. Neuville is the author who specialised in this topic. Concerning wages and purchasing power, we refer to the publications of the VUB-*Centrum voor Hedendaagse Sociale Geschiedenis* (Centre for Contemporary Social History), with P. Scholliers as the driving force: *Loonindexering en sociale vrede*, Brussels, 1985. The evolution of purchasing power of wage earners in the period of economic depression was researched by B. Coppieters and G. Hendrix (*BTNG*, XVII, 1986, 3-4). For the spatial aspects of the social question, we can refer to the *BTNG* thematic issue on working class accommodation in the 19th century (VIII, 1977) and, for the more recent period, to: *Barsten in België. Een sociale geografie van de Belgische maatschappij*, Berchem, 1990. BTNG also dedicated a special issue (1990, 3-4) to the problem of migrants with relation to the labour market, and A. Martens provided an introduction in: *Buitenlandse minderheden in Vlaanderen-België*, Kapellen, 1985. G. Vanthemsche and E. Deslé both published on employment policy before the First World War (*Tijdschrift voor Sociale Geschiedenis*, X-1985, 1; XVI-1990, 1). The former author also made an in-depth analysis of unemployment: *Werkloosheid in België*, 1929-1940, Berchem, 1989. The cooperatives were the topic of a *BTNG-RBHC* thematic issue (1991, 1-2).

Research into strikes resulted in a number of contributions on the 19th century and the early 20th century (*BTNG*, XIII, 1982, 2-3; XIV, 1983, 3-4; XIX, 1988, 1-4; XX, 1989, 1-2) and a synthetic study: J.L. Degee, *L'évolution des luttes ouvrières en Belgique*, Liège, 1980. R. Gubbels and M. Molitor treated a number of important social conflicts of the 1945-1961 period: *La grève, phénomène de civilisation*, Brussels, 1962, and also covered the 1969-1975 period: *Les conflits sociaux en Belgique*, Leuven, 1976. V. Feaux made a film about the events of 1960-1961: *Cinq semaines de lutte sociale*, Brussels, 1963, while A. Meynen discussed the social and economic background of this strike in a few articles (*BTNG*, IX, 1978, 3-4); J. Neuville and J. Yerna, *Le choc de l'hiver 60-61*, Brussels, 1990, published in the *Pol-His* series. Overviews relating to the 1980s are lacking. The strike of September 1983, however, did receive some attention in *Contradiction* (1984, 39) and in the writings of E. Niesten (Berchem, 1984). A well-documented overview of more recent trade union developments can be found in J. Cottenier and K. Hertogen, *De tijd staat aan onze kant*, Berchem, 1991.

Research into the history of the social consultation model has seen major advances in recent years, among others thanks to D. Luyten and G. Vanthemsche (ed.), *Het sociaal pact van 1944. Oorsprong, betekenis en gevolgen*, Brussels, 1995; G. Vanthemsche, *De beginjaren van de sociale zekerheid in België 1944-1963*, Brussels, 1994; D. Luyten, *Sociaal economisch overleg in België sedert 1918*, Brussels, 1995. Its institutional aspects were covered among others by E. Vogel-Polsky, *La conciliation des conflits collectifs du travail en Belgique*, Gembloux, 1966, and in the collective work

Dertig jaar Belgische arbeidsverhoudingen, Deurne, 1977. Certain aspects of the crisis of this consultation model were tackled by authors such as J. Bundervoet and A. Martens. The *Hoger Instituut voor de Arbeid* (Higher Institute for Labour), the Leuven centre for labour sociology and *De Gids op Maatschappelijk Gebied* (ACW) regularly publish on the topic, and also the annual *L'Année sociale* deserves a mention. Finally, the subject was analysed along multi-disciplinary lines in *De sociale zekerheid verzekerd?* (Brussels, 1990, 2 vols.).

Immigrants and refugees have featured high on researchers' agendas in recent decades. Among the introductions to this subject: A. Martens and F. Moulaert (ed.), *Buitenlandse minderheden in Vlaanderen-België*, Antwerp, 1985; E. Deslé, R. Lesthaeghe, E. Witte, *Denken over migranten*, Brussels, 1993; A. Morelli (ed.), *Histoire des étrangers et de l'immigration en Belgique*, Brussels, 1992. With reference to policy, there are e.g. A. Rea, *La Belgique et ses immigrés. Les politiques manquées*, Brussels, 1997, and E. Deslé, A. Meynen, K. Vandenbrande, *Migrantenpolitiek in Brussel*, Brussels, 1997. In *Onbekend of onbemind ?*, Leuven, 1990, J. Billiet et al. research the attitude of Belgians towards migrants. F. Caestecker wrote the history of refugee policy in the post-war period (Brussels, 1992) and in the 1930s (*Ongewenste gasten*, Brussels, 1993), and also compiled an overview of the 1840-1940 period in English (New York, 2000).

Political tendencies, parties and pillar organisations

Thanks to the numerous books and articles by the late A. Simon, which we cannot possibly list here, we are particularly well-informed about the Catholic party in general. J.L. Soete in turn conducted a thorough study of the 1863-1884 period in: *Structures et organisations de base du parti catholique en Belgique*, Leuven, 1996. Yet also the most important constituent aspects have been researched in-depth. Concerning liberal Catholicism and Ultramontanism: H. Haag, *Les origines du catholicisme libéral en Belgique*, Leuven, 1950; K. Van Isacker, *Werkelijk en wettelijk land. De katholieke opinie tegenover de rechterzijde*, Antwerp, 1955; E. Lamberts, *Kerk en liberalisme in het bisdom Gent, 1821-1857*, Leuven, 1972; *De kruistocht tegen het liberalisme. Facetten van het ultramontanisme in België in de 19de eeuw*, Leuven, 1984; V. Viane, *Belgium and the Holy See, 1831-1859*, Brussels-Rome, 2001. On the position of the Church on the social problem: K. Van Isacker, *Averechtse democratie. De gilden en de christelijke democratie in België, 1863-1884*, Antwerp, 1955; R. Reszohazy, *Origines et formation du catholicisme social en Belgique, 1842-1909*, Leuven, 1958; P.-R. Broeckaert, *Predikatie en arbeidersproblemen. Onderzoek naar de sociale opvattingen van de seculiere en reguliere clerus in Vlaanderen, 1800-1914*, Mechelen, 1963; P. Gérin, *Catholiques liégois et question sociale, 1833-1914*, Brussels, 1959; S. Scholl, *Honderdvijftig jaar katholieke arbeidersbeweging in België, 1789-1939*, 3 vols., Brussels, 1963-1966; E. Gerard et al., *De kracht van een overtuiging*, Zele, 1981; *De christelijke arbeidersbeweging in België, 1891-1991*, Leuven, 1991; *Voor kerk en werk. Opstellen over de geschiedenis van de christelijke arbeidersbeweging 1886-1986*, Leuven, 1985; G. Kwanten, *Welstand door vereniging. De ontwikkeling van de christelijke arbeiderscoöperaties 1886-1986*, Brussels, 1987; P. Pasture, *Kerk, politiek en sociale actie*, Leuven, 1992; W. Dewachter et al., *Tussen staat en maatschappij, 1945-1995: de christen-democratie in België*, Tielt, 1995. The post-war progressive catholic movements are discussed in W. Beerten's work on the UDB (Brussels, 1990), in the anthology edited by M.T. Coenen and S. Govaert (Brussels, 1999), in J.L. Jadoulles' analysis of progressive intellectuals (Louvain-la-Neuve, 2003) and in *Left Catholicism*, 1943-1955, edited by G.R. Horner and E. Gerard (Leuven, 2001). On Daensism, there are among others: L. Wils, *Het Daensisme. De opstand van het Zuidvlaamse platteland*, Leuven, 1969 and F.J. Verdoodt, *De zaak Daens*, Leuven, 1993. Thanks to E. Gerard, we also have a reliable description of the Catholic party during the interbellum: *De Katholieke Partij in crisis*, Leuven, 1985, while G. Van Haver researched the reactions of Catholics to fascism in: *Onmacht der verdeelden* (Berchem, 1982). The publication of F. Van Cauwelaert's archives by R. De Schrijver (Antwerp, 1971) is also important for the study of the party in this period. On the Catholic youth and student movements: R. Aubert, *Organisation et caractère des mouvements de jeunesse catholique en Belgique*, in: G. de Rosa, *La Gioventù Cattolica*, Rome, 1972; L. Vos, *De ideologische oriëntering van de katholieke studerende jeugd in Vlaanderen, 1936-1940, BTNG*, VIII, 1977; L. Gevers, *Bewogen jeugd*, Leuven, 1987. 19th-century structures in the Church in Flanders were researched by J. Art from an interesting social-political angle (Kortrijk, 1977). H. Gauss studied the role of the Church with relation to written fiction (Bruges, 1975). On the attitude of the party in the school war during the 1950s: L. Haagdorens, *De mobilisatie van de katholieke zuil in de schoolstrijd, BTNG*, XV, 1984, 1-2. This topic is also extensively discussed in *Het Schoolpact van 1958*, edited by E. Witte, J. De Groof and J. Tyssens (Brussels, 1999). H. Coenjaerts et al., *De CVP-staat*, Berchem, 1979, is useful in connection with the more recent evolution of the party, in spite of the subjective approach and a number of factual mistakes. For the post-war evolution of the Catholic pillar, cf. M. Van Haegendoren and L. Vandenhove, *Het verdriet van Vlaanderen. Over de macht van de katholieke zuil,* Antwerp, 1985. Excellent historical and sociological contributions on the Catholic pillarisation are to be found in: *Tussen bescherming en verovering,* Leuven, 1988; H. Righart especially researched the realisation of the pillar (Boom, 1986). In connection with the secularisation of the pillar: D. Seiler, *Le déclin du cléricalisme,* Brussels, 1975, and J. Billiet and K. Dobbelaere, *Godsdienst in Vlaanderen. Van kerks katholicisme naar sociaal-culturele kristenheid,* Leuven, 1976. With L. Voyé, K. Dobbelaere published several articles on the further secularisation of the pillar (among others in *CH-CRISP, Tijdschrift voor Sociologie*). Moreover, there were publications of biographies and memoirs of prominent Catholic politicians relevant to the period in question: H. Haag, *Le comte Charles de Broqueville,* Brussels, 1990, 2 vols.; K. Hoflack, *Theo Lefèvre,* Antwerpen, 1989; J. Smits, *Gaston Eyskens. De memoires,* Tielt, 1993, 2 vols.; L. Moyersoen, *Baron Romain Moyersoen en politieke problemen van zijn tijd,* Aalst, 1986. Biographies have also been published of P. Van Zeeland (by V. Dujardin and M. Dumoulin, Brussels, 1997), J. Duvieusart (by V. Dujardin, Gerpinnes, 2000), J. Pholien (by F. Carton de Tournai and G. Janssens, Bierges, 2003), A. De Schryver (by G. Kwanten, Leuven, 2001), P. Harmel (by V. Dujardin, Brussels, 2004). The memoirs of A. De Staercke, published by J. Stengers and G. Kurgan, also contain interesting data about the post-war period (Brussels, 2003).

Our knowledge of the liberal party has also seen a considerable increase in recent years; we will mention this general overview: A. Verhulst and H. Hasquin (ed.), *Het liberalisme in België,* Brussels, 1989. Apart from this, there was also the publication of *De liberalen van 1846 tot 1996,* Brussels, 1996. These works have been complemented by a number of articles and works on certain aspects, especially as far as the 19th century is concerned. In *Revue de L'ULB,* 1963-1964, J. Stengers focused on a few ideological aspects and J. Bartier published several articles on 19th-century liberalism (e.g. T. Verhaegen, *La Franc-Maçonnerie et les sociétés politiques,* in: *Revue de L'ULB,* 1963-1964). P.T. Verhaegen has also had his biography written (Brussels, 1996). Starting from a number of brochures, A. Erba tried to reconstruct *L'esprit laïque en Belgique sous le gouvernement libéral doctrinaire, 1857-1870,* Leuven, 1967. There is plenty of excellent information on liberal education policy thanks to J. Lory's *Libéralisme et instruction primaire (1842-1879). Introduction a l'étude de la lutte scolaire en Belgique,* 2 vols., Leuven, 1979. In *Geuzengeweld,* G. Deneckere talks about 19th-century anti-clerical collective actions (Brussels, 1998). J. Tyssens concentrated on the study of the entire philosophical left and the school war during the interbellum: *Strijdpunt of pasmunt,* Brussels, 1993; a general overview of the school question in the 20th century was published both in Dutch and in French (Brussels, 1997) by the same author. In *Het schoolpact van 1958,* mentioned earlier, there is obviously quite some attention for the different aspects of the school war. Most contributions to the anthology *Histoire de la Laïcité* (Brussels, 1979) provide a *status quaestionis* of historical research concerning the different organisations of freethinking Belgium. E. Witte dedicated a study to 19th-century freethinkers' associations (Brussels, 1977). With J. Tyssens, she extended the subject until the present in: *De vrijzinnige traditie in België,* Brussels, 1996. This topic is also mentioned in the catalogue *Tweehonderd jaar vrijzinnigheid in België 1789-1989,* Brussels, 1989, and in *Van wijsheid met vreugd gepaard,* about two centuries of freemasonry in Ghent and Antwerp (under the guidance of J. Tyssens, Brussels-Ghent, 2003). In *Passer en Davidster,* J. Koppen describes the battle of the German occupier against Jews and freemasons (Brussels, 2000). The biographies and studies of prominent liberals such as J. Vuylsteke (by J. Verschaeren, Kortrijk, 1984), K. Buls (Brussels, 1987), J. Hoste sr. (Ghent, 1989), P. Frédericq by C. Coppens (Ghent, 1990) and L. Augusteyns bij D. Vanacker (Ghent, 2008) also provide an insight into the liberal party and the Flemish Movement. The book in honour of M. Bots also contains articles on this subject (Ghent, 1995). H. Van Velthoven's work about J. Hoste jr. focuses on the London war period (Ghent, 2005). The evolution of the liberal parties since 1961 has also been described, among others in several *Cahiers* of CRISP and by J. Bouveroux, who also provided a concise overview of the recent evolution of the different Belgian parties: *Van zwarte zondag tot zwarte zondag* (Antwerp, 1996) and *Van zwarte zondag to paars-groen* (Antwerp, 2003).

Since the anthology *Geschiedenis van de socialistische arbeidersbeweging in België* was realised under the direction of J. Dhondt, much work has been done in this area, as may be seen in several contributions in *BTNG* (e.g. V, VII and VIII), in works by D. Deweerdt, *De Belgische socialistische arbeidersbeweging op zoek naar een eigen vorm, 1872-1880,* Antwerp, 1972; A. Mommen, *De Belgische Werkliedenpartij, 1880-1914,* Ghent, 1980; G. Vanschoenbeek, *Novecento in Ghent. De wortels van de sociaal-democratie in Vlaanderen*, Ghent, 1995; M. Liebman, *Les socialistes belges 1885-1914*, Brussels, 1979; M. Claeys-Van Haegendoren, *25 jaar Belgisch socialisme. Evolutie van de verhouding van de Belgische Werkliedenpartij tot de parlementaire democratie in België van 1914 tot 1940*, Antwerp, 1967; *Hendrik De Man*, Antwerp, 1972; J. Puissant, *L'évolution du mouvement ouvrier socialiste dans de Borinage*, Brussels, 1982; and in the annotated source publications concerning socialist leading figures: H. De Man and C. Huysmans (Standaard, Wetenschappelijke Uitgeverij, 1974-), each with extensive introductions. J. Craeybeckx (Mededelingen van de Koninklijke Academie voor Wetenschappen, Letteren en Schone Kunsten van België, Klasse der Letteren, Brussels, 1978) and H. Van Velthoven (*BTNG*, V, 1974) both studied the position of the BWP with respect to the Flemish Movement. A. Pletinckx analysed the BWP during the crisis years (*BTNG*, XIII, 1982, 4). The Kritak file: *Wat zoudt gij zonder 't werkvolk zijn? Anderhalve eeuw arbeidersstrijd in België*, Leuven, 1977-1981, should also be mentioned here. *25 jaar Links*, Leuven, 1984, has also been given attention. On the occasion of the 100th anniversary of the socialist party, several historical works were published. On the francophone side, we will mention a general overview (Brussels, 1985) and a number of monographs about the federations; on the Dutch-language side, there is *Eeuwige dilemma's. Honderd jaar socialistische partij*, Leuven, 1985. Relating to the socialist trade-unionism during and after the Second World War, the contributions of R. Hemmeryckx are worth mentioning (*Cahiers du CRISP*, 1119-1120), as well as his dissertation on the ABVV during the 1940s (Brussels, 2003); W. Steenhaut analysed the UTMI. In recent years, several biographies of prominent socialist figures have been published: M. Dumoulin, *P.H. Spaak*, Brussels, 1990; R. Devleeshauwer, *Henri Rolin, 1891-1973*, Brussels, 1994; J. Polasky, *E. Vandervelde. Le Patron*, Brussels, 1995; W. Geldhof, *Stockholm 1917. Camille Huysmans in de schaduw van titanen*, Antwerp, 1996; M. Mayné, *Eugène Hins*, Brussels, 1994. Also about Huysmans: *Het enfant terrible*, by J. Hunin (Amsterdam-Antwerp, 1999). With M. Galle and S. Loccufier as editors, a memorial collection about A. Van Acker was realised (Brussels, 2000). For quite a while now, the periodical *Brood en Rozen* has been providing the popularised distribution of these and other research results.

The picture of the Belgian Communist Party (BKP) is also gradually becoming more complete: L. Reyntjens, *De eerste kommunistische groepen in België en hun fusie tot de kommunistische eenheidspartij*, in: *Vlaams*

Marxistisch Tijdschrift, 6 (1971); R. Van Doorslaer, *De kommunistische partij van België en het Sowjet-Duits niet-aanvalspakt tussen augustus 1939 en juli 1941*, Brussels, 1975; M. Liebman, R. Van Doorslaer and J. Gotovitch, *Een geschiedenis van het Belgisch Kommunisme, 1921-1945*, Ghent, 1980; J. Gotovitch, *Du rouge au tricolore. Les communistes belges de 1939 à 1994*, Brussels, 1992. Belgian Trotskyism between 1925 and 1940 was researched by N. De Beule (Ghent, 1980), and anarchism by J. Moulaert, *Rood en zwart. De anarchistische bewegingen in België, 1880-1914*, Leuven, 1995.

The number of books and articles devoted to the Flemish Movement is considerable. We will limit ourselves to the most important ones: H.J. Elias, *Geschiedenis van de Vlaamse Gedachte, 1880-1914*, 4 vols., Antwerp, 1963-1965, and *Vijfentwintig jaar Vlaamse Beweging, 1914-1939*, 4 vols., Antwerp, 1969; A.W. Willemsen, *De Vlaamse Beweging*, I. 1830-1914; II. 1914-1940; III. after 1940 (vols. 4, 5 and 6 of *Twintig Eeuwen Vlaanderen*, Hasselt, 1974-1979); L. Wils, *Het ontstaan van de Meetingpartij te Antwerpen en haar invloed op de Belgische politiek*, Antwerp, 1963; by the same author: *Flamenpolitik en Aktivisme. Vlaanderen tegenover België in de Eerste Wereldoorlog*, Leuven, 1974, and *Honderd jaar Vlaamse Beweging. Geschiedenis van het Davidsfonds*, 3 vols., Leuven, 1977-1989; *Vlaanderen, België, Groot-Nederland. Mythe en geschiedenis*, Leuven, 1994. Other interesting works: *Joris Van Severen*, Leuven, 1994; B. De Wever, *Greep naar de macht. Vlaams-nationalisme en Nieuwe Orde. Het VNV, 1933-1945*, Tielt, 1994; H. Van Velthoven, *De Vlaamse kwestie 1830-1914. Macht en onmacht van de Vlaamsgezinden*, Kortrijk, 1982; E. Seberechts, *Geschiedenis van DeVlag*, Ghent, 1991; D. Vanacker, *Het aktivistisch avontuur*, Ghent, 1990; A. Vrints, *De Vlaams-nationalistische collaboratie in Antwerpen tijdens Wereldoorlog I*, Brussels, 2002; G. Leemans et al., *Vlamingen komt in massa. De Vlaamse beweging als massabeweging*, Ghent-Antwerp, 1999. M. Rooses (Leuven, 1981), W. De Broek (Ghent, 1984) and M. Reynebeau (Leuven, 1995) have also given their vision on the Flemish struggle. E. Witte analysed the political stance of Flemish literary figures in the 19th century (in: *Hoofdstukken uit de geschiedenis van de Vlaamse letterkunde*, vol. 3, Ghent, 2004). E. Gubin provided a balanced analysis of the Flemish Movement in Brussels for the 1840-1873 period (Brussels, 1979). Concerning the Brussels linguistic problem, we can refer to the relevant chapters in the anthology *Brussel, groei van een hoofdstad*, edited by J. Stengers (Brussels, 1979), and to several articles in the current publication *Taal en Sociale Integratie (1978-1993)* by the VUB *Centrum voor Interdisciplinair Onderzoek naar Brussel*

(Centre for Interdisciplinary Research concerning Brussels). It has been continued under the title *Brusselse Thema's* (1993-). In this series, it is worth mentioning separately: F. Louckx, *Vlamingen tussen Vlaanderen en Wallonië,* 1982, 5; M. De Metsenaere, *Taalmuur = Sociale muur?,* 1988, 9; and E. Witte (ed.), *Het probleem Brussel sinds Hertoginnedal (1963). Acta van het Colloquium VUB-CRISP van 20 en 21 oktober 1988,* 1989, I and II; E. Witte (ed.), *De Brusselse Rand* (*Brusselse Thema's,* 1, 1993), in which the problem of special facilities is discussed in-depth. In the same series, A. Detant investigated the linguistic legislation in the Brussels municipal institutions (1996), E. Witte studied those of Brussels Capital Region (1998) and J. Koppen et al. those in the municipalities with special facilities (2002). The series also extensively highlights the post-war period. This is also the case, albeit rather one-sidedly, in H. Todts, *Hoop en wanhoop der Vlaamsgezinden,* 6 vols., Leuven, 1961-1987; W.R. Jonckheere, *Jan Verroken,* Leuven, 1992. E. Witte and H. Van Velthoven compiled an overview relating to language and politics (Brussels, 1997), while H. Van Goethem analysed the linguistic situation in the judiciary (Brussels, 1990). Concerning the Leuven question, we can refer to H. Todts and W. Jonckheere (Leuven, 1979) and to C. Laporte (Paris-Brussels, 1999); the history of the split of ULB-VUB was analysed by J. Tyssens in *De Tuin van Akademos* (edited in cooperation with E. Witte, Brussels, 1995). The biographies by L. Wils of F. Van Cauwelaert (Antwerp, 1988, 2000) and by B. Van Causenbroeck of H. Vos (Ghent, 1997) also focus on the Flemish Movement. This is also the case for new studies about the Willemsfonds by H. Van Velthoven and J. Tyssens (Ghent, 2001) and about the Vermeylenkring by R. De Groof (Brussels, 2004). With the three new volumes of the *Nieuwe Encyclopedie van de Vlaamse Beweging* (Tielt, 1998), historical research on the Flemish Movement has also gained a solid reference work.

The Walloon movement is less well-represented in publications, even though research in recent years has made considerable progress. As far as Brussels is concerned, information can be gleaned from: *Taal en Sociale Integratie* (R. Van Alboom, E. Deslé, J. Tyssens, K. Deschouwer) and especially from C. Kesteloot, who, apart from numerous contributions, has also published her dissertation: *Au nom de la Wallonie et de Bruxelles français* (Brussels, 2004). The study centre J. Destrée regularly publishes on the Walloon movement; cf. especially: J. Destatte, *L'identité wallonne. Essai sur l'affirmation politique de la Wallonie, 19e-20e s.* (Charleroi, 1997). Also the CRISP publications (especially C. Kesteloot) cover the movement. In his recent study about G. Thone, H. Hasquin puts the Walloon collaboration in the spotlight. In the meantime, also the Walloon movement has its three-volume *Encyclopédie* (Charleroi, 2000-2001).

On the fascist movements during the interbellum in francophone Belgium, the following should be consulted: J. Stengers, *La droite en Belgique avant 1940, Courrier hebdomadaire CRISP*, 468-469, 1970; J.M. Etienne, *Le mouvement rexiste jusqu'en 1940*, Paris, 1968; J. Willequet, *Les fascismes belges et la seconde guerre mondiale*, in: *Revue d'histoire de la 2me guerre mondiale*, 1967, 17; E. Defoort, *Charles Maurras en de Action française in België*, Bruges, 1978; E. Verhoeyen and F. Uytterhaegen, *De kreeft met de zwarte scharen*, Ghent, 1981; R. Van Doorslaer and E. Verhoeyen, *De moord op Lahaut*, Leuven, 1989; M. Conway, *Collaboration in Belgium. Léon Degrelle and the Rexist Movement, 1940-1944*, New Haven-London, 1993; F. Balace (ed.), *De l'avant à l'après guerre. L'extrême droite en Belgique francophone*, Louvain-la-Neuve, 1993. For post-war and more recent evolutions of the extreme-right and racism, we refer to: W. De Bock et al., *Extreem-rechts en de staat*, Berchem, 1981; R. Van Doorslaer et al., *Herfsttij van de 20ste eeuw. Extreem-rechts in Vlaanderen, 1920-1990*; the contributions about Belgium in: H. De Schampheleire and Y. Thanassekos (ed.), *Gezichten van hedendaags racisme*, Brussels, 1992; H. Lepaige, *Le désarroi démocratique. L'extrême droite en Belgique*, Brussels, 1997.

The research into the so-called New Social Movements has seen a breakthrough in recent years, especially concerning environmental, peace and third-world movements. After the studies by P. Stouthuysen in *Res Publica* (1983) and in *CH-CRISP*, we have also seen the publication of: S. Walgraeve, *Nieuwe sociale bewegingen in Vlaanderen*, Leuven, 1994; S. Hellemans and M. Hooghe (ed.), *Van 'Mei 68' tot 'Hand in hand'. Nieuwe sociale bewegingen in België, 1965-1995*, Leuven, 1995; P. Delwit and J.M. De Waele, *Ecolo. Les verts en politique*, Paris-Brussels, 1996. The 2004 *BTNG* thematic issue (4), provides the most recent state of affairs. The women's movement is discussed in the series *Vrouwenstudies*, VUB, Brussels, 1988-, and also in the works of B. Marques-Pereira on the fight concerning the liberalisation of abortion legislation in Belgium (Brussels, 1989, and several *CH-CRISP*). E. Witte analysed the specific political aspects of this problem area (*Abortus, Vrouwenstudies* 4, Brussels, 1993); D. Deweerdt wrote *En de vrouwen?*, Ghent, 1980, with a history of the women's movement, and also provided a history of women in the First World War (Ghent, 1991); R. Van Mechelen covered the 1970s (Leuven, 1979) and has meanwhile updated the work (Ghent, 1996). On the francophone side, the historical contributions of E. Gubin should be mentioned, and also M.-T. Coenen, *La grève des femmes de la FN en 1960*, Paris-Brussels, 1991, and M. Denis and S. Van Rokegem, *Le féminisme est dans la rue. Belgique 1970-1975*, Paris-Brussels, 1992. L. Van Molle and E. Gubin have also realised a useful historical overview with *Vrouw en politiek in België* (Brussels, 1998). In *BEG*, a thematic issue in 1998 (4) was also dedicated to women and society.

Essential for the knowledge of recent evolutions of the party system, apart from a few general overviews such as K. Deschouwer, *Politieke partijen in België*, Antwerp, 1987, and M. Maes, *De ledenaantallen van de politieke partijen in België*, Leuven, 1988, are the periodicals we mentioned earlier: *Res Publica* and *Courrier hebdomadaire du CRISP*, which systematically follow the evolution of the parties. Useful additional information can be found in the politically oriented periodicals mentioned earlier.

Foreign affairs, military and colonial policies

R. Coolsaet provided a general overview of foreign policy in *België en zijn buitenlandse politiek, 1830-1990* (Leuven, 1998).

As far as the diplomatic history of Belgian independence between 1830 and 1839 is concerned, the only alternatives for this overview remain the older works of F. Delannoy and A. De Ridder. H. Lademacher discussed an important aspect in *Die Belgische Neutralität als Problem der europäischen Politik 1830-1914*, Bonn, 1971. J.S. Fischman concentrated on the London conference in *Diplomacy and revolution* (Amsterdam, 1988) and also N. Van Sas, *Onze Natuurlijke Bondgenoot. Nederland, Engeland en Europa 1813-1831*, Groningen 1985, provides a clear explanation of the problem. The Belgian-Dutch relations also get much attention in the proceedings (mentioned earlier) of the 1981 Colloquium.

C.-A. Tamse, *Nederland en België in Europa (1859-1871). De zelfstandigheidspolitiek van twee kleine staten*, The Hague, 1973, provides the necessary information on foreign policy in the mid-19th century, which can be complemented as far as trade policy is concerned with M. Suetens, *Histoire de la politique commerciale de la Belgique depuis 1830 jusqu'à nos jours*, Brussels, 1955. M. Dewaele published several articles about the period around the First World War. The period between the two World Wars has enjoyed quite some interest: S. Marks, *Innocent Abroad. Belgium at the Paris Peace Conference of 1919*, Chapel Hill, 1981; P. Van Zuylen, *Les mains libres;*

politique extérieure de la Belgique 1914-1940, Brussels, 1950; O. De Raeymaeker, *Belgiës internationaal beleid : 1919-1939*, Brussels-Antwerp, 1945 ; F. Van Langenhove, *La Belgique en quête de sécurité*, Brussels, 1969 ; D.O. Klieft, *Belgium's Return to Neutrality. An Essay in the Frustrations of Small Power Diplomacy*, Oxford, 1972; G. Provoost, *Vlaanderen en het militair-politiek beleid in België tussen de twee wereldoorlogen. Het Frans-Belgisch Militair Akkoord van 1920*, 2 vols., Leuven, 1976-1977; R.L. Schuursma, *Het onaannemelijk tractaat. Het verdrag van België van 3 april 1925 in de Nederlandse publieke opinie*, Groningen, 1975. K. De Volder analysed the German-Belgian relations between 1936 and 1940 (Handelingen Zuidnederlandse, XLVI, 1992). The period of the 'drôle de guerre' was extensively covered by J. Van Welkenhuysen (Brussels, 1988), while L. De Vos and F. Decat specifically focused on one crucial month in *Mei 1940* (Kapellen, 1990).

For the post-war period, we consulted, among others: J.E. Helmreich, *Belgium and Europe. A Study in Small-Power Diplomacy*, The Hague, 1976; L. Reichler, *Belgian Defense Policy*, Leuven, 1982; F. Van Langenhove, *La sécurité de la Belgique. Contribution à l'histoire de la période 1940-1950*, Brussels, 1971; O. De Raeymaeker, *De kleine landen en de internationale samenwerking*, Antwerp, 1947; by the same author: *Small Powers in Alignment*, Leuven, 1974; R. Coolsaet, *Buitenlandse Zaken*, Leuven, 1987; id., *De veiligheid van België*, Antwerp, 1983; *Klein land, veel buitenland* (1993). P. Stouthuysen analysed the politicisation of Belgian security policy, 1945-1985 (*In de ban van de bom*, Brussels, 1992). Y. Vanden Berghe published about the Cold War, and M. Van den Wijngaert et al. provided an anthology on the topic: *Oost west, west best* (Tielt, 1997).

Insight into the colonial policy of Leopold II is provided by G. Kurgan's *Léopold II et les groupes financiers belges en Chine*, Brussels, 1972, while his Congo policy is mainly explained in works by J. Stengers. We will mention e.g. *Congo, mythes et réalités*, Gembloux, 1989 and *The Congo Free State and the Belgian Congo*, Cambridge, 1969; *Le Centenaire de l'Etat Indépendant du Congo. Recueil d'Etudes*, Brussels, 1988. The negative aspects of colonialism were mainly stressed in: D. Vangroenweghe, *Rood rubber*, Brussels-Amsterdam, 1985, and in: A.M. Delathuy, *E.D. Morel tegen Leopold II en de Congostaat*, Berchem, 1985. Concerning decolonisation and later evolutions, we mainly relied on: C. Young, *Introduction à la politique congolaise*, Brussels, 1968; B. Verhaegen, *Rébellions au Congo*, Brussels, 1968-1969; I. Schalbroeck, *Belgisch Congo. De dekolonisatie van een kolonie,*

Tielt, 1986; A. Huybrechts et al., *Du Congo au Zaïre, 1960-1980*, Brussels, 1982. Useful introductions, finally, are: R. Cornevin, *Histoire du Zaïre des origines de nos jours*, Brussels, 1989; J.L. Vellut, *Guide de l'étudiant en histoire du Zaïre*, Kinshasa, s.d.; J. Gérard-Libois and J. Heinen, *Belgique-Congo*, Liège, 1988; and G. de Villers, *De Mobutu à Mobutu*, Paris-Brussels, 1995.

The monarchy and politics

Also in this field, A. Simon has been groundbreaking, analysing the policy of Leopold I in-depth in several books and articles. G. Janssens and J. Stengers (ed.) realised *Nieuw licht op Leopold I and Leopold II* (Brussels, 1997). Leopold II's policy was mainly studied in the light of his Congo policy (cf. supra). Albert I's position was analysed in e.g. *Actes du colloque Roi Albert*, Brussels, 1976 and summarized by J. Willequet (Brussels, 1979) and in: M.R. Thielemans and E. Vandewoude, *Le Roi Albert au travers de ses lettres inédites, 1882-1916*, Brussels, 1982, and L. Schepens, *Koning Albert, Charles de Brocqueville en de Vlaamse Beweging tijdens de Eerste Wereldoorlog*, Tielt, 1982. Data and interpretations about the Royal Question were mainly gleaned from *L'An '40* (mentioned earlier) and from: L. Schepens, *1940. Dagboek van een politiek conflict*, Tielt, 1970; A. de Jonghe, *Hitler en het politieke lot van België*, Antwerp-Utrecht, 1972; J. Stengers, *Aux origines de la question royale: Léopold III et le gouvernement. Les deux politiques belges de 1940*, Brussels, 1980. A detailed and balanced history of the Royal Question has been compiled by J. Velaers and H. Van Goethem: *Leopold III, de koning, het land, de oorlog*, Tielt, 1994. For the eventual resolution of the question, cf. P. Theunissen, *De ontknoping van de koningskwestie*, Kapellen, 1984, and V. Dujardin, *Entre régence et royauté*, Brussels, 1995. C. Koninckx in turn described Leopold III's diplomatic qualities in *Diplomaat voor de vrede*, Sint-Niklaas, 1987, and M. Van den Wijngaert sympathised with the king in *Een koning geloofd, gelaakt en verloochend*, Leuven, 1984. A synthesis of the entire question can be found in J. Gérard-Libois and J. Gotovitch, *Léopold III, de l'an 40 à l'effacement*, Brussels, 1991. In a *CRISP-Courrier*, J. Gérard-Libois already shed some light on the conflicts that the Royal Question would cause in the post-war CVP (1969-1970). Another analysis of the role of the monarchy can be found in J. Stengers, *Koningen der Belgen van Leopold I tot Albert II*, Leuven, 1997. *Monarchie en macht. België en zijn koningen*, provides a solid introductory overview (Brussels, 1992). The death of Baudouin and Albert II's access to the throne also led to a few publications: H. Le Paige (ed.), *Questions royales*, Brussels, 1994; L. Neuckermans and P. Van den Driessche, *Albert, koning na Boudewijn*, Leuven, 1995; C. Koninckx and P. Lefévre (ed.), *Boudewijn. Een koning en zijn tijd*, Tielt, 1998.

The media and politics

Mainly thanks to the *Interuniversitair Centrum voor Hedendaagse Geschiedenis* (Inter-university Centre for Contemporary History), Belgium is probably the country with the most complete press history. For the political aspects of the press, not only the many press catalogues of a certain region or city are important, but especially the press monographs published by the Centre since 1958. By way of example, we can mention the ones relating to the 1830-1848 period by A. Vermeersch (1958, 4), concerning the press during the First World War by M. Leroy (1971, 63), concerning the Flemish press in the 19th century by M. De Vroede (1960, 12) and about the Christian-democratic (P. Gerin, 1975, 80) and socialist press during the interbellum (1974, 75). Thanks to the Centre, the *Journal de Bruxelles* and *La Réforme* were thoroughly analysed (1965, 36, 39; 1972, 64). Yet also outside of the Centre, monographs were published focusing on the political role of the press. A few examples: E. De Bens, *De dagbladpers tijdens de Tweede Wereldoorlog*, Antwerp-Utrecht, 1973; E. Witte on the *Moniteur belge*, 1830-1845 (Brussels, 1985); G. Durnez on *De Standaard* (Tielt, 1985); W. Vandaele on the Volksunie press (Antwerp, 1984). Concerning radio and the political evolution, cf.: J. Putzeys, *Radiostrijd tussen de twee wereldoorlogen* (*BTNG*, XXV, 1985); G. Boon, *De Belgische radio-omroep tijdens de Tweede Wereldoorlog*, Wommelgem, 1988, and *Omroep en politiek* by J.C. Burgelman, who studied the broadcasting organisation and the party-political power strategies in the 1945-1960 period (Brussels, 1990). In connection with more recent evolutions, we consulted, among others, numerous *CRISP-Courriers* on the media (mainly by E. Lentzens) and R. Campé et al., *Radioscopie de la presse*, Brussels, 1975; H. Verstraeten, *Pers en macht*, Leuven, 1980; J. Op de Beeck (ed.), *Omroepen in de woestijn*, Leuven, 1985, and *Omroepen in Europa. België*, NOS, Hilversum, 1990; E. Witte, *De breedte van het scherm*, Brussels, 1994; J.C. Burgelman, D. Biltereyst, C. Pauwels (ed.), *Audiovisuele media in Vlaanderen. Analyse en beleid*, Brussels, 1994. Recent relations between the media and politics are analysed in several contributions to the VUB series *Media en Maatschappij*; there was a separate publication on the media and 'black Sunday' (M.

Verkouter, *Een mythe van papier*, Brussels, 1994). E. De Bens compiled a more recent history of the *Belgische pers* (Tielt, 1997).

The state reforms after the Second World War

Apart from the numerous *CRISP-Dossiers* and *CRISP-Courriers* dedicated to this topic by J. Brassinne and others, we consulted the following works in the composition of the related chapter: R. Senelle, *De grondwetsherziening 1967-1970*, Brussels, 1971; P. De Stexhe, *La révision de la Constitution belge, 1968-1971*, Brussels-Namur, 1972; J. Gilissen, *De derde grondwetsherziening*, Antwerp, 1974; J. Van Rompaey, *Essai de synthèse de l'évolution de la réforme de l'état en Belgique de 1961 à 1979*, in: *Bijdragen en mededelingen betreffende de geschiedenis der Nederlanden*, 1979, 94, 3; A. Méan, *La politique de papa*, Liège, 1989; P. Berckx, *Honderdvijftig jaar institutionele hervormingen in België*, Antwerp, 1990; M. Uyttendaele, *Le fédéralisme inachevé*, Brussels, 1991; A. Alen and L.P. Suetens (ed.), *Het federale België na de vierde staatshervorming*, Bruges, 1993; *Le fédéralisme. Approches politique, économique et juridique*, Brussels, 1994; N. Jacquemin en M. Van den Wijngaert, *O dierbaar België. Ontstaan en structuur van de federale staat*, Antwerp, 1996; J. Clement et al., *Het Sint-Michielsakkoord en zijn achtergronden*, Antwerp, 1993. A. Alen and his staff keep updating the series with analyses of recent reforms. Concerning Brussels, we refer to E. Witte et al. (ed.), *Het Statuut van Brussel*, Brussels, 1999. The Flemish Parliament was also the subject of research, first in M. Goossens' *Dertig jaar Vlaams Parlement* (Brussels, 2002) and then in *Levende democratie* (Brussels, 2004, edited by N. De Batselier).

List of Abbreviations

ABVV-FGTB	Algemeen Belgisch Vakverbond Fédération Générale de Travail de Belgique General Federation of Belgian Labour
ACEC	Ateliers de Construction Electrique de Charleroi Electrical Construction Workshops of the city of Charleroi
ACIB	Association Catholique de la Jeunesse Catholic Youth Association
ACOD	Algemene Centrale der Openbare Diensten General central of public services
ACV-CSC	Algemeen Christelijk Vakverbond Confédération des syndicats chrétiens Confederation of Christian Trade Unions
ACVW	Algemeen Christelijk Verbond der Werkgevers General Christian Federation of Employers
ACW	Algemeen Christelijk Werkersverbond General Christian Workers' Association
Agalev	Anders gaan leven To start living differently
AGC	Asahi Glass Company
AMADA	Alle Macht aan de Arbeiders All Power to the Workers
ANL	Armee de Libération Nationale Army of National Liberation
APIC	Association des Patrons et Ingénieurs Catholiques Association of Catholic patrons and engineers
ARGO	Autonome Raad van het Gemeenschapsonderwijs Autonomous Council for Public Education
ASLK-CGER	Algemene Spaar- en Lijfrentekas Caisse générale d'épargne et de retraite General Savings and Annuity Fund
AVV-VVK	Alles voor Vlaanderen, Vlaanderen voor Kristus All for Flanders, Flanders for Christ
Benelux	Union of 3 neighboring countries: Belgium, the Netherlands and Luxemburg

BEP	Bureau voor Economische Programmatie Office for Economic Programming
BLEU	Belgisch-Luxemburgse Economische Unie Belgian-Luxemburg Economic Union
BRT	Belgische Radio en Televisie Belgian Radio and Television
BRTN	Belgische Radio en Televisie – Nederlands Belgian Radio and Televisioin – Dutch speaking
BSP-PSB	Belgische Socialistische Partij Parti Socialiste Belge Belgian Socialist Party
BTK	Bijzonder Tijdelijk Kader Exceptional Temporary Staff
BVV	Belgisch Vakverbond Belgian Union
BWP-POB	Belgische Werkliedenpartij Parti Ouvrier Belge Belgian Worker's Party
CAL	Centre d'Action Laïque
CCC	Cellules Communistes Combattantes Communist Combattant Cells
CCI	Comité Central Industriel Central Industrial Committee
CD&V	Christen-Democratisch & Vlaams Christian Democratic & Flemish
cdH	Centre Démocrate Humaniste Humanist democratic centre
CEPIC	Centre Politique des Indépendants et Cadres Chrétiens Political centre of Christian independents and staff
CERW	Conseil économique regional wallon Regional Walloon economic council
CIA	Central Intelligence Agency
CMB	Centrale der Metaalindustrie van België Central of Belgian Metal industry
CNAPD	Comité National d'Action pour la Paix et le Développement National Action committee for peace and development
CNCD	Centre National de Coopération au Développement National Centre for Development Aid
CNN	Cable News Network
Cocof	Commission communautaire française French community commision

Costa	Commissie voor Staatshervorming Commission for state reform
CRB	Centrale Raad voor het Bedrijfsleven Central council for companies
CVP-PSC	Christelijke Volkspartij Parti Socialiste Chrétien Christian People's Party
DeVlag	Deutsch-Vlamische Arbeitsgemeinschaft German-Flemish Workers Union
Ecolo	Ecologistes confédérés pour l'organisation de luttes originales Ecologists confederated for the organisation of original struggles
ECSC	European Coal and Steel Community
ECU	European Currency Unit
EEG	Europese Economische Gemeenschap European Economic Union
EMS	Europees Monetair Stelsel European Monetary System
EMU	Economic and monetary union
EPS	Europese Politiek Samenwerking European political cooperation
EU	European Union
Europol	Europees Politiebureau European police office
FDF	Front (Démocratique) des Francophones Democratic Front of Francophones
FLNC	Front de Libération Nationale du Congo National Liberation front of Congo
FN	Fabrique Nationale d'armes de guerre (Herstal) National war arms factory (in the city of Herstal)
GDP	Gross Domestic Product
GER	Gewestelijke Economische Raad Regional economic council
GNP	Gross National Product
GOM	Gewestelijke Ontwikkelingsmaatschappij Regional development company
IBRAMCO	Iranian Belgian Refining and Marketing Company
ID21	Integrale Democratie voor de 21ste eeuw Total democracy for the 21st century
IMF	International Monetary Fund
Indymedia	Independant Media Center

JOC	Jeunesse Ouvrière Chrétienne Catholic Workers' Youth
JSC	Joint Stock Company
KAJ	Katholieke Arbeidersjeugd Catholic Workers' Youth
KPB	Kommunistische Partij van België Communist Party of Belgium
KP-Vlaanderen	Kommunistische Partij van Vlaanderen Communist Party of Flanders
KUL	Katholieke Universiteit van Leuven
KVV	Katholieke Vlaamse Volkspartij Catholic Flemish People's Party
KWB	Katholieke Werkliedenbond, nu: Christelijke Werknemers-beweging Catholic Workers Movement
LVV	Liberaal Vlaams Verbond Liberal Flemish Union
MAC	Mouvement d'Action Civique Civic Action Movement
MNC	Mouvement National Congolais National movement of Congo
MOC	Mouvement Ouvrier Chrétien General Christian Workers' Association
MPW	Mouvement Populaire Wallon Walloon popular movement
MR	Mouvement Réformateur Reformist Movement
NATO	North Atlantic Treaty Organisation
NBB	Nationale Bank van België National Bank of Belgium
NCEE	Nationaal Comité voor Economische Expansie National committee for economic expansion
NCOS	Nationaal Centrum voor Ontwikkelingssamenwerking National Centre for Development Aid
NIM	Nationale Investeringsmaatschappij National Investment Company
NKB	Nationale Koninklijke Beweging National Royal Movement
NMBS-SNCB	Nationale Maatschappij der Belgische Spoorwegen Société National des chemins de fer Belges National Railway Company of Belgium

NMKN	Nationale Maatschappij voor Krediet aan de Nijverheid National Society for Credit to Industry
NSB	Nieuwe Sociale Bewegingen New Social Movements
NSJV	Nationaal-Socialistische Jeugd in Vlaanderen National-Socialist Youth in Flanders
NSKO	Nationaal Secretariaat Katholiek Onderwijs National secretary of Catholic education
N-VA	Nieuw-Vlaamse Alliantie New-Flemish Alliance
OAS	Organisation of American States
OCMW-CPAS	Openbaar Centrum voor Maatschappelijk Welzijn Centre Public d'Action Sociale Public Center for social action
OECD	Organisation for Economic Co-operation and Development
OEEC	Organisation for European Economic Cooperation
OF	Onafhankelijkheidsfront Independance Front
OREC	Office de Redressement Economique Office of economic rectification
PC	Parti Communiste Communist party
PCS	Parti Catholique Social Catholic social party
PRLW	Parti pour les Réformes et la Liberté en Wallonie Party for reform and liberty in Wallonia
PS	Parti Socialiste Socialist party
PVDA	Partij van de Arbeid Labour Party
PVV-PLP	Partij voor Vrijheid en Vooruitgang Parti des Réformes et de Liberté Party for Freedom and Progress
RAD	Respect voor Arbeid en Democratie Respect for Labour and Democracy
RBP	Raffinerie Belge des Pétroles Belgian Petroleum refinery
RIB	Renault Industrie Belgique Renault Industry Belgium
RMT	Regie voor Maritiem Transport Service for maritime transportation
RO	Royal order

RTB	Radio-Télévision Belge Belgian radio and television
RTBF	Radio-Télévision Belge Française Belgian radio and television francophone
RTL	Radio-Télévision Luxembourgeoise Luxemburg radio and television
RUG	Rijksuniversiteit Gent Ghent State University
RVA	Rijksdienst voor Arbeidsvoorziening State Service for Labour
RW	Rassemblement Wallon Walloon Rally
SALT	Strategic Arms Limitation Talks
SAP	Socialistische Arbeiderspartij Socialist Workers Party
SeP	Solidarité et Participation Solidarity and Participation
SFvB	Sociaal Forum van België Social Forum of Belgium
SHAEF	Supreme Headquarters of the Allied Expeditionary Forces
SHAPE	Supreme Headquarters Allied Powers in Europe
SP	Socialistische Partij Socialist Party
sp.a	Socialistische partij anders Socialist party differently
Spirit	Sociaal Progressief Internationaal Regionalistisch Integraal-democratisch Toekomstgericht Social Liberal party
SS	Schutzstaffel Protective Squadron
START	Strategic Arms Reduction Treaty
TAK	Taal Aktie Komitee Language Action Committee
UCB	Union Chimique Belge Belgian Chemical Union
UCL	Université Catholique de Louvain Catholic university of Louvain (French-speaking)
UDB	Union Démocratique Belge Belgian democratic union
UDRT	Union Démocratique pour le Respect du Travail Democratic union for respect for work

UHGA	Unie van Hand- en Geestesarbeiders A federation of unions
ULB	Université Libre de Bruxelles Free University of Brussels (French-speaking)
UN	United Nations
Unctad	United Nations Conference on Trade and Development
UNIZO	Unie van Zelfstandige Ondernemers Association of Independent Entrepreneurs
U.S.	United States (of America)
UVV	Unie Vrijzinnige Verenigingen Union of Freethinkers' Associations
VAKA	Vlaams Aktiekomittee tegen de Atoomwapens Flemish action committee against nuclear weapons
VAT	Value Added Tax
VBN	Verbond der Belgische Nijverheid Union of Belgian industry
VBO	Verbond der Belgische Ondernemingen Federation of Belgian Companies
VDB	Vanden Boeynants
Verdinaso	Verbond van Dietsche Nationaal-Solidaristen Union of Diets National Solidarists
VEV	Vlaams Economisch Verbond Flemish Economic Union
VFIK	Vlaams Fonds voor Integratie van Kansarmen Flemish Fund for the Integration of the Underprivileged
VGC	Vlaamse Gemeenschapscommissie Flemish Community Commission
VKW	Verbond van Kristelijke Werkgevers en Kaderleden Union of Christian Employers and Managers
VLD	Vlaamse Liberalen en Democraten Flemish Liberals and Democrats
VMO	Vlaamse Militanten Orde Order of Flemish Militants
VNU	Verenigde Nederlandse Uitgeversbedrijven United Dutch Publishing companies
VNV	Vlaams Nationaal Verbond Flemish national union
VOKA	Vlaams Netwerk van Ondernemingen Flemish Enterprises Network
VOS	Vlaamse Oudstrijders(bond) Flemish Veteran Movement

VRT	Vlaamse Radio- en Televisieomroep Flemish Radio and Television
VTM	Vlaamse Televisiemaatschappij Flemish Television Company
VU	Volksunie People's Union
VUB	Vrije Universiteit Brussel Free University of Brussels (Dutch-speaking)
VUM	Vlaamse Uitgeversmaatschappij Flemish Publishing Company

Person index

A
Acker, A. Van 223, 229, 230, 231, 232, 238, 240, 243, 254, 274, 465, 466, 487
Albert I 15, 138, 144, 150, 152, 177, 189, 209, 210, 493
Albert II 321, 441, 493
Anciaux 429
Anseele, E. 103, 106, 107, 147, 160, 173, 223
Astrid, Princess 444
Astrid, Queen 215

B
Babeuf, G. 51
Baels, L. 215, 240
Baets, D. De 95
Bara, J. 81, 82, 85, 464
Bartels, A. 31
Batselier, N. De 349, 426, 495
Baudouin I 15
Beernaert, A. 114, 119, 136, 464
Beers, J. Van 95
Bekaert, L. A. 145, 166, 329
Bertrand, L. 103
Beuckelaere, A. De 139
Biest, Alain Van Der 323
Bissing, M.F. von 145, 171
Boëll, G. 62
Boeynants, P. Vanden 280, 288, 466, 467
Borginon, H. 139, 201, 202
Borms, A. 174, 175
Bourgeois, G. 429
Bovesse, Fr. 188, 208
Brandt, W. 401
Brismée, D. 74
Broqueville, Ch. De 119, 138, 152, 153, 177, 464, 465, 485
Brouckère, Ch. de 463
Brouckère, H. de 61, 83, 84, 85, 463
Brouckère, L. de 109, 160, 210
Buisseret, A. 176
Buls, Ch. 95, 486

C
Calewaert, W. 266
Capart 381
Cardijn, J. 169, 170
Carton de Wiart, H. 113, 147, 152, 464
Cauwelaert, F. Van 132, 140, 153, 156, 164, 172, 184, 198, 199, 201, 484, 489
Cauwenberghe, J.-C. 341, 468
Churchill, W. 228
Claes, W. 295, 296, 307, 404, 423, 440, 467
Clercq, S. De 200, 201, 202, 203, 204, 475
Clercq, W. de 280, 288, 301
Cockerill, J. 62, 98, 99, 137, 165, 287, 353
Coëme, G. 404, 423, 467
Coenen, F. 75
Coenen, M.T. 484, 491
Coens, D. 262
Coghen, J. 43, 46
Collard, L. 254, 257
Collin, F. 213
Connerotte, J.-M. 324
Conscience, H. 57
Cools, A. 323, 426, 441, 466
Coppée, E. 62, 99, 165, 275
Coppieters, M. 349, 482
Coremans, E. 95, 132, 133
Coulon, N. 74
Crokaert, P. 157, 207

D
Daens, A. 112, 113, 330, 484
Darwin, Ch. 83
David, J.-B. 58
Decker, P. De 61, 83, 84, 85, 93, 463
Defuisseaux, A. 102, 103
Degrelle, L. 153, 157, 160, 198, 204, 205, 206, 207, 208, 475, 490
Dehaene, J.-L. 320, 326, 328, 382, 386, 424, 427, 436, 437, 441, 467, 468
Dehousse, F. 176
Delacroix, L. 146, 147, 151, 152, 178, 464
Delcroix, L. 323, 423
Denis, H. 73, 75, 491
Deschamps, A. 81
Deschamps, P. 90
Destrée, J. 158, 174, 489
Devaux, P. 48
Devèze, A. 152, 153, 163, 209
Di Rupo, E. 341, 426, 468
Dosfel, L. 131
Ducpétiaux, E. 31
Dutroux, M. 323, 324, 325, 326, 327, 331, 420, 430, 437, 441, 442, 444, 448, 478
Duvieusart, J. 242, 243, 244, 466, 485

E
Elias, H. 201, 202, 204, 205, 488
Elslande, R. Van 226
Empain, E. 62, 98, 99, 135, 151, 165, 275
Engels, Fr. 54
Erskine 228, 238
Extergem, J. Van 161, 190
Eyskens, G. 193, 200, 233, 241, 255, 275, 276, 277, 376, 377, 394, 436, 466, 485
Eyskens, M. 399, 467

F
Faider, Ch. 84
Franck, L. 140
Francqui, E. 152, 164
Fredericq, P. 140
Frère-Orban, H. J.W. 5, 48, 53, 56, 61, 62, 69, 81, 82, 463, 464
Fuss, H. 191

G
Galle, M. 380, 487
Galopin, A. 205, 213, 217, 236, 479
Gamond, I. de 116
Gaulle, Ch. De 401
Geens, G. 379
Gendebien, A. 31, 463
George VI, King 211
Gérard, M.-L. 193, 213, 493
Gerrits, L. 95
Gevaert, L. 130, 145
Geyter, J. De 94, 95
Goblet, J.A. 38, 463
Goethals, R. 95
Gol, J. 304, 314, 368, 379, 428, 467
Gravez, T. 89
Greef, G. De 73, 75
Gutt, C. 151, 212, 230, 232, 476

H
Hammarskjöld, D. 396
Hansenne, M. 304
Happart, J. 380, 381, 382, 383, 431
Harmel, P. 226, 252, 255, 376, 401, 402, 404, 466, 485
Helleputte, J. 110, 113, 115, 119, 124
Hemelrijck, M. Van 394, 395
Heremans, J.-P. 95
Herman, E. 292
Hersant, R. 445
Himmler, H 203, 204
Hins, E. 73, 75, 487
Hitler, A. 185, 201, 203, 204, 207, 208, 210, 211, 214, 216, 240, 493
Hoornaert, P. 175
Hoste, J. 164, 172, 486
Houben, R. 226
Humbeeck, P. Van 62, 89, 90, 127, 128, 464
Huysmans, C. 109, 133, 138, 140, 152, 153, 158, 161, 172, 173, 174, 190, 212, 223, 230, 466, 487
Hymans, P. 138, 163, 178, 180

J

Jacquemotte, J. 158, 161
Jadot, J. 164
Janson, P.E. 85, 105, 116, 147, 163, 465
Janssens, P. 426, 474, 478, 485, 493
Jaspar, H. 147, 150, 152, 175, 465
Jottrand, L. 31

K

Kabila, L. D. 400
Karel, Prince 229, 244, 248
Kasavubu, J. 394, 395, 396, 397
Kats, J. 52

L

Laet, J. De 95
Lahaut, J. 242, 244, 490
Lallemand 266
Langrand-Dumonceau, A. 62, 64, 479
Lanotte, J. Vande 345, 468
Lebeau, J. 463
Leburton, E. 261, 293, 377, 466
Leemans, V. 200, 217, 488
Lefèvre, Th. 226, 254, 256, 279, 374, 376, 451, 466, 485
Lenin, W.I. 158
Leo XIII 89, 110, 113
Leopold I 5, 15, 29, 30, 37, 38, 45, 46, 79, 153, 493
Leopold II 15, 79, 98, 127, 135, 136, 137, 492, 493
Leopold III 6, 12, 15, 144, 150, 159, 177, 183, 185, 189, 194, 209, 210, 213, 214, 219, 220, 228, 239, 240, 241, 242, 442, 493
Lilar 394, 466
Lumumba, P. 394, 395, 396, 397, 398

M

Mac Leod, J. 131, 133
Maelen, D. Van der 338
Maere, A. De 95
Mahieu 190
Major, L. 223, 239, 275, 289
Malou, J. 61, 69, 80, 87, 463, 464
Man, H. De 109, 161, 190, 192, 193, 194, 196, 201, 212, 222
Marchal, P. 430
Marie-José 214
Maritain, J. 226
Marshall, G. 239, 246, 248, 406, 451
Martens, A. 188, 189
Martens, W. 262, 295, 302, 306, 318, 378, 379, 380, 391, 399, 424, 436, 437, 467, 480
Marx, K 51, 54, 76
Mathot, G. 423, 467
Maurras, Ch. 156, 206, 490
Maystadt, Ph. 424, 468
Meenen, P. Van 31
Mercier, D. 127, 128, 138, 146, 147, 148, 153, 155, 156, 157
Michielsen, L. 266
Miert, K. Van 332
Mobutu, J. D. 16, 396, 397, 398, 399, 400, 493
Moens, W. 206
Montalembert, Ch. de 86
Montpellier, T. de 89
Motz, R. 163
Mounier, E. 226
Moureaux, Ph. 424, 467
Moyersoen, L. 225, 485
Moyson, E. 75, 92, 330
Muelenaere, F.A. de 38, 463
Mussolini, B. 157, 207, 208

N

Nemours, Duke of 27
Neuray, F. 177
Nolf, R. 164, 175
Nols, R. 375
Noppen, K. Van 323, 441
Nothomb, A. 80
Nothomb, C. F. 381, 428, 467
Nothomb, J.-B. 38, 40, 45, 46, 89, 463
Nothomb, P. 157, 158, 177

O

Ostaijen, P. Van 174
Otlet, E. 62, 98, 479
Overstraeten, R. Van 210, 244
Overstraeten, W. Van 161

P
Paepe, C. De 73, 75, 76
Peereboom, E. Van de 115
Peers, W. 266
Peeters, L. 391
Peirens, W. 260
Pellering, J. 74
Perin, Ch. 110, 368, 476, 477
Perin, F. 110, 368, 476, 477
Petrella, R. 335, 338
Philippart, S. 62, 71, 479
Picard, L. 156
Pierlot, H. 162, 211, 212, 213, 215, 228, 229, 238, 240, 245, 247, 465
Pillecyn, F. De 139
Pirenne, J 241
Pius IX 89
Pius X 128
Pius XI 169, 170
Potter, L. De 31, 463
Pottier, A. 111
Poullet, P. 118, 128, 144, 149, 155, 162, 179, 188, 465, 474

R
Raet, L. De 131, 134, 145
Reeck, H. Van Den 174
Renard, A. 197, 218, 275, 279, 368
Renkin, J. 113, 119, 151, 465
Rijswijck, Th. Van 57, 95
Rodenbach, A. 94, 131
Roey, E. Van 198, 207, 278
Rogier, Ch. 5, 38, 43, 45, 53, 55, 56, 61, 68, 69, 79, 80, 85, 93, 463, 464
Rolin 487
Romsée, G. 201, 203, 217, 475
Rooses, M. 131, 134, 488
Roosevelt, F.D. 192

S
Saeger, J. De 226
Saint-Simon, C.H. 51
Sap, G. 45, 198, 403, 431
Schollaert, F. 119, 124, 127, 136, 464
Schuind, G. 217
Segers, P. 157
Segers, P.-W. 437
Severen, J. Van 174, 206, 207, 488
Smet de Naeyer, P.J. de 119, 464
Snieders, A. 94
Solvay, E. 62, 98, 99, 100, 138, 164, 165, 275, 351
Spaak, P.-H. 160, 188, 190, 192, 193, 209, 210, 212, 223, 227, 233, 241, 248, 252, 256, 279, 374, 376, 397, 437, 451, 465, 466, 487
Spitaels, G. 295, 423, 440, 467
Stalin, J. 187
Stevaert, S. 426
Stillemans, A. 112

T
Terwagne, M. 158
Tesch, V. 62, 99
Theunis, G. 151, 152, 153, 179, 464, 465
Theux, B.T. de 463
Thone, G. 175, 490
Tindemans, L. 293, 294, 295, 377, 378, 402, 404, 436, 466, 467
Tito, J.B. 246
Tobback, L. 424, 434
Tollenaere, R. De 201, 475
Truffaut, G. 176

V
Van den Bossche, L. 263, 318, 439, 468
Van Rossem, J.-P. 431, 448
Vandenbroucke, F. 345, 348, 349, 423
Vanderkindere, L. 95
Vanderpoorten, A. 164, 467
Vandervelde, E. 106, 107, 116, 136, 138, 144, 149, 158, 160, 162, 178, 179, 192, 210, 465, 474, 487
Verhaegen, A. 111, 113
Verhaegen, P.Th. 48, 485
Verhulst, A. 261, 485
Vermeylen, A. 131, 140, 190
Verroken, J. 375, 489
Verschaeve, C. 206
Verwilghen, M. 325, 327
Victoria, Queen of Great Britain 45
Vigne, J.O. De 95
Vleeschauwer, A. De 212, 214
Vliebergh, J.E. 131
Vos, H. 36, 171, 172, 174, 190, 198, 201, 473, 474, 476, 477, 484, 489, 492

Vriendt, J. 133
Vuylsteke, J. 94, 95, 486
Vyvere, A. Van de 153, 464, 474

W
Watt, J. 42
Wauters, J 167
Weyer, S. Van de 38, 40, 463
Wiele, J. Van de 203
Wilhelmina, Queen 211
Willem I 473
Willems, J.F. 57
Wilson, W. 171
Winter, E. De 23, 210, 217, 276, 277, 282, 302, 368
Woeste, Ch. 67, 112, 146, 154

Z
Zeeland, P. Van 177, 186, 188, 189, 191, 193, 198, 465, 474, 485

Subject index

A
Abako party 394
ABVV 223, 224, 239, 274, 275, 278, 279, 289, 294, 295, 298, 306, 312, 328, 329, 333, 340, 344, 347, 487
Abwehr 202
ACOD 253, 277
ACVW 166
ACV 111, 155, 166, 169, 170, 191, 193, 195, 197, 276, 278, 289, 294, 295, 298, 305, 306, 312, 328, 340, 344
ACW 154, 155, 157, 169, 170
Advisory Committee for Bio-Ethics 268
Agalev 257, 404, 417, 426, 430, 434, 459, 460, 468
Agir 315, 432
Algemeen Katholiek Vlaams Burgersverbond 199
Algemeen Verbond ter Bevordering van het Officieel Onderwijs 253
Algemene SS 216
Algemene Vlaamse SS 203, 204, 205
Alliance Agricole 155
Amis de l'Exploité 161
Anti-Egmont committee 378
Anti-Socialistische Werkliedenbond 113
Anti-terroristische Gemengde Group 304
Anti-War League 192
APIC 166, 195
Arabisch-Europese Liga 431
Arbitragehof 263, 381, 384, 390
ARGO 262, 263
Army of Belgium 220
ASLK 70, 118, 165, 285, 474, 475
Association Catholique de la Jeunesse 157
Association de la démocratie militante 75
Association démocratique 54
Association pour la réforme electorale 81
Attac 338, 339

B
Belgian Catholic Church 91
Belgian Catholic Union 154
Belgian Church 28, 35
Belgian Lesbian and Gay Pride 267
Belgian Union 166, 223, 332
Belgisch-Luxemburgse Economische Unie 307
Benelux 16, 210, 247, 406
Blauwvoet 94
Blue Lions 371
Boerenbond 124, 125, 126, 155, 166, 198, 199, 251, 480
BRT 376, 446, 447
BRTN 376
BSP 224, 230, 239, 240, 242, 255, 257, 275, 278, 279, 282, 362, 364, 400, 401, 466, 467
BTK 295
Bureau voor Economische Programmatie 277, 284
BWP 103, 105, 107, 108, 109, 112, 113, 115, 116, 123, 125, 128, 132, 133, 136, 137, 138, 140, 144, 149, 154, 158, 159, 160, 161, 163, 168, 169, 172, 179, 186, 187, 190, 192, 193, 194, 196, 210, 212, 223, 224, 465, 486, 487

C
Catholic Action 157, 169, 170, 198, 200, 206, 207
Catholic Bloc 126, 199

Catholic Party 36, 49, 80, 87, 91, 94, 109, 111, 112, 113, 121, 123, 124, 126, 127, 131, 133, 148, 149, 150, 152, 153, 154, 156, 157, 163, 169, 172, 184, 187, 189, 197, 198, 199, 200, 202, 208, 221, 224, 225, 227, 229, 234, 237, 239, 243, 276, 362, 376, 452, 483, 484
Catholic Student Action 170
Catholic Union 149, 154, 155, 156, 162, 166, 169, 187, 294, 312
CCC 303
CD&V 427, 430, 460, 468
cdH 428, 460, 468, 469
Central Council for the Business Community 284, 308
Central European Bank 408
Central Freethinkers' Council 258
Central Office of Catholic Education 156
CEPIC 299
Cercle du Libre Examen 220
Charismatic movement 443
Chevaliers du Travail 106
Christus Rex 157
College ter Bestrijding van het Terrorrisme 304
Comité Central Industriel 166
Commissie voor Staatshervorming 389
Commission for Relief in Belgium 164
Communist International 187
Communist Party 161, 174, 183, 187, 190, 192, 219, 221, 238, 431, 487
Community council 379, 386, 387, 453
Congo Reform Association 136
Council of State 381
Court of Arbitration 263, 381, 384, 390
CSC 111, 295
Culture councils 261, 377, 446
Cultuurpactcommissie 261
CVP 112, 199, 200, 225, 226, 229, 230, 233, 240, 241, 242, 243, 244, 249, 251, 252, 253, 254, 255, 259, 260, 261, 262, 265, 266, 267, 278, 279, 299, 300, 356, 362, 364, 366, 371, 375, 376, 377, 378, 380, 381, 382, 394, 400, 402, 417, 420, 421, 423, 427, 428, 429, 434, 436, 438, 459, 460, 466, 467, 468, 484, 493

D
Davidsfonds 94, 189, 198, 251, 362, 363, 366, 488
DeVlag 203, 204, 205, 216, 488
Dolle Mina 265
Dutch Culture Commission 378

E
Ecolo 404, 417, 426, 430, 444, 459, 460, 461, 468, 469, 490
Enterprise council 284
European Commission 326, 335, 408
European Community 393, 409
European Economic Community 16, 281, 406
European Monetary System 407, 408
European Political Cooperation 409
Europol 409

F
Fédération des Associations et des Cercles 155, 199
Federation of Catholic Circles and Conservative Associations 87
Financière Intermills 292
Flemish Community 318, 454
Flemish concentration 198
Flemish Council 139, 318, 379, 380, 460
Flemish Cultural Council 261
Flemish Legion 204
Flemish north-south movements 336
Flemish Socialist Party 103
Flemish SS 203, 205
Fonds voor Industriële Vernieuwing 295, 296
Force Publique 395
Forges de Clabecq 329, 330, 408
Francophone Community Council 379, 386, 387
French Community Council 453
Front de la Jeunesse 299
Front démocratique des Francophones 266, 372, 373, 375, 376, 377, 378, 381, 390, 413, 428, 429,

434, 449, 459, 460, 467, 468
Front des Francophones 257
Front Movement 140, 171
Front National 315, 432
Front Party 172, 174, 179, 201

G
Gemeenschappelijke Actie 95, 239, 257, 275, 409
Gemeentekrediet 70, 472
Gestapo 203
Gewestelijke Ontwikkelingsmaatschappijen 284, 377
Group-G 220

H
Help U Zelve 163
Hitler Youth 204
Hoog Comité van Toezicht 323
Humanistisch Verbond 257

I
ID21 429
Indymedia 335
Inquiry Commission 136
International Brigades 210, 218
International Monetary Fund 333, 399
International, First 75, 76, 101, 103
International, Second 109, 132, 158, 161
International, Fourth 162
International, Third 161

J
Jeune Droite 80
Jeune Europe 395
Jeune Garde Socialiste 161
Joint committees 164, 167, 193, 196, 233, 252

K
KAJ 157, 169, 170
Katholiek Verbond van België 154
Katholiek Vlaams Verbond 154
Katholieke Verenigingen en Kringen 154, 157
Katholieke Vlaamse Landsbond 156, 199
Katholieke Vlaamse Studentenbeweging 170
Kolendirectorium 280
Kriegsmarine 205
KUL 40, 48, 50, 206, 264, 376
KVV 199, 200, 201

L
Labour Bank 160, 173
Labour committee 119
Landsbond der Christelijke Mutualiteiten 155
League of Nations 179, 180, 208, 210
Légion Nationale 175
Liberaal Vlaams Verbond 132, 163, 173, 253
Liberal Congress 48, 54, 83, 108, 162
Liberal Flemish Federations 94
Liberal Party 5, 49, 53, 54, 56, 61, 66, 76, 80, 81, 82, 84, 85, 91, 94, 102, 109, 115, 116, 132, 152, 162, 163, 173, 256, 362, 365, 366, 368, 369, 376, 423, 425, 428, 431, 459, 485, 486
Liberal People's Association 132
Liberal Young Guard 163
Libre Pensée, la 84
Ligue de l'Enseignement 162, 253
Ligue de la Réforme Electorale 103
London Conference 29, 491

M
Marie Mineur 265
Meeting Party 80, 93, 94
Militärverwaltung 195, 202, 203, 204, 205, 206, 213, 214, 216, 217
MNC 394, 395
Mouvement des citoyens pour le changement 428
Mouvement Ouvrier Chrétien 169, 257
Mouvement Populaire Wallon 279, 368
Mouvement Syndical Unifié 197
MR 429, 460

N
Nationaal Centrum voor Ontwikke-

lingssamenwerking 336, 337
Nationaal Comité voor Economische Expansie 277, 284, 289
Nationaal Comité voor Vrijheid en Democratie 254
Nationaal-Socialistische Jeugd in Vlaanderen 204
National Bank of Belgium 68
National Central 111
National Committee for Aid and Food Supply 138, 164
National Company for the Restructuring of Textile Manufacturing 296
National Congress 5, 19
National Crisis Fund 167
National Investment Company 280
National Labour Conference 186, 231, 284
National Labour Council 284
National Legion 203
National Service for Economic Recovery 193
National Union for the Restoration of Grievances 91
Nationale Commissie voor Ethische Problemen 266
Nationale Koninklijke Beweging 219
Nationale Maatschappij voor Krediet aan de Nijverheid 165
Nationale Raad van de Steenkolenmijnen 280
North Atlantic Treaty Organisation 247
Nouvel Europe Magazine 299
NSKO 255, 261
N-VA 366, 427, 429, 430

O
Organisation Todt 205
Oslo Group 210

P
Parti Catholique Social 199
Parti Socialiste Républicain 103
Partisans 93, 218, 238
Peace Movement 323, 403, 404, 405
Persgroep 445, 446
Peuple, Le 75, 161, 241, 445
Planbureau 284
Police 26, 53, 54, 72, 108, 115, 174, 205, 207, 208, 216, 217, 235, 238, 242, 278, 280, 288, 303, 304, 314, 315, 324, 325, 327, 341, 347, 375, 389, 398, 409, 440, 441, 442
POSA units 303
Prévoyance Sociale 107
Pro Vita 265
Progrès, Le 106
Provisional Government 19, 41, 43, 463
PS 103, 108, 116, 146, 158, 160, 183, 188, 192, 196, 201, 204, 208, 216, 224, 256, 323, 362, 365, 368, 433, 445, 467, 487
PSB 224, 255, 257, 282, 362, 368, 372, 466, 467
PSC 208, 225, 251, 252, 253, 254, 255, 260, 261, 262, 265, 266, 267, 299, 300, 303, 362, 364, 373, 376, 381, 382, 400, 427, 428, 436, 459, 460, 461, 466, 467, 468, 469
PVDA 102, 431
PVV 256, 262, 300, 301, 365, 428, 459

R
Rassemblement Wallon 257, 368, 459
Regional Council 377, 379, 386, 387, 389, 460
Regionale Uitgeversmaatschappij 445
Renault 329, 330, 331, 332, 333, 340, 341, 342, 409, 452
Respect voor Arbeid en Democratie 299
Rex 149, 153, 157, 183, 184, 187, 197, 198, 199, 204, 207, 209, 216, 229, 237, 243, 458
Rijksdienst voor Maatschappelijke Zekerheid 231
Rijksuniversiteit Gent 84, 131, 133, 264
Rode Leeuwen 371
Roularta 446
RTB 376, 446
RTBf 376, 447

S
Sabena 399

School Pact 7, 12, 15
Scild en Vriend 94
Secret Army 220
Social and Economic Conference 284
Social Impulse Fund 319
Social Polytechnic 170
Socialistische Arbeiderspartij 45, 198, 403, 431
Socialistische Gemeenschappelijke Actie 275
Société Générale 30, 42, 43, 45, 46, 62, 68, 98, 99, 135, 138, 145, 147, 151, 152, 164, 165, 205, 213, 217, 218, 275, 292, 301, 351, 395, 399, 407, 447, 479
Solidaires, les 74, 75
Solidarité et Participation 260
Solvay 62, 98, 99, 100, 138, 164, 165, 275, 351
SP 224, 257, 259, 262, 301, 306, 323, 349, 356, 365, 366, 380, 382, 384, 404, 423, 425, 426, 428, 459, 460, 461, 467, 468, 469, 487
Sp.a 338, 345, 349, 357, 426, 430, 460, 468
Spirit 24, 37, 57, 87, 110, 111, 121, 139, 141, 152, 157, 194, 196, 223, 224, 225, 231, 255, 349, 366, 378, 382, 426, 429, 430, 446, 460, 468
SS Sturmbrigade Langemarck 205
SS Sturmbrigade Wallonia 207
State reform 17, 189, 190, 196, 283, 368, 389
State Security 103, 441
States-General 21
Stichting Technologie Vlaanderen 312
Sturmbrigade 204, 205, 207
Supreme Headquarters Allied Powers Europe 16, 126, 309, 324, 329, 330, 345, 349, 350, 351, 355, 401, 409
Supreme Headquarters of the Allied Expeditionary Forces 228, 229

T
Taal Aktie Komitee 364, 371
Trade Union Commission 107
Treaty of Maastricht 404

U
UCL 264, 335, 376
UDB 224, 225, 229, 465, 484
UDRT 299, 431
ULB 187, 264, 376, 489
Unemployment funds 121
Unie van Hand- en Geestesarbeiders 212
Unie van Vrijzinnige Verenigingen 257
Union Minière 135, 152, 395, 398
United Nations 157, 245, 246, 247, 248, 335, 343, 395, 396, 405, 473, 475

V
Vaste Nationale Cultuurpactcommissie 261
Vatican 28, 35, 36, 37, 38, 85, 86, 90, 112, 169
VBN 227, 277
VBO 166, 282, 344, 345
Verbond van Coöperaties 155
Verbond van Kristelijke Werkgevers en Kaderleden 345
Verdinaso 197, 206, 207
Verenigde Feministische Partij 434
Vereniging van Socialistisch Onderwijspersoneel 253
Vermeylenfonds 362, 363, 366
VEV 130, 145, 166, 198, 281, 300, 345, 364
VFIK 318, 319
Vivant 428, 460, 461
Vlaams Actie Comité voor Brussel en de Taalgrens 364
Vlaams Belang 357, 425, 432
Vlaams Blok 315, 316, 320, 330, 357, 366, 369, 378, 388, 389, 429, 430, 431, 432, 444, 449, 452
Vlaams Front 171, 174
Vlaams Handelsverbond 166
Vlaams Liberaal Verbond 164
Vlaamse Katholieke Landsbond 132
Vlaamse Televisiemaatschappij 446, 447
Vlaamse Uitgeversmaatschappij 445
Vlaamse Volksbeweging 364
Vlaams-nationaal Zangverbond 198
VMO 364, 431

VNV 157, 183, 184, 187, 189, 197, 198, 200, 201, 202, 203, 204, 205, 206, 207, 209, 217, 229, 237, 243, 362, 364, 366, 488
VOKA 345, 346, 348
Volksbond 113, 132, 154
Volksunie 257, 261, 362, 364, 365, 366, 371, 494
Volksverbond 75, 154, 362
Voorpost 431
Vooruit 75, 106, 159
VOS 36, 171, 172, 174, 190, 198, 201, 473, 474, 476, 477, 484, 489, 492

W
Waffen-SS 204
Walloon Council 386
Walloon Region 329, 369, 379, 451, 453, 468
Warsaw Pact 400
Wehrmacht 202, 215
Willemsfonds 94, 163, 164, 261, 362, 363, 366, 489
Witte Brigade 219, 220
Witte Brigade-Fidelio 219, 220
World Social Forum 336, 338
World Trade Organisation 333, 334

Y
Yser pilgrimage 172, 364, 366

Z
Zivilverwaltung 216
Zwarte Brigade 205